LEST WE REGRET

LEST WE REGRET

by

DOUGLAS REED

JONATHAN CAPE
THIRTY BEDFORD SQUARE
LONDON

This book contains approximately 135,000 words which, in order to save paper, have been compressed within 338 pages. There are many more words on each page than would be desirable in normal times; margins have been reduced and no space has been wasted between chapters. In the less stringent conditions of peace the book would extend to some 448 pages.

BOOK
PRODUCTION
WAR ECONOMY
STANDARD

FIRST PUBLISHED SEPTEMBER 1943
SECOND IMPRESSION MARCH 1944

JONATHAN CAPE LTD.   30 BEDFORD SQUARE, LONDON
AND 91 WELLINGTON STREET WEST, TORONTO

PRINTED IN GREAT BRITAIN IN THE CITY OF OXFORD
AT THE ALDEN PRESS
PAPER MADE BY JOHN DICKINSON & CO. LTD.
BOUND BY A. W. BAIN & CO. LTD.

CONTENTS

AUTHOR'S NOTE

I WOULD be grateful if people in many parts of the Empire, who have received no reply from me, would read this book as an acknowledgment of their letters, a token of friendship reciprocated and an answer to their questions.

I was forced to choose between continuing to write books or entering into a correspondence so great, that it would have occupied all my time. Most of these letters share a common theme — anxiety for the future, however our victory in this war may appear — and this book is a joint reply to them. The clear road beyond victory, for which we long, is still not visible.

That is why I chose for my title the words *Battle in England*, from a letter written by a young officer who served far away from this, his native island. The letter was not sent to me; it was quoted in the House of Commons. One sentence vividly expresses the thought that prompts this book:

'We still feel out here that *the ultimate battle is being won or lost in England.*'

And so it is. With victory, the battle for our future will only begin. The years 1919-39 are close enough for us to remember that.

My publisher thought that the title I chose would confuse readers, who would expect from it a book about the military battle of Britain. The cover, therefore, bears another title: *Lest We Regret.* The theme of the book, nevertheless, is that 'Battle in England' which will have to be fought and won in this island, after the war, if our future is not to be lost.

I have interpolated in the text several quotations from letters to me; they were so apt to my theme that I have used them to illustrate it.

PART ONE

GREAT ARGUMENT

TO FRIENDS AND FOES

> It is the land that freemen till
> That sober-suited Freedom shows;
> The land where, girt with friends or foes,
> A man may speak the things he will. — TENNYSON

EVEN good things come to an end, and this, gentle reader (forgive an outmoded salutation; to be abreast of the courtly times I ought to call you 'sucker' if you applaud me and 'rat' if you do not, but being a writer called rabid I love 'gentle reader'), this is the last of the books with which I have goaded and coaxed you, one nearly every year, since 1938. This opening sentence gives any I may vex an opportunity such as comes only once and I make no charge for it.

(But neither rejoice nor lament too soon, gentle reader. If you will allow me a moment to change my literary clothes, I shall soon reappear before you in another guise.)

Of its kind, alone, is this book the last. It is the end of my modest fore-sight saga, which I began in 1938 with a book called *Insanity Fair*. Great were my expectations then. Foreseeing this war, I thought I might avert it — with a book. O young man in a flurry! I foresaw then that little time remained before a thing might happen, which would leave this country the choice between capitulation without a fight and a war began in the worst imaginable circumstances for itself, and this thing was, the abandon-ment of a little country far away, called Czechoslovakia. Many chances to avert the war, were already gone; this one remained.

To-day, those thunders of yesteryear dwindle, and *Insanity Fair* and its three children go their rounds, soon to be joined by this, the fourth and last. I did not guess, when I began, that I should write more than one book, or suspect how much personal satisfaction I should reap, in spite of the disappointment of the hope which inspired the original book.

For the first time in my life, excluding the war service which I shared with millions of others, I cast from me thoughts of money, security, a career and the future, and acted from a patriotic impulse too strong to be thwarted. Yet the financial calamity I feared, like Shaw's disasters, never happened: in place of the calling I reluctantly gave up, I gained a better; and I surprise myself by the pleasure I still derive from having punched on the nose the craven imp, 'Safety First', and said the thing I would and the thing I knew. In that listless England, I 'did something', the most I could, and if this was but a book which has now joined the legion of others it was mine own. If I could plant the seed of adventure and the ideal of upholding what you think right at all costs, in any youngsters' minds to-day, by writing this, I should be glad, for I know that they would gain by it.

Enough is enough. I gather that I do not bore others, but refuse to bore myself. Not for me, to outstay my encores (and I once saw even that happen, at the Scala in Berlin, when an English band leader was so clamantly applauded that he gave an encore, then two, five, ten encores, turning between each to ask 'Do you want any more?' until the audience became silent, then restive, and finally called 'No, no more!').

Prognostication is the thief of time, and I have other things to do. Because I believe our future salvation can only come from, through, or be taken from us by our Parliament, which robbed us of the last victory, I shall try to enter that building, where voices for England speak so seldom and so often for all else. When peace comes, I want also to go abroad and write of what goes on there, in the hope that the people of this country, if they are accurately informed, will not let themselves be hoodwinked again.

But first, this book, the last of its line. It is a fitting finish to the logical sequence. *Insanity Fair* was an urgent warning of the imminent outbreak of war. *Lest We Regret* is an urgent warning of a greater danger, the approaching outbreak of peace.

This statement was greeted as a jest when I made it to a luncheon audience in London. The English take their leisure sadly and like to beguile it by listening to a speaker with whom they disagree while eating food which disagrees with them. Between indignation and indigestion, they have a grand time. They pay much for a bad meal and nothing for a good speaker (the odd belief prevails that the hotel-keeper deserves payment for his wares but not the speaker).

But this was no joke! To-day millions of people have their every want cared for; to-morrow, they will need to fend for themselves. To-day all have work; to-morrow, each will have to seek it. To-day the young people take no thought for the morrow; to-morrow, they must think hard for the day. To-day, all clearly see their task, to win the war; and think they see clearly how to accomplish it, by serving. To-morrow, they will wish to live in peace, found families and prosper, but will they see the way to achieve that? To-day is filled with the adventure of war; to-morrow will be filled with humdrum.

Such, at least, was the last peace. It was *not* peace. It was worse than the last war, worse than this war. These words protest against being written, yet they are true. The last peace, which was to endure for ever, held for twenty years. Twenty years of mass unemployment, derelict areas, a decaying countryside, growing disbelief and despair; twenty years, during which the men who came back from the last war saw their victory wantonly thrown away, while the rising generation lost faith in the future and the new war approached.

That was the peace of 1919-39. That is the world to which the boys and girls will return unless they make it different.

That is where I and this book come in:

Having a son, a fighter pilot who got his wings at the age of eighteen, and a daughter who, after serving as an A.T.S. private in a mixed anti-aircraft battery for twelve months, now has a commission, I have come in contact during the past three years with a great number of the ordinary rank-and-file of the young generation. I feel convinced that these intelligent, deep-thinking boys and girls are *not* going to leave the making of the new world to anyone but themselves, when the war is won. Because I feel this — having listened for hours to their endless talks and discussions about the things that matter (freedom, simplicity, beauty, love, and, above all, *right thinking*) — I wish with all my heart that you would write something to show that we have a belief in, and an appreciation of them and all they are doing.

From a woman of Glastonbury.

An inspiring text! What writer would not be fired by such prompting? This letter, and that from which I chose my first title, set me to write

Lest We Regret. The same hope inspires it that produced *Insanity Fair.* Though the war was not averted, the peace may yet be saved. I seek to help towards this by a book. For 'these intelligent, deep-thinking boys and girls', if indeed they 'are *not* going to leave the making of the new world to anyone but themselves when the war is won', will need to know, when they step into Civvy Street, what snares and delusions await them, how England was misled into a new war, and how England was misgoverned in the inter-war years. That is essential; good intentions are not enough paving for Civvy Street.

The generation of the last war may thus come into its own — by telling its sons and daughters what to do and what to beware of and by saving them from another twenty years of creeping and paralytic disillusionment.[1]

Ever since we first went on two legs, mankind has been divided into those who seek to learn from yesterday's disasters, and those who cry, let to-morrow take care of itself. If we were not born with organs of procreation, the wise men would be those of the second group, but as we produce children, I think them fools. True, Horace taught men to avoid inquiring what is to be to-morrow, Cicero thought ignorance of future ills more useful than knowledge, and the wisdom that Omar found in the wine cup was, not to fret about to-morrow. But the empires these busy thinkers lived in declined: their philosophy is that of the slave; its fruits are the knout, the galley and the concentration camp. For to-morrow becomes so quickly to-day, and we live twenty-four thousand days!

I prefer a modern philosopher, by name Winston Churchill, who said, 'the use of recriminating about the past is to enforce effective action at the present', and 'we cannot say the past is past without surrendering the future'. If only his practice kept to that precept! He now says, 'the past *is* past', but his first thoughts were better ones. For our future *was* surrendered once, by saying 'the past is past', and we were only saved as a man might be who is cut down from the gallows before he chokes.

Our future can be surrendered again for that very reason. The present

[1] Already a generation is forming to which this talk of 'the twenty years' may convey little, since its members were too young to feel the sense of betrayal, frustrated idealism, and increasing despair which the Chinese, Abyssinian, Austrian and Czechoslovak episodes, to chart only the peaks, caused in their parents. One way to gain a vivid glimpse of the period is to read two plays which I mentioned in another book: Priestley, *Time and the Conways* (Heinemann, 1937), and Somerset Maugham, *For Services Rendered* (Heinemann, 1932), and to picture oneself fifteen years from now, in the place of some of the characters.

odds are, that it will be surrendered. None of the bad things that caused this war has been changed. 'The past is past,' said the culprits, and they surrendered our future.

That is the first thing to have in mind when you start off, best foot foremost, down Civvy Street. Without understanding that, you can accomplish nothing because you do not know where you are going. You may be intelligent and deep-thinking, you may be greatly resolved 'not to leave the making of the new world to anyone else', but your resolve will be vain.

You need not make a new world, anyway, but only a better one of this delightful planet, which offers everything a man could wish, and in particular of this beloved island. Your best years will be before you, if you make them so; they will be your worst if you surrender them to others. Youth, in my experience, is not a happy time. The best years are after thirty-five, when achievement begins. But the most galling bitterness is, to fight a good fight, to shape your career, your family, and your contribution to immortality, and then to find everything you have built destroyed by others.

Down Civvy Street, lie 1950 Corner and 1960 Square, and they can be blacked-out, fear-stricken, and bombed, or gay, busy, and full of light and life. The one certain way to come to another Slough of Despond, is to say 'the past is past' and to surrender the future.

So I now set out to make a map of Civvy Street, compiled from experience, for those who do not remember what befell before or know what to beware of. Will it avail?

To me and a lot of other people you appear to have a lot of what are known as the right ideas. But it is perfectly useless merely to keep pouring books out about it all, for the very reason that you yourself have stated; that a certain freedom does still exist so far as the matter which may be published in books is concerned. The result is that much 'controversial' language may be used and the effect on the public is made less as the years go by. You may have conquered the book world, but it really counts for little. A nice juicy book on sex would probably do the same. The pen is *not* mightier than the sword. The right voice in the right place might be. Why don't you make a bid to go into Parliament?

From a Gunner officer.

Keep on. You are doing more good than you think. You sometimes suggest that you feel a sense of wasted effort, in spite of the great circulation of your books. It is not true. The truth is taking root and spreading, and you have helped more than you know.

From a woman assistant in a chain store.

Who knows which of these views is right? It is irrelevant, because I believe in trying, and this is my present way of trying, and because some of those 'intelligent and deep-thinking people', when they enter Civvy Street, may prefer a fight for the future to the surrender of the future.

For now, implacably, peace — with all its horrors, if it is to be the peace of 1939 — moves towards us. When it will reach us, none can tell, as this war is being waged. I think we could have knocked out our enemy in 1941, at that cataclysmic moment when the Germans were thrown back from Moscow in the middle of an appalling winter, and in every German mind tolled, like a double knell of doom, the thoughts of 1813 and Napoleon and 1918 and the Kaiser. If I could see any way by which we now might lose, I would hedge, but, short of an invincible resolve not to win, I can see none. Somehow, somewhen, seemingly much later than need be, we shall prevail, and then will come peace. What the end of that will be, if the 'intelligent and deep-thinking boys and girls' relapse into the apathetic indifference of 1919-39 I have foreshadowed in another book.[1] The question now is, how shall we avoid that?

Our men in the Middle East are thinking and talking about their families at home, of what sort of post-war world there will be and what place they will occupy in it.

From a broadcast by Mr. R. G. Casey, British Minister of State in the Middle East.

Well, they will have one advantage above all price, if they will but use it: the experience of 1919-39. In 1919 this book could not have been written because none suspected the hidden reefs on which the peace was wrecked, or dreamed of navigation so culpable that we should run on them. They are all still there, those reefs, but now we know them, and this book is meant to show them.

It is meant to be a Baedeker of 1943-63, an itinerary of the coming twenty years drawn in the light of those other twenty years. I want to

[1] 'A Brief History of the Next War', in *All Our Tomorrows*.

take the reader step by step, through the years after this war, showing him as he goes the pitfalls into which we fell in the past. In future, far more people than before, because of bitter experience, will closely watch foreign affairs; here is a handbook for them. It is designed as a chart for constant reminder of the rocks and shoals which, between 1919 and 1939, they did not suspect; or a road-map of these coming years, with the signs now in place (DANGER — CONCEALED TURNING — LEVEL CROSSING — and the like) for lack of which the last peace was wrecked.

'Freedom, simplicity, beauty, love, and above all, right thinking.' None of these things will be waiting in Civvy Street. They do not thrive in wartime, they droop. They can be regained by people who are ready, not only to die for England, but even to live for England; by people who long for something more invigorating than a lotus-eater's paradise of 'peace and prosperity', but also something less wasteful and stupid than war and austerity, every twenty years.

The battles of this war, unhappily, are nothing. Think of the battles of the last; what do they mean to-day? The battle that means something, the battle in England, will begin when the boys and girls return to Civvy Street.

When they have won freedom, once again, from the menace of foreign conquest, they will find much less of freedom at home than there was when they went away. Will they even fight to recover what has been filched? Politicians, leader writers, professors, magnates and managing directors begin to murmur, No, and to make plans accordingly. The letter from which I have taken my text, says Yes. If they do not fight, how ludicrous were these two wars.

> For Freedom's battle, once begun,
> Bequeathed by bleeding Sire to son,
> Though baffled oft, is ever won

says Byron. A strange man; a great poet who spent his fortune, his health and his life fighting for the liberation of Greece — which is again part of our cause to-day, and how valiantly the Greeks fought! His private love affairs so shocked the England of his day (and possibly would similarly shock the England of this day, where the people have thronged to see a play about the rape of a kidnapped girl by a maniac) that it declined to bury his body in Westminster Abbey ('we know of no spectacle so ridiculous', wrote Macaulay on this subject, 'as the British public in one of its periodical fits of morality'). About a hundred years later, a Mr. Chamberlain, who compelled a small nation to capitulate to a predatory great one, was interred there. The moral of the story is that the English veneration for an alderman is eternal and unchanging. The questions it raises are: What is freedom, and what, morality? The comparison offers another illustration of the meaning of the battle of England to come and of the types of Englishmen between whom it will be fought.

Enough of freedom remains in England still for me, in beginning to tell of this battle in England, to borrow Byron's couplet:

> Without or with offence to friends or foes
> I sketch your world exactly as it goes.

CHAPTER II

'SOMETHING CONSTRUCTIVE!'

IF we are to go together through the piping times of the new peace, gentle reader, we must understand each other. We shall not, if I say, 'let's avoid this pothole or pitfall, into which we fell in 1919, or 1929, or 1939', and you reply 'Prophet of gloom, cannot you suggest something *constructive?*'

The Gadarene swine (which animals I hereby thank on behalf of generations of writers) were accosted during their headlong rush by a swineherd, who said, 'Er, wouldn't you be helping the peace effort better if you turned about and went the other way?', to which their leader, accelerating, squealed in reply, 'You are a destructive critic; can't you sometimes suggest something constructive?'

Transform the swine into chargers, put British cavalrymen on their backs, send them galloping into the Valley of Death, and you have — what? An imbecile mistake, and a court martial of the senior officers responsible? No: that would be destructive criticism and recrimination. Instead, you say 'the past is past', surrender the future, and call it Glory.

This is idiotic, and as a method, applied to the affairs of a great nation, it palls.

... I was *terrified* of war, because first of our son and secondly of every other mother's son. I believed Chamberlain and his party were doing all they could to prevent war – infuriatingly stupid of me and mentally lazy too, but few people had your opportunities of knowing and plenty of dope was given to us, *but* I swallowed the dope because I wanted to. I know that now. I would not face up to the sin and folly of 'appeasement'. I hoped and hoped and hoped it would work and at the Munich time I honestly believed that Chamberlain's effort was wonderful. I still think you are not fair to him. I said, thank God for Chamberlain. Lots of mothers and wives and sweethearts did.

From an officer's wife in India.

The most staggering proof of human gullibility I know is the fact that the declining British birth rate, which was an ominous feature of the inter-war years, rose after Munich. It shows at least that the roots of decline lie in spiritual things, not in a small purse, and that only new hope, not cash inducements, can bring revival. People who seek the future after this war should bear that pathetic example of credulity in mind. It should cause them to study public affairs more closely, to watch, instead of indiscriminately idolizing, the politicians of the moment, and to remember that the things they are told are usually untrue.

Anyhow, having said all that when everyone was applauding, now that he is dead, a broken-hearted and discredited man, when it would be so easy to heap blame on him I know I was an insignificant one of the millions who made it possible for him to carry on his appeasement policy, and I shoulder the blame with him and say 'Please, no recriminations'. Churchill and Co. said 'no recriminations' a little bit because the old school tie code says 'Don't kick a man when he is down'. But I add, please tell us what we can do *afterwards*. I am sure there will be an afterwards of construction in Britain, though things are looking black enough out here and some of us may never see England again. . . .

From the same letter.

The writer of this letter wishes to say 'the past is past' without surrendering the future. It cannot be done. I do not know the state of Mr. Chamberlain's heart when he died. Discredited he was with me, long before that, and I said so as vehemently as I could, knowing that the most constructive thing he could do for England would be, to resign. But in what sense was he 'discredited' otherwise? He was high in the government, and would be to-day if he lived. He kicked Czechoslovakia and England's honour down; but he was *up*. He benefited under the old school tie code, which is, don't kick a man when he's up. His associates are still high up.[1]

How is anything to be 'constructed' if the foundations which were rotten are not to be repaired? The same men who smugly said after Munich, that 'the humpty-dumpty Czechoslovakia, once knocked over by Hitler, could not have been set up again even after a victorious peace', now tell us we fight for Czechoslovakia, Yugoslavia, Greece, Holland, Poland, Belgium and Norway, and promise that all these nations shall be free. A jellyfish might as well hope to grow a spine, as this island to reach a secure future while such standards of loyalty and truth prevail in our public life.

The condition of mind revealed in the letter I have quoted is our most dangerous enemy. Wishing will *not* make it so; thinking might, but such people refuse to think. They ask for 'something constructive', but really mean: Tell us that all will be well if we jog along in the old rut. It will not.

Yet these people love England, and want what we all want: a better England and an enduring peace.

You are very scornful of the old and we are old, but we are desperately anxious if and when we win this war that we should put all the energy, brains and goodwill left to us to make no mistake this time about winning the peace, and we know a good many others of like

---

[1] Memories are so short and people grow so fast that I here explain briefly what the word 'Munich' signifies; people who to-day are old enough to serve, and are called on to serve as a result of the thing that was done at Munich, begin to ask vaguely, 'What *happened*, at Munich, exactly?' In September 1938 Hitler, after other experiments in aggression which were condoned by the British Government, turned on Czechoslovakia. This country was ready to fight, as was Soviet Russia, and stop the rot. The official policy of the British Government, that is, the proclaimed policy on the strength of which the electors returned it to office in 1935, was to stop aggression. Mr. Chamberlain flew three times to Germany, and after the last flight to Munich, forced the Czechoslovak Government to surrender part of its territory to Hitler, intimating that Czechoslovakia would receive no British support if it resisted. The territory involved contained the Czechoslovak defences. Without it, rump Czechoslovakia was as defenceless as we should have been after Dunkirk without the English Channel. It was obvious that, after a pause, Hitler would seize the rest. In view of the mass of information which, for five years before that time, was supplied to the British Government, it is impossible to believe (1) that Mr. Chamberlain really thought that the peace was saved by the surrender of Munich; (2) that he did not know that the ultimate outbreak of war, through that surrender, would find us in a much worse situation than if we accepted the challenge then, and (3) that he did not know that a stand then might have averted war altogether.

mind, if we could find someone to suggest a constructive policy that might help to make Britain a happier, more comfortable and less ugly place for ordinary men and women to live in.

Who wants more than that? But we cannot have it without making those changes which our past disasters command. To hope that the same men, or their kind, and the same methods will win the peace, is to yield to the delusion which caused the birth rate to rise after Munich. The beginning of 'something constructive' is to perceive that. Otherwise, you start out blindfold into Civvy Street.

Incidentally, I am not 'scornful of the old'. I have always been resolved to grow old one day, and should be foolish to abuse my to-morrow's self from respect for myself of to-day. The oldness I dislike is a habit of mind, something given to men in their cradles in England. They are born old, these people. The damage is done a few weeks after conception, when father says, 'Are you *really*, Joyce? By Jove, I must put him down for Marlchester'.

In that moment, another good man is lost, and a few months later another veteran enters the world. Hopelessly handicapped before he was born, he begins that long travail of qualifying for a pension which will take him, by way of a public school, a University, Parliament and the Cabinet, to the implacable oblivion of Westminster Abbey, where he will never be heard of again.

Parental and pre-natal influences will ruin him. As soon as his aged mind begins to work, he will comprehend that, with or without merit, he will always move up because he was put down, for Eton. In the illusion that he is having a grand life, he will be hostile to all who were not put down for Eton because he will fear that they might raise claims for unmoneyed ability. Being taught from the start that his own upward progress could only be retarded if he were to annoy those above him, he will never kick anyone who is up.

Such are the old men of all ages, who led us in the inter-war years, and still hold us in the grip of the machine they have devised, for monopolizing the machinery of government.

To attack age as counted in years, is stupid, for the spirit is a sword which stays bright, if it be tended, no matter how shabby the scabbard becomes. Lloyd George's last great speech, when he demanded the retirement of Chamberlain just before Dunkirk, was made at the age of seventy-seven; Shaw's imaginary conversation between the King, the Prime Minister and the Archbishop of Canterbury at the time of the abdication, was written at eighty; and both of these reached the highest peaks of ability and intellectual vigour.

True, we grow older as a nation, and should mend this, but an aged state of mind, not one of physical decrepitude, holds us in thrall. It is as prevalent in the young as the elderly. The three words, 'fear of change', best define it, and it is as common in the slums as in the mansions. But in the mansions it is more dangerous, for there the weal or woe of the slums is made.

Consider Richard Hillary, a handsome young man who did not fear death, yet feared 'change'! One of the few to whom so many owe so much, he rode gaily into the Battle of Britain, was badly burned in his aeroplane, as by chance was I in the last war, and has since been killed. One of our best, he wrote a good book about the war (*The Last Enemy*, Macmillan, 1942). A man of wit and valour. A man enlightened enough to make fun of the intellectual standard required of our rulers: he went to the university, he said, determined, without over-exertion, to row himself into the government of the Sudan, that country of blacks ruled by Blues, where his father spent many years.

And yet! What a gulf was fixed between this man and his fellow Englishmen! 'Apart from the scholars', he said, he and his generation at Oxford came from the 'so-called better public schools'. They were held together by 'a somewhat self-conscious satisfaction in their ability to succeed without apparent effort'. (Given the pre-natal entry for Eton, neither ability nor effort are necessary for success.) To 'the scholars' (unless these came from Eton) they scarcely spoke; 'not, I think, from plain snobbishness, but because we found we did not speak the same language'. Through force of circumstances, the scholars had to work hard and were 'conversationally uninteresting — not that, conversationally, Trinity had any great claim to distinction'.

How can a man's conversation prove uninteresting if you do not speak to him? 'The scholars' conversation', adds Hillary, 'might well have been disturbing.' His attitude, and his friends' 'might seem reprehensible and snobbish', but he believed it basically to be 'a suspicion of anything radical — any change, not a matter of class distinction'.

You perceive, gentle reader, what the awful thing was that this brave, good looking and witty young man feared, what he meant by 'anything radical, any change'. He feared and meant an unmoneyed man at a university! The secret of our decline, which we have yet to arrest, is contained in these words.

Hillary's generation 'knew that war was imminent', and were convinced they had been needlessly led into the crisis 'not by unscrupulous rogues, but worse, by the bungling of a crowd of incompetent old fools'.

Yet the thing they feared more than death was 'any change' in the exclusive order which made such bungling not so much possible as inevitable! Then what do the survivors think to-day, when the same 'crowd' rules? Is dislike of 'the scholars' still their overriding obsession? Are they still too suspicious of anything radical, any change, to save the peace? The 'crowd of incompetent old fools' were but the men who, a few years before their own time, similarly rowed their way into the seats of the mighty from the same colleges, who also did not speak to 'the scholars' because they feared 'anything radical, any change'. Is this war radical enough for them? Would the collapse of the Empire or the conquest of this island seem radical to them?

'Mr. H. G. Wells', wrote Mr. Winston Churchill once, 'was born in humble circumstances into an island community where great statesmen had broken down the barriers of privilege and caste, and where wise laws enforced by vigorous Parliaments kept open the paths that offered careers to talent.'

A strange statement! How many of the 'open paths that offer careers to talent' led men with talent, but without money and the public school and university qualifications, to office in Conservative governments between the two wars? The fingers of one hand would be enough to count them. How many such sit in Mr. Churchill's own government (apart from the Socialist hostages)?

Short of a governmental ban, which exposes you to that same ridicule which you invite the world to bestow on Hitler, you cannot keep down great writers, great artists and great composers. These are careers for which talent equips, which money will not buy, into which public schools and universities cannot force you. Men born to money seldom excel in these callings, and I think this is the reason for the English detestation of artists. True, suppression *has* been tried, by some of those wise governments: Mr. Churchill was banned in his day, a government veto was put on the broadcasting of a dinner given to Shaw on his seventieth birthday, and for many years the Lord Chamberlain suppressed one of our greatest playwright's plays, *Mrs. Warren's Profession*, in the London which now flocks to see rape on the stage. However, only imprisonment or hanging can prevent a pauper, with pen and paper, from writing his thoughts, and Mr. Churchill probably accorded too much praise to 'wise statesmen and vigorous Parliaments' when he suggested that, but for these, Mr. Wells's novels would not have been successful.

'Something constructive!' How difficult to offer anything constructive to minds so solidly cast in this mould, to minds which wish a building to be made secure while perpetuating the defects which made it collapse.

I do want to ask you if your next book could be constructive for a change. Can't you, with your enormous knowledge of the world and of the men and women in it, suggest how we may build up all our to-morrows on a happier and a better scale. I have read your last book with the greatest interest and with piercing amazement that such a state of things can exist — but it leaves you shattered, disillusioned, despondent. Is everything rotten? Surely there must be some good thing somewhere, some sound cornerstone on which we can start to build again?

From a woman of Tadworth.

For any ejaculation's sake, gentle reader, forget this interjection, 'something constructive!', before we start out in search of 1953 and 1963, unless you really wish to construct something. No button exists that you may press to ensure great riches, a pleasant surprise, and a meeting with a dark man. No magic will secure your future without any exertion on your part. If a book can help, this one shall. Reject what I suggest, if you will ('I don't think it would work' is being much used, Sir or Madam), but please do not listen to what I propose and then say 'why don't you propose something?'

For I have made all the constructive suggestions in their day. The two constructive suggestions, when I first wrote, were that we should avert this war by a military alliance with Russia and the most urgent and most substantial increase in our armaments. Either would have sufficed. *Both* were the official policy of His Majesty's Government, repeatedly proclaimed by its leaders from the front of the stage; *both* were opposed and thwarted behind the scenes. That is the darkest mystery of our times and the greatest danger to our future.

The many suggestions in this book all merge into that greater and paramount theme: *the need to find a way to prevent future governments, secure in a great majority obtained by promising the people one thing at an election, from doing another after the electors' vote has been given.*

The words in italics contain the riddle of our past and the key to our future. I beg you, gentle reader, to study them; they are few and simple and both our to-morrows depend on your understanding them.

After the last war, which left the graves of our dead 'girdling the world', to quote King George V, an Imperial War Graves Commission was set up. Its latest Report contains an eloquent sentence:

> Reports have been received of family or private graves where the first burial was the father killed in the last war and the second burial a son killed in the present war.

I suppose the same thought will leap to everybody's mind who reads this, that came to mine: who will occupy the third place in that grave?

On this, our companionable journey down the years to come, we may meet, at 1960 Corner or thereabouts, the grandson of that father, the son of that son. I hope we may find him in good heart, and going cheerfully towards a secure future; I do not mean secure in the sense of so much a week or even of eternal peace, but of release from disillusionment, cynicism, and trust betrayed, of faith in his time, his country and his leaders. I hope we may find that he has recovered the belief in honour, humanity, the dignity of man and the high motives of his native land which were taken from his father and grandfather, and that we may have helped to that.

I was born in a Liverpool slum and spent six years in Canada. Age thirty, married, factory hand in Civvy Street, and the possessor of a burning desire to help improve conditions as I know them. I have followed fairly closely the situation that you describe and have a maddening feeling of impotence when realizing how little so many of us were interested in the powers that were shaping the things to come. I believe enthusiasm would not be lacking if enough people could be led to realize the greatness that could be Britain. I know of many who would gladly do all in their power to make or help make Britain really great, in the truest sense. The spirit of adventure is not dead among the

English. Dormant it may be, but a lead in the right direction would resurrect the spirit of the pioneer.

From an R.A.F. aircraftman in India.

So, gentle and indeed beloved reader, unknown friend in many lands, sender of good wishes and tokens and gifts from near and far, sharer of the deep feeling for this country and its kindred countries overseas which caused these books to be written, here is 'something constructive'. The blackout still holds us in its thrall, and not the physical blackout of this war, but the spiritual blackout from which our leaders, who might be possessed of demons, will not release us. Here is an attempt to throw a light into the future of

This strange conglomeration of imbecility, genius, futility, achievement, paganism, Christianity, beauty and hideousness known as England. England! The very word is a poem, but how sadly and badly the metre has gone wrong and how truly the poets can rewrite it if only they wake up and apply their eyes, brains and hearts to organize success.

From a woman of Reading.

PART TWO

FREEDOM LOST!

GOD'S ENGLISHMAN
(to Adam Wakenshaw)

WHAT sort of people have we become in 1943, as we prepare again to return to Civvy Street? 'This happy breed', Shakespeare called us, in his inspired and enraptured panegyric about 'This precious stone set in the silver sea, which serves it in the office of a wall, or as a mote defensive to a house, against the envy of less happier lands'. The events of 1940, when we waited in baffled surprise for the invasion which never came, show how precisely he told the truth even in his most lyrical moments.

Because of his accurate portraiture, he must have been right, when he wrote that we were a happy breed. I think this was a happy land, when the lads and lassies danced round the maypole or gaily brought the harvest home, when the countryside was common to all and water pageants enlivened the Thames.

The words do not fit to-day. Staunch, dour, dogged, suffering much and complaining little if you like, but 'a happy breed' we are not. The machines destroyed much of the beauty of our country and our way of life, and we have not yet found the means to revive it in spite of the machines: to make the motor-tractor and the garage and the factory as much part of a pleasant English symphony as were the plough, the barn and the mill. That is the goal we should set out to reach, in Civvy Street.

We shared with the French the brunt of the first world war, and have borne ourselves the brunt of the second. Some fathers and sons already share one grave. The avid picture papers, those chattering parakeets in our dark jungle, show us other fathers, who survived that war, and their sons, serving together in this one. 'Fighting for freedom', we become daily more enchained by the bans and taboos which men who sit at desks devise because this 'work of national importance' is the industry by which they live, and they know no other way but this to feed their self importance, multiply their subordinates, puff out their authority, increase the paper mountain and prolong their sway. We move with dull resentment towards the Servile State, of forty million ciphers regimented by a million Bumbles.

And yet the stock endures. After one hundred and fifty years of relentless misgovernment and two world wars, it is as sound as ever, and this depressing picture could be changed, by the wand of patriotic revival, as quickly as the transformation scene in a pantomime.

With twenty despondent years behind them, their beliefs and ideals shattered by the contradictory words and deeds of a generation of politicians, with no light to guide them but their inherited idea that this island and the empire built by their forefathers should keep together and remain unconquered, these islanders, outarmed, outnumbered, ill-equipped, have fought a fight that should astonish the world when all the figures can be counted and all the stories told.

Backward through Norway, Belgium, France, Greece, Crete, Malaya, Burma and Libya, always backward but never beaten; manning a bleak outpost in Iceland and garrisoning tropical Madagascar; holding the seas; smashing down the enemy in the air; it is a fantastic story, for these islanders are not very many and they have borne the brunt.

Within a few months of Dunkirk, while our island still slowly repaired its defencelessness, the armies of General Wavell in Libya, and of General Platt and General Cunningham in East Africa, fighting always against vastly greater numbers, smashed the Italian empire and captured some 350,000 men. The decision to reinforce our armies out there, while this island was in such plight, appears staggering in retrospect. (Writing in an earlier book I gave too large a share, as good friends from the desert told me, to the Imperial troops, in those astonishing victories. When our own men return they will find that, since the Ministry of Information was set up, our information is meagre. Only long afterwards were the excellent official accounts published which showed the part played by men from this island.)[1]

They are tough, these islanders. Not even the age of prosperity, the last century, which has so defaced and disfigured our land and warped our physique, has broken them. I remember them in the last war, in my

[1] *Destruction of an Army*, and *The Abyssinian Campaign*, H.M. Stationery Office, 1942.

own platoon — miners, bow-legged and squat from their labour, under-sized, scarred by the coal-chips, dour and bitter in their slavery to old King Coal, men whose forefathers were driven by theft from the good land they tilled and the good air they breathed. Their spirit should have been broken. They were unbreakable — and they were volunteers.

To-day again the spirit of these men 'wrests prodigies of valour from the wronged flesh', as C. E. Montague wrote, who with relentless eyes described them: battalions of colourless, stunted, half-toothed lads from hot, humid Lancashire mills; battalions of slow, staring faces, gargoyles out of the tragical-comical-historical-pastoral edifice of modern English rural life.

Between the wars even worse things were done to these men, so that the travelled Englishman was shocked by their appearance when he came home. The young Germans were physically far better: these were the 'starving German babies' of which we heard in 1919 (and shall hear again in coming years). The babies which really starved, from mal-nutrition of the mind, were the English babies; of them, a writer in *The Times* just before this war, who took the then fashionable view that much was admirable in 'The Things' which we now ostensibly fight against, said: 'The contrast in physique between Englishmen and Germans between the ages of fifteen and twenty-five is amazingly in Germany's favour.'

Of these British heirs of the years 1919-39 (the pitfalls of which we now strive constructively to avoid as we go through the Civvy Street of to-morrow) William Shirer wrote: 'These prisoners were a sad sight. What impressed me most about them was their poor physique.'

Or go back to 1912, when an American, Price Collier, said in *England and the English* (a most sympathetic book about this country): 'Look at the people who swarm the streets to see the Lord Mayor's show and where will you see a more pitiable sight? The beef-eating, port-drinking fellows in Piccadilly, exercised, scrubbed, groomed, they are well enough to be sure; but this other side of the shield is distressing to look at. Poor, stunted, bad-complexioned, shabbily dressed, ill-featured, are these pork-eating, gin-drinking denisons of the East End. Crowds I have seen in America, in Mexico, and in most of the great cities of Europe; of India and China I know nothing. Nowhere is there such squalor, such pinching poverty, so many undersized, so many plainly and revoltingly diseased, so much human rottenness as here. This is what the climate, the food and the drink, and man's rule of the weaker to the wall, accomplish for the weak. It is one of England's ugly problems and deserves a chapter to itself.'

I could long continue with such quotations. They present a true picture, though long training for battle in this war has made an improvement in physique. These conditions were the result of bad housing, bad feeding, bad education in matters of health, and lack of opportunity for fresh air and physical exercise.

Could anything be more constructive than the resolve, at the beginning of Civvy Street, to alter this? It is unworthy of us. We stand, at this moment, on a high peak in our history. Our reputation in the world was never so great. The prodigies these men have wrested from the wronged flesh have wiped from the minds of mankind the memory of Munich and everything that went before.

Once more mankind looks to us as their hope in years to come, their only hope for a free life. French peasant women run to open the doors and let the light stream out, when they hear the R.A.F. (I remember looking down from my aeroplane on November 10th, 1918 and seeing the Belgians wave long-hidden flags to us.)

The Serbs would not fight in their mountains, but for us. The Greeks, who with hatred in their hearts watch the Germans and Italians strutting about Athens, put their hope in us. The Hollanders rejoice when a British bomb destroys their factories. The Norwegians exult when a British aeroplane attacks Gestapo headquarters in Oslo. South American Republics loosen their relations with Germany and Italy because of us. Germany's satellites, Hungary, Roumania, and Bulgaria, grope towards the safety-exit — renewed communications with us. 'England', they tell themselves, 'will listen when we say, we could not help it, Germany made us fight.'

Never was such opportunity ours. Fresh from Germany, Howard K. Smith, in *Last Train from Berlin* (Cresset Press, 1942), says: 'It is true to say that England has never been more popular on the European continent than she is to-day.'

Five years ago, at the time of Munich, it would have been true to say that England was never more unpopular. The change has been brought about, not by the politicians but by the fighting man from this island — the man, or his son, who after the last war was turned into the street when magnates closed the shipyards to eliminate competition, the man whom absentee mineowners threw out of the mines, the man who was paid thirty shillings a week for labouring from dawn to dusk on the land, the officer who was axed, the ex-officer who was forced to peddle vacuum cleaners.

Is the opportunity they have won to be wasted again? At home, in this island, everything points to this. It is 'constructive' to demand that this should not happen and to propose how it can be prevented from happening.

In *Retreat in the East* (Harrap, 1942), O. D. Gallagher says: 'I would like to say now, talking as a South African, that in the eleven theatres of war where I have worked as a reporter in the past seven years I have seen no troops show such courage of various types as the troops from Great Britain. Whether it was fighting a hopeless offensive against impossible odds of men or material; whether it was fighting a disheartening, long delaying action without prospect of a single victory; whether it was in the mad heroism of a smashing attack to force a victory; whether it was courage in private matters, not allowing themselves to be worn down by nagging anxiety about wives or sweethearts left to their own devices at home thousands of miles away — whatever courage the war called for, these men found it within themselves. Courage is their birthright. The rather uninspiring man in drab clothes who filled the cities of Great Britain, who breathed air contaminated by industry, who nervously said, 'O I beg your pardon!' if he accidentally brushed against you in a crowd, is not the man he was. He is a tough guy now . . . see the square-jawed men of the Commandos, the sunburned men of the desert, the confident men of the air forces, and the men of the sea. They are the men of Britain reborn . . . their day comes!'

A tribute true in every word save the last ten. Their homeland has *not* been reborn. The contrast between their fighting achievement in foreign fields and the spiritual anarchy in this island remains as incongruous as it was in the last war. At home, the spirit is still that of 1919-39. No single thing has changed, and Mr. Churchill, like all his predecessors, has denied the need for change by saying 'the past is past'. Their day will *not* come unless they claim their heritage and fight a battle in England for it when they return.

The shabby body they inherited, the tortured flesh, has improved through service. They can see to it that their children are not thrust back into that poor flesh-and-blood tenement which shocked visitors to this island.

The men who bore the brunt, and who will return, are their own worst enemies. For the healthier flesh is still inhabited by the downcast spirit bred in the inter-war years. The antics of our statesmen in those years, the repeated breach of promises made to our own people, have left these men bewildered and loath to think or talk about 'politics' — a word which only means the nation's housekeeping, their own welfare, and their children's future. The two new forms of adult education which the last quarter-century has brought, and which none escape, though all should now train themselves to resist them, greatly helped to produce this spiritual ailment. If *The Decline and Fall of the British Empire* should yet come to be written, broadcasting and the films would deserve a long chapter in the story of the blame. These two have become instruments of mal-education and may do much to make the returning men yield themselves slavishly to another twenty years of delusion ending in a new war. Their reform, their liberation from alien and meretricious influences should be a first objective of the battle in England.

This low state of mental health is a great menace to us in the coming journey through Civvy Street. If these men cannot nerve themselves to try and understand *why* the events of 1919-39 came about, they will surrender their own future, degrade themselves into voting-donkeys to be duped by the dangling of any carrot at election time, and plant the seeds of the war after this.

The women of England could do much to rouse their men, when they return to Civvy Street, from the obscene apathy of the inter-war years and from the passion for being gulled which caused them to put on a performance of *Idiots' Delight* at the time of Munich and even to produce more babies.

A war correspondent, Philip Jordan, writing from Tunisia about the British infantryman, said: 'He is the greatest soldier in the world. In this war I have seen, among others, British, German, Russian, American, French and Japanese at war, and I have not the slightest doubt who is the best . . . the British soldier is the best, and best of all is the often forgotten infantryman . . . a lot of them are stupid men because of the environment in which they have been brought up, and their vocabulary must be the most limited in the world . . . they are men on whom the waves of twenty years of political unrest have broken and who, even though their average standard of intelligence is a disgrace to the rich country which underfed and now conscribes them, know more than their fathers did and have the same innate shrewdness . . . the modern soldier is a citizen, not always perhaps a very bright one'.

All who have moved among our troops know the truth of this. The cult, or habit of ignorance is discreditable to men who fight so well, and will make them, when they return to Civvy Street, fair game and sitting shots for the unscrupulous, unless they can be moved to attempt the greatest adventure of all — the adventure of thinking, learning and understanding a little about their own affairs.

I do not like the nationalization of the deity and am usually repelled by talk about 'God's Englishman'; Germans speak of 'God's German', in Liberia people probably talk about God's Liberians, and we are all supposedly God's chillun anyway, Eskimos, Hottentots, and all, whether we wear shoes or not.

But at the threshold of the future, let us give the name, for once, to an Englishman, Adam Wakenshaw. A good name and a good man. Take him as typical of the man England produced in these last twenty years, the man whose spirit even that England could not kill.

After that last war, when the land for heroes was receiving its returning sons, Adam Wakenshaw ran about in Newcastle and sold newspapers. He wore no shoes, because he owned none. Later he became a miner, and when he was at work, lived with his wife and child just round Starvation Corner. When he was out of work, since he would neither draw the dole nor get into debt, he hawked things about the streets. When this war came he was called up, sent to Libya and, when his arm was blown off, continued to fire his gun at the enemy until he died. For this he was awarded the Victoria Cross. When the Lord Mayor of Newcastle went to inform his widow, she was out, being gone to the Town Hall to ask help of the authorities in obtaining shoes for her seven-year-old son.

The perfect short story! Like father, like son; England, from war to war! It even has a sequel. When the officers of Wakenshaw's regiment announced that they would supply coupons and cash for some shoes, an official, that is, a man sitting in an office, announced that this would be An Offence.

31

About 1955, we shall meet this boy in Civvy Street. He will be about twenty. I hope we shall find that he has always worn shoes, because they are necessary, in town life; that he has something in his head and never lacked something in his stomach; and that he enjoys, not so much 'security', but the feeling that his country likes him and that if he works hard he can get ahead.

God's Englishman! He is no picture-book hero, and unhappily he is better when he is told what to do than when he is left to himself; that is why he is good in war, ineffective in peace. He is the exact opposite of the independent-minded Englishman of legend.

He has now a better chance than ever before, to make his own country, that sorely misused and misled land, worthy of the things he has done for it and of the almost divine renown he has won for it again in the eyes of all other Europeans. If he relapses into indifference when he sets foot in Civvy Street and we sink back to the depths we touched between 1919 and 1939, we shall not rise again.

He can prevent that by becoming as good and combative a citizen as he is a warrior.

CHAPTER II

WHERE ENGLAND STOOD

ONE glorious afternoon in October 1940 — what a golden summer and autumn that year brought, and what a waste! — I drove out of London to rid myself for an hour of the feeling of fear and taut expectation which lay over the city, as if vultures wheeled between a clear sky and a friendly sun and ourselves.

This was at the height of the London *Blitz*, a word which the Londoners borrowed from the Germans to describe the air assault. They were apter than they knew. Indeed, they were as wrong as they habitually are in the use of foreign phrases or the description of foreign things, for they took it from *Blitzkrieg*, and this term, which means war conducted with the speed of lightning, was only apt until Dunkirk. By the autumn of 1940 the war was clearly not to be a *Blitzkrieg*, and the Germans, ruefully realizing this, were already coining a mouth-to-ear jest to mock their leaders: '*Es kommen sieben Jahre Blitzkrieg*', or 'We are going to have seven years of lightning war'. But as the word *Blitz* by itself denotes not only rapidity, but also something stabbing and striking from the sky, the Londoners chose the perfect name for their ordeal. 'The Blitz' cannot be bettered.

The great city was partly depopulated, so many people were gone. The theatres were closed, and the restaurants that remained open were half-empty at night. By day, the sirens sent flocks of frightened people running in all directions. I shall not forget the afternoon when I walked through Hyde Park and an infernal din of guns and bombs suddenly shattered the air, and, before me, a man huddling a child to his breast dashed madly across the road to take shelter beneath — a tree! Overhead, twenty-two German bombers passed, slowly, low and in formation, and the barking guns rabidly strained to reach them like a pack in full cry after a fox, but they flew on, not one within my vision was hit.

London still struggled vainly to cope with the destruction. The débris lay about for days, the streets were shut where unexploded bombs lurked. The blessed change which the spring would bring, was impossible to foresee; only increasing desolation lay ahead, you felt, and what would London look like in six months more?

And in all minds, unspoken but clear to read on every face, was the thought: as soon as dusk falls, the sirens will sound, and then we shall hear that humming sound, and the first bombs, and the guns, and then the fires will bite into the sky, and the fire-fighters will go by, with their clanging bells, through the empty streets — we must get home before it starts! So, in the afternoon, the trek would begin, the great queues would form at the bus-stops, and others at the underground stations, and soon London would be empty as the grave. Life would stop and death would take its place.

The sun shone on my native city, which thus waited for its nightly ordeal, as I drove through St. John's Wood and Golders Green and Tally-ho Corner, and Barnet, which I remembered as a place still rural, whither I went bicycling in my boyhood, to spend rapturous hours at the ancient Horse Fair. I found again that London has no end. No matter how far I went, I thought, I would only come to more houses and more shops.

Then I reached a place where the road ran between two old inns. One faced towards London, and by it I left my car. Then I walked across the road to the other. It turned its back on London, and on the further side was a little courtyard, with a great oak tree to shade it, and below that a rough bench, where the gaffers, once upon a time, would sit, with their mugs of beer, and talk, their day's work done.

None stirred. One moment, I was among the millions, the next, I was alone in the world. I sat on the bench and looked in astonishment at the scene before me. London was cut off as by a knife. Here, some super-human power might have intervened to say, 'Hold, enough: London shall go no further'. The green land fell away in quiet meadows and woods heavy in the heat, to a hazy and shimmering horizon, many miles distant. Not a bungalow, not a chimney; only, among the dark curves of a far-off copse, the hard cone of a steeple, a landmark which the men from these parts, through the centuries, took with them in their mind's eye when they marched away to follow Marlborough, or to fight Napoleon, or to be shipped, peasants driven from their acres, to Australia, or to seek freedom in Canada, or to trudge through the morass of Passchendaele. Clattering into the silence, like coins into a plate, came the immemorial sounds of the countryside: a hen clucked, a rook cawed, a dog barked.

Perfect peace. The contrast between what lay behind my back and what lay before me cut so sharply into the imagination that it hurt. I felt like a man who sat on the edge of one world and looked into another. This could not be real: it was a vision. I would have liked to get up and walk into that vision and keep on walking and never turn back.

The warmth of the old bench seeped into my legs, the gnats danced beneath the oak, and the film that town life draws over human eyes cleared from mine as they refreshed themselves in that lovely scene. Here was a little fragment of the lost poem, England, not spoiled by man, not reached by war. During a century and a half, these fragments have become fewer and fewer, and further between. Sitting by the inn, for an hour, sunk in warmth and beauty and quiet and thought, I tried to reconstruct the poem from its fragments, to recapture the metre and the lilt. . . .

A nostalgic longing for a past that you did not know, an unreasoning belief that it was better than the present, is stupid. As men grow older, they think the old times were good because they were younger then. But a careful examination of those times, and a reasoned conclusion that much *was* better then, is different.

That much was better in England, we prove by our books and advertisements and calendars. If we wish to show a foreigner what we understand by the word England, which stirs something deep within us, we seldom show him anything that England has produced since 1800 — unless it is a battleship, a tank, or an aeroplane. We take him back to what remains of 'unspoiled England' — to the old cathedrals and village churches, the manors and oast houses, the views which have not been ruined, and even (save for a few masterpieces about the genteel villadom which grew up during the last century) to the old poets and painters. We do not show him a factory, coalmine, derelict area, slum, a litter of inter-war Council homes, or a multi-storeyed apartment house. We built better then, before we somehow went wrong. England was merrier, and the breed happier.

Where *was* that wrong turning? Among many causes which combined around 1800, to produce the things we see to-day, the greatest was the Enclosure of England, which altered our whole way of life for the worse, depopulated our countryside, bred our overcrowded cities, and changed a race of people, rooted in the land, to one of narrow-visioned townsmen who have lost their native lore.

To-day, few people know what the word 'Enclosure' even signifies, though the thing it means has warped the life and fortunes of their land. The well-disciplined school-books tell them little. They are unconscious of something which affects every moment of their being.

I did not realize it until I began to travel. Then, when I returned from abroad, I was baffled by the hedged-aboutness of England. I saw nothing like it elsewhere. Each time I came back, it puzzled me more.

I could not tread my native heath, or go anywhere save by road — unless I travelled long distances to some spot yet free, like the New Forest or Dartmoor. In other countries I could strike out whither I would, right or left, when I left the town behind me. Here, barbed wire, railings, fences, hedges, walls, and trespassers-will-be-prosecuted boards met me at every turn. I lived, once, deep in the countryside, and for miles around was no field or wood which I might enter. On all sides was derelict land, but it was guarded as if it were Eden itself; I might not use it.

C

'Freedom' is a jewel of many facets, and an important facet, though not the greatest of all, is a man's freedom to roam and know his own country. That the road is so often called 'the open road' in England, is something of deep meaning. Only because all else is shut, do we need to lay stress on the openness of the road. In this matter, England is the least free country I know.

This is the fruit of Enclosure. That anything so monstrous could be done to a country, at the very time when enlightenment and the lowering of barriers were in the universal air, with so little resistance then and so little realization of it now, is bewildering. Tennyson was out of date, or dealt in dreams, when he wrote, about 1850, of 'the land that freemen till, the land that sober-suited freedom chose', for freemen no longer tilled it then. They were driven from it, by Parliament-sanctioned pillage, and those who protested were often sent to Australia as convicts!

The rich men who did this hardly foresaw that factories would rise like mushrooms from the earth, during the century that lay ahead, or that these would rapaciously demand hordes of despondent men, uprooted from their native acres, to toil in them. They acted only from immediate greed.

Yet they could not, had they known, by any one other stroke have done so much to produce that unhappy throng, crowding towards the towns, the coalmines and the areas subsequently to become derelict. They made the man of the tortured flesh and retarded mind, who nevertheless has given back to England, if England will but grasp and keep it, the leadership of the world in 1943; the man who soon will come back to the native land he may not own, unless he be rich, or till, save as a tenant.

The same kind of people govern us now that governed us then. Their own governing motive is 'deep suspicion of anything radical, any change'. Yet they brought about the most radical change in our history and the most disastrous in its effects; the face of England bears the scars, the breed the wound.

The pretext, 150 years ago, was that Enclosure would redeem the English countryside from decay. The result, in 1939, was described by a British Minister of Agriculture. During a 200-mile tour of derelict farms, which left him 'amazed' (for, although his job was to know about the land, he did not know 'that such a thing could happen in England to-day'), he saw hundreds of acres of one-time fat meadows and well filled barley fields choked with nettles and thorn bushes; he was told of fifteen thousand derelict acres in Suffolk alone; he saw the site of 'a pleasant seven-bedroom mansion, where the owner once lived, but which has now disappeared, nobody quite knows how or where. People have taken it away piecemeal in motor cars, hand carts and perambulators'. On the other hand, he saw, during that tour, many more thousands of enwalled acres, empty parklands, reserved for the use of owners often absent and seldom active, where once were busy cottagers and thriving smallholders.

To-day people become a little interested in their country and eager to know what has happened to it. They should study the story of Enclosure. When the whole trend of Europe and of the young American Republic was to liberate the masses of mankind from serfdom, when this universal impulse even brought about Revolution in France, a revolution in the opposite direction was accomplished in this country with the connivance of Parliament. It did not greatly stir the surface of the times, and has left hardly a ripple on the conscious mind of Britain!

At the very moment when enlightenment was dawning, this kind of argument was used to support the theft of the land: 'The use of common land by labourers operates upon the mind as a sort of independence ... when the commons are enclosed, the labourers will work every day in the year, their children will be put out to work early, and that subordination of the lower ranks of society which in the present times is so much wanted, would be thereby considerably secured.'

More than half the cultivated land of England, before Enclosure, was farmed on the common-field system, and the landless farm labourer was hardly known in the villages of England. Compare what these men, whose land was to be taken from them, themselves thought about it, and the picture they painted of the future, with the arguments advanced in excuse of it and with the actual results:

The Petitioners beg leave to represent to the House of Commons that a more ruinous Effect of this Inclosure will be the almost total Depopulation of their Town, now filled with bold and hardy Husbandmen, from among whom, and the Inhabitants of other open Parishes, the Nation has hitherto derived its greatest Strength and Glory, in the Supply of its Fleets and Armies, and driving them, from Necessity and Want of Employ, in vast crowds, into manufacturing Towns, where the very Nature of their Employment, over the Loom or the Forge, soon may waste their Strength, and consequently debilitate that great Principle of Obedience to the Laws of God and their Country, which forms the Character of the simple and artless Villagers, more equally distributed through the Open Countries, and on which so much depends the good Order and Government of this State.

From a petition against enclosure by the inhabitants of a Northamptonshire village, 1797.

A gruesome glimpse of the century and a half that lay ahead!

About a fifth of the total acreage of England was enclosed between 1760 and 1840, and the old village community of freemen (freeholders, tenant farmers, cottagers and squatters) all sharing rights to common land, which went back to our earliest history in this island and which neither Romans nor Normans destroyed, was broken up. Until that time, any man might hope, by his own labour, to acquire property and rise in his village. From that time, we inherit the most unhappy of beings, the landless farm labourer.

What *was* Enclosure? Often it was simply a petition to Parliament bearing the signature of one big landowner for authority to put a fence round some piece of land until then shared by all. For long, he was not obliged even to inform his neighbours of their impending eviction!

Thus was Westcote in Buckinghamshire, enclosed in 1765 on petition of the most noble George, Duke of Marlborough; Waltham, Croxton and Braunston, in all five thousand six hundred acres, in Leicestershire, by the Duke of Rutland and the local parson in 1766; and hundreds more. The smallholder's only hope of succour was to reach and move the heart of a Parliament packed with great landowners and as distant from and daunting to himself as the Court of the Last Judgment.

In Parliament these petitions were laid before Committees of Members from the districts where Enclosure was proposed — the cronies of the petitioner! Often, petitions affecting the enclosure of thousands of acres, and the fate of hundreds of freemen, were rushed through in a week or two. Parliament passed an Act giving the Duke of Leeds power to work mines and get minerals, from the land thus to be confiscated; how ignoble, in view of that beginning, was the indignant debate in the House of Lords in May 1938, when the proposal was made to reconvey to public owner-ship the coal that lies beneath our once fair countryside. In that debate, a noble Marquess, complaining of 'disadvantages in the democratic principle, one of which is apparent now', fervently upheld 'the sanctity of private property'!

'Sanctity', the dictionary says, means 'purity, inviolability, holiness, sacredness, solemnity.'

Thus did dukes and squires put fences round commons or waste land, a vast expanse containing villages and cottages and land formerly shared by all. What remains of the English village of old shows that it was the flourishing home of a thriving and hopeful community. When the land was enclosed, 'consent' was only needed from proprietors! The cottagers and squatters who did not *own*, but yet *enjoyed* freemen's rights to the land from days before the Druids, were overridden roughshod and evicted.

Indeed, this was, a hundred years before its time, the Soviet system of confiscation, used by big landowners (instead of officials calling themselves 'the State') against the 'freemen who tilled the soil'.

It was not infrequent to decide upon the merits of a Bill which would affect the property and interests of persons inhabiting a district of several miles in extent, in less time than it takes me to determine upon the propriety of issuing an order for a few pounds by which no man's property could be injured.

Lord Thurlow, Lord Chancellor of England, in 1781.

The manner in which a large part of England was taken from the many and enclosed by the few was simple and is staggering to look back on. Recent history contains nothing to compare with it. A petition was 'accepted'; that is, the petitioner's friends in Parliament passed it for him. Then, Commissioners, who were appointed by the Enclosers even before they presented their petition to Parliament and were often the lord of the manor's own bailiffs, arrived to put a fence round that 'certain proportion of the land which has been assigned to the lord of the manor in virtue of his rights and the owner of the tithes'. The power of the Commissioners was absolute. This happened in the England in which Pitt was Prime Minister, who declared 'it is the boast of the law of England that it affords equal security and protection to the high and low, the rich and poor'.

Thus were men who, like their forefathers, for a thousand years, enjoyed the right to till and use the land, driven overnight from it by Act of Parliament. Very rarely, and then usually by chance, a Member tried to check the worst abuses. For instance, Sir William Meredith in 1772 proposed that the assent of a Committee of the whole House should be made necessary before a clause was put in any Bill to make 'an offence' punishable by death: he accidentally overheard the lord of the manor and his friends, in a Committee room of the House, unanimously agree to insert in the Bill, which would make law of their own pet petition, a clause making opposition to it a capital offence!

The real motive behind the Enclosure Acts (as distinct from the professed ones of patriotic concern for the future of English agriculture and the welfare of the countryfolk) is vividly revealed in the *Carlisle Papers*.

This publication contains the letters of one George Selwyn, M.P. He was Chairman of the House of Commons Committee which considered, and reported in favour of a petition for the Enclosure of King's Sedgmoor, in Somerset, in 1775. This land, said the selfless petitioners, was of little value in its then state, but could be greatly improved by enclosure and drainage. A Bill was accordingly prepared by a Mr. St. John, brother to that Lord Bolingbroke who coveted the land in question, and it was approved by the Committee of which Mr. Selwyn was chairman.

The truth of the transaction is exposed in Selwyn's public letter to Carlisle: 'Bully has a scheme of enclosure which, if it succeeds, I am told will free him from all his difficulties ... I cannot help wishing to see him once more on his legs.' And again: 'Stavordale is also deeply engaged in this Sedgmoor bill, and it is supposed that he or Lord Ilchester, which you please, will get two thousand pounds a year by it. He will get more, or save more at least, by going away and leaving the moor in my hands, for he told me himself the other night that this last trip to town has cost him four thousand pounds.'

Faro was played for high stakes in those days. The letter shows clearly that Selwyn was as little interested in the salvation of Sedgmoor by drainage, as he was in ploughing up the moon. He meant to help his friends, who would help him if he needed help, or were in debt to other friends; for Bully was in financial trouble and Stavordale owed money to Fox, who owed money to Carlisle.

Thus were the common lands of England shared out round the gaming tables of Piccadilly and St. James's. Thus were the high walls and tall fences built, which meet the wayfarer's eye when he leaves the English village in search of the English countryside to-day. The Parliament was one of landlords; its permanent officials pocketed about £120,000 in fees in fourteen years for assisting the Enclosure Bills through; where, at Westminster, was the English freeman to find a friendly ear? 'The sacred rights of property' counted for nothing when the property was the poor man's mite. Said the despoiled English countryman: 'Parliament may be tender of property; all I know is, I had a cow and an Act of Parliament has taken it from me.'

The 'freeman who tilled the soil', the man who inherited from immemorial times the right, if he could buy, build or rent a cottage, to enjoy the use of commonly-held land, the small farmer, cottager and squatter with a title, unwritten but rooted in antiquity, to a share in his native soil: all these were left the choice between becoming hired farm labourers, seeking work in the towns, or emigrating.

Go to an alehouse kitchen of an old enclosed country, and there you will see the origin of poverty and poor rates. For whom are they to be sober? For whom are they to save? For the parish? If I am diligent, shall I have leave to build a cottage? If I am sober, shall I have land for a cow? If I am frugal, shall I have half an acre for potatoes? You offer no motives; you have nothing but a parish officer and a workhouse! Bring me another pot![1]

To-day, we hear that State doles 'will destroy the spirit of adventure'. It was destroyed then, when 'cottages were pulled down as if by an invader's hand, and families that had lived for centuries on the land were driven out. Ancient possessions and ancient families were swept away'.

But this first consequence was not the worst consequence. The ultimate result was still more disastrous. Enclosure killed the spirit of a race. The petitions against it which are buried in the *Journals* of the House of Commons are the last voice of village independence. The unknown commoners who braved all threats and sent their vain protests to the House of Commons that obeyed their lords, were the last of the English peasants. Such as they were in Gray's mind when he wrote of 'some village Hampden that with dauntless breast the little tyrant of his fields withstood'.

Thus was merry England killed and joyless England born. How sardonic a jest that the House called 'of Commons' should have destroyed the English commons! And how mocking a paradox that John Yeoman,

---

[1] *The Annals of Agriculture*, ed. Arthur Young, London, 1784-1815, vol. xxxvi, p. 508.

when he went to fight 'for freedom' against Napoleon, should already
have lost the second cornerstone of freedom: the right to enjoy his native
land. (Of the first cornerstone we will talk in the next chapter, gentle
reader.)

Alone among the men he fought with or against, he was deprived of
that. The French and the Germans both have it to this day and are never
likely to lose it. (The Germans under Hitler passed an Act making farm-
holdings hereditary and inalienable and no future German government,
unless it be one under alien influence, is likely to tamper with this.)

Thus John Yeoman was, in this respect, the least free of all the men who
fought Napoleon. (In 1854 he was sped to the far Crimea with talk of
giving back his commons: 'Commons for Heroes!' When he returned,
no more was heard of that. By the time John Yeoman, clerk, mechanic,
unemployed miner, came to fight for freedom in 1914 and 1939, he no
longer remembered that he ever was a yeoman, and this kernel of freedom
was not even mentioned among 'The Things' he fought for.)

Thus the year after Waterloo saw bread riots and the firing of ricks and
barns. The English began to emigrate, and the enclosing squires began,
in Parliament, to pass laws against poaching. The common lands became
the stupendous game preserve which they now are. About the time John
Yeoman was told that he would be enslaved if Napoleon landed in England, Parliament fixed the penalties for poaching at hard labour, flogging,
or transportation. In the year following Waterloo, when freedom was
made safe for a century, a Bill went through Parliament, without debate,
which imposed the maximum penalty of transportation for seven years
on any person found unarmed but with a net for poaching in enclosed
land; and in some of the subsequent years one in seven of all criminal
convictions in England were convictions under these Game Laws!

In my council-school days, in London, I was mistaught that Australia
was first colonized by British 'convicts', and consequently regarded the
first Australians I met, in France, with awe and respect. So subtle is the
poison which still runs in our veins from those times. For what was the
crime for which many of those men who were shipped oversea were
convicted? That they sought to defend their ancestral right to live, work
and eat! By no twisting of the human code did they do wrong. They
were of our best.

Because that spirit lives on in their descendants of to-day, these are freer in their being and bearing than we. Because of that inherited passion for freedom, they spring so quickly to our side when we are in danger. They still are freemen of the land; they may go or farm where they will. They think they inherit this from us and love us for it. They do not realize that we have lost something so precious, or that this loss causes the caged, restrained, inhibited manner which the Englishman has come to wear.

Just after Waterloo, thousands of these dispossessed husbandmen were sent to Australia, many of them boys under eighteen, and some of these for life. Who sent them? The enclosing squires, jealous of their pheasants, were also magistrates and sentenced them. Of these benches Lord Brougham said, 'There is not a worse constituted tribunal on the face of the earth, even that of the Turkish Cadi'. Any who used arms in their defence, when attacked by gamekeepers, were hanged.

Ah, that was an England, when, midway between Trafalgar and Waterloo, Romilly carried a Bill through the Commons to abolish the death penalty for the theft of five shillings — and in the House of Lords the Archbishop of Canterbury and six other bishops helped to reject it! But no doubt that archbishop was strong on the subject of Sabbath observance. (The Son of Man, should He come to earth again, would often fail to recognize his disciples.)

In 1943 we fight again 'for freedom'. England is a great enclosed park sprinkled with suburbs — for the villages, bereft of their 'bold and hardy husbandmen', have become small samples of the big towns. All the other peoples who fight with us have the thought of their land, their native acres, at the core of their motives, and all will return there. John Yeoman alone will not.

In 1942 an all-wise government admonished us to 'spend our holidays at home', and since we might go hardly anywhere else, the advice was easy to follow. For many people this meant confinement to the kitchen parlour, for if they might not go to Blackpool or Southend, only the street, the pub, or the berailinged local park remained. The countryside, even if they could reach it, was closed, save for our dear open road.

The patriotic stop-at-homes, however, were promised as reward, 'ample facilities for out-door recreation'. But that very thing has been lacking since Enclosure. So the Minister of Agriculture 'appealed' to landowners, and particularly to 'owners of mountains and moorlands', to

43

'permit reasonable access to their property'. The modest man's life, limb, property and family were at the unrestricted disposal of the Government. Only this humble request could be made to the present-day successors of the squires who enclosed. Whether any Englishman trod a mountain or moor as a result, we may safely doubt.

For fifty years, in this free country, a Bill to gain for the descendants of John Yeoman 'access' to his native mountains was regularly thrown out by Parliament. In 1939 it was suddenly allowed to become law — but in such a form that in practice nothing has been changed; and during the war enclosure and restriction have been carried even further.

The emperors of Austria were also archdukes and counts of so much else that their titles filled a page. The grandees of Spain decked themselves in flowery chains of titles. Oriental potentates call themselves the Son of God, Daughter of the Moon, Lord of this, that and the other. I know no title so grandiloquent and arrogant as, 'Owner of Mountains and Moorlands'.

In this country you may ask an ordinary looking man his calling, and he may reply, 'Oh, I own mountains and moorlands'. And if you then say, 'Sir, what of that humble, forlorn, impoverished and sickly looking fellow over there? Would you permit him briefly to use one of your mountains — not a big one, of course, but one of your smaller and partly worn mountains?' he will answer, 'Not on your life, Sir. I am putting a railing round it'.

When the South Africans may not climb Table Mountain, or the Australians be forbidden to use Sydney Beaches, they may realize how confined we have become since Enclosure. Consider this picture of conditions near two of our greatest cities, from an article on the Access to Mountains Bill by Professor Joad:

A person visiting the Central Station at Manchester on a sunny Sunday morning might well suppose that the city was in fear of invasion, and that an exodus of refugees was in progress. He would be wrong. Looking closely, he would see that all the supposed refugees were reasonably young and vigorous; in fact, they were not refugees at all, but only ramblers escaping from Manchester. From 7.30 onwards the station is alive with them. Rucksacks are piled on the platforms; hobnails clink on the stone; sandwiches bulge from the pockets of tweed coats. By half-past nine the station is empty; the trains have taken them away to Edale and Chinley for a day on the Derbyshire moors. From each of the great northern towns there is a similar exodus. It is, I submit, impossible not to regard this exodus with approval. Taking them by and large, our northern industrial cities are the ugliest agglomerations of brick and mortar with which mankind has ever defaced the surface of the earth, fitting monuments to the mean spirit of trivial profit-making which engendered them. For a hundred years men and women stayed in these places because they must, worked in them, played in them, and on Sundays, when piety forbade games, lounged in their streets and waited for the pubs to open. To-day hiking has replaced beer as the shortest cut out of Manchester.

Between Manchester and Sheffield there are some 215 square miles of moorland. A great belt of spacious country, empty save for a few moorland villages. Some parts, as where Kinderscout raises its ugly head some two thousand feet above sea level, are grim and bleak: others are a spread of bracken and purple heather cleft by deep valleys with fast-running streams. This country is in the highest degree exhilarating; it tones up both spirit and body and, appropriately, it lies in the heart of the most thickly populated area in England — stretching on the east to the gates of Sheffield and the urban agglomerations which sprawl over the south of Yorkshire, on the west almost to Manchester and the teeming populations of the cotton towns. It would be difficult to imagine a more admirable playground for these close-penned city folk, as invigorating as their towns are depressing, as wide as they are cramped, as beautiful as they are ugly.

Yet of the total area all but 1,212 acres is closed to the public; 109,000 acres are in private ownership and sacred to the preservation of grouse; 39,000 acres are owned by local authorities some of whom mysteriously debar the citizens whom they are supposed to represent, from access to the land of which, as citizens, they are owners. Over all this stretch of country the hand of the keeper lies heavy. Walkers are frowned at by notice boards and everywhere trespassers will be prosecuted. On Sundays hundreds of walkers are carefully shepherded along the public footpaths. In the whole district there are only twelve of these which are over two miles in length, and on fine Sundays you will see a continuous file of walkers following one behind the other for all the world as if they were a girls' school taking the air in 'crocodile'.

What a picture! I know no country which can offer one distantly comparable with it.

Enclosure has produced results worse even than those which the 'bold and hardy husbandmen' foretold. Nowadays this dog-in-the-manger disease is not confined to the group with which it began. It has spread through the whole community. Every little local Bumble's ambition is to put a railing round something; it makes him feel important, and he encloses the pieces of greensward, the public parks, which alone remain to the English from their great heritage of commonly-shared land. Hence our fortified parks, an English monopoly; anywhere else it would be thought mad to put a hideous iron fence round that which is meant for all. Consider this ludicrous picture from the daily press:

> Though railings surrounding Ashton Park, Preston, have been removed for war purposes, the gates are locked at night. Boys collect at closing time and tell the park keeper not to lock himself in. But it is no joke. It is a formality that must be carried out so that the town does not lose its rights of closure when the park is enclosed again.

'The town' must not lose 'its rights'! What is the town but the towns-people? Who but they have rights in the park, the last place they may go to? Why *must* it be enclosed?

But the thing goes even further. It leads to the enclosure of the little squares in which London abounds, places which might relieve much of the surrounding ugliness. They, too, were imprisoned, and behind a cur-tained window a watchman, the representative of the 'Committee of Management', kept jealous watch to see that no child played on the grass or puppy on the paths.

Came the war, and the railings were removed. Now the Committees, resolved to have these monstrosities restored immediately peace breaks out, complain in the newspapers of the affront done to those who 'pay for the upkeep' (a shilling a week from each householder) by the sight of citizens using the paths or sitting on the seats in a warm noonday hour.

The mania has infected the very descendants of those who were driven from the land. The Englishman's ambition seemingly is to acquire a little house and garden and enrail it. The railing keeps nothing out and nothing in. The dog jumps over or squeezes through; the burglar steps across. But the sight of his railing apparently makes the Englishman feel, in a small way, like those who benefited from the great Enclosures, like a little lord of the manor. 'Freedom' is come to mean, to him, the liberty to imprison himself.

Enclosure, I wager, is chiefly to blame for the way the Englishman has enclosed his spirit. He moves through the old books and tales as a man, forthright, plain-speaking, independent, intolerant of petty oppression. Nowadays he encloses himself; he immures his spirit; his instinct is to repress his emotions and his thoughts; he hedges. And 'to hedge' is the precisely apt word. He is enclosed.[1]

Such are the effects of Enclosure, and they grow ever worse. The few who profited claim that all has been for the best. The Marquess of Salisbury, in propounding *Post-War Conservative Policy*, affectionately quotes another peer, Lord Stamp, as 'showing' that 'the average man at the end of the nineteenth century had become four times as well off as his predecessor at the beginning, and the same development has continued into the twentieth century, including the decade before the present war'.

Medical records, certainly, show that we are far healthier than we were. But the argument collapses when the infallible test is applied. We have ceased to multiply. Englishmen no longer wish, as their forefathers wished, to bring many children into a world in which they will be four times as well off. For many years, even after Enclosure, we increased exceedingly. Belief in the world, and faith in the future, were hardy plants, not easily discouraged. Now, they droop.

Does any sign offer that, after this new world war for freedom, a spirit of freedom will prevail; that the land will be liberated, at least that part which once was commonly shared; that an Englishman will be free to climb a mountain? For Enclosure only works one way. The small man's fence will not avail him if the squires wish to hunt across his acre. Remember the Devonshire man who twice asked the fox hunters to keep off his poultry farm, where he sought to make a living. 'Silly, futile and

[1] An American, Claude C. Washburn, wrote in *Pages from the Book of Paris* (Constable, 1910): 'In France the individual is the unit; but in England the unit is the whole. The individual rights of which the Englishman is so proud are only material rights that affect his bodily comfort; of genuine personal liberty he has no conception. He may walk the streets in almost complete safety from physical attack; but he has thrust upon him from childhood the cold formalism of an established religion. The precincts of his property are rigorously protected against aggression; but socially he himself is born into as iron-clad a system of slavery as has ever existed. Rich or poor, of high rank or low, he is classified at birth as a member of a caste in which not the individual but the type is the reality ... Suggest to an Englishman an act that would be an infringement, however slight, on a class to which he does not belong; he will not reply, "I cannot do that because ...", but simply, "That is not done". The system is perfect. Nor does the Englishman want it changed. I can find no analogy for the willing pride with which he accepts his bondage. Imagine all the negroes of the South rising as one man at the time of the emancipation, crying "We will not be free", and turning in anger on President Lincoln, and you have but a feeble likeness to the attitude of the English towards their would-be liberators; for the negroes were only stupid children, while the English are a race of men, enlightened, "progressive", almost civilized indeed, one would say. . . .'

unreasonable', his request was called, and when he shot a hound he was prosecuted and heavily fined.

To-day, under the threat of starvation, the English countryside thrives again within its Enclosure. No scrap of land that will grow food must be wasted, we are told.

The fox destroys much food. It could be quickly exterminated. Hunting has never exterminated the fox. It is not meant to. It is the pastime of the wealthy and the foxes are jealously preserved for it. The Minister of Agriculture was asked 'whether he was satisfied that foxes were being as rapidly and economically exterminated by foxhunting as they could be by any other method; and, if not, whether he would instruct masters of foxhounds that they must either show better results or cease to operate during war time?'

Listen to the reply: 'The answer to the first part of the question is, Yes; the second part therefore does not arise.'

The history of Enclosure shows that the English squires were the first Bolshevists. They were Reds. They seized the land of others. It was the most galling and debilitating thing ever done to the English spirit. It is vain to think of 'constructing' a better England after this war unless the causes of our present plight are first realized. This is foremost among the things that should be changed.

Of our two great parties, the Labour Party behaves towards this paramount question as a tame elephant might behave to a wild tiger. The other Party, which alone is politically vigorous, is directly descended from the enclosing squires, with their faro debts, and has not changed its mind since 1800.

The Marquess of Salisbury's *Post-War Conservative Policy* puts its heaviest veto on 'the nationalization of agriculture'. Well, this Party took the land which was not theirs. That part of England, if they could ever look beyond class, they would liberate; they would still hold enough, the bulk. That would not be 'nationalization' but restitution and the amendment of a criminal misdeed.

The Minister of Agriculture grew quite heated when he was urged to check staghunting in war time.

It is a monstrous paradox. If freedom exists at all in the minds of men, this country is the home of it, and men who love it are unitedly on our side to-day, because they know they cannot win or regain it, save with us and through us. When we win, they will get *this* freedom. The bold and hardy husbandman of France will blithly work on his plot, liberated from the watch of alien masters. Even our enemy, the bold and hardy husbandman of Germany, rid of the interference of Nazi officials, will gladly till his freeman's land again. The bold and hardy husbandmen of Serbia, Holland, Czechoslovakia, Belgium, Greece, Norway, Poland, will re-enter into the enjoyment of their fields. We alone are shorn of *this*, the half of freedom.[1]

. . . The sun stepped down, and the shadows crept out from the oak. The premonitory hush of evening gathered over the peaceful scene. In the inn behind me, mugs and glasses clattered, as all was made ready for the labourers who would come when their work was done.

I needed to go, because soon dusk would fall, and the blackout, and the sirens, and the noise in the air would follow, and I must be back before then. First, I went for a moment into the little church hard by. The most utter peace I ever knew filled its cool nave. I looked at the memorial to the dead of the last war; beneath it lay a few fading flowers. I read the long list of vicars stretching back far to Thomas de This and Wilfrid de That in Norman times. Then I noticed that one part of the old church was newly restored, and different from the rest. I found a tablet which told that in the last war a Zeppelin bomb fell on this very spot and brought down part of the ancient tower.

Even here! Even in this peace! These two wars, I thought, would follow you into the deepest glade of the darkest forest; you would find an unexploded bomb there, or a crater.

I took the car and drove back, still musing on the enchanted scene I thus discovered. As I came into the town the crowded buses were hurrying to their suburban destinations, the people streaming into the underground stations, or going, with their bundles, to some vault or cellar. Emptier and emptier were the streets. With the thickening dusk, the traffic lights took on a jewel-like brilliance. I reached Portland Place and, while I waited for the red light to change, the sirens called. I put the car away, and as I walked home the first bombs fell.

Another day was over, and a daylight dream of England.

[1] An excellent account of Enclosure is given in J. L. and Barbara Hammond, *The Village Labourer* (Longmans, Green & Co., 1911), and I am indebted to this book for much valuable information.

WHERE ENGLAND STANDS

WHERE does England stand, within its still unbroken citadel, as it approaches peace and the greatest opportunity in its history? The long siege has been withstood; through the sally-ports surge those men, of whom the Duke of Wellington said, 'Yes Sir, they may be small, but none others fight so well'; they converge doggedly upon an enemy whose dream of world conquest fades; in the streets where we Mafficked and Municked, the crowds will sing and dance and cheer again.

Shall the colours peel from that picture again, as we walk down Civvy Street? Shall we find it, marked '2s. 6d.', in a tarnished gilt frame in some dusty junk shop at 1960 Corner, as we go through the years?

Just before the German invasion of France, I went to the Imperial War Museum. Here was a Haunted House, a place where the ghosts of a million men and countless million hopes walked. Banished to oblivion in Lambeth, it was an eerie place, the shabby sepulchre of an idealistic generation. Here, in pictures that attracted great crowds in 1919, were 'the boys' going over the top on the Somme or floundering in the mud at Ypres, the Royal Flying Corps pilots setting out in Morane Parasols, the old uniforms and equipment — things as dead and meaningless as battle-axes and arquebuses.

To-day again this little island has saved the way of life on this planet as we know it. Our world may be small; if you consider the universe and the planets as a limitless sea with a few fish in it, it is indeed a very small plaice. But it is important for us. This island vanquished, and neither the decapitated empire nor America would have escaped conquest. That would have meant a new order in this world and by no stretch of imagination which we can reach, a better one, whatever our present lot.

Where do we stand now, who live in this insignificant and supremely important fragment of earth, the British Island? 'The boys', when they come back, may see in some little local picture theatre, if it then still goes the rounds, a film *Mrs. Miniver*, which will show them their island during the siege. It was made far away and the players do not speak the

English of this land. Hollywood, which showed Vienna during the last impoverished years of its decline as a place of gay uniforms, countesses, wine, song and lilac, now shows them England besieged: a place where well-poised feudal squires and squiresses emerge from their Enclosures to deal firmly, tactfully and kindly with the Blitz and with a chorus of half-witted yokels.

How sick am I of this picture! While our islanders fought all over the globe, the Ministry of Information produced in their honour a series of short films called *Into Battle*. The first was about friendly aliens in a non-combatant unit! Among some fine types of men in it, I recognized one who followed, in a certain foreign city, the second oldest calling in the world. By no standard, can such a picture deserve pride of place in this island.

The means of implanting the suggestion that we are second-rate are now so great, and the films and radio so subtly spread it, that the native character, already sorely injured by Enclosure, may be further undermined. Two American soldiers once asked the Brains Trust what thing they might take back with them to America, which could count as 'typically English'. The answers were: 'A bottle of English beer'; 'Some crumpets'; 'Mr. Winston Churchill, but we can't spare him'; and, 'the English word, "quite".'! Such was the distillation of English culture.

A piece of an English railing might be an answer. Only one real answer exists, and all those lips should promptly have given it: a set of Shakespeare. Because Shakespeare is the greatest writer living or dead, and you might, in a book, describe everything England means to us, and to the world, in this present climacteric of the world's history, by borrowing from his words.

It is sinister that this is the *only* answer we can make. A Frenchman, a German, a Hollander, a Norwegian could offer many answers even to-day. We have lost so much that we have nothing else that is typically English. True, by diving into the past we might find something: a Sheraton chair or a Chippendale cabinet, a picture by Constable or Crome, pewter, homespun. But to-day? A piece of Wedgwood, perhaps, or a bulldog? Certainly not a film about England during the siege; that, we import! We cannot export an enclosed estate or a derelict area. No, the only answer is Shakespeare, who lives to-day as he lived centuries ago.

We might offer the world the *voice* of England, but it is silent. This voice we hear is not the voice of those who toil, or fight, or serve, and long to better our island lot.

Since this great new thing, broadcasting, was made the monopoly of the politicians of the day — after the war, a Free English broadcasting station should be set up somewhere abroad — only the mealy-mouthed and the tongue-in-cheeked may enter there. That hour in the week, after the Sunday evening news, when more people than at any other time settle themselves to listen, was once filled with broadcasts that sought to invigorate and stimulate, to contribute to an improvement in our affairs. Now we rarely hear any but those who know how to speak long and say little, to embroider verbiage with flowery compliments to men in office; it is like the uttermost hell, where sinners are condemned to listen for all eternity to interminable aldermen.

Compensation for the lack of anything to listen to, at this upward end of the broadcasting scale, was offered when 1943 began. We were permitted by the grace of the song pluggers to hear, at its lower extremity, the sound of gastric wind being expelled from the human body, or a lifelike imitation.

The song (of whom or what was it typical?), was broadcast often enough for listeners to accustom themselves to this new level of taste and public enlightenment. Then second thoughts seemingly set in at broadcasting headquarters, for 'Right in der Fuehrer's face' was broadcast with silent gaps in the places which this sound previously occupied. The Press, which overlooks nothing of importance, indignantly told its readers that the B.B.C. was now refusing 'to blow Hitler raspberries'. Came the dawn, and another day in the life of England. I love to picture the ladies and gentlemen of the Board of Governors banning questions about Enclosure, for instance, while raspberries are blown across the overladen air.

With all this sealing of lips, save for the purpose of blowing raspberries, the spirit of England at home is astonishingly different from that which our fighting men show in action and which the world now salutes again. Outside the fortress, are staunchness, dogged endurance, valour and resolve; within, are repression, self-seeking, babel and trivial talk. The broadcasting monopoly, which is enormously wealthy, entrenched in privilege, and commands the entire talent of the country, should be the spokesman of the nation, because it speaks to the whole world. How can we give of our best, from within the island fortress, save through it?

Once the Brains Trust was asked, 'If you had six months to live, how would you spend them?' One Brain said he would gather round him choice wines and food and fill himself with them. Another said he would spend the time 'in a mortal funk'. This at a time when our men, on land, on all the seas and in the air, face death as their daily lot!

The Brains Trust itself grew restive in the shackles that were put on it and some of its members clamoured for the raising and widening of the debate. At that, another member complained that 'the highbrows' were trying to ruin the Brains Trust, that we were fighting, after all, for 'lowbrows' and democracy, and that the Brains Trust must be kept 'lowbrow'. This diverting argument was most typical of our island to-day. The brain lives behind the brow, and lowness of brow was a chief characteristic of the first men who went on two legs. It may be studied in any monkey house. I love to picture the perfect Brains Trust, completely browless and simian, discussing questions of freedom, honour, culture, art, and civilization.

The contrast between the British achievement in the world, during the last three years, and the spirit of the home island, as it is evinced in the only way it can express itself, through our broadcasting, is staggering in its incongruity. It shows that the worthiest battle remains to be fought when this battle is done: the battle for the spirit of England.

The beginning and end of that battle is, Freedom. A battle for anything else, in England, would be worthless. But a man must understand what he strives for. How would a simple man define Freedom, the thing we have not?

Freedom is a thing of innumerable facets, but split it, and it has but two halves. The first is the half we have lost, the freedom to enjoy and use a part of our native land. The second half is the greater half, because the first half rests on it.

It is, freedom from wrongful arrest and wrongful imprisonment.

Given these two things, a man is as free as he need wish to be on this planet; the rest is for him to make. Freedom of speech, assembly, religion, contract, and the rest, are smaller facets. These are the two halves of the jewel.

The first half was taken from us through Enclosure. The second half, the only basis on which freedom can be built, we kept through thick and thin. Now it has been taken from us, with the connivance of the same Commons which enclosed the free lands, by men who say they will give it back when the war is over.

We should not rest until that first half of the jewel is taken from the safe and restored to us, and then we should set out in search of the second half.

The danger is, that few realize the worth of this priceless thing. Everywhere I went before this war, I found that, while the English reputation sank like a declining sun, from China to Abyssinia, from Austria to Czechoslovakia, this thing still gave the Englishman a feeling of superiority over others. They shared that feeling. Here, they thought, walks a free man.

In no other country I knew obtained, in our full measure, the law that no man might be arrested and held without immediate publication of the charge against him, or imprisoned without open trial. In France, Yugoslavia, Hungary, Italy, Roumania, Greece, Bulgaria and Germany, the policeman, magistrate or judge, in greater or lesser degree, might detain and intimidate men, and delay or falsify the processes of the law, so that no man felt free. Cash and corruption entered largely into the system, and often justice and the police were but instruments of victimization wielded by persons in office.

In the Scandinavian countries, Holland and Switzerland, which seemed to me the happiest and best-run in Europe, an order akin to ours prevailed. But I hope to do them no injustice in saying that this priceless right existed, in the same degree, in no country but ours.

It gives the poorest man a feeling of ultimate dignity; he is not quite an outcast. It was envied in us, far beyond wealth and possessions, by people in other lands. Until 1939, we might promptly and proudly have told any stranger, who asked what he might take away that was typically English, 'Take a copy of the Habeas Corpus Act'. He would immediately have understood and agreed.

Wrested from tyrants during centuries of struggle, this became the half of our jewel of Freedom, and we kept it even when we lost the other half. If the legendary Englishman looked the whole world in the face, this was why: he neither owed nor feared any man; and this was his chief title to the respect which awaited him when he went abroad. Simple people often do not know the value of old heirlooms and cast them away. If they understood, they would not agree, even in a world war, to yield this right, save under the most stringent safeguards. These do not exist to-day.

For centuries we kept that half of Freedom, but only by dint of a battle in England that seldom paused for long. Those who fought for it, fought for all mankind, for Freedom went out from here; but for them, the serfs and slaves would not have been liberated, and the other facets of Freedom, which were presently added to the rough stone, would never have been cut. One after another, they fought for this through the centuries, and when they died, saw that the Battle in England still went on. Without them, we should have lost it long ago.

Consider William Cobbett, who for forty-five years strove, with raging anger, against the things which were to be done to England between 1800 and 1943. He saw them all before they happened. With Enclosure going on around him, he rode his Rural Rides and clamoured against the spoliation of the countryside which he foresaw as clearly as if the future opened to him, against the human hives which were being allowed to sprawl and straggle over the land, and particularly against 'The Wen', his prophetic name for London. His was a lone voice; but he never ceased to cry, and was heard. But for him, we might have lost the greater half of freedom a century ago.

Cobbett was *not* merely an angry and antiquated old farmer who thought the country must be going to the dogs because the whole world was not given up to the cows. Cobbett was not merely a man with a lot of nonsensical notions that could be exploded by political economy; a man looking to turn England into an Eden that should grow nothing but Cobbett's Corn. What he saw was not an Eden that cannot exist, but rather an Inferno that can exist, and even that does exist. What he saw was the perishing of the whole English power of self-support; the growth of cities that drain and dry up the countryside, the growth of dense dependent populations incapable of finding their own food, the toppling triumph of machines over men, the sprawling omnipotence of financiers over patriots, the herding of humanity in nomadic masses whose very homes are homeless, the terrible necessity of peace and the terrible probability of war, all the loading up of our little island like a sinking ship; the wealth that may mean famine, and the culture that may mean despair; the bread of Midas and the sword of Damocles.

In a word, he saw what we see, but he saw it when it was not there. And some cannot see it — even when it is there.[1]

Cobbett gave his whole life to the battle in England, and above all to those two vital objectives: the freedom of the land, and freedom from wrongful imprisonment. He fought for them in England, in France during the French Revolution, in America just after the American Revolution, and again in England. He never faltered, was furiously decried, greatly loved, and treated those two impostors just the same. He lived for England, and, could he have been listened to, our way would lie clear before us now.

This man, the son of a small farmer ('who, when a little boy, drove the plough for twopence a day, and these, his earnings, were appropriated to the expenses of an evening school'), became a great master of the English language, wrote incessantly and insuppressibly, and commanded a huge audience. When he was twenty he enlisted in a regiment of foot, and before he was thirty, jumping over many heads, became its sergeant-major during service in Nova Scotia. On his discharge, having gained knowledge of what went on in the regiment, he accused some officers of peculation from regimental funds, but then, suspecting the court of connivance, fled to France, and afterwards to America. When he returned, eight years later, he was famous, through his writings; he was wooed by a Tory government and offered the editorship of a government newspaper so that he might, for a comfortable salary, laud all that was done by authority and lampoon all who protested.

He refused, and began to publish the weekly *Political Register*, the most famous independent journal of the next thirty-five years. Sometimes the politicians, sometimes the mob, attacked him. He was fined for criticizing the Government's treatment of Ireland. His windows were smashed.

Half-way between Trafalgar and Waterloo, Cobbett angrily protested against the public flogging of British soldiers under a guard of German mercenaries. The things that happen in England! He was fined a thousand pounds and imprisoned for two years. In prison, and after he came out, he continued to write, for another seven years, as a fierce and independent critic who could neither be corrupted nor cowed.

[1] I am grateful to the executrix of the late G. K. Chesterton, and to the publishers, Messrs. Hodder & Stoughton, for permission to quote this extract from his excellent book *William Cobbett*, 1925.

Then came the crisis. The Government took powers of wrongful arrest. It suspended the Habeas Corpus Act and introduced the Regulation 18B of its day. Cobbett, the chief prey, escaped to America.

He returned a popular hero, and until he died maintained his robust and independent criticism of public affairs, when he thought this necessary. When he was nearly seventy, the Government tried once more to break him by bringing him before the Court of King's Bench on a charge of inciting rural disorders. He defended himself and the charge collapsed, covering the Government with ignominy. During his last years, when he was an Independent Member of Parliament for Oldham, they abandoned hope of intimidating this honest and turbulent Englishman, who would not suppress the fears he felt for England as he saw the seeds of decay being planted.

But for such a man, and his like, we would not for so long have kept our peerless right of freedom from malicious arrest and wrongful imprisonment.

To-day Cobbett's fight has to be fought again, if we are to check the retreat from Freedom and win the battle in England. Even the gods might hesitate to claim the power now wielded by one man, to imprison others; and its great danger is that none ever knows how it may be used to-morrow. The Minister who employs it to-day is not ruthless; but he himself, before he received it, laid stress on this peril. He does not know how any successor may use it, yet refuses to relinquish it. Ah, the difference between words and deeds, between Opposition and Office!

Once this power is used, the extremists are avid for its continuance, because they hope to wield it to-morrow. *The Daily Worker*, released from suppression, calls for 'the rats to be put behind bars', that is, for people whom it dislikes to be put away. Two other London newspapers, so swiftly does this rot spread, now currently recommend that all sorts of persons unsympathetic to them should be imprisoned. The disease infects the middle parties, those which abjure us to 'fight for Freedom'. In the Commons and in the Press, lickspittles and lackeys 'call the attention of Mr. Morrison' to the activities of someone they do not like. Put this man away, they mean: I dislike his views. They call themselves Conservatives, Socialists, Liberals, Democrats.

The present Minister has reduced the number of people thus detained from the original 1,817 to about 500. We know now that many innocent people were put away. In our parlous plight of 1940, when good reason offered to suspect treachery, but among persons much higher placed than these obscure individuals, the gaoling of hundreds of people without charge or proof may have been excusable. Now that we are invulnerable it is inexcusable. Some of them have been imprisoned for years, uncharged. They should be charged and tried, or released.

The unanswerable argument against this thing is that every time an arrest under it has been tested *at law* it has been found wrongful in some way. These tests have been few, because they can only be applied when a man has been released and is free to use them, and then only if he has money enough for enormously expensive actions. But the result has always been the same.

We now know that the Home Secretary, who is required to have 'reasonable cause' for believing a prisoner to be of hostile associations, may consider the statement of some secret informer enough, who will not be punished for perjury, if his information later be found false, because his testimony was not made 'on oath'. The anonymous letter-writer is thus promoted to the status of a servant of the Crown!

Consider those few cases. Mr. Ben Greene, after nearly two years' imprisonment, succeeded at great cost in obtaining from the Home Secretary the statement that the allegations against him 'might be regarded as withdrawn'. When his solicitor, by threatening a question in Parliament, elicited the name of the secret informer, who immediately withdrew his allegations, this proved to be a German subject. He is immune from retribution.

Remember Cobbett, and the flogging of the British soldiers at Ely under German guard!

Then, Mr. H. S. L. Knight. When he claimed damages for wrongful dismissal, he was an R.A.F. aircraftman whose commanding officer was 'completely satisfied of his loyalty' and who recommended him for a commission. Mr. Knight was put away for six months and summarily dismissed, in result, by his employers. After his release, when he was in the R.A.F., he was only able to make his case public by using the 'wrongful dismissal' issue to bring it before the courts.

He was denied damages, the Court finding that his employer was 'frustrated' by his arrest from fulfilling the contract. *But* Mr. Justice Hilbery said that Mr. Knight was completely cleared of any misconduct that would have justified his dismissal and that his arrest was due to 'tittle-tattle'!

Consider the facts. He was put away on suspicion of Nazi sympathies. The 'evidence' against him consisted of (1) a letter referring to his 'appalling Communistic views' from a colleague whose testimony the judge 'rejected completely'; (2) some scraps of conversation reported by a woman typist who said in court that she was 'irresponsible and temperamental', broke down, and ran out weeping; and (3) a statement (contemptuously dismissed by the judge) from 'Mr. W.'. We may not know who Mr. W. was. He was a Jewish refugee from Germany and thus entitled to this new privilege of laying anonymous information, with impunity, against British citizens!

Mr. Justice Hilbery's judgment in this case was either ignored or given inadequately by the British Press, which claims to speak for British citizens. It is to my mind one of the most excellent in our recent history, and reveals one of the most flagrant injustices committed in the name of national interests in our time. The judge ironically referred to the unnamed enemy alien informer 'whose name has not been stated because we know that the giving of such names may lead to all sorts of very dreadful consequences to innocent persons who may remain behind in Germany' — but who was privileged with impunity to denounce and have imprisoned an innocent British subject! The testimony of this anonymous poltroon, said the judge, 'amounted to absolutely nothing'; 'I can find absolutely nothing at all in that evidence which even slightly savours of any sort of misconduct'. Of the evidence of a woman who boarded at the same guesthouse as Mr. Knight, he said 'Her evidence resulted in absolutely nothing'. Of the evidence of the hysterical woman clerk (who said Mr. Knight had made a motor-car journey over a road built by Hitler in Bavaria, which happened to have been built by an Austrian Republican Government in Austria!) he pointed out that she broke down in the witness box, and said her evidence, 'riddled as it is with inaccurate statements of fact, when examined has nothing in it'. The evidence of another secret informer, when it was now tested in open court, he 'rejected without the least hesitation as unreliable'; he was 'satisfied that this witness had a wholly warped and perverted view of the plaintiff'. Of the wrongfully imprisoned man himself, the judge said, 'The Plaintiff gave his evidence like an honest man and I think he gave his evidence to the best of his ability accurately'. The plaintiff's *dismissal*, he said, was not justified. What then of his *imprisonment*?

This fantastic case would have moved the Members of a decent Parliament to wonder how many other unknown people are detained through anonymous slander, and to demand reform, but no. Five days after this a Mr. Watkins of Central Hackney declared in the House that 'these hundreds of people . . . are all guilty in varying degrees'.

Then a Mr. Thomas Wilson, who was put away for eighteen months and ruined by this imprisonment and the cost of his attempts to gain justice. He, too, found a way to bring his case into court after release, and stated that he 'raised the matter in an attempt to maintain some of the few rights remaining to a citizen'. (Under the Bill of Rights every citizen has the right to appeal to the King's Bench Division, but a petition which he sent was prevented from reaching the Court. He applied for the Home Secretary who imprisoned him, Sir John Anderson, to be committed for contempt of Court.)

This is what Mr. Justice Humphreys said:

There is no more important duty attaching to the Judges of the King's Bench Division than that of looking after the liberties of British subjects, and where one of those subjects has been committed to prison not by an order of a court of law but as the result of the opinion of a Secretary of State in the peculiar circumstances referred to in Regulation 18B, which only apply in war time, he has an inalienable right to ask that his case should be considered by that Court, and the Court is bound to consider whether he was being detained in custody legally or illegally. If any case should be brought before me hereafter in which any person — I care not how high his position or how great his fame — be found to have interfered with the right of one of His Majesty's subjects, I think that I should have no difficulty in putting into force, with the assistance of other members of that Division, the great powers of the King's Bench Division of imprisoning such a person for contempt of Court. Sir John Anderson himself knew nothing about the matter. But something happened for which Sir John has thought it his duty to apologize to the Court because it was done by an official of the Home Office, and the Court is glad to have that apology. The applicant chose to send an application to the Court himself. The document is irregular in form, but is a clear request to the Court from a person in custody to have his case considered. It is a perfectly proper document, in respectful language, desiring that if it was thought that he had done anything wrong as a servant of the Crown, he should be put on trial in the ordinary way and should not be detained indefinitely without a possibility of proving his innocence. That document was not dealt with at the prison. It was sent to another department where it was the duty of somebody to censor it. I cannot conceive any reason why such a document should not see the light of day. There is nothing improper in it. Someone, whose name the Court has not got, and whose position it does not know, intercepted that document and did not forward it to that Court to whom it was addressed. That official thought that it was not the proper way for the case to be put before the Court. It was no business at all of that official to form such a conclusion. It certainly was a piece of great impertinence on his part to take on himself to do what he did.

Mr. Justice Tucker, concurring in this judgment, together with Mr. Justice Wrottesley, said in some future case it might become a matter of great importance to decide what was the position if a Secretary of State said: 'Somebody in my department informs me of certain facts and I am not going to tell you what his name is.'

This judgment may make a man cry, 'There are still judges in England'. For in other lands, all know arrest or imprisonment without trial; but few know such peremptory rebuke as this to official misusers of authority. The pity is that the Judge limited his warning to 'next time'.

In this case again you see the anonymous poltroon. This man, whose name not even an English Court of Justice could wrest, was an official. Such as he, when they are criticized, are protected by Ministers in Parliament with the words 'The honourable Member is attacking men who cannot defend themselves'. Yet these men may secretly denounce British citizens, or deny them their rights, and with impunity.

These few cases already make a grave indictment against Regulation 18B and the way it has been administered, and an uncorrupted House of Commons would by now have compelled a change. Add to them the memorable judgment of Lord Atkin who in the House of Lords dissented from four other Law Lords to say:

I view with apprehension the attitude of judges who, on the mere question of construction, when face to face with claims involving the liberty of the subject, show themselves more Executive-minded than the Executive . . . it has always been one of the principles of liberty for which, on recent authority, we are now fighting, that the judges are no respecters of persons and stand between the subject and any attempted encroachment on his liberty by the Executive, alert to see that any coercive action is justified in law. In this case I have listened to arguments which might have been addressed acceptably to the Court of the King's Bench in the time of Charles I. I protest, even if I do it alone, against a strained construction put upon words with the effect of giving an uncontrolled power of imprisonment to the Minister . . . I am profoundly convinced that the Home Secretary was not given unconditional authority to detain.

Add this last judgment, from the case of a Mr. Frank Arbon and a Major Alexander de Lassoe, D.S.O., M.C., who did not complain of their detention, but that, in breach of the instructions issued by the Home Secretary, the conditions of their imprisonment were 'punitive' (that is, those of convicted persons) instead of 'custodial' (that is, those of persons detained but neither charged nor tried, and therefore not proven guilty). Lord Justice Goddard said:

In the case of a detained prisoner, a prison officer is always present, while in that of a remand prisoner the officer is only within sight, but not within hearing. That, I am told, is in accordance with the directions of the Prison Commissioners. This raises a question of grave importance. It is a strange state of affairs that, had the plaintiffs in the present case been charged with an offence under a statute, they would have been entitled to interview their solicitors out of the hearing of a prison officer, as might a prisoner charged with murder, rape, or any other crime. Yet, as they had not been charged with any offence, that privilege was denied them. The law has always protected most jealously the confidence of communications between solicitor and client, and it is repulsive to me as a Judge to learn that that confidence is being violated, for that is what it amounts to.

In these quotations, gentle reader, you have seen, at work in England, the evil thing they know abroad. The root of the only real liberty we have left has been gravely impaired. After this war, extremist parties will be turbulently active, and will find ready hearing among disappointed people, as they found after the last war. It is mad to do, in the name of 'Freedom', the very things they would do if they could. It gives young people no choice between policies, programmes, methods or ideals. It 'force' is the new clarion call, they will choose the most forcible. 'Beating the Nazis with their own weapons' (or the Communists) has invariably failed wherever I have watched it, from Dollfuss to Carol. It invests the people who suffer from it, such of them as *are* revolutionaries or traitors, with glamorous appeal when they come out.

Apart from that, it is wrong. It is a new attack, now as in Cobbett's day, on the last British liberty, the one on which alone we could build. It is not insignificant because to-day it hits few people, and these have few friends. Forces are at work in this country, now, which would fain use it after the war to destroy us.

It is unnecessary, and alien to everything we call British. If it is not checked now, the battle in England will have to change it. In other countries, I was often startled by the immediately depressing effect which this thing has upon the population. Overnight, mouths shut, eyes veil themselves, and men withdraw into a shell of miserable caution. To some extent this has happened here.

It must be stopped, so that we can get back to the one sound basis of Freedom — Freedom from wrongful arrest. On that, by means of decent debate, you may build anything. By violence, no matter how small the beginnings, you can only destroy.

We have retreated further from Freedom than most people are aware; indeed, nearly the whole way. No happiness awaits us along that path, but only worse misery. Regulation 18B, until it is revoked, is a noose suspended over the heads of a multitude who do not think themselves threatened to-day — in fact, the whole nation.

Liberate the land, and restore our ancient freedom from wrongful arrest, and we may yet find our future.

PART THREE

FREEDOM REGAINED?

FIRST THINGS FIRST

WE approach Civvy Street, gentle reader, and look towards 1950 and 1960 with the eyes of 1918. Early in that street, a wrong turning will entice us and we must be alert to avoid it if, this time, we are to reach a place where we may 'construct something'.

We want to reach, and build, not Liberty Hall, but Freedom's House. Its walls are, freedom from capricious arrest, and freedom to use and enjoy our own land; for is it not absurd, to read that this professor or that politician have been made 'Freeman of London', or 'Freeman of Edinburgh' when Englishmen are not freemen of England?

But first things come first, and before the walls comes the foundation. The foundation is: foreign policy.

The words seem to baffle many people. Yet foreign policy is but the ordering of our relationships with other countries. Those neighbours, Mr. Brown and Mr. Jones, so conduct their relations that Mr. Jones does not throw rubbish over the fence and Mr. Brown does not enter Mr. Jones's house without permission. That, between States, is foreign policy.

Our foreign policy — I mean the one we *should* pursue, the foundation for our house — is simple. Stupendous skill in pursuing a wrong policy while deluding the people that you follow the right one, is needed, to fail in it, and the achievement of our successive governments in bringing us to the present war is the eighth wonder of the world. If I were to see a man perform the Indian rope trick with the North Pole I could not be more astonished than I am by that fantastic feat. Only foolishness in a dimension as infinite as space, or knavery, could account for it. But if certain sections or combines or groups prove to have made great gain from this war when the fog of it lifts, of power, or territory, or raw

64

materials, or cash, the events of that nightmare prelude, 1919-39, would become explicable. For this reason, those events cannot be studied too closely.

Many English people seem to feel physical pain when urged to consider foreign policy. Yet it is easy to understand; its object only is, to prevent the conquest of this island by a foreign foe. This is the foundation of our house. Each time that foundation is shaken, cracks appear in the walls and ceilings of the house. Look back to the Napoleonic wars and Enclosure; to the 1914 war and DORA; to the present war and Regulation 18B; and then look forward to the future.

We in this island hold a position of such enormous strength in the planet that, supported by the kindred countries oversea, we could ensure peace in the world indefinitely. The battlefields of time are strewn with the litter of a thousand wars, and churchgoers who sing of an age 'when wars shall be no more' may privately think this an absurdity. Yet my statement is true. Whether wars *ought* to be no more, I am unsure; because I remember with what glee I welcomed the hope of adventure that 1914 brought and cannot honestly expect the nineteen-year-olds of to-day or to-morrow to feel differently. But I am sure that wars which imperil this island ought to be no more, and never need be again.

We have no cause to cast desperately about for a means to be secure, as have landlocked nations. We *have* security, unless we throw it away. As Shakespeare said:

> This fortress built by nature for herself
> Against infection and the hand of war;
> This happy breed of men, this little world;
> This precious stone set in the silver sea,
> Which serves it in the office of a wall,
> Or as a mote defensive to a house,
> Against the envy of less happier lands.

Yet this impregnable pass was sold in our time! That the enemy did not enter, is the one enigma more baffling than that of our foreign policy between 1919 and 1939.

We have, then, the most formidable natural fortress in the world. How may it be kept secure? We are not very many in numbers, but our natural defence, the sea, is so strong that it makes good that weakness. As long as we have a supreme Navy and a strong Air Force, we can prevent any enemy from conquering this island. We have the foundation for our house.

There is one exception: numbers against us so overwhelming, that not even the sea could redeem the balance. This could happen only if all Europe were united against us. That almost happened!

To prevent it happening, is where 'foreign policy' begins.

The people who live in Europe across the Channel desire peace founded on our strength, on the invulnerable position which nature has given us. They will only choose something else if we force them to. They look to us as their single hope of building their own house of freedom, because they know that the alternative is foreign conquest. But if they think we shall not defend our island, they will combine against us; for in that case each man's only hope of a future is, to stand well with the conqueror.

That is what nearly came about. Had Poland not resisted in 1939, and forced us to declare war, it would have happened. As it was, many European peoples joined with Germany. Czechoslovakia we ourselves forced to capitulate. Italy and Hungary joined with Germany willingly, Roumania and Finland reluctantly, Bulgaria docilely. France, in effect, did not resist. Greece, Yugoslavia, Norway, Holland and Belgium resisted. But in some even of these countries, and in Spain, groups of people formed themselves to fight for Germany, though we fought against Germany.

A Polish capitulation, or our abandonment of Poland, would have brought about a European coalition, ranked against us, which would have outweighed the value of our natural defence, the sea. This is the only result to which a foreign policy of withdrawal from Europe, of talking about 'little countries far away of which we know nothing', can lead. We cannot withdraw from Europe without either withdrawing from this island or living in it under foreign rule.

If we revert to that lunatic policy, the next war is already begun, or our future capitulation is certain. Then, since our fate is inexorably linked with that of Europe across the Channel, what must our foreign policy be?

Only one nation in Europe so much outnumbers us as to be moved repeatedly to attempt our overthrow, knowing that without this it cannot have even European conquest, for the other peoples will never stop fighting. It is Germany, and this will remain so for as long as we need consider.

These lusty people are separated from us only by the North Sea, or, when they conquer France, by the Channel. Were we separated only by a land frontier, we should now live under German rule. The sight of this little island, so near but so thwarting to ambitions for European conquest creates a perpetual temptation.

Thus our future is as implacably bound up with those of the other Europeans as is our long immunity with the Channel. We *cannot* make the best of all worlds and let Germany do what it will in Europe while hugging ourselves in safety upon this island. That would create a European coalition against us which not even the Channel could withstand. We should have had enough proof of this now.

What should our foreign policy be then? Simply to maintain that supreme Navy and strong Air Force and keep a wary eye on Germany?

No, that is not enough. One loophole still remains through which our life and liberty might ebb. We cannot survive without an alliance. It would have prevented this war.

The Russians are far more numerous than even the Germans. But Russia has only a big toe in Europe. It is an Asiatic State, too far from us to attack us, too swollen to covet what we have. You cannot attack another country across thousands of miles of intervening States and large expanses of water. Look at the map. Besides, Russia has an enormous empire; Germany seeks one. Germany is an outstretched fist, under our nose. Russia is a big word a long way off. (I do not take German ambitions amiss, and think people mad who ask 'But aren't there any *good* Germans?' meaning, are there none who are content only to attack Poles and Czechs and Serbs and leave us alone? No Germans are as bad as all that.)

A hundred and fifty years of recent history should now have convinced our people that we need the alliance with Russia and that we shall go wrong again in Civvy Street if we fight against this fact. Should we have beaten Napoleon, but for his catastophe at Moscow? Well, it would have taken much longer at the best.

In 1914 the Germans would have reached Paris and the Channel coast but for the Russian attack from the east which made them halt on the Marne. We would not have won that war in 1918 but for the Russian offensives of 1916 and 1917.

I believe we could have won this war in 1941, by striking with all our force at the moment (which must have been the most fearful in any German's memory) when Hitler's armies were halted before Moscow. Where should we stand now, but for the Russian counterblows of 1941, 1942 and 1943?

But we speak, not of past wars, or even this one, but of winning the next peace. For that, we need an alliance with Russia. We have made one for twenty years. The present war was bred in twenty years, The term should be extended to fifty years.

For Russia will not attack us. If we want to have war with Russia, we shall have to go to Russia, and we have done this twice, in 1854 and in 1918. The story of that last attack is sinister and a straight line leads from it through all the events which brought this war about.

I used to think that the state of dementia about Russia in which so many of my compatriots live, and which enabled them to be led blindfold into the present war, only reached back to the confiscatory days of 1918; and that earlier, when they were able to find invigoration in pictures of the Romanoffs in the *Tatler*, Russia was held in friendly regard here.

But even Tennyson, a hundred years ago, raved about 'that o'er grown Barbarian in the East', and possibly this helped to make The Boys in the Crimea feel that they fought for something, though who can guess now, what that something was? It was probably a 'crusade', a word our leaders invariably use about this war, in which the Turkish alliance is vital to us. If the moon were coloured red we should certainly have a strong anti-moon party in the House of Lords and all the stately homes.

History has tried hard to hammer into our heads the need for a constant alliance with Russia in the present condition of Europe. For this other great State *can* do us one mortal injury, and that is why it is a vital prop in our foreign policy. It *can* join with Germany, if we persist in fostering mistrust in our motives.

This, too, nearly happened. In Germany, a strong party has long favoured alliance with Russia as the only means of overcoming this country. If that had happened in 1939, it would have meant our instant extinction. That it did not, was not our achievement, but Germany's omission. Hitler stopped at a standstill agreement with Russia, and did not form the full fighting alliance. After this war, when Germany will twice have tried the other method of attacking both ourselves *and* Russia, with the result of defeat in both cases, the party in Germany to which I refer will be stronger than ever in its argument. Those people in the world, who then will still desire our downfall and be powerful enough again to mislead public opinion, will work to that end by estranging us from Russia.

Look back a moment, before we enter Civvy Street, on the things they did, on the monstrous web of delusion they wove about the British people.

People forgot it after the last war, but they know now the vital importance to us of having Germany engaged on another front when Germany fights us. And before this war began, Germany was faced by *three* fronts, not two. Germany was not even prepared to fight on *two* at that time; for that reason, the project for the standstill agreement with Russia, which would reduce the number of fronts to *one*, for the first two years of this war, already lay in Ribbentrop's drawer.

But the *third* front was decisive. While it remained the war could not begin. Not even Hitler would unloose it.

It was destroyed at the command of England, and English people in millions cheered their own imminent doom, which, eighteen months later, they would escape by a hairbreadth!

The *third* front was the coalition of the Little Entente, three States liberated or strengthened by the last war, Czechoslovakia, Yugoslavia and Roumania. The capitulation of Czechoslovakia, which the British Prime Minister brought about, destroyed that front. The vast quantities of arms now furnished to the German armies by the Czechoslovak State factory at Skoda; the fierce resistance offered even now by Serb guerrillas in their mountains to forty Axis divisions; and the help given to the Germans by the Roumanian armies sent to Russia; these show what was lost. At the time of Munich, all these, and the Russians, were ready to fight. This would have been a war of *three* fronts. Germany would not have begun that war. And the defeatists claim that we 'gained time'!

It is vital, for our future foreign policy, to understand that episode. Powerful people in this country who detested Communism (quite rightly), could not see that the one way to stimulate Communism in *this* country was to allow a war to come about in which Russia, *on whichever side*, would play a dominant part; and that the way to prevent the growth of Communism in this country was to avoid the war, which could only be prevented by an alliance with Russia. These people, if they care to look about them to-day, will see that they have more Communists in this country than ever before.

These people still pursue their dangerous illusion. It causes them, in my belief, to think the prolongation of the war a lesser evil than a victory mainly won by Russia. Opportunities have already offered to curtail and win it. Each time stubborn opposition has been raised to the seizing of them. As I write, the war approaches its fourth birthday and still we do not strike. When the great opportunity of 1941 offered, the call for action was stilled by rebukes to 'armchair critics' (though, at the time, more civilians than fighting men had been killed) and in 1942 the same demand was refused with protests about 'the impossibility of finding the ships' (though in November 1942 'the greatest Armada in our history' took American and British troops to North Africa). But another motive, animosity to Russia, was often clearly revealed.

The third front, which would have prevented the war, was wantonly destroyed. When we come to Civvy Street, these motives and these people will reappear; indeed, they still thwart us in reaching victory. Munich is the date to remember, and the golden rule, that in foreign policy honesty is the best policy.

First things first. Foreign policy is the foundation of our security, and you cannot clearly understand it without understanding those events. After the invasion of Prague, General Halder, who later became Hitler's Chief of Staff, spoke to German officers at the Staff Academy in Berlin. The text of his talk came to the hands of an able Polish officer who was engaged in Secret Service work. General Halder's subject (six months before the war began) was 'The Coming War'. He said, among other things:

> The situation in Central Europe has been entirely changed. The third front, which caused us so many headaches and threatened the heart of the Reich, has been destroyed once and for all. With the destruction of the Czechoslovak army of forty divisions, the Little Entente has in effect ceased to exist.

Thus was the war made while Britain cheered.

But, you say, after much toil, much misleading, and reprieve from annihilation, Britain has understood that simple problem. We *have* an alliance with Russia, for eighteen years to come. Our present leaders are not those who prevented it before; they see its importance.

Beware: at the very beginning of Civvy Street you turn into Gullible Lane. We made a similar alliance with France! Remember what happened to it, in twenty years, between 1919 and 1939. While the British people were told that it was impregnable, it was destroyed piece by piece, so that at the end, when it collapsed, we were all but buried in the ruins.

That is the final result of false foreign policy. Nevertheless, the lesson of those years is that the British people knew what foreign policy *should* be followed. Their instinct was as sure as that of the lioness, which from some inner prompting springs to defend her cubs, or of the primitive man who, he knows not why, seizes his club and goes warily, suspecting danger, to the mouth of his cave. Their instinct was so strong that every British Government, during those years, promised it would pursue the right foreign policy. The manifold devices of secrecy, anonymity and delusion enabled them actually to pursue the wrong one.

Then, how do we stand to-day?

Under Mr. Churchill, we have made an alliance with Russia for 'common action to preserve peace and resist aggression in the post-war period'. It is for twenty years. This war was brewed in twenty years. If we keep the alliance, we shall have peace at least until 1962. If its term were for fifty years, and we kept it, we should have peace at least until 1992.

Our Foreign Minister, Mr. Eden, has said (December 2nd, 1942):

There is no reason why any conflict of interest should arise between Russia and ourselves. That foreign policy [he said] was firmly based on history. In each of the great world conflicts, that of Napoleon and those of 1914 and 1939, we found ourselves on the same side and after each 'we drifted apart'.

(We did not 'drift apart' in 1918; we attacked Russia.) On the maintenance of the alliance, said Mr. Eden, 'lies the best chance of building a new and better international society after the war'.

Mr. Richard Law, our Deputy Foreign Minister, said (January 22nd, 1943):

If we and the other nations of western Europe fail to have an adequate understanding of Russia after the war, you will find exactly the same thing happening again — Russia will withdraw beyond her frontiers and she will become a tremendous question mark. It will be impossible then to find a political solution of any real stability. It is, therefore, absolutely vital that relations with Russia should be as friendly, cordial and sympathetic as they can possibly be.

All is well, then; the three men responsible for our foreign policy, on which the foundation of our future rests, our island safety, know what to do and will do it?

No. We do not know how long they will be in office, and anyway, we have repeatedly seen that if anonymous hands grasp the wheel and alter the course of foreign policy, the men on the bridge will not sound the alarm, but will keep silence, or will even profess that the course is still the true one, while the ship heads for the rocks.

Behind those official protestations, lies a silent but stubborn conflict in England, between those who want to get the war over and those who would sooner see its prolongation than a Russian victory, which now makes the course of the war enigmatic and enshadows our future after it — for, wriggle as you like, you will not have either early victory or long peace without that Russian alliance.

It is a tragic paradox. Those people in this island who cannot bear the thought of Russia brought about this war by wrecking the alliance which would have prevented it. They did not see that the one way to stimulate Communism *here* was to allow the war to happen: or did they see that, and desire it? Are they more subtle than we think, these hidden ones? They cannot see now that the one way still further to foster Communism here is, unnecessarily to prolong the war by holding back while Germany is engaged with Russia. Or do they see that, and desire it?

Our paramount interest, from every sound and patriotic point of view, is to get this war finished. Any who work against that work against us and our future, whatever their motives. But no doubt remains that the same hidden influence, which was able to prevent the Russian alliance before the war, so that the war came, is still most powerful in this country, and that a consequent confusion is spreading into our foreign policy again, which can only bring us worse misfortune.

Our leaders declare that no delay has occurred, in pressing on with the war. Well, it approaches its fourth birthday; we have not struck; our air-bombing, with its bouts of fierceness and long lapses, is still not the 'unprecedented ordeal' which Mr. Churchill last promised in June 1942; the commando raids have ceased, save for the inexplicable one on the strongest point of the German-held French coast, since Lord Keyes was dismissed from the leadership. Instead, our leaders, with much unction, tell us to expect 'a long war', as if four years of this misery were not long.

A long war is not necessary. We shall win it in 1943 if that 'unprecedented ordeal' from the air, so often promised, is imposed, and if we strike when it has done its work. In February 1943, the Royal Air Force for the first time delivered really heavy and continuous blows. The results were *immediate*. The most obvious terror at once became discernible, in the almost panic-stricken measures of the German leaders, the tone of their speeches, and — most important of all, gentle reader, for those who know how to discern what goes on in Germany — in the open allusions to 'a very serious situation' published in the wary Swedish and Swiss Press.

Then why do they speak of 'a long war'?

I do not exaggerate in saying this war might have been won in 1941, at that catastrophic moment when the Germans were halted before Moscow in the most appalling winter on record. You might question Litvinoff's statement made in New York in 1942 ('If German forces had been diverted from the Russian front in the winter of 1941, when the Russian army held the initiative, Germany would beyond doubt have suffered considerable if not a final defeat'). But you may now find the proofs in the words of Germany's leaders.

Hitler told the Reichstag, when the danger was past:

There was in the East such a winter as had been known not even in those parts for more than 140 years. In a few days the thermometer dropped from 0 degrees to minus 47 degrees and even lower . . . There was a general backward movement. I can say to-day that the process was extremely difficult. Added to our other difficulties was the psychological difficulty due to the defeat of Napoleon in 1812 . . . The temperature was one which could not be borne . . . Neither the German men nor the machines and other means of transport were suited to this kind of weather, which was at one place 52 degrees below zero, while the worst temperature in 1812 during the retreat of Napoleon was exactly 25 degrees below . . . It was necessary only in a few cases for me to intervene. Only when nerves were at breaking point, obedience wavered, or where a sense of duty was lacking in mastering the task, I made stern decisions in virtue of the sovereign rights which I believe to have received for the purpose from the German people. I did so with the utmost ruthlessness, and thanks to the sovereignty which the nation gave me we stood this winter and we accomplished the feat which broke down 130 years ago. . . .

Do you know what these words mean, gentle reader? Mass executions! What an opportunity we lost!

In May 1942 Göring said: -

> 1,500 kilometres and more we penetrated into the distant Russian space, and just at the time when a new mighty blow was to be struck a new enemy fell on us. Not the Russian divisions, not the Russian arms and not the Russian command. It was the elements which rose against us . . . such a winter as has probably never been experienced in the history of such struggles . . . The rapid rivers were frozen, swamps and lakes as well: one white blanket of death was spread over the endless land . . . The Russians succeeded in traversing the frozen rivers, lakes and swamps by night and in reaching our rear. The Russians in our rear in the north, centre and south! Partisan detachments blew up everything, waylaid the supply columns. Maddening cold almost froze our troops . . . The skin of their fingers stuck to their rifle barrels. The engines failed, could no longer be started. Tanks got stuck in the deep snow, one thing piled on top of another . . . Some of you have read the history of the great Corsican, Napoleon I, who retreated from Moscow in the Russian winter, his army being annihilated to the last man. There was one vast field of corpses at that time. Such thoughts could arise! Not all men are equally strong. Many a leader was bound to think of the cruel parallel of 1812 . . . We were happy when December had gone. When January passed, we said to ourselves 'Only another two months'. February, too, passed, and the front still held out, on the whole. Temperatures began to rise; we rejoiced . . . When spring came the Russians had not destroyed the German Army. . . .

And Goebbels, on New Year's Day of 1943, still gave thanks. The sigh of relief in his voice, as he looked back on that calamitous moment, and recalled the terrifying comparison with Napoleon, which all Germany then made, could be heard.

What a chance neglected! The instinct of this country, at that time, was as sure as ever. It itched to have at the Germans. The clamour was hushed with stern rebukes to 'fireside critics', uttered by people who in this war assuredly enjoy more comfort than any soldier and most civilians.

And now, they talk of 'a long war'. Indeed, in the light of that event, it is impossible to conjecture to-day, when the war may end.

The confused conflict of thought, about Russia, still thwarts us. Of how much misery has it been the cause!

The stubborn antagonism to Russia, in this country, is too strong to be ignored or denied. Indeed, it is open, and can be proved. The awful thing is, that antagonism to Russia means antagonism to winning this war quickly. But even to that, the people seem to have become accustomed. You would think that, with hundreds of thousands of their men in foreign captivity, they would feel strongly about it. I think they lose the power to feel strongly about anything.

The openly expressed antagonism ranges from the statement attributed to, and never denied by, a British Minister (of the hope that 'the Russian and German armies will exterminate each other, and while this is taking place we will so develop our Air Force and other armed forces that if Russia and Germany do destroy each other we shall have the dominating power in Europe') to the statement of a Conservative M.P.:

> I cannot forsee the military result of the German attack on Russia, but of this I am certain — the war of 1914 brought Bolshevism to Russia, the war of 1939 will drive it out. Russia has proved greater than any dogma. The Bear walks like a man again.

The Catholic Herald said:

> The military alliance with Russia was forced on us by necessity. A large section of our people, *including the Prime Minister*, regarded it as an unpleasant necessity . . . perhaps the disasters which have overtaken the cause of the Allied Nations in Russia may not be, in the long run, the unmitigated evil they may seem.

The Review of Foreign Affairs, with which several Conservative politicians are associated, said:

> We must remember that large numbers of the Russian people would regret it if we moved a single inch from our position: for many observers believe that, whatever the outcome of the war, Mr. Stalin will not survive it . . . The great calamity in which Russia finds itself is largely due to his disastrous policy. From every point of view, therefore, it is of supreme importance that by no means should we give the impression that we are in alliance with the Bolsheviks.

This was published after the alliance was signed. Lady Astor remarked that she was tired of hearing about Russia, and that after the war Russia would have to get into 'the British way of thinking'. (What may be Lady Astor's conception of 'the British way of thinking'? In a book called *Last Train from Berlin*, the American author depicts her, during a tea-party at Cliveden, as giving 'a one-lady show; she donned a feathery hat, crammed a set of protrusive false teeth in her mouth and gave us an "Imitation of an Englishwoman imitating an American woman"'. In a debate in the Commons on the proposed Foreign Service reforms, however, she said she did not believe there was any country which would not welcome 'a sound, intelligent Englishwoman' as a diplomat.)

If our delay in striking to win this war is quite unconnected with the powerful opposition which has been shown, to any blow which might mean, not only victory for us but also victory for Russia, this belongs to the major coincidences of history. It lends sinister meaning to the talk about 'a long war'. In its indifference to the lot of the British people, the protraction of the separation of husbands and wives, and the prolongation of imprisonment for our men in Germany, it is a masterpiece of callousness.

The root of it seemingly lies in the horrifying order of class antagonism in this island, which knows no bounds. I say 'no bounds', because all these classes, or money-groups, should set a boundary to class-mania; it should stop at the cliffs of Dover. Project it into your foreign policy, let it confuse you about the map of Europe, the size of the various nations there and their aims, and the possible threat to yourself, and you head for disaster.

The people in this island who allowed the war to come about, from this maniac fear of Communism, and now see, as a result of it, a more thriving Communist Party here than we ever knew before, seemingly wish to inflate this to the size of a real danger, by prolonging the war. They are as stupid as the others who now begin to call for us to strike at Germany, *not* so much in our own interest, which is, to finish the war, as because Russia is Communist. These people, in their turn, ascribe the Russian successes, not to Russia, but to the merits of Communism. A great problem, when we return to Civvy Street, will be to remove the fog from the eyes of these people; but the paramount danger comes from the people at the top end of the money-scale, who in this matter cannot be brought to see clearly, and will either bring a real Communist danger or a third war upon us.

This Greater War — the class war in England — inspires in me the feeling I might have if I were compelled to share a bed with a skunk and a squid. These two, wedded, might produce as pleasant an off-spring. To see so much misery born of so much stupidity, is an abject thing.

Unhappily, it runs from top to bottom now. The higher money-groups enclosed themselves within their fences; the lower ones have now enclosed themselves inside a hedge of passive resentment just as impenetrable. The initial sales resistance of a slum child, to beauty or freedom, is amazing; but with what widely opening eyes does it yield, after the first attempts!

That anything has changed, in England, in this respect, during a second world war, only those will believe whose thoughts are delivered to them, with the milk, in pictures and headlines. 'They feared the "low" and hated and despised the "stuck-up", and so they "kept themselves to them-selves", according to the English ideal'; thus wrote Mr. Wells in *Kipps*, many years ago. The 'low' and the 'stuck-up', in this strange island, hold the same feelings towards the in-betweens. The moon seems nearer to us than the ideal of each-for-all, in this land which 'must be free or die', and yet suffered Enclosure.

But in foreign policy, since we live in a tiny island off the European mainland, we cannot keep ourselves to ourselves, unless we wish to suc-cumb, in an orgy of mutual detestation, to a foreign conqueror. Our enemies and our friends choose themselves. Our indispensable ally, if we are to win this war soon and to have after it the peace we sorely need, is Russia, and this applies to all of us, whether we travel third, second or first class. It applies equally whether Russia is Bolshevist, Communist, Anarchist, Monarchist, Republican, Fantastic, Surrealistic, Masochistic, Fascist, National Socialist, Atheist, Deist, or Uncle Tom Cobbley. It applies even if every Russian paints himself green, stands on his head and sings Aztec love songs in Esperanto.

The most ominous and disappointing thing in this war is that, even after four years of it, when we so direly need peace, confusion about Russia should stand between us and victory. This can only happen, I surmise, because of one other thing.

We hear a lot nowadays about 'vested interests', a phrase which denotes the prolongation of some evil state of affairs by persons who stand to profit from its continuance. But war is the greatest vested interest of all. More people stand to gain by its protraction than by that of any other evil state of affairs imaginable. When thousands of men die each day, as in the last war, they cannot have their way. When a war drags on *without* heavy casualties, their position is very strong.

Masses of English people long desperately for an end to this war. They are the fighting men long separated from their women folk and children, the wives, and decent citizens generally. But there are many others who lose nothing by the war, who gain substantially by it. They may not consciously realize the fact, but they find life pleasant and experience no active yearning for an early return to peace. Manufacturers who reap great profits and workpeople who earn high wages; politicians who have selflessly renounced their salaries but receive far more than before in non-taxable 'expenses', and company directors who are exempt from income-tax because their fees are paid tax-free; the enormous army of officials who are exempt from service but enjoy accumulating privileges; the great legion of people 'reserved' to deliver lectures about poison gas, a weapon which, as the specialists know, will not be used in this war because it is ineffective: all these and many more, whether they realize it or not, have a vested interest in the war, and feel no vigorous urge to press for its ending.

Their existence, and the fact that our casualties have not yet been insupportable, combine to form a mass of opinion at least passively favourable to the dragging-on of the war. Their existence enables the confusion of thought about Russia to continue.

If we do not strike soon, and so break the stalemate, dangers will arise from this confusion which will make an almost inextricable tangle of the future. One new danger already looms up. Russia, being moved to even greater suspicion of our sincerity, begins to play with ideas of pressing into Europe, of occupying territory there for future safety! The Russians have already hinted broadly that they intend to keep that part of Poland which they entered when the Germans attacked from the West. Now they even encourage the formation, in Russia, by emigrants from Poland whom the Poles would certainly deny to be Polish, who themselves refuse to become Polish, of a sort of 'Free Polish' movement with the obvious aim of setting up something indistinguishable from a Soviet Poland in the other part of that country!

Do you perceive, gentle reader, to what endless complications this indeterminate policy towards Russia leads? Our honour is bound up with Poland. We cannot acquiesce in the partitioning of that country. We might not have won the Battle of Britain without the Polish airmen who fought with our own men. Their share in the victory was great: read *Squadron 303*, by Arkady Fiedler (Peter Davies, 1942), if you are not acquainted with it. Do we wish to be faced with the choice, when the war ends, between handing Poland over to Russia, as we handed Czecho-slovakia over to Hitler, or fighting Russia?

When we promised Russia 'all possible help' (at the German attack in 1941) we should have insisted on a clear understanding about Poland first, and then struck. Now, the shadow of new trouble grows out of this question.

Here *The Times* pops up again. *The Times*, on March 10th, 1943, just as Mr. Eden flew to America to discuss such matters, printed an article on 'Security in Europe' which greatly alarmed all the exiled Governments in London. It said, among other things, that

> The sole interest of Russia is to assure herself that her outer defences are in sure hands; and this interest will be best served if the lands between her frontiers and those of Germany are held by Governments and peoples friendly to herself.

Now, what sinister thing is this? Poland did not attack Russia, nor ever threatened any harm to Russia. Poland fought against Germany, and then was divided between Germany and Russia, for the how oftenth time in history. The thing *The Times* claims for Russia is exactly that which Hitler claimed for Germany in respect of Austria and Czecho-slovakia. Neither of those countries threatened Germany. The claim was a lying pretext for aggression and annexation, preparatory to a great war.

The Polish Government in London was officially told that the article in *The Times* did not represent the British Government's policy. But this rings an ominous bell in my memory.

On November 29th, 1937, *The Times*, of which I was the Corre-spondent in Central Europe, published a leading article which carefully launched the suggestion that Austria's destiny lay in union with Germany.

It caused a minor panic in the Austrian Government, which was only assuaged when, as the Austrian Chancellor himself told me, the British Government stated, on his inquiry, that 'there is no change in British policy in Central Europe' and that England 'would not permit any change in the *status quo* in these parts'. On March 11th, 1938, Hitler marched in. The British Government accepted the change without changing countenance.

On September 7th, 1938, *The Times*, in a leading article, launched a proposal for the cession of the 'fringe of alien populations in Czechoslovakia' to the Reich. A flood of public protests was the result. The British Government issued an official statement that 'the suggestion in *The Times* leading article ... in no way represents the views of the British Government'. On September 18th, 1938, Mr. Chamberlain presented an ultimatum to Czechoslovakia in the exact sense of the suggestion made by *The Times* on September 7th. The 'fringe of alien populations' was duly transferred to Germany at the British command, and the new war became certain. (I resigned from *The Times* at that moment, feeling that the knowledge and experience of a trained foreign correspondent were valueless to it.) Six months later, Germany took the rest of Czechoslovakia.

Now, in 1943, *The Times* makes a similar suggestion about Poland. The British Government repudiates it.

We may march towards even worse dilemmas, through this incorrigible and intolerable confusion in our foreign policy.

We cannot surrender Europe, either to Germany or Russia, without surrendering ourselves. Though Magdeburg is but Maidstone in German, and Pont l'evêque not much more than Abbotsford in French, none of us are ripe to give up nationhood, and we in this island do not wish to. Are we fighting this war for merely another Munich?

It is urgently necessary that we should clarify our relations with Russia, for the dangers multiply, as I have shown. We should insist on a clear and just agreement about Poland, and strike to win this war.

First things come first, and the first thing for us is foreign policy. Not only our island safety, but such liberty as mankind may ever win, in this mortal world, depend on it. In war-time, foreign policy is easy for Englishmen to understand. It is, to fight the enemy. When they return, they hand over the torch to the men who sent them, but did not fight.

Thus is the torch lost. Having fought, they should never take their eyes off it.

After the last war, men revived, and adapted to our times, the symbolic rite of the eternal flame, which was never allowed to go out, night or day. They thought thus to keep alive the memory and guard the faith of the million men who died in the last war. Somewhere, that pathetic flame probably still flickers, though it sank in 1935 and went out at the time of Munich. If the men who come back from this war could think of our foreign policy as that flame to be cherished, and not as two words which they but dimly comprehend, they might in good heart start on their journey and be sure that they would find a secure future, a happier breed and a freer land, in 1950 and 1960.

That will not happen if they leave their affairs, unwatched, in the hands of men elected to Parliament and then forgotten. The key to foreign policy is Russia. Even now, in the midst of the war, we threaten to lose it. We need to reach an arrangement with Russia quickly, as the price of the blow for victory which we should strike without further delay, about the frontiers of Poland; a land which we cannot desert if any faith at all is to remain in this country. After that, we need an alliance with Russia for fifty years.

On that basis, we may have the long peace we need. It is the first thing we need, and first things come first.

CHAPTER II

THE CHOICE OF ENEMIES

'A MAN cannot be too careful in the choice of his enemies,' wrote Oscar Wilde. 'Truth standing on its head to attract attention,' scoffed Le Gallienne, of such Wilde talk. But men will often only look at truth when you use some such device to attract their attention to it.

The jest, at all events, contains a major truth, for us. Germany, by the numbers of its people, their warlike inheritance, the ambitions these produce, and its place on the map, chooses to be our enemy. We cannot build a tight little island, unless we recognize the danger. One thing alone will make Germany our friend: our own strength, supported by a Russian alliance. This is sad for people who like, though they do not know, the Germans, and for those who dislike, though they do not know, the Russians; but it is true.

It will remain so when we return to Civvy Street, and for long to come. We are urged nowadays to read a Russian novel, called *War and Peace*. The book of our future is called, Peace or War? This is the answer to the question.

You may no more hope to abolish day and night, than to escape from this inexorable choice. We can only finish this war quickly, have enduring peace after it, make this island safe and hold the Empire together, if we realize that Germany chooses to be our potential enemy and that we must choose Russia for our indispensable ally.

That this war still goes on and that we have not yet won it, is in my belief due to the fact that international forces, whose interests are not ours, who do not care about our people or our island safety or our future, still seek to blind the British to this truth, and have substantial success. But these islanders will be mad if they allow themselves to be bluffed again, and their eyes to be diverted from the enemy who chooses himself. The delay in ending this war is already deeply suspicious, and can only profit international arms manufacturers and power-seeking groups. It places our future in jeopardy again.[1]

[1] Lord Keyes, whose project to seize Trondjem might, in the view of good observers, have saved Norway and inflicted a major defeat on the Germans early in the war, who has now been dismissed from leadership of the Commandos, which have been inactive since his retirement, stated in March 1943 that the Commandos could have been used to seize Tunis and Bizerta in November 1942, while the First Army moved up on land. As I write, our long pause in Tunisia, which is caused by the German hold on those two ports, threatens to prolong the war still further.

Rear-Admiral M. W. W. P. Consett, who was British Naval Attaché in Scandinavia during the last war, in 1928 published a book called *The Triumph of Unarmed Forces* (Williams and Norgate), which deserves close study by all who seek the causes of war. Its theme is, that while the British *armed* forces strove for victory, the British *unarmed* forces, such as finance and goods supply, helped Germany to hold out. The sub-title of the book is, 'An account of the transactions by which Germany during the Great War was able to obtain supplies prior to her collapse under the pressure of economic forces'. In his Preface, Admiral Consett says 'The war was prolonged far beyond the limits of necessity . . . From the very beginning goods poured into Germany from Scandinavia, and for over two years Scandinavia received from the British Empire and the Allied countries stocks which, together with those from neutral countries, exceeded all previous quantities and literally saved Germany from starvation'. The gravest facts are disclosed in this book about the way essential war materials from this country reached Germany through Scandinavia, thus 'prolonging the war'.

Admiral Consett quotes a protest of his own to the British Minister in Norway, in 1916, about the continued supply of lard to Denmark, which was thus enabled to release an amount

The coming of the war seems neither to have dispelled the illusions, nor checked the machinations, which caused it. The public is again being misled about the inexorable choice of enemies and allies. Even before we reach Civvy Street, we shall hear again the cry 'Don't try to keep Germany down' which was used, after the war began, by the late Sir Nevile Henderson. In my experience, the people who use such phrases care nothing for the weal or woe of Germans. They pursue other motives.

The Fair Dealers raised their voices in the last war, as we approached victory, and defeat advanced on Germany. A Mr. Walter Runciman, M.P., was then approvingly quoted by the German Chancellor as 'expressing the opinion that we should be nearer to peace if accredited and responsible representatives of the belligerent powers would get together in a small circle for a mutual exchange of views'. He was a member of the 'Lansdowne Group', which (at a time when Germany was everywhere victorious) advocated early negotiations to end the war. The proposal was repudiated by angry public protest. It seemed to die.

Did it, though? Twenty years later, in 1938, a Lord Runciman was chosen to visit a small country far away, which our politicians 'knew nothing about'. He recommended the surrender to Germany of that part of it which contained its defences. Mr. Chamberlain enforced the surrender by threatening to abandon Czechoslovakia to its fate; he thus destroyed the Third Front and the dam which prevented this war.

Thus we may prick our ears now, if we wish to hear the first sounds of the next war, in 1963, and prevent it.

In the summer of 1942 Lady Snowden spoke, in London, to the Anglo-Swedish Society. Before this war, she caused alarm and despondency

to Germany yielding enough nitro-glycerine for 600 tons of gun ammunition; as well as a letter from a Danish naval officer to himself expressing sympathy with him 'for having to live as you do amongst these people who are making fortunes in supplying your enemies with food when the officers and men of the British Navy are risking their lives in trying to blockade your enemies'. I have not seen the figures of our trade with Sweden published during this war, but the memory of Admiral Consett's invaluable book is awakened by an item published in an Australian newspaper on November 11th, 1942: 'A message from Stockholm says that the Swedish Stock Exchange had a Black Monday coinciding with news of the Allied landings in North Africa, when traders judged that early peace prospects were excellent. Shares in armament and subsidiary plants fell, many touching a record low. Some lost 50 points'.

The causes of war are important to detect. But the causes of the *prolongation* of wars, once begun, are equally important, and Admiral Consett's book gives the most authentic information I know of one of these causes. They are important to bear in mind when considering the strong opposition which always arises, in this country, to any public clamour for action which might *shorten* the war.

to hard-working British newspaper correspondents in Berlin, who fought to awaken this country to the impending danger. She went to Germany, and after 'five days' intensive search for the truth' there, wrote:

> There is no antagonism to England in this country ... On the contrary, there is an earnest desire on the part of Herr Hitler and his people for friendship with England, and if it should rest with him and them there would be no war ... But there is a sad and growing conviction that nothing the German spokesmen can say or do will advance by one iota those fraternal friendships which ... are so ardently desired if they can be honourably achieved ... The secret of Herr Hitler's power lies in his selflessness and his sincerity ... He is a simple man of great personal integrity ... I would not hesitate to accept his word when promised.

(Lady Snowden supported in 1917 the arguments of the 'Lansdowne Letter'). 'A great difference of opinion', reported the *Evening Standard* in 1912, 'has arisen about what she meant in her speech. Lord Sempill, who was in the chair, tells me he understood her to express the opinion that a negotiated peace was desirable "when the time is ripe". Lord Sempill says he agrees with this suggestion. But Lady Snowden, when I spoke to her, warmly denied the suggestion that she advocated a negotiated settlement. "There can be no discussions with the Nazis", she said, "and I said that at the luncheon. My exact language was, 'We cannot negotiate with men who have elevated bad faith to the status of a creed' "."

(A few Nazi leaders, 'guilty men', will disappear as the war goes on. That is irrelevant. The disappearance of the Kaiser benefited us not at all.)

'When Lord Sempill said he agreed with the idea of a negotiated peace', the *Evening Standard* continues, 'I asked him at what point he was prepared publicly to suggest the course he would like followed. "At the moment when the military situation is dominantly in our favour", he replied, "and when the time comes we want to benefit from the experience of the past — we don't want another Versailles." I then asked him if he would introduce a motion in the House of Lords on the subject. "Yes", he said, "and I am sure I could get a lot of support for such a motion".'

Seemingly we move, then, from the Lansdowne Letter of 1917 to the Sempill Motion of this year or next. But we have made an Alliance with

Russia which engages us *not* separately to negotiate with, or make any armistice or peace treaty with, *any* German Government.

'The old world is dead': thus Professor Carr, of *The Times*, ends his book, *Conditions of Peace* (Macmillan, 1942). What nonsense. We move in a circle, like a cat chasing its tail. The old world remains unchanged. The same mistakes are repeated in the same way, as if we were only born yesterday. The same futile phrases are used: they have not even been exchanged for utility phrases in war-time. They are mortally dangerous, for many people clutch gladly at a phrase of straw, instead of swimming further in the waters of thought and seizing a lifebelt of truth.

The worst of them all is, 'No Second Versailles'. I have challenged hundreds of its users, and never found *one* who had read the Versailles Treaty or knew how it worked. No treaty can be maintained if the victors are inflexibly resolved to allow the losers to rearm and make a new war; that was why this treaty now lies in ruins. It was in its main provisions the best treaty Europe ever knew. Never before were so many Europeans free to live their own lives.

Are we, then, when the din of war begins to be drowned by the pandemonium of peace, or even before, to repeat every mistake we made before, like blinkered asses on a water-wheel?

If we are, for what do such men die as Richard McLeod of Hull, who wrote to his mother before the bombing raid from which he did not return:

> If I am killed, I know it will be in the most glorious and Christian engagement to which it has pleased God to call a member of our house. You know how deeply I felt about Czechoslovakia. Judge, then, how much greater my feelings are when I know that this is for Britain. Despite all that lies close to my heart, I look upon this as secondary to the establishment of a life of peace and security for all the little races of the world for which we fight, and particularly the Czechs, who have filled me with admiration.

This spirit and this ideal are in danger of being betrayed once more. The lag in our prosecution of the war, the neglect of chances to strike and win it, become sinister. Confusion is growing about an issue which should now be clear: who is our enemy, and do we intend to defeat him? We have been promised that 'nine months' of 1943, which expire in October, will at last bring clarity. If they do not, we shall be thrown back into the miserable darkness of the pre-war years — when the British *people* clearly saw that Germany was choosing to be their enemy, but their leaders denied that this was so and retarded our armament while the self-chosen foe prepared!

WHODUNIT?

THE English have a passion for what they call thrillers and I call dullers. Whodunit? Was it murder, and by whom? Through endless pages they plough, in search of the answer to this problem. The motives which may lead to a murder are of enthralling interest. But death is final, and the process of unravelling afterwards is no more absorbing than the opening of a road to discover the cables beneath — an operation which always attracts many beholders.

But if they like Whodunits, let them take with them, as they go through Civvy Street in search of their future, the greatest mystery story of all time. It is our own story. But we are not dead; we live. The corpse stands up, and goes on again. We nearly died, though.

Whodunit? Who led us up the garden path; what footpads waylaid and nearly killed us? Why did they do this? Where and when may we expect to meet them again, in Civvy Street, and how may we thwart them? Who told us, this is the road to peace, and led us straight to war? Who took our savings, destroyed our businesses, and sent our sons and daughters away?

About 1950, you may come to the solution. That would be time enough, to foil 'Them' at Their next attempt.

Whodunit? The best detectives begin by searching for the motive. Find the motive, and you may find the assassin. And where may one look for the motive? Why, among 'the guilty men', Hitler and his grisly gang, of course: that is what the footpads will blandly say, when we meet them in Civvy Street again. They will hope, by that deceit, to lure us into another dark alley.

No. Germany held the bludgeon, but we needed first, to be delivered to the footpad. Then, whose was the profit?

I think the answer is: international bankers; their cousins, international arms manufacturers, with their offspring trades and kindred industries, particularly oil; and international power-seeking groups.

'The whole world will be much poorer after the war,' said the Chancellor of the Exchequer, Sir Kingsley Wood, on February 2nd, 1943. It is patently untrue. Wealth is transferred by war, not destroyed. The small man whose house and furniture have been destroyed, who was forced to close his business and go to fight, will be poorer. His neighbour, whose house and furniture were not destroyed, will own property many times more valuable than before; the big store which remained open when the little shop closed, will be richer.[1] The cost of an exploding shell or bomb is not blown to smithereens; the money lies to the credit of the manufacturer who made it. The ten shillings in every pound, which now are taken from our incomes, do not evaporate; they maintain the stupendously swollen legion of exempt officials. As in all these wars, some become richer, others poorer. No poverty afflicts the great bankers and armament syndicates: this is their harvest-time. A big book could be written about the enrichment of some and the impoverishment of others, during this war; and it should be called, 'Profit at Home!'

We begin to see the motives!

The Correspondent of the London *Times* came in to give me a report on the effects of the London protest to Hitler about rearming — a protest made after England and the United States have sold millions of dollars worth of arms to Germany.

The American Ambassador in Berlin, William E. Dodd, writing in his Diary on December 5th, 1934.

The British investor put more money into Europe than into the whole of the Colonies — more money into the Dutch East Indies than into the whole of British Africa.

Mr. Herbert Morrison, Home Secretary, on January 10th, 1943.

While ex-Servicemen sold matches and played barrel organs, the Big Five Banks were vieing with each other to see which could lend the

---

[1] In March 1943, land bought for about £75 an acre in 1913 was sold for £283 an acre, at Boston in Lincolnshire, while a house in that town which was worth about £150 before this war, was sold for £500. In the House of Commons, about the same time, Mr. James Griffiths, M.P. for Llanelly, reported that a house in London which was bought for £950 in 1939 was sold for £1,500 in 1942, that a cottage sold for £575 in 1939 was resold in 1942 for £1,075, and that houses *condemned* before this war are now being sold for £500 and £600. These conditions are now general in England.

most millions to the Hun. 'Put Germany on her feet', was the slogan and they certainly succeeded in that. Are we going to do that again? There has been a hint of it in some of the Foreign Secretary's speeches.
Lieut-Commander Braithwaite, M.P., Conservative, Holderness, in the House of Commons.

I saw something of those transactions. After Hitler came to power, and high-speed rearmament began, the German Government, like a policeman deftly slipping the handcuffs on a citizen, calmly shackled this country to the German war machine by withholding payment of a large amount of short-term loans, when they fell due. An arrangement was reached, called a 'Standstill Agreement'; the foreign bankers agreed to leave the money in Germany, interest being paid. These agreements were annually renewed. Each year the bankers from London arrived to talk things over, spent pleasant days in the Adlon Hotel, and departed, praising Germany's fairness in the matter. All knew that the capital sum was spent on armaments, and that these would presently be used against British soldiers.

British newspaper correspondents were not allowed to tell this story of Germany's rearmament, urgent warlike ambitions, and the way the new war was being financed. Some of these bankers were on the boards of great armaments concerns and of British newspapers. While the British journalists were prevented from telling the truth, these newspapers, and the politicians, told England that 'Hitler is a peace-loving man', and that those who said the contrary were 'warmongers'.

These sums remain in Germany. What part will they play, after the war, or even in shaping the future course of it? Bear them in mind, when the cry of 'Give Germany a Square Deal' goes up! (Readers should also consult Philip Noel Baker, *The Private Manufacture of Armaments*, Gollancz, 1936, and Bernhard Menne, *Krupp*, William Hodge & Co., 1937. They may also bear in mind that the three inter-war Conservative Prime Ministers all originated from the daughter-industries of the arms trade. When *Tory M.P.*, by Simon Haxey (Gollancz, 1939), was written, sixty Conservative Members were directors of armaments and allied industries.)

In the last war, things happened which aroused tempestuous protest from the outraged conscience of mankind. The Germans occupied the Briey Basin, a mineral-bearing district which lay between France and Germany and was rich in iron. The French never bombed it, or tried to put it out of action, though the Germans were using the iron for muni-

88

tions. The works belonged to the de Wendel family, which belongs to the greatest French munition manufacturers. The scandal became known during the war, and after it a stormy debate raged in the French Parliament. But it led to no result: the influence of the *Comité des Forges*, the French Federation of Heavy Industries, was too strong. The Frenchmen who were killed by the shells made from those ores, were dead! Conversely, German soldiers were killed by British shells, the nosecaps of which bore the mark 'KPz 96/04' (or, Krupp patent fuse), the patent fees having been credited by the British makers to the Krupp account. At little German goods-stations, the Krupp name and trade-mark were filed or ground off high-grade steel bars before they continued their journey to Switzerland (and France). British metal merchants made deliveries of iron ore to Rotterdam, in peaceful Holland (for Krupps). A French armoured cruiser stopped a Norwegian vessel containing 2,500 tons of nickel from French New Caledonia for Krupps, half of its cost already having been paid by Krupps; a French prize court declared the cargo to be contraband of war, but an urgent order from the French Government released it, and it was delivered to Krupps.

And so on, and so on. A long war, not a short one, could be the only desire of the people, in all the belligerent countries, who profited from such transactions. The same motive certainly prevails, among similar people, to-day. In that war, the Press retained much freedom in all the countries which fought; hence the exposure of such things. In this war, the Press has been muzzled.

Nevertheless, we know of a transaction in this war which trumps, in bestiality, even those of the last.

After the invasion of Austria, it became clear that Mr. Chamberlain and his Tory cohorts meant to help Hitler to destroy Czechoslovakia. At that moment, I remarked to a bewildered colleague, on a café terrace in Prague, 'This *can't* be stupidity; it must be treachery'. For this would (1) destroy the Third Front, which prevented Germany from beginning the war while it stood; (2) we should thereby hand over to Germany the Czech defences, and therewith, all Czechoslovakia; (3) we should throw away the *four armoured divisions* which the Czechs held ready to put against the German *five* (Lord Gort faced the Germans without even *one* fully armoured division).

But that was not all. The territory which we would compel Czechoslovakia to yield to Germany, contained the Skoda armaments works, at Pilsen, the arsenal of the old Austro-Hungarian Empire. Its war-time output would be prodigious. And British money was invested in it: a sound investment, if British foreign policy remained honest; but a mad one (we *then* thought) if British foreign policy handed it to Germany. How little we knew!

The Skoda Works were given by Mr. Chamberlain to Hitler. How many tanks and guns have the Germans made there, and how many of our men have been killed by them? The French laid much of the blame for their collapse on the Skoda-made tanks which the Germans used.

That is bad enough, but worse follows, in this chapter of our Whodunit? Truth becomes not only stranger, but beastlier than fiction. The picture of a British soldier being killed by a tank which our Government, while England cheered, forced the Czechs to hand to the Germans, is bad enough. But consider another picture: that of a British shareholder, during the war, receiving dividends on his Skoda shares, while his neighbour's son is shot down over Skoda by a Skoda-made gun or nightfighter! The R.A.F. were sent there!

This is what happened:

After Munich, the British conscience was soothed by the news that the British Government would lend what remained of Czechoslovakia £6,000,000 'for reconstruction purposes'. The stricken and amputated state was thus to be healed and helped on its feet again.

When Germany took the rest of Czechoslovakia, six months later, most of the £6,000,000 stood to the Czech credit in London. It was promptly blocked, so that the Germans could not get it. The British Government compelled the surrender to Germany of the Czechs' *own* gold, held by the International Bank in Basel, on the board of which we were, and still are represented.

What happened to the £6,000,000? Was it returned to the credit of the British taxpayer? No! The payment, out of it, of the claims of British creditors 'seemed reasonable'! The British holders of Skoda 6 per cent debentures received their money. The Treasury Order authorizing this was issued in March 1940 (when Mr. Chamberlain was still Prime Minister, Lord Simon Chancellor of the Exchequer, Sir Horace Wilson Head of the Treasury), a few weeks before the Skoda-made tanks crashed down on the British and French troops!

Inaccurate headlines like 'Dividends from Death' and accusations of usury draw the red herring of prejudice across the trail [wrote a financial expert in a London newspaper], Skoda debenture-holders are ordinary commercial creditors, and cannot in justice be treated differently from other such creditors. The suggestion that armament-makers are afflicted with a double dose of original sin reads a little queerly in these days.

The people who put their money in Skoda did so in good faith, and if Governments could be trusted to tell the truth and pursue an honest foreign policy, they even chose a patriotic investment. But the causes of war can never be removed if men may think, 'Well, come war, come peace, come victory or defeat, whether the weapons this concern makes are used for or against my country, I shall get my money'.

Nothing can justify the payment of interest to British shareholders in a business which now makes arms to kill their own countrypeople. They should lose that money, and thus learn the need to watch the actions of their governments. What objection could these debenture-holders feel to a new Munich Agreement or a new war, in twenty years time? Can any find decent congruity in the picture of these payments, being made by the British Government to shareholders in German-occupied arms factories, while our land is placarded with appeals to private charity for 'the R.A.F. Benevolent Fund'? Are the orphans of a man shot down over Skoda to depend on alms, while the State pays interest to shareholders in that same concern?

I hope some begin to perceive the real nature of the Munich Agreement, for their future after this war depends on their understanding it. The trouble with individual British investors in international arms concerns is not that they have a double dose of original sin, but a quadruple dose of aboriginal apathy; if they would watch politics as closely as they watch prospectuses, the British creditors of Skoda would draw their dividends to-day in a world at peace and without shame to themselves. But much original sin is in a Government which applies public funds to such an end at such a time.

This detestable transaction is the trueborn child of the Munich Agreement, and breathes the spirit of that pact now pronounced dead, but yet alive. This should be included in the history books, for the benefit of the growing generation. Two English children of to-morrow, if they were to ask the famous question of the last war, 'What did you do in the Great War, Daddy?', might respectively be told, 'I bombed Skoda', or, 'I drew my dividends from Skoda'.

The great question, 'Whodunit, and why?' takes on a sharp edge when these things are studied. The breakdown of the peace began with the Japanese attack on China in 1931. Our leaders wagged admonishing forefingers at the Japanese. During the next two years, fifty-three licences for the export of war materials to Japan were issued in this country. One big firm alone sent nearly £500,000 worth of arms during that period. America sent many times as much. These were but pickings. The real profits began when the Japanese were ready and soldiers from the West were sent to fight them. Heads I win, and tails you lose! British, Imperial and Indian soldiers paid the price, at Hongkong, Singapore and elsewhere; Americans, at Pearl Harbour. On the stock exchanges, they talk of 'making a killing', when they mean, to make money. Here, both were made.

Whodunit? The larger pieces of the puzzle fall into the places. We grow warm, gentle reader. We approach the motives and the culprits.

But what of the weapon? I think we have found it. Call it The Hidden Hand, or Anonymity.

The further you probe into these things, the more clearly you find that power to-day is wielded by men who lurk in shadow, whose instruments the politicians merely are, those public figures which you acclaim to-day and curse to-morrow.

Call these men, collectively, Anon. You may believe that a God exists, in heaven; then why not a demon, on earth, called Anon. Anon is many men, and we have seen the main groups to which they belong, in the realm of commerce. (Religion supplies another, and territorial ambitions, deriving from a book thousands of years old, another.) All are super-national; all pursue aims which cut through the interests of the communities of peoples called nations, or states, which they use as their instruments.

Only by assuming the existence of this non-national, anti-national, super-national, international demon, Anon, can I understand Mr. Lloyd George's words (April 7th, 1923):

Wars are precipitated by motives which the statesmen responsible for them dare not publicly avow. A public discussion would drag these motives in their nudity into the open, where they would die of exposure to the withering contempt of humanity.

You perceive, gentle reader, why our statesmen always say 'No recriminations', 'no scapegoats', 'no public inquiry', 'the past is past', 'no useful purpose would be served . . .', 'this information would not be in the public interest'.

Mr. Lloyd George is an authority. He was not 'responsible for a war', but he became responsible for conducting one. No greater expert, then, lives. Why 'dare' he not publicly avow these motives? If but one man, of his weight, would say all he knew, we should have peace for a long time.

He confirms my explanation, that hidden motives exist for these wars. But if the statesmen 'dare not avow these motives', they must be in the power of others, of Anon.

Let us make this thing vivid and comprehensible by considering one such man:

Hendrik August Wilhelm Deterding was born and died a Hollander. How many realized that, when they read some servile gossiper's paragraph about Sir Henri, or even Sir Henry Deterding? He received a British order, carrying a knighthood, for the great help he gave, in the last war, in ensuring our oil supplies.

He was extremely successful in the oil business, wealthy and powerful. During his life, most of the world's oil came under the control of two great concerns, one of which he led. The importance of oil should now be clear to the dullest. Next to a monopoly of food or drink, nothing could give the monopolist such power over mankind. (The oil monopoly seems to have been sometimes fiercely contested, sometimes tacitly shared between the two concerns.)

Little has been published in this country, about the political power wielded by the oil concerns. In America, several books have appeared. The law of libel, a formidable instrument for preventing the British public from learning that which it should know, has been used to prevent publication here. This is one reason for the prevailing ignorance on the subject; another is the subservience of the Press to such powerful interests.

One leading London newspaper, in the inter-war years, undertook to publish six articles explaining the politics of oil, the way they cut through national interests, and particularly their influence for peace or war. They stopped at the fourth article, and when the writer asked, why, the editor replied: 'The oil articles brought about my ears a very considerable whirl-wind, and if I were you I think I would lay off oil for a bit. It is too big a racket to handle safely.'

Here the reader may gain a glimpse of the inhibitions which work in newspaper offices, and infer for himself how far they are likely to tell him the truth.

But back to Deterding. In 1918 the British attacked Russia and occupied the Caucasus, the great oil-district of Southern Russia, where the two great international oil concerns held great interests (you may remark, gentle reader, that Hitler, who still hopes to gain our support, or at least our inactivity, while he is engaged with Russia, particularly attacks this region). The Bolshevists refused to disintegrate, and the British withdrew, leaving White Russians in occupation. In 1920, the Red Russians drove them out, and since that momentous day a large oilfield has been outside the ownership and operations of the international concerns.

This was confiscation! It was not worth the bones of a single British soldier, then or twenty years later. For that matter, the Bolshevists, who needed international help, eagerly sought an arrangement with the former owners. Conferences at Genoa and The Hague came to nothing. They were dominated by the vengeful figures of cosmopolitan oil magnates who, though not delegates to them, filled the big hotels around ('Anon', in the background!).

From that moment Deterding was obsessed with hatred of the Bolshevists. It is fair to say that he lived for the day when they would be overthrown (he foretold this as imminent, repeatedly), and the Caucasus oil be restored to its foreign owners. Being immensely powerful, he was able to press this aim in many ways. Several British newspapers became the mouthpieces of it. (Some may remember the placards, 'No Soviet Oil sold here!', which were distributed to garage owners.)

He was entitled to his opinion. The point is, that he was able to exert influence on *British* policy and politicians, though a new war on account of the Soviet oilfields was no interest of the inhabitants of this island. True, in one letter to the Press he accused the Bolshevists of 'not playing cricket'; but his birth, thoughts, feelings and interests were not British, but international.

His second wife was a Russian lady. They spent much time in Paris, and he spent large sums in training young émigré Russians there in the way they should go.

His third wife was a German woman. When the new war approached, and his dream of Bolshevist humiliation seemed to approach realization, he retired with her to an estate in Germany. There just before the war began, he died.

This is an important fragment of the story of Anon, of yesterday and of this war. Such a man could not feel that the safety of this island was the paramount thing, that an alliance with Russia was indispensable for it. He could only think of the oil of the Caucasus, and did not mind what soldiers died to get it, if it were only regained. He was but one of many who were powerful behind the scenes.

These things we did not know, last time we stumbled through Civvy Street, towards an avoidable war. This time, we know, and need to watch our step. We need to know who shapes our course, what hands are outstretched to alter it. The curse of anonymity is heavy on us. The structure of our public life has been built to prevent us from seeing what goes on behind the scene while, in front, a Minister stands and says, 'We realize that our safety lies in alliance with Russia and shall pursue that policy'.

The misery of this war should not be prolonged, or a new one brought about after it, because somebody's factory was confiscated in 1918. I object to the fact that, if my books were translated into Russian, no payment would reach me, and do not protest less strongly because my books are outlawed in Russia, and for that matter in Germany. I might write a book one day which *would* be published in Russia. My dues would be confiscated in practice, for I would not wish to visit Russia merely in order to spend, on hotels and meals, whatever roubles lay to my credit in a Russian bank.

I should violently object to this confiscation. But I would scarify any who urged that, for such reasons, we should encourage some other country to attack Russia or make war on Russia ourselves. That would imperil a much greater interest of mine, and my compatriots, than my earnings as a writer; it would imperil the safety of this island.

Perhaps this personal illustration may make a plain thing clear. It is the simple but vital principle which such powerful men as Deterding cannot understand, because their roots are international.

Such men were powerful enough, behind the scenes, to lead us into a new war, from which they thought to fetch private chestnuts. Consider once more, in this light, the events of 1935, when the war really began. We shall meet 1935 again, as we pass through Civvy Street, and we cannot construct something, in the future, unless we understand them.

In 1935 the British Government, alarmed by the protest of eleven million people, pledged itself to check aggression — and to prevent the coming war. The case in point, though it was in fact the beginning of this war, was the seemingly local episode of Italy's attack on Abyssinia. None of the experimental exploits, with which the warmakers probed the strength of the nations pledged to preserve the peace, could have been easier to check. Not even armed force was necessary. The coveted territory lay far away, across sea and desert. The aggressor's supplies could have been cut off knife-like, by the others combined, and led by Britain. He owned no oilfields, and drew his fuel supplies from the outer world.

Our hand, then, was on his jugular vein. We needed only to squeeze, he would release his victim, the world would applaud a British victory more famous than any gained in war, aggression would collapse in ignominy, peace would be safe for long to come. 'The oil embargo might clearly force the termination of hostilities', said Sir Samuel Hoare.

Oil! But, twenty years before, Caucasus oilfields were taken from the foreign holders. The aggressor, Fascist Italy, was anti-Communist!

Within a few months of the 1935 election, the British Government wrecked the oil embargo. In 1936, Mr. Chamberlain declared, amid oleaginous applause, that the very thought of an oil embargo was 'midsummer madness'. This war began.

The strength of these hidden men, who pursue their ambitions on our shoulders, could not be more clearly revealed. I have shown one, Deterding. We shall meet others, lurking in the shadow in Civvy Street. They are our enemies. The secret of their power is, Anonymity.

War, the red flower, grows from seeds planted in peace. The seeds are the 'motives which the statesmen responsible dare not avow'. These motives, then, exist *in peacetime*. It follows that the statesmen who *seem* to wield power, in peace time, are the instruments of hidden motives, deriving from hidden men. Mr. Lloyd George's words are clear, and we are entitled to take them at their full weight.

They show how dangerous is the habit of giving idolatry to Ministers of the day, which has grown up with this. This country has yielded to it thrice, in recent times. Mr. Baldwin, Mr. MacDonald and Mr. Chamberlain were built into idols by the Press, which is often controlled by persons unknown, and by the broadcasting machine, which is a government monopoly in our country alone (of lands professing to be democratic). The credulous saw heroic figures, which they worshipped. They suspected nothing of this hidden mechanism, these concealed promptings.

We have Mr. Baldwin's own admission that he deliberately misled the country to win an election. Mr. MacDonald's biographer says 'There was the dogged, unshakable loyalty of the miners and their wives; they simply could not believe that their idolized hero would be a traitor and a renegrade' (though he was these). Mr. Chamberlain's claim to idolatry is now open to examination. The method by which public idolatry is created may be seen in the statement of one of his Ministers, on the eve of Dunkirk, that he was a super-man, on whose model we ought all to be built. When Mr. Chamberlain was dead, the same speaker was asked, in a Brains Trust debate, who was the greatest orator of our day and at once replied, 'Mr. Churchill' (by this time, Prime Minister).

Whodunit? A great screen of anonymity has been built between the people and those ulterior motives of which Mr. Lloyd George spoke. They see only public spokesmen; they do not suspect what goes on backstage. If this continues, we shall re-enter Civvy Street blindfold, and never know where we go. Only this vast apparatus of anonymity, I believe as I look back, enabled the country to be drawn into this war. It takes a hundred forms: the Official Secrets Act, the Libel Act, and the blunt refusal to give names of officials responsible for grave misdeeds, who yet wield great power; the refusal of inquiry into national disasters; the withholding or deliberate falsification of information, without subsequent penalty; the anonymity of newspaper ownership or control; the concealment of relationships between Ministers or politicians and banking or armaments interests.

In this war the armour of anonymity, behind which these 'motives' work, has been immensely strengthened. Never was so much withheld from so many, as in this age of our Ministry of Information. The denial of information, under Mr. Churchill's leadership, has become more habitual than before.

More than once, in this war, Mr. Churchill has spoken of military disasters, which befell us, as the gravest in our history. Yet for the first time in our history, enlightenment about them is refused! ('In every previous war dispatches have been published' – Sir R. Glyn, M.P., in December 1942.) Information about Hongkong, Singapore and Tobruk has been denied. In the case of Dunkirk, alone, have the Commander's dispatches been issued. We know *what* happened; we may not know *why* it happened.

If you read these dispatches, you will find no justice in the relegation of Lord Gort, the Commander. He was made 'a scapegoat'. The blame belonged to others, who were not soldiers, into whose conduct all investigation is refused, with the cry 'No scapegoats'. Yet here, you might come to those 'motives'. Here, you might find Anon.

'No scapegoats'.[1]

This, the denial of responsibility, is Anon's most powerful shield and the cause of our troubles, past and to come.

The principle of non-accountability in all circumstances cannot be defended. Only behind this screen, can hidden men and hidden motives wreak their will. We reject this monstrous doctrine in every other department of our public life. When General Cunningham advised caution in Libya, he was deposed. Lord Gort, though he was blameless, was exiled to Gibraltar, after Dunkirk. General Auchinleck was dismissed when the battle went ill in Africa, and General Ritchie, too.

Of the real responsibility, the political responsibility, alone, may we never know anything. This makes nonsense of the rest, for it leaves Anon in power. What will it avail us in 1970, if we come to another Dunkirk, and a general is removed, while the men who armed his enemy and left him without arms or supplies, remain in office and cry 'No scapegoats'?

What will it profit us, that the Foreign Minister should in future be empowered to dismiss an unsuccessful Ambassador, if Anon dictates a policy which spoils the work of any British envoy?

Consider Sir Nevile Henderson, the last British Ambassador to Berlin.

---

[1] The method, of denying either inquiry or the public right to any information, has now seemingly become Government doctrine, and the citizen who continues to desire enlightenment about his own affairs may soon commit a penal offence, by the way matters go. In March 1943, as a result of the absurdly exaggerated blackout, to which I have drawn attention in several books, 173 people were crushed to death in a shelter accident. Mr. Herbert Morrison, the Home Secretary, announced that 'no good Londoner would want to look for scapegoats', and a public inquiry was refused.

No 'reforms in the Foreign Service' would have helped us, in this case. He was chosen for his post *because* he held certain views. I doubt whether any other senior member of the British Foreign Service could have been found, so blinded by prejudice that his sense of British national interests was hopelessly impaired. But for those who thought that Germany might be brought to attack Russia and regain the Caucasus oilfields, or those whose German-invested money was gone into the German war-machine, he was the ideal Ambassador. He was the worst possible one from any other point of view. Who prevailed, then?

The dismissal of generals, the talk of 'reforms in the Foreign Service', are but dust in the public eye, while anonymity and non-accountability remain at the top. If Anon retains power at the fountain-head of power, he can warp the work of ambassadors, thwart the efforts of generals, after this war again. But that is the situation, as long as 'No questions and no recriminations' is the implacable last word of every succeeding Prime Minister.

Because of this, we shall meet at the beginning of Civvy Street, not only the great barrier of Enclosure-in-everything, but a blackout: anonymity and non-accountability. Under its cover, the things were done which caused this war, and they could not have been done in the light. If they are to be left hidden, our future is beset with the same dangers.

Whodunit? Of our Ambassadors, only Sir Nevile Henderson has been allowed to publish a personal apologia, one of the most gravely mis-leading documents of our time. But the deviation in our foreign policy, which led to this war, was not the result of misinformation supplied by our Ambassadors, and the public is deluded again if it gains this impression from the much-vaunted 'Proposals for the Reform of the Foreign Ser-vice'. Sir Nevile Henderson, alone, was capable of gross misconception of affairs. The other British representatives were often men bred to an enclosed state of mind, who gave signs of physical pain if brought to-gether with any from without the pale. But they did not subordinate their judgment or patriotic feeling to caste prejudice or red-spots-in-the-vision. They were perfectly informed by their subordinates, and by the British newspaper-men, and perfectly informed the British Government.

While Sir Nevile Henderson was allowed to say his piece, the tale these men could tell has *not* been published. That would cut Anon's claws.

Our Ambassador in Berlin before Henderson was Sir Eric Phipps.

(Before *him*, was Sir Horace Rumbold, of whose plain warning, given a few weeks after Hitler came to power, I have written in another book.) Sir Eric Phipps wrote in *The Times* on February 3rd, 1943:

The idea seems to prevail that his Majesty's representatives abroad in the years preceding the war failed to keep H.M. Government properly informed of financial, political, naval, military and air force conditions in the States to which they were accredited. Was this really so? Only a Blue-book publishing their correspondence during those years can answer this question. When the late Sir Nevile Henderson returned from Berlin at the outbreak of war he was authorized to publish a volume which proved conclusively that every effort had been made by H.M. Government to maintain peace ... What the British public should know is whether H.M. representatives abroad warned their Government from 1933 onwards of the grave dangers ahead, and, if so, why those warnings were disregarded ... Diplomatists are being accused of living too sheltered lives; but was it not rather the public that was allowed to live in a sheltered world of illusions while H.M. representatives abroad struggled with grim realities? Our political system seems to need some reform whereby public opinion will be properly enlightened by politicians with sufficient courage to reveal the truth, however unpalatable, to the nation. Unless these wider and more essential reforms are also carried out it is to be feared that no great results will come from merely divesting the diplomat of his old schooltie.

That is the exact truth. I am strongly in favour of opening the Foreign Service, and *all* British service, to unmoneyed men from modest schools (the 'Reforms' which have been announced will not do this; they are a fraud). But all our ambassadors might be drawn from free schools, and they could accomplish nothing if their information were suppressed and ignored at home, and the British Government pursued a policy contrary to their reports; Sir Eric Phipps is completely right. (I only differ from this authority in one point. If 'the politicians' are too dependent on some secret tutelage to speak the truth, or are too cowardly, why should not an ambassador resign and warn the country? That, after all, is what I did in my small sphere, and I ran more financial risk than any diplomat.)[1]

[1] Lord Vansittart, who was permanent head of the Foreign Office for five years after Hitler came to power, who understood the German situation perfectly, whose counsel would have averted this war, and who occupied the post which, by all tradition, gives authoritative guidance in such major issues of foreign policy, revealed in March 1943 that in 1938, 'I was removed from my post because I was anti-German'.

Thus the ambassadors have been kept silent, save the one whose words can only mislead further. The curtain of anonymity is drawn ever tighter round the throne of non-accountability. Of the generals, one has spoken, but his words reached few. This was Brigadier-General J. H. Morgan, who served on the Commission sent to Germany, after the last war, to supervise disarmament there. Speaking in London on December 19th, 1942, he said that in 1923 he reported to the War Office, *but this was never made public*, that in his opinion, as a result of the investigations and our control, the Germany Army at that date, although limited by the treaty to 100,000 men, really consisted of 500,000 newly-trained men. 'In reply', he said, 'I was informed by the Director of Military Intelligence, "We think yours is a conservative estimate". Unfortunately, that was never told to the people or to Parliament and the world, and Germany was able to get away with it by spreading abroad the legend that she was totally and completely disarmed.'

In 1923! Sixteen years before the war began, and during every day of those years trustworthy information poured into the British Foreign Office. Behold, gentle reader, the curtain which is kept between you and the truth.

Of our admirals, one, Lord Chatfield, an erstwhile First Lord of the Admiralty, wrote in March 1942:

> The true story of the causes of our lamentable defence position in 1938 is known to few. I am one of those few. I have written that story and one day it will be read; but it would not be altogether desirable for the nation to read it to-day.

He is wrong. Nothing could be more desirable. Hushing-up only leads us to worse troubles. In November 1942 he published the first volume of his Memoirs, *The Navy and Defence* (Heinemann). It tells the story of the last war. The second volume, which should contain that essential knowledge of 'the causes of our lamentable defence position' in the present one, has not been published. 'The causes of our lamentable defence position'; 'wars are precipitated by motives which the statesmen responsible for them dare not publicly avow'; his words and Mr. Lloyd George's look like first cousins.

Lord Hankey, who also could better serve this country by speech than by silence, wrote, of Lord Chatfield's Memoirs, 'It is to be hoped that

Authority will not hold up too long the appearance of the second volume'.

Senior air officers, too, have told me of their urgent warnings about the strength of Germany, their appeals for aeroplanes to be built.

Mr. Herbert Morrison, speaking to America, once said: 'The British people saw sooner than their Government that Hitler and his gang were thugs who had to be stopped.' It is not true. The British people could not *see* that, because the evidence was falsified and kept from them. If they now believe little they hear, that is the reason. They *felt* that, yes, but they were not allowed to *see* it.

I have given, in four books, a mass of evidence to show that our governments were fully informed of German rearmament and warlike intentions, and of the certainty of war if the foreign policy which our situation demanded (quick rearmament and a Russian alliance) were not pursued.[1]

And what was the result of it all? We were brought to disaster and Dunkirk, and only survive to-day, in my opinion, because the enemy, inexplicably, did not strike.

Even when the war began, that hidden something still held us down. We did not strike to help Poland, we did not bomb Germany, we did not fill the gap in the Maginot Line. As to that, a most sinister piece of evidence has just come to light.

The Maginot Line, behind which the similarly deluded French people were told to feel themselves secure, stopped short of the coast. The gap was mainly held by British troops. About December of 1939, British war correspondents returning from France told me that this gap was not being adequately fortified. They could make none listen, in London, they said.[2]

[1] The search for the sinister powers which brought this war about reveals that precisely the same thing happened in America! For the American ambassadors, unlike the British, have now been allowed to speak. An astonishing document is the White Paper, called *Peace and War*, issued by the United States Government on January 2nd, 1943, and published in London by H.M. Stationery Office. It contains a mass of warnings, covering a period of many years before the war, from United States envoys all over the world! The most amazing is the warning delivered by the American ambassador in Tokyo (of Japanese plans for a surprise attack on Pearl Harbour) on January 27th, 1941, ten months before the actual attack occurred! A few days before the attack, he urgently recommended especial vigilance at Pearl Harbour. The attack found an unguarded naval base, unwary garrison and unready air force! Of this a Republican leader, Senator Vandenberg, said, 'Our failure to be on the alert at Pearl Harbour approaches the infamy of treason'. The same words could be spoken in this country.

[2] French officers noticed the same thing; see Arthur Koestler's *Scum of the Earth*, p. 157 (Jonathan Cape, 1941), 'Perhaps "they" didn't want the gap closed', says a young French officer. 'Who are "they"? 'I don't know . . . I only know what I saw.' German officers also noticed this. See de Polnay's *Death and To-Morrow*, p. 91.: To him [a German colonel]

Now important information about this grave affair has been published in Johannesburg. Colonel Deneys Reitz (then Deputy Prime Minister of South Africa and now South African Minister in London) and Mr. R. G. Casey (then a member of the Australian Government and now British Minister of State in Cairo), after a visit to France, made *direct representations to Mr. Chamberlain*, in December 1939.

This is what Colonel Reitz says:

> It was clear to me that humanly speaking the Maginot Line was impregnable, but the rest of the French and British line, beyond the Maginot fortress, struck me as a very different proposition. ... Mr. Casey and I both served in France in the last war and were well acquainted with the conditions holding in this region. We were greatly perturbed by what we considered *the lack of preparation* against a German assault. Even in the Maginot Line itself the French commanders were busy night and day reinforcing the line by concrete strong points to the rear, whereas in the rest of the French and British line we thought the defences were *wholly inadequate*. So strongly did we feel this that we decided to make immediate representations to the Prime Minister of Great Britain, Mr. Neville Chamberlain.

Colonel Reitz then quotes, in confirmation, a letter from Mr. Casey to himself, from which the following is an extract:

> My dear Reitz: I spoke to Eden about our seeing Chamberlain about our visit to France. He says such a visit would not cause any embarrassment and is speaking to the Prime Minister in order to arrange it ... The simple fact that we wanted to convey was that we sincerely believed the 25-mile line now held by the British Army in France was dangerously deficient in concrete protection for troops and arms and that this belief was more than emphasized by our visit to the French sector, where day and night efforts are being made to reinforce by concrete in depth the already formidable concrete defences. The French army commander, General Conde, stated and emphasized over and over again that he would never be satisfied that he had sufficient concrete and that it was the only answer to the modern weapons of the tank and air bombardment. Finally I would be prepared to say that I

the quick German successes in Flanders and in France were as much a mystery as to me. Several times he asked me how it was possible that the French and the English did nothing to prevent them. Germany had shown in Poland her methods of warfare. The Polish campaign was but a dress-rehearsal of the May offensive. He, the professional soldier, was very much perplexed by it.'

felt myself obliged to bring this matter prominently to the notice of my Government. I am, yours sincerely, R. G. Casey.

Colonel Reitz then continues:

We duly saw Mr. Chamberlain and I remarked at the opening of the interview, Sir, if you will pardon a vulgarism, the Germans will go through the French and British lines like a dose of salts. Mr. Casey and I then proceeded to explain to him what we felt to be the shortcomings of the French and British defence lines beyond the Maginot Line. Mr. Chamberlain gave us no definite reply, but promised to obtain reports of his military advisers. Obviously, on my return to South Africa, I could not mention these things; but I feel that after this lapse of time no harm can be done by stating what actually took place.

When, in September 1939, Mr. Chamberlain, who in September 1938 promised 'peace in our time', declared war, he said: 'There is only one thing left for me to do: that is, to devote what strength and powers I have to forwarding the victory of the cause for which we have to sacrifice so much.'

Not even that promise was kept. Two of the great Dominions knocked — as how many British representatives and newspaper men abroad knocked for years before — at the door of 10 Downing Street, with their urgent warning, in December 1939. In May 1940, the Germans came through the unclosed gap 'like a dose of salts'.

This is the gravest evidence yet disclosed about that dark period, 'the astonishing seven months', to quote Mr. Churchill's words, who has refused inquiry into it.

Mr. Eden has said, 'Every word that has been said about the shortage of equipment suffered by the British Army in France is fully justified', but associates himself with the denial of inquiry.

A well-known political writer, Mr. A. J. Cummings, recently said: 'The really entertaining book will have some such title as *The Idle Months*, or *Time is on our Side*. It will lift the curtain on that extraordinary and mysterious period between the declaration of war and the German *Blitzkrieg* in Western Europe. Who, if he has the knowledge, will have the courage to write it?'

(I would write it, but it would not be 'entertaining'.)

'We cannot say, the past is past, without surrendering the future.' Yet Mr. Churchill now says 'The past is past'.

What was the final balance?

The British Army in France was authorized to surrender. (Lord Gort's Dispatches.)

In this country was 'not even one fully trained and fully equipped division'. (Mr. Eden, October 23rd, 1941.)

In this country were 'less than 100 tanks'. (Mr. Churchill, December 15th, 1942.)

In this country were, how many fighter aeroplanes? We have not been told that, but the Americans often know more about us than we, and the *New York Herald-Tribune* of December 17th, 1942, said there were 'only three squadrons of fighter aircraft intact in Britain'.

The present head of our Air Force thought 'all was up'.

(£1,500,000,000 was voted by Parliament for arms in 1937.)

The War Minister of the time, Colonel Stanley, after a rest, has been restored to the Government as Minister for the Colonies. Many other Ministers from the Governments responsible remain in office.

If any reader who knows my other books will add the material contained in them to this, he will see the shape of a terrible indictment, which cannot be ignored unless our future is to be put in jeopardy.

The pass was open. The foe did not enter. When he attacked, three months later, many new aeroplanes, of our own making or American supply, were ready. That he did not come in June is inexplicable. He could have destroyed the Navy at a cost, heavy, but worth the prize: world domination. If we are not to have one word of explanation of that, if the men who did this are to govern us for another twenty years, what prospect does Civvy Street offer?

All is to be hidden behind the curtain of anonymity. A future Prime Minister, while we are kept unarmed and our enemies prepare, may again tell us in 1964 or 1965, as Mr. Baldwin told us in 1934 and 1935, that 'no country within striking distance of our shores will be allowed to outarm us in the air', that 'Germany is not approaching equality with us', and the like more, and all his colleagues may connive, knowing that responsibility for any calamity may be waved aside with the words, 'No recriminations!'

We deserve better than that, but shall not get it without a Battle in England. For Mr. Baldwin has retired to earldom, Mr. MacDonald and Mr. Chamberlain are dead, but the machine they built lives after them and has been left intact.

Whodunit? We may see now, if we will, that these men were puppets. We have dimly perceived the shapes of other men, behind, to whose gain this war works, or whose obsessions it feeds, or whose plans it furthers. We may be pretty sure *who* did it. We can detect *how* they did it: by using the weapon of anonymous power, by working in the blackout.

Our political system seems to need some reform whereby public opinion will be properly enlightened by politicians with sufficient courage to reveal the truth, however unpalatable, to the nation.

This diagnosis (of Sir Eric Phipps) is exact. These wars could not happen if the truth were known to, instead of being concealed from the country.

How may we thwart Anon?

Members of Parliament, if they lack the native courage to liberate themselves, should have the shackles of dependence struck from them by revival of the olden and golden rule that they may accept no paid employment, in any form, from the Government or its associated monopolies. They should be forbidden to sign a pledge of unquestioning obedience to Party orders, which falsifies any pledge they make to their electors. They will not find the spirit to press for these things, after the degrading effects of the past eight years, and should be prompted to it by the return of a large number of militant Independent Members.

The discussion of our fighting forces, on which our safety ultimately rests, should be accompanied, at the presentation of Defence Estimates to Parliament, by a report on the actual expenditure of money from previous Estimates (the mystery of the £1,500,000,000 voted in 1937 remains buried beneath the doctrine of non-accountability and non-accountancy). The pretence that this is 'not in the public interest', and might be useful to foreign powers, is a fraud. The knowledge that we are *strong* would deter them in warlike ambitions. Statements, such as those of Mr. Baldwin which I have mentioned, which exaggerate our strength, which are false, but which delude the British public, encourage them to make war, did much to produce this one, and are certainly *not* in the public interest. The heads of the Services should attend the Defence Estimates debate in the Commons, and testify to the accuracy of the information given.

The Government should annually lay before Parliament, and this should be published without curtailment in the Press, an exact statement of British foreign investments. Investments within the Empire should be encouraged, and a fixed ratio set. Investments in foreign countries should be forbidden for the armaments and allied industries, and banking loans similarly debarred, unless our defence position is proved, by the production of authentic information in public debate, to be secure, and the Russian alliance is firm. The public cannot satisfy themselves that these conditions exist unless accurate information about foreign policy, armaments and investments is supplied. Deliberate misinformation about these subjects was the means by which the public was lulled into allowing this war to approach.

The Official Secrets Act should be amended so that it may no longer be used *against* the interests of the country by anonymous persons. (Diplomats or serving officers, for instance, who knew that official statements to the country about relative British and German air strength were untrue, would have been intimidated by the threat of this Act, had they resigned and warned the country.) Ambassadors, serving officers and civil servants, should not be placed in conflict between their loyalty to the country, which is paramount, and their allegiance to the Government of the day — since we now know that Governments of the day wilfully misinform the country.

The most dangerous gap is that indicated in Sir Eric Phipps's letter: 'Did H.M. representatives abroad warn their Government from 1933 onwards of the grave dangers ahead, and if so, why were those warnings neglected?'

How can a government of the future be prevented from pursuing, from some ulterior motives, a foreign policy contrary to the wish of the country and to the information supplied by its own representatives? A check in this can only come from the revival of an independent spirit in Parliament, the present abject plight of which is our greatest danger. This, again, can only be produced by Members independently returned to Westminster for the specific purpose of exposing and mending the abuses which have grown up there.

The independence of the Press should be restored, and the quickest way (but one closed now, like most useful things) would be to issue an independent newspaper. Every newspaper should be bound, by law, to publish the names of its proprietors and board. To-day, the power behind the Press is anonymous. One newspaper came into conflict with the Home Secretary, and the names of its proprietors were published. *More than half* of them were men whose names could not even be ascertained by a visit to Somerset House and consultation of the register; they appeared simply as 'Somebody's Bank Nominees'! Thus, the power to tell millions of people things, each day, is vested in people who conceal their identity. The Home Secretary stated that he possessed 'the power' to make the newspaper divulge their identity, and by saying this he used a powerful weapon, not to compel their disclosure 'in the public interest', but to make the newspaper *desist from criticizing the Government* (which happened). As far as the common weal was concerned, the anonymous owners might continue hidden.

This is important. From much experience, of the way public opinion may be misled and malformed, I know that an essential measure towards the cleansing of public life in this country is that the people who buy and read newspapers should know who those are that not only print and sell them, but express violent opinions, and arrange the information they print according to their own purposes.

Another thing which injures the public interest is the hidden influence of 'the advertisers' on newspapers. (I have shown how it worked in the matter of oil-politicians.) If newspapers represent themselves as organs of public opinion, these inhibitions should be removed. A 'censorship in the interests of truth' should take the place of the many subtle interferences with it. This could be achieved by simple legislation to restrict advertisement revenue to a decent proportion of newspaper income. Without this, and the disclosure of proprietorship, newspapers become the instruments of Anon, whose ends may or may not be ours.

Above all, the shield of anonymity which stands before the Civil Service should be removed. At the time of Munich, the British public suddenly learned that a man whom it hardly knew even by name, Sir Horace Wilson, was playing a leading part in an issue which was, literally, of life and death for many English people. A public inquiry, and a full report, is needed into the powers which the Civil Service have come to wield in anonymity. It is indefensible that men completely unknown to the public should wield all manner of undefined and unrealized powers, in the country's most vital affairs, and that, whatever mistakes or misdeeds they may commit, they remain cloaked in anonymity.

All these things, and many more, go to make the demon Anon in this country, who was as guilty of the war as the puppet Hitler, behind whom stands a German Anon. If the people of our island *know* what is going on, they can be counted on to see that wars are prevented, or that they are in good state to fight them if they come. The great edifice of falsehood and secrecy which has been built around our affairs, prevents them from forming a judgment, and it has clearly been raised for that purpose. It should be torn down, when the Battle in England is joined.

Whodunit? I think we have found the footpads, international men; and their motive, monetary or territorial gain; and their weapon, anonymity. If we fall into the hands of these thieves next time we pass through Civvy Street, we shall deserve our fate.

CHAPTER IV

THE RE-EDUCATION OF ENGLAND

As our prospects in the war improved, mainly through the resistance of the Russians, a murmur began in this country, and grew into a chorus, of the kind which usually presages something evil for us. After the war, said these voices, 'Germany must be re-educated'.

Germans, that is, are to be made *good*! We shall teach them how to behave; teach them, that to oppress small nations is wicked, but that the Hoare-Laval Pact and the Munich Agreement were virtuous; impart to them our renowned code of fair play.

Fun is fun, but this is a serious matter, and at first I suspected a misprint. The urgent need, obviously, is to re-educate England. But these announcements accumulated; clearly the speakers knew what they said, if not what they talked about.

Then I perceived the nigger behind this woodpile (for queer motives always prompt such pious proposals). He popped up in a report of 'a week-end conference of the British Social Hygiene Council'. The name suggested a body formed to combat venereal disease. The debate, however, was not about such ailments. I still wonder what 'Social Hygiene' is.

The report said that 'Young scholars, psychologists and social reformers are being trained in America for the job of remoulding the mind of German youth after the war'. This, it added, was revealed by the chairman, Miss Maude Royden. A German doctor, escaped from the Nazis, to become a naturalized British subject, was 'behind the plan'. After 'sounding people in England', he was gone to America, where 'his schemes are shaping'.

Behold the figure of one we know, the 'friendly alien' from Germany and Austria! If his 'schemes' should ripen, he is to take charge of 'the mind of German youth' after the war. The same idea then appeared in other quarters. A German newspaper published in London said:

Those Germans who to-day apathetically allow everything to take its course, will slowly find the way back to civilization. Their children will have to be brought up on lines which wise European humanists will set down.

Next spake the Vice-President of the United States, Mr. Wallace, in the same sense. Mr. Wendell Willkie answered in words which I cannot better:

Any post-war effort to police the education of our enemies, after the tradition of conquerors, will produce only resentment and hatred, and I shuddered to hear a member of our Government plan such a thing. Education must grow out of and carry on a native culture. To determine the nature and manner of their own education is the right of men everywhere. [1]

This scheme, which takes shape behind the scenes, is seemingly one to force on the Germans an educational system operated by returning emigrants. This is no interest of ours; our interest is, to keep our island safe, and to build a house of Freedom here in a world at peace. A quick way to breed a new war would be to use the strength we shall have, at the peace, to enforce such schemes as this. It would implant in German minds deeper resentment even than a permanent occupation; and a permanent occupation would at least ensure peace.

One way alone offers to re-educate Germany in the sense we desire: to

---

[1] Unhappily and ominously, the United States Government, according to *The Times* of April 10th, 1943, is 'preparing to co-operate with other Governments of the United Nations on the re-education of post-war Europe'. A Dr. Ralph Turner, of the "cultural relations division of the United States Department of State", said the American Government was "not trying to formulate a programme in this educational matter", but was "*preparing to support a programme of private agencies which could be made part of a United Nations programme*".

maintain a British Navy and Air Force stronger than the German, a substantial Army, and a Russian alliance. Given those things, we need not choose teachers for German children. Without them, we may send thousands, but we shall still have war. Any man who still thinks the Germans can be 'educated' to leave us alone, if they think they can beat us, is a fool. Those who wish to 'educate' them do not even think of that: they seek power in Germany, under our wing. Brains in a comely woman have been called superfluous, and in a homely one, inadequate. The Germans think likewise about this kind of 'education'.

In Civvy Street, about 1960, I fear we shall meet men of pious mien who will say, 'Don't bother to go on. Germany is re-educated now, you have nothing to fear, and you may hand over your armaments to An International Union! Come for a ride along Apathy Avenue to Fool's Paradise'. Beware: those are the confidence tricksters.

Because English people, alone among Europeans, find these simple things hard to understand, England sorely needs re-education. Germany knows what it wants, and how to get it, if others allow. Our people hardly know how to keep what they have.

Re-education begins at home, and a perturbing revelation of tomorrow's Civvy Street was opened when the man who is now charged with our schooling joined in this ludicrous chant about 're-educating the Germans'.

This is Mr. R. A. Butler, who is the living embodiment of all our problems. We shall often meet him, in Civvy Street. Englishmen hardly know his name, but his family's place in the Tory encampment is so strong that none but himself could prevent him from becoming Prime Minister. If he should not reach that office, the reasons will be similar to those which might cause the Royal Academy reluctantly to reject an oil-painting containing neither colour nor outline, save those needed to portray an old school tie. The good Lord Simon's shivering cronies, in his far-off Oxford Union days, said he 'might have been more impassioned'; they would have been lost for words to fit Mr. Butler.

Here is the scion of Enclosure. He *is* President of the Board of Education, and thus should have charge 'of the mind of English youth', after the war. He *was* Deputy Foreign Minister, before this war, and thus has an exceptionally intimate knowledge of the mal-education of the English. His office was, to inform the House, and through it England, about Foreign Affairs. Never was so little enlightenment imparted in so many words: the proverbial silent man, Calvin Coolidge, at least gave accurate information when, asked what the sermon was about on his return from church, he answered 'Sin', and further asked, what did the preacher say, replied 'He was against it'.

Mr. Butler, 'with complete calm, succeeded in feigning ignorance and giving nothing away'. His reticence largely contributed to the mis-information of the British people, which enabled them to be drawn into this war. When he was promoted, he remarked that his inability ever to divulge any information, as spokesman for Foreign Affairs, was a source of sorrow to him. The statement was seemingly ironic; but real woe and suffering for the British people were the result.[1]

Mr. Butler, then, who is now Minister of Education, is the most typical product of the England which needs re-educating. He told the Commons in December 1942, in answer to a Liberal who wanted the Government 'to concert with the Allied Governments measures for the re-education after the war of the youth of Germany': 'I am in touch with the Ministers of Education of certain of the Allied Governments and they have this question very much in mind. The re-education of the youth of Germany is a task of which I recognize the importance.'

Mr. Butler was not entrusted with *that* task. (Labour Members displayed an unusual feeling for reality by asking, 'Will the Minister catch the young Germans before he tries to educate them?', 'Has the Minister thought how many youths there are in Germany who require this education, and how many teachers will be required to educate them?', and 'Will the Minister see that lectures are given to the Nazi youth after the war, showing how we built up our Empire and how to avoid these perils?')

The man who has charge of *English* education is on a slippery path, and would drag us with him, if we allowed.

---

[1] In his new office, Mr. Butler displays anew his unique talent for withholding information about our vital affairs. Innumerable questions have not extracted from him any indication about his education proposals for *this* country, or whether they will leave the class-order in education and opportunity unimpaired. Asked for an assurance that he would at least produce these proposals 'during this century', he merely answered, 'I hope so'. In February 1943, horror of horrors, he announced that he was considering the preparation, for the instruction of European minds after the war, of 'history books of an objective character'. When *English* school books contain an objective account of Enclosure or the 1935 Election, we might think of writing history books for Europe!

The re-education of the English is the vital thing. First, in the sense that they should neither be denied information about their own affairs nor lulled with misinformation: in this paramount department of education, Mr. Butler's record does not promise well. Second, in the narrower sense of schooling; in this, Mr. Butler has at least *promised* well. He has stated the need for 'greater opportunity and social equality after the war'.

All politicians speak so, during a war; it counts as good for the spirit of the troops. But what needs to be done, assuming that he will practise his precept?

Education in the sense of schooling, that sheltered period of the Englishman's life before his mind is warped by the two mighty instruments of adult mis-education (the broadcasting monopoly and the alien near-monopoly of the films) has been ruined by Enclosure, which was continued into Education. The schools, too, were ring-fenced, and we call these enclosed schools, public schools. A narrow gate leads into them, marked Money, and a narrow gate leads out, marked Opportunity.

By no other means may an Englishman advance, unless he buys-and-sells things or enters one of the artistic callings, which money cannot regiment. A few unmoneyed youths, by abnormal diligence and persistence, may slip through the little side-entrance marked Scholarships; but even then, 'the scholars are not spoken to at Oxford'.

Thus the affairs of the country, and all the public Services, remain in the hands of the Enclosers. Such other talent as might benefit the nation is denied access. One government after another, in the inter-war years, consisted almost exclusively of men who displayed a piece of striped textile which said, 'I may be foolish, but by Gad, my father was well-to-do enough to send me to Rugtonchester'. You cannot exclude nine-tenths of a great people and find only good leaders among the remaining tenth.

For of what need we be ashamed, in our past twenty-five years? Solely, of our leadership. Since the people of this island again began to take a hand in our affairs, and that hand held a weapon, we have climbed to a higher summit, in the world's esteem, than we ever reached before. The danger is, of another climb-down: that The Boys, when they come back and hand in their uniforms, will listlessly yield the leadership of our affairs, once more, to the men and the methods of the thrice-discredited past, and thereby surrender their future.

From a certain amount of experience with the British soldier, I know how many will say, when they get back, as they said in 1918, 'Well, that's over and done with' — except that they will have learned enough cynicism to add 'but you wait until those bloody politicians muck it up again!' To a few glorious exceptions it will occur that it's up to them to do something about it, but oh, how few!

From a letter from an officer in the Grenadier Guards, serving in the Middle East.

This state of mind, of the volunteer-serf, our people should cast from them like a plague-infected garment. What is 'Politics', the word they fear? 'Politic', says the dictionary, means 'shrewd, sagacious, especially in policy; adapted to promote the welfare of the state'. 'Politician': one who is interested in, or occupied with politics.

Every man should be a politician, in this sense.

The mal-education of England, Enclosure-in-everything, from the land to opportunity, has produced the island of which Ascot is the portrait in miniature — the Enclosure, with the top-hats, and outside, the milling mob. On the last Ascot Day before this war, I was in the English countryside, near that racecourse. Around, the land lay in that state of grey neglect which so many castebound, foxhunting Ministers of Agriculture deplored, but did not remedy. The war was near, and already burdened the air. But the lanes were busy. Each cloud of dust was barely fallen, when a new one was stirred, as the shining limousines flashed by. Inside them, silk hats, and frocks from Paris.

And now? The old order is changed?

Major Sir J. Lucas asked the Minister whether London taxicab drivers are instructed to refuse fares to Newmarket and other race meetings; the Minister replied that there is at present no regulation under which taxi-drivers in London or elsewhere can be instructed to refuse fares to any particular destination (June 1942). 'A bookmaker's appeal against a conviction and sentence of three months' hard labour and a fine of £200, for travelling to Newmarket by car for the St. Leger, was allowed; he was also allowed twenty guineas costs' (September 1942). 'A bookmaker's journey by car to Newmarket was ruled "essential" by the magistrates at Harlow, and he was found not guilty of causing motor fuel to be unlawfully used; he said his firm had heavy commitments on the St. Leger, no less than £300,000 being invested on the day before the race.'

The old order, which the mal-education of England produced, which would have led to the conquest of this island, but for the enigma of Dunkirk, has not changed. It caused the loss of large portions of our Empire.

That story, you may find in many books. Read the tale of the *Tuans Besar*, the self-enclosed big-businessmen of Singapore, in O. D. Gallagher's *Retreat in the East* (Harrap, 1942). It was repeated in Burma, next door; read how the *Burra Sahib* shut their minds within the Mingalodon Golf Club, near Rangoon, until the enemy entered:

I say, excuse me, but you woke me up in the middle of the night. You came crashing past my bungalow, making a *terrible* noise. I thought it was enemy action. I jumped out of my bed into the trench. Would you please not do it again, or I shall have to inform the Committee. This is a quiet country club. We know there is a war on, but we try to avoid as much of the unpleasantness of war as possible.

The picture, which all those descriptions gives, is one of a society in decadence, self-enclosed against every new idea and all new blood, living for tennis, bridge, dancing, cocktails and the tittle-tattling picture-papers from home, hostile to enthusiasm and energy, breeding few children, and concerned only, when one was toilsomely produced, to put it down for Eton.

The few thousand British officials and merchants who made their living out of Malaya were out of touch with the people ... Whether the British administration of Malaya will in future be adjudged a success or failure, the fact remains that the majority of the Asiatics were not sufficiently interested in a continuation of this rule to take any steps to ensure its continuance.

Ian Morrison, *Malayan Postscript* (Faber, 1942).

The story was told often enough *before* the war, though none would listen. Here you see British society in a Chinese 'treaty port' as long ago as 1922:

Perhaps the conversation was less varied than the courses, for guests and hosts had seen one another nearly every day for an intolerable number of years and each topic that arose was seized on desperately only to be exhausted and followed by a formidable silence. They talked of racing and golf and shooting. They would have thought it bad form to touch on the abstract and there were no politics for them to discuss. China bored them all, they did not want to speak of that; they only knew just so much about it as was necessary to their business, and they looked with distrust on any man who studied the Chinese language. Why should he unless he were a Chinese Secretary at the Legation? You could hire an interpreter for 25 dollars a month and it was well known that all those fellows who went in for Chinese grew queer in the head ... They wore their evening clothes a little uneasily as though they wore them from a sense of duty to the country rather than as a comfortable change from day dress. They had come to the party because they had nothing else in the world to do, but when the moment came that they could decently take their leave they would go with a sigh of relief. They were bored to death with each other.

W. Somerset Maugham, *On a Chinese Screen* (Heinemann, 1922).

But this Enclosure overseas was not a colour one, not the simple contrast of black-and-white, brown-and-white, yellow-and-white. It was the reproduction, far away, of the order in this island, which has produced the repressed spirit now common to all classes, or money-groups of English people.

It begins with Englishmen. Contemplate it, in a book published in Australia:

Tribute should be paid at once to the British and Dominion women in various parts of Malaya who so quickly provided canteens for the Australian soldiers when they reached the country, and gave up so much of their time to operating them ... It should be mentioned, however, that no voluntary effort was made before the arrival of the Australians to make easier the lives of British garrison troops, some of whom had been in Malaya for four years. The British Tommies were sore about this preferential treatment of the A.I.F., and rightly so. A prophet so lowly as a British private soldier had very little honour among his own people in Malaya in pre-war days.[1]

[1] From *The Story of the Australians in Malaya*, by Gilbert Mant, an Australian War Correspondent (the Currawong Publishing Co., Sydney). Mr. Mant, in his valuable book, confirms other reports of the State of Singapore:

The Malays in Burma, of whom there were more than 2,000,000, as a race maintained a disinterested neutrality. The truth of the matter is that the native races were completely indifferent regarding the Allied cause. Without actively opposing it, they had little cause to love the British regime of the type Malaya enjoyed, and felt that if Japan won, it would mean merely a change of masters ... Australian private soldiers were refused admittance to the Raffles Hotel in Singapore, and to such European clubs as the Selamgor at Kuala Lumpur and the Sungei Ujong at Seremban, though many of these volunteers were respected members of exclusive Australian clubs and carried letters of introduction to the

Not colour-against-colour, then, or Pukka Sahib against untouchable, but Englishman against Englishman. Men from the Dominions might be invited into Englishmen's castles, because they have not Enclosure, in their own lands, and one is as likely to be eligible as another. The Englishman must be kept out, until you know from which drawer of the Enclosure chest he comes, and whether it is the one with the striped tie in it.

The picture is akin to that which 'the British Colony' offered in many European capitals, and even in London itself, where the colony called Society, between the wars, led a similar existence of enclosed vacuity, among eight million Britons.

During the Second World War, London was even enclosed against the British soldier! I do not exaggerate; this is but another facet of the thing Gilbert Mant observed in Singapore. An order forbade serving British subjects from spending their leave in London! Imperial, American and foreign soldiers were not thus debarred; I should like to see anybody try. They went to London as pins to a magnet. The British soldier might only go if his family were there, or he evaded the regulations. Even if he were stationed at Dover, and his family lived at Dundee, he was made to travel homeward by a roundabout route which deprived him of hours of hard-won respite.

When American and Imperial troops arrived here, citizens were rightly encouraged to lavish hospitality on them. But I have known English villages where all doors were open to a man from overseas, and English

secretaries of affiliated clubs in Malaya. In Australia at this time such well-known clubs as the Royal Sydney Golf Club, the Union Club and others were extending hospitality to British Malayan judges and civil servants who were members of affiliated Malayan clubs . . . In all parts of Malaya the cultured class of Indians and Chinese had first-class clubs of their own and many Australian private soldiers soon found that here they were indeed welcome . . . No more biting commentary on the European outlook in Malaya can be given than to mention that Australian soldiers, banned from their own clubs, were accused of 'lowering British prestige' by mixing so intimately with the Indians and Chinese in their clubs . . . Unquestionably there was an acute class consciousness and a moral flabbiness amongst the Europeans in Malaya. Here snobbishness ruled supreme. A British Resident was an official and social god. The *Tuans Besar* were minor gods, with many worshippers. This is not an attack on the European civil servant, the rubber and tin man in Malaya. They were all Michael Arlen's 'charming people', and, through lack of official guidance, the events after the outbreak of war with Japan left them in a rather pathetic daze. They saw their whole world collapsing round them; not only material bomb damage, but spiritual damage. Many lost everything they possessed. The whole thing to them was fantastically unreal. They walked around, bewildered, unable to understand the castastrophe . . . It is impossible to escape the conclusion that the Europeans in Malaya, as well as in other parts of the Far East, led preposterously spoilt, artificial existences.

soldiers, stationed alongside them, never entered a stranger's house. This neglect of the man who has borne the brunt, who in Mr. Churchill's words 'will at once be sent to the other side of the world', if the European war ends before the Asiatic, produced a pathetically comic episode in London. A newspaper proposed that the Americans should be allowed to beguile their leave by being given access to 'the roofs of tall buildings', from which they might contemplate the bomb-broken vista. The suggestion was applauded, and presently heads with American caps on them might be seen, speck-like, on those roofs. I modestly suggested that British soldiers, and perhaps even a native Londoner or two, under armed guard if necessary, might be allowed to look down on London, and later an obscure notice said that these lowly ones, too, might become freemen of London's rooftops, for a moment.

Will any gainsay me, that the re-education *of England* is the pressing need?

The English have been under the impression that they were genuinely liked abroad; because they had money to spare and were easy-going, because they liked travel and could make themselves at home wherever they were, they thought they were popular. It has been something of a shock to them to discover in the course of this war that this was a delusion. Now, I think it will be admitted that they have many good qualities; but they are not good mixers and they are shy. It is pathetic sometimes to see them in a foreign country trying to ingratiate themselves and succeeding only in rubbing the inhabitants the wrong way. We are accused of snobbishness; and the charge is justified; it is perhaps our worst defect. It may be that it is natural to the English character; for it must not be supposed that it exists only in the upper- and middle-classes, it is just as strong in the working-classes. The wife of the skilled workman will hesitate to associate with the wife of an unskilled workman; and I know myself of a case in Bermondsey where a very nice, pretty girl was looked down on by the family of her husband, a printer, because she came from a street that was considered mean, though to my eyes there was not a particle of difference between the shabby little row of houses her husband's family lived in and that in which her own family lived, and they were less than a mile apart. But the snobbishness of the well-to-do has certainly been fostered by the exclusiveness of their education. The public school — which in the United States is called private school — has been for more than a century a characteristic feature of English life and many good people are of the opinion that the better qualities of the English are due to its influence. It is generally believed (though I think erroneously) that the Duke of Wellington said that the battle of Waterloo was won on the playing fields of Eton. Now it is evident that parents will no longer be able to pay the sums it has cost them to keep the boys at these expensive schools, and already many of them are at their wits' end to keep going. They can only survive if they become once more what they were founded to be, public schools in which rich (such rich as there are) and poor can share the same education. They have outlived their usefulness, and I think it will be all to the good if, as the labour leaders desire, they are transformed into the same sort of institutions as the lycées of France and the gymnasiums of Germany. When all are educated together, rich and poor, highborn and lowborn, the class consciousness which is the great obstacle in the way of mutual comprehension must surely disappear. Whatever the origins and circumstances, boys in the same school, doing the same tasks, playing the same games, are equal; and I think it permissible to hope that when they grow up, whatever their conditions in after life, they will preserve a sense of the essential equality of all men which they learnt unconsciously at school. And it may be also that when the English of this particular class, instead of spending their most impressionable years herded with other boys, spend them at home, going to school for the day, when they mix with boys of all sorts, they will lose that shyness that gives so many people who don't know them the false impression that they look upon themselves with excessive complacency. Then they will more easily gain the goodwill that their sterling qualities merit.

Thus wrote Somerset Maugham, fresh from the disaster in France, in *Strictly Personal* (Heinemann, 1942). The diagnosis contains only one fault. He appears to argue that the public schools should be reformed because people will no longer be able to afford to send their sons to them. That is irrelevant, and not true. Early in the war, delusion about 'the new poor' may have been possible; now, we know that we shall have as many war-rich after this war as after the last. Not on that account, but to make the unhappy breed happy again, do we need a change.

For we have tried the order of life based on Enclosure, and the first-, second- and third-class compartments in all things, and know whither it brought us and will again bring us, if we do not alter it. What has it bequeathed to us? When peace comes to be made after this war, the

Government will be full of men, who wear the 'Enclosure' button in their lapels, who all repeatedly foreswore and denied The Things for which they now, incessantly, shriek that we must fight.

Will any voter know for what he votes, or be able to put any faith in his future, if he returns those men to office again?

The class system in Government, built on Enclosure, has proved its badness from top to bottom — for those few from below, who were let in, were as loath to break with it as those on top. They were dazzled by promotion from third to first class; the comfort of those cushions seduced them, and the feathers entered into their spines.

Not alone the German lust for conquest caused this war; that could have been checked. Graver milestones in our downhill story were Mr. Baldwin's election of 1935, Mr. Eden's resignation of 1938, and Mr. Churchill's retention of 'the guilty men' in 1940, and in each of those episodes the sinister influence of the exclusive class order can be seen.

Mr. Baldwin would *not* have 'lost the election', had he told the country the truth. But if he had, it would have been better for an incompetent Labour Administration to dither about in foreign affairs for a couple of years and then ignominiously give way to a strong Conservative one, which would have had time to prevent the war. His ruling motive was, at all costs to keep Labour out, and the country's interest suffered.

Mr. Eden resigned on an issue of honour and principle in which he was proved a thousand times right, and if he had followed it up, many of the best Conservatives, Socialists and Liberals would have joined with him to prevent the war. But, after the resignation, he only called for 'unity'; that is, he urged the country further to support the policy he would not be associated with and the leaders he refused further to follow! This was an astounding thing, and can only be explained by the imprisoning influence of Enclosure. (Mr. Duff Cooper, also, to judge by his book, *The Second World War* (Jonathan Cape, 1939) seemed to be shocked by his own temerity after a resignation which counts as one of the few brave deeds in those abject years.)

Mr. Churchill, in 1940, could have gained the support of the entire country for any reform he wished. To-day, the same men ride on his shoulders who for years decried him, and many of the men who supported him are outside the pale.

The re-education of England presses, indeed. In this matter, on which our life depends, the great Dominions could teach us something. They love us. Why? Listen to a French Canadian priest, Father Sabourin, who went with the Fusiliers Mont Royal to Dieppe:

We did not cross the Channel to fight for England, but we believed that we were going to fight, with England, for Canada. I do not come to say that I do not love England. I say that we fought with England, our ally. Why should I not love England? Because she still permits me to say my prayers on my knees each morning? Because she permits me to say Mass each morning in my church? . . . I will make a declaration, an act of faith still greater. At this moment I infinitely prefer to be a loyal British subject, I prefer infinitely more that it be England which guards my liberties rather than be under the sovereignty of no matter what other country in the whole world, and from that I do not exclude, alas, even France. I know, as you do, that the English Government is Protestant. Is it your fault that you are Catholic? Is it their fault that they are Protestant? Then, leave it to Providence to do what it has to do. But I do not want to rid myself of the idea that if I have all my liberties in my country, I owe it to England. In spite of the fact that the Government is not of the Catholic faith, I still prefer to be governed by the Anglo-Protestants there than to be under the control of Hitler, or of Mussolini, or of any other guardianship whatever, when Protestant England leaves me, a French Canadian, the right and entire liberty to practise my faith, to speak my language, to maintain my traditions. It was for that that we fought at Dieppe.

They love us, then, for the priceless thing we gave them. They do not realize, detestable paradox, that we have lost much of the thing we gave. They, and their example, could give it back to us.

For these men from the Dominions are freer than we. Their feeling of freedom does not spring alone from the freedom of which Father Sabourin spoke, freedom of religious practice. That, even we still have. It springs from two other things. Their lands are free. Their opportunities are free, because their schools are not enclosed.

They have their political evils, their slums. But in those two great things they are free, and they rightly see the guarantee of this freedom in the strength of the British Navy and the continued safety of this island from foreign conquest. They do not remark, until they have lived here long, how much of freedom we have lost, through the enclosure of the land and the schools, since their own forefathers founded the Dominions on our island freedom.

Inspiration may be obtained from a newer, fresher world. My father, for instance, was born a poor farmer's son in the remoter parts of Nova Scotia. From this humble origin, he succeeded in educating himself and becoming, in course of time, a reasonably prosperous medical practitioner. This was not done through State-aided grants or scholarships, but rather by his own efforts at self-help in 'working his way through college' — by working in the vacation and earning sufficient to pay his fees in term-time. There was nothing unique about this: the same thing is done by many young men in Canada to this day.

'Odysseus', *Safer Than a Known Way* (Jonathan Cape, 1941).

That is the thing we gave the Dominions, have lost ourselves, and must regain, so that Mr. and Mrs. Wiggins of Wigan may say, over the baby's cot, 'Let's tell him when he's older how he may by his own exertions become a doctor, lawyer, engineer, artist, singer, or civil servant — how he may make himself useful to the country and himself'. To-day, Mr. and Mrs. Wiggins, having inherited only the taint of keeping-themselves-to-themselves, and knowing they cannot pay public school fees, say 'Poor little chap, we wish we had *the money* to give him a chance in life. Have you filled in your football coupons, Dad? We might *win* something.'

'Odysseus' continues:

Young men of every type, origin and class, *should* have this opportunity to rise in the world by their own efforts. *Equality of opportunity* is the vital ingredient — the health-giving vitamin, so to speak — of a healthy human society. Its importance tends to be overlooked; but it is the kernel of the whole problem. For equality of opportunity you need, first of all, a decent level of wages — so that a young man can earn sufficient to pay for an advanced education, or alternatively set himself up in an independent business, if he so wishes; you need a truly democratic system of education, i.e. for rich children and poor children both to go, side by side, to the same schools; you need an entire absence of class feeling. These conditions are not present in England despite all our talk of freedom and social justice; they are not present owing to the low level of wages in the first place and to the prevalence of social and class prejudice in the second — the latter being reflected particularly in our system of education. The State-aided grants and scholarships that take their place are more of a sop to the social reformers than a genuine attempt to tackle the problem at its root. The chances of a child obtaining a first-class education and a consequent entrée to a higher grade of society without substantial financial help from parents are small; his chance of success in any walk of life is smaller still if he is of humble origin — if he has not been to one of the correct schools. It is only the occasional man of genius who is able to overcome this latter handicap — a handicap considerably intensified over the course of the last twenty years. This system, and the short-sighted political outlook it has engendered, have brought our country to the verge of destruction; clearly, if we are to ensure our survival, it must be altered in the most radical fashion.

Thus a man whose parents found opportunity in a Dominion, who himself looks at England with widened vision. Our order of Enclosure and Exclusion has produced, at the top, a ruling class of proven incapacity, absorbed only in maintaining the outworn distinctions of wealth and position and thus blind to the greater interests of the land; if you look back at its performance, during the past twenty-five years, you may exclaim, with Dr. Johnson, 'Why, Sir, Sherry is dull, naturally dull; but it must have taken him a great deal of pains to become what we now see him. Such an excess of stupidity, Sir, is not in Nature'.

At the lower end of the scale, it has produced those men who fight so staunchly, who have restored our name to the zenith of fame, but whose 'average standard of intelligence is a disgrace to the rich country which underfed and now conscribes them'. By inserting a punctured disk into the petrol feed of a motor-car, you may ensure that it can only move slowly. This has been done to the minds of our people. Why train our minds, they think: no opportunity offers, to use them.

Thus we breed the type of fourteen-year-old who wrote this letter to a London newspaper:

> I have learned very little from my nine years of schooling. Do you know I can't even speak correct Enlish? I know nothing of Shakespeare although I have many of his books. I can't understand them. Nor can I speak any language or do mathematics. Much as I would like to know all these things I haven't had the chance. In fact, I am generally ignorant.

(An even worse product of mal-education was the reply printed by that newspaper: 'This grousing ignoramus wants to blame education which taught him to read, because he cannot read Shakespeare. He cannot understand it, though there are dictionaries available for sixpence. He is "generally ignorante" in the midst of the finest school continuation system in the world. Heavens alive! He's not worth educating.')

I have the utmost sympathy with this boy. I felt exactly as he feels, when I left school at thirteen. I felt the prompting to learn and achieve, but could see no way. All doors were closed. To widen the mind and improve the body, choose a career and train for it: these things were only for the moneyed. Later, I did find ways; but when I look back I see that luck helped me, and how many others can count on luck?

When we set foot in Civvy Street, we shall at once meet this enormous obstruction built across it, this money-filter placed between the people and the service they might render themselves, the community and the country: the enclosed schools, with their monopoly of opportunity.

What do schoolmasters themselves think of it:

... The public schools represent and perpetuate a great social cleavage. There are two 'nations' instead of one. There is no community or fellowship between them and the rest of us. If we are to have that democracy to which we are all paying lip-service, then our educational system must be conceived and built to promote it. The social problem is bound up with the education system.

> The headmaster of an East London School, Parmiter's, writing to the Press in February 1943.

Mr. Harold Nicolson gives as three of the virtues of the public schoolboy: humility, tolerance and a sense of responsibility 'towards those who are less fortunately situated than himself'... Ten years teaching in small public schools and some little contact with them during a headmastership of twenty years in a country grammar school left me with the impression that the most obvious characteristic of the public schoolboy is exclusiveness... the opposite of those three qualities. The spirit of exclusiveness is fostered in many ways. The public schools have their own Headmasters Conference, Year Book, schools examination; they have regulations against the admission of tradesmen's sons from a neighbouring town; they play games only against other public schools. ...

> Mr. R. Williams, writing to the Press in February 1943.

The enclosed schools always boasted that they formed *character*. We do not strive to produce academicians, they said, but Men Of Character, fitted to rule. You cannot produce an article of quality, from a mould, if quality is not the condition of the stuff you put in. But quality is *not* the condition, only money. The flaw is in the mixture, not the mould. The result has been, that the most patent fault, in the men who ruled England between the wars, was lack of character. They cared less for truth than victory at an election, less for honour than a temporary advantage, less for England than Enclosure.

It is a rotten order. But the English do not like to root out even a rotten thing. They prefer compromise. That may be good, if it does not lead them to perpetuate grave evils from fear of 'anything radical, any change'. Fear of *violent change* is good; fear of reform is imbecile. The simplest way to reinvigorate England is to reform this system. Give every man equal opportunity, for his children, and the future is secure. None need think this a revolutionary, or even a new proposal. I only echo the words of all the great men, from Mr. Churchill and Mr. Butler on. The difference possibly is, that I would do this thing, if I could.

The Headmasters Conference (the league of the enclosed schools) is presided over by the headmaster of Winchester. (Much power, privilege and wealth in England is in the gift of this college alone, for the benefit of babes unborn whose parents say: 'Let's put him down for Winchester'.)

The headmaster of Winchester said (January 1943):

The policy of the Headmasters Conference is (1) That the schools should be made accessible to parents who would at present be unable to afford the expense.

The headmaster of Rugby said (November 1942):

The public and boarding school must remain, but not as a backwater or pleasant tributary, as it is at the moment. The money qualification must go. We and our critics object to that with all our hearts.

The headmaster of Aldenham (January 1943) expressed a wish that 'every school in the country should become a Christ's Hospital'. (The method of admission to this school, roughly, is that the same tests of intelligence and character are applied to each potential pupil, and the fees charged are in proportion to his parents' income-tax return. This is better than the order prevailing at the enclosed schools, which is that of a highly-priced ticket of admission entitling the bearer, without further ado, to a front stall in England for the rest of his life.)

Mr. Butler, who is intent on re-educating Germany, was more cautious, in October 1942: 'Just as our political system has become democratic, people are looking for an extension of that system into the field of education. We have to build a system that will give equivalent opportunities to all, by degrees . . .' and so on and so on.

The statement that 'our political system has become democratic' has the same relation to fact as a poem would have which sang the fragrance of Gorgonzola cheese.

From the headmasters, then, we might hope for some help; little, because behind them lurk the Boards of Governors. From Mr. Butler, representing the Party that adores Enclosure, we may expect none.

What do the plebs suggest? The National Association of Schoolmasters, in September 1942, rightly called the enclosed schools 'the most exclusive employment agency in the world' and bluntly demanded that they be swept away, 'as the virtues of the public schools training for leadership are incompatible with democracy'.

If the others do not go far enough, these go too far. Such windy phrases often kill a good cause, in England.

What should we then do? (and bear in mind that Germany, after defeat, will retain from the National Socialist interlude a great reform in this vital matter. It is unreasonable and exasperating that the vanquished alone, in these successive world wars, should taste any of the fruits of victory).

The best answer I have seen came from an unmoneyed schoolboy, one Eric Michael Davis, a Sixth Form student of Leeds. He said, most rightly, that class hatred is not felt against the public schools by ordinary schoolboys. (This is not a matter of class antagonism at all, but only one of a healthy ambition to be able to serve the country and the community, and rise in the public service. If hatred exists, it is at the top, among the shadowy boards of people who control the enclosed schools and all the advancement which is in their gift.)

What the poorer classes want, he said, is not that the public schools should be standardized, but that there should be *enough opportunities for the poorer classes to be educated*. A good reform to that end, he said, would be 'the abolition of a limited number of scholarships being awarded each year: in their place *all* students who gain a certain number of marks show-ing that they have reached a certain standard, should be awarded a scholarship, irrespective of the *number* of students attaining that standard each year'. This, he continued, should apply particularly to university scholarships. At the moment, 'the greatest hatred is not against the rich man, but against the education authorities' (he does not know that they are the same). 'We see students being paid for to go to the universities, whilst we, who have passed the same examinations as they, and perhaps more, are unable to go to the university. Those who say, "Abolish the rich man's privileges" should rather say "Add to the poor man's privi-leges". We want the standard of education made higher, and not lowered.'

He means, the poor man's *opportunities*, not *privileges*, of which he has none, but apart from that mischoice of a word the suggestion is admirable. What does a poor man's son gain, through a scholarship, if all the few places at public school or university are filled before he qualifies? Give him the knowledge that, if he reach a set standard, he will reach a public school or university, and you plant at once the seed of energy and hope in our frustrated breed. You bring about, at a stroke, natural selection and the ascent of the best. If a man, knowing that these things are within reach of diligence, fails to attain them, he can only blame himself. Oppor-tunity was his, and he missed it. But to-day, Opportunity is denied him.

Here you have wisdom out of the mouth of a sixth form schoolboy. He does not say 'Abolish the public schools'; the schoolmasters might learn from him. He does not say, 'Slam the door, marked Money, and open another, marked Merit'. He says, 'Open a second door, marked Merit, and let merit pass through without hindrance, as money passes through the other'.

I would never cry 'Abolish the public schools', or envy any, who pine for it, the chance to be photographed against a muddy wall at Eton or in a grotesque straw hat at Harrow, though these pictures have been among the most telling used against us, in this war, by German propaganda. Pre-serve them, increase their number — and admit to them and to the universities any boy who attains a certain standard. That is the key to our future.

But one paramount thing needs to be understood. This is *not*, first and foremost, a matter of schools, schooling and schoolmasters. It is a question of *opportunity*. The public schools to-day hold a monopoly of preferment; only those who pass through them (save for the insignificant quota of scholarship boys who are 'not spoken to at Oxford') may rise to the higher ranks of the State service. Either the public schools must widen their doors, and allow unmoneyed youths who attain a set standard to enter, and pass up the stairway of advancement beyond; or they must relinquish that monopoly, and the State service must be thrown open to all who reach that standard. This is the bottleneck that must be broken.

Do not keep your gaze, gentle reader, on the front door to those schools. The back exit, the one marked 'Advancement only by this door', is more important. That is the place where unmoneyed talent, energy and spirit are turned back, and only money is allowed to share in the conduct of our affairs.

Are these few schools, 'governed' by little groups of anonymous people, to retain, after this war, the monopoly of governing England? Is the word 'Rugby' to be essential, on Tom Brown's application, if he aspire to become a general, admiral, air marshal, ambassador, high civil servant, leading barrister or judge, or Minister? Is he to remain condemned, without it, to rise no higher than warrant officer, lawyer's clerk, chief petty officer or archivist? If so, an entrance door marked Merit must be opened.

Only through this reform can we come to a happier England, to a reinvigorated land, and to a foreign policy, cleansed of class antagonism, which will keep this island safe and enable a house of Freedom to be built within it. We might as well aspire to paint the moon green, as to re-educate Germany by means of 'wise European humanists' who wish us to transport them, on their backs, to power in Berlin.

Re-education begins at home.

CHAPTER V

FOUR ENGLISH FREEDOMS

I HAVE set out to show, before we venture into to-morrow's Civvy Street, how we lost Freedom and may regain Freedom. We have come to the edge of a steep place; we should retrace our footsteps, to the place where we went astray, and resume the agelong march of English mankind which we thought to follow in fighting the war of 1914-18.

My experience, of that war, the years which followed, of many countries, and of this war, has shown me no better definition of Freedom than the simple one I have given: a man's freedom not to have his body imprisoned, unless he is a proven wrongdoer, and to use and enjoy his native land.

Those are simple aims to reach, and a vigorous public opinion could quickly achieve them. Nowadays, say many, English people are not interested in these things. They are bored with them, and listless. They would sooner submit to forceful guidance, without question; they come to like a command, and do not much care who gives it. What they cannot bear, is to struggle with thought:

> Living, as I do, in or near one of Britain's 'mightiest cities', I have had an opportunity to observe appalling conditions at first hand, but the most appalling thing is the apathy of the average citizen with regard to these conditions in their own country, no, even in their own city or village . . . But I feel that the few sane men in the country deserve support. My husband, who is in the army, agrees with me on this point and I will see that my baby son does also, if I possibly can.
>
> From a woman of Glasgow.

> There are, it appears, hundreds of thousands of young men who still do not know why they are fighting and what they want to get from the war. The majority of fellows in our lot are in just such a position and they don't seem to have the inclination or energy to do anything about it. And we are supposed to be 'the cream of the nation's youth' and to have received an advanced education. I myself joined the R.A.F. for something better than a return of the old existence after we have won the war.
>
> From an Aircraftman serving in South Africa.

Do our people then, of their own aimlessness rather than the blindness or malice of their leaders, drift towards a state of comfortable slavery such as that of the people of Shihr, in Southern Arabia, where, as the Delhi correspondent of *The Times* related, the Sultan of Mukalla set free a slave as punishment for spreading defeatist rumours?

If it were so, I would rather walk alone on the other side of that street than with the throng. If it were so, our plight between the wars would be bliss compared with the plight to come. Are our men, who fought so staunchly, so weak-kneed that they will prop themselves against the first wall of glum indifference in Civvy Street, and think of nothing better than the next meal, opening time, I must get some cigarettes, what's on at the pictures and what's on the radio? I do not believe it, and in this one thing am not open to conviction.

Our men, when they return, if they do not mean to prove themselves dullards in the peace they have fought for, should first restore our charter of liberty, the Habeas Corpus Act, and then set free some of the land. On that basis, they may build a free and better island.

The Archbishop of Canterbury once defined 'four freedoms' which this country needed. They appeal more than the 'four freedoms' of something called An Atlantic Charter, for instance, 'freedom from fear'! That is a tall order, and to my mind a meaningless one. Shall we cease to fear cancer, for example?

The Archbishop said:

> There are four requisites of life which are provided by nature, even apart from men's labour: air, light, land and water. I suppose that if it were possible to establish a property claim upon air, somebody would have done it before now and made people pay if they wanted to breathe what he would then call 'his air'. But it has not been possible to do this. Unhappily it has been found possible in the case of both land and water, and we have tended to respect the claims that have been made by owners of land and of the water flowing through it, in a way which subordinates the general interest to the private interest of those owners. I am not myself at all persuaded that the right way to deal with this question is by the nationalization of the land, but I am quite sure that we need to assert the prior interest of the community in respect to land and water with a vigour of which our recent political history shows no trace.

This was followed by loud wailing about 'churchmen interfering in politics'. People of like mind did not protest, but applauded, when another Archbishop looked upon the Munich Agreement, that despicable transaction, and said it was good. Yet that was 'interference in politics', as our men presently found, who reeled backward through France before the weight of the Czech-made tanks.

Air, light, land and water! Put those four freedoms on the basis of legal protection against wrongful arrest, and you have four English freedoms, so well founded, that you may say, this land is free!

'It has not been found possible to establish a property claim on air!' What man would say this, who ever saw a slum. And that applies to light, too. (In war time they even contrive to deprive us of light. We should light up the sky, when the aerial enemy comes; instead, we black-out ourselves. Not for lack of devotion to the example of the ostrich, has the daylight sky been preserved to us. I do not suppose I shall be visited by an official bearing a copy of the Official Secrets Act, if I say that some great minds would have liked to put a wall of smoke around us when we were attacked by day, so that the raider might know just where we hid.)

Freedom of air and light, we can only achieve by the better building of our houses, streets, towns and cities, and particularly by the abolition of the slums (which have been made worse by the war). These two freedoms belong to a later chapter in this book.

Land! You have seen, gentle reader, by what means that part of the land which belonged to all was taken, and what is the title to that 'respect' which 'the owners of land and the water flowing through it' claim for their possession of it. This freedom should be achieved by restitution and the liberation of much land, still commonly-held, which in practice has been enclosed by petty officials.

Water! The rivers were enclosed, too. 'Washed by the rivers, blest by suns of home', sang Rupert Brooke in his lovesong to England. He was lucky, if he was washed by the rivers.

I have bathed in many rivers abroad, and never found one I might not bathe in. Here, they are usually imprisoned. The 'fishing rights' bring in large rents. In thirty-five years of English life, I have bathed in only two English rivers. The thing is inconceivable in any other country I know.

The first occasion stands out like a glorious oasis, when I look back, in the desert of a London boyhood which stretched until I was nineteen and went soldiering in France (where I was washed by many rivers). The memory is as vivid as to-day's sunlight. I tasted a delight never dreamed of before. I was sent, one year, for a brief holiday, to a farmer in Amersham, which then was rural, and spent spellbound hours watching him feed the pigs or turn off, with fascinating speed, the legs and rungs of cottage chairs, on a lathe in his barn. Between-whiles, I wandered down the lane, turned into a field path, and came to a bathing pool, at a place where a narrow stream widened! Memory can recall no hours to compare with those. To-day, I believe London has swallowed Amersham, or nearly. If I went there, I doubt whether I should find the farm or the pool.

No wonder that our young men go gladly to war. The Londoner becomes ever more brickbound.

> One in four of the population of this island is now squashed into the greater London area . . . It cannot be right that the best blood of the country districts and of the pre-war distressed areas should have been drained away.
>
> Mr. Hugh Dalton, President of the Board of Trade.

Indeed it cannot be right. But it can be righted. Of forty million people, ten million herded together in Cobbett's 'Wen'! How right he was, over a century ago, as he rode out of the tiny London of his day into the enclosed countryside and, turning in his saddle, looked back and raged. Are we, in twenty years time, to be twenty millions in Greater London, and look out from our brick prison on a countryside of walled-in parks, derelict fields, golf links, roadhouses, foxhunters, racecourses, reserved rivers, advertisements for purgatives, 'Tea' and 'No Trespassing' notices, all enclosed by barbed wire?

Between the wars, a Scot, A. G. Macdonnell, wrote a book called *England, Their England* (Macmillan, 1933) about the southern part of our island. Those should read it, who have not. Though written as satire, it gives a true portrait, and not a caricature, of the crazy way of life we developed between 1919 and 1939.

During this war, the countryside has revived, and once again the politicians cry, like the raven, Nevermore! But their words ring false at every test; they are feeding-stuff for the voting-cattle. In the midst of this war, the spoliation and disfigurement of the remaining countryside go on.

For instance, a great hydro-electrification scheme has been introduced for the Central Highlands of Scotland, one of the last potential holiday grounds left to Britons north and south of the Border, and laws have been introduced to enable the power stations to be built, the dams to be made, and the stark parade of pylons to begin, through the forests and over the hills. Much monies, the initiators say, will accrue. And the native Highlanders, of whom all but 300,000 have in course of time been driven from their ancestral land? Will they be better off? Listen:

> It is in our view plain that the general provision of electricity to crofters or fishing hamlets throughout the Highlands for domestic and small power use is quite impracticable, the cost of transmission and distribution being prohibitive in relation to so small a demand.

The countryman, with the pylons stalking past his croft, may continue to burn a candle or sit in the dark. If he were made too comfortable, where would the cheap labour come from for the great factories, which are to be fed with power, and thrive, on the Caledonian Canal and Cromarty Firth? Profit is the only standard. If this spirit prevails, what likelihood is there that the beauties of this area will be spared?

While our ears are filled four times a day with threats of starvation and admonitions to grow food on every inch of land that will produce anything, great stretches of countryside are being torn up and left derelict in a rush for quick profits. The same Minister who makes those appeals, by whose authority 'bad farmers' are turned from their land, allows it. Powerful interests gain from this short-term profit-making and long-term ruination, and that, in England, is alway final.

This happens in several counties, but chiefly in Northamptonshire, where over 3000 acres (an area greater than the City of London) have been torn up, pillaged, and the débris left for posterity. Here are the words of a Governmental Committee (Lord Kennet's) written four years ago:

> For lack of foresight, for lack of organization, year by year, this part of our land is being reduced to and left in a state that no one can see without shame.

For lack of scruple, rather. That was before the war, before the scales fell from our eyes and we suddenly saw (so the politicians say) the mad crimes wreaked on our land. It still goes on.

Beneath the fields of Northamptonshire lie valuable iron ores. Formerly, labourers took off a few feet of soil, extracted what ore they could, and levelled the ground again. Then came Progress. Great steel monsters, with jaws which reach 60 and 70 feet into the ground, tear it up and throw it away, scoop out the ore — and then go, leaving lines of hideous humps and dumps that stretch for miles, where once was green land. The soil is not put back and levelled. Nothing grows on those pyramids. The profit has been taken; the chapter is closed.

A fantastic picture that a mad artist might have painted of a landscape in the moon.

L. F. Easterbrook.

In other countries, they put the soil back, after the ores have been removed, and the land heals. But with us, the landowners pocket their money, the iron companies sell their steel, 'the cost of restoration would be more than the land is worth' — the captains and the kings depart, leaving a devastation behind them as horrifying as anything an invader could achieve. 'What is involved', says the Kennet Committee, 'is the fate of 80,000 acres — 125 square miles of countryside' (that is, about twenty-six times the area of the City of London.)

'In vain doth valour bleed, while avarice and rapine share the land', said Milton. Our Government is equipped with every conceivable power to dragoon and harass the humble citizen, and order every act of his daily life, down to the knob of coal he must not burn and the half-sheet of paper he must not waste ('An Offence! Penalty, imprisonment!'). It does nothing to hinder *this*. Hitler could not have devised a better way to lay waste our countryside.

(But a Norfolk farm labourer who thought it wrong that his local Agricultural Soviet should plough up *common* land, used as a children's playground, while leaving other good but not common land alone, so that he cut the barbed wire round a golf course and planted onions on the greens, was heavily fined.)

When the Minister of Agriculture, in his search for that home-grown food which would save the lives of our ships and seamen, asked the Hampshire War Agricultural Committee to find him more arable land, because more food *must* be grown, they replied that the only remaining land was a piece of 10,000 acres in the Test Valley already exempted by himself, through 'a compromise' with the owners of 'the fishing rights'.

This was once rich herbage, grazed by cattle, but after the last war, when agriculture fell into decay, the owners sought other ways to earn money from it and presently made much more than farming would have brought them. 'Wealthy sportsmen', those typical figures of England, Their England between 1919 and 1939 (was not an outsize photograph of Mr.

Chamberlain, with rod-and-net, the chief exhibit in the British Pavilion at the Paris Exhibition?) were ready to pay 'up to £200, or even more, a mile, for the fishing rights'.

While small farmers could be told to plant potatoes here and turnips there, or be thrown out of their farms, this land was left alone. England might not 'waste bread'; but no crops might grow on these waterlogged acres. The ordinary citizen's two-seater, waiting in the garage to take him to Brighton one fine day, might be taken; indeed, almost anything might be taken from him. 'The compromise' was inviolable. This land was left waterlogged, weedy and overgrown, for the benefit of 'the fishing'.

Thus spoliation and enclosure go on. 'Never again', unless our order be changed, is clearly to be 'Once more'.

The present Minister of Agriculture counts in the inner coteries of politics (for nowadays our politicians are almost unknown to the general public) as a vigorous administrator and possibly a future Prime Minister. He said, in October 1942:

> British agriculture was sadly neglected before the war. The neglect was worse than anyone dreamed possible ... Much of our countryside was dying. Peace was desolating the land faster than war. With the war, the whole situation for British agriculture changed in a flash ... Some Power has wrought a miracle in the English harvest fields this summer, for in this, our year of greatest need, the land has given us bread in greater abundance than we ever knew before ... Nearly all we have had to do with farming for war can be of permanent value when peace returns. It will not have to be scrapped and destroyed when the whistles blow for the armistice. [Why *will* they use that ill-omened word, Armistice?] On that day we shall at any rate have our land and our people. We have the soil, the climate, and the men needed to make British agriculture not only an efficient industry, but an inspiration to the world, as indeed it was a century ago.

Thus Mr. Hudson. 'Peace was desolating the land faster than war'! And the desolation that now goes on in Northamptonshire? 'We have the soil'! Who has the soil? Who has that part of it which was our people's heritage 'a century ago, when British agriculture was an inspiration to the world'?

An earlier Minister for Agriculture, Sir Reginald Dorman-Smith, returned from governing far Burma, contemplated the same transformed scene, and said:

I have seen downland which was derelict almost groaning with grain. I have seen vast acres of common land with grand crops of potatoes and oats. Last time I saw that land it was smothered in bracken and other foulnesses.[1] When I came back, my first sight of Britain was from an aeroplane and I found it hard to believe my eyes. Rural Britain has been transformed. To those of us who have fought for long years to enable our land to perform its proper function it is just like a dream come true . . . I know the fear which, while not preventing him from throwing himself wholeheartedly into his job, is present in many a farmer's heart: the fear that after the war Britain will forget and farming will be forced to undergo the agonies of the last post-war period. I do do not believe that will come to pass.

And the devastation of thousands of acres in Northamptonshire, *during* the war? The 'foulness' of the Test Valley?

There is no health in these words and promises. No 'miracle' has been performed here, no 'dream' has come true. The country wants food and those who work the land have been enabled to grow and sell it. But the land, though it thrives again, is still imprisoned.

Here is a good job for men to do who come back from the war, a job that can and should be done: to make England, Their England. England, Our England. To prevent a new abandonment of the land to 'bracken and other foulnesses'. To prevent the ruination of any more of it. To prevent the enclosure of any more of it. To redeem that which has been wantonly spoiled. Above all, to regain that part of it, for the use and enjoyment of our people, which was taken by theft, sanctioned at Westminster, to pay gaming debts. To build four *English* freedoms in a land green and pleasant again.

That is a good destination to strive for, in Civvy Street, and a worthy objective in the Battle in England.

---

[1] The small relic of our land which is still 'common' to us was indeed smothered in foulnesses, and often still is. The reason is, that petty local authorities, who since the days of Enclosure tend to ape the enclosing gentry, like to forbid the use of the remaining commons. If not watched night and day, they enclose them. By chance, I happened on a case in Sussex, where a local commoner was summoned for' causing three horses and two goats' to be grazed on Lindfield Common In Contravention Of A Cuckfield Urban District Council By-Law! Not even for this, may the few remaining commons be used nowadays! The criminal, in this case, was stout-hearted enough to challenge the village despots' right to forbid commoners from using commons. When I last heard of the case, counsel was ploughing through Latin documents of the times of Charles the Second, and had already discovered long buried treasure in the form of 'rights of commonage and common pasture'.

PART FOUR

BATTLE IN ENGLAND

CHAPTER I

IN CIVVY STREET

One day I sat at a window in Piccadilly and read the two letters which set me to write this book: the one from a young officer fighting overseas who said, 'We still feel out here that the ultimate battle is being won or lost in England'; and the one from a mother who said, 'I feel convinced that these intelligent, deep-thinking boys and girls are not going to leave the management of the new world to anyone but themselves when the war is won'.

I thought about them a lot, and then took up a newspaper. A loud headline said, 'Demobilization will be slow after the war'. I laid the paper down, and looked out into Piccadilly and the Green Park.

Two French officers passed; with lively gestures, they helped a voluble debate. Across the Green Park grass, went a tall British sailor with a girl in red, arm-in-arm, her head turned up to him, his down to her; a pretty picture. The American soldiers strolled by with loose gait, and were briskly passed by a pair of short and buxom girls in the blue of the women's Air Force. A lean, languid and sexless being, probably male, in white-striped black suit, black hat and umbrella drifted incongruously to its club, a derelict pleasure craft among the men and women of war. A fat and red-faced woman in a shapeless fur coat, with a tea-cosy on her head, was followed by three lithe and laughing girls, bare-headed.

Bless you, pretty compatriots, I thought, looking at them affectionately, for discovering your hair and how to tend it; when I came home from foreign parts, of yore, your heads reminded me of rookeries, and if, by some process I cannot understand, we have gained this much from the war, it is a great deal. Indeed, this is worth fighting for, for Hitler himself never did anything worse than the things you formerly did to your hair.

They split, to make way for a tramp who shambled between them, his head bent, his eyes searching the pavement, his shabby legs bearing him towards the barns and hedgerows. Was he happy or abject, this man, I wondered, free or enchained? Without a side glance he passed the wooden shelf, built on stout legs, which some compassionate clubman, on a day, put to ease the overladen porters, toiling with their loads from Covent Garden. I remembered a starry night when I went along Piccadilly with someone who was in fractious mood, so that I picked her up, and sat her on that shelf: 'This is where men put their burden', I said, 'you stay up there awhile, until you are easier to bear.' Through the trees I saw pieces of the Victoria Memorial and Buckingham Palace. A lorryload of soldiers clattered by. How little the scene was changed, I thought, since 1918.

1918! Demobilization! I fell into a daydream. Piccadilly and the Green Park vanished, I saw a forlorn winter's day and a country road that ran, gleaming in the rain, up a hill somewhere near Grantham. In a muddy field at the top, was a wooden hut, which I entered. A calendar hung on the wall; it showed the date January 16th, 1919. At a table planted on the bare boards sat a young captain. No ribbon on his coat, no wound stripes on his sleeve; 'I suppose you've been sitting here all these years', I thought automatically, and a feeling of antagonism stirred within me. (I wonder if men feel that to-day?) He signed a paper and handed it to me, a thing the size of a letter. 'Certificate of Demobilization', it said. I folded it and put it in my pocket, went out and down the hill. A drab and dreary world lay before me, and vanished disconsolately into a mist which rubbed out its edges. Nothing clear, nothing sharply defined, no destination beckoning.

I stopped, and took out the paper again. This flimsy thing, then, in my hands, was Victory, Freedom, the world safe for Democracy, the land fit for heroes — all I fought for. Glad adventure, eager curiosity, a uniform, faring forth, trudging to the trenches, leave, wounds, hospital, fighting in the air, good companions, fear, boredom, more wounds, more hospital, bully beef and biscuits, crashes, four years — here was the net result, on paper: my life and freedom.

I did not feel free. My uniform was no longer mine; I must buy clothes, and clothes were dear. None would provide my next meal: I must earn it. None would tell me when to get up, where to go and what to do: I must decide that. No more would others think for me; I must think for myself. During part of the four years which lay behind me, I loved the war and wished it would never end; during the later part, I loathed the war and dreaded the peace. Now, peace was come. I folded the paper again and put it away. The rain increased. The road before trailed uninvitingly into the mist. No life stirred. I went on.

Thus I mused, looking at Piccadilly and the Green Park, when I must have fallen asleep. The daydream became a real dream, for suddenly I found myself back in the wooden hut on the bleak hilltop. The same captain sat at the table. But the date on the calendar was changed. It said January 16th, 194-; I could not read the last numeral, because the leaf fluttered in the draught. Anyway it was Nineteen Forty-Something. I was still twenty-three, and in my dream this seemed quite natural. I took the paper, and saw the words, 'Certificate of Demobilization', written across it.

So this is demobilization, I thought, the thing I have thought about so long, and sometimes longed for and sometimes feared. This is the Thing I have been fighting for, this sheet of paper. The rush to join up, in 1939; the retreat to Dunkirk (I hope old Jack, whom we were forced to leave because of his shattered leg, was looked after by the Germans); the evacuation; the Battle of Britain; that tank attack at Tobruk; wounds; hospital; the sand; the heat; the cold; the dive-bombers; no mail and I wonder what Milly's doing at home; no leave; fear; boredom; good pals; the landing in Europe — they all boil down to this.

I folded the paper and put it in my pocket, and went out.

The dank, unfriendly road fell into the mist. At the side of it stood a middle-aged man, who seemed to wait for something.

'Good day', he said, as I approached.

'Good day', I said, looking at him doubtfully, for his face seemed familiar. 'Er — do we know each other?'

'Of course', said he, 'I am Yourself.'

'Why, of course you are', I said, 'you are Myself. How stupid of me. I knew I'd seen you somewhere. You look well.'

'Tolerably so, thank you', he said, 'where are you going?'

'Going?' I said. 'Now, where am I going? I've hardly thought about it.'

'Ah, that's a great mistake', he said, quickly, 'the mistake most of them make when they come out of there' — and he pointed to the hut. 'That's why I stand here and speak to them. Now, where *are* you going?'

'Well', I said, feebly, 'I suppose, to 1950 and 1960 and a career and a family and a home and all that. At least I hope so.'

'Vague, but not bad for a start, with qualifications', he said approvingly. 'Now I've been that way before, and it's a very difficult road to find. You won't find it by yourself. You'd be surprised, how difficult that road is to find. No signs, all manner of wrong turnings, snares and pitfalls without number. I went astray scores of times. And the mist is thickening. I'd better come along with you.'

'Well, if it's not troubling you', I said, uncertainly.

'No trouble at all', he said, cheerfully, 'that's why I wait here.' We started off together. 'Now, how do you feel?'

'I feel a bit lost', I said, 'like a lamb that's wandered from the fold.'

'I know, I know', he said, 'that's how I felt. You've been fighting for your country, and now you've to fend for yourself. And you won't find many good shepherds on this road.'

'Are you one?' I asked.

'I am resolved to be', he said, 'by crook or by hook.'

'You see', I explained, 'I feel a sense of sudden flop. Now that we've won this Thing that we were told to fight for, peace, it turns to ashes in my hands. I feel, in a way, that I've led an ideal life for four years. I never needed to take any thought for to-morrow, because others thought for me; yet all the while I felt that I was serving a great cause, that I was a fine fellow. The radio, the newspapers and the politicians told me so day and night. As soon as this was put into my hand' — and I showed him my demobilization paper — 'I felt that I was a man without a task or mission, and one who, at that, must look after all his own wants. I feel suddenly unwanted; I seem to belong nowhere, and I don't think that's right, after my service. From now on, all I've to do is, to fight for myself. I miss the feeling of each-for-all and all-for-each, which my service somehow gave me — now the hurly-burly's done.'

'Now the battle's lost and won', he said, smiling. 'You know Shake-speare?'

'A bit', I said.

'Now listen to me', he said, stopping abruptly in the middle of the road and buttonholing me with my own forefinger, 'that's the very first and worst of the wrong turnings. Now you see how you would have gone astray, but for me. Why should you lose the feeling of service, of having a task or mission to accomplish, simply because those who until now told you what to do have cast you out? If you only serve when one man tells you that you are called up, another that you are to go to the front, and a third that you are to charge the enemy, that is not so much service as slavery. Why should you claim any merit for your service, if you only did what you were ordered to do and could not refuse to do? Any fool can obey an order. Now that you set out for Civvy Street, you feel adrift, because you have no one to command you and no battle to fight, save your own personal struggle to exist, and you do not feel that to be a great cause. There is a gap.'

'Yes', I said reluctantly, 'that's about it, I expect.'

'That's where they all go wrong', he said, urgently, 'they not only take the first wrong turning, they set off on the wrong foot. They all come out of that hut thinking, Well, the hurly-burly's done, the battle's lost and won, now we'll crawl into the first hole we can find in Civvy Street and forget about the country. We'll no longer be one of millions, serving and fighting for the country, we'll be each man for himself and the devil take the hindmost. We'll leave the country to something called The Guvverment; we call the man we work for The Guv'nor, so the Guvverment must be something really great. Why should we worry further about the things we fought for? The Guvverment will look after them. So you see, Yourself', said Myself, looking at me earnestly, 'nearly every man who comes out of that hut a freeman puts his mind into bondage as he comes through the door. He thinks, there's nothing to fight for now. Instead, he should say, Ah, the fighting's done now, but the battle just begins. Any dolt can obey an order. But it takes a man, as he comes through that door, to say, now I'll start fighting, of my own free will and in my own free right, for the things I believe in, for this country, and for its future, and I'll never stop, while I live, whether I'm alone or one of a crowd. Don't you see, that gives him a destination and an ideal and a hope? They wouldn't need *me*, to show them the way, if they thought that. That would give them the feeling of an even greater task and mission. That would destroy their delusion, that Service means going when you're called up.'

'Um', I said, 'I see what you mean. A kind of Battle in England.'

'That's right', he said eagerly, 'A Battle in England, a Battle for England. Start out with that idea, and you don't feel a sense of slump or flop, when you leave that hut.'

'It sounds invigorating', I said, 'but how? What can one do? A man

141

feels so small, so helpless, so alone, so much harassed by the need to earn a livelihood, so much overwhelmed by the powers of frustration that enclose him.'

'Oh, rats', said Myself, 'he only feels like that because he has never tried to feel different, because he shuffles out of that hut thinking, the Battle's over, instead of, the Battle now begins. But I'll tell you all about it on the way.'

'Good', I said, 'I'm open to learn.'

'That's all you need', he said, 'let's shake on it', and he stretched out my arm.

I shook my hand. 'Let's go', I said, and we started off. . . .

CHAPTER II

WHEN THE BOYS COME HOME

I WANDERED through 1919 as through a thickening wood. Victory was come, and peace, the glorious Things we so long fought for. I, and all the others who survived, were home again. The world safe for democracy and the land fit for heroes lay before us. In Paris, was a march of triumph to the Arch of Triumph. In London, I watched the Guards come home, and the V.C.s go to a tea-party at Buckingham Palace, and the Unknown Soldier drive by.

Yes, this was no illusion. Here it was, the thing we wanted, yet none seemed to want me. When I came home feet-foremost, during the war, women threw roses into my ambulance, a girl kissed my bandaged face as I was carried on a stretcher into a hospital. Now the thing we strove for was in my grasp. Yet when I opened my hand I found it empty.

I meandered about, went into a teashop, bought an evening paper and opened it. Joe Smart, it said, beneath big headlines, was once again ahead of all other revue-producers with a big idea; his new show, Dope and Glory, at the Rhinodrome, contained a chorus of ex-officers!

I went along and bought a seat. There they were, The Boys. Their names were printed on the programme, in the order of their appearance, so that you might identify each of them: Lieut. Jones of the King's,

Captain Smith of the Queen's, Lieut. Brown, M.C., of the Prince of Wales's, and Captain Robinson, of the Duke of York's Own; the chorus boys of 1914-18, come back. They marched about, backstage, while a girl sang:

> Good-bye, khaki,
> We're gonna put you in the addick,
> Good-bye, khaki,
> You've made the world so democraddick,
> We've been true to you,
> We'll give all due to you,
> So long and cheerio, and now we're through with you . . .

They marched off, in khaki, and came back, in scarlet, blue and gold, swords and bearskins, to deafening applause, and they saluted with their swords, and marched off again, to draw their four-pounds-a-week while the show lasted, and the girl kissed her hand to the audience in payment for the thunderous cheers.[1]

'So long and cheerio, and now we're through with you . . .' They disappeared into the wings, into Civvy Street and the future. The future, which would see music hall comedians asking each other, 'What, you were an officer? Have you dyed your British Warm yet?' (Loud laughter, for many of them could not afford an overcoat.) The future, which would see the bemedalled out-of-works pushing piano-organs round the streets of London. The future, which would cast away in every town and village in England, like stranded fish, such men as Captain Grafton:

It is 'the Captain's' chief tragedy (though he does not know it) that he survived the war, which was not only the climax of his existence but, probably, the only part of it that Nature qualified him to justify . . . His type is one that must be recognized in the aftermath of every great war in history. Shakespeare knew his peers and drew them incomparably . . . He is a spare man, just short of fifty — though he feels (and thinks) like a boy — with thin hair plastered down by some kind of fixative that conceals its greyness, and a toothbrush moustache clipped short with the same object . . . He usually wears khaki shirts, with a zigzag gunner's tie, and cord riding-breeches, covered in winter by a greasy

[1] The day after I wrote this I read in my morning newspapers that a V.C. of this war, discharged with a pension granted for *one year*, was appearing on the music hall stage in uniform to earn money.

trench-coat or a British Warm. The remnant of the service tradition shows itself in his too limited vocabulary still embellished with war-time slang ... and in his attitude towards politics and life in general, which is that of a puzzled schoolboy, nursing a grievance against the changed values of these degenerate days, yet constrained, out of soldierly pride, not to make a fuss. It is difficult, of course, to see the way in which everything for which he and his friends fought and suffered is going to rack and ruin without active protest. But the old guard can still pack up its troubles and do its bit. Captain Grafton does it, with a solemn sense of duty, at meetings and armistice-day parades of the British Legion (when he puts on his medals) and also as Scoutmaster ... He feels more important, happier and more 'like himself' on the rare occasions when he dons a black shirt and a belt and sets off with a loaded cane in his hand to parade with the North Bromwich Fascists. Then, at least, he feels that England has need of him ... A pathetic, if not quite admirable figure — poor Archie Grafton with his attempts to maintain the old military smartness, his perpetual anxiety to do the soldierly thing and live up to the code of the ante-room ... His life virtually came to an end in 1918, and nothing less than another war can resuscitate him — by which time (if the dreadful thing come) he will be too far gone to be of very much use. Like everybody else who served actively in the war, he is a wounded man, and a sick man, too. . . .

Ah, poor Archie Grafton, and his neighbour, Mr. Rudge, the orphan of Enclosure:

Mr. Rudge cannot, like Captain Grafton, be described as an inter-loper. The Rudges have staked their claim to belong to Monk's Norton in a good many square feet of the graveyard's surface. At the time of the Civil War (or the Rebellion, as Miss Abberley calls it), they owned the Goodrest Farm. Now all that remains of their landed property is the small-holding of fifteen acres which Mr. Rudge inherited ten years ago from a second cousin. . . .[1]

The picture is exact and is drawn with a melancholy humour. But decay is not comic.

Don't let it happen again. 'They' will do it again, if you let them, but yours will be the fault. For yours is the power, who won the glory.

Come back to a Battle in England, not to a life of living death, spent in

---

[1] I am grateful to Mr. Francis Brett Young and to Messrs. William Heinemann for per-mission to quote these lines from his *Portrait of a Village*, 1937.

a declining countryside, supported by doles or pensions, spoiled by a feeling of eternal frustration. Claim and use your fullest rights of citizenship.

Come back to fight, and not to follow. Interest yourself in and inform yourself about the affairs of your country. Keep away from extreme parties, which only offer worse enslavement, by even worse misrulers. But immerse yourself, as a matter of right and daily duty, in the thing called Politics — which is, the state of your island.

Instruct yourself, by reading, about the condition of your Parliament and your Parties, so that you may detect the means which are used to deceive you. Arm yourself with the weapons of reason and debate, and sharpen them upon the knowledge which any man, who is not idle or a dolt, can acquire. Gather round yourself men of like mind, and thrash out, with them, the problems of the day. Choose one of them to stand for Parliament as an Independent, under the pledge that he will accept no Party allegiance; or stand yourself, and let your friends go from house to house, to persuade the voters that some new men, who are not merely the sausages turned out by The Party Machine, are needed in Parliament, to watch over our affairs in the coming years.

Do not die on your feet, like Captain Grafton. If you were able to fight with a rifle or a tank, you can fight with your mind and your love of this country. Train yourself to find the falsehood in political speeches and the newspapers, so that you may enlighten those about you; this is the greatest task of all. Combat the dullard's, the slave's, the traitor's lazy objection that 'You can't do anything about it', 'It wouldn't work,' 'I don't know anything about politics,' 'They'd get you down'.

These are the people who will destroy England, if you let them. This state of mind will be your greatest enemy, when you come back. Resolve to destroy it by contempt and ridicule; and, to that end, *inform* yourself of what goes on.

Learn, and be ready to tell others, who 'They' are. For these weakwits, these self-made serfs, are right, in their dull apprehension that hidden forces now work to oppress them and mislead them into war. After two World Wars, the evidence is too strong to be denied. But it is *not* impossible to learn who They are, how They work, and how to thwart Them.

This is what patriotic men can do, each in his own circle, and it is a better undertaking than to meander downhill for the rest of your life, in angry, befuddled but impotent ignorance, like the Captain Graftons, and, when your instinct tells you that They are about to take your future from you again, to traipse off to the nearest town in a black shirt, or a red one.

Do not, when you come back, lay the weapon of the spirit aside, with the uniform and the other equipment, but keep it, and keep it sharp. Do not give your thoughts entirely to Getting A Job And Holding It, for by that means you pawn your future; and They will wreck it for you again. It will not avail to Get On With The Job and Leave Politics To Them.

The instinct of the British people is sound. They knew that this war was being brewed for them, but could not rouse themselves to prevent it. They are right to-day in feeling that they are held in the thrall of powerful forces which prepare further misery for them.

They are only wrong, in their miserable acceptance of this, as of some enchainment which they cannot throw off. This is where 'the boys', who come back, can reinvigorate England, if they do not lay aside the weapon of the spirit. For they will have made England famous again, they will have travelled far and widened their vision, they will be fit and vigorous; they can seek out, detect and frustrate 'Them', if they do not become like Captain Grafton. They can *make* their future, and not let others mar it.

Sir Stafford Cripps, on February 6th, 1943, said he noticed 'with some distress, a growing tendency in our country to view the future with a certain degree of hopelessness and of almost sour disillusion'. He correctly diagnosed the feeling of the country. He has contributed to it. Only yesterday, people hoped they would find in him, at last, a man who would fearlessly say in Parliament the things that people feel. His acceptance of relegation to a routine department, where he is little heard or seen, has disappointed this hope, like so many earlier ones. He could help us more by leaving office and speaking from a different platform every night.

He said that public confidence, in improvement after this war, showed signs of weakening just as victory approached. Doubts were creeping in; privilege and selfish interests were busily preparing to cast the future in the mould of the past.

Then he said:

Indeed, it is almost commonplace in these days to hear the most confirmed advocates of change expressing the view that 'They' will never really implement the promise of a new Britain or a new world.

Who are these mysterious people referred to as 'They', who are apparently looked on as the veriest broken reed of a hope for the future? 'They' is not the language of a democracy or even of the class-struggle. 'They' is the language of dictatorship and defeatism of the common people. We must put aside all such subservience within our democracy and speak instead of what 'we' want and 'we' will do or insist upon being done. But in order that 'we' may be effective to make 'Them' do what we wish, we must understand not only the problem of the future but also the lessons of the past.

But 'They' do exist, and Sir Stafford Cripps was wrong, and the British instinct is right, if he implied that they do not.

You need only to recognize 'Them'. I have tried to show who they are. The first of 'Them' is the order of moneyed privilege, in this country, which began with Enclosure of the land, continued with Enclosure of the schools, and has been completed with the Enclosure of all opportunity, advancement and preferment. This has produced the repressed spirit of England, the sagging spirit which is our greatest enemy, for it delivers us, ready-made tools, into the hands of the rest of 'Them'.

The rest of 'Them' are powerful forces of many kinds, none of which have their roots in this country, but spread all over the world, and these pursue their aims, through us, our Enclosed order, and our armed strength, or our foreign policy, without regard to our island interests. To-day, they may think it will profit them for us to be weak; to-morrow, that their ambitions will be best served if we make war. They command mighty means to mislead and misinform us, to tell us we should disarm or rearm, connive in aggression or make war against aggression.

The individual men who go to make this manifold man, Anon, are no better or worse than other men. But their interests reach beyond frontiers, and They therefore know no frontiers, no nationhood. Their interests are not *ours*; but they wield great power in our land, over our policies. They have their spokesmen in Parliament; and if any of these spokesmen chances to be a political leader, the other members of his Party are *sworn* to follow him, so that the island interest is already forsworn.

This is the stranglehold, on our native interests, which can only be broken by the appearance in Parliament, for a term long enough to smash it, of Independent patriots. But Their greatest weapon is the Press. In this matter, I am as good a judge as any man, and I say that our newspapers, with few exceptions, are the enemies of truth, and of our future, in this country to-day.

These international forces compose jointly 'Them'. They are, in the main, international bankers; international arms trusts; international oil suppliers; Zionists; and the more extreme elements of international Jewry, working from all countries, for which Zionism is too small a name.

'They' wait, in Civvy Street. Begin your journey, in that street, with the feeble habit of averting your glance from them (and all too many Englishmen are prone to this, in real streets of plaster-and-asphalt, among their flesh-and-blood fellow beings) because you think them too strong for you, and your future is already mortgaged. Look at them, watch them, ask about them, inquire their names, study their activities, learn how to forethwart them, and Civvy Street lies clear before you, leading to a secure future and a better England.

For their strength lies in anonymity. Tear aside the screen, expose them to the light of day, and their strength is gone. This is why it is sinister that British Governments protect the method of anonymity, with every means in their power. . . .

> Good-bye, khaki,
> So long and cheerio, and now we're through with you. . . .

sang that grinning girl. The curtain came down. I went out, into Civvy Street, in search of the future. I thought of it only in terms of employment, work, achievement, and when I found it, 'They' took it from me.

I did not know that 'They' existed. Given that knowledge, I would have been alert, and so might others have been. This time, 'the boys', when they come back, and those who grow up here, may know. They may know that Civvy Street has two sides, both of which they must know and watch — Hard Work Side and Politics Side, which in the inter-war years was the shady side, the side on which 'They' lurked.

Don't let it happen again. It need not and will not, if you keep the weapon of the spirit, when you hand in your other arms, and return to a Battle in England.

CHAPTER III

WHEN THE GIRLS COME HOME

I KNEW two girls, in London, in 1913. One was very pretty. She never married. That war left too few men to go round, and although you might have expected a husband to find her in spite of that, she was missed, by some mischance, and joined the class of the Miss Sheldon-Smiths,[1]

whose ages varied between thirty-one and twenty-four. Their only brother, the heir to the family's embarrassments, was killed at Gheluvelt. They are all three unmarried and likely to remain so. Their tragedy is that the generation in which they might reasonably have expected to find husbands of their own kind was eliminated by the war; and the fact that they are more class-conscious than the aristocracy seems likely to keep them single.

The other girl was married three times, between the wars. This does not disprove my statement about the insufficiency of men; it would happen to some women, if only three men were in the world, and all her husbands were married at least twice.

When I came on leave from France in 1915, in the first glory of my officer's uniform, I met them both, and blessed the chance; I was glad to be able to bask in their admiration of it. It was grand. Given a million guesses, on that sunny day, my imagination would not have stretched enough to picture the fantastic thing that happened twenty-eight years later, in 1943. I met the same two, in Piccadilly. I was in civilian clothes. They were both officers in the A.T.S.!

'Well, well', I said, to the thrice-married one, 'this is where I get my own back on the posters of the last war. What are *you* doing in the Great War, Mummy? Come on, let's go and celebrate this. All the nice men love a soldier. We didn't want to lose you, but we thought you ought to go, and with all our might and main we shall hug you, squeeze you, kiss you, when you come back again. On Saturday I'm willing, if you'll only take the shilling, to make a woman of any one of you. I do hope we meet a private, so that she'll have to salute you. How is the spirit of the troops?

[1] Francis Brett Young, *Portrait of a Village* (Heinemann, 1937).

Still excellent? Is all quiet at Weston-super-Mare, or wherever you stand guard?'

'Shut up', they said, 'we've heard it all before. How *are* you, citizen Reed? It *is* good to see you.'

'I expect you say that to all the men', I said, 'but come on. This deserves to be honoured.'

So we went, along that street which my feet so often trod, in peace and war, in lean times and fat, and came presently, for it was noon, to the selfsame table where we three sat together and refreshed ourselves, all those years ago.

'This is an extraordinary thing', I said, 'I feel like Mr. Bultitude in *Vice Versa*. Here we sat, you two and I, that other time, and I was an officer and you were civilians and you sunned yourselves in my reflected glory, and I bought you lunch, and now here we sit, and you are officers and I am a civilian, the glory is yours and the shadow mine, and you are going to buy me lunch. . . .'

'Oh no', they said promptly, both together.

'I might have known it', I said bitterly, 'I have been lured here under false pretences. The more it changes, the more it is the same. When there is only one man left in England, and you have taken from him every right and wrong with which he was born, when you are all Field-Marshals and he peels the potatoes for your meals in the mess, when you are both Prime Ministresses of England, wearing trousers habitually and carrying an umbrella always, you will still expect that one last man to pay for your lunch. Justice is not, in this world', I said gloomily.

'Cheer up', they said. 'We'll buy you a cocktail.'

'I wouldn't drink one of those wartime compounds, which neither cheer nor inebriate but only poison, even if you gave me the price of it in addition', I said. 'I'll eat your health, in Spam, 1943, honourable and gallant ladies both, and may your pips never grow less.' Then I turned to the thrice-mated one. 'And you, Second Subaltern Defoi', I said, 'what will you eat?'

'I *wish* you'd remember my name', she said, 'that was my second husband.'

'I wish you'd never married at all,' I said, 'I've never been able to catch up with them since. Now let me see, what is it? I know. It's Firstleigh.'

'That was number one', she said, 'it's Drymal.'

'Of course it is', I said, 'and how is he? Where is he?'

'Oh', she said, hesitating slightly, 'He's . . .'

'Not another word', I said hurriedly. 'Tact is my mainspring, but I warn you, I shall never be able to remember Forthleigh, if you think to take that name next. From now on I shall call you by your maiden name.'

'All right', she said, quickly, 'what is it?'

'Er — oh lor!' I said. 'Look here, it isn't fair, I'm not a human filing cabinet, Barbara. She can't expect it, can she, Peggy?' I appealed to the other one.

They both smiled. 'Well, you remembered those all right', they said.

I asked them how they came to be soldiers. Barbara owned a prosperous business in Mayfair, which was destroyed by a bomb. She would not receive compensation until after the war, and but a fraction of the value then, when the cost of beginning again would be at its peak. Peggy was secretary to a Harley Street specialist who went into the Forces. Both laboured under a feeling of uselessness and cut-adriftness and went into the A.T.S., where they met.

I turned the talk to the future, and tried to draw them out. They seemed vague, planless. They didn't know this, they supposed that. Barbara expected she would start another business, when the war was over. Peggy assumed she would drift into a job. They enjoyed their life, when they were in camp, but when they were on leave longed to be back with the things and people they knew, and dreaded the return to duty, until they were back.

Indeed, I found that, like 'the boys' in the last war and too many of 'the boys' in this one, they made no effort to think out the future at all. They thought of it only in terms of individual competition for a livelihood, and not at all in terms of our island safety, of enduring peace, and of a happy breed. But I held the talk to the barrack-square of this topic; I put myself in command, drilled their thoughts and made them go the way I desired. So we talked, something in this wise. . . .

'How do you like women's rights, now that you come to share all but one of the wrongs of men?' I asked them.

'How do you mean, all but one?' they said.

'Why, don't you see', I said, 'you have now gained everything but one thing. You may vote, become a Minister, practise as a doctor or barrister, wear uniform, rise in rank. The one and only thing now denied you is to share a soldier's grave with a man. But I am sure that our mis-leaders will arrange for you to be granted that uttermost boon in the next war, if you wish to have it that way. So you see', I said, 'the removal of the immemorial hindrances which were laid in the way of women, has brought you almost everything you want. Our good War Graves Commission has recently reported that sons, killed in this war, have now been laid to rest alongside their fathers, killed in the last. This is the only place yet denied to you. Throw your imagination forward another twenty-five years, and picture such a grave being opened to receive — a granddaughter, killed in action! Are you pleased with the progress which women have made, in your time?'

Peggy smiled. 'The awful thing about you', she said, 'is that you put things in such an odd way, that I never know whether you are joking or not.'

'I have to do that', I said, 'because I can only make you listen at all, and think a little, that way. People in this country are trained to recognize, as truth, only lies dressed up, and now hardly know truth when they see it. I mean what I say. Can't you see it? It's as plain as a flagstaff and right in front of your noses. Your mothers wanted to right the wrongs of women by sharing the rights of men. They got what they wanted, through the first World War. You, their daughters, have inherited this "Equality with men", which they fought for, in the second World War. You want "Equality with men", yes? Is that what you want?'

'We suppose so', they said, vaguely.

'Then, sweet friends of my youth', I said, 'do you not see that you have but one thing still to gain, if that is all you want, if "Equality with men" is the summit of your ambition, if you cannot raise your eyes to a higher view of your world than that which a female worm would see.'

'Well, get on', they said. 'What *do* you mean?'

'Why, that your own low-sightedness', I said, 'and the guile of those who wish to destroy us, is causing you to look at a lie dressed up as truth and think it truth, when the truth is something different. For you will agree with me that what women really want, and men too, for that matter, is not to share a soldier's grave with a man, or even to have their husbands and sons laid in such a grave, or yet to be denied a man at all, but to share a bed with a man, to marry and have children and live useful lives.'

'You always talk like that', they said.

'I do', I said, 'I call a bed a bed. But that *is* truth. You won't deny that that is what women have mainly wanted since the world began and are likely to want as long as the world lasts?'

'No', they said, 'we won't.'

'Well, then', I said, 'after this war, not only the boys, but also the girls, will come back, and enter Civvy Street in search of the future. In our country alone were the women taken from their husbands and homes and lovers, in such numbers. The Germans did not do that, at any rate until the catastrophe of Stalingrad, when the war was three and a half years old, and I do not think they will, at this stage, be able to enforce it, in any large degree. I think they looked to the future of their nation, whether they lost or won this war, and were wiser than we, or our leaders. I think a very deadly blow was struck at the roots of English life, by this action, and we shall not see its full results for some years to come, and those will be the years when some seek to bring about a new war. But anyway, it was done, and soon the girls will come back. Now I ask you, Barbara and Peggy, jolly old Second Subalterns, as the imbeciles Bones and Bertie Wooster would have said, what hope will remain for our future if they come back to wage a kind of civil war, and a most uncivil war at that, against the men with whom they must marry and breed?'

'What should they do, then?' they asked.

'It's obvious', I said, 'what they want, first and foremost, is what the men want: the safety of this island, and within it, our House of Freedom, so that we may build a better future. They then may look forward to happiness. What on this planet will it avail them, to yield to the deluders, and think only of gaining "Equality with men", if, while they fix their eyes on that, the peace is stolen from them again, their homes and families are broken up again in another twenty years' time, and both their men and themselves taken to fight?'

'Don't you think we *ought* to have full equality?' they said.

'But of course I do', I said, 'and you *have* it. You are pushing against an open door. I believe this island contains more women than men, and you have the vote. No office is too lofty for you to reach, no reform can be withheld which you demand, if you use that power. Let me give you an example. In November of 1942 one of your sex in Parliament, Mrs. Tate, drew attention to the fact that civilian women, injured through enemy action, received lower compensation than men. Now this was an obvious injustice, and a simple thing, which all could understand. It cannot be defended. Immediately the Members of Parliament, those men *and* women who are sworn to vote for *any* Governmental policy, however injurious to our interest, began to grow uneasy, because they fear the electors more than anything in the world, and knew, that in so clear a matter the people could not be bamboozled. They began to look anxiously over their shoulders at their constituencies — and this is another proof of the thing I try so hard to explain, the great power which the voters possess, if they would but make their minds clear about the matters in which they should use it, and how to use it. The result was that no less than 95 habitual Yessers voted for Mrs. Tate's proposed reform, and against the Government. I feel sure that, in consequence, this injustice will be mitigated.'[1]

'Well, that sounds good', they said.

'Yes, it sounds good', I said, 'but in fact it isn't. It is the best example I know of the false trail which women are following. For what *was* the issue, simplified to its clearest point! If one of their legs were blown off, women wanted to receive as much money for that banished limb as would a man. Well and good. But what do they *really* want? They want both their husbands and themselves to retain *both* legs, to live in a secure island, and one progressively improving its domestic lot.'

'Um, we see that', they said.

'And that is why', I said, 'they are allowing themselves to be led along a wrong turning, that will bring them to fresh trouble, when they fix their thoughts on this misleading catchword, "Equality with men". It is a secondary, not the foremost thing, and it is something they already have, if they take it. What they *want*, most of all, if they would realize it, is peace after this war, so that they may live happily with their men. That, they can only have through a sound Foreign Policy, a cleaner Parliament, and a freer Press. That is why the few women they have sent to Parliament have done them great disservice, by showing energy *only* in the campaign for "Equality with men" or, in a few cases, in some cause, such as the admission of large numbers of immigrants to this island, which is actually dangerous to their own future.'

'What should we do, then?'

[1] Sure enough, the Government gave way!

'When the girls come home', I said, 'and are called on, by dazzling promises of "Equality with men", to instal a new Parliament at Westminster for another five or ten or twenty years, let them ask these candidates, what policy they propose to uphold in Foreign Affairs, and whether they intend to pledge themselves to follow the orders of their party leaders if, *after* the election, they pursue a different policy; what attitude they will take in Parliament about the activities of organized international powers which try to exert influence on our policies; whether they will insist in Parliament on obtaining information about the powers which control our newspapers, about the foreign activities of our armaments concerns and the activities here of foreign armaments and oil enterprises; and the like more. In short, they should refuse to be deluded by promises of "Equality with men", which they can force *any* Member to press for, and only vote for that man, who will show them how he proposes to work for our safety and peace, and who will pledge himself to resign and bring about a by-election if he sees these things endangered. That is what the girls should do, when they come home. It's the same thing which the boys should do, those boys who will be the fathers of their children and of the other boys and girls who will be sent away "to fight for freedom" in twenty years' time, if *these* boys and girls allow it. . . .'

'Well', they said, as I paid the bill, 'it was grand to meet again.'

'It was indeed,' said I, 'but remember how impossible this meeting would have seemed to us, in 1915. Don't let us live on a descending scale of hope and faith. Each of you is now a leader, of lady troops. Talk to your girls, try and make them think as Englishwomen. Show them that the radio, the pictures and the Press, to-day, are their enemies, the instruments of delusion. Try and bring them back to a wise, a native, a patriotic state of mind. Make them feel that their present service is a small thing, that the real Battle in England will begin when they set foot in Civvy Street, that they can do more for us in this island there than they ever can in your huts and on your gun-sites. Don't let them meander along, drooling "There's a long, long trail a-winding, into the land of my dreams", when so many lie in wait to lead them to a nightmare.'

We went out and parted at the corner of Bond Street, and I saluted them both.

'Good Heavens', they said, 'you mustn't do *that*! It's against *all* orders.'
'Is it?' I said. 'I was always a rebel. What do you think I fought for freedom for, in the last war? This is a free country, ennit?'

CHAPTER IV

SNAP!

DECEMBER 14th, 1918, said the calendar on the wall of my hut in France. The Armistice (which was to last for just twenty-one years) was five weeks old; the echoes of the cheering were hardly still. The Boys were not yet come home; they were in France, Italy, Russia, the Balkans, Mesopotamia, Egypt, India, or somewhere else, far away.

No matter, at home their interests were being well cared for. The Victory they won was being invested for them. They looked homeward and saw an Election. 'We will hang the Kaiser', 'We will squeeze Germany till the pips squeak', 'We will bring the war criminals to justice', 'We will banish war for ever', 'We will build homes for heroes in a land fit for heroes to live in'.

The politicians said these things, and the newspapers echoed them. The Boys breathed again. All was well. Their victory was not in vain. The war to end war was over, their representatives at home were making the world safe for democracy, all save a million of those who went away were still alive, and those now due to come back would not be able to say that England had failed them.

It was the Snap Election. During the war of 1914-18 the Parties, joined in Coalition by their own vote, prolonged the life of the Parliament of 1911 three times, from five to eight years (just as the Coalition has done this time). On November 25th, 1918, just *fourteen days* after the Armistice, they dissolved Parliament, which would otherwise have expired on January 31st, 1919, when a few of The Boys would have already returned, and the hysteria of November 1918 would already have dwindled a little.

They would not wait even for those few weeks. Who cared what happened to the Victory which The Boys won, or to The Boys? The politicians must hasten to cash in on *their* victory. Seats must be made safe for Members. 'Vote for the Government that won the war'. Parliament was dissolved on November 25th, 1918, before the rumbling echoes of the last gun were dead. The Snap Election was held on December 14th, 1918. Mr. Lloyd George's Coalition was returned with a majority of 472 Members, out of 707, and of the 472, 334 were Conservatives.[1]

The *political* victory was won, the military victory thrown away, and the peace lost, while the deluded people still nursed tender feet and sore throats from the rejoicings of November 11th, 1918. The Snap Election was over. Snap! went the jaws of the Party Machine. They closed on what? On the Kaiser? On the War Criminals? On Victory? Peace? Freedom? Homes for Heroes? Work for All?

No, they closed on the people of this island, who, thus duped, were put in a strait-jacket of impotence, which was only relaxed while the next war was being prepared at election times. At each of those infrequent opportunities they were induced to put their head between the jaws again. Snap. . . .

That is the trick, by means of which a democratic machine may be used to dupe the people and lead them into a new war.

Within four years of the Snap Election, Mr. Lloyd George, the War Winner, was dismissed by the Conservative majority. The era of three Tory Prime Ministers opened, Mr. Bonar Law, Mr. Baldwin and Mr. Neville Chamberlain, with the lamentable interludes of their puppet, Mr. Ramsay MacDonald.

Now the same process begins again. Our present Parliament was elected in November 1935, and was due to expire in November 1940. The war came in September 1939, and in 1940, 1941 and 1942 Parliament prolonged its own life, so that it is now due to be dissolved in November 1943. If, before that, Germany has capitulated, it will hold a Snap Election. If Germany still fights, it will probably renew its existence by another year, and then dissolve and hold the election when victory comes, or is obviously imminent.

The Boys in either case will not be here. Mr. Churchill has promised, on their behalf, that if the war with Japan still goes on they will im-

---

[1] At the subsequent elections, between 1918 and the present war, the number of Conservative Members returned, out of 615, was 347 (1922), 258 (1923), 415 (1924), 260 (1929), 472 (1931), and 387 (1935). For eighteen of those twenty-one years, the Conservatives enjoyed large majorities.

mediately be sent across the world, all the King's Forces! No doubt the radio will enable them to hear the good tidings from home: 'We shall exact full retribution from "All Nazis and Quislings"', "We shall make war impossible for all time", "We shall find employment for all and make this island fit for The Boys and The Girls to live in", "When they come home, we shall provide social security for all", "We shall begin a great programme of public works and reconstruction. . . . "'.

The only question is, will the Coalition (called, to-day, the National Government) appeal to the country, or will the two great Parties compete? The signs are, that the device of 1918 may be used again. The Coalition may present itself to the country as 'The Government that won the war, led by the Man Who Won The War'[1], and would probably flutter the pages of the Beveridge Report before the electors ('A Land Fit For Heroes To Live In') as the proof that the welfare of this island is safe in its keeping. The Labour Party has shown that a share in office tempts it more than the bachelordom of Opposition. If it decided to go to the country as a Party, the Conservatives would offer themselves not only as the Men Who Won The War, but also as the champions of the Beveridge Report, and say, 'Even the Socialists couldn't give you anything more Socialist than this!' And if by some freak of the moment it obtained a majority, a dire prospect would open for this country,

The odds are on a Snap Election held by the Winston Churchill National Government (instead of the Lloyd George Coalition), and the electors would be expected to forget that many of The Men Who Won The War are also those who actively promoted its coming.

Two or three years later Mr. Winston Churchill, if he stoutly held to the alliance with Russia or set about to prevent the loss of the peace, would be cast aside, as Mr. Lloyd George was cast aside, and the Conservative Party would resume open control. At any subsequent election, brought about by reviving public uneasiness, some trick would be found to lull the electors for just as long as was needed, to hold an election.

This is the course of events to come, if the people of this island do not set themselves to understand the way the political machine has been deftly thrown out of gear, so that it works only for their delusion. The prospect of another twenty years of political captivity, stalemate and

[1] In March 1943, Mr. Churchill, in a national broadcast, indicated that this was in fact his intention.

stagnation, with who-knows-what cooking behind the scenes, now opens to them unless they learn the trick and the way to thwart it.[1]

An exact simile is available for the method by which a majority was always obtained from the voting but unthinking adults of this island between the two wars, the method by which the next majority will be sought.

It is, the seduction of a woman under promise of marriage.

It is plain Lyceum melodrama. The villain makes the promise. The electorate yields. The promise, of a certain course in policy, is immediately broken. The people are left with the offspring, war.

The most flagrant example is the 1935 election, which was won through the promise, without which the protesting electors would not yield their honour, of 'collective resistance to acts of unprovoked aggression'. The betrayal was already planned, and was perpetrated immediately the country gave the vote.

The baby was this war.

But exactly the same trick, in various forms, *was played at every election between 1918 and 1935*.[2] Precisely the same deception is now being prepared, for the next election.

[1] 'National Government' (or, 'Coalition Government') is a spoil-sharing pact at the electors' expense. Members of Parliament, by 'agreeing to abstain from controversial matters', betray their pledge to him and his interests. Individual members, however, like the method. During this war, through the distribution among the docile of offices, employment, privileges, perquisites, invitations to broadcast-on-condition-of-saying-nothing, petrol allowances, journeys abroad, and the like, the life of a Member has become so blissful compared with that of the citizen or fighting man, that many would like to perpetuate the 'One Party Parliament'.

If that befell, we should emerge from the war with a Parliament of Yes-Yes men similar to Hitler's Reichstag of SS men. We have invariably received the exact opposite of what we have fought for or been promised, since 1914, and it was obvious that, if we only defended Freedom with all our might for long enough, this proposal would be made.

Commander Stephen King-Hall, M.P., in a letter to *The Times* in February 1943, says he has 'long believed that we are in a state of crisis which demands the application in our politics of the principle of national government'; that 'there is no likelihood for a long time to come of the crisis abating to an extent which will make it sensible to go back to the party-government system . . . We may never go back to it'. These words are indistinguishable from many speeches made by Nazi leaders, in 1932 and 1933.

This would further exclude the people from Parliament and prevent them, in any circumstances whatever, from being able to exert influence or control upon it. If this 'One Big Party' project is realized, this country may confidently look forward to an even graver deterioration in our public life and the conduct of our affairs, than we experienced in 1919-39. The return of sufficient Independent candidates to Parliament would checkmate it; they could exercise there the duty of watchmanship which enough Members of Parliament seemingly would gladly surrender in return for material advantages.

[2] The facts should be known even to the shortest of memories, but I refer readers to two chapters, 'A Snap Election', and 'How a Nation Was Hoaxed', in L. Macneill Weir, *Tragedy of Ramsay MacDonald* (Secker and Warburg, 1938).

One other thing, than the promise, is necessary, for the trick to succeed. Each time the seduction and betrayal are accomplished, a spectator is present, who must either denounce the seducer or become a conniving accomplice. The spectator is Parliament. How are the spectator's silence and acquiescence, in the betrayal, procured?

This is the enigma which so long bewildered us. We, the audience, always saw that witness of the betrayal, lurking behind a tree, and expected him to denounce the villain. We wondered why he kept his lips sealed. He *looked* an honest man. Lyceum melodrama, we felt, was failing us. *This* was not in the good old tradition.

That is the man we have to get at and reform, if we are to bring the play back to the better tradition: the Member of Parliament. He presents himself to us as an honest man, who only wishes to go to Westminster to watch over the promises that were made during the wooing.

He is already forsworn. He is the villain's bondman.

That is the secret of our tragedy, and will be the cause, if our future is taken from us again. These men pledge themselves to do *whatever* their Party leaders may tell them, *after* the election, after the electorate has yielded! But the *leaders*, as Mr. Lloyd George has told us, are subject to 'motives' which 'precipitate wars' and which they 'dare not avow'. How, then, can the *Members* watch over the fulfilment of the promise that is made, to gain the votes, if they are, by written or implicit pledge, bound to follow these leaders in anything they do?

This was the evil partnership, of misleader and sworn accomplice, which the British people desperately tried to break by the Peace Ballot (a national call for armed force to prevent aggression) in 1935.

Labour candidates at an election are only adopted as candidates by that Party when they sign a pledge in no circumstances whatever to vote against a Party decision.

Conservative candidates at an election do not sign a pledge, but in practice accept exactly the same bondage; the methods of enforcing it are more subtle but equally stringent: and consist of exclusion from office, ostracism and expulsion.

Thus Conservative and Labour Members, once they have induced the electorate to return them, go to Westminster, *not* as honest witnesses resolved to ensure that the promise of wedlock is kept, under which the electorate yielded the vote; but as men sworn not to question the subsequent conduct of the seducer.

The methods by which this dishonourable acquiescence is obtained, in the Tory Party, have been described in many books, including *What of the Night?* by Watchman, a Conservative M.P. (Hamish Hamilton, 1940) and *Guilty Men* by Cato (Gollancz, 1940).

Of the Labour Party, Lord Wedgwood, in his *Testament to Democracy* (Hutchinson, 1942), says:

> The charge made against Members of Parliament which is probably best founded and most serious, is that they show so little independence and do always as they are told. Party discipline tends ever to become more strict, and the penalties for the breaking of Party Rules ever more formidable. No aspirant may become a candidate for the Labour Party, either for local Councils or for Parliament, without solemnly undertaking to obey the Party Rules. Till this undertaking is signed the candidature will not be endorsed at headquarters. The Rules are that one may not vote against any decision come to by the weekly meetings of the Party M.P.s. One may abstain from the vote and speak against the Party view, but the Labour M.P. or Town Councillor must not vote against the Party decision. That I hold to be an infringement of the rights and duties of Members of Parliament. Party decisions of this sort in old days were not numerous; they are now frequent, *and the rule is being silently extended to cover all decisions that have to be made by the pro tem. Party leader on the spur of the moment in the course of any debate.* I could never have joined the Labour Party had this rule been in practice in 1919. It is a surrender of conscience, reason and duty which ought to be intolerable to any Member of Parliament. Members of Parliament are not instructed delegates; they are there to hear, weigh and decide, according to their own judgment, every issue put before them. The coercion of these Rules is a first step in the direction of Fascism and Naziism. [Lord Wedgwood[1] might have added 'and Communism'.] It sets Party before country, force above reason, debate becomes useless, and electors are betrayed.

Professor Edward Hallett Carr (of *The Times*), in his *Conditions of Peace*, says:

> The supremacy of the Party machine, dominated by economic interests, has been a conspicuous feature of British democracy in the past twenty years. It has been exercised in the constituencies, where

[1] Lord Wedgwood was a member of the Commons for thirty-six years, before his recent translation to the Lords.

the Party candidate for a promising seat is chosen no longer — except on rare occasions — by representatives of the electors, but by the Central Party machine. It has been exercised still more effectively in the House of Commons, where individual members are subject to ever stronger pressure to obey the dictates of the Party Whip. The process thus becomes a double one. *A Member of Parliament is elected not on personal considerations or by the choice of his constituents, but as the agent and nominee of a Party; except on increasingly rare occasions, he votes not as his conscience or as the supposed will of his constituents dictates, but as the Party decides. The fact is notorious . . . a serious corollary of these developments is their effect on the quality of human material which enters Parliament and attains promotion to ministerial rank.*

The method, then, is that of the seduction of a woman under promise of wedlock, in the presence of witnesses supposedly honest, but actually suborned!

The leaders, whom these witnesses are thus pledged to obey, are actuated by 'motives' which 'precipitate wars' and which they 'dare not avow'!

Thus the choice which confronts the electors, at an election in our island to-day, if two main parties compete in it, is, to choose between posting a letter in one of two pillar boxes, from neither of which a collection is made. When these two Parties coalesce, the number of pillar boxes is reduced to one, and there is still no collection. Since the pledges to the people, given at an election, mean nothing, because of that overriding pledge given to the Party, the country is left without any check on the Government between elections. The British people did once try to hold Parliament to its electoral pledges. This was in 1935. Consider the events, of that year, when this war really began; we cannot construct something, in the future, unless we understand them. We shall encounter 1935 again as we go down Civvy Street. It will call itself 1955 or 1965.

In 1935 the efforts of the men who worked to bring about the war, and the desperate anxiety of the British people to prevent it, both reached their highest vigour. The *instinct* of the British people for what threatened, was as sound as that of a ferret for a rat. They produced, of their own strength and free will, a gigantic bid to save the peace from the wreckers.

The Peace Ballot of 1935 was the one action in those inter-war years, which might revive faith in the ability of free men and women, thinking as individuals, to thwart a criminal design, and prevent an unnecessary war. It failed, or rather, it was foiled; but it has bequeathed to us a basis on which to construct something for the future. We only need to learn *how* it was foiled, so that the wreckers may be foiled next time.

Nothing in our history becomes us so well as that gallant attempt of the people to guide the rulers. No other nation can point to so valorous an effort. We know that we can fight in war, as volunteers or conscripts; we do not need to reassure ourselves of that every twenty years. In 1935 people tried to show that they could think and live for England in peace, a much higher aim. Men and women thrust aside the Party machine, spurned intimidation and inducement alike, and said to the politicians, 'You are steering for war. Change the course *now*, or we will dismiss you'.

This Battle in England, was *won*. The Party machines waged a counter campaign of scurrility and lies which has never been equalled: 'Party politics of the lowest kind', said the renegade Socialist Prime Minister; 'The Blood Ballot', shouted the Tory press; 'wilful deception of the people', said the Liberal Foreign Minister. They raged in vain. For the first time the delusion-machine was beaten. Seven million people voted for collective armed resistance to aggression.

For the first time, England spoke. The Government bowed to the storm. Overnight the foreign policy of isolation and war was changed to one of resistance to aggression and peace as demanded by the Ballot. On that issue, elections were held, and a thankful country returned a chastened government with an enormous majority. On that mandate the Foreign Minister went to Geneva and promised a rejoicing world 'resistance to aggression', while fifty other countries jubilantly allied themselves with us. England's name never stood so high as on that day, when the people compelled their leaders to do what they wanted and what the world knew was right. Even to-day, when all the Adam Wakenshaws have lifted England's name to a new pinnacle, it does not stand quite so high as it then stood; the world remembers what came after!

Once entrenched in power, the British Government resumed the condonation of aggression until the new war was certain! The annexation of Abyssinia, was already privily arranged when the election was held! The British people did not produce the strength for the second national protest, which would have overthrown these misleaders.

It is the blackest story in our history. The Parliament elected in 1935, in that glowing moment of hope, still sits to-day. The Government still contains most of the Ministers of that time, men who swear to-day what they forswore yesterday.

But the Peace Ballot of 1935 has at least exposed the trick. We now know that the country *can* check its leaders, when it sees that they are misguiding it, and that they will bend to the country's will. We also know, since that event, that they will only *pretend* so to submit for as long as they need to win an election, that they regard such elections as an irritating break in the placidity of political machination, and that they will return to the false course once the election has been won.

We need, then, to devise a double-check, for next time. It is not enough to organize a Ballot, for the Parties will return to their evil ways, no matter how strong the Ballot proves the nation's will to be, when the voting is over and they are safe in office for another term of years. The next Ballot must include a safeguard; the intimation that if the Government, once returned, and pledged to a certain course, betrays that pledge, a second Ballot will be held, and organized with even more vigour than the first, and that this will be supported by *a number of by-elections*.

The second clause is vital. Government, Parties and Parliament cannot ignore *that*. Here is the means to keep a constant check on the country's policy and safety. Essential to it is the return, at future elections for twenty years at least, of a large number of Independent candidates, pledged to refuse party bonds, and pledged also to resign and bring about by-elections if any divergence threatens, from policy as proclaimed at a general election, in any issue of paramount importance.

Such watchdogs in Parliament would reinvigorate it, force the Parties to return to cleaner methods, and provide the brake-and-accelerator, which the country could apply if the Government went too fast in a wrong direction or too slowly in a right one. It would give such people as those who made the gallant bid of 1935, the means to ensure that a similar national protest made in similar circumstances in the future, could not be contemptuously disregarded once an election was over. It would give the nation an eye and an ear and a voice *between* elections, in a Parliament now filled with placemen sworn to obey their leaders even when these betray national interests. It would fill the hole into which the high hopes of 1935 were disdainfully thrown once the election was won.

Given such watchmen in Parliament, the Peace Ballot of 1935 would have been a battle won, because the war would have been averted. The men who initiated it did not think far enough ahead to provide a safe-guard, against the sabotage of the people's will *after* the election. One of them wrote to me:

> What you say about the frustration of the years since the last war is true. I was one who watched with concern events as they unfolded, and the feeling that I could do nothing to stop the mistakes I saw being made was terrible. Only once did I succeed in doing something. I conceived the idea of the Peace Ballot[1] and started it here in X from whence it spread, and what was the result? The Tories paid lip service to the astonishing result, won their election, and then went right against the wishes of the people who voted in that Ballot. The people voted for collective action against aggressors and for state ownership of the arms industry. They never got anywhere near either of them.'

I have shown why; they did not devise a safeguard.

If the present system continues, of electing to Parliament men who make promises they cannot fulfil, because they have privately accepted an over-riding authority, our future can only become darker. The opportunities, which it gives, for unseen forces to wield power behind the political scene, to dominate our island life, and to work against our national interests, are too great. While it continues, none, who are not ready to surrender the future, should vote for a Party candidate without obtaining the public pledge that he will not sign such a written undertaking, or yield to an unwritten one, when he returns to Westminster. No election meeting should be allowed to open or close without this question being put, and any candidate who refuses to cast off that bondage should be denied the vote.

But the only sure guarantee of smashing this evil practice, which would deliver us in chains to those who may wish to wreck our future again, is to send at least a hundred Independent Members into the next Parliament.

This is a reform which must be made and which those people who help-lessly ask, 'What *can* I *do*?' can *do*. They can understand this thing, which is simple, and they can abolish it. As long as it continues, they are en-slaved, and no electoral promise means anything. It is the main cause of our present plight and can yet bring worse calamity on us.

---

[1] Which proposed, not 'Peace at any price', but collective resistance to aggression and State control of the armaments industry.

Unless people perceive this spanner which has been thrown into the works, the next election will be the first step in the destruction of their future. 'Vote for the Men Who Won The War', the radio will shout. 'Enduring Peace and Social Security', the Bondmen will speciously promise. 'All is well' the newspapers will clamour. Snap, will go the jaws of the Party machine, and bang will go the promises and the future . . . .

. . . December 14th, 1918, said the calendar on the wall in my hut in France. 'Election time in England to-day,' I thought vaguely, 'that's good. Lloyd George and his men are looking after us. They'll see that the Kaiser and the War Criminals are punished, that the peace is won, that the slums are abolished and the countryside revived, and England made a place of home and beauty. I wonder why they call it a *Snap* Election', I thought, 'I don't understand what they mean by that.'

I do, now. And so may you if you read.

CHAPTER V

PEACE, THE GRAVEYARD

1921, and London. At last I was come to a small job. I sat in a cellar in Fleet Street and typed letters for a few pounds a week. After the long spell of unemployment, this was comforting. No advancement offered but the coins in my pocket were solid. I rattled away on the typewriter, went to the pictures or a music hall in the evening, meandered about Kew Gardens or Hampton Court on Saturday afternoons and Sundays.

Life continued. I knew a girl. . . .

From vague promptings of dissatisfaction, nevertheless, I answered advertisements. A famous authoress, who needed a secretary, asked me to call. I only remember her eyes, which were astonishingly blue. She lay on a sofa, and her husband hovered around. She lived in Kenya. She offered me the job. Life on a ranch; experience, adventure, a fine climate (as I now know), travel. I asked to think it over. I went away and thought. The pictures and the music hall; the aimless but easy existence; my mother; England, which I loved; the girl. . . .

I refused. I look back on the incident with horror. I can hardly believe it. I climbed back into my rut and fixed my eyes on the ground. The strength of the intangible something — inertia, I suppose — which held so many Englishmen of my generation in its grip is almost unbelievable. I tell the story, because I hope that it may help others. How many others have done the same, rejected all that life and the world offer?

To-day, I would not wait for the offer of a job. I would get on a ship and go, because I know that a man can get some kind of work anywhere, if he means to, and because I have found that nothing is so good, as to go away for a time, travel the world, feel the gap between your eyes widening and your mind opening and your knowledge increasing. I would go *anywhere* that was open — anywhere in Europe, the Dominions, Africa, anywhere at all.

Soon after that episode, I took another job, for I was seemingly not quite inert and kept on trying, in a vague way. Then I was sent to Paris, and though I did not refuse, I went reluctantly. I recall now, when I seek to detect the motives which caused my mood, that I was still in the grip of an infatuation, to which the men back from four years in France were especially subject: England was Home, and nothing else in the world could be so good and lovely, and somewhere in it, sometime, I should find A Little House and A Little Garden.

Though I did not aspire to live in one of a row of semi-detached houses, each exactly like the next, my dream was not much loftier. It was the most limited ambition a man can have, though I invested it with a romantic glamour: a roof and some food. The dullard's vision: a cottage with roses round the door. I needed thirty-five years to grow out of that weak project, which in effect was, to build my own little Enclosure in the land of Enclosure, call it my castle, and settle down in it, to grow old and die. The golden coins that life gives us to spend are so few, but threescore and ten, and yet I, like many more, wanted to put them in a stocking.

After six months, I was recalled from Paris. I came home gladly! Ah, to be back in England, and the pictures, and Kensington Gardens, and the Empire on Saturday night, and the trips to Box Hill, and the shops in Regent Street, and the strolls by the Serpentine, and the fortnight at Shanklin, and the crystal set, and a lawn-mower and clippers and a bird-bath, and somewhere, in the distance, The Little House and The Little Garden, and the girl. . . .

Gruesome, is it not? I have shown the worst skeleton in my cupboard, and the thing which shames me most. How I should loathe myself of 1921 if I met myself, in 1943! You, I would say, are the sort of man who makes better men despair of England. What the devil are you doing, wasting your life like this? You, with your paltry amusements and your trivial occupation and your petty preoccupations and your little dream house and your small ambitions. For Heaven's sake, I should say, shake yourself, and get up and get out, into the world, and live. Go into politics. Go into Parliament. Get on a ship, as steward, go anywhere you like, work first at that and next at that, travel around, until you feel you know something and are alive and can do something useful.

I came back to England, gladly. I did not think I should leave England again. While life oozed by, I thought of a brick coffin — The Little House. . . .

You have just seen, gentle reader, the man who will surrender our island's future again, unless you and I can awaken, enliven and inspirit him. That we may be able to do it, I am encouraged to hope by this passage in a letter from one of you, a middle-aged English North Country-woman:

> I hate slums, dirt, squalor and jerry-built bungalows (incidentally I live in one myself), and that's why after the war I was dreaming of a nice old, long, low, white house in the heart of the countryside, where I could enjoy peace and beauty. Now, I am beginning to realize that's just what we have *not* got to do. It is we commonplace folks who have got to get things done. . . .

As a penitent sinner, who came through the valley of living death which that existence was, as a man who saw the calamity to which this country was only brought through public lethargy in this island, and one who hopes that from such experience we may save our future, I would like to post myself in sackcloth and ashes at the entrance to Civvy Street, and say to every man and woman who approaches it:

'Keep out of the rut and spurn the groove. Do not tie yourself to a small job and accumulate burdens on your back. Do not rush to own a radio, an arm-chair and a parlour, and make yourself for years to come the slave of hire-purchase. Own as few things as you can, for the tyranny of small possessions is intolerable. "A young man married is a young man marred". Well, that contains much truth, but is not worth saying, for none will take counsel in this matter. But if you must take a wife, choose one who will come with you, with a knapsack on her back, to Kenya or Capetown, or Canada, or Queensland, or Christchurch, and will set to work with you to build a future there. If you can't find one such, take none, but wait. Don't crawl into a little job and a little house, waste yourself in trivial pursuits, give yourself up to the narcotics of picture-houses and radio, encumber yourself with little worldly gods, obligations and responsibilities, and shut your eyes to all that goes on in your country and in the world, outside your four walls. Do not live like a snail, which crawls painfully about with a little house on its back, asking nothing better of life than a little lettuce, and thinking itself secure within a castle which, the next moment, They will destroy. (They, in this case, are the sharp-beaked thrushes, which are very anti-snail.) Get out into the world. You will increase your value to others and your enjoyment of yourself a hundred times as quickly, if you know something more than the life of the little garden, the parlour, the eight-fifty to town, the radio, the pictures, the football pools and the football results. You'll have a grand life, and you'll feel twice as large round the chest and twice as clear in the head, and you'll help to revive and reinvigorate this island and this Empire.'

That is what I would say. Perhaps we, of the last generation, have some excuse. Who would have believed, in 1918, that such things would happen as the next twenty years brought? But the new generation has no excuse. The man who, after this war, returns to Civvy Street, knowing that in twenty years he may be called again, his house destroyed or his business ruined, his sons and daughters taken, even his little car or radio or refrigerator seized — the man who, knowing these things, comes back and looks no further beyond his nose than the acquirement of the little house, the little business and the little car, puts himself, his family, all he owns, and his future in pawn.

The human appetite for possessions, in view of the short time we spend on this earth, is curious, and if beings on any other planet are able to observe our doings they must often be doubled up with laughter by our efforts to acquire things from which death will soon separate us. How much of the blame for this war, I wonder, was borne by very rich men, some trifle of whose wealth was taken by the Bolshevists, or who feared that the Bolshevists would come and take their all, so that they used all their power to establish Germany as A Bulwark Against Bolshevism, and to prompt Germany to attack Russia. I recall at least three such who then lost all their possessions, which they previously moved about from one country to another, through death, after the outbreak of this war, but before they even knew the small consolation of Hitler's assault on the Russians!

The loss of small possessions, through two of Hitler's successive invasions, first made me realize what a nuisance they are, at any rate to a man who wishes to keep moving. I still suffer from their tyranny, because I own many books, which I cannot discard, and as these weigh more than iron bars, they are a pestilential hindrance to travel, when I am allowed to travel. I know of a man whose untimely end was due to the tyranny of his belongings, and his tale will serve here as a cautionary one.

After several years in Europe, he pined for home comforts and caused his furniture, which was stored in England, and already disturbed his dreams, to be sent to Paris, where he was stationed. He furnished a flat, and then was ordered to Switzerland. Again he went through all the long process of finding a flat, having the furniture packed, transported, examined at the customs, delivered, unpacked and set out. A few months later he was sent to Vienna. Once more, he sought a flat, the furniture arrived, the heavy bills were paid, and within six months Hitler invaded Austria. My acquaintance was transferred to Budapest, the furniture was packed, and remained in Vienna, awaiting his instructions to forward it. The turbulent summer of 1938 followed, when war seemed imminent. By now the tenant of a flat in Budapest, he spent a more miserable summer than most, for his furniture would travel down the Danube, if he ordered it to be sent, and he saw it caught between the fire of armies entrenched on the banks, and riddled with bullets. Then the good Mr. Chamberlain procured peace in our time, and the furniture travelled to Budapest. A year later war broke out. For a time the furniture, and its owner, were spared. Then, in 1941, the Germans invaded Yugoslavia, where he happended to be at the moment. He could have made a last-moment get-away, but was harassed by the thought of that furniture, in Budapest. He stayed, and the widening German net found him in it. He returned to Budapest, was there interned, and died of pneumonia.

So, gentle reader, when you set out in search of a wider and fuller life than this island can afford, travel light, that you may be free. Keep your indispensable belongings within the limits of a suitcase or a trunk. Hire, but do not buy, what you want: a house, a flat, furniture, a car; and hire it by no more than the month. But the same modest counsel holds good, within limits, if you stay in this island. We shall not know, for ten years at least after this war, whether They will seek to destroy again in ten years more everything that has been built up, and until we know that, it will be absurd for people to spend their energy, once more, in putting up cockshies for others to knock down. So I would say, if you have money to spend, spend it on travel, on the acquiring of wide experience.

Of one thing I feel sure. We fight this war, we are told, for 'four freedoms'. If we find, after this war, that all sorts of obstructions and bans are placed on the freedom of people to travel or to emigrate from this island, that will be the plainest sign conceivable, that this second war was but a stage in a process, and that worse things impend; that the process itself is one of the gradual confinement of the people of this island, which could only lead to their eventual subjection to foreign rule.

Travelling about the world, I have seen that innumerable opportunities offer to the people of this country, especially within the Empire, but also in foreign countries, for those who seek them, and my experience is, that those who fare forth are happier men than their stay-at-home fellows. They are also more enlightened. If only a tenth of the people in this country knew the States and peoples of Europe first-hand, as the tiny group of Britishers knew them who lived in those countries between the wars, we could not again be led into a needless war, or inveigled into any other policy injurious to our native interests. The sum of knowledge within the country would be too great.

If this book comes into the hands of any men and women who return to Civvy Street with the desire to preserve their country from a new war, I would say to them, do not seek, in this island, the peace which is that of the graveyard. Make peace an adventure. You cannot serve your country better than by leaving it, at any rate for a part of your life, not as a way of escape, but as a means to gain understanding of the perils which threaten it.

You will find life a thing of infinite zest, instead of a dull corridor with tiny windows. You will come to understand your own land better by studying other lands. You will see what they do better than we, and what we do better than they. You will be able to form an opinion worth having, because you will have a standard of comparison. After some years, you will come to look back on your narrow and enclosed way of life in England with some resentment, and even revulsion, and you will set yourself to change these things when you return; or, if you stay abroad, you will be better equipped to play your part in raising a happy breed.

In short, the dream that boys have, when they see a great ship, white and gold, sailing off to foreign parts, is one of the few dreams that may come true. The things they picture to themselves do exist, at the other end of the journey. Move about in this world, and you may live on an ascending scale of happiness, not on a level plane of routine, or on a down gradient of declining ambition and energy.

To learn to know the world, is within the reach of all, who are ready to work, and to save a little. The only thing that could hinder it would be some barrier erected by our own rulers, who do so many sinister things. To prevent that, should be one of the first resolutions of men and women who return to Civvy Street. Those who oppose current proposals for 'Social Security' complain that they would destroy 'the spirit of adventure' in England. How can such a spirit thrive, if those who would venture forth are hindered from doing so, and how can our Empire thrive if this continues?

To make peace an adventure! That is something worth living and fighting for. To return to the peace of the graveyard, and with downcast head plod along the rut, is the sure way to new trouble.

. . . Five years, I then spent in England, and was glad to be in my rut. In 1927 I was ordered to Berlin. I was loath to go. The witch's spell, the dream of the little house and the lawn-mower, still lay on me: I confess it, for the discouragement of others. Then I pulled myself together, and told myself that I was a fool to reject opportunity for the sake of this rural vision, which was a sort of compound dream distilled from Constable's pictures and phrases about a green pleasaunce and snatches of romantic poetry and Gray's 'Elegy' and 'The Village Blacksmith' and old coloured prints. I went to Germany.

For three years the ache for England lay in me, and I itched to return. Then I suddenly realized that I was sleep-walking. I awoke, with a start, from my dream, and saw it was a bad dream. After thirty-five years, my spirit sprang to life within me.

THE EXAMPLE OF FRANCE

Why, everything I loved was within my reach, I needed only to stretch out my hand, and instead here I lay and dreamed of a cottage-and-roses-round-the-door. Lakes, forests of fir-trees, snow-capped mountains, blue seas and blue skies; foreign cities, strange peoples, new tongues, different ways; knowledge, experience, understanding; all these were around me, and I pined to plant myself, vegetable-like, in some rural suburb, and mow the lawn, and listen to the radio, and go to the pictures!

The change was sudden and startling. I have briefly described how it came about, in the hope that some may profit by it, curtail their hesitations, and grasp at the unending adventure which peace may be.

CHAPTER VI

THE EXAMPLE OF FRANCE

Even victors are by victories undone
— JOHN DRYDEN, 1631-1700

Woe to the conquering not the conquered host
— LORD BYRON, 1788-1824

DECEMBER 1921. Tiny tinselled flakes of snow glittered in the crisp evening air of Paris. The street lights sparkled like diamonds in a jeweller's shop window; in this twilight hour they shone brightest. I stood in the big doorway of the house, in the Boulevard des Italiens, where was my attic, and talked with Jean, the chauffeur, my neighbour. We could just see the noisy traffic of the Rue de l'Opéra.

I was getting into my stride, in Civvy Street. The leanest times lay behind me (and the worst, I then thought, little dreaming of 1933); three years of unemployment, peddling things from door to door, and abject occupations. Now I was come to something better.

Jean approached middle age. Four years in the trenches and three wounds lay heavy on him. I could not understand him. I thought all was well with the world again; he was bitter, in 1921! He did not believe in the future. He thought all the bloodshed and suffering were wasted, that the Germans would soon make a new war. He thought *Messieurs les*

Anglais sought to get France down and rob France of its victory. I thought he was mad. All on a December evening in 1921.

Jean-Marie Jones joined us. He was what we call in English a *commissionaire* at a bank. His long fair hair was brushed back, his silky moustache reached nearly to his ears. Women often glanced at him sideways; he looked good in his neat, blue uniform. His wife was a Frenchwoman, of gloomy mien and vixenish temper, of whom the gossips, on the ascending floors of that house, confidently said that she often planted the famous horns on his well-shaped head.

He was the child of the Entente Cordiale. His mother was French, his father English. He spoke the idiom of Belleville and Bermondsey with equal fluency. His life was spent in equal parts between the two countries. He told Jean, in French, bawdy tales of his exploits as a factory hand at Leicester, and me, in English, the story of his conquests in Calais, where he once owned a garage.

He umpired our debate. He joined with Jean and cursed *Messieurs les Anglais* in biting Parisian slang; and when I told Jean that the perfidy of England was a French illusion, he nodded approvingly and, knowing that Jean understood no English, said, 'That's right, tell the bastard off'.

My French was a great joke with him because once when I was his guest at dinner and his wife gave a *pouf* of satiety, I asked whether she were *pleine*. No, they both said, shaking with laughter, she was not pregnant. I thought I might have hurt them, because, for all her reputed diligence in this respect, she was seemingly incapable of attaining such a condition and they wanted a child; but their merriment was whole-hearted.

Englishman, Frenchman and Anglo-Frenchman, we discussed the future, while the little snowflakes begemmed the hard, dry air. Jean looked with brooding eyes towards the Rue de l'Opéra, scowled so much that his moustache withdrew into the grooves in his face, and imprecated, in 1921. Ah, the politicians and the corruption, and the Germans are starting again, and mark my words, Monsieur Reed — he shook an emphatic forefinger — *Messieurs les Anglais* . . .

It is unfortunate [said Mr. Greenwood, the Labour leader, in the Commons on February 16th, 1943], but true, that there exists in many quarters in the country and among members of the Forces an atmosphere of cynicism tinged with bitterness which might be dangerous for our future . . . it will be a bad end to the war if those who have in their various ways secured victory return to eat the bread of disillusionment and live among shattered hopes and discarded, unfulfilled promises.

Such things are often said, by peers, politicians, prelates and newspapers. Seemingly none of them realize that they breed this despondency.

If they wish to uplift the sagging spirit, they can. The causes are not unknown. Starkly confronting us, at the beginning of to-morrow in Civvy Street, is the example of yesterday's France, by which we may learn. Victory is always more dangerous to the victors than to the vanquished.

The reasons which led to the abject decline of victorious France were the same which led us to Dunkirk. The only difference was, that the French lacked a last ditch, an English Channel, behind which they might rally.

Our position, after this war, will be like that of France in 1918. We shall be victorious, tired, sorely tried. But we are richer by the French example; we need not sag, as France sagged, if we purify our public life. The cleansing can only come from below. The politicians, and those behind them, are too set in their ways to change of their own will. Every man who returns to Civvy Street should bear in mind the example of France.

The seeds of despondency were planted even during the last war. They began with the miserable treatment of the French soldier. He was the least of men in his own stricken land. He was paid a halfpenny a day. He felt inferior. He fought as bravely as any, and shed his blood more copiously. Yet his rulers seemed bent on breaking his spirit. Foreign soldiers thronged his country and all were wealthy compared with him.

In our House of Commons, on September 10th, 1942, when the disproportion between the pay of our men and that of American and Imperial troops was mentioned, Sir Stafford Cripps sought to justify it by recalling the plight of the French soldier in the last war and saying the disparity in pay 'did not jeopardize comradeship or the power of collaboration'.

He is wrong. This thing soured the Frenchman's spirit. It embittered him, and justly. Moreover, he was tormented by the thought of his womenfolk, and again, with reason. Colinette, all too often, was not waiting by the poplars, or longing and watching, where the long white roadway lies. She was in the *estaminet*, with the British soldiers.

In this war our men have been put in a similar position. The British soldier, even if he has not been sent overseas, has been separated for years from his wife and children. He may have been overseas for even 'five, six or seven years' (Sir James Grigg, War Minister, on February 16th, 1943) but be denied leave 'because of the shipping situation'.

While the things continue, which break up family life and breed despair, such words are useless as those which the Bishop of Salisbury uttered on February 17th, 1943:

> There is absolute degradation of moral standards. There are married women and girls with no sense of morality — girls of fourteen and fifteen. Women whose husbands are away and who are heedlessly disloyal to them...women who say, 'He is away overseas, he has his little fun, so why should I not have mine?' I have no record of the number of young girls who are ruined at an extraordinary early age — I cannot say, before they understand, but before they can appreciate the hideousness of the dangers.

How senseless to rail at the victims and ignore the culprits. This is but the repetition, in England, of the thing that was done to France.

Human beings usually prefer, if they have the chance, to lead decent lives, to be loyal, found homes and families. But they feel that 'They' will not allow them to keep their ideals, that life slips away, that they must clutch at any illusory happiness or any fleeting amusement, while they may. Nothing can be more destructive of faith (and if it continues, the churches may be quite empty in another twenty years) than for priests continually to reproach the people with *sexual* immorality and to ignore the immorality of the things which are done to them.

The regeneration of a large part of our younger womanhood, which during this spiritual blackout tends to lapse into waif-and-strayhood, is among the first objectives of a Battle in England. It cannot be achieved by sermons about sexual morality, while the roots of despair are driven deeper.[1]

[1] Waif-and-strayhood among young people is a sign of spiritual despair always seen in countries which pass through bad times. It was prevalent in Russia after the Bolshevik revolution, and in Germany after the last war. In our wealthy land, it is inexcusable and can only spring from a lack of civic responsibility. The newspaper reports about this generation of waifs and strays which rises in England, are deeply significant. During March 1943, two of these pathetic children passed, shadowlike, through the columns of the Press. One was an eight-year-old boy of Bristol, who did not know a bath when he was shown one and tried to step into it fully clothed. He lived 'among the ruins of bombed buildings and ate food from

In this country the British soldier mixes with soldiers from oversea who receive several times as much as himself. Envy is a thing which the British hardly know; nevertheless, injustice rankles, and the thought of it lingers. It was made more unjust in 1942, when a White Paper was published by the Government, which sought to show that the British soldier was much better off than he actually is. Of it, Major Milner of Brighton said in the Commons:

> It is a tissue of lies from beginning to end, an utterly and completely fraudulent document . . . in the sense of what it conceals or admits. If this document had been produced by a commercial gentleman in the City of London he would have got seven years at the Old Bailey . . . I hope the usual cloak of anonymity which surrounds Treasury officials will not be allowed to cover up the rascal who is responsible for it. Let him be dragged out into the daylight and strung up to the nearest lamp-post, where he can enjoy the scorn and derision of the soldiers he has so misrepresented.

The cloak of anonymity was left round this man. His action seems to spring either from dislike or contempt of the people of this country. Those members of Parliament who express alarm about the current feeling of cynicism and bitterness did nothing to expose him. Yet this spirit is the product of such repeated blows to patriotic self-esteem.

By similar means was despondency planted deep in the French mind. Do our leaders *wish* to repeat the process here? Another unpleasant resemblance exists. In the last war we claimed the right to try by British courts martial British soldiers charged with offences against French subjects or property. I cannot conjecture why the French Government agreed, but think they did wrong. Many cases were tried, from petty things to rape and murder, and justice was roughly done. (But I think the sentences were remitted when the war ended.)

pig bins'. The other was a nineteen-year-old girl of some education. She lived with a French-Indian soldier of the Canadian Forces in wigwams which he built for her on a Surrey common. Her only possessions were a crucifix, a Bible and a rosary. She did not smoke or drink. On the wooden supports of the wigwam she carved simple prayers. Her letters to the man (who could not even read them) show a being gentle, religious, and idealistic. 'I would not blame you one little bit if you did not want to marry me, because I am really too young and old fashioned to be married. I regret what we did because it is wicked . . . oh, the smell of burning wood, the loveliest smell in the world'. This girl was murdered, and her body buried on the common by the man. Much of the current radio and film entertainment, and newspaper material offered to these young people might have been devised with an eye to their corruption: for instance, such songs as 'You can't say no to a soldier . . . you've got to give in . . . he's got a right to romance', and so on.

This was another blow to the self-pride of the French. In this war, a similar request was made by the American Government and accepted by our Government. This island is not partly occupied, as was France; law and order prevail. The agreement, made between the two Governments, was presented to Parliament in August 1942 with the demand for immediate approval. One member said he 'never remembered the Government coming to the Commons with an actually concluded agreement', in the next breath he said any criticism would be 'impertinent'. One Law Lord, Lord Atkin, expressed some misgiving; (he alone has protested against the capricious use of the power of arrest under Regulation 18B).

This was unique. Our ancient law is, that the King's courts alone may try crimes alleged or committed in this country by no matter whom. Why do our rulers so easily surrender the good things in our heritage and so tenaciously cling to the bad ones? The right to sit in judgment on the citizens of another country, in that country, is usually exacted only by a conqueror. (As practised by us in Egypt and China, indeed, the arrangement is called 'Capitulation'. We have during this very war renounced such rights in China!)

Who can guess why the demand was made or granted, in this now secure island? Our judges and courts of law are good. We were given no explanation. Charges of the gravest importance to British citizens (including murder and rape) have been tried by American courts martial; they have been most casually reported in our Press, when they have been reported at all. Responsibility for law and order, and even behaviour, as far as the American troops are concerned, has been transferred to the American military authorities.

Those of our public spokesmen who express such loud concern about the dejection of the native spirit offered no resistance, make no comment. Yet such things gall people; they feel they are not staunchly represented. Issues of deep principle should not be lightly decided.

Many other things have been done which add up to make the British citizen-soldier feel inferior. The spirit which inspires these things seems to me to be malevolent, unless it is the product of the dusty offices and corridors, where no sound human feeling can thrive, in which the unknown men work who do them. One of them was the announcement that officers of the last war, who were promised the retention of their rank, would be called up as privates in this; it is unique in the world.

Another was the ban on visits to London. A grave one was wing-stripping in the Royal Air Force. This seems tantamount to degradation (in the old drumming-out ceremony, epaulettes and buttons were torn off). I know, from flying experience, that some men who fly *have* to be rested. In the last war, the wings were never taken from them; in this, they are, when they are 'grounded'. Many officers serve in the Air Ministry and other R.A.F. headquarters who never even gained wings.

In the same spirit, of spiteful refusal to yield any tribute to past service or present self-esteem, was the Air Minister's rule that serving soldiers, sailors and civil defenders who flew in the last war may not wear their wings. Because the last war was the first air war, these badges are treasured beyond gold or jewels by many who won them and now serve again. No reason, other than a malicious one, suggests itself for this ban, which was devised, like the others, by anonymous men. As for Parliament and the Parties, their feeling about men who serve was indicated by the Vice-Chairman of the Tory Party when he said that his Party does not much care about adopting candidates from the Forces.

Things which rob the citizen of the feeling that citizenship and service entitle him to any right or respect,[1] depress the national spirit and breed that bitter cynicism which led, twenty years after 1918, to the collapse of France.

Consider another such action. After the loss of rubber-bearing lands in the East, a Member of Parliament proposed that tyres should be taken from laid-up motor cars 'to help the war effort'. The argument is admissible that the loss of our rubber supplies makes such seizure necessary, although it strikes at the most deserving class of the population: the fighting men, who are away, and the elder citizens at home who, though they may serve, are denied by some petty official the use of their cars, although the newspapers prove how many unworthy people are still allowed to use them.

An order empowering the seizure of tyres was later announced. It contained something else: The power to seize *all laid-up motor cars*!

No single member or newspaper protested or asked the reason! Our sources of motor-car supply were not lost! The industry works night and day, exclusively for the Services. Why were Mr. Smith's two-seater

[1] A Member of Parliament, a Mr. Driberg, who has served in neither war, in a debate about the persons imprisoned without charge or trial under Regulation 18B, stated that 'honourable and distinguished service' in the last war was 'quite irrelevant' in claiming charge and trial for the captives; those who serve in this war may note the implication.

and Mr. Brown's limousine to be seized? These are about the last things they retain of their pre-war possessions. In them they hoped to take that longed-for holiday 'after the war' when they returned, or were allowed to buy petrol again. Those millions of idle cars, lovingly stored in their little garages, represented many Englishmen's dreams for the future.

None even asked why this was done. The cars have not yet been taken. If they are, a new privileged class will be created in the island to which the Boys return. The class of those allowed to ride in motor cars! For many people have kept and run their cars. These are either petty officials, or those who obtained from a petty official the certificate that their work is 'of national importance'; the description covers more activities than charity ever covered sins.

When the war ends, these people will still own and run their motor cars. The man who went overseas, or the man at home whose labour was simply to support his family, rear his children, keep his business going, and do duty at night as a Home Guard, Observer, or Air Raid Warden (the man whose work was *not* of national importance) will be left without one, if those cars are taken.

Any who are good at figures may compute the wealth that will accrue to the motor-car industry, if these cars are taken, and they might care to investigate the business associations of Members of Parliament, and of officials in the competent Ministry, who devised this regulation. An entirely new market would be created for this industry, once rid of all the old cars which otherwise would be made to do for another five years. Freed from that competition the price of new cars need know no limit after the war, and the number of potential buyers would be similarly increased.

The Conservative Party has held power for twelve years on the anti-Socialist appeal alone. Here is a measure, enacted though not yet enforced, by an overwhelmingly Conservative government which would give swollen officialdom the status it enjoys in Soviet Russia; where money means nothing, but official employment carries with it the things that money can buy elsewhere.[1]

[1] 'There are several million bureaucrats in Russia of greater or lesser importance. They comprise a social class which is as distinct from the masses as the English nobility is from the cockneys, and they enjoy the same privileges as the upper classes of other nations . . . A successful bureaucrat in Moscow lives about as well as an American with a salary of about £2000 a year, though his actual income is only about £600. He may have a two- or three-roomed apartment in a big Moscow hotel near the Kremlin, complete with marble walls,

If the cars are taken, this will be indistinguishable in its results from Communist and National Socialist practice. (How our newspapers jeered at the millions of Germans who, before the war, were induced to subscribe to the 'People's Car', only to find that the war intervened, the cars were not delivered, and their money went into the war machine.)

Such things breed 'cynicism and bitterness'. I have before me a page of the *Daily Mail*, of July 8th, 1942. On one side is a big headline: '1,300 ex-officers seek in vain for job'. The report beneath says that in April 1942 1760 officers, rejoined for this war and then discharged on account of age, were seeking work. The writer, Mr. Geoffrey Simpson, estimated that the number, when he wrote, was nearer 3000. He quoted the Labour Ministry as saying 'The problem is a small one; after all, it involves at the moment only 1300 men . . . It is difficult to find suitable employment for ex-officers . . . Army officers "axed" and thrown on to the labour market can expect no special facilities in their search for civil employment'. (On August 7th, 1942, the Director of Public Relations at the Ministry of Labour, a Mr. A. S. Frere, stated in *The Times* that the best service which many of these discharged officers could give would be 'to accept training for manual work in munitions factories'!)

On the same page is another big headline, 'New check on aliens'. The report which follows quotes Mr. Justice Croom-Johnson, in the High Court, as urging the police to watch the activities of

people of nationalities that have sought succour and assistance here at a time when we are fighting for our lives in the greatest war in history. Of the 60,000 German and Austrian refugees, adds the report, only about 500 are out of work. Many have found lucrative jobs — £1200 a year as chemists, £700 a year as factory managers, £12 a week in skilled war work . . . apart from the highly paid and skilled workers, there are waitresses among them earning £6 a week (in salary and tips) *while the girls whose places they took are earning only half that amount in war factories. . . . London has a special Labour Exchange for Germans and Austrians.* Once the Ministry of Labour has vetted their credentials, a wide choice of jobs is open to them. Yesterday, there were jobs advertised in this Exchange for a second chef, a factory manager, floor waiters, dental mechanics, laboratory assistants.

grand piano, and bath-room. His rent for such an establishment, if anything at all, is nominal. At his disposal, day and night, is a chauffeur-driven limousine, which he retains so long as he remains in office. . . .' From an article by Walter Graebner, an American correspondent, in the *Daily Mail*, January 13th, 1943.

'No special facilities', then, for our own ex-officers. 'A special Labour Exchange for Germans and Austrians'! 'It is difficult to find suitable employment for ex-officers'; 'a wide choice of jobs is open to Germans and Austrians'.

This attitude is anti-British and anti-patriotic.

I foresaw this thing in the second of these five books. Now it goes even further than I feared. These aliens came here under specific pledges, given in Parliament, (1) that they would not stay, (2) they would not become a burden on the island tax payer, (3) they would not be allowed to compete unfairly with native labour. They are now (1) allowed to stay indefinitely, (2) are maintained by the British taxpayer if unemployed, (3) may take employment vacated by a British man or woman called away, (4) are exempted from compulsory military service, (5) were exempted from all civil defence duties until recently, when some talk was heard about using them for fire watching, (6) are under no obligation to yield their employment to returning British citizens.

This is the worst thing I have seen done to any country. Tories and Socialists, from Mr. Baldwin and Sir Samuel Hoare to Mr. Bevin and Mr. Morrison, have joined to do it.

Since I last wrote, this great wrong has been made even worse. Of recent months, British citizens of both sexes have been cast without mercy into prison if they refused to take employment, less congenial or worse paid than their own, or far away, to which they were 'directed'. Working men who have found jobs in factories may be forced back to coal mines at lower wages, or imprisoned; British working girls may be forced to take inferior posts far away from home, or be imprisoned. The newspapers continually report such cases. Many posts thus made vacant by the threat of imprisonment have been filled by aliens who are actually of enemy nationality! On March 19th, 1943, Mr. Bevin, the working-class representative who is Labour Minister, announced that British workers thus evicted from their jobs have no legal right to regain them after the war!

In a long experience of many countries, I have met nothing to compare with this. Not one Member of Parliament has protested against it.

Similar things destroyed the spirit of France. The Frenchmen who came back from the last war were made despondent by the conditions they found: the flaunting wealth of the profiteers, the rottenness of politi-

cal life, the influx of aliens. Where were the fruits of victory for them?
They could believe nothing they were told. Was not the Maginot
Line, later, the biggest hoax in history?

France was held in a vice of political corruption and anonymity. No
envoy from another planet would have recognized the signs of victory
in this dejected land and its cosmopolitan capital, where a Frenchman
passionately kissed the hand of a strange lady in a café exclaiming, 'Pardon,
Madame, but I have been so moved to hear you speak French'.

The queen of the crazy carnival was Miss Josephine Baker, a handsome
negress of many physical attractions; if any of these were unknown to all
France, they were few and small. Miss Baker was safely conveyed to
Morocco, after the disaster, and a picture in miniature of the France
which our politicians seemingly wished to resurrect may be gained from
this report published in December 1942:

> La Baker is in Marrakesh and has been seen driving in an elegant
> carriage drawn by two bay horses, and with servants in attendance,
> through the picturesque market place, with its snake-charmers,
> mountain warriors and traders.[1]

Once during those years of creeping despair, while the new war was
being cooked, the soul of France revolted. The English spirit made its
effort through the Peace Ballot of 1935; the French rioted in 1934, aim-
lessly, not knowing what they wanted or how to get it, but moved by the
violent impulse to end their torment, somehow.

Stavisky was not a Frenchman. His roots lay in Eastern Europe. In
the France of 1919-39 he was important. He was head of the pawnshop at
Bayonne. Do not picture a furtive booth in a mean street. French pawn-
shops are Government establishments. Their resources are limitless, for
the credit of the Bank of France and the State supports them.

Stavisky, a high municipal official, therefore, made a large fortune by
raising loans on the valuables pawned with him. (If any wished to redeem
a fur coat or diamond ring, Stavisky would recover it from his banking
friends.) With the money thus gained, he promoted companies and soon
his finger was in every French financial pie.

Here, again, was Anon, the man who wielded hidden power. In 1933

---

[1] For a picture of the state of France in those twenty years, read E. E. Cummings, *The
Enormous Room* (Jonathan Cape, 1928); Elliot Paul, *A Narrow Street* (Cresset Press, 1942), and
de Polnay, *Death and To-morrow* (Secker and Warburg, 1942).

a newspaper exposed him. As he brought no libel action, it began a great campaign.

Thus, quite suddenly, the public saw the thing it suspected and detested, but never before could lay hand on. Anon's activities were revealed. This was Corruption; the outraged country seethed. Fresh accusations appeared each day, and the Prime Minister, Chautemps, was forced to act. He ordered (he *said*) Stavisky's arrest. Stavisky 'committed suicide'; he could have implicated too many others.

During the days that followed, the rottenness of French parliamentary and political life was laid bare. The Mayor of Bayonne was arrested. The Minister of Commerce, Dalimier, resigned. Stavisky's cheque book was produced and convicted the great Tardieu, and the head of the State theatre, the Comédie Française, where Stavisky's leading lady played leading lady. The Minister of Agriculture was involved. Several Members of Parliament shot themselves. Judges and bankers disappeared. The Prime Minister's niece committed suicide.

Then came the little more which was too much. The public exposure showed that a political party was in Stavisky's pay: the Radical Socialists (who were not Socialists, these names mean nothing in French politics). Their leader was Daladier. When Chautemps ignominiously resigned, Daladier was appointed Prime Minister!

The nation's self-control snapped. The people were impoverished by taxation; the way their rulers lived was now disclosed to them. Shopkeepers, clerks, officers, war veterans, workers, Fascists, Communists, surged into the streets. M. Jules Romains, the French writer, sent a message from the Place de la Concorde to Daladier, saying: 'Whatever happens, hold on. This riot is absolutely unimportant. A little energy, and you can save freedom in the Republic.'

Freedom! Whose? O much-dishonoured word!

Twenty-two Frenchmen were killed by police bullets. Daladier resigned. An iron censorship was ordered. Never again might a Stavisky be exposed.

France never rose again, from that day, but sank into deeper despondency until the day of capitulation. By such means and such men was France broken. For your delusion, gentle reader, they talk of The Men of Vichy! They would restore that France!

This was the story of the nation which was bled white, for victory in the first World War. We should never forget the example.

Our public life is not yet so corrupt as was that of France. But it has deteriorated much in the last twenty years, and the dangerous period impends — the years after this war. Already the sale of honours is a known thing, proved and openly debated in Parliament. The payment of retaining fees to Members by industrial concerns is a thing generally known in Parliament which should be outlawed. We know, from statements made in Parliament by Tory Members, that Tory Members pay thousands of pounds for a seat. For what?

If 'They' exist, who work to destroy nations and make wars — and the evidence becomes too strong to ignore — their mightiest weapon is political corruption, and its handmaiden is anonymity. I mean, the anonymity of men who wield power in high Government offices and whose names are refused in Parliament, no matter what crimes they commit against the national interest, the refusal of inquiry into culpable misdeeds, the sinister withholding of information about public affairs 'in the public interest', the secrecy of newspaper ownership, and the whole machine of clandestine corruption.

The edifice of rottenness which Stavisky built in France could only be erected behind this curtain of anonymity. When *one* newspaper found courage to tear it aside, the structure collapsed; does this not recall Mr. Lloyd George's statement about 'the motives' which statesmen 'dare not avow', which, if they were laid bare, would 'die of exposure to the withering contempt of humanity'?

But immediately after the riots, *a censorship was imposed*. Censorship is the iron safety-curtain of Anon. From then on, France might be led, without further mishap, to disaster. No prying newspaper might again hinder the plot. Why, without that censorship some newspaper might have told the French that the Maginot Line was a hoax!

'Censorship' is a weapon used by those who hold power *against* those they claim to represent, not in the interest of these. That is important to remember. Behind this screen, evil things may be done. The only censorship which would serve our interests — the safety of this island and domestic freedom — is the one we lack, 'a censorship in the interests of truth'. A stealthy censorship against the truth was used to make this war inevitable. The Battle in England should begin by destroying anonymity in our affairs. Indeed, if the pernicious order, of power wielded in anonymity and irresponsibility, is not changed, our revival will be much hampered, and we may be led along the path which unhappy France was made to follow.

What a Calvary that has been! How many people in this sea-enclosed island realize that France has suffered more, in this war again, than any other? The entire country has been occupied, this time. Its good food and wines have been plundered. We sank a third of the French fleet; they sank another third, rather than aid the Germans. I hope our Government will one day publish the weight of bombs dropped by us on France and Germany; Brest and Lorient must be among the most heavily bombed towns in this war.[1]

But, worse than all that, a great part of young French manhood lies in foreign captivity. The French population, in 1939, was 42,000,000. Say the half were males, and a third of these, 7,000,000, males between 16 and 35. About 1,400,000 have for three years been prisoners in Germany! What a blow to the virility of a nation, what a burden on the future!

People in this country hear nothing of these 1,400,000 Frenchmen. They hear almost as little about the hundreds of thousands of British prisoners of war. Since General Giraud procured us the entry to French North Africa, and began to rearm the remaining French armies, so that they might resume the struggle at our side, our newspapers have only reviled him, and clamoured for the revival of 'French Democracy' (that is, Stavisky's France!) in Africa.

The best weapon with which people may equip themselves, for the coming journey through Civvy Street, is understanding of what happened in France. Another book which will help them is *One of our Pilots is Safe*, by Flight-Lieut. William Simpson, D.F.C. (Hamish Hamilton, 1942). The author was shot down, in an obsolete bomber, on the day the Germans attacked. He crashed in flames, was rescued, suffered long agony, and is now disfigured and crippled. His terrible story of French misery, starvation and enslavement becomes a glorious one, because a ray of hope for the future of the French nation shines out of it, in the resolve of the common

---

[1] For a revelation of the state of some minds in this country, I commend readers to study any debate in the House of Commons about our air-bombing. They will find that voices are invariably raised in protest against the bombing of our enemy, Germany, *but that no voice has ever been raised to protest against the bombing of our prostrate friend, France, or even to express compassion.* Even the French seemingly welcome this bombing, so indestructible is the human longing for liberty, but if this palliates our assault, it does not vindicate so callous an attitude towards our captive friend.

people to rid their country, first of the hated invaders, and then to see that France is never again betrayed by dishonest politicians and inefficient generals. The author says that they now bitterly regret their indifference to the way the country was misgoverned by successive regimes, admit that they took life too pleasantly and irresponsibly, and are deeply conscious of the shame attaching to their inglorious military defeat.

· The example of France shows us, who will soon return to Civvy Street, how a nation, bled dry by war, callously maltreated even during that war by its own rulers, and left listless by victory, may fall an easy prey to unscrupulous men and sink into despair. A dark sign of the present, and one ominous for our own future, is that our rulers seemingly exert themselves to restore, in France, the very order which caused those disasters (and we have been refused inquiry into our own similar ones). We need to remember, in Civvy Street to-morrow, what happened to France yesterday, and to be alert.

. . . I said good night to Jean, that night in December 1921, and to Jean-Marie Jones, and went to bed. Presently I returned to England, and saw them no more.

Ten years later, I was in Paris again. Bitterness and cynicism had grown apace, but the foreign tourist saw them not. He saw only the man with the dirty postcards, the brothels, the all-night bars, the clashing dance bands in their glittering alcoves, the bawdy picture-shows, the prostitutes — and he called all this 'Gaiety'! This scum on the surface, and his own superficiality, lay between him and the impoverished, bewildered, fearful, hard-working people of Paris. He saw, not Paris, but a nude revue; not France, but a dirty postcard.

But I revisited other haunts and old acquaintances, and was shaken by the embittered disbelief I met. At a cabaret, one renowned for its acid satire, I found that Jean's venom, against *Messieurs les Anglais*, was as soothing balm, compared with the things which now were said. (By that time, ten years of British nagging about 'the French hatred of the Germans' lay behind us, and also the premature withdrawal, compelled by us, from the Rhineland, which, as I wrote in the first of these books, 'advanced the date of the next war by five years'.) The things I heard that night, about my own country, made me angry but anxious.

I next saw Paris a few weeks before the calamity. I blame myself still because, with all my experience of the eve of disaster in other countries, I did not, or would not recognize it in France. But I believe all others allowed their hearts similarly to mislead them. The underlying loveliness of Paris, and the feeling this bred in them, were too strong. They would not believe in the impending doom.

Yet it was unmistakable. It was terrible. On the surface all was the same; like skaters on thin ice, moved the elderly politicians and bankers, with their young, befurred women, the man-with-the-postcards, the jazz-drummers in their 'smokings', and the brothel touts.

But underneath was an awful unease, fear and confusion. If you ignored it by day, you could not at night. For the French Government imposed no blackout, but a spectral, blue-grey order of dimmed lighting. It was the fitting illumination for the final act to which they brought France. The streets emptied early, and in this ghastly twilight Paris looked corpse-like. I shudder now, when I think of it. In those deserted streets, marched the ghosts of millions of men. Overhead, in the darkness, the vultures waited.

I returned to England. On the night when France collapsed I was in a London theatre. The orchestra played the Marseillaise. I saw a British naval officer's head, as he stood at attention, sink on his chest. When it was over, young actresses tripped down from the stage and danced the polka with the playgoers.

A few weeks passed, and on the radio I began to hear the voices of the deluders. 'The last time I saw Paris', they drooled, 'her heart was young and gay ...' 'Paris will be gay again ...', they moaned.

Gay! I have shown you how gay was Paris, in those years. Do we fight to force the French to resume that way of life?

The example is there. We may learn from it. Every man should carry the picture with him, in Civvy Street to come.

Don't let 'Them' do it to us, when you come back. This is worth a Battle in England. This *is* 'worth fighting for'.

CHAPTER VII

THE HOUSE THAT JERRY BUILT

1922. Westbourne Grove in London. If any aspire to visit a grove, let them go to this one, and then look up the word in the dictionary.

Peace was already four years old. I could hardly believe it; the four exciting war years stood out, in my memory, like coloured pictures among photographs, but these four years of struggle, disillusionment and humdrum merged, in retrospect, into a patternless, grey blur.

I slept hard, after Victory came and sharply reminded me that a man needs a roof. I slept hard during the war, too, but that was different; dignity was in the firestep of a trench, dugouts, bivouacs, tents, the open ground, French farmhouses and old châteaux. These dingy back rooms, with their grasping roomwomen (why 'landlady', for bed and breakfast's sake?) were squalor, dependence and misery. Shall I ever forget those mean lodgings in Salisbury and Tunbridge Wells and Westbourne Grove! One early morning, mounting a pitch-dark stairway to my attic, I passed a madman standing on the landing; I did not know until the next day that he was there, yet my hair rose on my scalp in the blackness as I passed him. But that is another story. . . .

Now, in 1922, I thought of marrying. The Little House remained a dream. Four walls and a roof for the day were difficult enough to find. Those who made the great war fortunes bought up the manors, mansions, villas and houses. What remained was being shared out among the returning men, and a new group of fortunes was thus being made. For the uttermost farthing was wrung from the generation which fought, and now sought its future.

'Wise statesmen', of course, passed laws to prevent the need of the home-seeking millions from being exploited. These were used, as the laws against black market operations have been used in this war, as perches, by the birds of prey. The 'rent control' laws were riddled with loopholes. Any usurer who owned a tumbledown house could fill his moneybags by charging either 'key money' to the distraught aspirant, or, if a lump sum could not be extorted, by asking a crushing rent.

Furnished dwellings were free from even the pretence of control. The home-seekers, most of them men back from the war, owned neither the furniture nor the money to buy any. Cheap furnished quarters would have been a godsend to them, but the sky was the limit for the rents of such. Thus they were forced to find empty rooms and yield themselves into the clutches of hire-purchase.

Demons might have devised the implacable process by means of which they passed from one financial servitude to another, until the new war was ready. For the first ten years, their backs were bowed beneath the burden of rent. Then building began to overtake demand and rents cheapened. The houses that Jerry built, and scattered over England, are the horrifying monuments to that age of grab-and-get-rich, each-for-himself-and-the-devil-take-the-hindmost, Good Old Neville, and roll on, the new war.

Enough of them are already become slums. But people lived in them who struggled to build a future for themselves and their children. If we must pay these heavy rents, they thought, let us at least become owners of our little houses. So, while the 'estates' quickly bred the signs of slum-dom, great palaces arose in the cities: the palaces of the 'building societies'.

In the little houses, the ageing men of the last war doggedly plodded towards Householdership. How many actually owned their homes when these were bombed, or their sons were sent to Singapore, or Mr. Dodger of the Labour Exchange, with his paper cuffs and paper forms and self-importance, ordered their daughter to go to a factory at John o' Groats? From the last war to the next war, their noses were kept to the grindstone by the weight of rent and hire-purchase. Small wonder, that they saw nothing ahead of them.

In 1922, when I thought of marrying and the peace was four years old, I found some rooms in a house in a dreary square north of Hyde Park. It was built in the last century for some well-to-do City man, or as the town residence of some rural squire. It began with the area and dark basement for the servants, rose to dining-room and other rooms on the ground floor, to drawing-room and other rooms on the first, best bedrooms on the second, nursery and children's bedrooms on the third, and maids' rooms on top. The interest on the purchase price paid by its owner may have been £100 or £150: I can only conjecture. By the insertion of flimsy partitions it was now divided into 'maisonettes'. This was one of the many loopholes in the 'Rent Control' law. The house must have brought in £800 or £1000 a year to the elderly bachelor who owned it. Its thousands of neighbours were earning like incomes.

I obtained two third-floor rooms, divided by partitions to make four. The rent was £2 15s. od. I earned £5. Until I earned more I kept afloat by double labour; one post occupied me from 9 until 5.30, by day, and the other from 7 until 2 at night.

Thus were The Boys, when they came home, made to carry a back-breaking burden. When it began to lighten, and they began to feel themselves free men, the new war broke. . . .

To-day, this happens again, like other evil things. Past experience might have been rubbed out with a sponge. Yet human credulity cannot be asked to believe that those lessons have been forgotten. The forces of avarice are so strong that it is *meant* to happen again.

Soon, if our leaders mean to win this war and set about to do it, the home-seekers will surge into Civvy Street. Last time, they were promised 'homes for heroes' in 'a land fit for heroes'. This time, they are promised social security. But firstly, social security is a myth, unless this island be made secure; secondly, it is a myth unless they can find decent homes at fair rents. The level of rents in this country staggers foreigners who come here.

The ground is clear for another decade of exploitation. To-day's Rent Restriction Act contains just those loopholes which made rent control ineffective after the last war.

It applies only to dwellings which were let unfurnished at the outbreak of war. The home-seekers will be far more numerous than the number of dwellings, and the surplus will be at the usurer's mercy. The extortionate owner will be free to do what he wishes with a house that was not let in September 1939. He may do just what my elderly bachelor did in 1922, and thus draw an income of £1000 from a house that costs him £100 or £200.

The greatest evil of all, the 'furnished rooms' racket, is like to flourish as it flourished in 1919 and after. A few sticks are enough to make a dwelling 'furnished' and any rent may be asked. True, it must not be 'extortionate', but the onus to prove this is on *the tenant*, who must incur the cost of prosecution and risk an adverse judgment. Lawyers know that tenants, hard pressed to find quarters, will not undertake this. The thing is a fraud; those who have no furniture are left at the mercy of exploitation.

A still graver abuse impends, this time. You may charge what you please for a broken-down caravan, tin shanty or wooden hut on a vacant plot of ground. This method of exploiting the need into which people have been cast may produce worse conditions in England than after the last war. In December 1942 the children of a woman who lived in a converted bus near Shrewsbury were burnt to death when it caught fire. At the inquest, she said she paid fourteen shillings a week for this habitation. No law protected her. Near Blackpool there is a colony of dilapidated wooden shacks and caravans, worth about £10 each. Elderly widows and old age pensioners live in them. One widow, with an income of 28s. 6d. a week, paid 12s. 6d. rent. The only lavatory was 200 yards away, and she was charged 3d. a week for its use. The nearest water, from a tap, was 200 yards distant. The furniture was a table, chair and bed. She could not afford 'to rent a room in Blackpool'. Similar conditions existed in the other hovels. The rents ranged from 10s. to £1.

While the country resounds with controversy about 'social security', the law ignores such things as these.

Some millions of houses were built between the wars (350,000 a year, latterly). Since this war began, hardly any have been built. 250,000 have been destroyed or made uninhabitable by bombing. The Minister of Health has already 'authorized Local Authorities to issue licences enabling slum houses to be reoccupied'. As a result 100,000 people, 'at a low estimate', are living 'in houses which three years ago were condemned, and 200,000 more in houses which would by now have been condemned'. In some districts 'there is now dangerous overcrowding'. He has 'little hope of anything substantial being done to relieve the present serious shortage of houses'.

And according to the Minister of Labour, 'there have been 1,800,000 marriages since the war and few of these newlyweds have yet got homes'. He added words which sound familiar:

> These working people are slaving to earn a new world. They shall get it. There must be no jerrybuilding of houses for the workers when this war ends, no ramshackle thrown-up jobs that make slums in twenty years.

THE HOUSE THAT JERRY BUILT

What do such words avail if, during the ten or twenty years when those new houses are being built, the home-seekers are to be the defenceless victims of extortion; if their health and their children's health is to be imperilled, and their spirit daunted, by ten years of rent-squeezing for the enrichment of a few? (In 1919 only 715 houses were built in England and Wales, and in 1920 less than 30,000.)

This yawning gap, between the present and the distant future when houses will be abundant again, is the gap from which the extortioner will fill his purse. That is the primary evil. The second is that of the houses themselves when they come to be built: they should not again be ugly little prisons for their occupants, and eyesores for the beholder.

The president of the National Federation of Building Trade Employers, a Mr. Leslie Wallis, in February 1943 said:

> We want to avoid the calamity which befell our industry after the last war, when anybody who had a little money bought a ladder or two and started building because there was nothing to stop them. Some awful rubbish was built then.

'Nothing to stop them'! Those are the important words. In this country, there is to-day something to stop the modest, hardworking, and patriotic citizens from every normal and useful action or ambition. There is *still* 'nothing to stop' the exploitation of the great mass of people who have served and sacrificed, through rent extortion and jerrybuilding. This makes nonsense of the fair promises of our rulers. If they do not propose to do anything 'to stop them', they only beat the air with windy phrases. Either they are incorrigibly inert, or they are resolved not to check the freedom of the free foxes in the free henroost.

These are two matters of the first importance, and are yet easily remedied. They do not need a new ministry and 20,000 more officials to be set right. Two simple laws are needed; one to put a fair limit on the rents chargeable for furnished quarters; the other, to fix minimum conditions for new houses, and their indispensable dovetailing into greater plans framed in the overriding public interest, which is, the need for light, sunshine, air, public services and the beauty of the general scene. Any man should have the right to buy land and build a house on it. He should not have the right to build one which is ramshackle, insanitary, mean, of obsolete design, or spoils the neighbourhood on either side.

From laws of this kind we seem far, and men of goodwill who make plans for the improvement and beautification of town and countryside after this war, work without a foundation.

A great opportunity lost in our history was that, to build a better London after the great fire of 1666. The plan was made, but was wrecked by people impatient to make quick profit out of their own plot, without regard to the general scene or the lot of the Londoners. The result was the chaotic inner London we knew.

A plan to create new beauty from to-day's ruins was drawn up by the Royal Academy. It is on public sale, and presents a picture of a stately and dignified city, a joy to the beholder. It was viciously attacked. An anonymous writer in an anonymously-owned newspaper lampooned 'The Vistamongers' (a few days later, he complained of the lack of 'strategic vista' in our military enterprises) and said 'This country must not be allowed to get into the hands of cranks . . .' A vista is a pleasant thing; I see no sense in thus deriding beauty. Similarly the plan was violently criticized because it was 'A Plan', prepared by 'Planners'. But in human life, people habitually make plans — to marry, breed children, repair their houses, or improve them. We become so mad, that even the word 'plan' may be held up to our deluded people as something foul.

Nothing more has been heard of the plan for London. We do not know whether it has been discarded, or whether any hope remains that so simple a need as the improvement of London, when London comes to be rebuilt, will be met by our voluble leaders.

The same holds good for the entire country.[1] The picture is one of chaos and delay. Sorely-tried Plymouth, where 40,000 houses were destroyed and 150 acres of built-on land razed, has an energetic City Council and City Engineer and appointed an expert as Consultant, to help 'prepare a plan of the future Plymouth'. All the good ideas are in it. But:

Although efforts will be made to discourage piecemeal developments,

---

[1] Three reports about rebuilding and replanning after this war, the Barlow, Scott and Uthwatt reports, have been made to Parliament, and three expensive ministries set up. The Government has taken no decisions about any of these reports. Local Authorities everywhere are held up in their own plans because they do not know what governing principles, if any, are to be laid down. In March 1943 the Minister of Health, Mr. Ernest Brown, seemed to foretell a new era of indiscriminate building and uncontrolled disfigurement when he urged Local Authorities not to wait, but to look around for areas suitable for housing and go ahead with their plans for building on them.

*there is no local power to prevent an individual owner of a site using it, if he
can obtain the necessary licence for labour and material.*

A great city, laid waste, one of our most famous, one which rings a
bell in every Englishman's heart. A great plan for its rebuilding (and how
unworthy had Plymouth become, like London, of its great past!). But,
'no power'!

This 'power' can only be given by Parliament in London. None
could be more usefully given than the power to prevent another period
of rent extortion and jerrybuilding; and to enable the towns and cities
to plan their rebuilding. In the process of 'taking powers' to deprive us
of every liberty, nothing is forgotten. Why are things neglected, so vital
to our future happiness as these? Who profits by withholding them?

The same story comes from all over the country. Birmingham,
Southampton, Liverpool, Manchester, all talk of 'rebuilding', make
'plans' — and do not know whether they waste their time or not.

Jerry Builder, were he able to get labour and material, would be as
free to-day as he was before to put up a roadside-café-amusement-palace-
and-filling-station of corrugated iron painted red next door to a Saxon
church.

Above all the 'furnished rooms' racket has begun again. If it is not
checked, it will reach villainous extremes when The Boys come back. In
January 1943, a correspondent of *The Times* was offered 'the choice
between a two-roomed furnished flat in Edgware Road at 7 guineas a
week, as a special favour, and a three-roomed furnished flat in Park Lane
at 14 guineas a week; the furniture in each case represented the barest
minimum, and the rentals asked were probably three times in excess of
1939 furnished rentals'!

The first test case showed how the law, which professes to prevent rent
extortion, in practice encourages it. At the end of 1942, four tenants of
a block of flats at Richmond, who were paying rents between £78 and
£96 a year, received demands for increased rent, accompanied by a
declaration that the 'standard rents' (that is, the rent charged at the outbreak of war, which must not be raised) were £210, £240, and £250!
The company owning the house (in such cases, the defendants enjoy the
additional protection of anonymity, since 'the company' is sued and their
names are not published) contended that the onus of proving the 'standard
rent' (that is, the rent charged on September 2nd, 1939, or at any subse-

quent first letting) *lay on the tenant*. The tenants formally charged the defendants with making a false statement about the standard rent. The company refused to produce proof! The 'maximum fines' were imposed on this company. They were of £10 each!

To place on the tenant the onus of proof, of the rent charged several years ago, when the tenancy may have changed several times, obviously makes a farce of the law, which thus, in practice, operates in favour of evasion. Only a most stout-hearted tenant, and one with money to risk, can venture to appeal to law in such conditions.

To say, in these conditions, as our Tory Chancellor of the Exchequer says: 'We shall all be much poorer after the war', is deliberate mockery. Any man who owns any kind of house, hut or hovel will be very well off, unless the law be changed.[1] As it stands, those who seek a roof and four walls will be his helpless victim. And when he has had a picking, the jerrybuilder will claim his.

You perceive, gentle reader, that usury, extortion and profiteering continue for many years after a war; indeed, when they become difficult a new war seems to develop. They go on now. But the birds of prey will begin their real feast when The Boys come home and are delivered into their hands — unless they realize that they return to a Battle in England, and not to a rest. These were The Things we fought for last time; to-day, once more, they are The Things. Here at home, other men hold power than in 1914-18; but their acts and omissions are the same. . . .

Three years, I spent in those abjectly depressing rooms. Then I found an empty house, outside London, eight years after the war ended. It meant a long daily journey to my work, and next to rent, the heaviest burden on the backs of the men who returned from the last war was that of fares. I could not afford the whole of this house. So, still dreaming of the day when I would own A Little House, I shared it with another family.

It was misery. After eighteen months, thanks be to Providence, I went abroad. For the first time in my life, I found decent quarters.

Even then I did not abandon the dream of The Little House. In 1931, having saved a little money, I bought The Little House in England,

---

[1] In the House of Commons on March 16th, 1943 Members reported that the forbidden 'key money' was already being charged again, that houses divided into makeshift 'apartments' or fitted with a few sticks of furniture were earning many times their rent, that houses, even *condemned* houses, are changing hands at double and triple their pre-war values.

through a proxy. I never did a more unwise thing. When I came on leave I went to look at it. It was a typical product of the jerrybuilding decade which followed the rent extortion decade. All the meanness of which the human spirit is capable was expressed in its niggardly rooms and grates, its tiny triangle of fenced-in wasteland called a garden, its outside plumbing, its lack of privacy for anyone living in it, its obsolete kitchen, its narrow windows, and its row of neighbours all exactly like itself. It was everything I hated. I sold it forthwith at a substantial loss.

I have shown you the prospect which Civvy Street offers to men who come back to anything but a Battle in England. None of these things has been changed. The rent squeeze and the jerrybuilder await them, as they awaited them in 1918. Both these evils could be easily remedied, through the Battle in England.

CHAPTER VIII

ESCAPE!

1929. The coast of Ceylon, washed by the deep blue waters of the Indian Ocean. A stone's throw from the shore, a tiny islet of red granite rock, crowned with the plumes of palm-trees, that look like ostrich feathers. A page from the *Arabian Nights*; a mirage materialized; a dream come true; an emerald set in pink coral; a gem, just an acre and a half in size, bedded in turquoise.

A man, a French count, with greying hair and a deep furrow between tormented blue eyes. Children from a mainland village bringing him offerings of flowers, which they drop at his feet. One of them singing a Sinhalese poem in his honour; honey-coloured limbs, gleaming bronze in the light of lanterns, against the drop-curtain of a velvet twilight. Around, gardens: all the flowers of the tropics, dahlias and gladioli from Holland, England and Australia, antirrhinums, carnations, petunias, verbena, phlox, Michaelmas daisies, golden rod. Tropical birds, twittering and chattering. A rockery, a pergola, a loggia, a peacock balcony. Terraces, an Italian Garden, a Lover's Walk. An eight-sided white house, with a domed central hall, 'The Hall of the Lotus', lined with panels of inlaid wood dyed dull gold and brown, the dome supported by eight squared pillars of Wedgwood b'ue.

All that done — the rough stone cut and polished and made into a perfect jewel — in eight years. Paradise regained, 1937!

The war had taken everything from me. It had made *table rasé* of my life. I had to begin a new life or die. My soul was a *grand blessé*, covered with the wounds of the past, which the present refused to heal. Worn by too much suffering, it was dying from want of nourishment. The whole of my being, both physical and moral, had lost its object in life. Paralysed, inert, it was incapable of effort, because I had lost even the desire of effort. I was flickering out in a living death, a life worse than death, because it had no longer the confidence of hope. I was suffering from the terrible disease which seems to have gripped the whole of humanity since the war: Fear. I heard the call of the East, and incapable of any resistance, searching in vain for a last remedy, I answered the summons. To the East I came to recover my lost desire of effort ... When, I asked myself, shall I have the strength to master fear — to dare to face the future? To rebuild, on unsuspected foundations, the edifice of my new life, with materials as yet unknown to me? I must wait, I must seek, but with the recovery of the desire to live I feel, I know, that I shall find them, for I already feel the revival of hope which engenders faith in the future. It is to the East that I owe the reawakening of the desire of effort; it is to my gardens of Taprobane that I owe the strength which has enabled me to transform the desire of effort into the reality of action, thanks to the happiness and peace which they have given me....[1]

Long ago I lived in a château, a gem of French Renaissance architecture, once the abode of kings. Its lofty walls were covered with delicate lace-like traceries and carvings, the like of which I discovered by chance on some of the ruins of the buried city of Polonnaruwa. Its steep slate roofs, mellowed by centuries, were broken here and there by gables and windows; its large round towers, built for artistic effect, not for war, were reflected in the waters of the wide, lake-like moat in which forty-pound carp, so old that moss grew on their backs, gambolled and rose to the crumbs of bread thrown to them each day at noon. The château had a park of two hundred and fifty acres, avenues of

[1] I owe gratitude to the Comte de Mauny and to his publishers, Messrs. Williams & Norgate, for permission to quote these extracts from his sad and significant book, *The Gardens of Taprobane*, 1937.

poplar trees and weeping willows, and a river, the Indre, threading its way across meadows carpeted with buttercups and meadowsweet. Its 'period' furniture and pictures were a lesson in French history. How exquisite it all was! ... How I loved the little manor-house of my childhood ... I can hear to-day the Angelus bell ... That indeed was my home, for there every detail contributed, by its history and associations, to the making of a home, even to the grass field with its stone monuments, on which was engraved, together with that of Du Guesclin, the name of an ancestor who fought victoriously against the English in the battle of Pontvallain. My home was made of my love for it and my pride was that I was able to call it my own. It broke my heart to leave it, and I felt that I had lost a treasure which could never be replaced ... Why bother about the past and the future? Thinking of them won't retrieve our mistakes of the past, nor will it help us to control the future. ...

The waves of the Indian Ocean were dying at my feet. The red cliffs encircling the bay, crowned with jungle trees, reminded me of Devonshire, and my thoughts wandered back to an English September. ...

A stranger wrote and asked to be allowed to visit my gardens and I invited him to lunch ... I expected to see a man of middle age, but to my surprise a very pretty, perhaps too pretty, and very young individual was ushered into the loggia. He — or perhaps I should say 'it' — was dressed in white: silk trousers, with a dozen pleats round the waist, a silk shirt of gossamer thickness, open at the throat, with sleeves cut short above the elbow, and white socks and shoes — in short, a vision in white. Wavy hair, brushed off the forehead; china-blue eyes, shaded by long, curled lashes; plucked eyebrows, very red lips, and perfect features ... Very young people, such as this specimen, having lost all sense of proportion, rush headlong to the van of the movement, and try to preserve the illusion that they are enjoying its abuses. It is during this moral and social evolution — or, more truly, this revolution — that the relics of what is called civilization decline irresistibly towards decadence. The intoxication of drugs becomes nothing but a drug; immorality gives way to amorality, and innocence to guilt — taking to courses which are often criminal, according to the law, lest it should be derided. Shame being non-existent, sins are merely faults ... This youngster, a mere boy, suddenly told me the whole story of his young life, of its utter failure, through the lack of moral sense and backbone, and he seemed to experience an uncanny pleasure in doing so. His family had disowned him, he had no home, and by indulging in every caprice, he was trying to forget both ... He was squandering what was left of a large fortune in going round the world, in search of *l'introuvable*, and he intended to end his travels at Hollywood, where — miserable, deluded child — he was bent upon finding a market for his beauty in the rôle of a *jeune premier*, and on becoming a world-famous film star ... Taprobane, rid of an incubus, breathed more freely when he was gone. ...

I look beyond my kingdom and I see what is called the world. A world revolving in circles, like a merry-go-round at a fair. How complicated, how tawdry, how paltry and despicably small it seems, compared with my world, so simple and great! ... A grotesque show, were it not so tragic in its worldwide consequences. Pygmies, playing at being giants, playing at danger, as children playing with fire, while the world — like the Rome of Nero — is bursting into flames ... Idealism is dead. One blushes at mentioning the word. We destroy all that we touch, because to build is for us to destroy. Fed with poison, we die of inanition, and our world is dying, slain by us. Victory becomes a shameful defeat, of which we are not merely the victims but, above all, the instigators and organizers. Where is our younger generation? It is not in the breach. I should doubt its very existence were it not that the atmosphere of the world reeks with the fetid and acrid odour of the fruit that is rotten before it ripens. I shall soon witness the breaking of the monsoon, when the artillery of heaven will thunder and its flood-gates will open; with the infernal tumult of a second deluge it will come, roaring like a lion, but bringing in its trail fecundity. The sea, maddened by the storm, the waves mountains high, will rush to the assault of the Isle of Dreams. They will break on the rocks, but will not shatter them as they foam with rage, and despite their roaring will not shake the island. The trees will wail, wrung by the wind, and the roofs groan under the deadly embrace of the elements. I, alone on the Isle of Dreams, in the submission of impotence, my heart thumping in anguish, swayed between terror and hope, can only wait — wait until 'His will be done'.

So written in 1937, on that islet. In 1942, you might see the book which contains these passages marked down in price, on the London bookstalls. It is one of the most vividly illuminating of our time and ordeal, but made small appeal to the generation reared on *How Awkward for Miss Blondish*.

The monsoon broke. By 1940, the old château in France rang with the clumping boots of German invaders. By 1941, the Japanese claw hovered over the Isle of Dreams. It has not closed its clutch, yet. But no end offers to the age of fear....

Escape! Here were two who tried to escape, each after his fashion: the middle-aged nobleman, descendant of so many French knights and squires, fleeing from the infamy of the time; the vagrant boy, spoiled, un-anchored, drifting towards suicide or an embittered old age.

How many others have built an Isle of Dreams! It is the vision of The Little House, into which you may creep and hide, so that none may touch you; the safe refuge for which a middle-aged Englishwoman thought she longed, who wrote to me:

> I have been hoping, after this war, to leave my jerrybuilt bungalow for a long, low white house, but I now begin to see that that is just what we must *not* do.

Escape is an illusion. Not even at the North Pole may you find it. A bomb will find the little house, or invaders will tramp into it, or the most implacable enemies of all, the men who make these wars, will reach a long finger into it and hook out your husband or son or daughter, as little Jack Horner put in his thumb and took out a plum.

You *cannot* run away from this thing, because it is *inside* you. It is, fear. The only way to liberate yourself is to overcome it, to face 'Them', to advance towards them instead of trying to hide from them, to tear their shields aside and smite them.

The moment you do that, you find hope again, and vigour; the spirit is reborn, because you attack the thing you fear. This lonely man in the Indian Ocean, who went nearly to the other end of the world, sat alone on his islet with fear, the thing he tried to escape. He would have been happier, I think, had he stayed in France, and fought there against the things he foresaw, had he fought a Battle in France, a battle for the future. When you take up the battle, the feeling of enslavement, oppression, impotence, fear is gone. Turn and fly: and it goes with you, like your own shadow, all your ways and all your days.

To-day, in our country, you may meet the fellows of that harassed man and all the many others who, between the wars, vainly sought Escape. We only live, they say to me, to get away from England after the war. We see no hope left, of improvement. Why should any such hope offer, I answer them, if you are so cowardly or so foolish — and they are taken all aback:

My husband is in the army and loathing the war. He is so sick of the whole darned racket that when it is all over we are packing up and going to a paradise where he will be able to rest his weary nerves. We are taking our two little sons, one aged three and the other one, to a remote part of Central Africa where we can live in wild seclusion on practically nothing. . . .

From a woman in South Africa.

I want to ask, do you intend doing anything constructive to alter the present state of affairs, when the slaughter has ceased? If so, I might help . . . It was my intention, if I survive, to cut myself adrift from my fellow maniacs and spend the rest of my life more or less with nature, for I realize that even with my supreme ego I can do nothing to alter a world peopled with 99.9 per cent mentally deficients.

From a naval officer at sea.

I have still so little hope of this country getting rid of the racketeers that when the war is over I intend to take a single ticket on the first boat to South Africa, where I may be given a chance to start again.

From an army officer who was wrongfully imprisoned
without charge or trial; who was able after his release,
by ruining himself, to prove his innocence; who then
joined the ranks and was quickly chosen for promotion.

These are but three of very many such despairing cries. Does the dispersal of the English impend?

Consider, again, the fantastic case of the 38-year old Londoner who, in 1942, stole a sailing-boat at Looe, in Cornwall, and set out in it, in the midst of war! His astounding project was, to land in German-occupied France, work his way somehow through to Spain and from there to Portugal, and then to find a ship for Brazil, 'with the hope of starting afresh'. He thought thus to find freedom and his future, to escape from misery and fear. I wonder how much he did, beween the wars, to slay those two demons. He was captured a few miles out to sea.

Strange, how far men will go in search of the wrong way, when the right way lies before them. For you may transport your body to Baffin-land, but you cannot separate your spirit from it, and all the misery and fear lie in the spirit. The things the spirit fears are not physical ones. Only by standing where you are, and giving fight, may you free the spirit and feel again that life is good, and the world a good place to spend it.

In the Battle in England we shall need to fight hardest against those who would yield to despair, desperation, or simple apathy, and those who would escape.

A variation of the request for 'something constructive', which some make to me, is that for 'a lead', which others raise. It might be flattering if it were not stupid. Have we not known enough leaders, from Adolf Hitler to Neville Chamberlain, enough wonderful men who will make all our to-morrows secure without any further trouble to ourselves? Why, I have been trying for five books to say that leaders should *not* be blindly followed and idolized, but watched, checked, spurred, and called to account. The most famous lead in history (and again I thank those beasts) was the one given by the foremost swine at Gadarea.

Beware of leaders! I propose to do exactly what I commend those to do who are good enough to pay attention to me: to throw myself into the Battle in England as an independent citizen, who wishes to lead none but hopes he may convince some that his way is right. I believe in debate and reason, not in sheepish obedience to any straw man whom others behind the scenes may put up, for the delusion of the mob.

'A lead', 'discipline', 'loyalty to The Leader'! Those are the old tricks. Any fool, or any slave, can play follow-my-leader; it saves the pain of thought and leads always to the same ends — domestic enslavement and foreign war. We need something new. The only new thing that offers, that has not been tried, is the raising of a generation which will think for itself, educate itself in public affairs and learn how to conduct them; which will deliberately devote itself, as individual men and women, to the study of our affairs, detect the means by which they are thwarted and ruined, and find the ways by which this can be changed.

Do any wish me to design a new shirt, or think I would?

Our problem is not so difficult. Despotic and autocratic rule, through Kings, Regents, Soviets, Nazi Dictators or Fascist Grand Councils, I have found repugnant everywhere I have seen it. Parliamentary rule is best, but its weakness is that it can so quickly be made rotten, by the corruption of delegates and the Press. These, however, are detectable and remediable things, which the evils of a dictatorship are not. To remedy them you need two things: to awaken and enlighten people to the means by which rottenness is produced (they must be shown *where* the spanner has been thrown into the machinery); and to stimulate in them the energy to mend these abuses.

Of all the Parliaments I have seen, ours is the best, because the number of parties in it is small, and it has always contained a few independent men through whom the truth might out, who joined to make formidable outcry when our vital interests were assailed.

But the rottenness of our Parliament has now gone too far. The future was put in pawn on the day when an inquiry was refused into the events leading to this war and Dunkirk. Things lie behind that which cannot be kept hidden if our future is to be safe, and some of them are already known. This is not a matter of recrimination, but of surrendering the future. A public investigation and a pronouncement of public ignomy are the least of the guarantees for our future, which should be claimed. If that is not claimed, it means that there is nothing which cannot secretly be done to our country, with immunity and impunity.

Our Parliament is like a clear pond on which the scum has gathered. It is like that reach of the fair River Test, of which I spoke before, where reeds and weeds and silt and all other foulnesses have not only been allowed to gather, but encouraged, so that a few £250-a-rod men might fish there.

New parties will not cure this. What benefit do a new Party and a new 'Programme' offer, if the new men, like the old ones, are privily sworn to obey Party orders, after the election, whatever happens, and no matter how these may conflict with pledges publicly made or with the national interest?

This mortal wound in our life will only be stanched and healed by sending to Westminster a great number of Independent Members, publicly sworn to conditions which will ensure one paramount thing: that they shall remain independent, and accept no secret bondage. A straight line leads from the obedience to which all Members at present pledge themselves, to the refusal of inquiry into the origins of this war and our disaster at Dunkirk; and this straight line, prolonged after the war, would lead to our downfall.

These are simple things to understand, not difficult. Any man or woman in this island can learn of them, verify them, and challenge a Party candidate with them. Thousands are in a position to stand as an Independent candidate at an election, or join with others to advance one. By this means, they may escape into a secure future. By turning their backs on these things, and seeking Escape, they make themselves the captives of despondency and fear.

... 1930, in Berlin. A dentist, called Ritter, took a busman's holiday; he summoned another dentist, to pull all his own teeth. He sought Escape, and this was his first preparation.

The ordeal of those years, the hopelessness of the future, overcame him. He did not stand and fight, study the troubles of his country, learn by whom they were caused, and set about to destroy these. He fought no Battle in Germany. He left the field to the enemy. He fled.

He took a woman friend with him, and went to an uninhabited island in the Galapagos Group, in the Equatorial Pacific. Berlin, Germany, the world and the future terrified him: he would build on that island old Omar's paradise — a little bread, the wilderness, And Thou!

He thought of everything. Toothache, he need no longer fear. He took the right tools, clothing, equipment, provisions; the minimum of everything, but still enough. He built himself a log cabin, tilled and fenced some ground, planted things which grew.

He was safe, with his companion!

He was not. Perhaps he might, in that spot, have survived the monsoon, the hurricane, or even the world tempest, who knows? But he died. How, I do not know, for only fragments of the story came to me. That was a pity, because it was an absorbing story: it should be fully written one day, as a warning to Escapers.[1] I regret that I have not the full truth of it, and am not even sure whether he died a natural death before those others came to his island.

For some came, men and women, or a man and a woman, or women and a man — I am not certain. Anyway, a triangle was formed, or it may have been a quadrangle, or some more complicated geometrical figure. Even in that remote and lonely spot, was no peace. Shots were fired, I think, or daggers flashed, or was poison used? Death came again, more than once.

---

[1] After I wrote this, I found that some details of this fantastic and fascinating story are given in William Albert Robinson, *Voyage to Galapagos* (Jonathan Cape, London, 1936), but the manner of Dr. Ritter's death is not fully explained, though a reasonable theory is advanced for the other deaths which occurred on the island or near it.

It was an extraordinary story, but my files and notes and cuttings were twice lost, when I hopped about Europe, trying to keep one hop ahead of Hitler, and I cannot tell the whole of it.

But that was the broad outline, and I know the moral, at least. Escape proved an illusion for the German dentist, as for the French count.

Study it, and you may see the way to the Battle in England. No escape offers — not to a desert island, or a distant country, or a little house, or to the radio or the pictures. The only escape lies in a good fight here in England, with the weapons of the spirit, and for the future.

CHAPTER IX

THE EXAMPLE OF GERMANY

Man learns little from victory,
but much from defeat — *Japanese proverb*

JUNE 1931. I sat in a pleasant garden, beneath trees, at a table. The white road ran past, and opposite an abundant cornfield climbed a gentle slope. In the distance was pithead machinery and a slag heap. I was on the out-skirts of Essen. I looked, and wondered why we, in England, do not marry industry and agriculture, town and country, like this, instead of setting the one to rape the other. How unlike the Black Country, was this picture, and yet the same things were wrested from the earth here, and a great city, bigger than Sheffield, lay close by.

Sheffield is in the heart of our wealthy island and I knew what it looked like. A place where a roof of smoke rested on tall chimneys, squalor stalked in mean streets, idle men loitered round Labour Exchanges; and where these conditions were apathetically accepted as the unchallengeable levy that industry, miscalled Prosperity, imposed on a land once green and pleasant.

In Essen was unemployment, too, but the scene was not like a plate from *The Rake's Progress*. Here were light, air and sunshine; ugliness was combated as the common enemy of all, rich or poor, busy or idle; and underneath was not apathy, but a bitter struggle for the future.

At my table sat two men and a girl; the Nazi leaders of Essen. I was there to inquire into the strength and aims of these Nazis, and at that table I first realized that, if they came to power, they would make a new war. They said so. I did not then believe they would gain power. I put faith in Grand Old Men, of whom my newspapers told me that Hindenburg was one, in the words of British Prime Ministers, and in the things I read. The men who soon will return to Civvy Street, and those others who now grow up here, should bear in mind this picture of an Englishman, eleven years after Victory in the last war.

I sat with Kurt von Adel, ex-captain, Hans Schultze, ex-serjeant major, and Greta Loring, who was Schultze's friend and the chosen leader of Nazi girls in Essen. I was startled by the venom of these men. They were bitter and cynical, yes; but these qualities were positive, not negative. They were more desperate than despairing. They were the opposite to Jean, my neighbour in Paris. They did not repine, on a bed of disillusionment; they worked and organized, night and day. Their driving power was the thought of defeat suffered and revenge to come: the prizefighter's ambition to come back. Jean's father, and even Jean himself, felt that same impulse in 1914; the defeat of 1871 provided it. After 1918, they felt within themselves no vigour, to fight for the victory they won. They let it be taken from them.

Von Adel, lean and ruthless, and Schultze, red-faced and brutal, still lived mentally in the trenches before Verdun. They throve on hatred. They hated their own Socialists and Communists first; and after them, the English, not because their native dislike of the English was greatest (their supreme detestation was kept for Czechs and Poles) but because the English island was the chief hindrance to a German European Empire.

Von Adel spoke frankly of the next war. The last war, he said, was a picnic compared with the spectacle Germany would stage next time. Schultze said contemptuously that Germans refused to be confined in a peaceful paradise of lowing herds and dairyfed prosperity, a super-Denmark. The girl looked at me inscrutably and said little.

In the ten years that lay behind, von Adel never ceased to fight, after his fashion, for the kind of Germany he wanted. He was among those who shot the Separatist leaders in Speyer, and for this reason was now a Nazi leader. Schultze was a typical serjeant major, with a passion for desk work. His job was to keep a card index of the local Socialists and

Communists, with their addresses, occupations, associations, and any weaknesses he could learn, against the day when he would dash about in a lorry and hurl them into a concentration camp. He was uneducated and secretly venerated von Adel, to whom he appealed, as we sat in the sun, saying 'Herr Hauptmann, it can't be very long now before we get our Third Reich, can it?' 'Very soon', said von Adel brusquely.

I smiled inwardly; I did not imagine that within eighteen months this beefy Schultze, whom I thought comic, would be able to slake his animal instincts on his own people. Von Adel's answer made him happy and, in slang that grated, he talked of the things he would do to his enemies. He kept in his pocket snapshots of himself, taken with a Hohenzollern Prince who wore the Nazi uniform, and proudly displayed these at every opportunity.

'Tell me, Herr Doktor', said von Adel to me in his clipped Prussian, 'Will your country try to keep Germany disarmed?'

'No', I said, truthfully. I was sure this stupid ban (stupid, when once you withdraw your army of occupation) would be cancelled, or would collapse. That did not worry me, because we only needed to maintain a supreme Navy and a strong Air Force, and this would thwart the ambitions of the von Adels and Schultzes, I knew; I could not then imagine British governments which would fail us in so vital a matter.

They were much pleased by my answer. Knowing what I thought I knew, I was inwardly amused at their satisfaction. They ordered some good Rhine wine and became jovial. They seemed to see a pleasant prospect, in its sunny and sparkling depths. . . .

Jean fell into despondency, when he saw Victory filched from him by his own leaders. Von Adel and Schultze yielded to desperation, a different thing. The prospect of regaining something you have lost seemingly gives more vigour than the holding of what you have.

Another danger that confronts us, as we re-enter Civvy Street, is that we may again breed a desperate generation in Germany, and, this time, in France too. We shall do this if we treat France, not as a reviving ally, but as a conquered enemy, and we have made a grave mistake already, by using our armed strength, in French territory, to promote the restoration of the corrupt regime which led France to disaster.

We have already seen one example of desperate French youth: Bonnier de la Chapelle, the unhappy boy who shot Darlan. He was the French counterpart, in 1943, of Schlageter, the young German of 1923; the miserable lad who feels that something is intolerably wrong with his country and who sees nothing he can do, save shoot someone.

Bonnier de la Chapelle shot Darlan at the moment that admiral decided he could serve France by helping the Anglo-American landing in North Africa. Darlan's aid was beyond price for us. Young Bonnier de la Chapelle, who hoped for 'a new France' from the impending expulsion of the Germans and Italians, thought that Darlan was to be used, by others, to re-establish the rotten French order of 1919-39. Our spokesmen in Parliament and the Press have tried hard to justify that belief. He faced his death without flinching.

In Germany after the last war, a generation which could have been won for peace was driven to desperation because no outlet for its hope or energy was offered by any save the extreme parties, Communist and Nazi, and these were the instruments, respectively, of a foreign power and of the warmakers inside Germany.

No political party followed a patriotic policy and also one of social justice and wider opportunity. The Nationalists stood for the old school tie and war; well, thought the young German, if we are going to make war, we don't want to make it for the officer class, the brutal serjeant major and the cannon fodder — the National Socialists offer us something better than that. The Socialists stood for government by Trades Union, without national ideals; why, the young German asked himself, should this one vested interest rule over us all, students, artists, doctors, lawyers, shopkeepers, artisans? The only great party of the middle, the Centre, was Roman Catholic; this, again, represented a sectional, not a national interest, and the Roman Catholics form only a third of the German population. The Communists stood for no more war, confiscation, and international brotherhood as practised in Moscow; well, thought the young German, if we are to have peace, we don't want that kind of peace.

No party offered the young German the possibility of working at once for peace, for the revival of Germany, and for a juster social order in Germany. Some offered one, some another, but none offered all of these things. As many Germans are born with a taste for war and conquest, the National Socialists, exploiting the motive of revenge, were given a great chance. True, they could not have succeeded without a Hindenburg to unlock the door to power. Here was Anon, whose instrument old Hindenburg was.

In this country, the party which claims to monopolize patriotic feeling, the Conservative Party, held power almost without a break between the wars; it left us nearly defenceless in a crisis, and at the same time stubbornly opposed all lowering of the barriers of privilege and all widening of the gates of opportunity. Is to-morrow's British generation to find its spiritual home in this Party? Our dilemma remains, that the other one is worse, in its narrow sectionalism. We seem very far from a British, a patriotic, party. We too may breed a generation torn between despair and desperation, if the years after this war are to be filled with spiritual torment.

A good picture, of the tempest which raged in the minds of growing Germans, before 1914 and between 1918 and 1939, is given in a chapter, 'The Secret in the Deeps', in Otto Strasser's book, *History in My Time* (Jonathan Cape, 1941). Readers may find in it, not only another of the causes of this war, but also guidance for our own future. Of the things which seethed below the surface Strasser truly says:

> The political parties, the Government departments and the news-paper offices felt and knew nothing, and would even in 1932 still know and feel nothing, and the emigrant leaders of the German Republic, even in 1937, as they looked back, would still consider their results a strange and unaccountable happening.

This is true of our country to-day, where so wide a gulf is fixed between our politicians and the mind of the people.

To win the peace we need to do three things about Germany. The first is, to let Germany feel the destruction which Germany has again wreaked in Europe but as yet hardly knows within the German frontiers. We can do this by the mighty air assault so often promised by our leaders. In a recently published book, *Volcano Island* (Geoffrey Bles, 1943), Mr. J. M. Spaight, formerly Principal Assistant Secretary at the Air Ministry, says:

> Already there are available bombers capable of smothering all the key plants in Germany. Let us get on with the job. To say that it can-not be done is nonsense. It has never been attempted on the scale which is possible now.

If the war ends without this repayment of damage done, we shall again plant the hope of revenge in the German heart.

The second thing is, to exact retribution for crimes committed from the German leaders, and not to let them escape again. This vital issue has already been gravely blurred, and the future complicated again, by the British Government's declaration which lent the nature of an exclusively Jewish vengeance to any such retribution. This would give any new Hitler fuel with which to stoke the fires of German resentment for a century.

The third thing we need to do to win the *peace*, is to remain stronger than Germany at sea and in the air, after the war, and to cherish our alliance with Russia.

If, instead of doing those things, we simply set out to restore in Germany (as we seemingly wish to restore in France) an order, the memory of which is universally detested, we shall encourage the growth of new ambitions of revenge. For what residue will remain, in the mind of the German generation now growing, from the years of National Socialism?

One of the last books to come out of Germany gives the answer. Joseph C. Harsch, in his *Pattern of Conquest* (Heinemann, 1942), says:

> There is of course a good deal of militarism in the younger German generation. But the real aspect of Nazism which appeals to them has been the purported break from the relics of both social and industrial feudalism. The average young German considers the abolition of the colourful students' corps of the old Universities to have been an important advance. The members of those corps had the same advantages in the pre-Nazi Germany that wearers of the right school tie enjoyed in pre-war England. It was a badge of class which denied opportunity to the non-wearer. Nothing else Nazism has done for the younger generation compares, in importance to them, with this removal of social obstacles to individual advance. Elimination of Jews from the competitive field gave them an immediate, tangible, but short-lived and relatively limited increase in opportunity. But the importance of opening up all avenues of advancement to youth from the lower classes, far exceeds, in the long run, this limited gain ... Nazi care for the material well-being of youth is as fine a thing as the dishonest political indoctrination of youth is bad. The health and physique of the new generation is an imperative challenge to the big democracies, which have too long put short-sighted industrial profits ahead of the well-being

both of youth and the working class ... The path has been opened to the advancement of the new generation, and promises, with much more sincerity than is realized in the outside world, to produce in the future real equality of opportunity founded on ability. This offer of equality of opportunity is the key to the loyalty of the new generation, as the careful regard for the welfare of labour is the explanation of labour's passive acquiescence. These two great segments of the German population have been given tangible and real benefits of which they are aware ... There are elements of challenge within Nazism and the German bid for world power which will leave their mark on the world. Many established privileges will be liquidated in the heat of the effort to overthrow Hitler which can never be re-established. Hitler's greatest source of strength is the equality of opportunity for youth in Germany, which is a new thing for that country. Those who overthrow him must recognize the importance of equality to the vitality of any society.

In that sober and excellent analysis, you may see the secret in the deeps of to-morrow's Germany. The Germany pictured in these words, is the Germany in which false policy, on our part, would breed a new generation of desperation. National Socialism, in wooing young Germany, has given it one thing which we sorely need in this country. We should be mad to destroy that and set the adult Germans of to-morrow thinking 'Hitler was not so bad after all. At least he gave us wider opportunity; our enemies have taken it from us!' That would be the way to breed von Adels and Schultzes again after this war.

... I met von Adel and Schultze twice afterwards in Berlin. Once was in 1932, a year before the Nazi triumph. Von Adel was accompanied by a youth of eighteen, a tragic representative of the desperate generation. He was an unmoneyed but educated lad, who could not afford to go to the University and saw no hope of a career in that Germany. He was a scrap of the human flotsam and jetsam that drifted about the scummy surface of Berlin. I was to become used to much which once revolted me, and did not need Schultze's information, imparted with a wink after the other two left us, to divine the relationship between this unhappy boy, Walter von X and von Adel. Von Adel was a homosexual and he kept von X, who was a male harlot. At an earlier period, von X would have inspired in me a physical nausea. By that time I knew so much of Berlin that my feeling for him was of compassion. I was richer in experience, and realized how little of the fault, in such cases, is often borne by the victim, and how much of the blame by his times, his rulers, and his exploiters.

Walter von X was a goodlooking lad. Berlin was full of young homosexuals who provoked contempt, but somehow contempt refused to come, when called for, in his case.

I saw him once again. I walked along the Kurfürstendamm, one day in 1934, and met him. I was surprised by the change in his appearance. He was bigger, fitter, no longer effeminate and mincing, but self-confident. He told me that he joined the Labour Corps as a volunteer and loved the life. He was now an officer. He was not afraid of work, then! I wondered whether I would ask him something. I decided I would. 'How is von Adel?' I said. He looked at me and smiled. 'I don't know', he said, 'I don't do that any more. *Das mache ich nicht mehr.*'

He was mad for National Socialism and Hitler. 'I've got an aim in life now', he said, 'I had nothing from my life before. It was all the same to me, *mir war alles gleich*. I feel that I have just been born'.

Poor dupe. What a choice was his: to drift round Republican Berlin as von Adel's property, or to give his soul to Hitler! We shook hands and parted, and I watched him go, with swinging stride, towards the Gedächtniskirche.

Where can he be now? Dead, perhaps, at Stalingrad? Watching the end of his dream from a barracks in France? Sitting at a desk in Berlin and falling back into his old ways, from disillusionment?

Who knows? He was of the generation of desperation. Our interest is, to prevent, not to promote, the appearance of another such. The way to promote it is, to be weak in our conduct of the war, infirm of purpose after it, and malignant in our treatment of Germany. The way to prevent it is, to be hard-hitting in our conduct of the war, resolute of purpose and strong in arms after it, justly severe towards guilty leaders, and to abstain from destroying any good thing they may have done amongst much evil.

Think on Germany in this light, gentle reader, as we go through Civvy Street together in search of our future. We must not only know our enemy, but know how to treat our enemy, so that he may not live on a festering hatred of us after the war and fall on us again at the first chance.

But the greatest lesson which the example of Germany offers us is, that victory breeds languor and laziness, and defeat, virility and effort; so that we need *to watch ourselves* even more than we beware of others.

CHAPTER X

'ALL NAZIS AND QUISLINGS'

1935 and Berlin. From a café terrace looking on the Tiergarten I saw a tall man in officer's uniform striding briskly towards the War Ministry. I knew him. He was a former neighbour of mine, in the days before Hitler came to power: the Oberleutnant.[1]

He was the war hero who enjoyed such renown in that apartment house in the Kantstrasse because he once appeared in the Allied list of war criminals. He was of 'the guilty men' of the last war. I told of him in another book. Now that the Republic was dead, he was happy and prosperous again. His uniform fitted him well. The next war would not be long to wait. All was well with his world once more. How he must have smiled when he thought of that list of war criminals! I watched him, lean and upright, turn smartly into the Bendlerstrasse. . . .

In this war, my Oberleutnant is probably an Oberstleutnant, at the least. I wonder if he has repeated his exploits of the last war, when he distinguished himself by shooting Belgian civilians.

The promise of 'retribution' was made last time. It was kept; let none deny this. Our troops held the Rhineland, and this compelled the Surpeme Court of Germany to try some of those guilty men, prove them guilty and sentence them.

The heaviest penalty imposed on any of those accused by the British Government was ten months' imprisonment. The total of *all* the sentences passed on these was *twenty-two months*. Hundreds of British subjects have been imprisoned longer than that in this war without charge or trial.

Most of the accused simply pleaded that they acted under orders. Those who gave the orders either remained quietly in Germany or went to some neutral state; none molested them anywhere. Our politicians were no longer interested, the electoral fruits of their promises having been plucked, and gladly pointed to the sanctity of international law, of which the laws against extradition are an important part.

The refusal of inquiry into the things that were done in *this* country to

[1] See the chapter 'Crime: *And Punishment?*' in *All Our Tomorrows*.

promote the war and weaken our defences, and the repudiation of responsibility for them by the men who did them, makes the talk of 'retribution' in this war sound ludicrously insincere. Nevertheless, we should know whether it is meant, or whether this cry is merely used to scourge the passions of the people when they have been misled into a war. At the least we should this time ascertain whether we have been deliberately duped so that we may approach the future with clearer minds about our own leaders.

Mr. Churchill promised that 'Quislings and traitors' would be handed to their fellow-countrymen for judgment. But these are puppets. How about the guilty Germans? Lord Simon stated on October 7th, 1942, that 'the successful conclusion of the war should include provision for the surrender to the United Nations of war criminals'. But what of those neutral countries; what of the Swiss, Swedish, Portuguese and Spanish extradition laws? Lord Simon on February 18th, 1943, laid emphasis 'on the need to insist on the surrender of war criminals at the signing of the Armistice and before fighting finally ceases', and said the war crimes would be best dealt with either by National Courts (that is Polish, Norwegian and the like) empowered for the purpose, or by military tribunals 'which have the great advantage of speedy action'.

What are the prospects, then, that retribution will be exacted, in a form which would make us safer in Civvy Street to come? I think, none. These vague statements suggest that a few unimportant catspaws may be lynched or executed and that the guilty men will go scotfree.

The same pernicious spirit, of discrimination between people of high rank, however guilty, and humble individuals, however little guilty, seems to govern this question, as that which causes so much injustice in this island.

The war appears to be conducted as a game, from the rules of which members of the Enclosure, on no matter which side, are exempt. Such terms as 'traitor', 'Quisling', 'defeatist', 'Fascist' and 'Fifth Columnist', seem only to be used for the delusion of the masses on both sides of the fighting front. Their passions have to be kept boiling, and their gullibility stoked.

Consider Hess, one of the guiltiest of the guilty men. All information is still refused the people of this island beyond the two scraps contained in statements by Mr. Churchill and M. Stalin: that 'Hess came here firmly believing that he had only to gain access to certain circles in this country for what he described as "the Churchill clique" to be thrown out of power and for a government to be set up with which Hitler could negotiate a magnanimous peace'; and that 'the reason why Hess was sent to England was to try and persuade the British politicians to join the coalition against the Soviet Union'.

Since then, information has again been refused — on November 17th, 1942, eighteen months after Hess landed — by Mr. Richard Law, our deputy Foreign Minister. The only news about him which has been extracted from the Government is that he is being treated as a prisoner of war (although all humble Germans who came here secretly by night have been executed) and that, when other German prisoners of war were put in chains, he was spared this.

How many people in this country realize that the truth, nevertheless, is now out? It was published in the Nazi newspaper issued in Stockholm, which prints only information instigated by the Propaganda Ministry in Berlin. The only thing this story does not tell is, why the British people have not been told the truth. It was obviously published in the hope of warding off 'the measures' (which Mr. Churchill and President Roosevelt long ago announced, but for which we still wait) 'to divert German strength from the attack on Russia'. It appeared at the moment a new German assault on Russia impended (in October 1942).

(For the enlightenment of readers, I interpolate that the fact that Hess is a captive and this country has not joined with Germany against Russia does not suffice to make his mission 'a failure'. As long as we do not strike at Germany, but hold aloof and allow Germany to assail Russia un-molested, it has neither failed nor succeeded; or in other words, it may be called a half-success or a half-failure. This is why the Soviet Government, when the truth was printed in Stockholm, demanded that Hess should be tried; the British Government refused. The 'measures' have been promised again for 1943. Their importance for us, is not that they would help Russia, but that they would bring this war to an end, which is presumably a British interest.)

The Nazi article stated that Hess's flight was not his own independent enterprise, but part of Hitler's policy, and was directed towards an alliance with Britain. 'Naturally' Hitler wished to protect himself against any miscarriage of the plan, and therefore agreed in advance to repudiate all knowledge of it and to give his repudiation additional plausibility by punishing persons who helped Hess to leave the ground. Hitler could not accept as final Britain's refusal to make peace after the defeat of France, and interpreted Britain's refusal to take the step as due to weakness. Therefore Hess was to offer to England a profitable agreement in the form of an alliance to make war on Russia, as the result of which Germany was to receive the Ukraine and the Caucasus oil regions, Japan was to receive Siberia, and the rest of Russia was to be split into separate homogeneous states. Britain's share, which was to be 'guaranteed' by Germany, was the retention of the Mandated Territories, especially in the Middle East, but Germany was to receive back her former colonies. Hess was sent because he was Hitler's official deputy. Also, as he was a proficient airman, he did not need a pilot, and was able to avoid the inconvenience of intermediaries. Hess was to inform the British Government that he came as Hitler's messenger, with full authority, and Germany's public repudiation of him was devised because obviously it was desirable to throw dust in the eyes of the outside world. Englishmen 'were thought to be gentlemen' who would understand and approve, or at least would allow Hitler's emissary to return and not to betray the Fuehrer's frank proposal, but they interpreted the Hess mission as a sign of weakness, and Mr. Churchill did not waste a day, but told Stalin everything immediately and kept Hitler's deputy a prisoner.[1]

We now know as much as we need to know about Hess. You may examine the story from every conceivable angle, but you will not find any reason *favourable to the interests of this country*, why the British people should not have been told the truth. Indeed, we now know everything but the most important thing of all: why information has been withheld from us.

Everything that could be done, has been done, to discourage the public from even thinking about Hess, and about the most important event in this war. Is all the talk about 'guilty men' and 'retribution' blatant falsehood? Are the prime movers in all this in reality completely exempt, and are they joined by a fellow feeling which reaches across all frontiers? What could create more of the 'bitterness and cynicism' which our politicians deplore, than that?

[1] In the absence of any war-winning British blow, Hitler (on February 24th, 1943), twenty-one months after Hess's flight, evidently thought that Hess's mission might yet succeed, for in a proclamation to the Germans he foretold that 'Germany's present enemies will in the end turn Nazi and join Germany in her war against Bolshevists and Jews'.

The signs point to it. Consider the case of William Joyce, nicknamed Lord Haw-Haw. A member of Parliament and a newspaper writter have recently stated that he will be hanged after the war. In November 1942, another Englishman began to broadcast even more violent diatribes from Germany. He is Mr. John Amery, the son of a member of the British Government. Anon suppresses all public references to him. The newspapers ignore him. He is not mentioned in our House of Commons. He is protected by the fellow-feeling of the members of Enclosure. Yet in Brixton Gaol, according to a Member of Parliament, lies an unfortunate man who is there for no other reason than that a relative of his is in Germany, that he is 'the younger brother of my brother'. His brother is William Joyce!

What justice is this? A man who helped Hitler in his rise to power, with money and in other ways, was Ernst Hanfstaengl, who came to this country before the war in circumstances which, again, we have not been allowed to know. He was interned when war began. Then, for some reason, he was handed over to the United States Government, which has seemingly released him. At all events, he has been writing articles in the American press. What hidden influence lies behind this transaction?

But the worst case is that of Prince Paul of Yugoslavia, a declared enemy of this country, who usurped dictatorial powers and tried to lead the protesting Yugoslavs into the war on the side of Germany and against this country. In March 1941, he sent his Prime and Foreign Ministers to Vienna to sign Yugoslav membership of the Axis pact. At this price, Yugoslavia could have enjoyed the preferential treatment which the Hungarians, Slovaks and Bulgars have purchased.

The Yugoslav *people* rejected clemency bought with dishonour in one of the most heroic gestures in history. When the 'Quisling' ministers returned to the 'Quisling' prince, they dared not appear in the streets. The people turned on prince Paul, drove him out, and enthroned the boy king Peter. Within a few hours, German bombs killed 26,000 people in Belgrade.

This prince is now our guest and is vehemently defended in Parliament whenever his name is mentioned!

I can write with knowledge about Prince Paul. He became Regent of Yugoslavia when King Alexander, his cousin, was murdered at Marseilles in 1934. From the moment he began to govern, he was detested by the Yugoslavs, who instinctively mistrusted him.

His palace outside Belgrade lay within great grounds, and around these lay thick hedges and barbed wire defences. If you passed, on the road, you would be startled by sudden movements and you would then see that hordes of gendarmes were concealed in the bushes. This prince lived within a hedge of gunmen. His fear of 'the Reds' amounted to obsession. I recall the hopeless gesture with which a British Minister in Belgrade once spoke to me about that. From the moment of his advent, the shadow of what would happen in 1941 lay heavy on Yugoslavia. The soul of the people revolted against a man who, their hearts told them, was a traitor.

I recollect how British newspaper correspondents were prevented from telling readers at home the real feeling of the Yugoslavs and from exposing this prince. This man, in effect, declared war on us, and then found that the people he ruled, in trust for his dead cousin, spewed him out. This man, in Mr. Churchill's words 'They swept from power', because he sought 'to lead them into a shameful heritage'.

Here, then, is an arch-enemy. He lives, according to Reuter's correspondent at Nairobi, 'in a house formerly occupied by an American millionaire in the loveliest part of Kenya. A British major, a retired provincial Commissioner, lives with him, and the house has a police guard which does not interfere with the Prince's liberty. He frequently goes to Nairobi, according to the Press reports, stays there at the leading hotel and hunts big game with the British major.

Who, if not such as he, are those 'traitors and Quislings' who, according to Mr. Churchill, are to be handed to their fellow countrymen for judgment? This is one of high rank and connections. This is what Mr. Richard Law, Mr. Eden's deputy, said of him on November 12th, 1942:

> The honourable member has represented Prince Paul as being a kind of ravenous tiger who, if he was not put in a cage, might overthrow the whole of the Allied Powers. The fact is that Prince Paul is a weak man, who would never overthrow anyone. The reason why he was sent to Kenya last year was not because this powerful, fierce tiger had to be kept in a cage. It was simply that he had to be got out of the way so that he would not fall into enemy hands, and could not be used by the Axis for their own purposes ... he was put in Kenya because it was

thought better to have him out of the area; because if he had been in that area, being not a strong man, but a weak man, he might, without meaning it, have been used as a pawn by the Axis Powers.

Such words make meaningless nonsense of the pledges about 'retribution'. Who shall, then, be tried? Is social rank the only test? (On March 22nd, 1942, Mr. Churchill again spoke of 'bringing to justice the grand criminals and their accomplices'.)

'Used by the Axis for their own purposes . . .' This man *signed* the Axis pact! 'He might, without meaning it, have been used as a pawn by the Axis Powers . . .' This man *sent* his Ministers to Vienna to sign the alliance with the Axis! That was why the people he unhappily held in his hand rose against him; he betrayed the trust of the dead king, and *led* his people into 'a shameful tutelage'; he has the blood of Belgrade on his hands.

Mr. Law's words provide a grim illustration of the disease which seemingly attacks our Members of the House of Commons when they exchange opposition or a back bench for office. I know, from first-hand experience, that they completely falsify the picture. The inference is that the promises of 'retribution' only apply, if at all, to obscure, friendless and uninfluential people. This is the story of the last war over again.

Mr. Law was among the young Conservative Members who rebelled against the misleadership of Mr. Chamberlain before Dunkirk, so that he at long last withdrew, and the evidence we now have is more than sinister enough to justify their courageous uprising then. In that great debate of May 7th, 8th and 9th, 1940, he said:

In the last few years I and every honourable Member have witnessed one or other prominent Member of the Government — the Prime Minister, or the Chancellor of the Exchequer, or the Lord Privy Seal — come down to the House and stand at the Box in the midst of the wreckage of some policy or other, in the midst of some defeat or other, and explain that there was nothing that could possibly have been done . . . To be associated with policies which always end in defeat and frustration, does not lend strength to your hand when you tackle new policies from a different angle. . . .

Now, Mr. Law stood 'at that Box' and spoke in the spirit of those others all too many of whom still sit alongside him. He spoke as Mr. Baldwin, Mr. Chamberlain, Sir John Simon, Sir Samuel Hoare, Lord Halifax, and all that company would have spoken. If, in the midst of this avoidable war, which was chiefly brought about by such misinformation of the public, so false a picture of one of our enemies, and one of the men who brought Europe to this pass, may be given to the House, our future is very dark.

We approach Civvy Street again. Seemingly we are to find at the very outset one of the sources of 'bitterness and cynicism' we met there last time. A main aim of the Battle in England will be, to restore truth to our public life, for the insincerity of public pledges, declarations, promises, and utterances in general becomes too blatant to be borne.

... I watched the Oberleutnant disappear in the direction of the War Ministry, that day in 1935. I could never look at him without feeling anger and revulsion. I could not forget those wantonly murdered Belgian civilians.

I wonder what tales he will have to tell his cronies after this war, the guilty man!

CHAPTER XI

THE BREED!

This happy breed of men ...
This England!
— SHAKESPEARE

OUR breed does not to-day show the qualities which led Shakespeare to call it happy. I have tried to show how its happiness was stolen and how it could be restored. Foremost among the necessities is, that it should breed again. The breed has ceased to multiply.

Enclosure, the decline of the English countryside, the spread of derelict areas, the growth of squalorous towns, one exhausting war and the approach of another have been the cause of this effect. Another great problem awaits in Civvy Street. We shall not find the happy breed again until we solve it.

About the time the bells did not ring in the New Year of 1943, an old

English lady died, a Mrs. Emily Whiting. She left 156 descendants. She was born in 1849, when the defeat of Napoleon seemed long since to have set life firmly on its hinges. The effects of Enclosure and the drift to urban impoverishment, were not realized, when she grew up. She was one of triplets. Her own family, of two sons and five daughters, was not thought large when she raised it. One daughter bore twenty-two children; the total of grandchildren was seventy-five. Seventy-three great grand-children, and one great-great-grandchild were alive when she died.

This was a belated projection, into the doubting England of to-day, of the blood and spirit of the older England which, whatever its troubles, felt no misgiving about the value of existence and the pattern of the future. It wanted to live, and to give life. It believed that life on this planet would become better; that wars, though they might not cease, would become less frequent; that inequality would gradually diminish and opportunity slowly broaden; that tyranny, oppression and injustice would dwindle.

To-day, this belief has given way to disbelief. That, and not the lack of 'family allowances' causes the thing we now face for the first time since we emerged from the caves: the halt in breeding.

In 1801[1] we were 9,000,000 people, in England and Wales; in 1850, 18,000,000; in 1901, 32,500,000; and in 1940 about 41,000,000. But even the slower rate of increase during this century, has not been due to natural multiplication, but to the fact that fewer babies die at birth and adults live longer. Natural increase has ceased. Thus we have, at present, a stable population, containing an increasing number of ageing and a decreasing number of young people, which will begin to decline when these two compensating factors have spent themselves.

We know, from our own experience and that of France and Germany between 1919 and 1939, that the twenty years after a great war are the dangerous time. The victors incline to a listless despondency, which leaves free scope to the machinations of 'Them', and the vanquished tend towards desperation. Just when we shall need our greatest strength, then, we shall be a nation predominantly formed of old or ageing people, tired from two great struggles, and bearing on bowed shoulders the burdens left by these.

That dangerous period is now inevitable; no future revival can fill the gap left by the unborn children of 1919-39, and the task, of tiding the

[1] See Richard and Kathleen Titmuss, *Parents' Revolt* (Secker & Warburg, 1942).

nation over those critical years until the results of a revival in breeding become apparent, is probably the greatest in our history.

Few we shall be, in any case, when the dangerous years begin. That is our legacy from Messrs. Baldwin, MacDonald and Chamberlain. But that is no reason to relapse into lethargy, to sleep while the story of decline and fall is completed for us by others in a third chapter. If the spirit revives, we shall still be enough to hold our own until the breed begins to multiply again. The danger is, a sagging spirit during those years when we shall have fewer young people than ever before, and more old ones; for among the aged, for some inexplicable reason, is found the weakness which applauds a Munich agreement.

Sir William Beveridge has foretold that by 1960 we shall be 'in a panic about the population of this country'. The only proposal that has been made, to avert the danger and the panic, is 'family allowances'. A sponge would be as useful to stop a leak. Family allowances have been tried in many countries, without success. This catchword is dangerous, in our perilous time, because people's gaze may be diverted by it from the *real* cause of the halt in breeding, which is not monetary, but spiritual — fear of the future.

Our ancestors, who bred so lustily through the centuries, were poor, but not *afraid*. Why should they have been, when any man who could rent a cottage or build a hut might grow enough food on the adjoining acre for any family he founded?

How can that impulse be revived, without which the survival of a free British island and the British Empire seems impossible? Every time we approach the British problem from a new angle, gentle reader, we come to the same conclusion; and that is because this conclusion is inexorable, inescapable, and right.

Ensure the safety of this island, restore our basic freedom from capricious imprisonment without trial, widen the doors of opportunity so that un-moneyed young men and women may reach the higher service of the State, liberate some of the land, preserve the thriving countryside we have made in this war, do away with slums and derelict areas, resume emigration to the kindred lands overseas; in short, mitigate the evils of Enclosure, frustration and class segregation, without abolishing anything, and you will revive a happy breed.

But you will not do it by family allowances. You will never induce people to resume breeding by the payment of so-much-a-week, whether it be the eight shillings proposed by Sir William Beveridge, or the five shillings proposed by the Government. The money might relieve poverty. I do not believe it would produce one more child. The decline in fertility, in our country, has been greatest among the moneyed classes and in the residential counties. Its roots are not want (impoverished nations show the highest birthrate to-day) but fear of the future.

A cash inducement is no substitute for the natural wish to have children, which can only be restored by the revival of faith in the future. A pathetic proof is the increase in the number of conceptions, in this country, after Munich.[1]

The British Empire offers convincing proof that the roots of decay are spiritual. In 1859 the decline of the Maori race, still suffering from despair caused by the British conquest, was so rapid that experts foretold their extinction about the year 2000. By 1871, they estimated, the number of Maoris would be 45,000; in 1900, 29,000; in 1928, 19,000; in 1956, 12,000.

The end of the Maoris was held to be so certain that Sir John Logan Campbell, when he bequeathed Campbell Park to the City of Auckland, left a legacy for the erection of a memorial to the vanished race. The memorial was completed, but happily has not been dedicated, because the reason for it has disappeared. The Maoris themselves were resigned to their fate, saying: 'as clover killed the fern and European dog the Maori dog . . . so our people will be gradually supplanted and exterminated by the European'.[2]

The decline of the Maoris continued until 1896 but was less serious than all foretold, and the recovery since then has confounded all anticipations. By 1901, the numbers were 45,000, and in 1936, 82,000. The Maori birthrate in 1939 was over *forty-six per thousand* against a white birthrate of 17.29. The Maori population at present increases at three times the rate of the white. No 'family allowances' operated here. The Maoris are still an impoverished race, and their future presents the New Zealand authorities with a grave problem. Nevertheless, the return of confidence in the

[1] In Germany alone, before this war, was the birthrate sensibly raised by family allowances. But the inducement was not a few shillings a week; it was a whole series of preferences which gave large families the status of a privileged class. Even this did not prevent a steep fall when the war came, and an even greater one when the hope of victory vanished.

[2] I am indebted for this information to the Rev. G. I. Laurenson, of Auckland, and to Miss Vera Dowie, of the Women's Service Library, Oxford, through whom Mr. Laurenson's paper came to my notice.

future was enough to produce this astonishing result. The Maoris thought their future was gone when the white man came. They felt no joy in life, and did not wish to transmit life. As time passed, and they were neither oppressed nor massacred, their spirit revived. The episode proved that the influences which prompt a people either to commit race suicide, or to breed, are spiritual.

The right influences can be restored to the people of this country, by rulers wiser than were those of the past twenty years. If they should be as unwise, and the people should tolerate such unwisdom, our to-morrows would be fraught with despair.

The only alternative theory would be that the growth or decline of races is governed neither by material nor spiritual causes, but by some impulse which we do not comprehend at all. If we were to yield to that dangerous explanation the prospect would arise that not only the British people, but the entire white race is in decay; that not only *the Decline and Fall of the British Empire* impends but the *Decline of the West* (the name of a book published during the last war by an outstanding German, Oswald Spengler. He feared the submergence of white civilization).

In my belief, his theory of a process of disintegration which cannot be averted, is wrong. No *need* exists for this thing to happen. The decline we have seen in the last thirty years was brought about by bad rulers; and they were all too often the tools of powerful international interests whose machinations and manipulations were not suspected by the people. Thus the events of the past twenty-five years were ominously true to Spengler's gloomy picture of the future. For our halt, or decline in fertility, is shared by nearly all the *white* races of the earth, and this is all the more reason why we should take the lead in altering it; the world asks nothing better than for us to set an example. In Europe, only Poland, the Netherlands, Italy, Bulgaria and Portugal have in recent years reported a birthrate slightly more than sufficient to maintain population numbers; and in the Empire New Zealand, Canada and South Africa.

But the Asiatic nations multiply prodigiously! The 390,000,000 inhabitants of India, over whom we rule with a handful of our forty-something millions, to whom we promise self-government if they behave, increase at the rate of 5,000,000 a year! The 180,000,000 Russians, of whom the overwhelming majority are Asiatics, seem likely to increase to 250,000,000 or more during this century, so quickly do they breed.

The 490,000,000 Chinese still rapidly increase by all accounts. These three together already account for half the human race! They are all very poor peoples, who would think you mad if you spoke to them about 'family allowances'.

These figures vividly show the importance of restoring the happiness, and therewith the fertility of our breed. You cannot entirely ignore numbers, in ruling an Empire that spreads all over the world.

I believe only one European people showed prolific fertility between the wars, the Poles. The reasons are plain to see: the liberation of their country, the enjoyment of their own land, revived hope in the future!

The lesson is clear. To think that we can save the future by the payment of five shillings a week is more audacious than to tell the tides to cease flowing. In this matter of the breed, which cannot stand still or retreat if it is to survive as more than a subject race, we come again to the root of all evil: the unhappy domestic order of our island, its class antagonisms, which confuse its foreign policy, and the bitterness and cynicism these breed.

That could quickly be changed, if the men and women who come back will fight for their country in peace. Only a revival of faith in the future, will set the breed breeding again. Do not be bluffed by talk of 'family allowances.[1]

CHAPTER XII

A TALE OF THREE MOTHERS

In the summer of 1942, three English mothers drowned their babies.

These were dire tragedies, but they do not appear here on that account, for much worse things happened in the England which, as Mr. Herbert Morrison said, 'is as happy at war as it was in the three years before 1939;

[1] The birthrate showed some increase during the last quarter of 1942, but this is probably an artificial and partly unhealthy increase due to reasons which are generally known and need not be mentioned here. The continuing improbability of any real and healthy revival of fertility was indicated by the Government's failure to prohibit the owners of houses and flats from refusing to take tenants with children. It is obvious that such devices as 'family allowances' can have no effect while such heavy discouragements as these, which breathe an anti-social spirit, may be inflicted on parents, and Governments, invested with every 'power' known to man, plead that they have 'no powers' to mitigate them.

a righteous and courageous policy is a great inspiration to a nation in days of hazard'.

In Colchester, a woman who for many years lived with a man to whom she was not married, killed herself and her six young children when she found that she was again pregnant. At Birmingham, a man of sixty-nine, whose six sons served overseas, whose old-age pension was ten shillings and whose fifty-eight-year-old wife earned thirty shillings a week, passed his nights with her in an air raid shelter, and awoke one morning to find her dead at his side. A woman of forty-five, the mother of ten children, left her sixty-three-year-old husband, and the eldest daughter, aged fourteen, to look after the home, while she joined the W.A.A.F., and the logical disasters followed. A baby of four weeks was found in the manger of a paint-and-plaster Nativity in a Catholic church at Leeds. A Swiss chef at a West End Hotel in London, committed suicide 'from worry at the amount of his work and the large number of banquets he was needed to assist in preparing.'

Such things, I opine, point to sadness of the spirit, as did the story of the woman who for nine years went from job to job with the mummies of her four illegitimate babies in a suitcase, and the other who lived alone with the mummies of forty dead cats. This is not fiction; these are fragments from a year's English happenings.

However, other people agreed that this was a happy land; for instance, the woman who wrote to a Sussex newspaper to say, 'The fact that "Jerusalem" was the favourite hymn of our late beloved George V, who evidently dreamed of the ideal community (as far as it is humanly possible to attain it, which probably could only be in a land like Britain), should be sufficient to commend it to every woman'.

The three mothers who drowned their babies belonged to those who were not happy, whose unhappiness even sprang from the war, unreasonable creatures! The human tragedy reaches its darkest depths when a woman kills the child she has borne; the denial of a life just given at such cost in suffering, can only come from uttermost misery of the spirit. A politician might do better to study such things, than the result of a division, the plaudits of a newspaper, or the atmosphere of the smoking-room in the House.

What these three mothers did is only incidental to this tale. They all did alike; the point is, what happened afterwards to each.

Two were working-class women, good wives and mothers. The first took four of her children and threw three into a pond. The fourth escaped. She then threw herself in but 'came to and found herself hanging to a branch'. She was charged with murder; found guilty but insane; and sentenced to be detained 'during His Majesty's pleasure'. All who knew her spoke most highly of her.

The second woman threw herself and her baby into a river. She was dragged out, unconscious. The baby was dead. In spite of this deed, I think every British soldier would revere her. Four days earlier, she learned that her husband was killed at Singapore. Before he went overseas, he said: 'Good-bye, dear. If anything happens to me, don't take up the struggle alone. Follow me every mile of the way. We love each other too much to be parted. Bring the baby with you.'

She was charged with murder and found guilty. The black-capped judge sentenced her to be hanged-by-the-neck-until-she-was-dead, adding the Jury's plea for mercy and his own opinion that the sentence would not be carried out. 'You are the victim of the lusts of the war lords of the world', he said. No newspaper, that I saw, bothered to report the sequel. Presumably she now faces lifelong imprisonment.

The third woman was not insane, nor was her husband dead. She was an officer's wife, related to people of title and rank. She drowned her baby and reported that the deed was done by a stranger. Later, she admitted the act. Her husband, who was on foreign service, never saw his son. When she appeared before a bench of local justices, prosecuting counsel (the spokesman of the public interest) said the case 'was one of a young woman suffering from mental exhaustion which resulted in fits of depression and despair consequent on childbirth, and in one of such fits she took the life of her baby'; 'no-one could do otherwise than feel the utmost sympathy for this poor girl'. Thereon, the local justices found that there was 'no evidence to support a charge of murder', and thus, when she appeared before a criminal court, the charge was merely that of causing the death of her infant son while the balance of her mind was disturbed by the effect of childbirth. Prosecuting counsel (the spokesman of the public interest) said 'there was no dispute that when the offence was committed she was not in her usual state of mind'. Well-to-do relatives offered to look after her. The judge 'approved of these suggestions'; she was bound over 'and immediately discharged'.

Such is the tale of the three mothers. My feeling for each is of compassion but what conceivable justice was there in the differentiation that was made? Why should two humble women, one of whom was insane while the other was moved by motives so much more comprehensible, have been subjected to the whole abhorrent ritual of a murder trial, *if the third was not*?

Sir William Jowitt, when he was Solicitor-General, broadcast the declaration that our law is alike for rich and poor. It is not. None, who judge fairly, would assert that, when they read the tale of the three mothers.

Enclosure, in England, was effected with the help of the local justices, who were often enough the fellow-squires of those who coveted the land, or even coveted it themselves. Fielding knew them, and in *Joseph Andrews* depicted the lawyer who assured Lady Booby that 'the laws of the land are not so vulgar as to permit a mean fellow to contend with one of your ladyship's fortune. We have one sure card, which is to carry him before Justice Frolic, who upon hearing your ladyship's name, will commit him without any further question'.

The institution of the 'unpaid' magistrate is rotten. No person charged with an offence should be brought before any but a trained, professional and paid magistrate or judge. To assume that the ownership of land, managership of a successful football club, or proprietorship of a prosperous business, fits a man to sit in judgment on his fellows, is absurd, and we should loudly reprobate the system if it existed, not here, but abroad. To give any local notable, any big frog in a small pond, such power, is wrong.

A still greater evil is their power to intervene at the source of justice, to reduce the charge on which a prisoner is 'committed for trial' before a judge, in favour of some local clansman. The first two of the three mothers, who were working-class women, found no compassion in them.

We have, in fact, class justice, of which this is a recent instance. It is another of the problems we shall meet in Civvy Street.[1]

[1] An episode of 1942 provided grim comment on this system of 'unpaid magistrates'. A Devon magistrate, aged sixty, shot a girl of twenty-two and then himself. The verdict at the inquest was 'murder and then suicide, while of unsound mind'. The verdict of murder could not be avoided, for the dead magistrate killed another human being. But many people lay in prison who were sentenced by this murderer, or were 'committed for trial' by him. What could be graver? Hence the saving clause, that he was 'of unsound mind'. But was he of unsound mind when he sentenced or committed them? Then every case, in which he ever sat in judgment, should be retried. And what when the same problem arises, not about a local

In an address to the Devonshire Club in 1943, Mr. Justice Birkett recalled the famous case of Elizabeth Canning in 1753 to show 'the great advance which has been made in the administration of justice in Britain during 200 years'. That was a clear case, he said, when an innocent person was sentenced to death; in his own lengthy experience, he never knew a case in which he was satisfied that an innocent person was convicted.

That is true (with the important reservation that for nearly four years now people have been put away *without* trial and that several have been proved *innocent* when their cases were subsequently brought before a judge). Our Courts of Law do not convict innocent persons save through human fallibility. But they, and still more the unpaid magistrates, do deal out different justice to persons accused of the same offence, which is nearly as bad. I would engage to rout any lawyer, however notable, who sought to show that the law is alike for rich and poor.

This is a bad thing, which becomes worse in wartime, and which men of goodwill should work to alter when they return to Civvy Street. The justice which the courts mete out, only reflects the spirit in which the land is governed, and this spirit has been worse in the present war than in the last. Though we have conscription and compulsion, inequality of service and of sacrifice is more blatant now than then.

I told, in *All Our Tomorrows*, the story of a miner who was badly injured in the pit and told his son, before he died, at all costs to get away from the mine; the son obtained other work, but was ordered, on pain of imprisonment, to return to the mine and lower wages, and within a few days was killed in the pit, on New Year's day of 1942. Mr. Ness Edwards, M.P., told in Parliament of a collier who was sent back from the army to work in a South Wales mine, was killed at midday on the fifth day after his return, and from whose pay the colliery company deducted a half-day's wages for his last day under, if not on, earth. Miss Hilde Marchant gave

magistrate, but about a High Court Judge? In the summer of 1942 such a judge was found drowned. The circumstances pointed to suicide. But a verdict of suicide 'while of unsound mind' would have raised problems about his judgments while alive, sufficient to cause heart failure to the entire legal profession. Thus, 'an open verdict' was returned, which means, no verdict at all. His judgments may stand. On how flimsy a basis our whole judicial edifice rests! To make matters more complicated, this judge sat in the divorce court and was an extremely devout Roman Catholic. The Roman Catholic Church refuses to recognize divorce, but counselled him to accept the appointment! Incidentally he was a wit, and liked to tell the story of a Hollywood film star who was married nine times and built a great marble sarcophagus for her own reception after death; she begged a famous poet to write her epitaph and inspiration supplied him with one in four words: 'Asleep — alone — at last!'

this picture of a strike of young miners in 1942: Looking from the train as it approached Swansea, she thought 'there has been some bad bomb damage here', for mines and sheds stood in rows of decay, while girders poked through green fields like iron skeletons. But 'no bomb explosion wrecked this industrial valley, this was the slow rust of peace'. She spoke with a nineteen-year-old miner, Glen Griffiths, brought back from well-paid employment in a factory to work for £2 10s. 0d. in the mine, while the village girls, his schoolfellows, earned £3 10s. 0d. and £4 in the munition works. When his elder brother said, 'it will all be closed down after the war, we will all be out like you', he replied, without bitterness, 'a good thing too brother, for this is torture. We will get away then when they don't want us. They will let us away, for this is punishment here'.

Compare these things with the statement made by Sir Kingsley Wood, the Conservative Chancellor of the Exchequer, that £66,450,000 compensation for coal royalties was to be paid in cash to the coalowners!

The worst thing 'They' have done, under cover of this war, probably is, the imprisonment of such men in derelict areas and coalfields where, in peacetime, they were not allowed to work. Socialist leaders and trade union chiefs, admitted to the Government Enclosure, have been employed to do it.

Tragic is the hope, which these young men express, that peace may soon bring idleness to the coalfields again so that they may escape. They do not see that the same misleaders seek to close even that door. Many Socialist leaders have proclaimed the need for 'the continuance of control' after the war. They mean, that men shall not be allowed to escape from the hideous captivity of the black regions.

The best thing for them, and for England, would be for such men to get away, to return to that part of the good land which should be liberated, or seek a better lot overseas. Even that outlet was denied them before the war. Emigration was hindered. Is that evil practice to be renewed? Is the emptiness of the Dominions to be perpetuated, while we have mass unemployment? Could lunacy go further?

One law for the rich, another for the poor: the phrase is old, but it continues true.

Recently several rich men have announced that they would give great houses and estates 'to the nation'. (Whether any part of such land formerly belonged to the nation and was taken by Enclosure, I do not know, in these cases.) The newspapers loudly applaud their generosity, but examine the facts:

The houses are 'given' with valuable contents. No public access to them is mentioned. Indeed, a condition of the 'gift to the nation' is, that the owner and his descendants shall remain in occupation as long as they wish! 'Such an arrangement', the public reports continue, 'is customary under the scheme of the National Trust for preserving estates of especial beauty or interest with the former owners continuing to live in them, subject to limited public access.'

Access? To what? Why, *the grounds* are 'given' in the sense that 'they will in due time be open to the enjoyment of the public, under such conditions as may be found to be desirable'. This seemingly means that people may be allowed, by way of a turnstile and a uniformed porter, to stroll through the grounds once or twice a week at some future time. The gift to the nation diminishes as you examine it. But that is not all:

'Where the donor and his family after him are to remain in occupation they gain by the consequent saving in taxation and death duties, but the nation also benefits by the endowed preservation of the beauty of the estate.'

Now, that is enlightening! 'The nation' has been 'given' something; what, is not clear. But 'the donor' obtains most substantial compensation for his 'gift'. He continues to live in his house and enjoy his grounds subject to the 'limited public access' to the grounds, which may come about some day. He continues, henceforth as heretofore, to pay his housekeeping expenses and the upkeep of the grounds; this seems no extravagant generosity.

But he is relieved of the taxes he would otherwise pay on them and of the death duties which would have to be paid at his death, or the death of his descendants! Truly is it more blessed to give than to receive, in England. Seemingly we breed yet another privileged class, of those exempt from taxation and death duties, if only their property be great enough.

The owner of a detached villa at Croydon standing in an acre of ground, should clearly present these to the nation and allow his neighbours occasionally to stroll round the garden. He will save himself and his heirs a lot of money.

The transaction strikingly resembles the other practice, by means of which prominent members of the Government party are exempted from the back-breaking taxation of war time, being granted large and non-taxable allowances for 'expenses' while, amid the plaudits of the Press, they patriotically forgo the taxable 'salary' of their offices! It resembles, again, the current practice of making 'tax-free' payments to company directors, managers, and the like. Such evasion makes nonsense of 'Finance Acts' which purport to raise the general level of taxation in the interest of 'the war effort', and of the claim that 'the burden of sacrifice' is equally distributed.

Lawyers blandly explain that the 'Finance Act' of 1941, which raised basic income tax to ten shillings in the pound, 'contains nothing to prevent anybody from entering into new "tax-free contacts" (and thereby immunizing himself from taxation). Thus, the solicitor of a famous brewery company, at the annual meeting in 1942, informed the shareholders that they might continue to pay nine directors their £15,000 free of tax. The cost to the company (that is, to the tax-paying shareholders and tax-paying beer drinkers) would be £30,000, but it was all perfectly *legal*. Conservative ministers refuse to interfere with this practice, and mock their hearers when they proclaim that 'we shall all be much poorer after the war'.

In the same way, the sentences which have been passed, under emergency legislation, on humble and obscure people, are often ferocious. The contrast between them and the toleration which is given to selfish effort to profit from the war, becomes in consequence more revolting.

For instance: In Norwich an elderly scissors-grinder was given seven years' hard labour for stealing goods worth £45 10s. od. from bomb-damaged houses. In a Manchester cellar, a gang of forgers, many of whom bore alien names, began a large-scale conspiracy against the State; they produced 100,000 counterfeit clothes coupons, and a Board of Trade official, after the trial, said that in another two months all clothing coupons would have needed to be called in. The longest sentence was of four years, and most were much less. A 'company director' from Bucharest, who sold coloured water at a high price under some high-sounding name, and was previously convicted ten times for the same offence, was fined £20. A poor woman who threw away some stale loaves was sent to prison for 'wasting bread'. When the London mansion of one of the millionaires of the last war was burned down, and firemen found an enormous store of tea, sugar, hams and other rationed goods, the newspapers fawningly reported, 'All this was legitimately acquired before the war by Lord X; there is no requirement to dispose of it, or any question of confiscation.'

Though not much public resentment is evinced about these things, their injustice is realized and causes the bitterness and cynicism which prelates and politicians lament. It sometimes even produces a protest, to the surprise of those who sit comfortably in the seats of justice or of power; for instance, the Old Street magistrate, who in deference to many appeals cancelled a month's imprisonment which he inflicted on a elderly woman, in ailing health and nearly blind, for harbouring her deserter son. He said he was 'staggered at the public's generosity'.

So much injustice, in war time, yields small hope that a mood of equity towards all will arise, after the war, among those who hold power and wealth. Between the wars, the obsession with money made England a land of pirates, buccaneers and freebooters. Each for himself, and the devil take the hindmost. The hindmost were, the derelict shipyards and coalmines, and the throngs of forgotten men around them.

Victory, in the last war, was a Guildhall banquet for the few and hunger for the many. The spirit of those times seems to live on in the following reports of two municipal banquets held in London in 1942:

Attlee, Bevin, Alexander, Lyttelton, Grigg, Eden, Bracken and Leathers, bowed in turn to the Lord Mayor. So did Dill, Paget, Portal and Pound — and the Chairmen of the Big Five Banks. Once again, as of yore, the guests sipped turtle soup in what was otherwise a war-time meal. And, once again, the City's gold plate came from the safe to decorate what remains of aforetime glories. . . .

The Daily Herald.

The Prime Minister, smiling and debonair, was in high spirits when he spoke yesterday at the Lord Mayor's Mansion House. It was a good war-time meal and a cheerful occasion. 'We are in the presence of glad tidings', said the new Lord Mayor, as he looked upon the happy faces of Cabinet Ministers, civic dignitaries and leading business men. . . .

The News-Chronicle.

Cheerful occasions; the chairmen of the Big Five Banks and leading business men; turtle soup and glad tidings; gold plate and happy faces!

Where, in this picture, are the men who have been separated for years from their homes and families, the widows, the wives who do not even know whether they are wife or widow, the women whose husbands for three years have lain in foreign prison camps, or the orphans of the Blitz?

But the worst injustice is that which particularly revolts, because it thrives in the midst of so much strident clamour about sacrifice and service and 'the war effort', at a time when so many poor and friendless people are so harshly dealt with for the smallest offence. It is the thing called profiteering in the last war, and black marketing in this.

I recall with what bitterness, as a man vainly seeking occupation after the last war, I saw the flaunting wealth of those who became rich through it. Many now sit in the highest places. When this war began, we heard much speechifying, in the sense that 'no great fortunes would be made this time'.

Great wealth has been transferred again this time, from the pockets of the patriotic, hard-working and long-suffering citizen, to those of the avaricious, and much of it has passed through the Black Market: the term we now use to cover all transactions which aim at obtaining an illicit share of things supposed to be equally shared, or at selling such at a profit.

If the newspapers report truly, the rigorous penalties, of which we heard so much in 1941, have remained on paper. They frequently tell of ruthless sentences on obscure people who have done some small wrong, but they have recorded no single case of really heavy punishment awarded to some illicit practitioner who operates in a *big* way. Sentences of imprisonment are rare. Where heavy fines are imposed, the culprit may work these off at so-much-a-day, in relatively short terms of imprisonment and emerge with his ill-gotten gains untouched! In some cases, the defendants have filed petitions in bankruptcy immediately after fines were imposed, and the government has refused to take action when the fact was pointed out that, unless alternative sentences of imprisonment were awarded, this made nonsense of the whole law.

Thus were the mocking birds allowed to alight comfortably on the very thing that is supposed to frighten them. Shakespeare had a word for it:

> We must not make a scarecrow of the law,
> Setting it up to fear the birds of prey, —
> And let it keep one shape, till custom make it
> Their perch, and not their terror.

Our laws against black-marketing offences have indeed been so applied that the birds of prey perch on them; the story of the last war repeats itself.

Illicit profit-making, in wartime, or the illicit gain of a greater share of some commodity than all are supposed to enjoy, is a particularly evil thing because of the way it spreads that cynical spirit among the public which our public spokesmen profess to find unreasonable. When attention has been called to inadequate sentences or evasions, the Government has always replied that it cannot interfere with 'the course of justice'. This answer was given in its classic form when a Member proposed that the Board of Trade should be empowered to appeal against what he rightly called 'derisory and fleabite penalties'. Sir William Jowitt, who was then Solicitor-General, and who broadcast the declaration about the impartiality of British justice between rich and poor, rejected this proposal, saying 'it would break the proud tradition that the Judiciary are free from interference by the Executive'.

In plain English, that means: the Government makes the laws, the judges administer them, and the Government must not tell the judges to apply them rigorously or leniently, for that is a matter for each judge.

This leads to an instructive case in point, for Sir William Jowitt (by that time Minister for Reconstruction), together with two Conservative M.P.s, an admiral and other persons of position, was in September 1942 charged at Canterbury with 'breaches of the Feeding Stuffs Rationing Order'.

Counsel appointed (by the Director of Public Prosecutions) to prosecute in the public interest, said 'The object of the Feeding Stuffs Rationing Order is to secure that everybody receives his or her share of the animal feeding stuffs'. The customer was bound to surrender coupons for his purchases to the dealer; the amount for which the dealer received a buying permit from the Ministry of Food depended on the number of such coupons which he handed in. Some of these dealers, said Counsel, 'obtained far more feeding stuffs than they were entitled to have' and 'misled their customers by delivering to them far more than their coupons entitled them to receive'. (Observe the curious wording of this last phrase.) As a result, 'a number of highly respectable people quite inadvertently committed breaches of the Order'. He was of opinion that they 'neither knew nor realized that they were receiving those excess quantities'. This, he knew, was no defence, but as he thought they were the victims of the dealer, he was *instructed* not to press for penalties.

All the defendants save one pleaded guilty. Small fines were imposed. Sir William Jowitt said he did not know of the excess delivery. He left the running of his farm to his bailiff, and 'I have always been taught that it is very bad policy to keep a dog and bark yourself'. (Sir William Jowitt, an eminent lawyer and former Solicitor-General, would know far better than any ordinary citizen that ignorance of an alleged offence is not a plea recognized by the law.)

The point that interests me is the statement of the attorney who represented the Public Prosecutor 'that he was *instructed* not to press for penalties'. If the Government (as Sir William Jowitt stated in Parliament) may not instruct or in any way use influence on a judge, for the stricter application of the law, surely none, not even a Director of Public Prosecutions, should instruct counsel to use influence by 'not-pressing for penalties'. In theory, the judge remains free to inflict what penalty he thinks right, but in practice, a judge is hardly likely to inflict the same penalty when the prosecutor says he is instructed not to ask for penalties, as he would, if the prosecutor were to use all his talent to obtain the strict rigour of the law.

No equity shows in this. I drew the attention of that Member of Parliament who protested against 'derisory and fleabite penalties' and who received the answer which I have quoted, to this case. His answer would have surprised me if I could any longer be surprised by the things our Members of Parliament do. He said, in effect, that the defendants in this case were only tried before a court because they were 'prominent persons', and 'a withdrawal of the prosecution might have been misunderstood'. Otherwise they would just have received 'a warning, as in so many similar cases'. 'In this case, at least', he concluded, 'the law was not impartial as between the high and the low!'

He meant (he who once protested against 'derisory and fleabite penalties'), that the high were *more* rigorously treated than the low would have been! The facts which were published do not support this opinion. The statement by counsel, that he was 'instructed not to press for penalties', should not be made, when 'prominent persons' are concerned, if the impartiality of the law towards all is to be asserted. Such impartiality is the soundest basis that can be laid for the life of a happy community. It is always difficult to attain, but disbelief in it greatly helps to corrode the spirit of the community.

I began with the tale of three mothers, who all did the same thing, but were most differently treated by our courts. They, too, are the symbols of something that is wrong in England; something which is dangerous for our future, and which we should work to alter, when we enter Civvy Street in search of the future.

CHAPTER XIII

THE CHILDREN OF ISRAEL

FEBRUARY 1939, in Prague. 'One of our Rabbis here', said Doktor Farisy, 'is preaching in the synagogues that Hitler is the Jewish Messiah, because he will cause all those countries of the world to be opened to the Jews, which now are closed to them.'

'The Jewish Messiah!' At the words, a horde of vagrant thoughts, doubts and questions, that long roamed about in my mind, fell into ordered ranks, and I suddenly saw their shape and meaning.

I turned to look at Doktor Farisy's Jewish profile, sharply etched against the white streets through which we walked. A heavy coating of snow made the turrets and gables and alleyways of Prague look even more Hans Andersen-like than ever. It was a lovely picture, spoiled by the feeling of fear that infected the air (for in another month Hitler would come).

We spoke of ways and means of getting out of Czechoslovakia, of Europe. Few spoke of anything else, in those days. Doktor Farisy was born in the Hungarian part of old Austria-Hungary, now become part of Czechoslovakia, and might have argued, according to the day, that he was Austrian, Hungarian, Slovak or Czechoslovak. He was none of these; no drop of such blood was in his veins. He was a Central European Jew. The newspaper for which he wrote, though it claimed to speak in the name of 'Czechoslovakia', employed only such as he: I knew all his colleagues, and they included no Gentiles. If these men were rootless, in the places where they lived, it was because they practised exclusion.

His eyes were set on Kenya, in the British Empire. He wanted a letter of introduction from me to a friend of mine there. Knowing that he would cling, in that Colony, to the method he and his fellow Jews used in Prague, I felt no duty to help him, for I saw in it the same danger to British nationhood, though in other than military form, as the one I knew in Germany. But I liked him personally and gave him the letter.

Sometimes fog suddenly lifts and reveals, in stark clarity, an object hidden before: a tree or the like. So it is on occasion, I find, with things that others say to me. As a knife needs a grindstone, so a mind needs the touch of another mind.

This was the result of Doktor Farisy's words. My disordered thoughts fell into pattern, like the pieces of a kaleidoscope. In the years that followed Hitler's coming, I knew something about the Jews, but did not realize it. The clamour raised by the Nazis against the Jews, which much exceeded the things the Nazis *did*, and the far louder echo of this in the world, blinded people to the truth of what happened, and for a time even confused me, though I was a close observer. Now, in Doktor Farisy's words, I suddenly saw something which I long looked at without perceiving.

'One of our Rabbis', he said, 'is preaching in the synagogues that Hitler is the Jewish Messiah. . . .'

Was *this* to be the final epitaph on Hitler: that he was the Jewish Messiah?

If so, how would the interests of my own country fare? I turned to Doktor Farisy with a whetted interest. . . .

We British approach the climax of the Second World War and the middle of the tortured twentieth century, and strive to retrieve our future from all this misery. In soberly considering the Jews and Jewish ambitions, and the relation of these to our British interests, one great fact stands out like a mountain peak, in the confusion: that a Jewish triumph is all that remains of our victory in the First World War.

When the Second World War began, German disarmament was gone and Germany was mightier in arms than ever before: Germany was mightier in territory than ever before; liberated Czechoslovakia was gone, and liberated Poland and Yugoslavia were about to go, with many other countries; reparations were gone; our security was gone; not even the faint aftertaste of victory remained in our mouths. The only thing that remained from that great struggle, with its millions of dead, was, and is, the Jewish National Home in Palestine, which we promised to build in the midst of that first war. It alone survives. The Jewish spiritual centre exists, with its population of nearly half a million. A Jew may now be born in Palestine and pass through an all-Jewish kindergarten, school and university without speaking anything but Hebrew; work on a Jewish farm or in a Jewish factory; live in a great all-Jewish city; read a Hebrew newspaper and visit a Hebrew theatre.

That is the sole achievement of British arms (save for the conquest of German colonies in Africa, which we did not need) remaining from the Great War. The origins of the Greater War are mysterious enough, and our own future when we have won it still obscure enough, for this fact to lend great probability to the words of the Rabbi of Prague; and it justifies deep misgiving about the clamour raised by many public spokesmen and public prints which, through its violence, tends to make this new war appear to be one waged primarily for Jewish aims.

For appetite grows with eating, and if the demands which are being made by or on behalf of Jewry in this war were gratified, the prophecy of Prague would be fulfilled, and ten or twenty years from now we might, looking back, see only the peak of a second Jewish victory rising from the chaotic memory of the Second World War — and we might then well be worried about the imminence of a third! In 1917, the demand for a National Home in Palestine, with which we too unconditionally associated ourselves, was a lofty one enough; but to-day that satisfied ambition is already contemptuously dismissed as a thing of no account, and much greater things are demanded.

Indeed, the public debate bids fair to develop into a competition among *all* the Powers engaged, friend and foe, to allot large portions of this planet to the Jews! Consider the fantastic stage which this competition has reached. No longer is the aim a National Home *in* Palestine, but *all* Palestine, and much more. Lord Wedgwood, the foremost non-Jewish Zionist spokesman in this country, has proposed the creation of a Greater Palestine for the Jews, existing Arab States to be destroyed and partitioned between the Jews and Turkey (*Testament to Democracy*, Hutchinson, 1942). No sooner did the Eighth Army chase the enemy from Cyrenaica, Libya and Tripolitania than Sir J. Wardlaw-Milne, M.P., proposed (*The Times*, January 24th, 1943) that these lands should be made available 'as another home for the displaced and oppressed Jews of Europe'. Goebbels announced (on March 14th, 1943, while the British

Press asserted that the Jews were being 'exterminated') that Germany 'is not opposed to *the creation of a Jewish State*. This world problem must be solved, but the solution may be carried out *by humanitarian methods*'. The heads of the Anglican, Methodist and Presbyterian Churches of Australia (*British* emigration to that Dominion, with Government assistance, was *stopped* before this war) urged the Australian Prime Minister (on March 10th, 1943) to 'set apart a considerable area of Australia as soon as circumstances permit for refugee settlement' (they adduced 'the particularly shocking German persecution of the Jews'). General Smuts, on March 17th, 1943, suggested to 'a deputation of South African Jewry', which waited on him, 'a confederation of Semitic States in the Middle East to solve the Jewish problem'.

These were but a few of the proposals which were made, for Jewish territorial expansion, but *at the same time* a most vigorous campaign was waged to claim for them unrestricted access to *other* countries, and full rights of citizenship there, or rather, superior rights to native citizens there, for the invariable assumption was, that these incoming Jews should be exempt from military service, but eligible for all employment, and that the denial to them of immediate naturalization would be intolerable cruelty. (For instance, a correspondent of *The Times*, on April 8th, 1943, reported that he knew of three young German Jews who came to this country and built up a business here, which became highly prosperous, through Government orders, when the war began; he described the refusal of naturalization, while British manhood was away at the war, as an insufferable injustice.)

The result of all this is that, as the war approaches its fourth birthday, and we draw nearer to Civvy Street, the aims and claims of Jewry have been put on the pinnacle of public debate, and the clamour about them drowns all other. While the sufferings of our own people may have hardly begun (for the great slaughter of the last war has mercifully not yet come upon us), Jewish demands tend to monopolize discussion, and are marked by an extraordinary duality and duplicity. Unrestricted movement from country to country, and preferential treatment in each, is demanded by the vehement champions of this cause; but at the same time separate national territories, the bounds of which seem to grow from day to day, and which can only be acquired through British arms, are claimed for this race, the numbers of which are given in the reference books as about 15,000,000 (or approximately the population of a small country, far away, which we knew nothing about: Czechoslovakia).

We witness the largest ambitions ever expressed and pursued in the history of the world. Here is something which cannot any longer be denied open discussion: it affects every Briton's to-morrows. When the tone of the present public discussion, and the demands which are raised on behalf of Jewry, are studied, the meaning of the words uttered by the Rabbi of Prague becomes clear.

This is a matter to be examined in a spirit of the most sober objectivity. It is not a question of the goodness or badness of Jews, but of Jewish ambitions, and the effect of these on British interests. Much of the blame for this war lies with those people who were blinded by a sneaking admiration for Hitlerist methods to the German danger, or by a deep fear of Communism to the indispensability of the Russian alliance. People who yield to any unreasoning animosity against the Jews are similarly misled and dangerous. They need only to know what the Jews are, what they want, and how this affects our future. Our leaders have brought us to a perilous pass by supporting *two* conflicting Jewish aims, about which Jewry itself is divided: the claim for equal rights of citizenship *and* the international, territorial, even Imperialist ambition. That confusion must be ended, or we shall come through it to endless troubles.

I have no hostility to the Jews, nor have I found any in the British people. As we go down Civvy Street, in search of the future which was denied us after the last war, we shall encounter forces which strive for power, or territorial conquest, in our world: great nations like Germany and Japan, financial interests like banks, oil undertakings and armaments trusts, and religious organizations like the Roman Catholic Church and Jewry. All pursue aims which reach *across frontiers*, and thus may conflict with our paramount need, the safety of this island.

This is no matter of prejudice; we have the right to discuss whether they will profit or injure us. Our interests and those of organized, international Jewry are not identical, and if I, gentle reader, am much alone in saying this to-day, that is because our politicians and newspapers have come to a dangerous state of infatuation or bondage. The files of British Parliamentary debates and newspapers show that objective debate was formerly common. About 1926, G. K. Chesterton remarked that, by some hidden means, this open argument was being stealthily curtailed.

People, he said, were still allowed to express general impressions about their country, until they came to the case of the Jews; but there the tendency was to stop, and anybody who said anything whatever about Jews as Jews 'was supposed to wish to burn them at the stake'.

Anon has proved most powerful in this matter. To-day, the most substantial arguments are dismissed by the asinine braying of 'Yah! Anti-Semolina!' (or whatever the lunatic saying is) and our entire, once public-spirited Press yields to this servile stupidity. That is not good enough. This repression of free speech in *one* question alone will have to stop.

A large number of Jews has been brought to this country by two Tory Prime Ministers, two Tory Home Secretaries, a Socialist Home Secretary and a Socialist Labour Minister. They were exempted from military service, but allowed to take any kind of employment. They were even given preference in employment, because our own men and women were sent to the Services and factories, or imprisoned if they objected, and employers engaged these newcomers, believing they would not be so taken. We have as much right to discuss this, as our relations with Russia, housing or the Beveridge Report. This concerns *us*.

These Jews should have been received only on condition that they took no employment vacated by a British subject (indeed, the Government gave this promise, but broke it) save under the legal obligation to surrender it to a returning British subject out of work (which legal safeguard the Government refuses), and that they should share the burden of military service (which the Government also declines to impose on them, pleading that they are technically 'enemy aliens', though they are numerously employed in the Ministries and the B.B.C., where they have access to vital military information!).

A very serious statement was published in a London periodical, *The Economist*, in 1939. It caused Sir Abe Bailey, a warm supporter of the Jews, to utter an emphatic warning. It was, that 'the average refugee is more helpful to the community than the average Englishman, whether the standard is monetary, capital, industrial skill or intellectual attainments'.

Hitler never said anything more hostile. This statement gained importance when Mr. Brendan Bracken, who was Managing Director of *The Economist*, became Minister of Information. No Member ever asked whether he shared the view expressed in his periodical. But the Ministry of Information, and the B.B.C., have been foremost among public employers in recruiting Central European Jews. I know, from many sources, the bitterness this causes, among qualified British subjects.

A pledge was given in Parliament that aliens would not be employed, in such Departments, in preference to qualified British subjects. I was in a position to know that the statement was incorrect. A question was put, and the pledge was then reduced: British subjects would be given preference 'provided they were suitable in other respects'. A pledge thus qualified means nothing. This is the beginning of the thing which always starts, when the Jews arrive: exclusion, as practised by Doktor Farisy and his colleagues in Prague.

'The "boys" did not or could not settle down; their jobs had been filled long ago by the people at home.' This was written, by a Jewish author, about the Hungarian soldiers who returned to Hungary after the last war. He is now in this country, and has been enabled, by our Government, to take any job he wishes. 'The Jew must be better in every respect than the Gentile if he wants to attain the same result, and win the same recognition.' These are also his words. The claim is not true. I have nowhere found the Jews cleverer than the Gentiles, or more stupid. They attain immoderate power through the strength of their cohesion, the cement of which is an age old anti-Gentile teaching. The weakness of the Gentiles, few of whom know the Mosaic Laws (of which Hitler's racial laws are the copy in brown) is that they do not realize this.

But if that is the source of Jewish strength, its main instrument is the infatuated Gentile, who is more Jewish than the Jews. From these, we suffer sorely. They are the stupid Gentiles of Jewish anecdote. Infatuation for a half-comprehended cause may drive a man to rabid bigotry.

In this country, examples of such infatuation fill the newspapers. Some are truly grotesque. Here are two:

In the Commons, on August 6th, 1942, Professor Hill 'asked the Minister of Labour whether he is aware that a number of foreign refugee dentists are at present unemployed; and whether, in view of the shortage of manpower, he will cease to reserve further dental students from military service until these refugee dentists are absorbed'. (Our own lads, that is, should be removed to make room for aliens! When the Minister, in reply, cautiously spoke of 'the need to maintain the future supply of British dentists', Miss Eleanor Rathbone said the 'excuses' which were given were 'really untenable'.)

In the *News-Chronicle*, on January 12th, 1943, Mr. A. J. Cummings, quoting Mr. Vernon Bartlett and the *Observer*, asked why our Government permitted the removal of 5000 Italians from Abyssinia to Italy 'without insisting on the release of Jews in at least equal numbers from Axis countries'. (According to the War Minister, on September 8th, 1942, Italy then held 15,500 *British* prisoners-of-war. Should the doctrine then obtain, even in respect of our captives, that 'the average refugee is in every way more helpful to the community than the average Englishman'?)

Those who should lead public opinion often seem to wish the people of this country to think that they regard this as a war fought chiefly for Jewish ends. The confusion is increased by the astonishing factor that in many of the countries involved in this war the Jews *alone* are exempt from military service: for instance, the Jews *in* Germany and the German-occupied countries, and Jews *from* Germany in this country. (Poles and Czechs *in* Germany are conscripted for the German army; Poles, Czechs and many more in this country, by their own exiled Governments; Englishmen in America for the American army, and so on.)

How many such Jews have come here? Public statements vary so much that they bewilder. Mr. Churchill, on April 7th, 1943, spoke of 150,000, up to the present. *The Times* of April 3rd, 1943, spoke of 250,000 *before the war*, claimed that by taking employment here they were 'making a valuable contribution to the war effort', and recommended that all who desire it should be given naturalization. According to Lord Cranborne, in the House of Lords on March 23rd, 1943, they are still coming at the rate of 10,000 a year. (Before this war, our unemployed were between one and three millions; in March 1943 Mr. Bevin reported 100,000 unemployed; on April 7th, 1943, Mr. Dalton, President of the Board of Trade, said 'We can never hope to have continuously 100 per cent employment after the war . . .') Sir Herbert Emerson, chairman of the Central Committee for Refugees in Britain, said in September 1942, '54,000 German and Austrian refugees are doing war work in British war factories and on the land' (this takes no account of those who have entered the Ministries, the B.B.C., the theatrical, medical, dental and other professions, and business and industry). No British figures have been given for the Jewish migration to the Dominions; but South Africa announced in November 1942 that 53,000 refugees reached the Union in 1941 and 1942 alone, 10,000 were given Government-assisted passages to

Australia in the last pre-war year alone, and large numbers have gone to Canada. As to the Colonies, Mr. Churchill stated that 21,000 'refugees from Poland' were being distributed between Uganda, Tanganyika, Northern Rhodesia and Nyasaland (the figure is large enough entirely to alter the structure of the white populations of these British Colonies). Even in August 1939 Sir Abe Bailey, a lifelong friend of the Jews, expressed deep misgiving about the displacement of British stock in South Africa by Jewish immigrants, and this was before the new influx began and native South Africans went off to the war.

According to the reference books, which in this matter are poor guides, the United Kingdom contained 300,000 Jews in 1938. The figure gives as little picture of Jewish activity and influence, even at that time, as an acorn gives of an oak. A fair inference is, that the Jewish population of this country and the Empire is well on the way to being doubled. The newcomers are in the bulk Central European Jews, that is, those of the most marked racial and religious characteristics.

If this were an influx of Icelanders, no problem would arise. We should absorb them, and the new blood would do us good. These people will not allow themselves to be assimilated. Their religion outlaws them if they marry non-Jews, and in the main they cling to this law, usually disinheriting disobedient children. British courts of law have upheld this disinheritance clause of Jewish wills.

The refusal to intermarry is their law, not ours. The Jew, not the Gentile, builds the Ghetto wall. In 1911, one Steinie Morrison was tried for a murder, the scene of which lay in the Jewish immigrant quarter of London; of the fantastic figures which appeared in the witness box, the author of the story of the trial, Mr. H. Fletcher Moulton, said:

> Truly the Russian Jew lives here as an alien — not in the sense that his interests or sympathies belong to any other country, but because he carries his Ghetto with him, a Ghetto whose gates enclose a life which we neither know nor are capable of understanding.

The Jewish Community in this country before the war was not large enough to imperil national interests. While the great core, of any Jewish population, remains armoured in its racial exclusiveness, some always find the possibility to retain their fierce tribal faith and yet to love the land they live in. This is practical compromise, a plant which flourishes in our soil. They keep their self-made Ghetto, but in the daily walks of life are able to adapt themselves sufficiently to the needs and beliefs of the people among whom it is built, for them to be able to say 'I am a Jew, and yet feel for England'.

These are the Jews, of long sojourn here, whom most of us know. I served with one in the trenches, lay next to another in hospital, and flew with a third. They were different, because they would not be the same, but I would have fought, and still would fight, against any third party who sought to make any differentiation between them and us.

These people come to a painful conflict of mind when some happening in the world starts a new mass-movement of Jews. Some (those who may rightly claim to be 'British Jews') know the immemorial trouble that will follow, and refrain from clamouring for the new immigration. But those at the hard core of organized world Jewry, the high priests of the fiercely exclusive and inflexible tribal faith, use all their power (and their power is great) to promote it. It may be laudable in them; but it affects our interests, and we need to discuss it.[1]

The interests of those national communities which are called on to receive the newcomers in their midst, are ignored. Admission is passionately demanded, and once given, is written off as a triviality. We have accepted 150,000 or 250,000 immigrants in this country and have helped

[1] This is what happens: 'One day, a Polish Jew in his caftan abandons some overcrowded ghetto and presents himself at the Hungarian frontier. A gendarme stops him. He is not desirable, this gentleman in the caftan. But from the threshold of his house Jacob, Abraham or Levy sees his co-religionist in the hands of the gendarme. "Alas, Master of the World" (he says to himself), "What, another Jew! We are already too many here. Why doesn't he stay in Poland, plague take him." And while he mutters this to himself, his slippered feet are already in movement and carry him irresistibly towards his brother in distress. The voice of blood and religion speaks louder in his heart than that of his own interest. It has spoken thus for centuries, and never weakens. Jacob, Abraham or Levy approaches the gendarme, and says: "He is a relative of mine, my guest. Leave him alone, he will stay with me." Once more the miracle! The Jew crosses the frontier!' (From J. and J. Tharaud *L'Ombre de la Croix*, Andrew Melrose, 1918.) This is the most revealing book I know, about the great reservoir of Jews in Eastern Europe from which we are now urged to accept a new influx. It is written with deep tenderness for the Jews, and I assume the authors to be Jews. On its literary merit alone, I should have expected this book to have become known all over the world, but the only English translation is still little known and hard to come by. The prevention, by manifold means of the circulation of books which reveal the life of the Jews, even when they are written with such warm sympathy, is a grave aspect of the whole problem, and contributes much to public confusion. The same authors wrote an equally illuminating and excellent book about the Jewish regime of 1918-19 in Hungary, called *Quand Israel est Roi*, Paris, 1921. The newspaper which began to publish this work was threatened with the loss of its Jewish advertisements unless it suppressed the later chapters. The one-sided bearing of the British Press to-day, which refuses all objective discussion of the matter, is attributable to similar influences.

unnumbered thousands more to go to the Dominions; we have spent millions on them, opened all employment to them, and spared them from military service. These are privileges *unique in history*. Yet the foremost champions of the Jewish cause in our Parliament, Lord Wedgwood in the Lords and Miss Rathbone in the Commons, and many others, repeatedly abuse our 'ungenerous' bearing. In a current pamphlet, we are even called murderers for not transporting all the Jews of Europe to these shores.[1]

The first Jewish influx is here. It is the first result of the war. Wiser administrators than those who promoted it should in future watch that this new section of our population does not obtain, at the cost of the sorely-tried and long-enduring people of our island, an improper share of wealth, power, land and privilege.

But now something even more dangerous to our nationhood, our island and our empire impends. This is an attempt to transplant an even larger number of Jews from Central Europe, to transfer to our backs the greatest problem of Europe. The hospitality, shelter and privileges we have already given are dismissed as of no account.

The people we are required to accept are, in the main, the Jews in Poland, that great reservoir from which world Jewry and Zionism are fed. What sort of people are they? The answer is found in the words, written before this war, of a Jew, M. Stefan Litauer, who is now closely connected with the Polish Government in London:

> There is no other country which suffers more from the burden of the social and economic consequences of the Jewish problem than Poland. No other country has such a high percentage of Jews . . . they constitute 10 per cent of the total population of the Polish Republic . . . At the conclusion of the Great War, when the Peace Treaties invoked the right of national self-determination, and nationalist ideas captivated all races, *the idea of Jewish nationalism began to gain ground among the masses of Polish Jewry*. This growing Jewish nationalism was *a check even to that*

[1] A typical example is given by a Jewish writer now in this country who was granted, first entry and then naturalization, and after receiving these boons wrote the following: 'Guarantees have to be produced for the maintenance of the unfortunates, and if at last a bone or a dry crust in the form of an entry permit is thrown to them, the stipulations, provisos and reservations are so numerous that it is almost worthless. Kind-hearted ladies accept highly-educated, cultured women as domestic servants, and treat them as they would never dare treat humble maidservants born in Britain; protected by the police regulations, they can keep the victims in their proper places.'

limited process of assimilation which was going on before. During the years from 1921 to 1931 the Jews in Poland underwent a colossal change. While at the census of 1921, out of a total of 2,849,000 persons of the Jewish faith, 2,111,000 declared themselves as Jews not only by race but also by national consciousness, and as speaking Yiddish, whereas 738,000 regarded themselves as Poles and gave Polish as their mother tongue; at the census in 1931 out of a total of 3,114,000 persons of the Jewish faith, 2,733,000 *declared themselves as Jews by national consciousness and as speaking Yiddish, whereas only 381,000 regarded themselves as Poles.* This process has been growing rapidly during the last few years. *Thus a bare 6 per cent of the Jews in Poland are united with the Polish nation in their hearts and thoughts, and 94 per cent, forming a body of over three million people, regard themselves as an alien element.* No wonder, therefore, that the Poles look upon the Jews as a factor weakening the development of Poland's National forces and standing in the way of a sound social evolution of the country. *Only by the greatest possible reduction in the number of Jews, especially in the towns, can the Jewish problem be solved. The Polish Government must therefore aim at a solution of the problem by a large-scale and planned emigration of the Jews.*

These Jews *felt themselves alien;* they were becoming more so; the problem could only be solved by sending them elsewhere!

Now, we are invited to receive them. That is no *solution* of the problem, but merely its transference to British shoulders. They would remain as alien here as in Poland; they wish this. Even 'the limited process of assimilation' of 1900-14, *declined* during the inter-war years. This quotation explains the nature of the problem more convincingly than any words of mine could. The effort to transfer it to our account is being made with such vigour and clamour that it confuses the issues at stake in the war, and makes its very origins suspect. Those who pursue it, with such noisy disregard for our native interests, are to blame for the growth of a feeling that the war is being waged primarily for Jewish ends.

In November 1942 a great campaign began about the 'extermination' of the Jews. At that very moment, the prospect of our victory first loomed distinct. The Eighth Army conquered in Libya; Italy showed signs of distress; the Germans failed to take Stalingrad; that Germany would be beaten, possibly even in 1943, became clear (and I wrote a play foretelling Hitler's disappearance).

Victory, then, approached. If it came, and found those Jews still in

Europe, they would remain there. If they were to *leave* Europe (if 'the problem' was to be solved by transferring it to *us*) they would need to come away before Victory arrived. Also, the British Government had suspended immigration to Palestine. The 'extermination' campaign began. The power which this particular interest wields over our public spokesmen and Press stands revealed as gigantic. Some newspapers gave more space to this matter than would be devoted to any other in any circumstances which I can imagine. The word 'extermination' was printed billions of times. It was used habitually, without flinching, by Ministers, politicians and the B.B.C. Any who care to keep note of the things which were said, and to compare them in a few years' time with the facts and figures, will possess proof of the greatest example of mass-misinformation in history. All sound of the suffering of the non-Jews who are Germany's captives was drowned.

Contemplate a British newspaper office, in peace. On the Editor's desk lies a cable reporting the statement of a Rabbi in New York that a hundred Jews have been massacred in Warsaw. The Editor forthwith telegraphs to Mr. Jones, his correspondent in Warsaw, to confirm the report. Mr. Jones investigates, and replies that it is untrue; it goes into the wastepaper basket. Or he says it *is* true, and it is published. But other Englishmen, beside Mr. Jones, live in Warsaw. If the published report is untrue, they will protest; other newspapers will expose the malpractice of this newspaper, in printing false news; Mr. Jones will lose his job. Innumerable checks exist *in peace* on the accuracy or inaccuracy of published statements.

Now come to the same Editor's room in war. The same cable lies on his desk. Warsaw is in enemy hands. The cable comes from New York. No means exist to verify or disprove it. The Editor, if he print it, should advise his readers to withhold judgment until verification is possible. But such journalistic scruple seems dead. The report is published as authentic news.

(I give this glimpse of the mechanism of a newspaper because I find that most people are more ignorant of it than they are of parthenogenesis, and for the better understanding of what follows:)

Before November 1942 none ever suggested that the Germans practised racial discrimination *in cruelty*. Jews and non-Jews suffered alike; but as the non-Jews were twenty times as numerous, their suffering was as much more, as the whole is greater than the part. Indeed, the *New States-man* remarked that 'Hitler subjected the Jews of Germany to every imaginable form of insult, robbery and oppression' (he subjected many more *non-Jews*, all over Europe, to the same things) 'but he did not slaughter them'.

Now, when the war was over three years old, like a bolt from the brown came this news that he *was* slaughtering them, and they must therefore be brought to England! How, if they were exterminated? That point was ignored; the word 'extermination' was deliberately chosen. It means 'to root out, destroy utterly'. (If that is not clear enough, the *New Statesman* said: 'Hitler is engaged in exterminating the Jews of Europe, not metaphorically, not more or less, but with a literal, totalitarian completeness, as farmers try to exterminate the Californian beetle'!)

We were told, then, that the Jews were being 'exterminated', and we must therefore receive them. We are entitled to examine the truth of this, since it is the basis of the claim made on us, mainly on behalf of those Jews in Poland who most tenaciously hold to the teaching (expressed by the Chief Rabbi in London) that 'the mission of the Jew is first of all to be a Jew'. (Hitler has used those very words about Germans.)

The claim was, that something *different* was being done to the Jews, something *more* than the non-Jews suffered: 'Nothing else in Hitler's record is comparable to his treatment of the Jews', the *News-Chronicle*; 'For Hitler the Jews were and are the first and principal victims of a frenzied malice manifest in his earlier outpourings as an irresponsible political agitator', *The Times*; 'Upon this people, the Jews, the fury of the Nazi evil has concentrated its destructive energy', the Archbishop of Canterbury; 'The worst cruelties are reserved for the Jews', the Bishop of Chelmsford; 'The persecution of the Jews is, however, unique in its horror; it is deliberate extermination directed against, not a nation, but a whole race; this is a horror unprecedented in the history of the world', the Archbishop of York.

These statements are untrue. I saw Hitler's work with my own eyes, from the day he came to power until the eve of this war. Nineteen-twentieths of the inmates of his concentration camps were non-Jewish Germans; nineteen-twentieths of his victims outside the German frontiers are non-Jewish non-Germans. This distortion of the picture has gone on since 1933. I felt misgivings about it then, when his first cruelties were practised, and I noticed that the Jewish share of the whole was being put out of all proportion in the foreign Press.

But now the *suggestion* has been crystallized into a definite *statement* which I would not dare challenge if it could be upheld: the Jews in Europe are being 'exterminated'. You must not use this big word unless you mean physical extinction. What was the evidence, first that 'extermination' was ordered, and second, that it was carried out?

(1) *The Times* of December 4th, 1942, spoke of 'a memorandum compiled by underground labour groups in Poland' which stated, 'one of the war aims of Hitler's regime, and one which has been publicly proclaimed by its highest authorities, is a complete extermination of the Jews'. The Archbishop of York said on December 9th, 'The extermination of all the Jews in Poland has been decided on and will be carried out'. The *Manchester Guardian*, on December 11th, spoke of some 'evidence available in London' that 'a plan was proposed to Hitler last June that the Jews [in Poland] should be exterminated by Christmas . . . He hesitated for a time but soon relapsed and decided to gratify his lust for cruelty by adopting the original proposal . . . One need not suppose that Hitler has signed an actual order for the destruction of the Jews, which is strongly reported but at present unconfirmed'. *The Times*, on December 12th, said 'Hitler has boasted of his intention to eliminate every Jew in Germany under his yoke'. Mr. Eden, on December 17th, spoke of 'Hitler's oft-repeated intention of exterminating the Jewish people in Europe'. *The Times*, on December 21st, quoting 'a statement issued by the Allied Information Committee', said 'Himmler, after a stay in Warsaw, issued an order that half the Polish Jews were to be killed in the course of a year'. The Archbishops of Canterbury, York and Wales, in the name of all the British Bishops, in January 1943, stated, 'The extermination already carried out is part of the carrying into effect of Hitler's oft-repeated intention to exterminate the Jewish people in Europe, which means in effect the extermination of some 6,000,000 people'. The Roman Catholic Cardinal of Westminster and the head of the Salvation Army associated themselves with such statements, which were repeated innumerable times in the radio and Press. On January 9th, the *New Statesman* said, 'In July of 1942 Himmler gave the necessary orders for extermination on a continental scale'.

(2) On December 4th, Mr. Vernon Bartlett wrote, 'According to

cables from Dr. Stephen Wise, President of the World Jewish Congress, and Dr. Chaim Weizmann, President of the World Zionist Organization, confirmation has now been received of an order issued by Hitler for the extermination of all Jews in Nazi-occupied countries before the end of the present month' (then how could they be rescued?). 'The number of Jews who have already died cannot, of course, be estimated with great accuracy. In the opinion of the World Jewish Congress roughly two million out of the three-and-a-half million Jews in Poland have been murdered by the Nazis since the outbreak of the war'. Almost on the same day, the World Congress, according to *The Times*, 'issued a statement on Nazi massacres of Jews in Europe showing that of the 7,000,000 Jews who normally live in the territories now under Nazi occupation, 1,000,000 have been cruelly done to death'. Mr. Harold Nicolson wrote in the *Spectator* of December 25th, 'In order to assuage his insane hatred of the Jewish people Hitler, with Himmler as his main agent, has carried out the murder of some 250,000 men, women and children in cold blood'. Mr. Harold Nicolson wrote in the *Spectator* on December 25th, 'In October 1940, the Germans interned 433,000 Warsaw Jews in a special area or ghetto which they surrounded with a high wall . . . For the month of October 1942, only 40,000 ration cards were printed'. (His clear inference, and he says 'there can be no doubt whatever of the facts', was that the number of Jews in the Warsaw Ghetto was reduced from 433,000 to 40,000 by 'extermination'.) The Jewish Labour representative on the Polish National Council in London reported, in March 1943, that 'only 200,000 Jews remain in the Warsaw Ghetto'.

Readers may compare these quotations for themselves. 'Extermination' *was* ordered; it was *not* ordered, but strongly suspected; it was ordered for *half* the Jews in Poland; for *all* the Jews in Poland; for all the Jews *in Europe by the end of* 1942. Two out of three-and-a-half million were already dead, on December 4th; one million out of seven million were already dead, on the same day; 250,000 were already dead, three weeks later. Thus spake our leading public men.

This was the factual basis of the most stupendous political and press campaign in my experience. I suspect that I am better informed about German affairs than many of the people who spoke thus, and I know of no 'oft-proclaimed intentions' or 'orders' to exterminate the Jews. Hitler is noticeably reticent on that theme. Any threats he has uttered cannot compare, in ferocity and iteration, with his threats to exterminate England, the British Empire, Bolshevism and other things. The only threats I know, which promised 'extermination', were clearly aimed, not at the Jews, but at the Czechs, Poles and Serbs, who are the *foremost* objects of German detestation. Such was Hitler's statement, on February 24th, 1943, that he would 'not spare *alien lives*', and its meaning was pointed two days later by Frank, the Czech 'Protector', when he said, 'Stalin could only enter Germany as a victor over the body of every single German *and over the body of every single Czech*'. The only authentic instance that I know (the Germans themselves announced it) of *local* extermination in this war, was the extermination of every Czech man, woman and child in the village of Lidice, where I once received most friendly hospitality. Similar, though smaller massacres have been committed on Frenchmen, Serbs, Norwegians and Greeks: the Germans published them.

The other evidence of 'extermination' consisted of two documents. The first was a Note sent in December by the Polish Government to the Allied Governments. According to the newspapers it began by drawing attention to 'the methods employed by the Germans in order to reduce the population to virtual slavery and ultimately to exterminate *the Polish nation*'. (The Jews of Poland refuse to consider themselves part of the Polish nation; but this Note was published under such headlines as 'Persecution of the Jews'.)

The second document was published in December, by the 'Inter-Allied Information Committee'; it gave 'a general picture of the persecution of the Jews by the Germans'. (This is seemingly not on public sale, and I rely on newspaper summaries, published under such headings as 'The Foulest Crime on Earth'.)

In respect of this document, and without disrespect to it, I must mention again that verification is impossible in war time. Its contents were published throughout the Press without any word of editorial caution. Here are two of its statements:

'Of the 86,000 Jews living in Yugoslavia on April 6th, 1941 (the day of the German invasion of that country) only 1000 remain alive; the rest have been brutally murdered' (a Sunday newspaper). I hope to recall that statement in a few years' time, when facts can be ascertained.

'On May 15th this year the German Governor of Belgium published a decree tantamount to an order of extermination of all Jews residing in

Belgium. Men from the age of 18 to 60 and women from 20 to 55 were obliged, on pain of removal to a German concentration camp, to accept any form of work offered them by the Labour Exchanges, no matter what their health, family obligations, or business.' (Several newspapers.)

If that is 'extermination', we are being exterminated in this country, by our Labour Minister, who wields similar powers. All non-Jewish Germans, Belgians, Frenchmen and the rest, are subject to exactly that German compulsion. If *that* is 'extermination', the Belgians were exterminated by a German Jew in the last war, Walther Rathenau, later Foreign Minister, who on September 16th, 1916, wrote to propose to General Ludendorff 'the solution of the Belgian labour problem, which can be achieved only if the 700,000 workers there are brought on to our domestic labour market without regard to questions of international prestige and even if the American Relief work should break down in consequence'!

Thus may credulous people be brought to believe that the thing they suffer themselves is 'extermination' for others.

Among other reports were these.

The *Daily Herald* of December 16th gave an extract from a speech by the chief Rabbi 'as copied from the manuscript'. It was to the effect that on July 27th, 1942, 500 Jewish women of a town near Kieff were ordered with their babies to a stadium where ('an eye-witness declares') German soldiers dressed in football clothes snatched the infants from their mothers' arms and used them as footballs, bouncing and kicking them around the arena. Of this report, Mr. Hannen Swaffer said 'Never since the days of the martyrdom of Christians in the Colosseum by Nero has such a story been told'. A correspondent of the *New Statesman*, who signed a Jewish name, remarked, 'May I, with a full sense of responsibility and of the possible opprobrium involved, say that I do not believe this story, and regard it as a fabrication from beginning to end. If anyone on the strength of this ventures to accuse me of pro-Fascism, or of any complacency in respect to the brutal manifestations of totalitarianism, I engage to flay his intellectual hide for him, however thick it may be'. (The *New Statesman* said, 'We agree with our correspondent in regarding this story as nonsense'.)

One London newspaper printed information 'from Moscow' that Hungarian Jews in bowler hats were driven in front of German troops in Russia to explode land-mines. Another, quoting a Rabbi in New York, stated that 93 Jewish girls in Warsaw poisoned themselves in a house rather than yield to German officers.

The 'evidence' about extermination clearly would not impress impartial judges. Nevertheless, no information conflicting with it was allowed to be published. A little is available, and I give two examples.

In Roumania in 1940, under King Carol, a wealthy Jew, Max Ausnit, well known in circles of international finance, was sentenced to six years' imprisonment for fraud and currency offences. After King Carol's flight, the Germans became the real rulers of Roumania, and a puppet government took office. The Germans installed Albert Göring, a nephew of the Marshal, as their representative on the board of Ausnit's chief enterprise, the great Resitza Iron and Steelworks. Soon after this, Ausnit was released and given an official testimonial, to the effect that his character was stainless, the charges against him having been made 'on purely political grounds'. This incident is hard to fit into the picture of 'extermination'.

'Extermination' was said to have been particularly ferocious in the Warsaw Ghetto. In 1942, a book about the German treatment of the Jews in Poland was written by a Jew, Mr. Simon Segal, for the Research Institute of the American Jewish Committee, and published in America. It covers a period earlier than that in which 'extermination' *allegedly* began, but gives so different a picture from the 'extermination' reports, which are unverifiable, that I feel entitled to allude to it. Of forced labour for the Jews, for instance ('tantamount to extermination', this was called), Mr. Segal says, 'Like all evils, the labour battalions and labour camps may have some favourable results. Young people who were never accustomed to manual work have been forced to work with their hands. In a free Poland they may become very valuable workers'. In spite of the terrible conditions, says Mr. Segal, the Jews carried on 'intensive activity in all spheres of life'. The Jewish Self-Help, from a headquarters in Cracow, operated 250 branches in various towns. It extended aid to individuals and distributed clothing, condensed milk and other food products. The Society for the Promotion of Health performed extensive medical work; the central organization for the care of children maintained orphanages. There was also 'much cultural activity'. In July 1941 the Nazis 'permitted libraries and bookshops to open'. 'Many public gatherings were organized in the Warsaw Ghetto in connection with the 105th anniversary of

Mendele Moicher Seforim and also in commemoration of Peretz and Bialik.' There were 'three Yiddish theatres and concerts are organized'.

A wide gulf obviously exists between this picture and that of 'extermination', and satisfactory evidence has not been given, that this gulf has been actually traversed.

The suffering which the Nazis have brought to Europe is appalling. It caused the embitterment of men like myself, who thought the last war was fought for an ideal, because it was foreseeable, and we who saw it coming clamoured, at enough cost to ourselves, to have it averted. But I have never been able to disguise from myself the fact that many more non-Jews than Jews thus suffered, or to suppress the question, why these proportions were falsified in the picture given to the greater world. Now that political demands of the first magnitude are launched, on the strength of this distorted picture, the thing becomes of grave importance to us. One great influx of Jews has already come to us. We are asked to receive another and to open Palestine for many more in breach of our pledge to the Arabs.

The perturbing thing is, that the campaign has revealed the British people, whose interests are also at stake, to be completely without representation, in this matter, in Parliament and the Press. Not *one* voice has spoken, to question the authenticity of the evidence, though this is riddled with contradiction; or to urge that British interests also should be borne in mind. All have clamoured that the Jews are being 'exterminated.'

Indeed, the only reasonable voice in all this tumult came from America, and it administered a much-needed rebuke to the boundless demands which were raised here. When the British Government, at the climax of the 'extermination' campaign, invited the United States Government to open discussions, the reply stated with uncompromising clarity the following opinions:

(1) The refugee problem should not be considered as being *confined to persons of any particular race or faith; temporary asylum* should be found for refugees *as near as possible to the areas in which these people find themselves*; (2) they *should be returned to their homeland with the greatest expediency on the termination of hostilities*.

In other words, the United States would not have the problem transferred to its shoulders; this country might, if it wished. Whether this cold douche of reason has restored our own rulers to a wiser mood, we cannot foresee, as I write. They seemed to be on the verge of placing on our backs the greatest problem of Europe.

The 'extermination' campaign, however, has already produced a result of the gravest importance for our future. This is the United Nations Declaration read by Mr. Eden on December 17th, 'that those responsible for these crimes' (that is, crimes against *Jews*) 'shall not escape retribution'.

Our failure to exact retribution after the last war is the second main cause of the present one. After this war, retribution will be even more essential, because the Germans have now reintroduced into Europe something which we thought banished: torture. In earlier books, I expressed deep misgiving about the hesitation of the British Government in stating its intentions in this matter.

But on December 17th the promise of retribution was linked *exclusively to the sufferings of the Jews*! No single word was given to the crimes committed against Czechs, Poles, Serbs, Frenchmen, Hollanders, Norwegians, Greeks, Belgians and the rest.

We have made no graver mistake. We formally tell the Germans, from our House of Commons, that anything they may endure at our hands will be solely on behalf of the Jews! The inference is that they may with impunity oppress, deport and murder Czechs, Poles, Serbs and others. We have lent our name to the threat of *a Jewish vengeance*! Do we *wish* to plant the seeds of hatred for us and a new war?

After that ill-omened declaration, the members, who have a supernatural gift for doing the wrong thing, unanimously rose and stood in silence. 'Such a scene has not been witnessed within the memory of man', gladly wrote Mr. Harold Nicolson. The words are inexact. Just four years before, these same Members rose as one man, not silently, true, but whooping and weeping. They applauded a disastrous deed, which made this war inevitable. We may expect no good from unanimous demonstrations in this interminably long Parliament.

For the Jewish vengeance is a thing known in Europe. The people of this too-sheltered island do not realize that. Europe has seen three recent examples of it, in Russia, Hungary and Bavaria.

How many recall, amid the clamour for 'A Jewish State', that our time has known *three* Jewish States? All save one vanished quickly, but the experience remains. Current events make it necessary to revive their memory, and to delineate the features of Jewish vengeance which were common to all. We should be mad indeed to force on Europe, in the name of 'retribution', conditions similar to those of 1917-20.

The early Bolshevists, of 1917-19, were predominantly imported Jews, not Russians, and the early massacres bore the signs, not of mob violence, but of vengeance taken by imported Jewish rulers. The Netherlands Minister in St. Petersburg (in a report to London which was published in a British Government White Paper *and then suppressed*) testified to the overwhelmingly Jewish and non-Russian nature of the first Bolshevist Governments, the leaders of which were shipped to Russia from other countries. In a report to a United States Senate Committee in February, 1919, the Rev. George A. Simons (who was Superintendent of the Methodist Episcopal Church in Petrograd from 1907 to 1918) said that of 388 members of the Bolshevist Government 371 were Jews, and 265 of these Jews from the Lower East Side of New York. *The Times* of March 1919 reported that 'of the 20 or 30 commissars or leaders who provide the central machinery of the Bolshevist movement, not less than three-fourths are Jews'. In 1920, 447 of the 545 members of the Bolshevist Adminstration were Jews. Jews predominated in government service, of all grades, and even in 1933 the *Jewish Chronicle* stated that 'Over one-third of the Jews in Russia have become officials'. In 1935 I saw this predominance of Jews in the Soviet service. The Jews formed a trivial proportion of the population, but monopolized officialdom, which is the equivalent, in this country, to monopolizing the best houses, food, clothes and motor cars.

(I do not refer to Russia of to-day, for I do not know the present situation, and the facts, like those about the Jews in Poland, are behind a high wall insurmountable in war time. An alliance with Russia is indispensable to our safety after this war. Whether Jewish paramountcy remains or has been reduced, my conviction is unshakable that our island safety demands a firm alliance with that country; it is the Russians who *fight*.)

Russia, whatever it is now, was then a Jewish State. 'Anti-Semitism' was immediately made punishable by death. That meant, that none might discuss the new régime, though it was unique in history.

Even human credulity cannot believe that the Russian chaos threw up all the best men, and lo, these were all Jews! In the pantomime a spring trap suddenly projects the demon king on to the stage; in Russia, obviously, a similar hidden mechanism was ready—and it dealt only in Jews, who came from abroad! These, again, worked only with other Jews.

It is proved by what happened elsewhere. In Hungary, new figures loomed from the mists of military collapse — and they were not Magyars, but Jews! Across the frontier, from Russia, came Kun, Szamuelly and Rabinovitch. They, too, set up an all-Jewish régime. True, they set a straw Goy in the President's chair, Garbai. But Béla Kun issued the death warrants, Tibor Szamuelly dashed round the countryside in his red train to execute them, Arpád Kerekes (Cohn) strung up the victims, Béla Vágó eagerly helped. 19 out of 20 leading men of this period were Jews. Budapest lay under a Directorate of five Jews, and a Jewish Public Prosecutor dispensed law.

This was the second Jewish State, the second anti-Gentile and anti-Christian régime. It collapsed under the weight of foreign hostility. The Jewish rulers escaped abroad. Its deeds were bloody — and bear the marks of anti-Gentilism. The 'Lenin Boys' did not kill Jews. Indeed, the régime bred resentment against the Jews, for these went too far. The Hungarians are devout, and though they listened to the attacks of the Political Commissars on Christianity, the country received a shock when a Jewish youth, Leo Reisz, spat on the Host during the famous procession of the Sacrament. (I should add that when I knew Hungary, between 1934 and 1939, the Jews were again more prosperous and powerful than in any other country I knew.)

The third Jewish State reigned in Bavaria from November 1918 until May 1919. Again, when Germany collapsed, Jews came from abroad to Bavaria and chose other Jews for their colleagues. Levine was the Jewish emissary from Moscow. Prime Minister was Kurt Eisner, another Jew. Others were Ernst Toller, Erich Mühsam, Gustav Landauer, and Königsberger:

> There was chaos in the city of Munich. The Spartacists . . . became more lawless than ever and the whole aspect of the city changed: instead of the peaceful Bavarians and a sprinkling of soldiers there were processions of women with terrible faces parading the streets waving red banners and calling for revenge; and there were sailors from the north, Russians in fur coats, Poles and Jews, until one had the impression of being in an Eastern town. The Bavarians, while easily influenced in

this disordered time, were themselves never cruel or violent; it was always their alien leaders, the professional agitators, who were the extremists.

From Henry Channon, *The Ludwigs of Bavaria* (Methuen, 1933).

This is the most important of the three Jewish régimes, for us to-day, because Adolf Hitler was in Munich during its rule. He did not escape from Munich and join the assembling anti-Bolshevist forces, like other patriots. He stayed *in Munich*, and was a soldier under the orders of the Jewish Red Government! *This period in his life has never been explained and is ignored in the literature about him.* Even more significant, and still less known, is the fact that one of his first acts as Chancellor was *to imprison Count Arco-Valley, who shot Kurt Eisner in* 1919! (This desperate young German officer, several times wounded and decorated in the 1914 war, wrote before his deed: 'Eisner is an anarchist and a Bolshevist Jew. He is no German, does not feel German, and he undermines every German sentiment: he is a traitor to his country. The whole nation cries out for delivery. My reasons for my action are: I loathe Bolshevism; I love my Bavarian countrymen.' Arco-Valley was hit by four bullets, but recovered; sentenced to death but reprieved; his fortune was confiscated for the benefit of Eisner's *two* widows! The only plausible motive that suggests itself, for Hitler's arrest of him, is the desire to remove witnesses of Hitler's conduct in Munich in 1918.)

This régime, like the others, was primarily anti-Gentile and anti-Christian. When threatened by assault from without, it arrested hostages, including women, from among the members of a small druidical sect (of the kind which always flourishes in South Germany). They were anti-Jewish, and anti-Christian! These were shot!

These things happened twenty-five years ago. But for this war they might have been forgotten. But the British Government, by the ill-omened Declaration of December 17th, 1942, has revived their memory. For those were Jewish vengeances.

If we befriend ourselves with such things (and they move behind the scenes again to-day) the events which led to this war will become more than ever suspect. Until 1918 none would have believed in those hidden men, and that hidden mechanism, which the end of the last war revealed. But it was there; the spring trap was set, and suddenly projected the demon king on to the stage.

None of those evil régimes could have been established but for the weapon of imprisonment (and execution) without trial. That alone enabled men, sent from New York to Russia, and from Russia to Hungary and Bavaria, to surround themselves only with men of their own kind and rule by terror. And that is the danger which Regulation 18B embodies, in this country. Since its powers were granted, a subtle campaign has been waged to have them put to new uses. They were first given for use against 'Irish terrorists' (what nonsense that sounds to-day), then enlarged for the benefit of 'Fifth Columnists' when invasion threatened (this now sounds almost equally silly). To-day, the reasonable precaution of 1940 has deteriorated into a régime of indefinite imprisonment for people whose very names are unknown, still less, of what they are accused. And during this later period a stealthy change has crept into the Parliamentary and Press debate about these powers. *Many speakers and writers now urge the prolongation of this régime and its use against any they dislike*; the debate becomes an anti-British one. This is the beginning of the evil thing I have described.

The weapon of wrongful imprisonment commends itself to some people on one ground alone: they would like it used for the suppression of that which, because they are too craven or too ill-informed to face debate and answer arguments, or because they pursue ulterior motives, they call 'Anti-Semitism'. They seek with this word to dismiss all honest native misgiving and would like to have imprisoned all who will not be deterred from expressing those well-founded misgivings.

The next step, if they could achieve it, would be a law, on the Bolshevist model in Russia, Hungary and Bavaria twenty-five years ago, 'against anti-Semitism'. The *Daily Worker*, immediately it was released from suppression, began to call on Mr. Morrison 'to put the rats behind bars,' and the same language has been used by a Member of Parliament who miscalls himself 'Independent' and by a newspaper which pays daily lip-service to Liberal Democracy and gives more space to the wrongs of the Jews than any other subject.

A danger exists here. I remember the Zinovieff letter and saw the Reichstag fire. In November 1942, the *Daily Worker* reported that cries of 'Perish the Jews' were used at a public meeting, and at once Jewish newspapers urged that 'Mr. Morrison should act'. The police officials who watched that meeting were too honest to connive and reported that no such words were used, so that the Government spokesman rejected the demand, which was then raised in Parliament, for 'steps to be taken' (which meant, that innocent people should be put away). But we cannot always count on honest men. Soon afterwards, a more serious thing happened. A bust of Lenin was found bedaubed with the letters 'P.J.', which are said to stand for 'Perish Judea'. The Soviet Ambassador made official protest.

I do not know my own face in a looking-glass, if I do not recognize in that the incident staged to further a political aim. We may open our newspapers one day to read of something graver than the bust-smearing incident. If we do, it will be the work of the hireling, the *agent provocateur*. A demand would then be raised to suppress all discussion of the Jewish question. If ear were lent to it, we should approach the plight of Moscow, Budapest and Munich in 1919.

Without antipathy against the Jews, but with their own interests constantly in mind, people should recall these things. They happened in our time, though not in our island; and this war, which was of such dark beginnings, produces the possibility that they might recur.

The same influence, hidden but powerful, works to confuse our foreign policy and our war aims:

In November 1942, British and American troops, superbly conveyed and convoyed by our Navy, landed in French North Africa, after secret talks with French leaders which ensured that little resistance would be offered, or none. This was a rare moment of glory in the war. Who can picture the resurrection of France without deep emotion?

The British people, for two years before this, were confused by much drivel about 'The men of Vichy' (among whom the only first-class professional traitor was our accomplice of the Hoare-Laval Pact, Laval). This was seemingly meant to divert their attention from their own Men of Munich, and from the dark omissions of what Mr. Churchill called 'the astonishing seven months of the phoney war' and of the astonishing seven years before. The men who were left with a prostrate France on their hands, and no Channel to save it, while its manhood was held hostage by the enemy, possessed one last hope: to temporize during the further development of the war, to hold the French fleet and French African armies as a threat over the German head, and to re-enter the war, with those weapons, if and when this became possible.

In November 1942 this happened. Darlan, a French admiral who never forgot the Anglo-German Naval Agreement of 1935, made behind the French back, saw the golden chance, facilitated our landing, and prepared to fight with us. He was shot, and died, a much-defamed man in this country.

General Giraud succeeded him, and, under his leadership, France re-entered the war. Giraud was violently belittled in our Parliament and Press. Here, misinformation reached a new peak.

Giraud is knightly in appearance and noble in deed. Few men can boast such a record. He may be compared with Bayard, and in the last war would have been a public hero with us. In this, misleaders of opinion bedaub his picture with dirt, for their own ends. But for his French troops, who held the Germans while the British and Americans moved up, and suffered heavy losses, our men would not, as I write, be in a position to drive the last enemies from Africa.

Henri Honoré Giraud is 63. Three of his sons now fight in Africa, for France and us. He belongs to the French officers, who like British officers, ambassadors and journalists, for years before this war vainly implored their Government to make known the warlike intentions of Germany and to hasten their armaments. In this country the men who thwarted them are still in power; and our policy towards France is seemingly bent on effecting the restoration of similar men there.

Giraud was captured in the last war and escaped to fight again. His renown was born then. In this war he *fought*; he was not of those who surrendered. He was taken, fighting in an armoured car, in the forefront of the fight, by Rommel himself. He was imprisoned in a German fortress, Koenigstein, on the edge of a precipice 150 feet high. The story of his escape, by means of a rope made from pieces of string and cord, belongs to the supreme achievements of the dauntless human soul — and he was not young! He reached France after fantastic adventures, and received a secret message telling him of the intended Anglo-American landing in North Africa. He went with a son and some officers in a rowing-boat to meet the submarine sent to fetch him, transhipped, in a flimsy rubber dinghy which bobbed about like a cork in the heavy sea, to a seaplane, and flew to Africa. (How people cheered when Mr. Chamberlain actually *flew* to Munich!) There he made possible the victory in Africa, the recovery of the Mediterranean, and the final triumph in Europe which are now in our grasp.

Giraud was abused and reviled in this island. In the Commons a Mr. Bowles, Member for Nuneaton, asked 'Do the Government agree that the people are not fighting this war to make the world safe for Girauds to live in?' The *Daily Herald* used the same sneer.

Could perversion go further? Thus is public opinion misled, about matters vital to our domestic liberty and foreign safety. What reason, outside a madhouse, could exist thus to treat a man who rendered us, his country and the world such service?

Once again, the reason was, the question of the Jews. When General Giraud agreed to receive British and American journalists, he was seemingly treated as the representative of a conquered country! The *Daily Express* reported that the first question asked was 'whether he would continue to discriminate against the Jews'. He was 'obviously nettled', said *The Times*. Well may he have been: this man who suffered so much was confronted by people who apparently thought, not of the recovery of France, of 1,400,000 French prisoners in Germany, or even of victory in the war, but only of this thing.

In the following weeks the entire British Press spoke as if French North Africa were conquered territory in which our commands were law. That French troops held the enemy while we prepared our attack, was news quite lost in this distortion of the picture. The British Minister sent to Africa said 'Our broad policy is that France shall be free to choose its own form of Government ... The attitude towards the Jews must be changed because the present attitude will never be acceptable to the British and American peoples'. What more blatant contradiction could be uttered, in two sentences? Are we to use our armed strength, everywhere we go, among friends or enemies, only in *this* cause?

Such a demand was made in the *News-Chronicle* of February 2nd, 1943. It said:

> General Giraud claims that 'the Jewish problem' in North Africa is a matter that concerns only France ... Everything else must give way, he says, to the need to mobilize the resources of France against Germany. Not so. The Allies are fighting for the validity of certain principles. One such principle is the right of the Jews to the privileges accorded to their fellow citizens. To deny them that right

is to accept the assumptions of Fascism. *Military action must conform to this acceptance of basic rights.*

Here, again, is the subtle perversion of the truth, by means of which the British people are deluded: that 'Fascism' means, not terror and war, but solely: measures to restrict Jewish influence, and that we fight chiefly against this. It is not true. 'Fascism' and 'National Socialism' are but 'Bolshevism' under other names. The enemy is *tyranny and terror,* sometimes used by all-Jewish régimes, sometimes by régimes which profess to be anti-Jewish, sometimes by régimes which ignore this question altogether. The 'thing' we *should* fight against is terror, as a means of usurping and holding power.

Thus another danger awaits us in Civvy Street. It is, this stealthy elevation, by every means of public delusion, of Jewish claims to the forefront of our war aims, where they do not belong, and the consequent threat, which this produces, to our foreign policy, on which our island safety depends, and our domestic liberties. We shall not produce a happy breed, here, by giving paramountcy to a cause which is not ours, but an international one: and we shall imperil our safety by it, for we shall produce greater hatred of ourselves than ever before, in the countries which after victory must become either our friends or enemies, if everywhere we go we use the might of our arms to enforce Jewish aims and claims.

If these were only 'equal rights with other citizens', none could demur. That is the high, and yet modest measure of human dignity which we *all* claim, which Tyranny denies. But Jewish aims go beyond that (witness the preferential treatment, over British citizens, given to Jews from Germany in this island during this war). They conflict with that unchallengeable statement of the rights of man.

What *are* the Jews, and their ambitions?

The Jews of the world are divided into three main groups: (1) more-or-less assimilated Jews (British Jews, and their like elsewhere); (2) 'Zionist' Jews (with a foreign policy and territorial ambitions); (3) International Jews, with boundless aims.

The first are the Jews who, in spite of their faith of tribal antagonism, find, through long sojourn and adaptability, the way to live on good terms with, and to promote the national welfare of, those national communities which have received them. These Jews claim only equal rights with their fellow-citizens, on the whole, and regard themselves as members of a *religion*, not a *race*. This is the smallest group; and (as the example of Poland shows) it tends to become smaller; while present British policy, by supporting wider aims, threatens to exterminate it altogether. Anything which promotes the belief that great Powers, like this Empire or the United States, are promoting the ambitions of the second or third group, immediately diminishes the population of the first group.

The second group contains those Jews, to whom the Jews of the first group in quiet times are often violently opposed, who pursue the aim called Zionism. These are organized, wealthy and powerful. They regard themselves as members of a *race*, and claim a home for it, in the place where this home was two thousand years ago, Palestine. It is now inhabited by others, whose immemorial home it also is. They can only rule in Palestine by dispossessing the present occupants, on the strength of title-deeds lost in antiquity. The claims of this group, then, go far beyond 'equal rights with other citizens'. Indeed, history cannot supply a precedent for this ambition. It is a political claim, involving territory, which *denies* the 'rights of citizens' already established there. We have grounds, not less substantial and more recent, to claim Saxony. This ambition is indistinguishable from that pursued by Mussolini in Africa, Hitler in Eastern Europe, or (I must add) by this country in Africa or India. Such ambitions, however, were realized, or attempted, by dint of Italian, German or British arms. The Palestinian ambition has been pursued through the use of *our* arms.

The third group of Jews are those who, as the events of twenty-five years ago showed, remain invisible until the moment of chaos, and pursue a greater ambition: exclusively Jewish rule in white countries, on the basis of laws outlawing 'Anti-Semitism' and the weapon of terror. Unlike the Zionists, who openly pursue their aims, this group is secret and unseen; but its existence was proved in Russia, Hungary and Bavaria in 1918-19. (None need waste stamps on telling me that 'Lenin was not a Jew'; I know that one.) Trotsky, Béla Kun and Levine were unknown to mankind, before they uncovered, and yet, when chaos arrived, they were suddenly there! The men they chose to work with them, the orders they set up, the laws they made and the things they did, cannot be gainsaid.

In quiet times, these three groups remain distinct. When wars come, populations shift, governments fall, and frontiers change, unrest and excitement spread through them all. Many members of the first group become uneasy, dreading change. Others, as ambitions become more hopeful, which seemed hopeless, move from the first group to the second, the second to the third (witness the baptized Peter Agoston of Hungary, who in peace wrote of the menace of Jewry to the Gentile world, and in chaos became Béla Kun's henchman).

We need *dislike* none of these groups. We need only *know* them, what they want, and how this affects us. Precisely this indispensable *knowledge* is withheld from us by a thousand stealthy devices. This is the danger of the attempt which is made, to prevent all open discussion of these matters.

A Socialist Leader (who is Leader of The Opposition, and thus seldom says anything, in the House) was reported by the *News-Chronicle* on November 2nd, 1942, to have told a Jewish audience in London that the next 25 years would see 'the fulfilment of their hopes'! (I doubt whether he told his electors that, in 1935. The current talk, then, was about Abyssinia.)

What are these 'hopes' which are to be fulfilled, and how do they impinge on *our* interests? Mr. Greenwood is an important man, and supposedly commits our second greatest Party. What does he promise in our name?

Are they the 'hopes' of those Jews who only wish 'equality of rights with their fellow-citizens'? Of those who want Palestine *and* 'equality of rights' everywhere else? Or of those who want untrammelled power, based on terror and anti-Gentile legislation (for that is what the early Bolshevists obtained, through their weapon, the Communist Party, in three countries)?

We are not told. So let us examine, severally, the three groups of Jews and see what their 'hopes' are.

The first is that of the Jews long-established by residence in all white countries, who were freed from discrimination during last century, when they came in most lands to enjoy that 'equality of rights' which was *then* depicted as their utmost desire. The highest places, in State service, professions and callings, were opened to them, and many climbed to these pinnacles.

This bred the first group, of absorbed, if not assimilated Jews: those who felt their interests to be vested in the country which received them, and worked for no exclusively Jewish aims, contrary to those of the land which became their home. (The great bulk of European Jews, the 3,000,000 Jews in the East, as I have shown from the testimony of one, never felt like this. From it came the Bolshevist Jews of 1918-20 and the immigrants who bred such discord in Germany after the last war. It includes those whom we are now asked to receive, in the name of 'extermination'.)

The first group of Jews was well defined, in the House of Commons on August 6th, 1942, by Mr. Lipson, the Member for Cheltenham. He opposed the proposal for a Jewish Army, which several rabid Gentiles advocated, and said he owned the advantage, over them, of being a Jew. (He pointed out that one of them supported the proposal in the belief that it would relieve Jews in his constituency from serving in the British Forces! You perceive, gentle reader, the need to watch your Member.)

Mr. Lipson, who often defends alone the best British and Jewish interests against non-Jewish Members of astounding ignorance, prejudice or dependence, and is in imminent danger of being pogromed as an anti-Semite, said that previous speakers 'expressed a view which to my mind is harmful in its conception'. This was, the repeated references to 'the Jewish *people*'. He submitted, with emphasis, that the Jews were *a religious community*. The anti-Semites, he said, argued that the Jews were a separate *people*, and thus justified discrimination against the Jews in various parts of the world. But

> this argument is also supported by the views put forward by the Jewish Nationalists, who also talk about a Jewish people. You cannot have the best of both worlds. You cannot at the same time say, 'There is a Jewish people, and therefore I am a member of the Jewish people and I want to get all the advantages and privileges that that carries with it' and also say 'I am a British subject, or a Frenchman or an American, with equal rights with other citizens'. Therefore, I feel that the Nationalists in their arguments are playing with fire, because they are proving the anti-Semitic case that the Jew is an alien in every country where he is. It is not true. In this country, thank God, we Jews enjoy the privilege of citizenship, the responsibilities of citizenship.

Mr. Lipson's speech contains the truth. Here is the 'British Jew'. He asks to receive no more, or perform less than we. No problem exists, with *him*. If this were all the Jews demand, all that our Governments intend to claim for them, all would be well. These, then, were *not* 'the hopes' which Mr. Greenwood promised to fulfil; the Jews already have so much.

So we come to the second group of Jews. Mr. Greenwood spoke to Zionists. He, leader of a great Party, promised, not what the Jewish *religious community* wants (in which Mr. Lipson included himself) but what the *Jewish people* want (who, as Mr. Lipson said, justify those self-defensive measures against the Jews in various parts of the world).

That is grave. What *do* they want, those Zionist Jews who count themselves 'a nation', and pursue territorial ambitions which can only be reached through British arms? If Mr. Greenwood was empowered to make this promise, we are committed to something gravely injurious to British and Jewish interests. This affects every British mother and mother's son.

Consider the birth of 'Zionism'. It was still a dream fifty years ago. Since then, one world war has brought it to fulfilment; a second now produces still greater ambitions. This opens sinister ways of thought, in the search for the origins of these two world wars, and I wish they were closed. It enshadows our future.

At the end of last century, the Jews were come to their heart's desire, if this was only the status which Mr. Lipson defined. But in 1895, Dr. Theodor Herzl, a Jew of Vienna, issued his pamphlet, *The Jewish State*, which called for the establishment of an independent Jewish State 'in some suitable territory (not necessarily Palestine)' (yet in 1903, when the British Government *offered* the Zionists Uganda, it was refused, at the instance of the present Zionist leader, Dr. Chaim Weizmann!).

A wave of enthusiasm went through Jewry everywhere. A succession of Zionist Congresses was held in the next twenty years, and when the First World War began, Zionism was an organized power, supported by much wealth, and able to press political aims of the first magnitude through our Parliament. *The Zionists at no time proposed, or admitted, that the Jews, if they obtained their own State, should yield any right of citizenship in other countries.*

The grant of full equality to the Jews in Europe, therefore, led at one immense jump to the claim of those rights and a Jewish State *as well*, Numerically strong nations have frequently conquered weaker ones.

The idea of Zionism was that a numerically weak 'nation' should conquer territory, through the political and armed strength of such great nations. At the same time, Jews should retain the right to become Prime Minister of Great Britain, Justice of the United States Supreme Court, Foreign Minister of Germany, Viceroy of India, Lord Mayor of London or New York, Prime Minister of France — anything and everything, everywhere.

The project is fascinating in its audacity. Most of our public leaders express sympathy for it, though none explain its full meaning thus.

Twenty-two years after the publication of Dr. Herzl's pamphlet, on November 2nd, 1917, Zionism gained its great victory. The British Government issued 'The Balfour Declaration', addressed to a private citizen, Lord Rothschild. It said:

> His Majesty's Government view with favour the establishment in Palestine of a National Home for the Jewish people and will use their best endeavours to facilitate the achievement of that object, it being understood that *nothing shall be done which may prejudice the civil and religious rights of existing non-Jewish communities in Palestine, or the rights and political status enjoyed by the Jews in other countries.*

Thus a British Government espoused the most audacious ambition in history: the conquest of Palestine and undiminished rights everywhere else! The Jews were to retain intact 'rights and political status' enjoyed elsewhere; the 'rights and political status' of the native inhabitants of Palestine, the Arabs, were *not even mentioned*. They were only to have their 'civil and religious rights'.

The pretext for this grave undertaking was, that it would win for our cause the Jews in Germany and Central Europe. It did not. They, like the established British and American Jews of *that* time, were happy in their countries, and were come to 'full equality of rights', of which Disraeli and Lord Reading, and many others were the proofs, living and dead. The Declaration was a surrender to the second group of Jews (behind whom lurked the third): those who sought to give the flesh-and-blood of territory to the doctrine of Jewish Nationalism. The Jews who were pleased, though not placated by it (for it only whetted their appetite), were the Jews of Poland and Russia and the more recent arrivals, from those parts, in America. If the Jews of Poland, between the wars, refused to feel themselves Poles, this was a main reason. From that day anti-Semitism has grown apace, for the Palestinian Arabs are Semites, and the campaign waged against them by the Zionists equals, in threats 'tantamount to extermination', anything uttered by Hitler.

The memory of the Balfour Declaration, and its fruits, can only arouse deep misgiving about the results to which the Declaration of December 17th, 1942, will lead.

In the last war, too, we professedly fought 'for the right of small nations to live their own lives'. The Arabs of Syria and Palestine lay under Turkish sway and were ruled by Turkish Governors. They looked enviously at neighbouring Egypt, where British arms ruled, true enough, but an Egyptian King reigned with a Council of Ministers and an Egyptian Parliament. They desired nothing better for themselves, and hoped for it, from the First World War.

Then they heard that something unique in history was to be done to them. The British conqueror would neither keep Palestine nor give it to its inhabitants. It was to be handed, without asking their leave, to a third party! What Arab could understand that? This was to be done in the name of a book written thousands of years earlier. With as much justice, the Arabs might claim to reoccupy Spain, which they held as long as the Jews ever held Palestine.

British troops conquered Palestine. The war cemeteries at Jerusalem bear witness. In the next twenty years, British officials there were left with an almost insoluble problem to solve. These are the words of the Mandate:

> The Administration of Palestine, while ensuring that the rights and position of other sections of the population are not prejudiced, shall facilitate Jewish immigration under suitable conditions.

This meant to the Arab that he was to be driven from his land. Jewish immigration rose from 30,000 in 1933 to 61,000 in 1935, and many more Jews entered clandestinely. Land bought from the Arabs for Jewish settlement was not allowed, under the conditions of the Jewish National Fund, 'at any time in the future, under any conditions whatever, to be alienated to anyone who is not a Jew'. The extreme Zionist, M. Jabotinsky, declared:

> We rely on European Imperialism ... Our Imperialism will flourish under the protection and support of any power, on condition that this power shall not show mercy to the Arab population, and that it uses an iron fist which will not allow them to move under it.

Mr. Asher Ginsberg wrote:

> The Jewish people are destined to rule over Palestine and manage its affairs in their own way without regard to the consent or non-consent of its own inhabitants.

Such words are indistinguishable from Hitlerist speeches, save in the substitution of 'Jewish' for 'German'.

The Zionist case was incessantly upheld in the British Parliament and Press, the subservience of which to this influence is a most dangerous sign of our times. Arab delegations to London came empty away; Royal Commissions went out, verified the need for Arab alarm, and returned to make proposals which were ignored. The Arabs were denied any means of stating their case. The Mufti of Jerusalem truly told one of the Royal Commissions, 'We have not the least power, nothing to do with the administration of the country, and we are completely unrepresented'.

For twenty years, British rule strove only to prevent the Arabs from gaining any kind of elected representation until the Jews were in a majority. The Legislative Council, promised in 1930, was never formed. In 1935 the British Government undertook to form it; the Arabs (who increased from 600,000 in 1918 to 925,000 in 1936, while the Jews increased from 53,000 to 400,000) were to have received seats in proportion to their share of the total population. Immediately, a violent Jewish outcry was raised in this country and America. A parliamentary debate followed, in which the Arab case was completely ignored — and the Legislative Council was postponed indefinitely. Mr. Amery, now a Minister, wrote that 'To go on refusing representative government until the Jews are in a majority is an almost impossible policy'. The policy has been pursued.

This policy produced, between the World Wars, an explosion of feeling among this people 'liberated' by us which *involved us in warfare similar to that waged by Mussolini against the Abyssinians, and which a whole Army Corps, with modern weapons, was not able to quell.* That event reveals the future dangers which will be brewed for us, if our leaders give improper prominence to Zionist aims. The radius of fellow-feeling for the Arabs of Palestine spreads far beyond the borders of Palestine; it reaches into Egypt, Saudi Arabia, Iraq and even India.

The power wielded by organized Zionism over the British Parliament and Press is only realized by those who have served the British Government in Palestine, or by writers who discuss *both* sides of the case. The lives of British administrators in Palestine were made so difficult by the knowledge that any effort to be just to both Arab and Jew would forthwith bring on them virulent attacks in Parliament, that they longed to reach the age of pension and retirement. They were ruthlessly pogromed for the smallest hesitation in yielding to every Zionist wish. Sir Ronald Storrs — whose book, *Zionism and Palestine* (Penguin Books, 1940, being a chapter from his reminiscences *Orientations*, Ivor Nicholson and Watson, 1937), gives an excellent account, written with painstaking fairness to both sides — says that after the Easter riots of 1921, 'I had to endure such a tempest of vituperation in the Palestine and World Hebrew Press that I am still unable to understand how I did not emerge from it an anti-Semite for life'. Indeed, since the Balfour Declaration was made, Zionism has become one of the greatest sources of anti-British virulence in the world.

To-day, the British Government is supposed to have perceived the danger which its actions in the last twenty-five years have brewed in Palestine, to have restricted land sales from Arabs to Jews, and to have restricted Jewish immigration to the figure of 75,000 for the five years 1939-44, after which 'no further Jewish immigration will be permitted unless the Arabs of Palestine are prepared to acquiesce in it'. But the 'extermination' campaign has now been opened, clearly with the aim, among others, of destroying this promise. If that happens, we shall provoke new hatred for ourselves. We may be prevented from hearing the Arab case, but the Arabs know for what purpose 'a Jewish Army' is proposed, and they remark that many Members of Parliament support the proposal. The bitter dispute in Palestine is only suspended, during the war, and after it will flare up, if British policy does not administer Palestine in future with more honourable regard for the interests of the native inhabitants. It is no interest of ours, to conquer foreign lands in the interest of others; and we already live under the reproach contained in T. E. Lawrence's words, in *Seven Pillars of Wisdom*:

> Honour: had I not lost that a year ago when I assured the Arabs that England kept her plighted word?

For what *are* the real aims of Zionism? They grow and grow.

Just as the grant of 'equal rights' in Europe produced the demand for a National Home, so the grant of a National Home now produces the demand for all Palestine, and more. Lord Wedgwood, that foremost spokesman of the Zionists in this country, in his *Testament to Democracy* violently attacks the British Administration in Palestine, saying it has hampered the Jews at every turn, left them almost unprotected among Arab looters, stopped their immigration, prohibited their land purchases, and taken in taxes 'the little money they saved from Hitler to supply Arabs who murder and a British Administration which denies them justice'. Jewish freedom has been sabotaged, 'crypto-Fascism' rules in the Near East and lurks in Whitehall. Whitehall would sooner the Jews drowned than landed in Palestine, and 'the mob of Arab plunderers and murderers use as their slogan, "The Government is with us"'.

(This is typical of Zionist references to Britain since the Balfour Declaration was made and the National Home established.)

Lord Wedgwood proposes a *larger* Palestine (embracing the Hauran, Transjordan and Sinai) as a self-governing State of his 'Democratic Federal Union', immigration to be unrestricted and Jewish police to keep order. Then the Jews 'would soon be in a majority', and the State would 'develop as peacefully and justly as the State of New York'. Lord Wedgwood would like the rest of Syria and Irak to be reoccupied by Turkey! America should either enforce this arrangement or take our place as Mandatory, 'for as Mandatory we have utterly failed, even though we have failed through treachery'.

That is, two Arab kingdoms created in fulfilment of our promise in the last war should be destroyed, Palestine, Syria, Transjordan and the Hauran handed to the Jews, and the Arab race enslaved and made homeless ('exterminated', perhaps) as a blow for democracy. Here is the printed, and even proud proposal that we should do something worse than we did at Munich, after the new world war 'for freedom' and 'for the liberty of small nations'.

At that rate, these wars cease to be funny. None need dismiss these words as fantastic, *because the only thing that now remains of what we built after the last war is the Jewish National Home in Palestine.* The new aim is *all* Palestine, and much more!

As this war progresses, Jewish aims tend to dominate the clamour. The newspapers which particularly lend themselves to this clamour (as you will perceive if you follow them closely, gentle reader) already attack all the other Things which we were urged and scourged to fight for. They uphold the power of capricious imprisonment, in this country. They deride and abuse Giraud, who resurrects France. They attack Michailovitch, who fights on in the Serb mountains. They attack Poland, on behalf of which we ostensibly went to war, and say Russia must have half of that country. Yet our honour is more deeply involved in this case than any other; we might have lost the Battle of Britain but for the help of Polish airmen.

The second group of Jews, then, the 'Zionists' who consider themselves, *not* as a religious community, but as a nation with territorial aims and speak of any who stand between them and these aims (in the first place, the Arabs) exactly as Hitler spoke of the Czechs and Poles, who wish to form a Jewish Army and whose aspirations have already involved us in one war — this section of world Jewry pursues ambitions going very far beyond 'equal rights with other citizens' and cutting very deeply into our interests. Only through us, can they attain these aims; they wish to use us, and yet abuse us. If you, gentle reader, take the pains to read the references made by Zionist spokesmen to this country, its officials and its soldiers, you will find in them charges of hypocrisy, treachery, bias, cowardice, and every meanness. I have enough to fill a book. Their power over the British Parliament and Press, nevertheless, has in the past been sufficient to prevent any view but theirs from gaining a hearing.

Indeed, Zionist ambitions, and the range of those who support them, widen so greatly, as we have seen, that they approach those of the third section of Jewry, which works in secrecy but has boundless aims. After the last war, we might have dismissed the thought of that invisible but powerful section as a nightmare. But to-day we cannot. The British Government's Declaration of December 17th, by identifying itself only with the aim of Jewish vengeance, has reawakened the memory of those days. Those three all-Jewish regimes of 1918 *existed*; that was no nightmare, and it cannot be scouted by the shouting of 'Anti-Semite'. Here, in our Europe, close at hand, only twenty-five years ago, we saw three, exclusive, all-Jewish, anti-Gentile, terrorist Governments. Peace, and the passing of the years, banished two of them and modified the third, I believe, which in any case is not our concern, but that of the Russians.

But now we have a world war again, with chaos lurking behind it, and need to be wary.

In my opinion, British interests are only compatible with those of the first group of Jewry, which desires equal rights of citizenship, and accepts equal duties. History has repeatedly shown that these form only a part of any one Jewish population, anywhere, and our interest therefore does not lie in promoting mass movements of Jews to this country. Our influence should be strictly confined to promoting the equality of citizenship for Jews in the countries where they now are, and should not be used to acquire for them in other countries that privileged status over other citizens which they too often work to obtain, and of which we have set a lamentable example in this country by exempting Jewish immigrants from military service while making them free of all employment vacated by native citizens who serve. As to the second group of Jews, the Zionists, the ill-worded commitment of the Balfour Declaration has involved us in an almost insoluble problem, but we should on no account be misled into doing more than to secure the National Home *in* Palestine, under the most rigorous trusteeship of the rights and interests of the Arab population. To promote both Arab and Jewish interests in Palestine is not an impossible aim; but the virulence of Zionist propaganda, and the extravagances of its innumerable spokesmen in our Parliament and Press, do more than any other thing to make it impossible.

As for the third section of world Jewry, the existence of which was clearly shown by those events of twenty-five years ago, and the continued existence of which many current signs indicate, its ambitions for exclusively Jewish rule, based on terror, are directly opposed to ours in every possible way.

. This is one of the major problems of our Civvy Street to come, one which seriously affects our future. The gravest thing about it is the way in which knowledge of it is withheld from the public, and open debate suppressed, by a thousand secret and stealthy devices, of which a great deal can be said, one day. Public discussion, however, will not much longer be denied, and will be more useful if it is conducted on a basis of authentic and impartial information than on one of ignorant prejudice.

For what is the present situation of this matter? The Second World War drags on, and after nearly four years of it, our leaders like to tell us blandly that 'a long war' yet awaits us. The people doggedly shoulder all burdens and tell themselves that one day victory will be won, and that after it The Things they think they have fought for will be honoured at a Peace Conference. They should know, from the experience of 1918, that victory may bring them the exact opposite of everything they are told to fight for. In this case, one major result of the war has already been achieved, under cover of the war and unnoticed by themselves. A great movement of Jews from abroad to this country and the British Empire has been effected. Through the compulsion of native citizens, to vacate their employment and fight or labour elsewhere, these exempt new-comers have been established here in prosperity, in breach of all the pledges which were made at their coming; and a move is now in progress to have them naturalized. The very thing has been done which was done in Germany, Austria and Hungary in the last war, and bred such discontent there. A Jewish writer from Hungary, now a naturalized Briton, whom I previously quoted, said of 1918 in Hungary:

> The Boys did not or could not settle down; their jobs had been filled long ago by the people at home.

Now, while we still toil towards victory and the peace conference, with ever-increasing burdens on our backs, two new aims are being pursued: the first is, to bring a second contingent of Jews from Europe to this country, while The Boys still fight, and similarly establish them here; the second, and in this our enemies vie with our own statesmen, is to establish a Jewish State, a thing different from and much greater than the 'National Home in Palestine' which is the sole remaining achievement of the First World War.

By the Declaration of December 17th, 1942, in which our leaders gave our name to the pledge of an exclusively Jewish retribution, we have con-jured up the memory of Jewish vengeances already experienced in Europe, and committed ourselves even more than by the ill-fated Balfour Declara-tion of 1917 to the cause of Jewish Nationalism or Imperialism, which is not ours, which directly conflicts with ours, which has already implicated us in one Arabian war, and which encourages settled Jews everywhere to feel themselves, not as citizens of the countries they inhabit, but as members of a nation with territorial aims.

Our policy has gone much too far towards identification with Jewish Nationalist aims, and this already confuses the entire picture of the war and of The Things for which it is actually being fought. Our foremost public spokesmen seem the victims of a Dervish-like obsession or infatuation in this question which blinds them to our own national and patriotic interests. In this matter, our policy needs to be rectified without further delay, and the intolerable confusion which has arisen to be cleared away, so that the people of this country may yet hope that they fight this new war for some native ideal and interest and for the cause of humanity — not for that of one power-seeking group as against another.

Readers may find some enlightenment in extracts from letters written to me by Jews belonging, as I classify them, to the three groups of Jewry, respectively:

I hate with a deep loathing these smug bandboys and impresarios, these black marketers, these fungoids who now, thank heaven, tremble once more in America, and their whole loathsome brood, but I beg of you please try to differentiate. Remember people like me, people of the East End who have 'taken it' side by side with your John Londoners and people who do love England sincerely and gratefully. Please don't condemn us all, though I suppose if Jews were to be condemned because of those about whom you write, then I too would be condemned — I stand by my faith.

From a British Jew, an officer serving in the Air Force.

Accept my best thanks for your book. As a Jew and as a Palestinian, I would wish that the truth, which you have found and laid down in your book, be known to the world. This truth is not pleasant, but good and useful; the more it will be known, the earlier the world will understand its own need for a Jewish National Home and for its completion, and the more we shall understand, what mistakes and blunders should be avoided. On the other hand, those Jews who did not yet understand the meaning of Jewish history, will learn from your book (and why) they *must* write off European Jewry and that they cannot 'invest' their thoughts in its preservation or even restoration.

From a Zionist Jew, formerly in Germany, now in Palestine.

The letter is flattering, but the writer may not fully appreciate my feeling that the interests of no people, either British or Arab, should be sacrificed to make a Jewish National Home. I think all could prosper together, but the rapacious and vituperative methods of Zionist leaders offer a great obstacle.

To Douglas Reed, the Enemy of England as well as of the Jews. The reply of the City of London to your *drivel* on anti-Semitism in your idiotic writings — the new *Jewish* Lord Mayor ! ! ! How pleased you must be — you fool!

Anonymous.

. . . 'Say that again', I said to Doktor Farisy as we walked through the streets of Prague, 'I didn't quite understand.'

'One of our Rabbis here', he repeated, 'is preaching in the synagogues that Hitler is the Jewish Messiah, because he will cause all those countries of the world to be opened to the Jews, which are closed to them now.'

Thoughts which long wandered at random through my mind suddenly fell into ordered procession.

'Do you know, Herr Doktor', I said, 'I've known that for a long time, without realizing it. Thank you for putting it into words. But my country will have to look after its own interests.'

'Why?' he said.

'You know very well that you haven't a single non-Jew on the staff of your newspaper', I said, 'and you'll do the very same thing in England, or Kenya, or wherever you go to.'

He looked at me warily, with veiled eyes, opened his mouth, and then shut it, without comment.

We walked on together.

CHAPTER XIV

ON HOLDING OUR OWN

We mean to hold our own — MR. WINSTON CHURCHILL

APRIL 1942. I went along the Strand, talking to a lovely and zestful companion. At last, we emerged from the worst of all winters — worse even than that of 1940. The air was crisp, the sun warm, the sky blue. London, the dreariest of cities when it waited aimless, confused, tired and lethargic for the war to begin, was now alive. The traces of bombing gave dramatic meaning to the scene. The air was rid of much of the smoke and petrol fumes. The streets were bright with uniforms, and brisk with the feeling of a common task and purpose. The war still lay in the doldrums, but the hope that will not be kept down any more than the rising sun, began to stir in all hearts again.

The news of Sir Stafford Cripps's failure to reach agreement with the Indians was just come, and another problem, which we shall encounter in Civvy Street, began to take shape. We passed a score of Indians, in khaki uniforms and khaki turbans. I thought, watching them, how great a thing this would be: to justify our rule in India, as we have regained much of the goodwill of the Afrikaners, won the allegiance of the French Canadians, restored hope to the Maoris, and paved the way, if we are wise after the war, even to reconciliation with the Irish.

The Indians were fine and soldierly figures, and their appearance won murmurs of admiration. (But so did the 'Kaiser's Bosniaks', those be-fezzed darlings of the Viennese. Proudly the Austrians watched those living Emblems of Empire, as they marched along the Ringstrasse in 1918; a few months later, they, Bosnia and the Empire were gone. We need not let such history repeat itself.)

While my shoes were cleaned, and the shoeblack told us of changes seen during thirty-five years at his pitch in the Strand, we watched the passing show. Some fine lads in battledress went by: 'Norge', said their shoulder-tabs. We saw the square-topped caps of the Poles, the Belgian tricolour in the cockade on an officer's cap, the long capes and gay képis of Fighting Frenchmen, Greek and Netherlands naval officers, some Czechs, even three Russian soldiers, and a few Americans, as yet uneasy in their uniforms.

Then a flying officer came to have his shoes cleaned. He was dark-skinned, and his shoulder tabs said 'Jamaica'. Few Englishmen know the Empire they love, and I for one am not stirred by the Imperial romanticism of a Kipling; I think it spurious. But the feeling of kinship and allegiance in peoples so far away, of which this was a vivid token near at hand, moves something very deep in me, and I suppose in others. The world has never known anything like the British Empire, or anything which could bring so much good to it, if we mend our ways after this war.

As we went along the Strand again, other names passed us, on the shoulders of men: Rhodesia, Malta, Cyprus, Newfoundland . . . And we saw, with glad surprise, for we knew the Australians were busy elsewhere, an Australian slouch hat. What memories it revived! Then we saw, in the Strand, Canada, New Zealand and South Africa; we did not go until we found them all.

A grand and glorious morning with the sun shining. The picture of the Strand faded, and I saw men from this island going out, long ago, in the great sailing ships, with love in their hearts for the land which denied them acres and opportunity, to found new countries far away; I saw their great grandsons coming back in the troopships. I saw them at Vimy and Gallipoli and Delville Wood, in Greece and Crete and Burma and Libya . . . .

To me, the greatest moment in this war was that which brought the prompt succour of the Dominions at the outbreak. They did not know how desperate was our plight, any more than the people of this island knew, and did not ask: they came. They have suffered as bitterly as we, and have more cause to complain than we, for, though they govern their own affairs, the course of the British Empire in foreign policy, in the great decisions which produce peace or war, is still set by the British Government, and here lay the blame. They could have said, 'This is your affair; you made the bed'. They did not. The tie held fast.

The British Empire was vindicated by its free children. I can never forget the new hope I felt, after nearly seven years of growing despair, when I saw those hats and shoulder-tabs from the Dominions.

To-day, some people, especially in America, announce that the British Empire must be broken up after the war. What, after such a demonstration as that! It was justified in 1939. The offspring lands held to us even in calamity.

> We have not entered this war for profit or expansion, but only for honour and to do our duty in defending the right. Let me, however, make this clear, in case there should be any mistake about it in any quarter: we mean to hold our own. I have not become the King's first Minister to preside over the liquidation of the British Empire.
> Mr. Winston Churchill on November 10th, 1942.

'We hold our own!' The phrase is badly chosen. We do not *hold* the great Dominions; they held to us. We cannot live without them. But that part of the Empire which we *hold*, we lost, where it was attacked. These are vain words then; we have to learn *how* to hold our Empire.

For what *is* the British Empire? This island is the foundation. Built on it, are four great columns, the self-governing Dominions of Canada, Australia, South Africa and New Zealand. Then comes the enormous superstructure: India, and scores of Colonies, Protectorates, Mandated Territories, and theoretically independent States where British arms actually rule.

When the island foundation threatened to crack, the four columns still held. The floor may be repaired yet. But the weakening was enough to upset much in the superstructure. Hong Kong, Singapore, Malaya, and Burma, all went. The British Empire was vindicated in its main component parts, those which govern themselves and by free choice held to us. In those places where *we* still exclusively governed and a hard test was applied, the structure broke (the reasons have been shown, earlier in this book, in quotations from many writers who knew those places in peace and war).

The lesson is clear. We did not justify our rule in those parts of the Empire *which we hold* — which do not hold to us of their own will. That which, in the Empire, we may call 'our own', held to us. That which we may by no means call 'our own', though we held it, did not hold to us. The faults in our way of ruling such lands and people, arise from our order of Enclosure and Exclusion in this island. The men who emerge from this filter go to distant tropical countries and create an Enclosure there. Within it, they reproduce the life they knew at home. They cannot or will not mix and merge, even with their own breed, still less with others. When the test comes, they are swept away, with their golf clubs, bridge circles, cocktail parties, illustrated weeklies, and the whole trivial paraphernalia.

'To hold our own', therefore, is a dangerous precept to take with us into Civvy Street. To maintain the British Empire, we need better methods. We return again to the beginnings of our problem. Consider the future from what aspect you will: you come back always to this island and its order of life.

Ensure our island safety, through foreign policy and armed strength, and the four imperial columns rest secure. Revive a happy breed, and you produce men vigorous and venturous enough to rule over the lands which are not our own, but which we hold, and which thus could be brought to see their happiness and prosperity in membership of the British Empire.

The problem is always the same and always simple. Our past rulers might have been possessed, by the way they worked against these plain rules and seemingly sought, by their every act, to imperil the firmness of our island base, the strength of the four Imperial columns, and the balance of the Colonial superstructure. Maintain all those, and you may keep the world at peace for an age. What influence, then, of malignancy or idiocy, worked to hinder emigration between the lands of the Empire?

The tie that held, in 1939, was that of blood in the main. Why cut the bloodstream, the source of life and allegiance? The great Dominions are empty of human beings. Each, save New Zealand, is larger than this island. All are lands of unlimited possibility. Canada is bigger than the United States (without Alaska), but contains only as many people as greater London. Australia and New Zealand *together* hold as many inhabitants as London, though they comprise as much territory as all Europe. The white population of South Africa, a land of abundant promise, is a quarter of that of London. Is that what 'holding our own' means: vast, unpeopled Dominions; inter-migration thwarted by all manner of devices; and, in this country, mass unemployment or forced labour?

Migration, or interchange, is the lifeblood of the Empire. To hinder it is so patently dangerous to the whole organism, that it becomes incomprehensible. But it appears even sinister when, during the absence of British and Imperial manhood at the war, a great move is made to transplant hundreds of thousands, or millions, of Eastern Europeans to this country and the Dominions! Here you see, behind the shining shape of The Things for which we supposedly fight, the shadow of The Things for which we may be actually fighting.

The prosperity of the Dominions, like that of America, was founded on the work of people mainly from this country, Holland, and the Scandinavian lands, who went out with little money and created wealth by enterprise and diligence. In those days, a man might move freely about his world. Between the wars, emigration was so much obstructed that the process almost stopped.

The condition, that a newcomer must bring a stated sum of money, was not the greatest obstacle. In olden times, most men saved something to take with them. The order of repression and discouragement, which has been built up in this country to-day, killed the spirit of enterprise in the rising generation.

But who can understand British and Dominion Governments which joined to prevent inter-migration? A main danger to our future is that of the halted breed, and a great cause of this, I conjecture, has been the hindrance of free movement about the Empire. A committee of our enemies could not have devised better means to enfeeble us and imperil our future.

During seven of the eight years before this war, emigration from this country almost ceased. Such movement as there was to the Dominions, was of *non-British* emigrants, and in one case at least this was the *direct result of British Government action.* 'Assisted passages' to Australia were suspended between 1930 and 1938! *When they were resumed, until August 1939, only 881 of the 10,992 persons who were helped to go to Australia were British! Nearly all the remaining 10,111 were Jews from Europe.*

A former British Governor of South Australia, Sir Henry Galway, testified in *The Times* of March 10th, 1940, to

... the disastrous effects of the Government's policy in this very important matter. If this policy is persisted in, it will not take more than a couple of generations before Australia's proud boast of a population with 95 per cent of British stock is silenced. One of the many evils resulting from the substitution of alien for British stock is that the industries are by degrees falling under foreign control. For instance, the sugar and peanut industries are already fairly well in the hands of the alien, while the fruit industry is going that way ... the average Member of Parliament is woefully ignorant on the subject of migration ... I humbly contend that it is up to the Government to do all in their power to save Australia from being swamped by people of alien race.

Sir Abe Bailey gave a similarly alarming report about South Africa, in *The Times* in September 1939. News of the same kind has come from Canada.

The average Member of Parliament is *not* 'woefully ignorant' on the subject of migration. He has become indifferent to the subject of British migration and is too susceptible to powerful and organized international interests which seek to promote *non-British* migration. The columns of Hansard for years past contain hardly any allusion to *British* migration.

The very pages burst with pleas for the admission to this country and to the Dominions of *non-British* emigrants.

This is an anti-patriotic thing. It is a direct blow at the foundations of the Empire, and one aimed at them by the elected representatives of our people during the absence of our men at the war. We cannot 'hold our own' by such methods; on the contrary, this means that we deliberately cast our own away. This thing, if it continues, will throw an unpleasant light on the origins of the present war. Here is another engagement in the Battle of England, which must be fought if the future is not to be darker than the past. We have seen that our Parliament will not help us unless it is made to; from some madness, or ulterior prompting, it seeks to cleave the bloodstream between this mother island and the offspring Dominions, and to fill the artery with an *Ersatz* fluid.

The Battle in England, against these anti-patriotic ideas, and against the international interests which foster them, will be bitter. It would be easier, if the Dominions themselves would help progressive and patriotic thought here:

> The Commonwealth Government is making plans to increase Australia's population from 7,000,000 to 20,000,000 after the war. Next to English-speaking people, people from Holland, Denmark and Sweden will be most welcome. Employment giving a decent standard of living could be provided for at least 20,000,000 people.
>
> A message from Sydney to *The Daily Telegraph*, January 1943.[1]

That is a very bright ray of hope (but if you will follow our Parliamentary debates, gentle reader, you will find no discussion of such things as this, but only a loud clamour about aliens). This is sound Australian and sound Imperial policy. This plan would achieve, at a single stroke, a great measure of betterment for Australia, this country and the Empire. It is a health-giving and patriotic idea, which would invigorate the breed in that far Continent, in this island, and strengthen the bond between. New Zealand, which shares the same recent memory of imminent peril, would follow suit. An Administration in this country, which was moved

---

[1] Mr. G. McCullagh, proprietor of *The Toronto Globe and Mail*, visiting this country in March 1943, said: 'I look forward to a period when Canada may become an outlet for a great migration of many different nationalities, but substantially British. There would have to be a well-planned scheme. Canada is a country with great material wealth, and can well become a great economic strength to the Empire. Its geographical position and friendly relations with America seem to place Canada in a unique position.'

by genuine Imperial and British sentiment, could gain the support of the Union Government in South Africa for a similar undertaking. As for Canada, the greatest Dominion, this is what a Canadian lady wrote in *The Daily Telegraph* on January 15th, 1943:

> Canada, my country, is very short of population. For the past two decades it has become almost static. After the war it will be less. We have become a 'two-child family' nation. In a small country this might be ideal; in Canada it is tragic. In recent years we have had little of the better type of immigrant from the British Isles, and if Canada is to remain British we shall have to have more of them, otherwise we must throw open our doors to all Europe once more. When the Beveridge Plan is put into operation the best of the younger generation will leave England, the independent, educated, enterprising and adventurously progressive will seek a free life elsewhere. I hope they will come to Canada; we need them; though, of course, most of the other Dominions will welcome them also. We shall not have any Beveridge schemes in Canada. There we must all stand or fall on our own merits, which is just what the Almighty intended we should.

Of what avail is it to speak of 'holding our own' while this vital question is ignored and our Parliament and Press champion only the cause of alien immigrants? We cannot hold our own island, much less the Empire, unless we reinvigorate the land, restore respect for British traditions, open the doors of opportunity, rebuild home and family life, revive the breed, check the drift to cynicism and resume intermigration within the Empire.

Our Government often proclaims what it will do after the war. It has spoken of 'four freedoms' which we are to enjoy. It has never spent a word, that I have read, on emigration. Will these 'four freedoms' then include the freedom which between the wars was nearly gone, which at the end was enjoyed more by aliens than by Britishers, to go to one of the kindred lands founded by their forefathers?

British governments, before this war, at one and the same time kept our island unarmed, and hindered emigration to the Dominions. Can any find rhyme or reason in that? It seems to add up to hatred of this island and its people; if it was not that, it was a thing of such mad idiocy that you may wonder what British governments are for and shudder at the thought that they seek to gain more power, and divest themselves still further of public control, after this war.

The story of our recent past makes it important that such words as 'we mean to hold our own' should be clearly defined. *How* do our rulers propose to ensure that our own shall continue to hold to us? They cannot do it without resuming inter-migration; or by preventing British and promoting alien migration.

Here is another foremost objective in the Battle In England. Revive a happy breed here, and encourage the resumption of breeding and inter-migration both in this island and in the Dominions, and we shall be fit to hold the lesser parts of the British Empire.

. . . We stood and watched the Australian in his slouch hat. 'How the girls loved those hats in the last war', I said. 'I love them *now*', said Lorelei. 'Here, come on', I said. 'Keep your Imperial enthusiasm within bounds. You are a piece of this old island, and not to be leased, lent, or let go. I consider my own hat most becoming.' 'Do you', she said, looking at it. 'Is that the one you bought in Prague?' 'It is', I said, 'the only hat that ever loved me, the one that was run over in Budapest and rescued from the sea by a Polish sailor at Gdynia, and bombed at a cleaner's in London, and found again by me on a salvage dump, and now that it has a hole in the crown, which parts from the brim, old ladies try to give me pennies in the street, but I never will desert this hat.' 'I love it', she said. 'That's better', said I. 'But I'd like to steal one of those Australian hats for myself, or one of these, look!' I looked, and saw a New Zealander, who came towards us. At the next corner stood two extremely good-looking Canadian Scots; their gaze told their opinion of Lorelei. 'Isn't it a wonderful feeling', she said, 'when you see these men from all parts of the world, and feel that they belong to us and we to them. I never *felt* the British Empire until now. You know how dull and blindfold we grow up in this country. To see them makes you feel so good and safe and part of something.' 'You're quite safe', I said brusquely, 'in my company, and you belong to me, as Glasgow to Will Fyffe.'

Then, just as we approached the doorway of Simpson's-in-the-Strand, two exceptionally tall, stalwart and handsome men, in dark blue uniforms came towards us. '*I say*', said Lorelei, 'what are these?' 'Australian Air Force', I said tersely, 'and if you don't stop talking British Empire now I'll make you pay for this lunch. The time is come to change the subject.'

She grinned and squeezed my arm. 'I love to rile you', she said.

CHAPTER XV

SOCIAL INSECURITY

DECEMBER 1942. I sat in a train, bound for Reading, and opposite sat a newspaper with two legs; the upper half of the forked radish was hidden behind those outspread pages. My eyes were unseeingly fixed on the football results thus displayed before me, and I came out of my reverie with a start when these columns suddenly collapsed, as if Samson pulled them down, and revealed a red face that wore a smile of foolish bliss.

'Social security', it said, 'that's what we want and we'll get it. They won't be able to play about with us after *this* war. The people will see to that. Social security!'

'Social security', I said, absent-mindedly, 'Ah, you speak of Bismarck's invention'.

'Bismarck!' he said, staring. 'What's Bismarck got to do with it?'

'Don't you remember', I said, 'after the 1870 war against the French, when Bismarck was getting Germany ready for the first world war, the German people grew restless, from an intuition of what was coming, and the German Socialist Party increased rapidly. Bismarck saw that they would have to be kept quiet, if the preparations for the next war were not to be disturbed, so he threw them a ball to play with. He called it "Social Security". Or rather, he called it "The Social Service State". But it was the same thing: you know, health and unemployment insurance, pensions, freedom from want, the whole bag of tricks. After Bismarck was sacked, the Kaiser took up the game, and the Socialists greatly enjoyed themselves, throwing the ball to him and having it thrown back to them. Meanwhile, the war simmered nicely on the hob, and was served up, piping hot, in 1914. The German Socialists voted for it. They stood up with all the others, when three cheers were called for the Kaiser, though they didn't actually cheer. The distinction was most important. Our own Socialists are good at the same kind of thing. Ah, dearie, dearie, me', I said, wagging my head sagely, 'that was a famous victory.'

'What are you talking about?' said red-face?

'Bismarck', I said.

'But I'm talking about the Beveridge Report', he said.

'I thought it was the same thing', said I.

He glanced at the communication cord. 'But I'm talking about Social Security', he persisted.

'So was I', I said. 'But I was *thinking* about the security of society.'

'What's the difference?' he asked.

'Just the difference between house and foundation', I said. 'A secure society is the foundation. Social security, if it exists at all, is a house which can only be built on that foundation. Try building one without laying a foundation: it will collapse about you. The trick has been played upon you twice already. Now you applaud the thimble-rigger as he sets his thimbles a third time.'

'I don't see that', he said, with a look of anguish.

'You are resolved not to', I said, 'or you will not take the pains.

'I get out here', he said, hurriedly.

'That's what they always say', said I. . . .

Picture to yourself, gentle reader, social security in its highest form. Imagine that you are a passenger in a sinking ship. You do not mind, because you are secure! You are locked in a watertight cabin with food, drink and oxygen to last you your natural life. When you die, you may say, 'Well it was a bit dull for me, but by Neptune I was Socially Secure! None can gainsay that!'

Imagine galley-slaves, beneath the knout, singing 'With a long, long pull and a strong, strong pull, all together for freedom, pull!' So does the clamorous chorus sound to me which we hear to-day. It is a nightmare of human delusion. While the foundations of our society are being undermined, they sing of the house they will build: 'Social security!'

But the foundations are being smashed — family life, truth, loyalty, faith and hope. This is worse even than the killing, in war: the ruination of the lives and faith of many who remain alive. This is the evil that lives after. It is the foremost reason why we cannot afford more of these wars, why the paramount need of this island for the next century, is peace.

If you wander through a maze, every wrong turning you take brings you back to the beginning; though you travel far, you advance not at all. To get out, you must find the *one* right way. That is our case. We are in a maze of anxieties about our future. All the turnings save one are false.

Only one way out, into a clear future, exists. It is, to make this island safe against any foreign enemy, first; and to build a house of freedom in it, second. Without that, the quest for social security is a false turning. Ignore the foundation, and social security is either a house of cards or a prison.

Thus the Beveridge Report, good or bad, is a secondary, not the foremost thing, and the public failure to perceive that is dangerous.

Let me give one vivid illustration of my meaning. The higher old age pensions which it proposes, are to reach their peak twenty years after its adoption. Twenty years was exactly the space of time needed to bring about this war! But what social security has an old age pensioner, or any other, in such a war?

Again, in twenty years, according to Sir William Beveridge, we shall be 'in a panic about the population of this country'. That is, we shall offer a more tempting prey than ever, to some predatory enemy, in twenty years' time, if our rulers continue to depress the national spirit, weaken the national will and neglect the national defences.

Then, how can you achieve social security, unless you make this island secure,[1] restore faith to its people, revive the desire to breed, and give them freedom to work and emigrate.

If these things were not done, the edifice of social security, before it was even completed, would be bombed, or the inmates of it would become the captives of a foreign conqueror. What security is that? Social security cannot be attained without national and Imperial security — and no Beveridge Report about national and Imperial security has been issued, nor can our governments be trusted to ensure it.

The Beveridge Report, then, is a secondary thing. Having made that clear, what are its intrinsic merits?

The number of people who have *read* it bears the same proportion to the number of those who applaud it as the number of people who have read the Versailles Treaty bears to the number of those who shout 'No second Versailles!' It has 300 pages and over 200,000 words. I never met a document so difficult to read and understand. Most of those who champion it unthinkingly conclude, from newspaper summaries, that they would profit by it.

[1] Sir William Beveridge shares this view about first-things-first; he said on March 3rd, 1943, 'I appeal to the Government to say that they will give priority to social security *after military security*'.

It contains one thing I want for myself: equal health and hospital services for all, particularly children. It contains two things I want for others: higher old age pensions, and the abolition of the victimization of the poor through insurance collectors.

Our first-, second- and third-class order in hospitals, is repugnant. I am not personally biased; I was only once delivered to the mercies of an English hospital, and became a first-class patient as soon as I recovered consciousness, being able to pay. But the health of the community is the greatest asset of the nation, and all should receive equal care. The cadging 'voluntary hospital' (with its money-box-rattling 'Appeal Secretary') is detestable, because the health of the population is a national, not a private or class interest. If after this war we could say farewell to alms, we should have achieved something worth fighting for.

I believe we should adopt the Swedish order, which excludes all differentiation. All hospitals there are State-controlled. Their revenue is obtained from two taxes, one levied by the State and the other by the borough in which the citizen lives. The State tax is a fixed percentage on income. The Municipal tax is levied according to income; thus, it cannot be evaded (like rates in England) by residence in a house below the standard of the individual's income. Treatment in the hospitals is alike for all. The only preference which money can buy, is a private room; the treatment does not differ. The cost of an operation on a boy's tonsils, for instance, would amount to about 1s. 6d. a day for as long as he remained in hospital. No operation fees are exacted, for the State doctor performs the operation.

(If I understand the Beveridge Report, it does not go so far as this. But this is a simple, yet ideal, arrangement.)

Equal care of the health of all children, is an essential part of the foundation of a secure society. The children are the nation's investment in the future, and the dividends this will pay depend very much on their health. Statistics, which are great liars, show that the health of children in this country was not inferior to that of children in other countries before this war. Their appearance belied such statistics. True, they were being liberated from typhoid, diphtheria and tuberculosis, but their teeth were appalling, and their bodies bore the same relation to human fitness, as derelict acres to thriving farmland.

The second good thing in the Beveridge Report is the proposal for higher old age pensions. The national interest commands unremitting care of the children. Every humane and decent instinct calls for the protection against want and distress, of those who can no longer work. The thing is better said than I can say it in this description of an old, husbandless, Cornish grannie, in Mr. A. L. Rowse's book *A Cornish Childhood* (Jonathan Cape, 1942):

> Her last years were made easier for her by Lloyd George's Old Age Pension. If anybody ever deserved 5s. a week after a lifetime of honest hard work, it was she; and if there was anybody to whom it was an inestimable help, it was she. The consequence was that she worshipped the name of Lloyd George — and quite rightly, too. The work of that remote politician away in Westminster, a mere name to her who knew nothing of politics and politicians — any more than any of us did — meant that much concrete security to her last years, so much for tea and sugar and bread and candles and coal and house-rent — there was little enough left over for meat. . . .

'The spirit of adventure' no longer stirs in old men and women. Nothing can be destroyed by alleviating their last years.

Thirdly, the Beveridge Report exposes the indefensibly high proportion of premiums-paid which is eaten up by the working costs of the great insurance companies. Of every pound paid in life insurance premiums by persons of limited means, seven shillings were swallowed wastefully in this way. (I believe the companies challenge the figure, but the ratio is undeniably too high, and the contrast between the squalid homes of the little insurers and the great palaces of the insurance concerns, is blatantly eloquent.) This, however, could be cured without nationalizing insurance. Simple legislation, setting an upper limit to the ratio of working-costs-and-premiums, would suffice.

The Beveridge Report also mentions the greatest abuse committed in the business of life insurance: the transference of millions of pounds, in pennies and shillings, from the pockets of the poor to the coffers of great concerns, through the forfeiture of premiums paid on policies which lapse. (The Beveridge Report deserves no particular credit for this revelation; the thing has repeatedly been exposed, and if it continues this is the fault of public apathy.) This great scandal has gone on for a hundred years unchecked, though simple legislation would stop it. Mr. Gladstone, in 1864, thought to shock the country by disclosing that one single company, in 1863, issued 135,000 policies and retained the premiums on *more than half of them* (70,000), on which payments were not maintained. Yet in 1929 the same company issued 811,545 policies, of which 444,829 (a larger proportion than in 1863) were forfeited through failure to maintain payment!

I have seen this thing at work. In the lean times after the last war, I rented a room from a poor widow, who was visited weekly by a jovial fellow with a little book and pencil, Mr. Wily. Mr. Wily knew these people. He would talk of the handsome sum they would draw if they were injured, and the fine funerals they would be given when they died. He called my old landlady 'Ma' and she, lonely creature, looked forward to his calls. Up and down those streets he went, collecting the twopences and threepences. Then one week, Ma would not be able to pay. 'That's all right, Ma', Mr. Wily would say, 'Pay me next week.' Next week, Ma could not find the fourpence or sixpence, and so it would go on. One day, Mr. Wily would suddenly say things couldn't go on like this, two shillings were owing now, he must have at least a shilling. Ma would be frightened and see visions of a bailiff or a policeman, and say she would pay next week. Next time Mr. Wily came, she wouldn't open the door. Mr. Wily, grinning behind his straggly moustache, would go his way. 'Insurance' of this kind became a mania with some of these women; they would run four or five small insurances at a time, and were always allowing these to lapse because they could not keep up the payments.

The British Parliament permits this. Not by its deeds, but by what it does not may you know it. Exposure by a Prime Minister and two committees achieved nothing; now the Beveridge Committee has again drawn attention to it.

But the main importance of the Beveridge Report lies in its proposals about unemployment insurance.

Again, it grasps the stick at the wrong end. If this island society is to be made secure, unemployment should be attacked first, and insured against afterwards. If mass unemployment recurs, Social Security is nonsense. It can only exist when men have the opportunity to *work*. To deny them that, and pay them for idleness, may be good or bad; it is not social security.

The Beveridge Committee was appointed to consider social insurance, which includes unemployment insurance. But the point is, that the Government has appointed no Committee to consider *em*ployment after the war!

Are we then to rest content with the former state of affairs, when millions were idle? For this reason, I smelt danger in the section of the Beveridge Report which deals with unemployment insurance. If a nigger was in the woodpile, it would be there. And indeed, I found this:

> Men and women in receipt of unemployment benefit *cannot be allowed to hold out indefinitely for work of the type to which they are used or in their present places of residence, if there is work which they could do available at the standard wage for that work*. . . .
>
> Men and women who have been unemployed for a certain period *should be required as a condition of continued benefit to attend a work or training centre* . . . the period after which attendance should be required might be extended in times of high unemployment and reduced in times of good employment; six months for adults would perhaps be a reasonable average period of benefit without conditions. But for young persons who have not yet the habit of continuous work, the period should be shorter; *for boys and girls there should really be no unconditional benefit at all; their enforced abstention from work should be made an occasion of further training*. . . .
>
> *Conditions imposed on benefit must be enforced where necessary by suitable penalties.*

That is compulsion and forced labour, as we now have it, introduced under pretext of the war and ostensibly only for the duration of the war. It existed in Soviet Russia and Nazi Germany. It is one of The Things we supposedly fight against. Young lads and girls *must* take what employment they are told to take, even far away from home; 'suitable penalties' will be imposed if they demur. 'Suitable penalties' can only mean imprisonment.

And *this* is Social Security! This is what the politicians mean when they speak of 'the continuance of control after the war!'

How many enthusiasts knew that this was in the Beveridge Report? It appears in Part II, on page 58. When the Report was issued, the public was benevolently advised, on account of its great length and complexity, to read a summary, *The Beveridge Report In Brief*, which contains 63 pages instead of 300 and costs 3d. instead of 2s.

Part II of the 2s. Beveridge Report, containing the proposals I have quoted above, does not appear in the threepenny report in brief.

In the great parliamentary and newspaper controversy about the report, I have not seen these vital proposals mentioned, though they are the most important things in it. They would impair our last remnants of liberty.

Here are no proposals to create *employment* and hope, for the young people of to-morrow's England, to get them on to the land, on to the sea, into the air, into the Empire. Here are but compulsion, labour camps, the abolition of free choice of employment and the threat of force.

Strange, that the people of this country, having been hoaxed so often, from the Zinovieff letter to the Gold Standard election, from the 'Save Abyssinia' election to the Munich Agreement do not become a little wary and examine what they are told before applauding. Their newspapers, without explaining this part of the report, lauded it as a model of 'advanced thinking'. Do people believe this? They were given a picture of a few Tory diehards implacably setting out to wreck a report which might be England's salvation. Did they not observe, then, that the Government itself called for this report and 'publicized it all over the world in a way that no report has ever been publicized' (Sir William Beveridge, on March 3rd, 1943). The Government broadcast the beauties of this report in scores of languages. Do people then really believe that the Government is opposed to the Report drawn up by a very old crony of Mr. Churchill? Do they imagine that the Government gave such vast publicity to the Report, merely in order to make itself unpopular?

The gullibility of the public is frightening. Nose-led by the Press, millions of people seemingly go about saying the 'vested interests and the old men are trying to wreck this wonderful scheme of social security, which would ensure our future. We will *force* the Government to give us the whole Report and nothing but.'

'They' *want* the Beveridge Report, or at any rate the proposals which I have quoted and which were omitted from the popular edition. What 'vested interest' would oppose forced labour, backed by imprisonment? (For that matter, you will find the same idea in Lord Salisbury's *Post-War Conservative Policy*.)

If this, the hidden barb in the Report, is swallowed with the tempting bait that surrounds it, the people of this island will find themselves hooked.

For this is Social Insecurity at its worst. This is the thing the blaring radio has implored us for over three years to overcome at the cost of everything we have: dragooning, regimentation, surrender to petty officials, and trades union tyranny. Do not believe that one party in Parliament is for and the other against *these* proposals. *Both* are avid for them.

Let any man or woman in this country who has been 'directed' to leave an employment, surrender it to another, often enough to an alien, and to take some worse paid employment, in some other place, on pain of imprisonment, consider whether that is Social Security. Social Security offers them that *after* the war.

Let any man or woman who has known the fear of unemployment consider whether, after the war, that fear will be greater or less, if he or she knows that the loss of a job will render them liable to compulsion to enter another trade, at lower wages, and to remove to another part of the country, on penalty of imprisonment. Let them consider whether they would then feel themselves socially secure.

This would be the end of personal freedom, and it is buried deep in the 200,000 words of the full edition of the Beveridge Report (which you, gentle reader, have not read, I wager). It is *not* contained in the popular threepenny summary which our paternal rulers prepared for your benefit. Think of this, before you yield to the enthusiasm of newspapers, whose proprietors you do not know, about 'Social Security'. If you swallow Social Security before this hook has been taken out of it, you are caught. You throw away what is probably the last hope for the future.

The proposals to which I have drawn attention mean that the two great parties which jointly govern us have their eyes fixed, after this war, not on the *promotion of employment*, which alone could mean Social Security, but on *the exploitation of unemployment*, which means social insecurity. No good for the future ever comes from the enchainment of the people, and the motives behind such measures are always evil. Such measures are the surest possible indication that new wars are being cooked behind the scenes. Any man who clamours for 'the whole Report and nothing but the Report', without gaining the written pledge of any candidate who desires his vote, that this hook shall be taken out of it, throws away his future.

The Beveridge Report, through no fault of its compilers, but possibly through the intention of those who appointed them, has done the country a disastrous disservice by fixing its gaze on 'unemployment', instead of 'employment' after the war, and in diverting public attention from the Government's failure to prepare *employment*. What we need, if we are to make our society secure, is employment, not a vast army of Bumbles engaged in distributing unemployment pay or imprisoning the workless. This is the paramount need from which the public mind is distracted by the fraudulent cry of 'Social Security'.

How can we have *employment*?

I tried, gentle reader, to make the Empire plastic and vivid in your mind's eye by showing this island as the foundation, the four great Dominions as pillars embedded in its safety, and the rest as superstructure.

Now let us build a plastic model of this island. Its safety and happiness rest on freedom from wrongful imprisonment and a liberated countryside, and on four other main foundation stones: the fighting services, the merchant navy, agriculture and coal.

Those are the four chief props. Make those strong and prosperous and the structure is secure. We cannot live without the fighting services, and they should be kept strong against the hour of need. We cannot maintain our Empire without a great merchant navy (of the sea *and* now of the air), which becomes even more vital in war; every effort should be spent to promote its prosperity. We cannot live, warm ourselves, travel or stoke our furnaces without coal; no care given to that industry would be too much. We cannot live happily in peace without a thriving countryside, and in war we may starve for the lack of it; it should not again be allowed to fall into decay.

These four things, together, spell employment, and the cure of unemployment. The problem of unemployment dwindles, and the problem of Social Security solves itself in a better way than by insurance, if they are done. Between the wars, all were neglected. That was the chief cause of unemployment and Social Insecurity.

Consider them separately. Firstly, the fighting services were starved (though we were told the opposite). The Navy was down to danger point, the Air Force below it, and the Army far below it. I have quoted the proofs of our plight after Dunkirk, when in my view we were actually defeated, but the enemy did not strike. We should never again allow the Navy or the Air Force to be less strong than any other in the world, and we should be content with the equality of only one other the American. The Army should be substantially stronger than we have hitherto thought necessary. Apart from the fact that this policy would have preserved peace (and as time passes the evidence accumulates that this was why it was not followed), it would have prevented one great part of our mass unemployment, which reached the figure of nearly three millions in 1932, when 60 per cent of all workers in shipbuilding and allied industries were out of work, and 46 per cent of all workers in the iron and steel industry. (Turn a deaf ear to proposals for our disarmament after this war, in whatever form they may be disguised. Beware Disarmageddon!) But, as part of the gradual loosening of the order of Enclosure, which is indispensable if a happy breed is to be revived in this island, conditions of service and possibilities of promotion for all ranks should be improved and widened.

Secondly. We have now learned, once again, the value to us of our Merchant Navy. But for it, we should have starved; without it, we could not contemplate the invasion of Europe which we shall have to undertake if we are to win this war. It was not so much neglected, as murderously assaulted. Large among the causes of this war looms the thing that was done in 1930, when rich men joined together and formed a company called National Shipbuilders' Security Limited (note the familiar words, and consider what 'national security' came of it), to buy redundant plants, dismantle yards, and resell the sites on the condition *that they would not be used again for shipbuilding*. No shrewder blow could be aimed at our island safety, or a greater encouragement given to any country that plotted to beat us through starvation. (Nine years after that was done, submarine warfare began again!) Within one year, and on the north-east coast alone, eight shipyards were bought up, closed and scrapped, and many more on Clydeside. Scores of thousands of shipwrights were thrown on the street. The Bank of England, 'our national bank', supported that transaction! It was called a measure to 'assist the shipbuilding industry'. Neither the seafaring nation nor the shipbuilding workmen were assisted; a few magnates profited. Now, under the stress of war, the Government has formed a corporation to reopen those derelict yards. The leading men in it are those who formed the buying-up and dismantling company!

Can any cite a madder or more evil thing. In that affair, too, you may see how unemployment and social insecurity are made, and employment and social security destroyed. To prevent such a thing from happening again, is more important than to make schemes for insuring against un-employment. This transaction produced a further large proportion of our mass unemployment, to swell that which resulted from the starving of the Navy, Army and Air Force. After this war, the public hand should retain at least this control of the shipyards, that none should be dismantled or cast into disuse again. That is more vital than the imprison-ment, if they refuse to leave their homes, of workers made idle by closing down. If any private owner feels unable to continue, the shipyard should be taken over by the State and operated with the owner as manager, if he wishes; for this is a national, not a private, interest. This episode clearly shows, like that of the insurance companies and the forfeited premiums, where the bounds of 'private enterprise' should be drawn; it should not be allowed to become legalized plunder, or to imperil our national safety.

After this war, a sister should be born to our Merchant Navy. This is civil aviation, the merchant marine of the air. The last war, which was the first air war, left us with the greatest air force in the world. Air travel and air transport were obviously to become the great new industries of the future, and we should have led the world in them, having so much experience, machinery, material and skilled labour in our hands.

Once again, 'They' intervened. Within a few months of the end of the last war, thirty thousand aeroplanes were thrown on the scrap heap, while good flying men were left to peddle vacuum cleaners. The Ger-mans, forbidden any military aircraft, raced ahead, and built a great network of efficient air transport lines that covered all Europe and then spread across the Atlantic. Our civilian transport lines were miserably treated, as were the shipwrights, the miners, the farm labourers, the mer-chant seamen. (An odd thing is, that even to-day our Prime Minister and other highly-paid people, habitually choose not British, but foreign pilots for their journeys.) Here an enormous field of employment, and of travel, adventure and enterprise, was allowed to go to weed, just like so much English farmland. The Germans, Americans and Dutch, left us far behind. British officials coming home from the Empire were wont to use foreign air lines because they were faster, more comfortable and better than ours.

In this island were 3,000,000 unemployed; here was a great vein of employment left untapped, and a new threat allowed to grow to our national security. To-day, that absurd position threatens to recur. The nation wastes its breath in argument about insurance against unemployment, instead of seizing the golden chances of employment which lie near at hand. For nearly two years 'a committee' has been 'considering' civil aviation. Something thwarts its work; it comes no further. Meanwhile, American air lines are spreading their services. Our production of transport and cargo-carrying aircraft has been relegated to the status of Cinderella. All the present signs are, that an unnecessary inferiority is being allowed to develop again.

But if that happens, it will be another great source of avoidable unemployment after the war, when it should be a gigantic field of employment and endeavour. Our present Under Secretary for Air, Captain Balfour, said in the House of Commons on December 17th, 1942:

At the end of the war we may be faced with two alternatives unless we safeguard the position as far as we are able. Either we shall have to contemplate closing down a large part of the aircraft industry, employing more than a million workers, and hope that the industrial market will be able to absorb and use the skill of those men elsewhere, or we shall have to continue building bombers and fighters for which there may be little or no use in the numbers that we shall be producing at the end of the war.

The words are enough to cause despair in the future of this country. Are we to start closing down, dismantling, dismissing again? If this is the intention, we can guess why the Beveridge Report was published, and why thoughts of unemployment, instead of employment, obsess our rulers.

But why? Why is the choice only between 'closing down and dismissing more than a million men' and 'building bombers and fighters for which there may be little or no use'? The third alternative is obvious. It is, to build a great merchant service and passenger service of the air, and to prepare for that *now*.

Air transport will be as vital to our Empire in future as the Merchant Navy always was and has proved again to be. Not only is it a means of employing hundreds of thousands of men, but it opens all those doors to travel, adventure, enterprise, the lack of which in England has so depressed the spirit of young men. The sea is in our blood; the air will have to be in our blood, too, if we are to survive. Our Air Force, when this war ends, will be as great as or greater than any in the world; and behind it lies the Air Training Corps, in which scores of thousands of youngsters have come to know the feel of the air, to think about flying, to raise their eyes above the level of the street, the pictures, the pub. We can become the greatest airfaring nation in the world, as we should be with such an Empire. This is opportunity in all its forms. Do our rulers mean to spoil that chance? In the past, most of us loved and lived for the Empire without ever seeing it. Air travel and air transport offer the means for it to become known to us all. This is not only a war-winning weapon, but, what is more important, a peace-winning one. It is being neglected, and the great chance is being allowed to slip through our hands once more. None cares for this vital matter. It is a part-time occupation of an Air Ministry which is obsessed with the needs of military aircraft. We need, at once, an Air Transport Ministry, and an Empire Air Transport Board, so that we, with the Dominions, may prepare now to take our place in the peaceful air when the war ends.

How grotesque, to talk of Social Security, of insuring against unemployment, when such an opportunity as this is ignored!

Thirdly. The other great vein of employment, which in the inter-war years became a source of mass unemployment, is the mining industry. 'Nationalization' is a word disliked in this country. But the right of coalowners, for whose profit men are in wartime forced down the pits on pain of imprisonment, should not extend so far that in peace they may close these pits and throw thousands of men on the streets to swell the throng of those who (under the Beveridge Report) could be told to go to some unfamiliar and still lower-paid work elsewhere. The coal industry is so vital a pillar in the structure of our land that the status and self-esteem of the miners should be the first care of any government, Tory, Socialist or Coalition. Instead of that, they have been miserably paid and shabbily treated. (This was the greatest weakness of England in the inter-war years, that the lowest wages and poorest conditions were reserved for the men who served the three most vital industries in the land — mining, agriculture and shipping. Merchant seamen have told me that even to-day, in war time, conditions of pay and service in British ships are inferior to those in Norwegian, Greek, Netherlands and other merchant navies.)

Fourthly. Agriculture furnished the fourth and last portion of the mass of unemployed. A good farmer told me, before the war, 'None but a fool would become a farm labourer in this country to-day'. These were the worst paid of all. They were lucky if they earned thirty shillings a week, for toiling from dawn to dusk. During the war, their wage has been raised to a decent level. Farmers and landowners have been guaranteed fair prices. A paramount necessity, after this war, will be, to maintain the revival of the land and not to let it lapse again into the state of grey decay which Ministers of Agriculture so eloquently deplored. This can only be achieved by guaranteeing a fair price level for farmers and a fair minimum wage for landworkers.

These are the four pillars on which *em*ployment could be built in England. They are all essential and complementary and vital both to our happiness in peace and our security in war. None are mutually antagonistic. If these four veins of employment were fully exploited, unemployment would remain the lesser problem which it formerly was; insurance against it would be simple and secondary. Add to those four things such large-scale schemes of emigration, concerted with the Dominion Governments, as that which the Australian Government has in mind, and the beginning not only of insular, but of Imperial revival is achieved.

These things, which so few people discuss, or even think about, are more important than Social Security, which is a blind, meant to divert the people's gaze from the real source of any misfortunes that come upon them. We do not need to have *un*employment. We can have *em*ployment, the only Social Security. Are there some who wish to deprive us of that, and who are they?

... He put his head through the window again.
'What did you mean by that about Bismarck?' he said.
'We were talking of Social Security, weren't we?' I asked.
'Yes, but what's it got to do with *Bismarck*?' he said.
'Have you a year or two to spare?' I said.
'Me?' he asked, in surprise. 'No, I haven't.'
'That's a pity', I said, 'I might have been able to explain it to you.'
The train began to move. He looked after me in great bewilderment.

CHAPTER XVI

NINETEEN-SIXTY CORNER

...We were come a long way together, uphill and down dale, Myself and I. He was a good guide. Having been that way before, he was able to lead me past many false turnings which I otherwise would have taken, to show me the right way when the road forked, and to tell me which, of those we met, were to be trusted or suspected.

I might have lost everything I owned right at the beginning, for I was sorely tempted to save my own feet by taking a ride, when I was invited by a wily-looking fellow with a megaphone, in the Snap Election Chara-banc. He said it would bring me where I wanted to go, but Myself, having been tricked before, held me back. 'Above all', he said, 'don't fall into that trap. Find your *own* way, and shun all who offer you a lift or a short cut.' Again, I would certainly have yielded, but for him, to the allure of Appeasement Avenue, a shady way, or to that of Social Security Street, a crooked turning. Both of these, according to the wily-looking man, who in my dream constantly reappeared and sought to beguile me, led to a delightful garden city, where mankind needed to do nothing but lie about in beautiful parks called Freedom From Fear, Freedom From Want, and the like, and listen to the radio.

It was not easy to pass these by, for the way we went was hard, at first, and uphill, and led between mean houses, and was peopled with harassed and distraught-looking men and women who, like myself, sought Nine-teen-Fifty Street and Nineteen-Sixty Corner, and beyond. I was much tempted to take those turnings, for everything was done to make them look pleasant and enticing, and they ran gently downhill, and the wily-looking man always cried eagerly 'This way, this way, you'll find 1950 and 1960 and the future down here. This is the shortest cut to 2000'.

But Myself dissuaded me each time. 'Don't believe it', he said, 'I *know*. I've been this way before, that's why I'm coming with you now. He's a fraud with his promises, he gets a commission on every man and woman he inveigles to go that way, and they don't get to the future at all. Down there, hidden, lies the Slough of Despond; I've seen it. Keep to this road.

This is the right road. It needs finding, and it's hard and uphill at first, but it gets better, much better, afterwards, and it's the only one that will take you to 1960 and set you on your course for Beyond.'

We even succeeded, much to the delight of Myself, in preventing many others from following the beckoning finger of the wily-looking man. They gazed longingly at those shady, easy, downhill avenues, but when they heard that Myself was come that way before, and knew all the wrong turnings and pitfalls, they fell in with us and pressed on. Then, suddenly, the wily-looking man became a crowd of wily-looking men, who shouted angrily after us, 'Yah, Reds, Whites, Blues, Vermilions, Warmongers, Pacifists, Cranks, Idealists, Fascists, Communists, Fanatics, Dullards, Intellectuals, Ignoramuses, Bolshevists, Diehards, Anti-Semolinists! ! !' This greatly worried our companions at first, but Myself reassured them, saying 'That's all part of the game. If they can't trick you, they try to frighten you. Keep on and you will be all right'. And at that, all the wily-looking men vanished, and there was peace.

So we pressed on, a goodly company now, and when we came to Nineteen-Fifty Street, our hearts lifted, for the ascent was less steep, the mist began to clear, the houses were better, the people held up their heads and looked happier, the children were healthier. We overtook many others, and these joined us; yet we were neither a mob nor a regiment, but patriotic pilgrims in our own good right, and nevertheless strong in our numbers and our knowledge of the thing we sought. Something warm and pleasant lay in the air. 'What is this feeling?' I said to Myself. 'Don't you know?' he said, 'It's hope'. 'Why, of course', I said, 'I remember, you and I knew it in 1914.'

On we went, and the way became ever broader, smoother, surer and more inviting. The mist was quite gone, now, and the sun shone on a land that was pleasant and often green. The road lay straight and clear before us; few turnings offered, and none would have been tempted by them anyway. We saw men demolishing mean streets, and other men, repairing hideous places where boards, which they uprooted and threw down, said 'Derelict Area'. We saw no fences, railings, or warnings against trespass; instead we saw an open countryside, a thriving land, with busy coalmines and shipyards, and at their gates a small sign: 'Ugliness and idleness, alone, forbidden!'

At last we came to a great open place, that might have been Trafalgar

Square, save that it was bigger and more beautiful; with a great green-sward that might have been Hyde Park, save that iron bars were gone; and a great river flowing by that might have been the Thames, save that no filth floated on it, no black squalor lined it, but on both sides ran a white embankment and noble buildings and gardens, and fine bridges crossed it, and on it pleasure craft plied, and everywhere keen and vigorous men and women and children went. Such things happen in dreams.

Myself stopped. 'Well, here you are', he said. 'You can't go wrong now. Just keep straight on. I shan't need to come with you any further.'

'What is this place?' I asked.

'This is 1960', he said. 'Go on as you've been going and you'll be all right. The way is clear now, but you'll meet the wily-looking man again. When you do, knock him down and look in his pockets. You'll find his contract there, and you'll see what he is really after.'

'Well, so long', I said, 'and thank you. You've saved us a lot of time and disappointment.'

'More than that', said Myself, 'I've saved you from Yourself. . . .'

I awoke with a start. Before me lay Piccadilly, the Green Park and the passing show: trees and green grass; khaki, navy blue, sky blue and drab. A barrage balloon rose above the trees; at the winch, busy figures worked. The hum of the biggest city in the world was in my ears.

My hand still held an evening newspaper. 'Demobilization will be slow after the war', said the headline.

KIND FRIENDS, ADIEU!

THE SUMMING-UP

I DID not dream, when I wrote the first of these books, that readers all over the world would accompany me through them. The things I wrote have nearly all been proved by events, but I can claim no especial prescience; chance made me a journalist, and this calling gave me exceptional opportunities to learn things hidden from others. Many other ways of informing the public exist, however, and the knowledge I gained was not rare enough, by itself, to cause these books to be so widely read.

If I may impart an open secret, the reason is that I, almost alone, write the things I know, through my profession, and believe in, through my birth and experience. People find in these books that which they should find, but do not, in parliamentary speeches and the Press. If the spirit and principle of yore animated the newspapers, the circulation of such books would be small.

The influences which work to suppress this, distort that or exaggerate the other, in the public prints, are now so great that none can obtain a fair picture of affairs from them. People feel this, and turn to the books of an independent writer. A curtain has been stealthily interposed between patriotic seekers after knowledge and the truth. The deterioration began in our time and has been quickened by two wars.[1] The newspaper free of shackles is as essential to the health of a country as the independent-minded Member of Parliament. The lack of both is a main cause of our spiritual ailments, of which 'bitterness and cynicism' are the greatest.

---

[1] The disease from which the Press suffers is also prevalent, by all account, in the Dominions. Colonel Stallard, South African Minister of Mines, said at Johannesburg in December 1942: 'The Press has fallen on evil days. The Press used to pride itself on freedom, in that editors without fear, favour or prejudice expressed individual views. They were a powerful and potent influence for good or evil in consequence. At present, not only in South Africa, but throughout the world generally, so far as I know, and certainly in the English-speaking world, the Press has become syndicalized in groups, and editors are no longer the free persons they were.'

According to my experience, this is a very mild statement of the position.

A book is a pasteboard-and-paper sandwich. Into this sandwich, I have put the knowledge and experience of thirty years, from 1914 till now. The sum of it is, a clear view of great dangers which beset our future. I have no wish to impart information for its own sake, and detest those who interfere with others and say, 'I only did it for your good'; they do more harm than any. Though my motive, when I wrote the first of these books, was not a monetary one (indeed, it involved the loss of a hardly-won career), it was nevertheless selfish. I merely took a long view of my selfish interest: I could not see any happiness in this world for me or my children unless my native country were either spared the new war, or equipped itself to win it.

I thought a mass of people must share this feeling, and found I was right. These books touched a vibrantly responsive chord, for the plain reason that very many felt as I felt, though of their feeling our Parliament and Press give no echo. The only antagonism they met (but it was violent) was directed against the parts of them which deal with the Jewish question. The arguments I raised were not met, or the facts questioned. The rebuke merely was, that I must not discuss the matter, and I do not agree. If a proposal were afoot, to bring a million Martians to this island, or to use British arms to establish a Martian National Home in Palestine, it would be freely argued, and the decision would rest on this unbiased debate. No community in the world should be exempt from scrutiny, when it demands boons from another.

An isolated reproach was that which minds in *rigor mortis* sometimes utter, that I 'criticized my own country' (as if I ought rather to lament the lack of lavatories in Liberia). One good Tory M.P., a loud champion of Munich, wrote that *Insanity Fair* did 'incalculable harm' to British renown in the world. If such as he but knew how much discredit *they* incur for us! I never before yielded to this temptation, but quote now a letter from an American officer: 'One other thing, *All Our Tomorrows* has done far more towards breaking down any latent friction in my mind towards the average English soldier than any of the pamphlets which I have thus far seen dealing with that important phase of our war effort.'

Well, how do we stand, at the end of these five books? What is the final content of the sandwich? What is the summing-up?

The ominous balance of the past is that the *causes* of this war, as far as they lie in this country, have been concealed. Dark clouds surround that unreadiness and defencelessness of ours; enough rents have been made in the curtain of secrecy for so much to become visible. If stupidity was to blame, no reason exists to shield it; it should be exposed so that future mistakes may be avoided. If worse than stupidity was at fault, concealment is a deadly blow at our future, for this would be a guarantee of new wars. That is why no man can give an honest answer to the request for 'something constructive'. If we knew why our defences were retarded to the point of national helplessness, we could build. If that information is refused, and to-morrow's men retain the secret power to do the same thing, we cannot.

That is the summing-up of the past, and you cannot escape it.

Now the war oozes to its end. The Casablanca Conference lies behind us and at it, according to Mr. Churchill, 'a complete plan of action' was formed 'which comprises the apportionment of our Forces as well as their direction, and the weight of the particular movements which have been decided upon; and this plan we are going to carry out according to our ability during the next nine months'.

('Nine months' takes us to October 1943. A fortnight later Lord Simon spoke contemptuously of the demand for 'a second front' as 'a catchpenny phrase'. What can Mr. Churchill's words mean but an attack on the enemy in Europe? Indeed, Mr. Brendan Bracken said a few days later, 'I can give you the assurance of the whole of the Government that we intend at the first possible opportunity to hit the Hun in various parts of Europe'.)

If words mean anything, then, and contradictory words mean nothing, we shall strike in 1943. If, simultaneously, the 'unprecedented ordeal' by bombing (promised by Mr. Churchill in June 1942) is imposed on Germany, we may win the European war in 1943. (For air-bombing at this stage of the war, gentle reader, is *a war-winning weapon* in our hands.)

It becomes high time that the war should end, for in this island the picture of injustice, of inequality of service and sacrifice, grows grave. *One day* in February 1943 brought the following four reports, which deserve comparison:

Mr. Bevin, the Socialist Minister of Labour, refused to extend compulsion for military service to 'aliens of military age at liberty in this country' (who are eligible for all employment). This, in practice, meant the continued exemption of Jews from Germany, Austria, Hungary and Rumania, as *allied* nationals are subject to conscription. It also meant that these aliens (by law, enemy aliens) enjoy an immunity shared by none other in this island or all Europe, friend, foe or slave. It is a unique example of privilege.

Mr. Brendan Bracken stated that of 2824 persons employed by the Ministry of Information, 644 were men between 18 and 41 and 805 women between 19 and 30; and that the B.B.C. employed 668 men between 18 and 30.

A Mr. X. and his company were fined £181 10s., or three months' imprisonment, for evasion of the price-control. A suite of furniture was sold to the company's head for £10 3s. 3d., and then put up for auction, where it fetched £52 10s. In all thirteen bedroom suites, four dining-room suites, and other furniture were thus disposed of, and the reader may calculate the approximate profit, and its relation to the fine imposed.

A 20-year-old English girl, Margaret B., who was ordered to leave her employment, her home and her mother, and go to a munitions factory, returned home, pleading that she was unequal to the work, her mother was ill, and the like. She was sent to prison for three months. Of this case, a magistrate said:

> The National Service officers are often merely clerks at the Labour Exchanges. They can peremptorily direct persons to go out of the district in which they live, take up work in distant factories, irrespective of personal dislikes and preferences, and of home ties of the kind which are normally recognized as good reasons for not leaving home. Never before in the history of this country has one small man in each district been given such enormous powers over his neighbour.

(All who know the West End of London will be aware how many posts, thus rendered vacant, have been taken by aliens. The Minister concerned, Mr. Bevin, is seemingly informed of these conditions, for he said in February 1943, 'Someone said that London is a luxury place. It is nothing of the sort. London is not walking along Oxford Street or Piccadilly. That is not London; that is a little fungus which has grown up in the middle of London. It is not Londoners who are there as a rule; very few Londoners are there at all'. Yet his Ministry promotes such conditions.)

Such is the daily picture of the Home Front. To a man who was at the other Front, in the first war, and detested these things at home, it has been instructive but depressing to watch them at close range, in the second war, and see that, if anything, they are worse now than then. They make ugly contrast with the spirit of the men who serve and fight, and with the highfalutin speeches about The Things they have ostensibly been sent to fight for.

For at the fighting fronts, our men merely prove that they can fight, and we knew that before. The causes of the war, however, in so far as they lie in this country, have been screened, and remain unchanged, and this is the reason for the spiritual uneasiness, the fear, which seethe beneath the surface. They may be forgotten for the moment, in the approaching tumult of victory, but they are there. People *know*, even if they will not admit to themselves, that victory, alone, is nothing; 1918 taught them that. And they know, even if they refuse to discuss this, that the men, the methods and the machine, which destroyed that victory and brought the new war, are still in power, in use, and in action.

That is what the Archbishop of Canterbury meant, though he may not himself have realized it, when he said, on March 23rd, 1943, 'Horrible as it is, we have to realize that multitudes of our people actually fear the return of peace more than the continuance of war'. This applies particularly to that large section of the population remaining in this island, which *gains* through the war, in wealth, privilege, and power to dragoon or imprison its neighbours. But it applies also to many who suffer through the war, and yet dread a return to the money-grubbing anarchy of the inter-war years, with its decadent ruling class and its idle millions, its 'building society' and 'insurance company' palaces and its slums and living death in them, its 'sound finance' on paper and its spiritual bankruptcy in fact, its rusting mines and rotting shipyards, its derelict areas and derelict acres, its foreign policy of noble words and craven deeds — its entire anti-British foolishness and knavery.

We may find wisdom in the words of a Chinese, and not a dead man, Confucius, but a living woman, Madame Chiang Kai-shek, who told a Chinese audience in San Francisco in March 1943 that she feared the Allies, after military victory over the Axis, may fight among themselves and lose the peace. She quoted the Hussites, those Czech Roundheads who successfully fought the German Emperor's Cavaliers, but allowed their own factional differences to culminate in self-destruction after victory. 'When these two factions had a common enemy they were united and strong against him', she said, 'but when they had defeated him they flew at each other's throats. Shall we avert a similar disaster and gain wisdom from this object lesson?'

Madame Chiang Kai-shek declined to come to England. I think I can guess why, but it was a pity.

How right she was! In the midst of this war, which should have sobered us, if anything will, confusion in this island, about our future, is worse than even it was between the wars. What is to happen at home; what is to happen abroad; you may vainly scan the Parliamentary debates and the Press for light or hope. In foreign affairs, our leaders of the spoken and written word seem only united about the wrongs and rights of the Jews; they attack or ignore Frenchmen, Czechs, Poles and Serbs, and yet these are inseparable from our honour, our faith and our future. In domestic affairs, the way is clear for even worse exploitation than was after the last war: slums which were to be condemned are inhabited, slums which were already condemned have been reoccupied, the supply of houses is millions behind the people's need, nothing has been done to prevent new slums being built, or the distress of the population from being exploited in another decade of rent-squeezing, house-purchase enslavement and furnished-room profiteering. They talk, not of creating employment, though the opportunities are boundless, but of exploiting unemployment, through the weapon of coercion; and this, if it is allowed, will again open the way to the rich man who, of his own will, decides to close a coalmine or a shipyard.

Yet these conditions, in England, were the cause of our troubles. Slums, unemployment, derelict areas, dismantled mines and yards, and a decaying countryside, breed a spiritless nation. When I wrote the first of these books, before the war began, many people refused to believe the things I wrote about our slums; seemingly they were born, with eyes, but without sight. In 1943 a book was published, *Our Towns: A Close-Up* (Oxford University Press). It was mainly the result of an investigation, carried out by the Women's Group on Public Welfare, among mothers and children 'evacuated' from the towns to escape the bombing. The authors warn readers that they must have 'a stout stomach', and give a revolting picture, or one for which no adjective is foul enough, of conditions in England.

Many of these unfortunate beings were degraded, a disgrace and a danger to this wealthy country. It was not their fault; the fault lay in the slums, the criminal exploitation to which they were exposed by landlords, hire-purchase and insurance concerns, and the conniving Town Council and Government. Dirt, vermin, disease, animal habits, foul mouths, lying, stealing, bed-soiling, betting, drink, football coupons, 'comic' papers, pawntickets, 'pictures', patent medicines — the story traverses the entire alphabet of misery and filth. How could they help it?

> Hundreds of thousands of families in all parts of the country have not a private closet, and there are areas where it is the exception for a family to have one.

This is the proud balance of a British Parliament which has sat for nearly eight years, as I write, and proposes soon, by posturing on the hustings as 'The National Government Which Won The War', and giving the electors no choice, to prolong its life for another five years — or ten — or twenty. . . .

In twenty years, this war was brewed. Our slums were essential to its cooking. The Boys, when they come back, should make time to attend a Juvenile Court, and see at what tender ages Englishmen and Englishwomen are hopelessly spoiled, in this country. Children are not intrinsically wicked. The root causes, as Mr. John A. F. Watson says in his valuable book *The Child and the Magistrate* (Jonathan Cape, 1942), are:

> Poverty and slums; disease and drink; immorality; indifference to religion; each of them conducing to that most tragic of all a child's afflictions — a broken home. These are the roots of evil.

The two things — our wretched order of class-segregation in this island, and the confusion in our foreign policy — hang inextricably together. Reform the one, and the other will cure itself.

How and where may we attack this tangle, hope to unravel it and straighten it out? As I think, only by reforming and cleansing our Parliament. That is where the obstruction lies.

We have but two Parties, that count. The Conservative Party, which annexes the claim to an Imperial patriotism, led us straight into a war in which we lost large portions of the Empire almost without a fight. The Labour Party, which claims to represent the working-class, was unable to avert mass unemployment, derelict areas, slums and the capricious closure of mines and shipyards.

The Conservative Party remains the monopoly of those who wish, first and foremost, to perpetuate the privileges of wealth and Enclosure. Two hundred and fifty of its Members are connected with the peerage, baronetage and knighthood; scores are bankers, company directors and landowners, newspaper proprietors and the like. The majority of them inherited wealth, nearly all come from one of a few public schools. You will find few working men in its ranks.

The Socialist Party is the near-monopoly of the great officialdom which the trade unions have become. It represents, not the working man, or Socialists, but labour 'organized' in those great unions which support so many officials. It is as 'conservative' as the Conservative Party, in wishing to conserve bad things in the interest of a *section* of the population. You *may*, in this party, find an old-school-tie or two, around the necks of a leader or two. You will find few small artisans or small employers, democratic Conservatives or conservative Socialists.

Where, in the Conservative Party, is a man to find a place who wishes to conserve the best traditions of this country but not the evils of Enclosure and the caste-system; to conserve the freedom of a man to make his own way and become rich, if he wishes, but not to close down a coalmine or shipyard, render thousands of men idle and imperil our national safety; to conserve the principle of private ownership, but not the unbridled licence of the slum landlord; to conserve parliamentary government, but not the doctrine of non-accountability and 'no recriminations'?

Where, in the Socialist Party, is a man to find a place who wishes to reform the educational system, but not abolish the public schools; to abolish unemployment, but not the freedom of contract; to abolish slums and derelict areas, but not to abolish private ownership?

And where, in either, is a man to find a strong and clear foreign policy? In neither. A man of civic and patriotic feeling, who knows no class feeling, or money barrier, can find no home in either of them. Each stands for the interests of a group, and these interests in both cases conflict with the interest of the whole.

The two Parties know this, and are also well aware of that carking question in the minds of the people: 'What of the future after the war?' That is why they now prepare, having tasted the sweets of office-sharing, to join hands, evade the need to offer the electors a choice between two policies, and jointly ride on our backs for many more years to come. The sectional interests they serve would thus be safeguarded; the interests of the nation would be lost. The Socialist Party is ageing and decadent; the Conservative Party is vigorous but castebound. The Socialist Party knows it is unlikely ever to gain a majority (without a new policy which it is too short-sighted to evolve), because the country, having been given various 'nest-eggs' by the Conservatives with this electoral aim in view, would again be stampeded by the cry, 'Your savings are in danger'. It makes ready to remain in sleeping partnership with the Conservatives at the price of a few jobs and the preservation of the trades union edifice.

The cost of this bargain to the country is seemingly to be Socialist complicity in the regimentation of labour — that is, not the creation of *employment*, but the exploitation of *un*employment. This is the device, most dangerous of all to our future, which peeps alike out of the Beveridge Report, the Marquess of Salisbury's *Post-War Conservative Policy*, and the utterances of innumerable Socialist politicians, that 'control must continue after the war': that men and women 'must not be allowed to refuse work, even in other trades than their own or in other places than their homes', and that 'direction' to new employment may be enforced by 'penalties'. The Socialist Party becomes a great vested interest, inimical to the rights of individuals and akin to any great capitalist concern in its disregard for these.[1] And the written pledge of obedience which is required from its representatives makes the real power behind this party as secret and difficult to detect as those 'motives' which, according to Mr. Lloyd George, 'precipitate wars'.

The political future, then, begins to take the shape of a pact between Conservatives and Socialists for the prolongation of office-sharing and

---

[1] This arrangement recalls the delineation of areas, in which muscling-in was forbidden, between the gangs of Chicago during prohibition, and is indicated in the following quotations:

Some of the big unions have carried collaboration with large groups of employers to such a point that their leaders are now impatient of the old conceptions of antagonism between capital and labour ... Many union leaders envisage co-operation with capital as desirable for the next decade or so, and they become angry with political warfare which postpones the share of power which they think this co-operation will give them. Some of them carry their anger to the length of wondering *whether Parliament is any longer worth while and they don't hesitate to put their views into words.*

Mr. Aneurin Bevan, a Labour M.P., on March 5th, 1943.

A suggestion that the country would be safer in the hands of expert trade unionists and first-class employers than in charge of professional politicians was made last night in Leeds by Mr. J. D. S. Highman, a Yorkshire trade union leader. 'The country', he said, 'does not run on politics, it runs on industry — the exports and imports of the country. Nobody is better fitted to govern, in my judgment, than those who run industry in all its spheres.

The Daily Herald, February 1943.

the elimination of public interference. You may imagine, gentle reader, how little likely the Socialists would be, in a Parliament without an Opposition, to draw attention to large sales of British arms to Germany, or British investments in German armaments. You may imagine how little likely the Conservatives would be, in a Parliament without an Opposition, to pursue a sound foreign policy, to give correct information about our affairs, or to restrict the licence of shipowners, coalowners and slum landlords to undermine our national interests.

A main cause of this war was the lack of a clear-sighted, patriotic and vigorous Opposition in Parliament. The Socialists behaved like children in foreign affairs, and in domestic ones saw only the interests of the trade unions. How much worse will our plight be after this war, if even *that* much opposition is to be bought out! Here a mortal danger confronts us at the very start of Civvy Street.

Before we sum up the future, then, let me say again, that we shall not have one unless we break that deadlock in Parliament, and we can only do it by returning a large number of independent men to Parliament, who will accept no Party ties, refuse to be denied information about our affairs, and bring about by-elections in a national emergency (such as that of 1935, which was inadequately met by the Peace Ballot). Such men would be the country's watchdogs in a House now corrupted almost beyond redress.

And their foremost aim, now or ten years from now, should be to obtain a public inquiry into our affairs in the years of phoney peace which brewed this war. Only when we come to that knowledge, may we safely hope to build the future. Many of the men who were to blame will by then be dead, though their deeds will live after them. Nothing need happen to the others. The publication of the truth would be enough ignominy. But it would be the guarantee, which we so sorely need, that It could not happen again. Without that guarantee, It *will* happen again.

On that essential basis, how might we build the future? This is how I would sum it up:

(1) Our safety depends first on our fighting strength and our foreign policy. We need to that end a supreme navy and air force and a strong army, and exact information about these should be given annually in Parliament. British investments abroad should be forbidden for armaments and allied industries, and regulated so that they flow preponderantly,

in a set ratio, to our Dominions and Colonies first, and to foreign countries only next.

(2) Our alliance with Russia, which will be essential to the equilibrium of Europe, should be extended to fifty years.

(3) We should restore the League of Nations exactly as it was, and fulfil its obligations, exactly as they were, for this would ensure enduring peace, given the two preceding conditions.

This is the most important thing of all, because a dangerous trap is being laid for us in this matter. Deluded people, who are the victims of phrases, tend to believe that 'the League failed', and they are wrong. The League of Nations was a simple and perfect instrument for ensuring peace, and was especially attractive to us because, through the withdrawal of one or two Great Powers, it was, in effect, a British-led League amply strong enough to prevent war. Its triumph would have been a British triumph, and from the moment of that triumph it would have become a universal League, with British prestige paramount. Its failure was a *British* failure; we destroyed the League, in 1935 and after, and some of the influences which misguided our policy in those years now peep through the curtain of history, as I have shown. Any who promise us future peace by promising us some new kind of international organization, cannot be sincere. If they intend to preserve peace, they can do it through the League (the framework of which still exists) and need no other organization. If, however, they propose some different international body, their motives immediately become suspect. In this connection, I commend any who are anxious for the future to treat with the deepest suspicion four phrases which are current to-day: An International Police Force; Federal Union; The United States of Europe; Abolition of National Sovereignty. All these new proposals, unless I do them an injustice, contain a common kernel which is mortally dangerous to our future. It is that, when our armed strength has won victory, we should hand over our armed strength to some international body, controlled by who knows what hidden powers. That would be the first step towards a new war. For only in that way could the *second* condition be brought about, which was essential to the making of this war: our defencelessness. I have explained that this was the *half* of the seed of the present war. Germany's warlike ambitions and armed strength were not enough, alone, to produce the war. Our unreadiness, to the point of defencelessness, was also essential to it, and to the schemes of those who desired war: and this was brought about, first, by our disarmament, and second, by the deliberate deception of this country by its own leaders, who told it that our rearmament was proceeding when it was not. Any who may seek future wars will know that this country will not again be gulled by appeals to disarm, and that it will not again be content to believe, without proof, even the statements of its leaders, that its defences are in order. The only way, then, to effect our helplessness a second time would be, to deprive us of our sovereign control over our own armed forces. This is the danger which lurks behind the specious proposals I have mentioned. Beware Disarmageddon in *any* form; if we want enduring peace, we can have it through our own strength and a League united around it. That would be, in effect, what we now have, and could have had in 1935: a League of United Nations. It would perpetuate peace.

(4) We should desist from imparting confusion to our Foreign Policy by lending the strength of our arms to the pursuance of Jewish *national* aims, since this breeds throughout Jewry, as experience since the Balfour Declaration has incontrovertibly shown, an ever greater number of Jews who discard the feeling that they are Poles, Germans, Englishmen or members of any other national community among which they dwell, and adopt the principle that they are members of a Jewish *people* or *nation*, with rights to a separate State, or even Empire to which they can only come through the armed strength of Britain or some other great power. They do not, however, yield the rights of citizenship, which have now been granted to them in these communities, but demand *both*, and this leads to an intolerable duality and duplicity of claims. British policy should be aimed to ensure for the Jews, as members of a *religious* community alone, 'equal rights of citizenship' in the countries where they dwell, and nothing more; or, if they are to have a National State, or Empire, that they should become citizens of it and aliens elsewhere. This is a major issue, which has already involved us in one minor foreign war and bids to involve us in others, and overshadows and distorts our foreign policy in a manner insupportable for the people of this country.

In this connection, the pledge given by the British Government, that immigrants brought to this country since 1933 would not stay here, become a burden to the British taxpayer, displace British citizens in the professions, callings and trades, or establish themselves here in prosperity during the absence of serving British citizens, should be *honoured*. The British Government's utmost endeavour should be, to see that these people return to their own countries and there receive 'equal rights of citizenship'.

(5) In our domestic affairs, Members of Parliament should by legislation be forbidden to sign pledges of unquestioning obedience to Parties which choose them as candidates, since such obviously override and invalidate pledges made to the voters at an election; and our whole present disaster is due to this secret and sinister allegiance.

(6) The principle of accountability should be restored, and legislation passed to compel the publication of documents, about the origins of such a war as this (in the manner followed, in this war, by the American Parliament), or of dispatches, about great military disasters. The country, under the present system, is denied all knowledge of the culprits and the blame by means of some cheap phrase. This is an indefensible arrangement, which is a main cause for our troubles, and is in effect indistinguishable from the methods of despotic and dictatorial government against which we supposedly fight.

In this connection a paramount need is to reduce, and eventually abolish, by law the practice of power-wielded-in-anonymity which has grown up in this country. Newspapers should be bound to publish prominently the names of their proprietors and editors, so that the public may know whose opinions they read, and what influences are likely to distort the information presented to them. Advertising revenue should be restricted to a modest proportion of sales-revenue, to prevent the acquirement of control, over the opinions and information presented, by anonymous third-parties, 'The Advertisers'. The proprietors of great concerns, similarly, should not be enabled to conceal their identity behind such names as 'The Venus Insurance Company', 'The British Imperial House-Purchase Corporation', 'The Patriotic Bank Holding Company', and the like. Persons who change their names should by law be compelled to print their original names in brackets in any such disclosure. The implacable doctrine of Civil Service anonymity, also, should be reduced; it is indefensible that men in the public service who wield great power over our national affairs should remain secret; the names of high permanent officials should be published with those of Ministers and their actions should be subject to Parliamentary debate, with reference to them by name.

(7) Certain industries of this country are inseparable from and indispensable to our prosperity in peace and security in war. These are merchant shipping, coalmining, agriculture, and (in the future) civil aviation. The neglect, or even the deliberate repression and discouragement of these (and the fighting services) were the main cause of both our greatest recent disasters: mass unemployment and the present war. Any 'Four Year Plan', or any plan at all, is useless which does not put the fostering of these four industries first among its proposals. The principle should be established, that 'private enterprise' cannot be allowed to go so far as the closure of mines and shipyards; that a fair level of wages and prices in agriculture must be set by law; and that the creation of a great merchant marine of the air is our first duty when the war ends.

(8) The principle should be established, that the problem of labour is one of employment, and not of unemployment. It should be attacked, first and foremost, through these four industries, which themselves are potentially able to employ such masses of workpeople, and on which many other smaller industries depend. The industries themselves, and the problem of employment, are both auxiliary to, and essential to our island security. As a safeguard against the exploitation of unemployment, the indications of coercion and imprisonment should be deleted from the Beveridge Plan, if it is otherwise to be adopted.

(9) Imperial security depends on our island security, and cannot be ensured while the Dominions remain empty. The whole structure of Imperial security hangs together, and cannot be better served than by a lively process of emigration from this country and of inter-migration between the Dominions and this country. The policy of British Governments (and presumably of Dominions Governments, too) for ten years before this war, was to hinder and even check such migration, and during the last of these years, to promote alien migrations. This is a direct blow at both our insular security and Imperial security, and should cease. The Dominions Governments, under stress of this war, have given clear signs that they desire a resumption of substantial British emigration after the war. This should be encouraged, partly by the assisted emigration of selected and trained candidates, but much more by the encouragement of independent emigrants who have saved a little money and are hardy and enterprising.

(10) The spiritual discouragement of the people of this country,

which is another great source of danger to its future, is largely due to the order of class-compartments and privilege which has grown up on the basis of Enclosure of the land. The locking-up of the land is also a permanent cause of repression and frustration, even when this is not realized by the sufferers. The liberation of the land, for the enjoyment of the people, should be pursued in every possible way, as part of a process for reinvigorating England. A survey of the remaining common land in the country should be made, and all prohibitions and vetoes which have been placed on the use of it by petty authorities removed; and such further small and stealthy enclosure should be forbidden in future by law. The practice of fencing and railing-off public places should be stopped.[1]

But that is not enough. The common land was once a large part of England and was taken by legalized theft. It should be gradually liberated. The survey should establish the extent of it. The word 'nationalization' is disliked in England, but the restoration of much of this land could be effected by means of a compromise. To-day, rich men 'give' their estates to the nation; actually they receive as much as, or more than, they give, because they are relieved of taxes and death duties, and remain in occupation, public access being small. (Parliament should demand from the National Trust, and publish, a simple statement of the area of land thus 'given' up to the present, and make access general by law; otherwise the thing is a fraud.) The area of formerly common land, now in private ownership, should be determined and this should gradually revert to public use and enjoyment, the present holders being remitted death duties and taxes on it, and remaining in possession of it for a generation. The settlement of smallholders and cottagers should be promoted, on a large part of it; and the remaining part restored to public enjoyment. This reform would do more than any one thing to revive the English countryside and to give the people of this island the feeling that they belong to it, than anything else.

(11) The Enclosure of education and of opportunity, through the system of public schools which hold a monopoly of high public employment, is another great source of social segregation, exclusion and frustration, and also depresses the tone of life in this island, and the spirit of the people. The public schools should remain, for those who prefer the order

[1] Recommendations containing points of resemblance to these were made, in March 1943, in a Report of the Nature Reserves Investigation Committee.

of two-nations-living-in-one-island. But exactly half the places in them and the universities (and more of these should be established), or else, exactly half the places in the commissioned ranks of the fighting services and in higher State employment, such as the Civil Service, the Diplomatic Service, and the Law, should be opened to unmoneyed youths, who attain a fixed standard at their schools, and are aware when they begin their schooling that they can so rise if they are diligent.

That is how I would sum up the future, if I could. If you, gentle reader, ten years from now, could look back and say, these things were done, you would be able to look around you at a happy breed and a happy England, and across the Channel, at a Europe, peaceful, respectful of us and grateful to us. In their hearts, they would every day of their lives wave flags to us, as those Belgians waved them to us, a British pilot and observer, from the streets of Mons on November 10th, 1918.

These things are good and simple things, which could easily be brought about. They would injure none, and benefit all, and give us peace and hope. They would destroy 'cynicism and bitterness'. They will not come about, of themselves. Our Parliament will do none of them, unless it is made to. Between us and them, stand secret pledges, secret men, hidden 'motives' which precipitate wars, and which 'the statesmen responsible dare not avow'. 'They' stand in the way. Public opinion, informed, enlightened and vigorous, could quickly change that.

I wonder how many people realize that we have, to-day, the thing for which we yearned, for which seven million Britishers voted, in 1935: a world united, under British leadership, to repel and punish aggression. We have it now, and that is why things go better with us; but for the betrayal of 1935, they would never have gone ill.

We *have* 'The League of Nations', armed, strong and punitive. We have now the thing that the soul of England called for, then; bear it in mind, gentle reader, so that you may know what you want in future, and get it. Our Navy, our Army and our Air Force are no longer English, British, Imperial; they are international, but they are British-led! Men of many breeds wear the navy blue, the sky blue, the khaki, with small differences of badge and brevet. When you hear that Polish airmen have bombed the Ruhr, that Norwegian ships bring us priceless oil, that French cruisers steam with ours in the Mediterranean, that Czech troops have shared an attack with ours, you see the thing that you might have had in 1935, without a war, to avert a war. That was the thing our leaders threw away, the thing we may have again to-morrow, the thing that Anon will wreck again, if he can.

One more thing. Anon will not seek to destroy us by disarming us, this time. He knows that the people would not submit to that. He will try to arm us, and deprive us of the control of our arms — by inventing some international body to which our 'sovereignty' must be surrendered. That would be fatal. The League of Nations was, in effect, a British League, based on our strength, glad of our leadership, dismayed at our desertion. You see before your eyes to-day, what it was. That is the thing we need to-morrow, and nothing else.

Ten years ago, I suppose, I began to think, though not then to write, these books: at the moment Hitler came to power in 1933. The new war immediately became certain — if we allowed it. The next six-and-a-half years, until it began, were years of deepening bewilderment and humiliation: it was, then, not only to be allowed, but actively promoted, by those British leaders who 'held the torch' for the million dead Britishers of the last war! For the nine months after that, between the beginning of the war and Dunkirk, I can find no word to describe my feelings. I knew, what none outside a small inner circle realized, that our line in France was not being made strong, that the gap was being left through which the Germans would come like a dose of salts. To-day, I see no other word than treachery to describe that, and as long as we are denied information, the suspicion can only become stronger.

Then, at last, we began to fight — at long, long last! What hope reborn was that, what an unforgettable autumn.

Yet to-day, I feel that the disillusionment of the last two years has been worse than even that of those eight years before; and in saying this I quote the words of another, an authority. The ecstatic moment of victory approaches, yes; but there is no *basis* to all this, because information about the seven poltroon years and the seven more than astonishing months has been refused, because the dark order, of power wielded in non-accountability, which brought about the war, and the seven months of inexplicable inaction, has not been changed. The only hope is, that the people of this country, those who are here and those who have yet to return, will fight a Battle in England to change them. Without that, their victory will be vain; they surrender their future.

x

323

To-day in England (and I thank the reader who suggested this excellent simile to me) 'we are like the characters in *The Three Sisters*, who are always going to Moscow — but never set out'. The only clear thing in our picture is the valour of our fighting men, who are at length allowed to fight and given good weapons. Everything else is confusion. Our Parliament, our politicians, our Press seem resolved to stand between us and a confident future. Our plight has been eloquently described by the Editor of *The Nineteenth Century*, in discussing 'our obscurantists', a word as good as any to describe these infuriating babblers-at-home who can perceive no native ideal or interest, no simple patriotic faith or clear way to ensure our safety after this war:

The unverified assumption and the facile conclusion as to the method [he says] and abdication as the purpose — these are the characteristics of the works we have examined and of all contemporary obscurantist literature — of the Editorials in *The New Statesman*, of recent books by Professor Harold Laski, Victor Gollancz, H. G. Wells, Commander Stephen King-Hall, Sir Richard Acland, Professor Julian Huxley, Mr. Edward Mousley, of at least four of the twelve contributions to *A Christian Basis for a Post-War World* (with an introduction by the Archbishop of Canterbury), of nearly all pronouncements on the subject of war-aims by leading members of the Labour Party, and so on and so on. Contemporary obscurantism is not confined to the Left. Professor Carr is not, as far as we are aware, a man of the Left, and views closely resembling his own are to be found in the editorial columns of *The Times*. Our Continental Allies who judge this country by the published word — and few have any other means of judging it — *are beginning to be appalled by what seems to them a peculiarly intractable and nefarious form of defeatism*. They are being persuaded that as soon as the power of Germany begins to crumble, they must place Great Britain before the accomplished fact of a Germany which will, by loss of territory, by deportation, and even by massacre, be rendered for ever unable to wage another war, for, unless they act at once and drastically, Germany will, if our obscurantists have their way, win the peace after having lost the war, and either go to war for the third time or become master of Europe without a war. Our obscurantists, for all their tenderness towards the foe, for all their condemnation of hatred, and for all their display of superior humanity, are doing the foe no good, are helping to intensify hatred and fear, and are inciting to ruthless inhumanity.

It is true that they do not represent the spirit of England. The heart of the nation is sound, but the head is muddled. Head and heart must work in unison, the sound instinct needs a fixed and clearly conceived purpose. Obscurantism has not only invaded the world of politics and not only dominates almost every discussion of war-aims and the nature of the peace. It has invaded the world of science, of art and religion, and has infected broadcasting. It is a denial, while pretending to be an affirmation, of all that is best in English life, it is an assault on the integrity of the sovereign intellect and on the heritage that has come down from Athens, Rome and Jerusalem. While employing the language of freedom, enlightened progress and victory, it is reactionary and defeatist in the direst sense. It would destroy an established world, regardless of the human happiness that would be buried under the ruins. It would build up a new world of colourless abstractions, a City of Dreadful Twilight, oblivious of the fact that the mere attempt to bring such a world about would mean revolution more frightful than any that was ever experienced. Revolution, and abdication more disastrous and shameful than defeat — these are the two things the obscurantists chiefly stand for. Let no one say they do not matter because they lack insight and foresight, because their ideas are confused and their books are dull. Alas, they matter a great deal. To attack them and to expose them has become a patriotic duty.

If I borrow the words of another, to end this book, that is not because I lack any myself, but because I think them among the most notable of our day. Here, one other writer at least has seen what lies behind the sham-holy and mock-humanitarian clamour of our Parliament and our newspapers, our prelates and our professors; the desire, conscious or unconscious, to destroy us, to weaken everything that is good in us, to strengthen our enemies, fail our friends, surrender our future, perpetuate our wrongs and deprive us of our rights.

The Gods may know how we have bred such leaders, and how they have come to such noisy authority in our English island. I do not. I only know that the picture I see in this country, the picture which all our foreign allies see, is one of maddening confusion in the public debate on the one hand, and simple valour among the humble people, on the other. 'The heart of the nation is sound, but the head is muddled.' How often have I written those very words, and the others: 'The sound instinct needs a fixed and clearly-conceived purpose.' The time comes when the heart of England will need to assert its supremacy over this muddled head, the sound instinct to insist on a firm purpose, or we shall yet be betrayed. It is a terrible thing for an Englishman, in this time when our men fight so staunchly, and have restored our renown to so high a peak, and when the simple folk endure so much, to see at home a condition of affairs which combines the worst features of German and of French life after the last war.

Now for the first time, as I reach the end of this last book, I think I perceive faint signs of awakening in England. People begin at last to stir and demur, to tell themselves that this war should be fought for the British future, and not for a third German war, or a Jewish Empire, or any other of the alien things which obsess our leaders, so that they tend completely to ignore the sufferings and anxieties of their own people. Perhaps, at last, the English spirit revives. That alone can save us.

What a great time it has been, what a pageant of staunchness, when you turn your eyes away from that dark political scene, towards the ordinary people, these wonderful people, who have every virtue but the courage to admonish their leaders. The whole world pays homage to *their* achievement; the whole world fears their leaders. The words of Madame Chiang Kai-shek, which I have quoted, are those which you may hear, gentle reader, if you care to inquire, from any Hollander, Pole, Frenchman, Czech, Serb, Norwegian or Belgian in this country. They have a deeper respect than ever before for the people of this country; but the policies of its leaders reduce them to despair. What *can* they think, when our Foreign Minister pronounces that the Munich Agreement is dead, and a leading newspaper (the one which chiefly championed that deed) promptly urges that Poland should be partitioned for the benefit of Russia; when voices are clamantly raised in Parliament against the bombing of Germany, but never against the bombing of France, Holland or Belgium; when Mr. Churchill and Mr. Roosevelt promise 'measures to divert German strength from the attack on Russia' and 'a complete plan of action to be carried out in the next nine months', and another Minister derides the 'Second Front' as 'a catchpenny phrase', and so on, and so endlessly on.

It is the same lunatic babel that we knew in the inter-war years. No wonder that Madame Chiang Kai-shek feared it; no wonder these others fear it. I fear it, and so, gentle reader, do you. That is why the

Archbishop of Canterbury spoke of those many people who 'dread the end of the war'.

If our people would produce the energy to impart their own spirit to their leaders, and to control their actions, we should have nothing to fear.

How staunch they are. A great parade of them passes through my memory. The taxi-driver who 'would hate to die in his bed' and drove through the worst of the Blitz: the bus-drivers who steered their cumbersome vehicles through that inferno; the train-guard in whose company I came from Bradford into King's Cross one early morning when the bombing was at its height — a walk across London to his home in Brixton awaited him; the R.A.F. pilot whom I saw shot down during the Battle of Britain, and his thumbs-up to the crowd when they fished him out of the Channel and brought him ashore; the Scots sea-captain in the inn at Dover, with the parachute of the German airman he shot down drying in the grate; the old lady I helped pull out of a bombed house in Paddington, who had an impediment in her speech, so that she said, indistinctly but emphatically, 'Oh, 'y 'oor 'oody 'ead!'; little Dorothy, who could have enjoyed the war, for she entertained the troops, but when the sergeant-air-gunner she liked was shot down, she rushed off to join the W.A.A.F. (if only more of the women with *living* men away from them were as loyal); young Molly, whom I thought empty, but she drove an ambulance all through the Blitz and was bemedalled for it; and all the hundreds of lads I have seen go off to the war in the air, at sea and on land.

With these people, if you could make them think, you could do more than conquer the world; you could keep peace in the world and make the world worth living in.

To the very many men and women of goodwill and deep care for their country, who have accompanied me through these five books, who have come all the way with me from 1914 to 1943, and have now even shared a journey with me to 1950 and 1960, I owe gratitude for much helpful information and invigorating comment.

If I do not take leave of them with a happy ending, that is because I think the phrase asinine, a part of the whole rigmarole of delusion, by means of which spines are softened and wits weakened in our time. Life has no ending but death, which few of us think a happy event. Indeed, the only thing we would have to complain of in this delightful and perfect planet, if 'They' were not, would be, that life is too short. But life only offers meaning if we think of it as an endless chain, in which birth and death are the links. In that infinite process, ending has no place. It is all beginning; with each new link, the chain begins again.

Not a happy ending, then, but a happy beginning. *That*, you *may* have, if you resolve, as the pandemonium of victory approaches, and we find that Civvy Street lies behind it, to fight a Battle in England for the future.

And with the wish, that we may join in that happy beginning, I thank you, most gentle reader, and hope that we may meet again, but not in *Insanity Fair*.

FOOTNOTE

THE lapse of time between the completion of a book and its publication, and the few blank pages at the end, give me the opportunity, as this one goes to press, to sharpen my argument, in the light of recent events, by adding this Footnote.

On the evening of May 12th, 1943, in a Sussex lane, I met a woebegone farmer. The weather continued cold and his crops would not grow; they drooped, grey and dispirited, in his fields. That night was warm, and when the sun rose on May 13th the scene in the fields was already magically changed; at eventide, when it went down, sturdy regiments of wheat and oats stood straight and strong, and grew almost as you watched. That selfsame day, May 13th, the newspapers contained the tidings of our victory in Africa. Not another local success, but complete and final victory; the Germans killed or captured to a man. I shall never forget that morning, with the crops reviving, the sun climbing happily into a golden sky, my farmer friend smiling broadly where he scowled the day before, and the exultant headlines in the newspapers.

At last! For the first time since Hitler came to power in 1933, daylight showed ahead. Victory beckoned. The Germans had suffered the two greatest defeats in their warlike history: those of Stalingrad and Africa. Now we had only to close our grip on the Mediterranean; squeeze Italy out of the war, who was ready and anxious to be so squeezed; strike unremittingly from the air at the German war-machine, which fortunately is compressed into the corner of Germany nearest to us, the Ruhr; land on the French coast; and victory would be ours.

Such will be the course of events in 1943, or early 1944, if we do these things. Shall we now do them, or will the dead hand intervene again, to frustrate our hopes? If the war should now drag on into 1944 and 1945 and 1946, perhaps into 1950, we may be quite certain that the enemy we fight is no longer Germany, or 'The Axis', but that invisible foe who was indicated by a significant phrase in Mr. Churchill's speech at Washington on May 19th, 1943 (after our African victory):

We have surmounted many serious dangers, but there is one grave danger which will go along with us to the end. That danger is the *undue prolongation of the war*.

Like Mr. Lloyd George (who spoke of those 'motives which precipitate wars' and which 'the statesmen responsible for conducting wars dare not avow'), Mr. Churchill points to the existence of dark and secret things, but does not reveal them.

This war already has been unduly prolonged, and in this book I have sought to detect the reasons by showing what powerful interests profit from its continuance. It was prolonged when we let pass the opportunities of 1942 and 1941. It was prolonged at its very beginning, in 1940 and 1939, when the British-held gap in the Maginot Line was allowed to remain unfilled during 'the astonishing months of the phoney war' (Mr. Churchill). To the accumulating evidence about that sinister period may now be added a book, *Infantry Officer* (B. T. Batsford, 1943) by a subaltern of the B.E.F., which went to France in 1939. It only contains 'as much of my experiences as the censor would pass', but includes this striking revelation about the 'phoney war' period (during which Australian and South African Ministers personally but vainly warned Mr. Chamberlain of the state of the British line in France):

During those eight months I don't think I took part in one field exercise, though I did construct a railway station yard, build a road, and turn a stream into an anti-tank obstacle. No, I'm wrong; not a complete obstacle. When it was half finished we left it to build the road.

The phoney war left this British island defenceless (though it was inexplicably spared). Australia (similarly spared) was left to face an imminent Japanese invasion with 'only ten tanks' (an official Australian statement); and the Australian Minister of Supply, Mr. Beasley, stated at Canberra on June 23rd, 1943, that 'the Chamberlain policy' was 'that the Dominions might have to be lost and then won back'. What, then, was 'the Chamberlain policy' about this island? Why was the gap in the Maginot Line left open? The question becomes more and more important for our future, as the event itself recedes.

Wars, then, may be, and have been 'unduly prolonged'. Now victory is within our grasp.

No sooner was our victory in Africa complete (the Germans, as I have often written, have a sudden and brittle breaking point, and collapsed in Africa just fourteen days after an unnamed Eighth Army general, in the *Daily Mail*, said 'There will be no quick and crushing defeat of the Axis forces; they will fight to the last man and the last bullet'), than the clamour against the bombing of Rome ('a crime', the Bishop of Lichfield), and against the bombing of Germany broke out in new fury.

For instance, Mr. Harold Nicolson has announced (in the *Spectator*) that if the only argument in favour of our bombing of Germany were that it would have the same effect upon Germany's internal resistance as was produced in 1918 by the blockade (that effect, I may interpolate, was the defeat of Germany) he would feel it to be 'better to have another year of military warfare than to achieve victory by bombing in the night'. Who is better qualified than he to say What We Are Fighting For? He is a former diplomat, a former deputy Minister of Information, a Member of Parliament and a Governor of the B.B.C. If he, then, is ready staunchly to face 'another year of military warfare', what serving soldier, sailor, airman, or wife of any of these should complain?

Ah, this England! Those of its sons and daughters who dread 'anything radical, any change' have no cause to fear. Not even the phrases change, from war to war.

'Another year of military warfare'! Well, enough people in this country might welcome the thought of many more such years, not only one, and dread the approach of peace. 'Big money has been made in the City this week. Diamond and gold shares have been moving up rapidly, and when business closed yesterday many brokers went home with that lightness of heart which comes with a comfortable increase in the bank balance' (*The Evening Standard*, June 26th, 1943). Compare this cheery item with the words of our Tory Chancellor of the Exchequer, Sir Kingsley Wood, on February 2nd, 1943: 'The whole world will be much poorer after the war'. Hard-working citizens will be much poorer, through taxation, the interruption of careers, and the ruin of businesses. But gains made on the Stock Exchange are free from taxation, like so many directors' fees and all increase in property values.

The long delay in bombing Germany is already chief among the causes of the undue prolongation of this war. (About that, too, we now have a piece of evidence. Major General Eaker, Commander of the American air forces in this country, speaking on June 10th, 1943, said that during 1942 Air Chief Marshal Harris, the head of R.A.F. Bomber Command, was asked about the effects of air bombing and answered caustically, 'I don't know. Why don't we try it some time?')

As I write, we are at last using this weapon to the full, with immediate results of the first importance. It is a war-winning weapon. One of the greatest battles of this war, and the one which for three years went all in favour of our enemy, was the unseen one which has been fought to hinder us in using it. If the dead hand successfully interferes again, this war will be unduly prolonged once more. But its undue prolongation will have an inexorable result: the loss of the peace.

The hidden mechanism of a war is not an agreeable thing to see when you place it beneath the X-rays. Since I finished this book, in which I have referred to the Skoda Works, the R.A.F. has been sent to bomb that great arms factory. The return journey was one of over 1,000 miles, and the bomber crews had to battle their way through the full fury of the German defences for the greater part of that distance, both coming and going. For Skoda is in Czechoslovakia, which, as Mr. Chamberlain said, is a long way away; he also said that he knew little about it, but the R.A.F. crews will now know quite a lot about it.

Our losses were heavy that night; indeed, our newspapers stated that the raid was the costliest excursion of its kind ever made by our airmen, and this was no wonder; writing in 1937, when Czechoslovakia was still free, I said that 'Czechoslovakia means you', and the relatives of the men who did not return, as well as the survivors who did, will now see clearly what I meant, and will, I hope, take pains to examine the records, in this respect, of candidates who seek their vote at the next election.

For the Skoda Works are in that part of Czechoslovakia which was handed to Germany at Mr. Chamberlain's command. The newspapers, which paid fervent tribute to the courage of our bomber crews, did not recall that fact; nor did they remind their readers that British shareholders in the bombed Skoda works, where our airmen found the flak so fierce, would duly receive their dividends, through the agency of the British Government.

Between compassion for our enemies and for the Jews of Europe, and indifference to the sufferings of the British people and the non-Jewish Europeans, which will grow more bitter if the war is 'unduly prolonged', the public debate in this island is one of confusion becoming worse confounded. Infatuation for, or subservience to the cause of Jewish nationalism produces excesses for which even a Government spokesman in the House of Commons on May 19th, 1943 was forced to use the word 'fantastic'. He alluded, among other examples, to the case of 'an aged Jewish couple in Berlin', much publicized in one of the hundreds of Jewish pamphlets now current. They were refused admission to this country, and this was depicted as another instance of British cruelty; all propaganda in this cause tends to take on a virulently anti-British note. Sanctuary in this country was claimed for them by their son, 'a naturalized Turk in Istanbul'. The son proved to be Krupps' agent in Turkey, a man who negotiated large sales of German arms to foreign countries!

Infatuated Gentiles, however, as always, far surpass the Jews themselves in extravagant demands. The *Catholic Times*, in February 1943, reported that a priest, a Dr. Bernard Grimley, vice-chairman of 'The Leicester Christian Council', at a public meeting in that city said, 'Let us offer the Germans Hess in exchange for 100,000 Jews. Let them have their submarine commanders back in return for Jews threatened with death'.

The Germans hold 90,000 *British* captives, to say nothing of Poles, Frenchmen, Hollanders and all the rest. The British prisoners-of-war, especially those whose homes or families are in Leicester, should appreciate this proposal, as should our sailors and merchant seamen the other suggestion, that captured submarine commanders should be returned to Germany. The *Catholic Times* said that this meeting 'had the support of Leicester's three M.P.s'. The electors of Leicester, especially those who have served overseas, or who mourn or pine for menfolk killed or captured, might care to ask these politicians, when next they stand at an election, on what conception of patriotism, or even of elected representation, they base such an attitude.

The affair of Hess bids fair to become a bitter comedy. How many people in this country now believe that this ringleader of the men we are taught to regard as fiends in human form, will be punished? In 1942 the British Government sent to the Soviet Government a solemn Anglo-American memorandum about the punishment of such guilty men, and asked for its views. The Russians have a sense of humour and replied, through an inspired newspaper article, 'If you are in such a hurry about bringing the war criminals to book, why don't you try the one you hold, Hess?' Whitehall hurriedly changed the subject.

Yet this is important. Hess becomes a public joke. Prince Paul of Yugoslavia, who sought to enlist Yugoslavia among our enemies and was driven out by his own people, is vehemently defended in Parliament when allusions to his conduct are made. The name of Mr. John Amery, who broadcasts violent attacks on us from Berlin, is never mentioned in the British Press. Seemingly persons of social rank, whatever their guilt, will not be held guilty. Yet an obscure British subject, one William Craven, 28 years of age, who wrote a letter to the German Legation in Dublin 'in the intent to help the enemy', has been sentenced to *penal servitude for life*, and will presumably serve that sentence!

What of the Empire? On June 23rd, 1943, the result of a popular canvass held in Canada was published. The questions put referred to the future of Canada. Of the people who were questioned, 49 per cent (or just under half) held that Canada should continue as a member of the British Commonwealth; 21 per cent, that it should become part of the United States; 24 per cent, that it should become an independent nation. Analysis of the result showed that those who wished to remain in the British Commonwealth were mainly 'Canadians of British ancestry'. (The emigration of such to Canada between the wars was discouraged in every possible way, either by intention or stupidity.) Those who wished Canada to be absorbed by the United States were 'Canadians of other origins'. (The emigration of such as these to Canada was promoted in the last ten of the inter-war years, and is still being promoted by the encouragement of Jewish mass-movements from Europe, during the absence of British and Canadian manhood at the war.)

Well might Dr. Trevor Owen, Archbishop of Toronto and Primate of All Canada, say, on May 2nd, 1943, that Canada hoped for 'several more million British immigrants after the war'. But the British Government, which sent no less than three Ministers to a 'refugee conference' at Bermuda in April, has announced no plans for British emigration to the Dominions, or for Imperial intermigration, and seems unconcerned about such things. And who will expect help in so vital a matter from our present Parliament, of which Sir Patrick Hannon, on May 13th, 1943, said 'Look around the House and see the condition of the Members. What a testimony we ourselves offer to the administration of the Ministry of Food – always cheerful, bright and happy. And if you make an occasional visit to their lordships in the House of Lords you see in them an abiding reflection of prosperity in the matter of nutrition'. (On August 2nd, 1939, a few weeks before the war began, Mr. Chamberlain moved to adjourn the Commons until October 3rd. The young Tory Member, Ronald Cartland, who was to fall among the first victims when the 'phoney war' ended and the Germans came through the open gap 'like a dose of salts', attacked Mr. Chamberlain for making 'a jeering, pettifogging party speech'. Sir Patrick Hannon, who, like Cartland and Chamberlain, represented a Birmingham constituency, made a bitter attack on Cartland, saying he wished to declare 'on behalf of the City of Birmingham their profound confidence in the Prime Minister and their devotion to his policy'.)

In the British Empire, and at its borders, the shadow of things to come looms up, while the war still goes on, or while it is 'unduly prolonged'. Sir Reginald Storrs, our foremost Palestinian expert, warningly remarked in the *Sunday Times* that the Jews 'have officially proclaimed their utter rejection of the White Paper' (by which the British Government pledged itself to check further Jewish immigration and to set up a *joint* Arab-Jewish State, as distinct from a Jewish one with the Arabs relegated to a state of subjection in their own lands) and that the Jews hold 'considerable armaments under their control'. General Nuri Said, the Prime Minister of Irak, in an interview published in the *News-Chronicle* on June 16th, 1943, expressed similar forebodings, saying 'At present there is only one cloud on the Arab horizon. That is the renewed agitation by the Zionists for a Jewish *State* as distinct from a Jewish *national home* in Palestine'. (The British pledge of 1917 was for a Jewish national home.) 'Arabs firmly adhere to the White Paper and demand that the British Government do likewise, for their fear is that *in a wave of sympathy for persecuted Jewry promises and pledges over Palestine may again become confused*'. And the Wahabi King of Saudi Arabia, in a statement published in June 1943, expressed the same misgivings, saying that 'the Jews cannot justify a claim to Palestine by recalling that they used to live there before the Romans conquered them, who in their turn were driven out by the Arabs 1300 years ago ... If the Jews need a place in which to live, there are countries in Europe, America and elsewhere that are larger, more fertile and more convenient to their interests'.

Even if this war should not be 'unduly prolonged', if it should now soon be ended, as it ought to be, British arms do not need to be drawn, through the might of finance, into a great new conflict in the Near East, in the service of a cause which is not our own. The grave subservience of our Parliament and Press to this cause, however, creates the danger that this may happen, and it is essential that our policy in the world should cast off the tutelage, in this respect, into which it has fallen, and should revert to the service of *British* interests.

Will the war be 'unduly prolonged'? Well, if we had struck in 1942 or 1941, our men would have met an enemy so desperately embroiled with Russia in the East that he would have been sore put to it to turn and face them in sufficient strength. But if they attack in 1943 (and we are promised this every day) they may find an enemy relieved of that mortal danger in the east, so that he will be able to bring scores of divisions from Russia to confront them in the west. Will Russia then open 'a second front' for *us*? In the light of this question, the sweethearts and wives of our men who will one day attack should look back on the clamour against invasion, which filled 1942 and 1941, and see for themselves how wars may be prolonged and victory made costlier.

Nevertheless, victory will have to come, later or sooner, and the signs are clear that it moves towards us — rather than we towards it. For thirty Conservative M.P.s have proposed (quite logically) the partitioning of Prussia after the war, and an indefinite occupation; thus did Conservative Members warn Mr. Lloyd George by telegram, at the last Peace Conference, not to be weak with Germany — and in 1938 they clamoured for the propitiation of Germany by the abandonment of small nations liberated in that war. Labour M.P.s demand in the House of Commons that the bombing of Germany should cease (they utter no complaint about the bombing of France, Belgium, Holland, Norway or Greece), they made similar demands about the naval blockade, towards the end of the last war — and in 1938 they clamoured that this country, the armed strength and foreign policy of which they did so much to weaken, should oppose the German aggressor with arms. And Mr. Herbert Morrison, who seemingly grooms himself for the Socialist leadership after this war, in all his speeches cries that, when we have defended Freedom With All Our Might, the only hope of future happiness for our people will lie in 'the continuance of control', in the submission of the workpeople to further dictation, by Mr. Dodger of the Labour Exchange, in the matter of the work they are to perform, the wage they are to receive, and the place of their dwelling. Thus do the present-day descendants of the liberated bondmen extol bondage as the means by which England may be made happy. They are as avid for power, for power's sake, as were the feudal barons and the captains of capital. But that way, quite certainly, lie new disasters and new wars.

Well may the British citizen, as the old phrases of 1918 and 1919 crop up again, feel himself like a man who sits in a picture-theatre and watches a continuous performance of the same film; and well may he mutter to himself, 'This is where I came in'.

With the best of goodwill, it is not possible to contemplate these things and say, that our situation to-day is clearer than it was towards the end of the last war, in which the victory of our arms brought us no security because of the infirmity of our policies in the following peace. M. Jan Masaryk, the Czechoslovak Deputy Prime Minister, in May 1943 said he was grateful to 'the British soldiers, those small, humble citizens who are capable of being the greatest heroes . . . As soon as the war ends they will modestly disappear into their little homes and cease to be glorious, and that is their greatest glory of all'.

He could not be more wrong. That would be their greatest, and irretrievable mistake, for, in the words of another of our allies, Commandant Kicq of the Belgian Army (April 1943), 'Seven out of ten Europeans feel that British policy after the last war towards Germany was responsible for the present war; they would be relieved if Great Britain promised, not to "Hang the Kaiser", but to ensure peace'.

That can happen again, if those 'humble citizens' withdraw, snail-like, into their 'little homes', and leave the care of British policy to such men as those who brought it to disaster between 1919 and 1939. In the words of Admiral Riiser-Larsen, Commander-in-Chief of the Norwegian Royal Air Force, 'While I have no fear of what Stalin would say or what Mr. Churchill would want to do when victory is won, I am afraid of what Britain will do and how you will look upon Germans, because you are too decent. You say vengeance and revenge belong to God, but it's no use threatening people with that when they don't believe in God.'

Are we then to have another Beanfeast in England, instead of the Battle in England which we need? The B.B.C., which keeps useful discussion of our affairs out of its broadcasts, though it blows raspberries to Hitler and tells the young girls of England that they 'have got to give in to a soldier', has now struck the note for the peace-to-come: 'We're gonna get lit-up when the lights go on in London.' Just that. A *tight* little island, for a day or two, and after that – who cares?

The decade, 1930-40, was, I think, one of the saddest and most abject in our history. That tragic comedy of errors, that pageant of human stupidity and cupidity, has been vividly depicted in a Voltairean masterpiece of our times which the greater public, I imagine, has overlooked: *The Thirties*, by Malcolm Muggeridge (Hamish Hamilton, 1940). Obtain it, gentle reader, and contemplate, with a wry and rueful smile, but with the resolve to learn its lesson, the gruesome picture of all our yesterdays.

Now we plough through The Roaring Forties. Nearly four of the ten years of the new decade are already behind us. Save for the peerless feat of our fighting men, their story already bears a grim likeness to that of the past. History in repetition, like a story too often told, becomes tedious; even stupidity palls in time, as a joke.

May we all, in 1950, look back on The Forties with a different feeling, and a prouder one – lest we regret.

July 9, 1943

Twayne's English Authors Series

Sylvia E. Bowman, *Editor*

INDIANA UNIVERSITY

Algernon C. Swinburne

(TEAS) 10

Algernon C. Swinburne

By JOHN A. CASSIDY

Indiana University

Twayne Publishers, Inc.　::　New York

To

Margaret and John

Preface

As is the case with most major Victorian literary figures, Algernon Charles Swinburne has had to wait until the middle years of the twentieth century for anything like adequate treatment of his life and work. To materials concerning him, more than to almost any other prominent figure of his time, Victorian taboos were applied with such rigidity that only with the publication of Professor Cecil Y. Lang's six volumes of *The Swinburne Letters* (1959-1962) have many hitherto suppressed documents been released to the world.

We now know much about Swinburne that we did not know before or could only guess at. And because of such studies as Oswald Doughty's *Dante Gabriel Rossetti* (1949), Helen Rossetti Angeli's *Dante Gabriel Rossetti* (1949) and *Pre-Raphaelite Twilight* (1954), Margaret Gilman's *Baudelaire the Critic* (1943), and James Pope-Hennessy's *Monckton Milnes* (1951), we are able more accurately to gauge the effect of others upon him and to recreate the artistic and philosophical climate in which he lived and wrote. Always, of course, we doff the hat to the great French scholar Georges Lafourcade, whose *La Jeunesse de Swinburne* (1928) and *Swinburne* (1932), dynamited the ice jam of reticence and started the flow of new information.

The purpose of this book is to throw as much light upon Swinburne's literary works as possible. Biography enters the picture only where it is indispensable to a full understanding of the writings. But because Swinburne's works mirror his life very closely and because his brilliant mind ranged far, wide, and deep for its fare, I have had to deal extensively with such matters as Pre-Raphaelitism, Positivism, and French aestheticism. To account for and explain the unmistakable traces of sadism and masochism in his works, I have utilized some of the most recent research of modern psychiatry in the area of abnormal sexuality.

My scholarly debts are many and my gratitude great to those who have assisted materially in the preparation of this book: Theodore A. Hill, M.D., psychiatrist, and Grace Harris Hill, psychologist, gave generously of their time and professional knowledge. Professor Stanley Pargellis and the staff of the Newberry Library, Chicago, provided library facilities and assistance which were indispensable. Professor Thomas Souter and Mrs. Mary Baker of the Indiana University Library, Miss Mary Zimmermann and Mrs. Veronica Szasz of the South Bend-Mishawaka Campus Library were helpful in providing materials through interlibrary loan. Assistant Dean Jack J. Detzler of the South Bend-Mishawaka Campus relieved me of other duties, thus making it possible for me to give more time to research and writing.

The Summer Research Grant from the Graduate Research Division of the Indiana University Graduate School, John W. Ashton, Dean and Vice-President, gave me time and opportunity to collect many of the materials used in this study.

JOHN A. CASSIDY

Indiana University
April, 1964

Acknowledgments

I am grateful to Messrs. William Heinemann Ltd. for permission to quote from the Bonchurch Edition of Swinburne's *Complete Works* and for permission to obtain and use microfilmed copies from the British Museum of the still unpublished juvenilia.

Acknowledgment is also made to the following publishers for permission to print copyright material:

To the Yale University Press for selections from *The Swinburne Letters,* edited by Cecil Y. Lang.

To the Oxford University Press for selections from Georges Lafourcade's *La Jeunesse de Swinburne.*

To the Modern Language Association for permission to use in a different form material from my article, "Robert Buchanan and the Fleshly Controversy," *PMLA,* March, 1952.

Contents

Contents

Chronology

1837 Algernon Charles Swinburne born April 5 in Grosvenor Place, London, first of six children of naval captain Charles Henry Swinburne, the second son of Sir John Edward Swinburne, and Lady Jane Henrietta Hamilton Swinburne, the fourth daughter of the third Earl of Ashburnham.

1849 Algernon taken to Eton by his parents and placed in care of James Leigh Joynes, tutor.

1853 Leaves Eton in August and, for no announced reason, does not return, though normally he should have stayed two more years.

1854 Permission to enlist in cavalry is refused by father. Tutored for Oxford.

1856 January, journeys to Oxford with father; entered Balliol College with Benjamin Jowett as tutor. One of the original members of Old Mortality, an undergraduate literary and discussion society under the leadership of John Nichol.

1857 Writes poems and essays for *Undergraduate Papers,* a publication taken over by Old Mortality. November—he meets Dante Gabriel Rossetti, Edward Burne-Jones, and William Morris, who are painting murals in Oxford Union; Swinburne is fascinated with them and Pre-Raphaelitism; he begins to write poems and plays in Pre-Raphaelite style.

1859 Learns doctrine of "art for art's sake" from Pre-Raphaelites, takes trips to London to visit Rossetti and others. The attention given to writing verse leads to poor academic record.

1860 Leaves Oxford under questionable circumstances without degree. Publishes *Queen Mother* and *Rosamond.*

1861   Goes to Mentone with family; goes alone on journey to Italy. Father grants him annual pension of £200 and permission to live in London. Visits Richard Monckton Milnes (later Lord Houghton) at Fryston; meets Richard Burton at Fryston; after meeting Burton he begins to drink more.

1862   Reviews Victor Hugo's *Les Miserables* and Baudelaire's *Les Fleurs du Mal* in *Spectator*. Review of *Les Fleurs* is first statement of "art for art's sake" in Engand. Begins long friendship with Hugo. Introduced to works of Marquis de Sade by Milnes. Moves into Tudor House in Cheyne Walk with Dante Rossetti. Defends Meredith's *Modern Love* in letter to *Spectator*. Quarrels with Richard Holt Hutton and ends connection with *Spectator*.

1863   Visit to Paris with Whistler. Association with Simeon Solomon. Death of Edith Swinburne. Swinburne goes to visit his cousin Mary Gordon; he falls in love with her; works on *Atalanta in Calydon*.

1864   Suffers disappointment in love affair with Mary Gordon. Leaves Tudor House; coolness toward Dante Rossetti. Elected to Arts Club. Visits Walter Savage Landor in Florence.

1865   Publishes *Atalanta* with dedication to Landor. Family moves from "East Dene" to "Holmwood." *Atalanta* achieves real success. Friendship with George Powell. Publishes *Chastelard;* it encounters adverse criticism. Angers Lord Houghton and Tennyson at Moxon's dinner.

1866   Praises Baudelaire at annual dinner of Royal Literary Fund. Publication of *Poems and Ballads* raises storm in critical press. Breaks with Moxon's and agrees to publish with John Camden Hotten. Publishes *Notes on Poems and Reviews* in defense of *Poems and Ballads*.

1867   Meets Mazzini in March; is persuaded by him to write poems for Italian freedom. Begins notorious affair with Adah Isaacs Menken.

1868   Publishes critical volume *William Blake;* poem "Ave Atque Vale" in memory of Baudelaire; ends his interest in "art for art's sake." Nearly drowned at Étretat.

1870   Assists Dante Rossetti in preparing *Poems* for publication.

Has trouble with Hotten over publication of *Songs Before Sunrise*.

1871 Publishes *Songs before Sunrise*. To "Holmwood" to recuperate from dissipation. Renews excesses in July and becomes so ill his father closes his apartment and takes him home. In October Robert Buchanan publishes anonymous article "The Fleshly School of Poetry," attacking Rossetti and Swinburne.

1872 Publishes *Under the Microscope*. Termination of friendship with Dante Rossetti.

1873 Hotten's death frees Swinburne.

1874 Concludes publishing agreement with Andrew Chatto and publishes *Bothwell*.

1875 Publishes *Essays and Studies* and *George Chapman*. Considerable association with Jowett.

1876 Letter to *Athenaeum* attacking Furnivall. In court because of Buchanan's suit over Swinburne's publication of "Epitaph on a Slanderer" and "The Devil's Due" in *Examiner*. Verdict in Buchanan's favor. Publishes *Note on the Muscovite Crusade* attacking Carlyle.

1877 Father dies in March; back in London by June with money from inheritance; unrestrained dissipation.

1879 Health considerably and steadily worsened by excesses; Swinburne in very poor health when, early in June, Theodore Watts takes him from his rooms to house in Putney. Publishes *A Study of Shakespeare* in December.

1880 Quiet life at "The Pines" with Watts. Publishes *Songs of the Springtides* and *Studies in Song*.

1881 Continues quarrel with Furnivall; publishes *Euthanatos* and *Mary Stuart*.

1882 Death of Dante Rossetti. Journey to Paris in November for five days with Watts; first and last meeting with Hugo. Handicapped by deafness.

1883 Publishes *A Century of Roundels*.

1884 Publishes *A Midsummer Holiday and Other Poems*.

1885 Publishes drama *Marino Faliero*. Exchanges poem "A Word for the Navy" for some of his old letters to Howell. Death of Lord Houghton.

1886 Publishes *Miscellanies* and *A Study of Victor Hugo*. First meeting with T. J. Wise. Quarrel with John Churton Collins.

1887 *Publishes* poem "The Question," attacking Gladstone and Parnell; also publishes "The Jubilee," *Locrine,* and *Whitmania.*

1888 Attacks Whistler and repudiates "art for art's sake" in article "Mr. Whistler's Lecture on Art." Attacks Gladstone in "The Armada."

1889 Publishes *Poems and Ballads, Third Series.* Attacks Parnell and the Irish in "The Ballad of Truthful Charles."

1890 Death of Sir Richard Burton and William Bell Scott.

1891 Writes "Eton: An Ode for the Four Hundred and Fiftieth Anniversary," but refuses invitation to attend ceremony. Publishes memorial verses on Burton and Scott and a birthday poem to Tennyson.

1892 Intense anger at Scott when *Autobiographical Notes* published; publishes "The New Terror" in reprisal. Publishes *The Sisters, a Tragedy.*

1894 Publishes *Astrophel and Other Poems* and *Studies in Prose and Poetry.*

1896 Publishes *The Tale of Balen.* Saddened by death of his mother and William Morris.

1899 Publishes "A Channel Passage" and *Rosamund, Queen of the Lombards,* dedicated to Mrs. Disney Leith.

1903 Seriously ill with pneumonia.

1904 Publishes *A Channel Passage and Other Poems.*

1905 Marriage of Watts (now calling himself "Watts-Dunton") to Miss Reich, Watts's secretary. Swinburne publishes *Love's Cross-Currents.*

1908 Publishes *The Age of Shakespeare* and *The Duke of Gandia.*

1909 April 10, death from pneumonia.

CHAPTER 1

The Paths of Orthodoxy

IN 1836, one year after his promotion to a captaincy in the British Navy, Charles Henry Swinburne married his second cousin, Lady Jane Henrietta Hamilton. Both came from old aristocratic families. Charles Henry was a younger son of Sir John Swinburne of "Capheaton Hall," Northumberland; Lady Jane was the fourth daughter and one of twelve children of the third Earl of Ashburnham, of "Ashburnham Place," Sussex.

Both families were in good circumstances and surrounded with rich traditions stemming from English history. Both had been warm adherents of the Stuarts. The Ashburnhams, however, forsook the cause long before the Swinburnes, who remained Catholic and followed the deposed James II to France, where some of them continued to live and be educated until the time of Sir John Swinburne, the poet's grandfather. When Sir John inherited the title, he renounced Jacobitism, anglicized both his religion and his politics, and won the practical reward of a seat in Parliament in 1788.[1]

Although some three hundred miles separate Northumberland and Sussex, intermarriage between the two families was quite common and had been so long before the union of Captain Charles Henry and Lady Jane. They, for instance, were second cousins by virtue of their maternal grandfathers having been cousins. Moreover the Captain's cousin, Sir Henry Gordon, was married to Lady Jane's younger sister.

I *Hadji*

On April 5, 1837, about eleven weeks before eighteen-year-old Victoria fell heir to the British throne, Algernon Charles Swinburne was born in Grosvenor Place, London. Shortly afterward, Captain Swinburne moved his family to the Isle of Wight, where

ALGERNON CHARLES SWINBURNE

he rented "East Dene," a luxurious home with at least ten acres of lawn rolling down to the seashore. On the east coast of Wight, near the village of Bonchurch, the site had distinct advantages. It was only about sixty-five miles from London, an equal distance from "Ashburnham Place" in Sussex, and just across Spithead Channel from the great naval base at Portsmouth.

Here Swinburne grew up with his four sisters and brother. A few miles further inland on Wight was the home of Captain Swinburne's cousin, Sir Henry Gordon, and his wife Lady Mary, Lady Jane's younger sister. Their only child, Mary Gordon, some three years younger than "Cousin Hadji," as they called Algernon, often joined the Swinburne brood as they played about the beaches and roamed the lawns around "East Dene."

It was an ideal place for a happy childhood; the only drawback was that the Captain was often away on naval duty, with only occasional leaves at home. This left Lady Jane to manage the home and rear the young. Hadji was, therefore, rather hopelessly outnumbered, living in a matriarchy and surrounded by four sisters and a female cousin. Edward, the youngest child, was not born until a few months before his older brother had left for Eton in 1849.

Lady Jane devoted herself to her children. Much of her time was taken up with their education. Earnestly religious, she guided the feet of her charges toward High Church Anglicanism. In the little school she set up and presided over at "East Dene," the Bible was read regularly. When Hadji's reading ability had progressed to the point where he could do so, he was often called upon to read portions of the Scriptures aloud, a task which delighted him.[2] With the personal involvement of his ancestors in England's past, Lady Jane found it easy to engage her son's interest in history. The novels of Scott were then at the zenith of their popularity; and she, like many Victorian parents, directed Hadji's attention to them with marked success. Dickens, too, was rising rapidly; Hadji was so taken with *Dombey and Son* that he acted out scenes from it.[3] From Dickens and Scott, Lady Jane took her pupil to Shakespeare and Moliere. As a proper Victorian lady she made certain that it was the carefully expurgated *Family Shakespeare* of Thomas Bowdler, the "Victorianized" Shakespeare tailored to fit the rigid niceties of the proper Victorian home. Lady Jane had had Continental training which gave her a good command of French and Italian. These she labored to pass on to her son, along with the love of both countries that had much to do with his literary career.

The boy learned with astonishing rapidity. Not only was he quick to comprehend and assimilate, but he rarely forgot. His memory was the kind that fills ordinary people with despair. Poems, for instance, that he had heard only once or twice, he could repeat verbatim long afterward. Had the rest of him only equaled his mind, he would have gladdened the hearts of his parents! But nature, in one of her compensatory quirks, had given him disadvantages to detract from his brilliance. His appearance was grotesque. His huge head, covered with carroty red hair, was out of proportion to his slight body and dainty hands and feet. The head rested upon a short, thick neck. His narrow shoulders sloped so as to be almost nonexistent. In size he was diminutive, and his voice, always high pitched, often rose with excitement until it became a screech. To make matters worse, from early childhood he was afflicted with a nervousness which caused his arms and hands to twitch as though he had St. Vitus's dance. When he walked, he had a bobbing, springing motion which made him noticeable anywhere.

One can imagine that when he appeared at Ashburton Place or for the longer visits to "Capheaton Hall," where old Sir John loved to gather his twenty-four grandchildren about him in the summer, members of both families must have looked at one another in amazement and wondered how and why this dwarfed, malformed fruit had appeared on their virile family trees. One can imagine too that his effeminacy, his delicacy, his lack of vigor and coordination stood out most glaringly when he attempted to take part in games with other children.

Towards such a child, a mother tends to be more than ordinarily protective; the father, knowing the stern demands of a man's world, can hardly conceal his dismay. An age gap of forty years existed between Swinburne and his father; not an impassable barrier, but still an obstacle to a close relationship. Add to this that the father was much away from home and boy, and we have another barrier. The two had been formed in different worlds: the Captain had begun his naval training at the age of twelve and had twenty-seven years of stern naval discipline behind him when Algernon was born; the boy, as has been seen, grew and took form in a feminine environment, indulged, pampered, and perhaps even treated as another girl.

Such straws are not conclusive but may be indicative. Because of the scarcity of reliable information about Swinburne's childhood and family relationships, we have to use whatever scraps are available to fill in the gaps with conjectures. That the relationship between Swinburne and his father was not one of sympathy and understanding is clear from a letter he wrote to William Rossetti on January 15, 1870. Defending Shelley against Rossetti's charge of unfilial treatment of his father, Swinburne takes pains to explain what he regards as Shelley's justification:

. . . I think you are rather hard upon him as to the filial relation. . . . I have no doubt that it may be said for Sir Timothy that his son was what Carlyle calls "an afflictive phenomenon" than that I was the same to my father before, during, and since my Oxford time; but I do not think you make allowance for the provocation given (as well as received) by a father, who may be kindly and generous, to a boy or man between seventeen and twenty-one or so, with whom he has no deep or wide ground of sympathy beyond the animal relation or family tradition. You will allow me to say that I am sure you can never have felt at that age the irreparable, total and inevitable isolation from all that had once been closest to the mind and thought, and was still closest to the flesh and the memory, the solitude in which one passes from separation to antagonism of spirit (without violent quarrels or open offense, but by pure logical necessity of consequence) the sense that where attraction gradually ends repulsion gradually begins, which many besides Shelley, and as affectionate and faithful by nature and temperament as he, *have* felt at that age.[4]

Swinburne is speaking of Shelley, but who can doubt that he is defending himself as well? He does not say how long before his "Oxford time" he was an "afflictive phenomenon" to his father toward whom he had an "antagonism of spirit." Perhaps he was not aware. Such aversions do not spring up over night, but are a slow, gradual growth. Sometime during boyhood he became aware that he and his father had almost nothing in common; and when, even before he went to Eton, he began to write and, with his sisters and cousin, to act out extravagant dramas, his efforts met with little understanding from his father, whose hobbies ran to mechanics and woodworking rather than to the arts.

Towards his mother his feeling was altogether different. Upon her he concentrated the affection that should have gone to both parents. She was his protectress, his tutor, his intellectual guiding light—the one who always understood and to whom he could turn for sympathy. The strong bond between them never weakened. Even after he lost his religious faith, she never ceased to believe that he would return to the religion of his childhood and, at every opportunity, she urged him to do so. Throughout her life she was the strongest single influence upon him; her death in 1896 left a void never to be filled.

All this brings us to a consideration of the matter which is central to Swinburne's life, character, and literary work—the question of his abnormal tendencies. There is no direct, positive evidence that Swinburne was a homosexual. Several of his letters to his Bohemian friends contain implications of this nature—as do some guarded references to him in the letters of William Bell Scott, Lady Trevelyan, and his mother. Still, implications and guarded references are not final proof. But whether or not he was a homosexual is not of the first importance to an understanding of his works. What is of the greatest importance is that strong traces of abnormal tendencies show up very clearly in his works and often are the factors which determine their fundamental character.

This matter is considered early in this study for a good reason. Recent research into homosexuality by a group of psychiatrists using case histories of over one hundred homosexuals they had treated as patients shows that the detachment of the father from the son either by absence or lack of sympathy is a factor which tends to encourage homosexuality and to prevent recovery from it.[5] Swinburne's father was physically absent until his retirement in 1857, when Swinburne was twenty; and he was detached mentally and temperamentally in the other ways we have noted. By all reports and evidence he was a good father who labored to understand and to do the right thing for his difficult son. But in Swinburne's mind he was aloof and unsympathetic, as the letter to William Rossetti shows. The psychological effect was probably just as baneful as it would have been if Swinburne's father had been what the son thought he was.

The same study of homosexuality shows that another factor often present in cases of abnormality is an overly possessive and indulgent mother, especially one who creates or encourages the impression that she alone loves the son and the father does not.[6] Under the circumstances Lady Jane could have unwittingly given such an impression, and her defense of her ugly duckling could have helped it along. Swinburne, of course, could have formed the impression, whether it was warranted or not. True or imagined, the total effect would have been equally harmful.

Although Swinburne found little in his father that he could idealize, for old Sir John Swinburne, his father's father, he had a profound admiration. Every summer the Swinburnes would journey to "Capheaton Hall" to spend several weeks in its romantic neighborhood. Lying less than forty miles from the Cheviot Hills and the Scottish Border, the residence and the countryside were rich in border history and ballads. Even more interesting than the countryside was old Sir John himself, an inexhaustible source of legend and history and a link with the romantic past. Born in France in 1762, the old patriarch was seventy-five when Hadji arrived in the family in 1837. The old man and his redheaded grandson soon discovered that they had more in common with each other than with their intermediate link, Captain Charles Henry, who represented a more unimaginative, plodding strain in the family. Swinburne bestowed upon Sir John all the love and admiration he denied his own father; and, since the grandfather lived until 1860, they had twenty-three years of association.

Sir John was the man that Swinburne wanted vainly to be. A dashing, romantic figure, goodlooking enough in his youth to be a movie idol in the twentieth century, he was a rebel and a republican who had been friends with Mirabeau and Wilkes. Moreover, he had a sensitive appreciation for literature which revealed itself in the many French titles in the library at "Capheaton Hall," in his presidency of the Literary and Philosophical Society of nearby Newcastle-on-Tyne, in his activities in the Society of Antiquaries, and in his close association with Leigh Hunt. His love of painting led to a friendship with Mulready and to pictures by Mulready and Turner for the gallery at "Capheaton Hall." To Swinburne he was a link with the Old France of pre-Revolutionary days, as well as with the bloody times of the Revolution when Paris mobs stormed the Bastille and beheaded a king. More important, he was a direct contact with such glamorous figures as Byron and

Shelley. A cavalier of the old school, he loved to ride to the hunt; and on one occasion he had had a shooting accident which blew out a piece of his skull and necessitated trepanning.

In a biographical letter to E. C. Stedman in 1875, Swinburne's only mention of his father is that he is Sir John's second son; then for some five hundred words he tells lyrically of the virtues and exploits of Sir John. Admiringly he says: "It is said that the two maddest things in the North country were his horse and himself; but I don't think the horse can have been the madder. . . ." [7] Telling of the old man's death at ninety-nine, he adds fondly and wistfully: ". . . he was most kind and affectionate to me always as child, boy, and youth."

In Swinburne's life Sir John stood at the head of a procession of older men to whom he turned for affection and guidance. After the grandfather came John Nichol, Dante Gabriel Rossetti, Lord Houghton, Benjamin Jowett, Walter Savage Landor, Mazzini, William Rossetti, William Bell Scott, and Theodore Watts-Dunton. Of all these, perhaps the truest and kindest was Sir John.

II *The River and the Flogging-Block*

Had Swinburne been a normal boy, nothing would have been more natural than for Captain Swinburne to have groomed him for the Naval College and a career like his own. But Swinburne was not a normal boy, and such a career was as far beyond his reach as the moon. The question was what to do with him. His ability and delight in learning were remarkable, his religiosity was pronounced, his flow of words when speaking on a subject near his heart was astounding. These added up to a career in the Church. A career in the Church necessitated a university degree. Eton, Oxford, and then the Church was the course planned by the parents.

The Captain and Lady Jane looked ahead with dread to the impact of the harsh discipline of Eton upon their rebellious, indulged little scion. To get him ready, they chose the Reverend C. Foster Fenwick of nearby Brook Rectory as tutor. Whether Swinburne had to endure anything like the brutal floggings dealt Bertie Seyton by Denham in *Lesbia Brandon* is doubtful. To get him ready for the heavy arms of Eton tutors, the Captain might have instructed Fenwick to lay on a few light floggings when

Hadji was lazy or defiant; but Lady Jane would have hardly stood for anything more.

Their concern was all the greater because Hadji was showing those signs of extreme nervousness that stayed with him throughout his life: the excitability; the trembling and jerking of the hands, arms, and, when seated, feet and legs; the rising of the voice to a screech; the seemingly uncontrollable gush of words. What would be the outcome when such spells came on him at Eton? Shortly before he left, Lady Jane took him to a specialist who advised that the condition was the result of too much "electric vitality," which if any attempt were made to stop it could have bad effects.[8]

Consequently, when the time arrived for Hadji to go to Eton in April, 1849, Lady Jane went along with her husband and the boy, even though she had to leave nine-month-old Edward to do so. One can imagine that her purpose was to make certain that Tutor James Leigh Joynes, in whose care Algernon was to be entrusted, knew to the full what the specialist had said so as to extend every possible consideration to this special case. Further aid was sought from Swinburne's cousin, Algernon Bertram Mitford, who, though only five weeks older, had already been at Eton three years, and whom the anxious parents asked to aid Hadji in his adjustment to his new environment.

Perhaps, also, Lady Jane privately asked Mrs. Joynes, the sympathetic, motherly wife of Tutor Joynes, to keep an eye on Hadji and to report to her from time to time on how he was faring in the severe, masculine environment of Eton. She effected such liaison years afterward with his landladies in London; she would hardly have missed the opportunity to have made such an arrangement with Mrs. Joynes. At any rate, the tutor's wife stood out in Swinburne's memory in an emollient light; for, when his mother wrote him in 1882 that Mrs. Joynes had died, his reply paid a grateful tribute to her "who was so infinitely kind to me, at an age when I most needed kindness."[9]

As anyone who knows boys could have predicted, Swinburne's career at Eton was a stormy one. His cousin Algernon Mitford (later Lord Redesdale) and Sir George Young, the only two students who are mentioned as having been close to him, insist that the other boys let him alone because of a certain quality about him that boded trouble for anyone who attempted to bully him. But one wonders if they were not simply trying to shield his memory in the time-honored tradition of British biography and in accordance with the code of "the old school tie."

Other reports are much more in harmony with Swinburne's character as reported in his adult life, and indeed as he himself displays it in his letters—as one whose intellectual snobbery and vanity led him to trample on the feelings and rights of others to the point of insufferability. Sir Edmund Gosse, Swinburne's first biographer, tells of his dumping a pot of jam on the head of a maid because he did not like the way she read Shakespeare to him and of his standing up in bed and spouting poetry in a wild manner, frightening a well-meaning attendant who brought him a dose of medicine.[10] By 1853, his last year at Eton, he had earned the nickname "Mad Swinburne," [11] and the head boy of one of the halls pointed to him and advised a group of new entrants to kick him if they got close enough—and, if not near enough, to throw a stone at him.[12]

The trouble was, of course, that the system at Eton was based upon rigid discipline at every turn of the way—discipline in studies, in deportment, and among the students themselves. Failure to prepare lessons well usually resulted in a flogging; insolence or bad conduct could mean the same thing. The flogging-block was an institution at Eton, an accepted feature of the school; floggings were administered publicly; and, by several admissions in Swinburne's letters, he was officially present on several occasions. The practice of "fagging," by which a younger boy became a servant of an older boy and could be flogged by him for careless performance of such duties as running errands, waking him in the morning, and serving him at meals was another Eton tradition. We have no information as to whose fag Swinburne was, which in itself may be significant of an unhappy relationship with an older boy that his family and friends have labored to conceal; otherwise Swinburne or his cousin Algernon Mitford would have alluded to his fagging experience. We have no such allusion.

All his life Swinburne rebelled at discipline of any kind. It galled him and usually sent him in the opposite direction from the one intended. To attempt to adapt him to Eton discipline was like trying to fit a square peg into a round hole; by no means was the effort successful, and both the peg and the hole bore the scars of the attempt.

One good result of his unpleasant experiences with other boys was that it made him reclusive and turned him even more to books for companionship. In his studies, largely classical with some mathematics, Italian, and French, he did well, though not brilliantly. The core of the curriculum was what it had been from medieval days—Latin and Greek. The old standbys in these two languages were read, translated, and memorized—this last to the tune of two hundred to three hundred lines a week; in addition, the boys wrote imitative exercises in the same sacred Latin or Greek as the originals. They were permitted, even encouraged, to read Shakespeare—but only for the purpose of rendering him into Greek.

Out of this, Swinburne acquired a good foundation in classical lore and literature which left a strong imprint upon his later writings. He also developed a feeling for the structure of language and the roots of words, as well as for the infinite variety of nuances and accents underlying all composition, prose or verse. From the imitative exercises, some of which still repose in the British Museum with Joynes' commendations on them, he learned much of the mechanics of prosody.

His love of French led him to increase his knowledge of that language so greatly that he won the Prince Consort's Prize for Modern Languages in 1852, though he gave his mother's early training more credit than he did himself or Mr. Tarver, his teacher at Eton. Tarver also introduced him to such works of Victor Hugo as *Le Roi s'amuse, Notre-Dame de Paris,* and *Lucrece Borgia.* So delighted was Swinburne that Hugo remained an idol throughout his life and exerted a profound influence upon Swinburne's own work. When *Les Châtiments* appeared, Swinburne caught from it both a hatred of "Napoleon the Little" and a great admiration for Hugo's power of invective—which had much to do with his own delight in hurling the thunderbolts.

Most of these efforts were in the line of duty and in obedience to the system. But his truly remarkable intelligence enabled him to do the required work in a minimum of time; then he devoted himself to a wide exploration of English literature, using Eton's excellent libraries to do so. In his four and a half years at Eton he gave himself easily the equivalent of a present-day college major in English. He did this reading entirely on his own initiative, for none of it was required. The Elizabethan dramatists were his chief delight, and he covered them thoroughly. He did not, however, neglect Chaucer, Spenser, Milton, Pope, Prior, Thomson, Young, Wordsworth, Coleridge, Keats, Shelley, Moore, or Landor. In Landor he discovered a kindred rebel spirit; like Hugo, he also became a lifelong idol.

But he did more than read and assimilate. He tried his own wings in imitative flights of poetic fancy. Even before he came to Eton he had written several bloodcurdling dramas. Now he turned his hand to another, called *The Unhappy Revenge* in imitation of Tourneur's *The Revenger's Tragedy*. The revenge in Swinburne's play is the betrayal of ancient Rome to the Huns by the heroine Eudoxia as a reprisal for the wrong done her honor by the Emperor Maximus. An extravagant piece of fustian, it shows little promise of what was to come. Few boys of twelve or thirteen, however, would have stuck with it for four acts, as Swinburne did.

We have one other piece of juvenilia from Eton days, "The Triumph of Gloriana," in honor of the visit of Queen Victoria and Prince Consort Albert to Eton on June 4, 1851. Quick to capitalize upon the occasion for pedagogical purposes, some of the masters issued orders that the boys were to memorialize the event in heroic couplets as a substitute for the regular weekly composition in Latin. Swinburne displayed exceptional powers in catching the heavy beat and general tone of the Age of Reason.

> *What Muse shall boldly raise a humble lay,*
> *To celebrate the glories of this day?*
> *When glittering myriads flock, a countless crowd,*
> *Confus'd, with hearts upraised and voices loud;*
> *A thousand shouts the spacious triumph fill'd;*
> *No heart, no tongue was then by silence chill'd.*
> *What means this pomp: and what this festal throng,*
> *That down the crowded way is borne along?*
> *'Tis Gloriana now her palace seeks;*
> *And in that single voice wide Albion speaks.*[13]

For two hundred lines "The Triumph" with its heavy, regular beat rolls on like a parade of caissons. Eton, "the Temple of

Loyalty," is Athens; rival Harrow is lightly ridiculed as "the Theban mountain," obscured and dimly seen because "wrapt in a mist." The classical motif is carried out with Wellington as Miltiades.

Despite its faults we have here something more than a school exercise. Although fettered in heroic couplets, the poem has an undersurge of power and music out of the ordinary—almost as though it were straining to break through the shell of eighteenth-century formalism into the freedom and lyricism of *Atalanta in Calydon* or the "Song of Italy." A poet was emerging.

In the summer of 1853, two or three years before he normally would have, Swinburne left Eton, never to return. Because Eton has never spoken on the matter, we still do not know precisely why Swinburne left. Gosse intimates that the trouble centered about Swinburne's rebellion against Joynes' discipline and about his loss of interest in his studies.[14] Obviously Eton did not appreciate him or realize that in him she had a future great poet on her hands. Because he got his work so quickly and easily, he was known as an idler. The headmaster bluntly told Captain Swinburne that his son was "one of the idlest boys in the school," a charge which Swinburne denied almost forty years later as "a beastly lie" [15]

There was no love lost between him and Eton; he and she were not at all in harmony, though they did bear with each other for four and a half years. He was not expelled from Eton: he finished the term apparently in good order, went home, and that was the end. What, then, was the reason?

Apparently the answer lies in the fact that adolescence brought with it abnormal tendencies toward masochism and sadism which in 1852-53 became so noticeable that the Eton authorities had to reckon with them. In a boys' school like Eton, the faculty and administration would certainly have known about and have been on the alert to detect the mental and physical disturbances sometimes accompanying adolescence. Because of Swinburne's delicacy and effeminacy, they could hardly have been oblivious to the possibility of latent sexual abnormality becoming stronger and more evident during puberty. Such symptoms manifested themselves all too clearly in his growing delight in flagellation.

In later years he confided to Lord Houghton his joy at being whipped at Eton,[16] and he wrote another friend and former

Etonian that the only two things he could like to see at Eton were the Thames and the flogging-block.[17] The tenor of the letter leaves no doubt that the block interested him far more than the river. To Houghton also he recounted with evident relish that for one notable flogging given him by Joynes he was permitted to soak his face in eau de cologne to heighten the pleasure.[18] This indicates either that Joynes was also abnormal or that he was playing along with the boy to discover the full extent and meaning of his strange reactions. I think the latter, for Joynes was so well thought of at Eton that he was later offered the headmastership and refused it.

The nature of the case once discovered or strongly suspected, Joynes would have been duty bound to report it to the administration. From that time on, Swinburne would have been under the closest surveillance by all his masters. Since the punishment of the younger boys was administered in public at the flogging-block and since in many of his letters and other writings Swinburne tells of his joy in watching floggings, he could have no more stayed away from the block than a pyromaniac could stay away from a fire. His joy there would have been equally evident and significant to alert eyes. Once they became certain of his affliction, the authorities had to get him out of Eton for his sake and for the welfare of the other boys and the reputation of the school.

We do not know whether Joynes or Provost Hawley wrote Swinburne's parents of their suspicions and described the symptoms, or whether Joynes told Mrs. Joynes to write Lady Jane that her son's nervous condition had become so seriously aggravated that he should not return to Eton after the close of the current term. The latter is more likely. In either case, the situation was handled quietly and tactfully out of consideration for the boy, the parents, and the school.

How much Swinburne may have known of what was happening to him emotionally and of its effect upon others is unknown. He never forgave Eton. In 1891, when the headmaster asked him for an ode in honor of Eton's four hundred and fiftieth anniversary, Swinburne wrote a formal poetic tribute to the old school's role in training England's great men. Later he chuckled with glee in a letter to William Rossetti at how he had flung "the name of their *other* typical naughty boy and disgrace to the orthodox traditions of the school full in the face of the authorities, who I *trust* will be in a due and proper rage (not for the first time, I should suppose) with both of us." [19] Shelley's was the only name mentioned in the ode.

Swinburne also wrote a burlesque of the formal ode, calling it "Eton: Another Ode." Like the formal ode, it is in rhyming triplets and in anapestic-heptameter; it ruefully, playfully sings of some of his experiences at the block, probably—as the saying goes—with more truth than poetry.

> *"Tell me, S[winburn]e, does shame within burn as hot*
> *(Swish! Swish!) as your stripes my lad,*
> *Burn outside, have I tamed your pride? I'm glad to see how it*
> *hurts you—glad—*
> *Swish! I wish it may cure you. Swish! Get up." By Jove, what*
> *a dose I've had.*[20]

Can we doubt that Swinburne's real sentiments were in the burlesque rather than in his formal ode? In Swinburne's mind Eton was synonymous with flagellation, a subject ominously delightful to him until his death.

CHAPTER 2

Oxford and the Pre-Raphaelites

FOR two and a half years after leaving Eton, Swinburne led a leisurely existence at "East Dene," "Northcourt," and "Ashburnham Place." In 1854 his desire to enlist in the cavalry for service in the Crimean War was thwarted by his father's firm veto. In 1855 his uncle, General Thomas Ashburnham, took him on a five-week tour to Germany, which left Swinburne rather unimpressed. Throughout the two and a half years, he dutifully tutored for Oxford with neighboring clergymen both at "East Dene" and "Capheaton."

Much more enthusiastic was his pursuit of his ambition to be a poet. Here he found a sympathetic ally in Lady Trevelyan, wife of Sir Walter Trevelyan of "Wallington," an estate a short distance from "Capheaton." Childless and thirty-eight years old in 1854, Lady Trevelyan was free to pursue her interests in painting and literature. Ruskin and William Bell Scott, the Scottish painter-poet who later became one of Swinburne's close friends, were often at her home during the 1850's. In her, Swinburne found one of the few genuine friends of his life and the first perceptive, understanding believer in his poetic genius. She encouraged him to write verses and then to bring them to "Wallington" to read them to her.

The interim was soon over. Oxford and the adult world lay ahead, and Swinburne, at nineteen, turned toward it eagerly. In the four and a half years he was to encounter some of the strongest formative influences of his life; there, he would adopt many of the leading ideas and develop some of the characteristics that were to loom large in his later career.

During these same four and a half years, the Crimean War would drag itself to a close, in 1856, the savage and unnecessary Sepoy Rebellion would run its course, and the situation between the Southern and Northern American states would worsen until the Civil War became inevitable. Britain's dread of the growing power of the French Emperor Louis Napoleon would manifest itself in her sympathy for the assassination attempt of Felice Orsini, and the cause of Italian freedom would be greatly enhanced by the French defeat of Austria in 1859. All in all, it was an interlude in which the world's stage would be readied for the great actors and events of the 1860's and 1870's.

I The Student of Balliol

On January 23, 1856, Swinburne and his father journeyed to Oxford, where Swinburne was duly enrolled as a student in Balliol College with the already prominent Benjamin Jowett as his tutor. Captain Swinburne later remarked that Jowett was not the tutor he would have preferred for his son, possibly because he thought Jowett too mild and sympathetic for such a mettlesome charge as Algernon, but in the long run the boy could not have done better. Jowett was already Regius Professor of Greek and soon to become Master of Balliol; today his is one of the great names in the history of British scholarship and of brilliant teachers.

Because he did not early discover Swinburne's genius, some biographers have censured Jowett for lack of insight, but the pupil, too, must share the onus. Jowett's Classicism may have rendered him unsympathetic to such an unrestrained Romantic as Swinburne, but Swinburne was antagonistic to anyone in a pedagogical robe. Jowett, like most college professors, was ready and eager to be a friend to any student; but he expected the student to make the first overtures. Swinburne did not make them. Later, when Jowett discovered that his pupil was being led into dangerous paths by the Pre-Raphaelites, he did all he could to effect a rescue, but it was too late. The master must have held himself somewhat responsible for the loss of his sheep; for in 1868, when he heard that Swinburne was in a dire plight in London, he came forward with an offer of friendship Swinburne eagerly accepted. For the next twenty-five years, till Jowett's death in 1893, his was a stabilizing influence—one of the comparatively few good influences in Swinburne's life.

During his first year at Oxford Swinburne became friends with John Nichol, four years older than he. Nichol was a transfer to

Oxford after four years at the University of Glasgow, where his father was professor of astronomy and where he himself later rose to the rank of professor of English literature. When they met in 1856 Nichol was twenty-three and Swinburne nineteen, not a great disparity in terms of years, but a wide gulf in terms of maturity, especially if the older man has the additional advantages of education and worldly experience. Nichol had such advantages. When they first met, Swinburne was a freshman greeting a cynical and witty upperclassman who had traveled, had met Mazzini, had adopted such republican principles as a belief in Italian freedom and a hatred of Napoleon III, and had rejected religious orthodoxy as puerile nonsense.

Through his reading of Hugo and perhaps through the influence of Sir John Swinburne, Swinburne already disliked Napoleon III and was sympathetic to Mazzini and the cause of Italian freedom. He was not yet ready to deny Christianity, but he was questioning it. So complete was Nichol's domination that in short order Swinburne became a rabid foe of Napoleon III, a devoted proponent of Mazzini, and a scorner of Christianity generally and of Roman Catholicism in particular.

None of these attitudes was unusual for the time, and the only one that would have been frowned upon by the Oxford authorities was the rejection of religion. Even that would have been reprimanded mildly because religious opinions at Oxford were at that time in a state of upheaval. Since more than half of the students were in orders or planning to be, theological matters came in for considerable attention in and out of the classroom. The aftereffects of the Oxford Movement and of the defection of Newman to Roman Catholicism in the 1840's still hung in the air at the old university. The persistent stream of young Oxfordites who followed after Newman gave rise to a suspicion in the country at large that Oxford was a hotbed of Roman Catholic subversion, of which the professors were the traitorous gardeners.

Actually, of course, the religious roads ran out of Oxford in three directions. The high road still led to Anglicanism, though one side of it favored High Church and the other Low; a smaller bypath led to Roman Catholicism; a third road—growing in importance—belonged to those who repudiated the Bible, Christianity, and all formalized religion, adopting in their stead a vague agnosticism which accepted the idea of a great creative force or principle, but ridiculed as childish the concept of an anthropomorphic deity.

The last was the road taken by Nichol and toward it he directed the steps of Swinburne. Evidently a most important step in the "conversion" of the neophyte was to convince him that his faith had been imposed upon him by his parents when he was too young to know better. In an essay written during his Oxford days called "The Limits of Experience," Swinburne remarks with complete gravity and certainty: "That much which is with us a matter of real and universal acceptance—much which has come to be regarded as intuitive and as it were indispensable to our existence and faculty of thinking—is indeed mere matter of experience and previous acquaintance removed beyond the limit of consciousness or memory, is an evident truth." [1] Listing ideas of power, love, liberty, and religion as among the items which lie beyond memory, he states that such concepts are imparted to the infant in his very early childhood by his parents. Religion is put at the end of the list as though he hesitates to touch it, but then he follows doggedly his reasoning to its bitter conclusion. As he sees it, there is no absolute conviction because there is no absolute truth. All his beliefs and convictions have been inherited—in his case they had come from a mother whose education and intellectual attainments were far below his because she had never had the advantages of the university. Since they are that and nothing more, why should he not now abandon them? Under the aegis of Nichol, abandon them he did and for life. In his famous letter to Stedman in 1875, he admits he has been brought up a "quasi-Catholic," but he denies that he had ever accepted the idea of a personal God. Therefore the loss of his faith has left him only with "a turbid nihilism," transformed after a time into Positivism, the worship of "the divine humanity, the ideal of human perfection and aspiration, without worshipping any God, any person, any fetish at all." [2]

This view, of course, was precisely that held by Nichol and countless other Victorian intellectuals who, shying away from the term "atheist," disdained any form of religious belief. Swinburne's reaction was more than disdainful; for the rest of his life he was an implacable foe of Christianity and seldom missed an opportunity to sneer at it in his writings.

At first glance this is surprising. Because his religion had come principally from his mother, toward whom his devotion never lessened, we would expect him to regard his lost faith with the gentle sadness that characterizes Matthew Arnold's religious poetry. Arnold, however, influenced by his father's developmental theory of history, regarded Christianity and other forms of religion as necessary and useful stages in the evolution of man's thought, much as he might have looked upon the Roman chariot in the evolution of transportation. But to Swinburne, all religions, and Christianity especially, were but gigantic hoaxes promulgated by tyrants like Napoleon III and the Pope to enslave the masses politically through religious superstition. Accordingly, he hated both the exploiters and their tools, the clergy. Instead of blaming his mother, he saw her as an innocent victim.

Another factor conducing to the loss of his faith was his growing awareness of his sexual abnormality. He knew he was not like other young men his age; if he did not know why, their sneers and jeers would soon have told him. His failure to develop normally must have been of such concern to both him and his parents that they must have sought the advice of a specialist like the one Lady Jane took him to before he went to Eton. One can imagine that, after talking with the worried parents, the good man took Algernon aside and told him that because of unknown factors of heredity he would never have the manly muscles, voice, appearance, or desires of other young men; that this was an affliction put upon him by God's will and one that he must bear prayerfully and patiently as a personal cross. One can imagine Algernon's initial shock turning into passionate complaint and then into savage denunciation of God for causing this affliction. When Nichol and atheism came along, he welcomed them. It was a senseless, nihilistic universe; his own calamity proved the point.

As a man thinks, so he is and so he writes. Nihilism is the poorest kind of basis for the artist. It is fatal to idealism, to optimism, to compassion, to hope. The long-range effect upon Swinburne's writings was to make them negative, pessimistic, and denunciatory. His muse was fated to fly with crippled wings. Where she might otherwise have soared over the mountain peaks, she did well to clear the tree tops.

Nichol's influence was increased when, in November, 1856, he gathered Swinburne and four other Oxonians in his rooms to form a literary-discussion group under the name "Old Mortality," a title based on the claim that all six members had at one time or another been close to death from ill health and were still frail. They soon won a campus reputation as revolutionaries. As organizer and presiding genius, Nichol set the tone. They met weekly in one another's rooms; read essays and poems, some original; and discussed literary matters. Their readings and discussions show clearly their unorthodox character. Nichol read an essay on Wycliffe; Swinburne read Browning's "The Statue and the Bust," with its unorthodox approval of adulterous love; his "The Heretic's Tragedy" and "Bishop Bloughram's Apology," both heavily satirical of religious hypocrisy; and Morris's "The Defence of Guinevere," which, like "The Statue and the Bust," flaunted Victorian standards of morality.

To read and discuss are well enough; but how much more satisfying it is to see one's views in print. Accordingly, the society established a magazine in November, 1857, and gave it the name of *Undergraduate Papers,* with Nichol, of course, as editor. They scurried around until they found a publisher who agreed to publish and sell the magazine, and even to pay small sums to the contributors. All that the brotherhood of Old Mortality had to do was to get it written and ready for the press!

The young reformers soon found that they had not reckoned upon the inexorable demands of a printing press. All too soon what had started out as a labor of love became only labor; after the third issue the members of Old Mortality ran out of enthusiasm. Editor Nichol, faced with the stern necessity of preparing for examinations for his degree in April, 1858, found that his editorial duties demanded more of his time than he could spare. *Undergraduate Papers,* in keeping with the name of the fraternity which had given it birth, expired quietly that spring.

II *The Influence of Rossetti*

Ironically, the greatest impact upon Swinburne at Oxford came from one who had no direct connection with the university—Dante Gabriel Rossetti, a London painter and poet. When Swinburne returned to Oxford from the Long Vacation in the fall of 1857, he found Rossetti there with Edward Burne-Jones, William Morris, and several other aspiring painters on a busman's holiday—painting murals on the walls of the Debating Hall of the new

Oxford and the Pre-Raphaelites

Oxford Union Society building. Rossetti and the Pre-Raphaelites had been well advertised to Swinburne through Lady Trevelyan, whose enthusiasm for them and their movement was of long standing and had been enhanced by her acquaintance with John Ruskin and William Bell Scott. With understandable eagerness Swinburne soon bent his steps to the Debating Hall.

Of such magnitude was Rossetti's influence upon Swinburne that a clear understanding of him and his works would be impossible without an extensive knowledge of the Italian-Englishman and his peculiar ideas. And to comprehend Rossetti fully, it is necessary to understand Pre-Raphaelitism, a term now almost synonymous with Rossetti, and the "art for art's sake" philosophy which he combined with Pre-Raphaelitism to form his own personal and artistic philosophy. We shall, therefore, deal with him at length.

A conglomeration of currents and crosscurrents, of rules laid down but frequently transgressed, of moods and enthusiasms, of various meanings to various people, Pre-Raphaelitism is neither simple to explain nor easy to understand. It originated in the spirit of rebellion against the authority of the Royal Academy which animated Holman Hunt and John Everett Millais, two young English painters struggling to win recognition in London in 1848. In that *annus mirabilis,* rebellion of all sorts was in the air, and no one should wonder that two young Bohemians caught the virus. Their grievance against the Academy was that they thought it ridden with formalism and hidebound with worship of old masters and old rules.

Their prescription to cure the Academy's ills was fashioned by Hunt, who was serious, earnest, and something of a philosopher. With the zeal of an evangelist, he agreed with Ruskin that all art should serve to bring the Kingdom of Heaven a little closer to earth. The painter, therefore, should begin with a "moral subject," one which would impress the beholder with a moral interpretation of some aspect of life, and then strive to put it on canvas just as he saw it and with almost photographic accuracy of detail. This last point he emphasized. At any cost, art must be true to nature and evidence such truth by meticulous attention to detail. The application of this prescription, Hunt argued fervently, would restore art from its moribundity under the hands of the Academy practitioners to a new and vital resurgence in the world of men.

Rossetti entered the movement quite naturally, for he was Hunt's pupil. He had too much of the gay picaro in him to be willing to dedicate his life to the teaching of truth through painting, but he joined with alacrity because he was a natural rebel against any kind of authority. He threw himself into the cause with zeal and rounded up several new recruits for the lark, including his brother William Michael, not a painter at all.

Great was the joy of the rebels when in the first volume of *Modern Painters* they found Ruskin condemning Roman artists for studying Raphael and for using his rules and reproducing his faults, instead of studying nature as Raphael had. The faults Ruskin objected to in the imitators of Raphael were, as Hunt saw them, precisely those of the Royal Academicians—the unnatural painting of figures, a slavish adherence to the outworn rules and methods of the "grand style," a false rendering of anatomy, a general disregard for truth, and an almost complete oblivion to the fundamental obligation of the artist to interpret the moral meaning of the life about him. Eagerly the English rebels adopted Ruskin's thesis and the name "Pre-Raphaelites," to which Rossetti suggested they add "brotherhood" as a token of the dedicated nature of their cause. So the Pre-Raphaelite Brotherhood came into being; the members swore secrecy and signed their pictures with the initials "PRB" after their names, more with a boyish desire to mystify the public than for any good reason.

So far, so good. But trouble came their way when, in 1850, Rossetti broke the oath of secrecy to let out of the bag the meaning of the initials and the purpose of the Brotherhood. Fully apprised of what these upstarts were about, the Academy rose in wrath and summoned to its aid the weight of authority and numbers. Because Hunt and Millais were better known, the full force of the tempest broke on their heads; but, by a quirk of criticism, Rossetti escaped almost completely and was even given a measure of praise in *The Times* for the poetry of his "Ecce Ancilla Domini." [3] To stem the tide, Millais succeeded in getting John Ruskin into the melee on the side of the Pre-Raphaelites on the ground that they were only practicing what he had taught. Even here the throw of dice was in Rossetti's favor, for, apparently hypnotized by Dante Gabriel's charm and air of authority, Ruskin hailed him as a Pre-Raphaelite chieftain and as an artist of outstanding merit.

The anger of Hunt and Millais at Rossetti for his betrayal of the secret meaning of "PRB" was all the greater when they saw him, a mere student, walking off with most of the honors and the chieftain's toga that should have gone to Hunt. But they were powerless to prevent it. With Ruskin's help and from a kind of natural magnetism from the Italianate connotations, the names "Dante Gabriel Rossetti" and "Pre-Raphaelite" became inextricably associated. Hunt and Millais felt certain that they had been cheated by that "sly Italian," as Millais' mother bitterly styled Rossetti, who, they were sure, had promoted his own interests at their expense.[4] Even though all the publicity had increased the popularity of all and raised the prices they could get for their pictures, the coolness among the three leaders grew so rapidly that the movement came to an end in 1852, at about the time the paper war against them subsided. By 1856 the Pre-Raphaelites had separated, each to follow his own pursuits.

Millais especially, though he rose to knighthood and the presidency of the Royal Academy, never forgave Rossetti. In 1896, though Rossetti had been dead fourteen years, Millais' rancor was still alive in his insistence that what Rossetti had practiced was not Pre-Raphaelitism: "His aims and ideals in art were also widely different from ours, and it was not long before he drifted away from us to follow his own peculiar fancies. What they were may be seen from his subsequent works. They were highly imaginative and original, and not without elements of beauty, but they were not Nature. At last, when he presented for our admiration the young women which have since become the type of Rossettianism, the public opened their eyes in amazement. 'And this,' they said, 'is Pre-Raphaelitism!' It was nothing of the sort. The Pre-Raphaelites had but one idea—to present on canvas what they saw in Nature; and such productions as these were absolutely foreign to the spirit of their work." [5]

This analysis holds more than a germ of truth. Though Rossetti's artistic principles and practices in many instances took their departure from Hunt's rationale of Pre-Raphaelitism, they departed so far that they became almost antithetical to the original. Hunt's insistence upon a moral purpose in theme and upon fidelity to truth in treatment meant nothing to Rossetti, who, as a complete Romantic in character and disposition, eschewed any form of discipline in life or painting. Much more fascinated was he with the emphasis of the Pre-Raphaelites upon the medieval scene and material which had come about through their absorption in the artists before Raphael, their adulation of Keats, and the widespread enthusiasm for things medieval in evidence on all sides in 1848, the Pre-Raphaelite natal year. Here Dante Gabriel was literally and figuratively at home. His enthusiasm for the Middle Ages was almost as old as his memory. The son of a Dante scholar, he had been brought up in a home haunted by the spirit of the great Florentine. The Dantesque influence was abetted by a boyhood love of Scott's novels which progressed to a later, even keener delight in the poetry of Keats, Browning, and Poe. From all these materials he created for himself a pseudo-medieval world of love, sin, and death—a world heavy with dark shadows and a sense of impending doom. Of course it was a world far removed from the real medieval world of history, but it was a world in which the neurotic Rossetti loved to dwell in fancy.

When Rossetti began to paint, quite naturally the pervasive influence of Dante and of the dream world which he—with Dante's help—had fashioned for himself flavored his works. No fewer than a dozen pictures are directly concerned with Dante or suggested by him, and the atmosphere and style are Dantesque. The paintings are heavy and dark, with little light; the faces are serious or sad, often in grief or pain, almost never with a smile or cheerful expression. The same dreamlike quality that hangs over the *Divine Comedy* marks Rossetti's paintings. They are steeped in a romantic ghostliness, a vagueness and unreality; and these qualities are achieved by the somber lighting, by the lack of sharpness and definiteness of line, and by the gloomy, tragic expressions on the faces.

A further departure from Pre-Raphaelitism came from Rossetti's almost psychotic sensuality. In real life he delighted in the role of Don Juan, and the procession of women who thronged through his life ranged from delicately spiritual Elizabeth Siddal to coarse, vulgar Fanny Cornforth.[6] Accordingly, in the greater number of his pictures woman is the center of interest. In compliance with Victorian taboos the women are always robed, but in such a way that more is often revealed than concealed. Invariably, too, the women are virginal and maidenly, with long, slender bodies; long, columnar necks; masses of luxuriant hair tumbling loosely about the shoulders; and sensitive, sensual mouths. Often he painted them with flowers—in their hair, or somewhere in the background—possibly a suggestion of virginity; but this virginity was waiting, expecting, yearning to be assailed. In accordance with Rossetti's observation that no woman is interesting until she has lost her virginity, he did pictures of some of the great prostitutes, adulterers, and adulteresses of history and legend: Rosamond, Lilith, Helen of Troy, Guinevere, Venus Astarte, Paolo and Francesca, and Tristram and Iseult.

By 1857, when Rossetti came to Oxford, he had added another ingredient to "Rossettianism," to borrow Millais' term. This ingredient was the idea that art had nothing to do with morality or moral didacticism and should be evaluated only on its merits as art. Diametrically opposed to the original Pre-Raphaelitism of Holman Hunt, this doctrine stemmed from Edgar Allan Poe's rebellion against the Victorian dictum that a poem should be judged by the moral truth it teaches. In this essay "The Poetic Principle," Poe states flatly that poetry should be evaluated only on its ability to excite and to elevate the soul. Such excitement and elevation are aroused, he maintains, only if the poem achieves real beauty. This attainment of beauty is the fundamental purpose of the poem, and any attempt to subordinate it to moral didacticism will inevitably militate against the creation of beauty.

Poe's essay was published in 1850, a year after his death. The idea was taken up in France by Théophile Gautier, who, in his book *Emaux et Camées* (1852), enunciates his version of Poe's theory, which he expresses as *l'art pour l'art*, or "art for art's sake." Influenced by Gautier, whom he called his "maître impeccable," Charles Baudelaire published a notable essay on Poe in 1852; and, because he was an art critic, he followed it with ample references to Poe's theory in his famous critiques, "Exposition Universelle de 1855" and "Salon de 1859." In the latter essay he paraphrases Poe by pointing out that a rigid adherence to truth is inimical to artistic beauty and by complaining that the French public demands truth where it should ask only for beauty in painting.[7] In the introductory essay, "Notes

Nouvelles sur Edgar Poe," to his translation of several of Poe's shorter works in his *Nouvelles Histoires Extraordinaires* (1857), Baudelaire—though he admits, as Poe did, that poetry might ennoble morals as a sort of by-product of its influence—insists that the prime aim of poetry must always be beauty. To attempt to make it subserve truth, science, or morality would prevent its attaining that sublime beauty which it must have if it is to elevate the human spirit to visions of the immortal and eternal— those beatific visions which Poe says are the ultimate goal of great poetry. Here, of course, is the aesthetic justification of "art for art's sake," just as the attainment of Heaven is the justification for religion. Only by serving art for the sole sake of art, say Poe, Gautier, and Baudelaire, can the faithful artist hope to create ideal beauty.

We pause here to point out, first, that Poe's idea was not completely original, for at least its essence is comprehended in Longinus' essay "On the Sublime," written in the first century A.D. Second, the great weakness of "art for art's sake" is that it is essentially Romantic and therefore essentially subjective. Divorced from Classicism or any other set of objective rules or principles, it trusts entirely to the artist's aesthetic tastes and perceptions to guide him in the search for and the creation of ideal beauty. However, if the artist is in any way abnormal, his artistic vision may likewise be distorted and may lead him far astray. So it was with Poe, whose fascination with the horrible often led him into morbidity. So it was with Gautier, who blended fantasy and the macabre to create the paganism of *Mademoiselle de Maupin,* the sensuality of *La Toison d'or,* the emphasis upon external beauty and workmanship and the indifference to morality of *Emaux et Camées.* So it was with Baudelaire, whose personal life of debauchery and taste for the erotic in art resulted in *Les Fleurs du Mal.* And so it was with Dante Gabriel Rossetti, who, hating all rules and discipline, leading a licentious and amoral life, and scorning all interference with his pleasure, was a "natural" for the new philosophy.

We do not know precisely how early Dante Gabriel embraced "art for art's sake" and added it to his peculiar brand of Pre-Raphaelitism. It could well have been in 1855, when he visited the Universal Exposition in Paris, in which Hunt and Millais were exhibiting, and for which Baudelaire wrote his famous critique with frequent mention of Poe and with liberal paraphrases from Poe's "The Poetic Principle." Rossetti had a sharp eye for anything new and significant in art or literature. Like most English painters, he kept abreast of what was going on in the art world of Paris. He could hardly have missed the essays of Gautier and Baudelaire with their interesting affirmations of the new philosophy. And, since Rossetti was a devotee of Poe, claiming that he had written "The Blessed Damozel" as a companion piece to Poe's "The Raven," he could have read Poe's essay as early as 1850 when it was first published. He could have formed his first acquaintance with the essence of "art for art's sake" then. Certainly, by the time he went to Oxford in 1857, Rossetti was an enthusiastic follower of the new philosophy.

A third point to bear in mind about "art for art's sake" is that Gautier, Baudelaire, and Rossetti did not confine it to their practice of the arts but carried it over into their personal lives. They did not say so, of course, but their reasoning obviously went like this: if the work of art is to be free from moral standards and values, why should the artist not also be unfettered by them? If his intuitions and his visions of beauty are to be his only guides in art, why should they not guide him in life also? In other words, why should he not be free to do as he wishes both in art and life?

In this connection we must remember that "art for art's sake" sprang from a rebellion against an overemphasized morality and against the philosophy of Utilitarianism, represented in England and America by the smug portrait of Queen Victoria; and in France by the ubiquitous image of Napoleon III. In the lengthy "Author's Preface" to his novel *Mademoiselle Maupin* in 1834, long before he read Poe's essay and adopted "art for art's sake," Gautier attacks Utilitarianism: "There is nothing truly beautiful but that which can never be of any use whatsoever; everything useful is ugly, for it is the expression of some need, and man's needs are ignoble and disgusting like his own poor and infirm nature. The most useful place in a house is the water-closet." [8] Even more far-reaching is Baudelaire's attack in his "Notes Nouvelles sur Edgar Poe" upon those who reason that because man is born good, his art should also be morally good. All men are not born good, Baudelaire insists, with his eyes upon some of the more macabre short stories of Poe; they are also born marked with evil, and it is both the privilege and duty of the artist to deal with this Satanic side of man and to express its beauty. Baudelaire's illustration of his own belief in the evil side of man is *The Flowers of Evil,* his book of poems first published in 1857, the same year as his essay on Poe.

Here again, of course, was justification for the artist personally to explore evil if he wished. Indeed, how could he portray it in art unless he thoroughly understood it? And how could he understand it unless he had experienced it in his own life? As we have noted, Gautier, Baudelaire, and Rossetti lived in open defiance of accepted moral standards and practices. As we have likewise noted, all three delved into the sensual, the animal, the abnormal sides of man's nature and presented them in connection with their work in painting, in literature, or in both. In Rossetti's case, the Satanic side of "art for art's sake" was ample justification for that medieval world of love, sin, and death that he created for himself, and for such paintings as "Bocca Bacciata" ("the kissed mouth") and "Found," the study of a London prostitute in her moment of greatest shame and agony. In his poetry he practiced the same philosophy in "Jenny," a compassionless meditation upon the life and character of a prostitute; in some of the more sensual sonnets of "The House of Life" cycle; in "Troy Town," a study of the pathological hatred of a scorned woman for her former lover; and in "The King's Tragedy," a study of murder and revenge. As in his painting, he had to be careful to disguise his real purpose from the ever-watchful and suspicious British Philistines. Britain was considerably less tolerant on moral grounds than was France, and Baudelaire's *Les Fleurs* was condemned by the French courts for immorality in 1856 and its author fined. Better, then, for Rossetti to go slow about publishing his poetry, and not to divulge his philosophy of art and literature beyond the circle of his immediate friends. Better to placate the British lion than to anger him; but, of course, if one could placate him by an apparent submission to his wishes while in reality one was slyly flaunting him and his absurd commands—why, all the better.

Besides being a painter and a poet, Rossetti was also an artist at befooling the British public. Sensing that the English inferiority complex toward Italian art and artists could be turned to the advantage of a clever Italian seeking to make his way in the arts, he rearranged his name from the baptismal Gabriel Charles Dante Rossetti to Dante Gabriel Rossetti. This was a shrewd move because it emphasized his Italianism and gave him a first name with the highest possible Italian literary connotations. Significantly, however, his family and close friends continued to call him "Gabriel" until his death and thus to write of him privately and publicly during his lifetime and after. His second step was to accent the Italianate in his appearance. Here nature aided him, for though he was one-quarter English, he was short in stature, inclined to be stout; he also had a swarthy complexion; heavy dark eyebrows over large, liquid dark eyes; and even in his late twenties a receding hairline that made him look ten years older. To these characteristics he added a heavy, drooping moustache and a chin-and-neck beard.

This was the man who, with a group of his young disciples he had gathered for the purpose, journeyed to Oxford to paint murals in the new Union building and whom Swinburne found there when he returned for the fall term. A good deal of "gush" has been written about the meeting between Swinburne and Rossetti. Some biographers of both treat it with awe and wonder, as though the heavens should have opened and prophetic voices been heard. They insist that Rossetti recognized almost instantly the genius in Swinburne and with admirable altruism determined to do all in his power to aid its development. What he actually saw before him was that which must have moved him to amazement first and then to silent laughter—an elfish little fellow five feet, four inches tall, of twenty who looked more like sixteen. If Rossetti did not know at the outset, he must have soon learned that Swinburne was of a wealthy, noble family—intelligence which would prick up his ears at the prospect of "tin," as he laughingly referred to money.

In short order Rossetti divined that he had in Swinburne a creature who was at the opposite sexual pole from himself. Whether Rossetti told the others we do not know, but he led the way in a program of jest and allusion at Swinburne's expense which must have been hard to take. In a letter to Rossetti in 1869, Swinburne outlined his plan for his *Tristram and Iseult* by detailing how Tristram would lay the groundwork for Iseult's seduction through tales of the sexual irregularities of other members of the

Court: ". . . but delicately, sparing respectfully the innocence of her who was to make the first and greatest scandal there of all in time—as in days past at Oxford, when we first met, you fellows might have respected my spotless adolescence. I don't say that you did." [9]

The effect of meeting Rossetti and his troupe of artists—William Morris, Edward Burne-Jones, Val Prinsep, and others—was electric. Swinburne was enchanted and lifted out of himself like the children of Hamelin when they first heard the fairy music of the Pied Piper. By this time he was surely aware that he was radically different from other young men. And he was filled with secret longings and desires that he had suppressed with shame because they were diametrically opposed to everything he had been taught. But here was a man with a philosophy that not only removed the shame, but encouraged him to express the longings and desires—in other words, to dare to be completely himself.

Not only the philosophy, but the man, too, fascinated Swinburne as no other ever had. Rossetti, had he wished, could certainly have been a great teacher. He had a hypnotic quality that made young men his devoted slaves and enabled him almost effortlessly and with a few words to so inspire them that the entire course of their lives would be changed. Burne-Jones, an Oxonian who also succumbed to Rossetti's charm, explained the effect of Rossetti's magic personality in an account that may well stand for Swinburne also:

He taught me to have no fear or shame of my own ideas, to design perpetually, to seek no popularity, to be altogether myself—and this not in any words I can remember, but in the tenor of his conversation always and in the spirit of everything he said. I remember that he discouraged me from study of the antique—the classical antique—giving as his reason that such study came too early in a man's life and was apt to crush out his individuality. . . . So what I chiefly gained from him was not to be afraid of myself, but to do the thing I liked most: but in those first years I never wanted to think but as he thought, and all he did and said fitted me through and through. He never harangued or persuaded, but had a gift of saying things authoritatively and not as the Scribes, such as I have never heard in any man.[10]

The phrases "taught me to have no fear or shame of my own ideas," "to be altogether myself," "to do the thing I liked most" all indicate that Rossetti preached the gospel of "art for art's sake" to his young followers. Swinburne's own testimony shows conclusively that his indoctrination into the new doctrine was by Rossetti. In a letter on October 9, 1866, to William Michael Rossetti, Swinburne explains why he ceased writing poetry in 1860 and 1861 to aid the cause of Italian liberty: ". . . it is nice to have something to love and to believe in as I do in Italy. It was only Gabriel and his followers in art (l'art pour l'art) who for a time frightened me from speaking out. . . ." [11] Later, referring to his unfavorable review of Hugo's *Les Miserables* in 1862, he says: ". . . I was just at that time . . . too much under the morally identical influence of Gabriel Gautier and of Théophile Rossetti not to regret . . . that a work of imagination should be coloured or discoloured by philanthropy, and shaped or distorted by a purpose." [12] The interchange of the given names of the two men is meant to emphasize the similarity of their influence.

Altogether, though Rossetti certainly gave Swinburne's literary creativity a decided stimulus, his influence was hardly the sort that a modern psychiatrist would have wished for him at this stage of his development. Rossetti and his thralls left Oxford by Easter, 1858—they never did finish the murals—but Swinburne made visits to London to sit at the feet of the maestro. To the neglect of his studies, the young Oxonian threw himself into the writing of poems and dramas dealing with medieval lore and imitative of those of Rossetti and Morris. With increasing boldness he gave vent to the abnormal promptings of his nature. By the end of 1859 he was giving so much time to writing poetry that he was in scholastic trouble. As a penalty for failing in examinations, he was rusticated in the early part of 1860. In June, 1860, he left the university for good without taking a degree and under mysterious circumstances which have never been cleared up. Jowett placed the blame on the Pre-Raphaelites. With greater precision he could have laid it squarely on the shoulders of the Pied Piper, Dante Gabriel Rossetti.

CHAPTER 3

The Oxford Litterateur

SWINBURNE'S OXFORD writings show very clearly his remarkable susceptibility to the influences upon him during these four and a half years. He was a complete romantic, and what he encountered in life, if it moved him emotionally and impinged upon his consciousness, was quite certain to come out in his writings. It is easy to discern the influence of Nichol and Old Mortality, of Oxford Classicism, of his readings in Hugo and Balzac. But Swinburne's much more profound reaction to Rossettian Pre-Raphaelitism and aestheticism is inescapable. The Oxford writings show him carried away with an unrestrained enthusiasm.

The Oxford works exhibit also many of the defects that mar the later works: the excessive delight in literary combat and the use of invective; the unreasoning, uncompromising hatred of religion; and the traces of sexual and psychological abnormality, together with an increasing boldness in giving free rein to the expression of his secret longings and desires—a boldness which, as we have noted, was the direct result of his conversion to "art for art's sake." Evident also in these writings of young manhood are the unmistakable signs of poetic genius and of the growth of technical skill and lyrical power. By no means was Swinburne a full-fledged poet when he left Oxford in June, 1860, but he was well on the way to becoming one.

I *Italian Freedom*

Swinburne's interest in Italy was intensified at Oxford through his contacts with Aurelio Saffi, lecturer at the Taylorean Institute, the Oxford center for modern language study. This former associate of Mazzini, an exile from Italy since 1849, was a firsthand source of information about the problems and troubles of Italy as well as the activities of Mazzini and the revolutionary party then struggling to throw off the yoke of the tyrants. Also through the young poet's adulation for Shelley and his enthusiasm for the poems of Browning, Italy had a claim upon his sympathy. The influence of Old Mortality raised his enthusiasm to a militant pitch.

Because it was always easier for Swinburne to hate than to love, his interest in Italian freedom centered on Ferdinand II, the Bourbon King of Naples, whose narrow escape from assassination in December, 1856, called the attention of the world to his tyrannical oppression of the people. In the essay "On Foreign Intervention," written in 1857-58 to be read before Old Mortality, Swinburne argued that, under extreme conditions, it was fitting and proper for one nation to interfere in the internal affairs of another. Ferdinand, he said, had created such intolerable conditions by treacherously abolishing the constitution and by doing all manner of injustices to the people, including imprisonment without trial of any who opposed him.[1]

Even more vitriolic is the attack upon Ferdinand in the "Ode to Mazzini," written in 1856-57. Stigmatizing Ferdinand as "the crowned serpent, skilled in many a wile," [2] Swinburne asks passionately in accents that owe much to Hugo's *Les Châtiments* and to Shelley's "Ode to Naples":

> *Shrinks not thy soul before the shame it braves,*
> *The gathered anger of a patient land,*
> *The loathing scorn that hardly bears to name thee?* [3]

Austria is anathematized for her share in causing Italian woes, but the secret villain—the behind-the-scenes plotter who connives at and abets the tyranny—is the head of the Church of Rome. Italy must bear the curse of slavery because she has remained in spiritual bondage to the Pope. Swinburne urges her to cast off the yoke of Catholicism so as to stand untrammeled and ready when the day of freedom dawns.

Despite its obvious faults and its imitativeness of Hugo and Shelley, the "Ode to Mazzini" is a remarkable achievement for a young collegian at the beginning of his sophomore year. Swinburne never published it, possibly because, conscious of the synthetic quality of the emotion which produced it, he considered it unworthy of the subject.

The second Italian poem, "The Temple of Janus," was camouflaged as a Roman poem. Written for the Newdigate Prize in 1857, both the subject and the rhymed couplet style were dictated by the rules of the contest. Even so, Swinburne cleverly managed to get in his licks for the cause of Italian liberty.

Janus was the Roman god whose duty it was to guard the gates of the city and the portals of the home. Depicted as two-faced, he shows his alertness by simultaneously looking both behind and before. Swinburne used this characteristic to plan his poem as a backward glance at the glories of the free Roman Republic, a present look at the slavery of Italy under the "crowned snake of Naples," and a forward vision of the same advent of freedom which he had prophesied in the "Ode to Mazzini."

The overall length of the poem is about four hundred lines. So long a poem in rhymed couplets in any but the most skillful hands would have inevitably produced a soporific monotony. But here again Swinburne exhibits a cleverness that is remarkable. He secures variety by inserting an occasional triplet and by closing the stanzas with Alexandrines; even more effective are the bursts of turbulent lyricism that are not Dryden, nor Pope, nor even Shelley. They are pure Swinburne.

What fault the judges found with this poem, we do not know. Such contests often produce strange results, and this apparently was one of them. Swinburne was passed over in favor of a student named Worley, whose only claim to fame is this coincidental connection with a great poet. Possibly the judges were of Tory leanings and did not enjoy the emphasis on liberty or the condemnation of kings and priests. Possibly, too, their classical ears were so attuned to the ponderous beat of eighteenth-century rhymed couplets that Swinburne's tripping rhythms and bursts of fairy music bewildered and alienated them.

The third and last of the Italian poems—until he returned to the theme in 1866—was "The Ride from Milan," written in honor of the obscure battle of Melegnano, fought on June 8, 1858, shortly before the much greater victory of Magenta, with which Swinburne may have confused it. Chiefly interesting because it shows that the Pre-Raphaelite influence had not completely uprooted his devotion to Italian freedom, it still marks a considerable lessening of his zeal. Sincerity is lacking, and the poem is more of a prosodic exercise than the vehicle of a powerful emotion. The center of emphasis is the rhythm and rhyme, exactly those of Poe's "The Raven," a poem which may have been brought to his attention by Rossetti, long one of Poe's admirers. Present also for the first time is an overdose of alliteration and an unfortunate diction that at times verges on absurdity.

A good argument could be made for including the Italian poems as a subdivision of the works done under the influence of Old Mortality. They are at least partially a product of the republican spirit fanned into flame by Nichol and his group; but, because Swinburne's interest in Italy and her problems antedates his coming to Oxford, a separate grouping is perhaps more appropriate.

II *Republicanism*

Actually, if we except the Italian poems, the only one of the Oxford pieces to result directly from the influence of Nichol and Old Mortality was the essay "Church Imperialism," and even this can be attributed partially to the effect upon Swinburne of Hugo's *Les Châtiments.* Appearing in March, 1858, in the third number of the *Undergraduate Papers,* this is at once an attack upon Napoleon III of France and an appeal to Roman Catholics everywhere not to follow the lead of the Pope in supporting Napoleon. Otherwise, Swinburne warns, the Catholic Church would be gravely injured, and such an outcome would be "an injury to all men."

His hatred of the French Emperor is genuine enough. After Orsini's abortive attempt to assassinate Napoleon III, Swinburne hung Orsini's picture beside that of Mazzini on the wall of his room, going through an almost daily ritual of dancing and bowing before them.

III *Pre-Raphaelitism*

Far and away the larger portion of Swinburne's writings at Oxford bear the unmistakable impress of Pre-Raphaelite influence. On November 10, 1857, only nine days after his first encounter with the Pre-Raphaelites, he was engaged in writing his *Queen Iseult,* his first Pre-Raphaelite work.[4] Though he had intended to complete the poem in ten cantos, he broke it off at the beginning of the seventh and left it unfinished, disparaging it later as "some awful doggerel on the subject of Tristram and Iseult." [5]

Inspired by Morris's "Defence of Guinevere," the "Haystack in the Floods," and possibly by "The Battle of Crecy," *Queen Iseult* runs to 1,103 verses and is Swinburne's most sustained effort up to that time.

The poem begins with a lengthy and unnecessary account of the parentage, birth, and upbringing of Tristram, who, at twenty, journeys to Cornwall, reveals himself to his uncle King Mark, and is commissioned by him to go to Ireland for Yseult. What follows is largely the conventional story but with some noteworthy exceptions. When Tristram and Yseult arrive at King Mark's court, Tristram's qualms at continuing the affair with his uncle's wife while he is a guest in the uncle's palace are overcome by Yseult, who comes to him barefoot through the snow (why she was not wearing shoes is not made clear) and carries him on her back to her own room. And when they are finally discovered and exposed, Yseult, in a scene reminiscent of Morris' "Defence of Guinevere," outfaces King Mark before all his knights and boldly denies her guilt, saying that, if she had ever been unfaithful to him, it was with the same knight who had exposed her. Frustrated, Mark has to suffer the laughter of the knightly audience and to accept their verdict of her innocence, though he cannot rid himself of suspicion. Sorrowfully, Tristram leaves Cornwall and makes his way to Brittany, where he somewhat reluctantly weds another Yseult, described as "of the white hands" to distinguish her from Mark's wife, who is "of the yellow hair." Though the new Yseult loves him passionately, Tristram has only a paternal feeling for her; and, on their wedding night, he refrains from touching her. Back in Cornwall, she of the yellow hair mourns for him, comforting herself that, if he ever returns, he will find her older, but still golden haired and as much in love as ever.

In such absurdities as these it is not difficult to see the curious compound of Rossettian sensuality and aestheticism and the all too evident traces of Swinburne's abnormality. The result is altogether grotesque, for the two elements are as incompatible as oil and water. In Rossetti's pictures and poems, the lady's loose, flowing hair is a sensual symbol, and nothing more. But Swinburne makes Tristram ridiculous when he shows him willing to die for Yseult's hair, and has him exclaim, when he is absent from his lady, that he "thirsted for one tress." The abnormality also shows through the fear of sexual contact with women which is symptomatic of homosexuality. Such an unmasculine reaction is evidenced in Tristram's being so timid that the more aggressive Yseult has to carry him piggyback to her room. And, in the nuptial bed with Yseult of the white hands, the doughty knight trembles when she creeps close and asks him to kiss her. Weeping, he prays to God while she goes to sleep, puzzled and still a virgin.

The best feature of *Queen Iseult* is a compactness and economy of expression notable by its absence from Swinburne's later works. The scenes are vividly described; the mood and tone are sustained. Here and there the story comes to life with an immediacy that could have been created only by an imagination that lived the scenes as it created them.

Also strongly initiative of the Pre-Raphaelite interest in the medieval are such poems as "Lancelot," which shows the knight torn between his conscience and his adulterous love for Guinevere; the fragment "King Ban," dealing with Lancelot's parents; and the "Rudel" poems, three short poems about the love of the medieval troubadour Jaufre Rudel for the Countess of Tripoli.

The poem "The Queen's Tragedy," written in 1859, is of special interest. The unnamed queen, who narrates the story, tells to the maids who hold her arms while she lies in bed the grim story of how the king and her baby were murdered by cruel men. Heartbroken, she relives the story of how they killed her husband, cut off his head, and nailed it to the city walls. Despite her pleas that she is not mad and that she will not harm herself if they free her arms, her ravings show her derangement. As the poem closes, she fancies the king is again by her side; and she promises that, if he will love her again as he did when they first met, she will blossom as beautifully and sing as sweetly as she did then.

If we place this poem beside Rossetti's "The King's Tragedy," completed in March, 1881, and published later that year,[6] the mystery of the identity of the king and queen is solved. Rossetti tells the story of the murder of James I of Scotland at the Charterhouse in Perth in 1437 by Robert Graeme and his men, despite the heroic efforts of his queen, the former Jane Beaufort, daughter of the Earl of Somerset and of Catherine Douglas, to save him. After the deed, the murderers flee to the Highlands before the king's men can seize them. Although the murder takes place in February, the queen keeps the king's body lying in state in Charterhouse Chapel till nearly the end of March, when the last wretch is caught and hanged.

Rossetti paints a vivid picture of the queen sitting and praying beside the bier all those weeks, giving no sign to anybody except Catherine Douglas. As Catherine brings her the news, the queen's face grows livid as she leans over and whispers to the dead king the name of the traitor punished. She falls to the floor with froth on her lips when the name is that of the archtraitor, Sir Robert Graeme. After the last traitor is hanged, she rises from her grim vigil, withered and wasted by her grief.

Swinburne's poem takes up the tale at this point, showing the queen's last haunted hour, her mind unsettled by grief and despair, doubtful of God's existence or mercy, yearning to be reunited with her murdered husband. We must admit that Swinburne's tragedy is not a tragedy as it stands, because the reader is not acquainted with the details necessary to establish the tragic thesis. Nor, for this same reason, as well as for the fact that the audience is never clearly described or permitted to become part of the scene, is it a good dramatic monologue.

Whose was the original inspiration to use this material—Rossetti's or Swinburne's? Because Swinburne wrote his poem twenty-two years before Rossetti, and because Scottish history and legend were much closer to him—"Capheaton" was only a few miles from the Border—than to Rossetti, he is the more likely choice. The reasonable conjecture is that Swinburne, during one of his frequent visits to London in 1859 and 1860, read his poem to Rossetti after first briefing him on the details leading up to the murder. Rossetti then filed the details, including the title, away in his memory, and resurrected them in 1880-1881 for "The King's Tragedy."

He should, of course, have given Swinburne proper credit. But he had completely broken off his friendship with Swinburne in 1872; and if his conscience gave him even a momentary twinge, he could have eased it by reflecting that he had used only that part of the material that Swinburne had not included, and that Swinburne had never deemed "The Queen's Tragedy" worthy of publication. The incident serves to show, however, that whatever the benefits were that may have attended the friendship of the two men, they were not always flowing in one direction. Rossetti did learn some things from the brilliant young Oxonian.

In an entirely different vein from "The Queen's Tragedy" are the seven sonnets that T. J. Wise titled "Undergraduate Sonnets" and published after Swinburne's death. Scholars have always considered them a mere poetic exercise, partly in imitation of Shakespeare (whose prosody they follow) and partly of Rossetti, whose translation of Dante's *Vita Nuova* sonnets led him to adopt the sonnet as one of his favorite verse forms. Swinburnians have always believed that the poet's love affair was with "Boo" Faulkner, the adopted daughter of London friends, whom he met in 1862 or 1863. But in 1858 Professor Cecil Y. Lang published an article containing the argument that Swinburne's passion was not for "Boo" at all—she was only ten in 1863—but for his cousin Mary Gordon.[7] My feeling is that the emotion was real and that the sonnets were probably written to Mary Gordon. Since she was only three years his junior and since they had been thrown together since childhood, he could well have been in love with her while he was at Oxford; or, another possibility, the sonnets might well have been written at any time after Swinburne left Oxford until the spring, 1864, when Mary Gordon apparently rejected him in favor of another.

IV Miscellaneous Poems

During the Oxford years Swinburne tried his hand at a wide variety of poetic forms and subjects, ranging from translations of Dante and Villon to ballads in imitation of the Border Ballads, a translation of the Catholic chant *Dies Irae*, and two sonnets titled "The Cup of God's Wrath," paraphrases of Biblical material. Since these are imitations and nothing more, there is no necessity for dealing with them at length.

Even less worthy of attention is the poem "The Death of Sir John Franklin" which Swinburne wrote in two mornings of February, 1860, while he was in rustication with the Reverend Stubbs of Navestock. A poem of about two hundred lines, it was written for a special prize of £50 for the best poem on the life, death, and character of Sir John Franklin, the explorer who had perished on an Arctic expedition. The result was a tedious poem in iambic pentameter with a loose rhyme scheme. We cannot escape the suspicion that Swinburne was more interested in the

£50 than in Sir John, for this is a mere poetic exercise like "The Triumph of Gloriana" of Eton days. As in the case of "The Temple of Janus," Swinburne saw the prize go to another. That Swinburne's offering dealt only with Franklin's death, to the exclusion of his life and character, and that its author had already departed Oxford under questionable circumstances may have cost him the victory.

V *The Dramas*

The active interest in the Elizabethan drama Swinburne displayed even before he went to Eton continued and grew stronger during the Oxford years, intensified to some degree by Pre-Raphaelite archaism and medievalism, even though the Pre-Raphaelites themselves had little interest in the drama as an art form. The result was three drama fragments—*The Laws of Corinth, Laugh and Lie Down,* and *The Loyal Servant*—all in the Elizabethan style and heavily indebted to Elizabethan plays and playwrights. The first of these, *The Laws of Corinth*—written in 1858 in imitation of *The Old Law* of Massinger and Middleton with some stylistic borrowings from Beaumont, Fletcher, and Chapman—is a fragment of one act and part of a second which centers around the love of Philocles, nephew of King Lysader of Corinth, for Erota, daughter of the aristocrat Antigonus. It is a maze of plot and counterplot told with such ranting and pseudo-Elizabethan fustian that we cannot regret that Swinburne carried this extravaganza no further.

To the second fragment, *Laugh and Lie Down,* Swinburne referred in a letter to a friend in 1874: "I suppose you can tell me nothing . . . of the *other* comedy attributed to C. T. [Cyril Tourneur] by Lowndes, with the charming title of 'Laugh and Lie Down.' I was so delighted with the name that in my last Oxford year I wrote in three days three acts of a comedy, after (a long way after) the late manner of Fletcher, under that title; but I shall take good care that this one never sees the light!" [8]

The nature of this fragment, written in 1859 and still unpublished, reveals clearly why Swinburne resolved to keep it hidden. Replete with flagellation resulting from abnormalities of love and sex, with uncertainties and mixtures of sex in which a man falls in love with a boy dressed as a girl, and with the question of another individual who may be a hermaphrodite, the play shows to what degree Swinburne gave free rein to his abnormal longings under the new freedom urged upon him by Rossetti, Pre-Raphaelitism, and aestheticism. As it stands, the play is a psychiatric document—a most significant item in a case history that leaves little room for reasonable doubt of one aspect of Swinburne's abnormality. Here, for instance, is the scene in which the page boy Frank confesses his love for his cruel mistress, the beautiful courtesan Imperia:

Imperia.   *I tell you, if you use me lovingly,*
               I shall have you whipt again, most pitifully whipt
               You little piece of love.
Frank.   *God knows I care not*
               So I may stand and play to you, and you kiss me
               As you used to kiss me tender little side-touches
               Of your lip's edge i' the neck.
Imperia.   *By my hand's hope,*
               Which is the neck of my lord Galeas,
               I'll love your beard one day; get you a beard, Frank;
               I were as well love a maid as you
               With such a child's cheeks.
Frank.   *Madam, you have pleasant hands,*
               What sweet and kissing colour goes in them
               Running like blood. . . .

    . . . .

    What makes you sigh still? You are now
    So kind the sweetness in you stabs mine eyes
    With sharp tears through. I would so fain be hurt
    But really hurt, hurt deadly, to do good
    To your most sudden fancy.[9]

The Loyal Servant, the last of the Oxford dramas and the most nearly complete of them all, consists of four full acts and the first scenes of the fifth. Probably written toward the end of 1859 and the beginning of 1860, it contributed in good measure to the academic disaster which ended Swinburne's Oxford career. It represents a backward turn in his dramatic development rather than a step forward; for, where the plot was original and the diction modern in *Laugh and Lie Down,* this play closely follows the plot of Marston's *Anthony and Mellida* and the dialogue is so affectedly archaic that it verges on absurdity.

VI *Literary Criticism*

In 1857 and 1858 Swinburne appeared also as literary polemicist and critic, the third of the roles he was to assume in his later career. Ordinarily, we would not amalgamate these two functions and designate them as one role, but in Swinburne's case criticism was inevitably and inextricably mixed up with polemics. It was also intertwined with his emotions, his likes and dislikes. Even when he set out to praise unstintedly the works of some friend, he rarely did so without giving some backhanded blows by drawing invidious comparisons to others he disliked. Thus in his *Notes on Poems and Reviews* (1866) he defended his own poems and sneered at those of Robert Buchanan. In his *Fortnightly Review* eulogy of Rossetti's *Poems* (1870) he found Rossetti's verse superior in religious sincerity to that of Robert Browning and Cardinal Newman. In his *Fortnightly Review* article, "Mr. Arnold's New Poems" (October, 1867), he lauded Arnold and disparaged David Gray. And he extravagantly praised the novels of Charlotte Bronte as greatly superior to those of George Eliot in his essay, "A Note on Charlotte Bronte" (1877).

This trait is evident in the first piece of published criticism he wrote, the article on Congreve in 1857 for the *Imperial Dictionary of Universal Biography.* After praising the sharpness and clearness of Congreve's mind, he says: "There is more weight and matter in Congreve than in any English Dramatist since the Restoration and at worst he is no coarser than his time. . . . As a comic writer he stands above the best who came after him, and beside the best who went before." [10] Now there is nothing intentionally polemical in these remarks, nor would they be likely to raise animosities when the writers who might have been offended by them were all dead at least a half century. But later on, when Swinburne drew similar invidious comparisons between living men of letters, ire and bitter recriminations were the usual result.

This comparative method is used in another early article,

"The Early English Dramatists," published in December, 1857, in the first number of the *Undergraduate Papers*. In it he is comparing Marlowe and Webster, whom he finds similar in their ability to plumb the profundities of human character, in their command of language, and in their abhorrence of insincerity. This essay is noteworthy because, only a few weeks after meeting the Pre-Raphaelites, he shows the impact of Pre-Raphaelitism in his praise of Marlowe and Webster for their adherence to nature. "Their style," he says, "has the simple and noble outlines of the great early painters of Italy and Flanders." [11]

Both the Congreve article and the essay on Marlowe and Webster are gentleness itself compared to the third essay, "Modern Hellenism," an attack on Matthew Arnold which appeared in the second number of the *Undergraduate Papers* in January, 1858. This one is Swinburne with his fangs bared. He takes exception to remarks Arnold had made in a lecture in the Oxford Theatre to the effect that the Athenians of the Age of Pericles were a more cultured and refined lot than the English in the Elizabethan times, and that, specifically, Sophocles and Thucydides were superior to Sir Walter Raleigh. Waving the Union Jack, Swinburne sneers: "It may be that we have been hitherto mistaken; but we must have more than the measured rhetoric of a lecture to prove that we must resign the heroes of our own history for the idols of Oxford Hellenism." [12]

The last of the undergraduate attempts at criticism is a critical burlesque called "The Monomaniac's Tragedy," published in the second of the *Undergraduate Papers* in January, 1858, and never reprinted. Purportedly a review of the poems of Ernest Wheldrake, "author of Eve, a Mystery," this is the first of several such burlesques which Swinburne perpetrated in his later career and used to ridicule people and ideas that moved him to derisive laughter. In the "review" he pretends to quote excerpts from Wheldrake's poems, but they are, of course, his own. In these quotations he is evidently ridiculing the Spasmodic Poets and two of their leaders, Alexander Smith and Sydney Dobell. Like the Beatniks of the twentieth century, the Spasmodic Poets believed they first must woo the poetic mood or trance, and that what came forth then was inspired verse, regardless of its absurdities. Swinburne satirizes such extravagances by having Ernest Wheldrake commit a variety of crimes in order to secure material for poetry which, when it comes, pours forth in ranting:

> *Oh! ah! oh!*
> *Ha! Ha! it burns me. Have I found him there?*
> *Nay, thou dead pain, it shall not alter thee;*
> *Tho' I hurled heaven into the reeling spume*
> *Of thunder-whitened ages, haled the moon*
> *At some red meteor's palpitating heels,*
> *A mangled residue of beams—what else?* [13]

This parody is at once criticism and delicious humor. More effectively than a whole volume of criticism could, it exposes the faults of the Spasmodic philosophy and practice—faults which have today relegated the Spasmodic verse to the limbo of forgotten literature.

CHAPTER 4

Life for Art's Sake

SWINBURNE'S first problem, when he departed Oxford in June, 1860, was to win his father's approval to go to London to try his luck in the literary world. Admiral Swinburne's reluctance (he had retired from the Navy as a rear admiral in 1857) to endorse such a scheme is completely understandable. After all, Swinburne's academic debacle had been brought about by his suceptibility to the aestheticism of Rossetti and his Pre-Raphaelites. Why permit him to feed on more of the same?

By this time the Admiral must have had at least strong suspicions of his son's abnormality. If Lafourcade's conjecture is correct that Swinburne's giving free rein to his secret longings led to "bacchic excesses" which forced Oxford authorities to request his departure, at least for the time being, then Jowett would have known the full story.[1] And, if Jowett knew it, he would have been negligent in his duties not to have acquainted the Admiral with full particulars. Furthermore, Admiral Swinburne had been in the British Navy for about forty-seven years; inevitably, cases of sexual abnormality among seamen would have come to his attention; and, as an officer, he may have had to deal with them. At least the common symptoms of such cases would be familiar to him, and he could hardly fail to perceive them in Algernon, in whom they were quite evident.

So the Admiral's consent was slow in coming, but it did come. In the spring of 1861 he gave his reluctant approval and an annual allowance of £200 to set his son up at 16 Grafton Street in London. Evidently, Swinburne's father nourished hopes that his son's literary enthusiasms would wane and that he in time might be persuaded to make his peace with the authorities of Oxford and take his degree. In any case, the annual caution money to keep his name on the roll of students was paid till 1878, the year after the Admiral's death.[2]

The hopes were vain and the money wasted. Once launched on the town, Swinburne was off like an uncaged bird. After all, he was twenty-four in the spring of 1861, and for the first time in his life he was completely on his own and had happiness at last. The guns were firing on Fort Sumter across the Atlantic, but they raised not an echo of interest in the former apostle of freedom. Fears were abroad that Napoleon might attempt what his greater uncle had never been able to bring off—an invasion of Britain— but that, too, caused little concern in one who a year before had clamored for Napoleon's assassination. English interest in Italian liberty was at a high pitch all about him; Swinburne's interest was centered on his own freedom. Life was too exciting, too full of endless possibilities to bother about other people's woes.

His career in London for the next six years was at least as harmful and disreputable as the Admiral could have dreaded. All things conspired against Swinburne as though a malignant fate dominated his life. Three separate factors operated so as to carry him almost to mental, moral, and physical disaster. The first of these was the continued, bad influence of Dante Rossetti and of other persons whom Swinburne met through him. Second was the equally bad effect of close association with Richard Monckton Milnes (later Lord Houghton) and, through him, with several other men whose influence was strongly negative. Finally, Swinburne had to endure the shattering blow of being rejected in love by his cousin Mary Gordon, who, so far as we know, was the only girl for whom he ever felt the passion of love. The cumulative effect of three such handicaps would be difficult for even a strong individual to withstand; for Swinburne, they were well nigh catastrophic.

I Rossetti's Disciple

In seeking London and Rossetti, Swinburne was reacting in a pattern now quite familiar to modern psychiatrists. Those afflicted with homosexual leanings have a marked tendency to move to large centers of population, where they can follow their abnormal longings without the constant fear of detection that threatens in smaller communities.[3] Although the large number of Swinburnes and Ashburnhams living in and around, or traveling through London, created some hazards even there, the very size and character of London offered more anonymity, and perhaps illicit opportunity, than any other British city. Likewise, in attaching himself to Rossetti, he was only doing what he would be expected to do in his circumstances. The sexually abnormal male often seeks an idealized bond or relationship with an older man who, he feels, takes a real interest in him.[4] Although he may not be aware of his own motive, he is of course only attempting to compensate for the lack of a normal father-son relationship.

As we have seen, Rossetti was neither an idealist nor an altruist. Despite his surface glitter and his admitted genius, he had little capacity for friendship. He used people for his own ends, diverting their money and influence to his own benefit when he could—as in the case of Ruskin and Morris—then casting them aside when they rebelled. Except in a few cases, his friendships did not last long because, sooner or later, his victims became aware of what he was doing. He attracted and fascinated young men always, but, when they began to question his impositions or his authority, the end of their association was in sight. Always he traded upon youth; older men saw through him too soon and too clearly, and even the young ones soon grew restive under his domination. Of him Val Prinsep said: ". . . like the dread Jehovah of the Israelites, he was a jealous God, and, from the moment he was not all in all to us, a gradually widening rift established itself." [5] To put it bluntly, Rossetti was pretty hard to take over the long pull, and anybody with spirit refused to put up with him.

Swinburne, however, was so bedazzled with hero worship that he saw no blemish in his idol. One of Hadji's weaknesses and virtues was that, where he gave friendship, he gave implicit and unquestioning trust. In return he expected the same generous friendship and trust. If in any way a supposed friend violated his high code of friendship, Swinburne's rage was fierce and unrelenting. So many betrayals did he suffer in the first half of his life, that he became increasingly suspicious and chary of friendship as he grew older. One of his greatest betrayals, he came to believe later, was at Rossetti's hands; and his bitterness toward the artist was commensurate with what his affection had been.

"And indeed the bonds between this poet and this painter were closer than any such statements can imply," says Ford Madox Hueffer of the friendship between Rossetti and Swinburne in the early 1860's.[6] At least they were from Swinburne's side. From Rossetti's? Rossetti had a cruel sense of humor which delighted to ridicule those under his spell. Swinburne had not been long in London when Rossetti asked him to pose with the voluptuous Fanny Cornforth for a picture which he promised would be used as the frontispiece for his anthology of translations entitled *The Early Italian Poets*. As Swinburne wrote Milnes on October 15, 1861, "Rossetti has just done a drawing of a female model and myself embracing—I need not say in the most fervent and abandoned style—meant for a frontispiece to his Italian translations. Two mornings of incessant labour on all hands completed the design; and the result will I suppose be, as everybody who knows me already salutes the likeness with a yell of recognition,—that when the book comes out I shall have no refuge but the grave." [7]

Biographers of Swinburne and Rossetti have always passed over this incident without comment, assuming, as Swinburne obviously did, that the picture was in good faith. Casting him in such a role was a mockery. Homosexuality is at least partially the result of secret, disabling fears of womankind;[8] the homosexual, therefore, shuns and dreads any close contact with members of the opposite sex outside his own family, a fact which so worldly a man as Rossetti must have known. Forcing poor Swinburne to remain in such a posture with Fanny Cornforth through most of two mornings was as diabolical a bit of torture as any ever devised during the Middle Ages.

This prank was not the last of its kind played on Swinburne by his beloved master. In 1867-1868, when the equestrienne Adah Isaacs Menken came to England, Rossetti urged her on Swinburne.[9] Rumor had it that he gave her £10 to seduce the poet and that she returned the money, confessing her failure. We wonder if he had made a like offer to Fanny to inspire her to her best efforts when she posed with Swinburne.

Such antics as these may have caused Swinburne some discomfort but hardly anything worse. Rossetti's Bohemian way of life, inculcated by precept and example during Swinburne's frequent visits to his studio in Chatham Place by Blackfriars Bridge and later at Tudor House did much more to Swinburne's moral fiber. Such visits became almost a daily occurrence after he went to London. It would have taken someone much more naïve than he not to have soon realized that the artist practiced in everyday life his philosophy of trusting his intuitions and impulses and of casting aside any and all inhibitions. With Rossetti, sexual expression was as necessary and natural as meat and drink, and it was treated as casually. It bothered him not a bit one day in 1852 to notify brother William Michael and Holman Hunt not to come to his rooms because Elizabeth Siddal was coming and he did not wish to be disturbed.[10] In the last years of his life he instructed Hall Caine not to leave his room and come down stairs when Mrs. Jane Morris was with him.[11]

Such restrictions were a necessary condition of friendship with Rossetti. As William Bell Scott puts it: All his close friends accepted "certain peculiarities in him. . . . placing him in a position different from themselves, a dangerous position to the man whose temperament takes advantage of it." [12] Following the usual pattern of Rossetti's friendships, Swinburne's affection for him cooled off appreciably in 1863 and 1864. After the suicide of Elizabeth Siddal Rossetti in 1862, Swinburne, Rossetti, and George Meredith went to live in Tudor House. In a relationship that left no room for doubt, Rossetti soon installed there the coarse Fanny Cornforth, whom Swinburne later referred to as "the bitch." [13] This was a "peculiarity" that Swinburne, who had a deep and abiding affection for Elizabeth Siddal Rossetti, could not accept. He soon moved out, and, though he and Rossetti continued to see each other occasionally, the old fealty was gone.

By that time, however, most of the damage to Swinburne was already done, but not all of it was the responsibility of Rossetti. Through him and those who orbited about him, Swinburne met several unsavory characters who helped along his deterioration. Among them were Burne-Jones, who encouraged his abnormal tendencies;[14] Simeon Solomon, the young Jewish painter who may have been introduced to him by Burne-Jones,[15] and who was or soon became a homosexual, for his letters to Swinburne indicate an abnormal relationship; Charles Augustus Howell, parasite, trickster, liar, and—according to William Rossetti's daughter, Helen Rossetti Angeli—one of several of Swinburne's friends who flogged him for his pleasure.[16] Through these men Swinburne met still other objectionables like John Camden Hotten, Savile Clark, and John Thomson, who was connected with and perhaps part owner of a sort of brothel in St. John's Wood, where Swinburne went in the late 1860's to be flogged by the beautiful and mysterious "Mrs. A." [17]

The induction into "art for art's sake" Rossetti had given Swinburne at Oxford was intensified and amplified after he came to London. In James McNeill Whistler, whom he probably met through Rossetti, he found a complete devotee of Gautier and Baudelaire. Having recently come from Paris, where he had been thoroughly immersed in the new philosophy, Whistler was an authority on both the theory and practice of the new doctrine. Swinburne was an inspired pupil. He broke into print as an apostle of the new artistic freedom on June 7, 1862, when his letter to the editor of the *Spectator,* replying to an unfavorable review of Meredith's *Modern Love, and Poems of the English Roadside* appeared in that journal. All schools of poetry, Swinburne argued, should not be circumscribed by "nursery walls," as the popular school of that day was. Any subject "worth the serious interest of men" should be treated in the adult fashion of the *Modern Love* sonnets.[18] He amplified and clarified his thesis in his review of Baudelaire's *Les Fleurs du Mal,* published first in 1857, later recalled and somewhat expurgated as the result of a lawsuit and fine of Baudelaire's French publisher. Republished in 1861, this was the subject of Swinburne's review in the *Spectator,* a magazine opened to him through Lord Houghton, who introduced him to editor Richard Holt Hutton, on September 6, 1862.[19]

In this article, the first important one in England on Baudelaire, Swinburne begins with a bold statement that art has nothing to do with morals or didacticism. Then, turning his attention to the verse, he praises it for the exquisite workmanship which "makes every subject admirable and respectable." [20] Warming to his subject, he goes a step further in praise of Baudelaire's philosophy of the beauty of evil. He finds the morbid subject matter of *Les Fleurs du Mal* fascinating because "It has the languid, lurid beauty of close and threatening weather—a heavy, heated temperature, with dangerous hot-house scents in it; thick shadow of cloud about it, and fire of molten light." [21] Even the most loathsome subjects, he finds, are made beautiful by the perfect art of the poet. Then he effects a synthesis of beauty and morality with a bold declaration that ". . . there is not one poem of the Fleurs du Mal which has not a distinct and vivid background of morality to it." [22] After quoting eighty-three lines from a number of poems, he completes the introduction of the British public to the French voluptuary by quoting from the "Litanies de Satan," which he acclaims "one of the noblest lyrics ever written." [23]

Swinburne's covert purpose in this article was to place the poems of the Frenchman before the British; his secondary object was to enunciate the principles of "art for art's sake" and to illustrate them forcibly from Baudelaire. Hence the too long and too many quotations from *Les Fleurs*. Hence, also, the farfetched equation of beauty with morality. (Even Baudelaire thought that Swinburne had gone too far in his praise, for he wrote the young enthusiast that he was not at all as much of a moralist as Swinburne seemed to believe.) [24] Swinburne's third purpose in this article was, of course, to execute a frontal attack upon British morality and religion. He did it deliberately and, I believe, with full awareness of what he was doing. Here he was going beyond his master, for though Rossetti practiced and lived according to "art for art's sake" and though he joked about the proprieties in private, he did not dare to do so openly.

To what extent Rossetti may have encouraged Swinburne to write this article, we can only conjecture. The painter was too enthusiastic a practitioner of the new gospel to have endeavored to dissuade him. The spectacle of a young Englishman of excellent family, educated in an English university, lauding a French pornographer and quoting his obscenities in a respectable English family magazine might well have appealed to Rossetti's cruel sense of humor. The fact that Swinburne was also presenting himself to his own people as a dangerous young man—something of a literary subversive who would bear watching—would have bothered Rossetti's conscience not at all.

In fairness to Rossetti, we may say that his influence on Swinburne was not wholly bad. Rossetti was a talented poet and a critic of no mean ability. In his early years in London Swinburne benefited considerably from Rossetti's criticism and inspiration. Even the bad influence Rossetti exerted upon Swinburne was not malicious. What he taught Swinburne was what he honestly believed and practiced himself, what he imparted to all his young disciples, Morris and Burne-Jones included. When he realized that Swinburne was carrying out his gospel so literally that his life was in danger, Rossetti was worried and perhaps conscience-stricken. But Swinburne's deterioration had gone so far, and Rossetti's influence over him had lessened to such a degree by 1865, that the painter was powerless to undo the harm he had caused.

II *Lord Houghton's Influence*

On the face of his position and his many accomplishments, we would expect Lord Houghton's influence on Swinburne to be good: politician, scholar, man of the world, biographer of Keats, patron of young men of genius, fellow student at Cambridge with Thackeray and Tennyson, social luminary, and *bon vivant* —here was a man with much to give in wisdom, experience, criticism, and influence to a talented young literary man trying to make his way in the world. But, alas, the total effect of Swinburne's relations with Lord Houghton was on the negative side. In fact, if Lord Houghton had deliberately planned to ruin Swinburne's character and reputation, he could hardly have done a more thorough piece of work.

Because he was older than Rossetti, held a much higher position of respectability in the world, and was a man from the same social class as the Swinburnes and the Ashburnhams, Lord Houghton's power for good or evil over Swinburne was nearly as great as the painter's. He lacked Rossetti's genius and personal magnetism, but he made up for it in his wide knowledge of the world and in his great personal influence. Swinburne could respect Rossetti as an artist, but he could never accept him as a social equal—and his unsavory way of life in his dingy studio was altogether another world from that of "East Dene" or "Capheaton." But Lord Houghton was widely known and respected as a friend of such people as Gladstone, Disraeli, Jowett, Carlyle, and Palmerston. Consequently, when Houghton gave his blessing to pornography or illicit sexuality, the effect upon his young friend was almost the same as if the Earl of Ashburnham or Admiral Charles Henry Swinburne had done so.

The harm Houghton did Swinburne was along three distinct but related lines of action. First, he intensified the young poet's abnormal sexuality by encouraging him to revel in pornography of all kinds and by placing in his hands books otherwise hard to obtain—like those of the Marquis de Sade. Many of these works dealt with flagellation, frequently a concomitant of homosexual-

ity; many of the letters between Swinburne and Houghton show
that the older man encouraged the younger one to dwell upon
such subjects. Second, Houghton influenced Swinburne to write
pornographic poetry and prose and to give full vent to aberrant
sexual tendencies, not, as Rossetti had, under the pretext of serving
art, but for the joy of such abnormalities. Third, Houghton took
a perverse delight in exhibiting Swinburne and his most offensive
poems before persons who would be most shocked by them,
usually people of prominence and influence, so that Swinburne's
reputation was considerably damaged in important quarters.
Because of Swinburne's subscription to Baudelaire's philosophy
of the beauty of evil and because of his own love of shocking, he
was willing to be exhibited.

The date of his first meeting with Lord Houghton is uncertain,
but it was probably in 1861. It could have been earlier, for both
men belonged to the Hogarth Club as early as 1858. In any case,
by 1861 they were on intimate terms. Within a few months,
Houghton was entertaining Swinburne at his country home at
Fryston, where his inordinate love of smut had led him to collect
one of the largest libraries of erotica in the British Isles. Here he
invited his especial guests and put into their hands the latest and
juiciest titles gathered from all over Europe. So paradoxical was
his nature that on one Sunday morning he paused long enough to
point out to his guests the exact location of his worst books and
then continued on his way to Fryston Church with Lady Houghton.[25]

We are aware that most men relish a salacious jest as long as it
is clever and contains real humor. After all, such humor springs
from man's rather laudable refusal to take himself too seriously;
it is his philosophical laughter at his own earthiness and human
frailty. And we freely admit that some of the supreme humor of
all ages is contained in jokes about those areas of experience not
properly mentioned in mixed company. But a wide gulf lies between humor and the sort of thing Lord Houghton delighted in:
the writings of the Marquis de Sade, for instance, whom Anatole
France called "notre fou." [26] Redolent of homosexuality and lust,
they are the excretions of depravity, and only a depraved mind
could find anything good in them.

The greatest single disservice Houghton did Swinburne was,
therefore, to introduce him to de Sade's works, probably in Au-

gust, 1862.[27] Outlawed in both France and England, de Sade's writings would be hard to find outside such a library as Houghton's, and for good reason. For instance, one of the worst of them is the "Dialogue entre un Prêtre et un Moribond," which combines unbridled lust and homosexuality with savage scorn and mockery of religion.

We can readily imagine Swinburne's delight in de Sade. This same intermingling of a denunciation of religion as hypocrisy and a reveling in abnormal sexuality was adopted by Swinburne and remained with him the rest of his life. One usually called forth the other, even in his private letters. More than any other factor, this obnoxious aspect of his poetry enraged the British public and brought down its wrath upon Swinburne in 1866.

That which fascinated Swinburne most in de Sade's works was the novel *Justine ou les Malheurs de la Vertu*. The story concerns Justine's trials and tortures at the hands of the homosexual Bressac and his valet, Jasmin. That she loves Bressac means nothing to him, nor does it temper the indignities he heaps upon her womanhood. He attacks and ridicules her religious beliefs, she being portrayed as quite devout. Perhaps the crowning atrocity of the novel occurs when Bressac puts a dagger into the hand of Justine and guides it into his mother's heart. *Justine* is crammed full of sadism, masochism, sodomy, incest, atheism, murder, and the same scorn of religion combined with abnormal lust that we noted in the "Dialogue." None of it was good pabulum for an erratic young fledgling only two years out of Oxford.

De Sade became an obsession with Swinburne and remained so until the end of his life. De Sade, whose very name is the root of the word *sadism*, and Lord Houghton brought out the very worst elements of Swinburne's nature and greatly accelerated his moral deterioration. In fact, Houghton became connected with de Sade in Swinburne's imagination—an association which suggests that more than a few similarities existed between de Sade's writings and Lord Houghton's private letters and conversation. In his letters to Houghton, Swinburne often addresses him as "mon cher Rodin." Rodin was the master of the pension of San Marcel, a house of the most questionable purposes and practices, in de Sade's writings.[28] Houghton obviously shared Swinburne's interest in flagellation, for in the same letter Swinburne says he is anxious to see the style of Houghton's flagellant fiction. This remark is in relation to chapters of a fictional work dealing with a schoolmaster's autobiography which both he and Houghton were apparently writing. In another letter to Houghton on February 3, 1863, Swinburne describes with ecstatic delight the proper way to flog a boy so as to raise red welts on his bottom,[29] and a week later he discusses the exquisite pleasure of being flogged in a room readied beforehand with burnt scents or in a grove of trees smelling of spring.[30]

These letters show clearly the damage done to Swinburne by his association with Houghton; they also prove beyond a reasonable doubt that Houghton had ominous traits in his own character that should be inquired into by his future biographers.

As in the case of Rossetti, Houghton's deleterious influence was increased by some of the people Swinburne met through him; but, because Houghton moved on a much higher social plane, their number was not so large nor their collective damage so serious as that done by the raffish hangers-on of the Pre-Raphaelites. The most outstanding of Houghton's acquaintances was Sir Richard Francis Burton (1821-1890), whom Swinburne met at one of Houghton's breakfasts on June 5, 1861.[31] Sixteen years older than Swinburne, a virile adventurer who had poked about the world in out-of-the-way places, Burton was perhaps overly fond of bawdry and alcohol, and he had a distinctly bad influence on Swinburne. The elder man encouraged Swinburne to the excessive drinking which soon became a major problem for him. Moreover, he introduced Swinburne into the sinister Cannibal Club, founded by Burton—whose travels had half convinced him of the benefits of anthropophagy—as an offshoot of the Anthropological Society.[32] For the club, which held its dinners under the symbol of a savage gnawing a human bone, Swinburne wrote the *Cannibal Catechism,* a parody of Christian prayer and religious teaching.[33]

Houghton's love of pornography led him to encourage Swinburne to write many of the most objectionable poems which later appeared in *Poems and Ballads* in 1866. Houghton then went about London spreading the word of the character of these poems. Houghton took a keen delight in bringing together at his home people of opposite tastes and ideas and setting them on each other. Swinburne and his poetry were surefire shockers for any but the most coarse Victorians, and Houghton made full use of his young protégé. At Fryston in the summer of 1861 he had him read his poems "The Leper" and "Les Noyades" before James Spedding, then Archbishop of York, and Thackeray and his daughters, who were in their early twenties.[34] Also at Fryston in November, 1862—this time with no women present—he paraded Swinburne before a company which included Lawrence Oliphant, the novelist, and Henry Adams, the quiet and intelligent young American serving as his father's secretary at the American Embassy and perhaps meant by Houghton to be Swinburne's foil on this occasion. In his *The Education of Henry Adams,* Adams gives a notable description of the occasion and of Swinburne:

The fourth was a boy, or had the look of one, though in fact a year older than Adams himself. He resembled in action . . . a tropical bird, high-crested, long-beaked, quick-moving, with rapid utterance and screams of humor, quite unlike any English lark or nightingale. One could hardly call him a crimson macaw among owls, and yet no ordinary contrast availed. Milnes introduced him as Mr. Algernon Swinburne.[35]

After telling how, at a signal from Milnes, Swinburne broke into a discourse lasting through the rest of the evening and far surpassing any conversation Adams had ever heard, the American describes with awe Swinburne's mental powers and the recitation of his poems "Faustine," "Four Boards of the Coffin Lid," and the "Ballad of Burdens," noting with curiosity that Milnes was "his most appreciative" listener.

Houghton's crowning exhibition of his "tropical bird" came at the Annual Dinner of the Royal Literary Fund on May 2, 1866. As chairman of this affair, Houghton asked Swinburne to be on the program. Swinburne, who very much disliked speaking before large groups, reluctantly consented and replied to the toast for the imaginative literature of England by reading in a shrill voice an essay on the reciprocal influence of English and French literatures. He paid special tribute to his old idol Hugo, and he gave considerable attention to Baudelaire and Arnold. This was a worse breach of conduct than reading his poems of morbid love to the Thackerays and to the Archbishop of York. For the guests at the dinner were strongly Tory and strongly patriotic, toasting the queen, the royal family, the Church, the Army and Navy, and finally the Royal Literary Fund itself—all preceding the toast to the historical and imaginative literature of England. To inject any praise of French literature into such an affair was hardly in good taste, but to extol such a rabid iconoclast as Hugo and such a morbid pornographer as Baudelaire was an abomination. In its account of the affair *The Times* gave the substance of the various responses to the toasts at length, but of Swinburne it said merely, "Mr. Swinburne having also acknowledged the toast, Sir R. Murchison proposed 'Classical and Scientific Education.'" [36]

Precisely what Swinburne said has to this day never been printed in full, though Gosse gives an excerpt from it in his biography. The speech remains locked up in the archives of the Royal Literary Fund. The report of *The Times* is the fullest contemporary account we have of the dinner. There, like Alice in Wonderland after she had drunk from the little bottle, Swinburne and his ill-fated speech are shrunk to an absolute phrase of seven words.

Houghton's apparent inducement to win Swinburne's consent to speak before the Annual Dinner was the consideration that his appearance would introduce him to an important and influential segment of the literary "quality" of England and would thus prepare for a strong reception of *Poems and Ballads*, to appear in a few months. But in April, 1866, Swinburne wrote Houghton a brief note mentioning his intention of praising Hugo, Arnold, and Baudelaire. Houghton, well acquainted with the atmosphere and purpose of the dinners, must have known that any mention of Baudelaire and Hugo would be as out of place as a guffaw at a funeral. Yet he did nothing to save the situation. Our conclusion must be that this was one more instance of his damnable practice of throwing opposites together in order to witness their embarrassment. Exposing Swinburne to the cold contempt of the Annual Dinner was even more cruel than Rossetti's having him pose through a long morning kissing Fanny Cornforth. It was also much more costly. The way was prepared for a strong reception of *Poems and Ballads,* right enough; but the reception was with critical brickbats.

Following the debacle that attended the publication of *Poems and Ballads* in 1866, Swinburne soon learned that Houghton was a fair-weather friend whose affection warmed or cooled with the rise or fall of Swinburne's popularity. From that time he had little love for Houghton, whom he and Burton referred to derisively as "the Thermometer," though to Houghton's face he remained formally civil. And after July, 1872, when Rossetti cut Swinburne's acquaintance completely, his bitterness toward the artist increased as, with the passing years, he realized how he had been duped and made game of. In a letter to Watts-Dunton in 1877, he joined Rossetti and Houghton together as being both unmanly and immoral.[37] When Rossetti died in 1882, Swinburne came forth with a formal poetic tribute in "A Death on Easter Day," probably more because of his friendship with William Michael Rossetti than for any other reason. When Lord Houghton died at Vichy on August 11, 1885, Swinburne was silent.

III *The Rejected Lover*

One final cause of the downgrade course of Swinburne's life from 1860-1866 was his frustration in his love affair with Mary Gordon, which we have already mentioned. We have no means of knowing precisely when this love affair may have begun, but we are reasonably certain that it came to a climax in 1863-1864. After the death of his favorite sister Edith on September 23, 1863, Swinburne went to "Northcourt," Mary Gordon's home, and stayed there till February, 1864. During this period he worked hard on *Atalanta in Calydon* while Mary played Handel's music on the organ. For recreation they rode about the country; in between times, he helped her with a story she was writing, *The Children of the Chapel*.

At some time before, during, or after this visit, she told him she was going to marry Colonel Leith. In "The Triumph of Time" Swinburne sings the sad song of this affair, though of course without mentioning names or giving telltale clews as to who his beloved was. Until Professor Lang's article of 1959, Swinburnians always followed the lead of the Gosse biography of 1917 and believed that the girl was "Boo" Faulkner, who, as Lang shows, was only a child in 1863.[38] Mary Gordon, on the other hand, was only three years younger than Swinburne, and in 1863 he was twenty-six and she twenty-two or twenty-three. Under the circumstances, it is entirely possible that a love affair between them could have come to a climax in 1863, especially in a family where cousinly marriages were frequent.

On the strength of what Swinburne says in "The Triumph" and of what Mrs. Disney Leith (Mary Gordon) says in the preface to

her biography of Swinburne, Professor Lang argues that Swinburne did not reveal his passion to her and that she, therefore,
did not suspect it. Here I am skeptical for two reasons. First,
Dickens and the other Romantic novelists to the contrary, women
have an extrasensory apparatus that tells them when a man loves
them, and I doubt that Mary Gordon, after the long years of close
association with Swinburne, was an exception. Second, if Swinburne had admitted that he had proposed and that she had rejected him, it would have been an extremely humiliating admission for one with his physical handicap to make, and it would
have necessitated an explanation as to why she turned him down
—an explanation he and she very probably did not wish to give,
or perhaps even to think about.

My guess (and in a case like this, one has to guess) is that
Swinburne proposed and Mary Gordon turned him down because information about his debility had spread through the family; and her father, mother, and perhaps she herself, all agreed
that there was no other course. In all likelihood they blamed his
misfortune on too much inbreeding. To have had more of the
same would have been to court even worse disaster. So she sadly
said no; and, rather than explain why, she makes the flat denial in
her preface.

There is no problem as to why he proposed. Nature does not
wish abnormality, and even the most sexually abnormal person
will from time to time experience impulses toward normalcy. But
if such impulses only result in frustration, the victim retreats further into abnormality. And Swinburne's subsequent life followed
this pattern. After returning to London, he rapidly completed
Atalanta and then plunged into *Chastelard, Poems and Ballads,*
and *Lesbia Brandon.* In his personal life he turned more and
more to such sinister figures as Howell, Solomon, and Thomson.
His letters through 1864 and 1865 show that his alcoholism had
increased as had his tendency to revel in abnormal sexuality. The
letters depict also a much greater absorption in the writings of de
Sade. "The poet, thinker, and man of the world from whom the
theology of my poem [*Atalanta*] is derived was a greater than
Byron," he writes to Houghton in July, 1865. "*He* indeed, fatalist
or not, saw to the bottom of gods and men." [39] And what de Sade
saw at the "bottom," the statement implies, was lies and hypocrisy.

When success finally came with the publication of *Atalanta* in November, 1865, Swinburne grew worse instead of better. On about November 25, 1865, Scott wrote Lady Trevelyan from London that " . . . he suffers under a dislike to ladies of late—his knowledge of himself and of them increasing upon him." [40] In *Chastelard,* soon to be published, Scott advised her, she would find evidence of this "insaneness of the impulses" which had now so excited Swinburne and driven him so to alcohol that both Dante Gabriel and William Rossetti felt he could not live long if he continued.

Alcoholism soon betrayed him into public disgrace. On December 13, 1865, he infuriated Lord Houghton by being late for an evening gathering where Houghton introduced him to Tennyson.[41] After the introduction, Swinburne turned his back on Tennyson and went into another room where he talked so loudly with Palgrave and George Lewes that he disturbed Tennyson and the rest of the gathering. Later, Houghton upbraided him and accused him of being drunk, as he probably was. At the Arts Club in February, 1866, Swinburne shocked the members by his "fearful language" and came near to being expelled.[42] In her last illness at Neuchatel in May, Lady Trevelyan asked Ruskin anxiously what he thought would be the final outcome of Swinburne's mad conduct; the only reassurance he could give her was that God had given him so much genius He would not let him perish —that Swinburne's good side would eventually triumph.[43]

But in December, 1866, things had come to such a pass that Swinburne was recuperating at "Holmwood," where the Admiral had moved his family from the Isle of Wight in 1865.[44] Thereafter the story was often repeated of the old Admiral's coming to take his son home to nurse him back to health and strength until the old man's death in 1877. From 1877 to 1879 there was nobody to perform this office until Walter Theodore Watts carried Swinburne from his rooms in an almost dying condition to the solitude of Putney in July, 1879. Gradually and persistently, Watts ruled out of Swinburne's life, one by one, the various parasites and noxious influences which had clustered about him since he first came to London. It was high time somebody did him this service; otherwise his death would have surely been an event of 1879 or 1880.

IV *Swinburne the Artist*

In addition to the harm done his character and reputation through his association with Houghton and Rossetti, Swinburne's artistic development suffered even more seriously. These were the years when he should have been finding himself and his proper place in the world and in the literary firmament. These were the years when he should have been learning to know himself; when he should have developed his personal philosophy of life; when he should have gauged his literary genius, its range, its capabilities, its limitations. These were the years when he should have pondered the world about him and fitted it and himself into the great sweep of history. This was surely the period when the artist in him should have burgeoned into strength and accomplishment.

For it is a truism that no artist can rise to the full height of his powers until his feet rest on the bedrock of a settled philosophy and until he feels confident of himself and of what he is doing. He must likewise find his own answers to the great questions of life. But Swinburne's vassalage to Rossetti and Houghton did much to prevent him from developing a personal philosophy or from engaging in a trial-and-error search for his own answers. Instead, he took their philosophies and their answers and labored unsuccessfully to distort his own individuality so as to conform to them. In 1861 George Meredith put his finger squarely on Swinburne's major weakness when he wrote of him: ". . . I don't see any internal centre from which springs anything that he does. He will make a great name, but whether he is to distinguish himself solidly as an Artist, I would not willingly prognosticate." [45]

To the end of his life, Swinburne never succeeded in achieving the "internal centre," or hard core of individuality, without which he could not achieve the greatness of Browning, Tennyson, or Arnold. Perhaps his physical handicap would have rendered such development impossible for him even had he not been dominated by Rossetti and Houghton, but we can safely say that he would have attained his mental, moral, and artistic maturity more satisfactorily and completely without their noisome influence.

CHAPTER 5

Literature for Art's Sake

NOTHING furnishes a better illustration of the reflective quality of Swinburne's writings than a comparison of the works produced from 1860 to 1866 with the course of his life and thought during those years. The hallmark of the Romanticist is his absorption in himself and his reactions to life—his experiences, his longings, his loves, his triumphs, his frustrations, his hatreds—and so it was with Swinburne. As he lived, he wrote. We can clearly discern the devotion to Pre-Raphaelitism, the increasing boldness with which he followed and practiced the tenets of French aestheticism, the consequent flaunting of the algolagnia in his nature, the passionate hope and longing of the love affair, and the bitter self-pity when he experienced defeat. We can discern also the progressive deterioration of his character, interrupted for a few months during which he rose to the lyric ecstasy of love, but resumed and hastened after his rejection.

Apparently, as the man deteriorated, the writing power grew. This phenomenon has led to the popular claim not only that, somehow, his genius required the fuel of dissipation to bring it to its brightest flame, but that when the tedious Watts-Dunton took charge and eliminated the dissipation, the flame subsided and, but for an occasional fitful glow, went out. This view I cannot accept. I believe the rise of his genius took place despite the dissipations, not because of them. Swinburne, after all, was at the time of life when artistic genius usually rises rapidly if the conditions of the poet's environment stir and excite him. And Swinburne, free of the restraints of home and Oxford, was greatly exhilarated by the impact of London and the brilliant minds he encountered there. Furthermore, he was profoundly moved by grief over the loss of his favorite sister Edith in the fall of 1863, and by his passion for Mary Gordon, which rose to a climax during his three months' stay at her home after Edith's death. These two events combined to rouse him from the opium dream that his life in London had become and to lift his genius to the heights of *Atalanta in Calydon* and to the best pieces of *Poems and Ballads*. The bitter hopelessness that took hold after he left Mary Gordon plunged him once more into the depths of algolagnia and led to that epic of abnormality, *Chastelard*, and to the worst poems of *Poems and Ballads*.

I   The Queen Mother *and* Rosamond

Written during his last year at Oxford and published toward the end of 1860, the play *The Queen Mother* strongly resembles Swinburne's earlier Elizabethan imitations. Queen Catherine di Medici, mother of King Charles IX of France, sets her maid of honor Denise to persuade the king to order the St. Bartholomew Massacre. Queen Catherine knows that the king is in love with Denise, but does not suspect Denise's complete opposition to the bloody scheme. When the Queen learns that Denise has instead tried to dissuade Charles from the atrocity, she has her imprisoned on the charge of poisoning the jester Cino.

The play reaches its climax in the Massacre, which Swinburne depicts with many bloody scenes. During the carnage, King Charles himself wounds a girl with his harquebus and then is grief-stricken when he discovers that it is his beloved Denise. The play ends with the perfidious Queen Mother completely successful in her diabolical schemes, yet she confesses that she feels a twinge of pity for Denise, now dead of her wound.

The chief fault with this play is that there is no central theme. Catherine is obviously meant to be the most important character as well as the mainspring that keeps the plot in motion. But Swinburne gives her no fundamental philosophy to account for her deviltry; she is not fanatically religious nor is she motivated by a profound hatred of the Huguenots, who have done her no harm. She desires and brings about the deaths of thousands of innocent people for no more comprehensible reason than that she is a villainess and must, therefore, engage in villainy. King Charles is a portrait only partially finished. Sadistic and admitted even by his own mother to be a weak fool, he shows pathos and nobility in his grief over the death of Denise. Perhaps the best character creation is the jester Cino, who parries and thrusts with such brilliant wit that we could wish Swinburne had devoted himself to comedy rather than tragedy.

He would have done a better play had he not been still laboring under the Elizabethan complex. Marlowe's mighty line in the heavy accents of blank verse style, with a labored attempt by Swinburne to imitate Elizabethan diction, only loads the play down with much verbiage. Had he written the play in prose and in the language of his own day, he might have had a stage success. But even with all its faults, it tells an intricate and interesting story well and carries the reader with it till the end.

Rosamond, also an Oxford product, was written and rewritten several times before it reached its final form. Based upon a twelfth-century legend about Henry II and Rosamond Clifford, reputedly the King's mistress, this is a dramatic poem rather than a drama. Because Rosamond was said to be buried in a convent near Oxford, Swinburne's interest in her may have come from his readings in the library and his walks through the countryside.

As Swinburne tells the story, a Pre-Raphaelite picture comes to life. Briefly, the plot centers around the love of King Henry II for Rosamond, with the third angle of the triangle formed by Queen Eleanor, whose jealousy and hatred drive her to seek revenge by poisoning her rival. Rosamond is the melancholy Pre-Raphaelite beauty of medieval times who is so carried away by a sensuous passion for the King that she is willing to sacrifice both her honor and her life for it.

Unlike *The Queen Mother, Rosamond* has a theme of "all for love," which is adhered to with some consistency. In all other respects, however, it falls far short of the other work, and its greatest fault is its lack of clarity. Because Swinburne assumes that his readers are familiar with the story, he omits such important details as Rosamond's labyrinthine bower and the use of the silk cord by the queen and her accomplice to penetrate the maze. Also in the first scene of the poem-play, Rosamond's companion Constance soliloquizes about her intention of betraying Rosamond; but, as we never see her again, we don't know whether she does or not. In several other passages the meaning is unclear. Most of this obscurity comes from Swinburne's deliberate imitation of Browning's style and technique in *Pippa Passes*. He succeeds so well that his story is even more of a puzzle than Browning's.

The distorted side of Swinburne's nature is evident in several references to flagellation: in the King's and Rosamond's confession that their love is composed of pain and pleasure; and in the extreme sadism with which the Queen torments Rosamond, seizing her by the hair and pinching her throat, before she finally forces her to drink the poison.

We may with justice consider *The Queen Mother* the first of Swinburne's adult works, but its many inadequacies place *Rosamond* as the last of the juvenilia.

II *Pieces for Periodicals*

Swinburne's five articles about Hugo's *Les Miserables* were published in the *Spectator* from April to September, 1862. He wrote each article as each part of the book was published, admittedly a poor way of criticizing a book. All the articles are highly laudatory, with here and there a slight objection or difference of opinion with Hugo. In the second article Swinburne makes it quite clear that his critical criteria rest squarely on the dogmas of *Ars Gratia Artis:* "Any book above a certain pitch of writing must be taken first of all to be a work of pure art. For we can bring no man's work to a higher standard. All the excellence of moral purpose in the world will never serve for salt to a thing born rotten." [1]

We can discern a clash within Swinburne between his great admiration for Hugo on literary and republican grounds on the one hand and his devotion to "art for art's sake" on the other. Though he couples Hugo's name with Shakespeare's and hails him as "the greatest master we have alive" and as "the one supremely great modern dramatist," he is clearly disturbed by Hugo's underlying moral purpose in *Les Miserables,* which is to drive home to his readers his conviction that all social ills can be cured by light and reason. Undoubtedly, Swinburne had Baudelaire's doctrine of the beauty of evil in mind when he wrote: "Besides, if the thing were possible, would it be a thing to wish for? To live in a world with the evil drained off would be a heavy and hopeless kind of life." [2]

Interesting to note are Swinburne's references to fictitious French poets and critics, Félicien Cossu and Ernest Clouet, in the articles in the *Spectator* for July 26 and August 16, 1862. Apparently, he was thus early preparing Editor Hutton for the hoaxes he hoped to put over on him in the following December. In both articles he quotes these two, deprecating their lavish styles but admitting some truth in what they say.

In December he sent in pretended reviews of Félicien Cossu's *Les Amours Étiques* and Clouet's *Les Abîmes,* both books as fictitious as the authors. *Les Amours Étiques* was purportedly a book of poems with such provocative titles as "The Sigh" ("At fifteen years I am no more a virgin"), "The Broken Wing," "A Night of Sodom," "Poor Girl," "Spasm of Love," and "Rictus." [3] Clouet's *Les Abîmes* Swinburne attempted to pass off as a book of essays on such matters as the relations of Joan of Arc with Gilles de Rais, an account of the *Fragoletta* of Latouche, and a lengthy eulogy of the Marquis de Sade.[4]

Swinburne's method was to quote lengthily from these two works, expressing his disapproval as he did so—a good dodge for getting them printed for the British public and the same scheme he had used in his review of Baudelaire. This time it did not work, though it came close. The article on Clouet was in galley proof before Hutton wrote Swinburne that the subject was obscene and that his tone was not so condemnatory as it should have been.[5]

Precisely what was Swinburne's object in this matter? Either he resented the strictures against French literature made by British critics and wished to pull their legs, or the article on Baudelaire had brought protests from so many subscribers that Hutton had expressed his displeasure to Swinburne, who took this method of getting even. Hutton and Swinburne were poles apart in their views on morality. In a note appended to Swinburne's letter to the editor of the *Spectator* defending Meredith's *Modern Love,* Hutton stated that he had written the original review which called forth Swinburne's disapproval.[6] In the review, Hutton had objected to the "wretched jocularity" of tone of some of the *Modern Love* sonnets and suggested that a better title would have been "Modern Lust." If Swinburne could have gotten one or both of his articles past Hutton, it would have made the editor look foolish because in a short time someone would have discovered that no such men or books existed.

It is highly possible that Hutton did not discover the hoax, but that some friend did and warned him in time to prevent the catastrophe. After all, an editor is duty bound to read and pass on copy before it gets into galley proof. He would hardly have neglected to do so with the contributions of such an erratic personality as Swinburne. Presumably, then, he had read and approved the article; and, had he not been warned, it would have appeared in the *Spectator*.

The evidence points to Lord Houghton as the friend in the case. In a letter on August 18, 1862, Swinburne asks Houghton if he can locate the missing last leaf of his article on Cossu, and elsewhere in this letter refers to "our common friend M. F. Cossu," indicating his sharing the joke with Houghton.[7] Houghton's warning to Hutton would be an obligation because it was through Houghton that Hutton had met Swinburne and accepted his work. The warning was probably accompanied by Houghton's request that Hutton not indicate to Swinburne his awareness of the burlesque but reject it as immoral. Otherwise Swinburne would have surely suspected Houghton, and Houghton was having too much fun with this odd genius to wish to lose him just yet.

Swinburne's practical joke was of course nothing short of journalistic treachery and an inexcusable betrayal of trust. Even had he succeeded, subsequent certain exposure would have ended his career with the *Spectator*. As it turned out, his career ended and a lifelong enmity sprang up between him and his former editor.

III Atalanta in Calydon

Although critics disagree about many things concerning Swinburne, they are almost unanimous in acclaiming *Atalanta in Calydon* to be one of the greatest of his works. Constructed on the rather obscure Greek legend recounted by Ovid in the *Metamorphoses*, and with the theme of man's helplessness to avoid an inexorable fate, this poem has a scope and magnificence absent in most of Swinburne's works.

What led him to return to the classical material, when since 1857 his attention had been focused on Pre-Raphaelite medievalism and, at least since 1859, on French aestheticism? When the poem was taking shape in his mind, from August, 1863, to February, 1864, he was away from London and Rossetti, first at "East Dene" and later with Mary Gordon at "Northcourt." Had his disillusionment with Rossetti that came when Fanny Cornforth moved into Tudor House brought a corresponding disillusion-

ment with Pre-Raphaelitism, and did he turn to classicism for relief? Or was it that in this poem he wished to deal with matters
concerning his relationship to his family and felt that the classical framework would provide a more noble vehicle as well as a
more effective disguise?

Whatever the cause, Swinburne selected a pre-Trojan War
Greek myth of a minor nature and clothed it with inspired verse.
When Meleager, the son of King Oeneus of Calydon and of
Queen Althaea, is born the three Fates are present. Clotho proph-
esies that he will have courage; Lachesis, that he will have
strength; and Atropos, that his life will last only until the brand
then on the fire is burnt to ashes. Althaea promptly seizes the
brand, puts out the fire, and hides the charred remains in a safe
place.

When Meleager approaches manhood, Oeneus sacrifices to the
gods; but, through an oversight, he neglects to include Artemis,
goddess of the hunt. After the fashion of slighted goddesses, Artemis takes her revenge by sending a huge boar to lay waste the
vineyards, olive groves, and farmland of Calydon and to fill its
people with terror. Meleager, determined to end this nuisance,
invites heroes from all of Greece to join him in the hunt. Among
those who respond are Castor, Pollux, Nestor, Theseus, Pirithous,
Peleus, Jason, Admetus, and Anceus. Noteworthy among them is
Atalanta of Arcadia, cared for by a bear in childhood, and now
an able huntress and a beautiful girl. Meleager falls in love with
her almost immediately, but his two uncles, Toxeus and Plexippus,
Queen Althaea's brothers and also in the hunting party, are
highly offended at the intrusion of an Arcadian girl into the masculine sport, and make such insulting remarks about her that
Meleager can hold his temper only with difficulty.

After the usual banquets and merrymaking, the hunt begins.
Hearing their calls, the boar rushes forth from the swamp and
attacks them. Jason's spear only grazes him. Atalanta coolly
shoots an arrow and wounds him, but not seriously. Anceus is a
casualty to the boar's fierce tusk before Meleager ends the fight
and kills the boar by plunging his spear into the beast and giving
it successive deadly blows.

The shouts of the others acclaiming his triumph die into envious murmurs when Meleager awards the boar's head and skin
to Atalanta. Especially angry are the jealous uncles Toxeus and

Plexippus, who interpret the giving of the trophies to the foreign Atalanta as an insult to their masculinity and to their country. Now they rush forward to snatch the trophies, vowing that no Arcadian will have these as grounds for taunts in the future. Enraged, Meleager slays them on the spot.

Ironically, the news of the tragedy comes to Althaea as she is making an offering of thanks in the temple for the slaying of the boar. Her grief for her beloved brothers turns into such anger at Meleager that she takes out the fateful brand, throws it into the fire, and watches it burn. Shortly afterward, another messenger enters with the tragic news that Meleager, unaccountably and mysteriously stricken as he and his triumphant party were making their way home, is dying.

Here Swinburne violates the Greek dramatic unity of place by shifting to the site where Meleager lies, surrounded by King Oeneus, Atalanta, and the others of the hunting party. Intuitively, Meleager knows that his mother has caused his death, but he forgives her because she, like himself, has only been the pawn of fate. Begging his kinsmen to remember his good deeds, he expires as the chorus solemnly intones the reflection that man cannot overcome the immortal gods.

As Swinburne tells the story, it has several points of difference from the version given by Ovid in the *Metamorphoses*, probably Swinburne's main source. Ovid tells it as an incident; Swinburne blows it up almost to epic proportions, nearly ten times the length of Ovid's tale. Ovid also makes light of the love strain. In Ovid's version before the hunt begins, Meleager feels a passion for Atalanta, but he resolutely suppresses it and centers his attention on the hunt. Swinburne makes the love factor the mainspring of the story—Althaea senses impending doom in her son's attraction to Atalanta, whom she finds unwomanly, and warns him against her; but he reminds her that he is a man grown, has proven his courage with Jason and the Argonauts, and has never seen a woman as "fair and fearful" as Atalanta.

Swinburne likewise has King Oeneus adding his voice to Althaea's, pointing out that Atalanta is designed by the gods for celibacy and is not the kind of girl who makes a good wife. Althaea begs her son not to bring about her death by perversely "following strange loves," but Meleager answers that he must live out his life as Zeus has planned it and regardless of the consequences. The chorus breaks in with a song prophetic of love attended by fate and death.

Before the hunt begins, in the ugly scene that takes place between Meleager and his uncles Plexippus and Toxeus, who sneer that his speech in praise of Atalanta is "woman-tongued" and will not slay any boars, Atalanta defends herself as living the life chosen for her by the gods, a life of unwed loneliness and childlessness; she promises that, when the hunt is over, she will leave Calydon forever.

None of this material is included in the *Metamorphoses*, but in Swinburne's version it darkens the sky and prepares the way for the tragic denouement. Here again are marked differences between the two stories. Ovid shows Meleager dying quickly and apparently without suspicion that Althaea has been the agent of his calamity, but Swinburne portrays Meleager as fully cognizant that his death is the result of his mother's wish and act. As soon as the messenger reports to Althaea that he has been stricken, the scene shifts again to the members of the hunting party as they stand about the expiring hero. There follows a climactic scene much like the finale of an opera, with the leading actors present —except Althaea—and each sings his own lines to his own music, but all blend into a harmonious whole with the chorus in the background. Atalanta regrets that she came to Calydon, Meleager consoles her by blaming the tragedy on fate, King Oeneus is grief-stricken at the loss of such a son, and the chorus intones a chant of the awful power of the gods. The trio and the chorus are succeeded by a long solo speech by Meleager in which he forgives his absent mother as the instrument of fate and calls upon her and his friends not to let his memory die among men. Then, turning to Atalanta, he asks her to kiss him, to mourn for him, and to let no man say his death was "woman-wise" and "dishonourable."

It is easy to read all kinds of autobiographical significance into *Atalanta* and undoubtedly much of it is genuinely there. The somber tone and the pervasive tragic gloom came from the painful loss of a beloved sister. Edith's death was the first break in Swinburne's immediate family circle; it placed him face to face with eternity and forced him to reexamine the course of his own life and his own negative philosophy. It gave him an epic view of himself in relation to the world about him which he had not had before and which may have been the result of his mother's pleadings at this time. For the rest of her life, his mother hoped and prayed that he would return to the religious belief of his youth. What could have been more natural than for her to have used these hours of grief to point out to him the folly of the life he had been living in London and its inevitable consequences?

If we accept Professor Lang's theory that Swinburne's love for Mary Gordon mounted to a climax and resulted in frustrating emotional defeat in the months following Edith's death, Swinburne's emphasis upon the love of Meleager for Atalanta is understandable on autobiographical grounds. Of course, Swinburne's concept of the story as a tragedy growing out of Artemis' desire for revenge and of her use of the boar and Atalanta as instruments of attaining that revenge necessitates the emphasis upon the love theme and its fatal aspects. But it neither necessitates nor explains the lyrical joy of the opening chorus, "When the hounds of the spring are on winter's traces," nor the closing scene of self-pity in which Meleager makes his final request of Atalanta:

> But thou, dear, hide my body with thy veil,
> And with thy raiment cover foot and head,
> And stretch thyself upon me and touch hands
> With hands and lips with lips: be pitiful
> As thou art maiden perfect; let no man
> Defile me to despise me, saying, This man
> Died woman-wise, a woman's offering, slain
> Through female fingers in his woof of life,
> Dishonourable. . . .[8]

The initial joy is too joyful for the purposes of Greek tragedy—but not for a young poet experiencing for the first time the delirium of love. The closing self-pity and the request for the girl to stretch her body upon his in a last embrace will hardly do for a Greek hero, but it would not be out of character for such a person as Swinburne—hurt, depressed, full of self-pity after his rejection by Mary Gordon—to have given release to his feelings in such a dream.

In this connection also, Swinburne's description of Atalanta as fearless, athletic, and beautiful in an almost masculine fashion is not out of keeping with a description of Mary Gordon, who loved to ride horseback with him and who is reported to have swum at seventy in the Arctic Ocean.[9] Notable, too, is the fact that after Swinburne's death, Mrs. Mary Gordon Leith did her utmost to carry out Meleager's request to Atalanta to "let no man defile me to despise me" by fiercely denying anything in any way derogatory to his reputation[10] and by publishing her memoir in conjunction with the carefully censored family letters to give substance to the image of him she wished the world to have.

Meleager's wish for Atalanta to lay herself upon him and to embrace him is only one of several bits of evidence about Swinburne's abnormality. Others include Althaea's warning Meleager that his "following strange loves" will "kill mine heart," [11] Meleager's description of Atalanta's masculine beauty with her "hallowed hair" and swift feet,[12] Plexippus' taunts that Meleager is effeminate ("a man grown girl").[13] The chorus's sadic description of the malignant gods who have created man only that they might take pleasure in his anguish is also in this direction.

> Who gives a star and takes a sun away;
> Who shapes the soul, and makes her a barren wife
>   To the earthly body and grievous growth of clay;
> Who turns the large limbs to a little flame
>   And binds the great sea with a little sand;
> Who makes desire, and slays desire with shame;
>   Who shakes the heaven as ashes in his hand;
> Who, seeing the light and shadow for the same,
>   Bids day waste night as fire devours a brand,
> Smites without sword, and scourges without rod;
>   The supreme evil, God.
> Yea, with thine hate, O God, thou hast covered us. . . .[14]

Can we doubt that this was Swinburne's passionate protest for his bereavement, perhaps for his frustrated love, and certainly for the malformation of his physical and mental being?

All such biographical factors are of prime interest to the biographer; our main concern is with the work. *Atalanta* is truly a great achievement. The theme of fate is superbly enunciated and executed with all the pieces blending into a splendid mosaic. Swinburne has turned Ovid's incident into an authentic and magnificent tragedy with a universal significance. Meleager is any man caught in the grip of forces he cannot withstand; Althaea is the tragic mother, filled with foreboding, who sees her child, heedless of her warnings, headed toward inevitable disaster. The weak link in the chain of events is her unmotherly act of sentencing her son to death for his defensible slaying of the two carping uncles, but this detail Swinburne inherited from mythology and probably felt he dared not change. Swinburne's title is also poorly chosen: the tragedy is Althaea's, not Atalanta's, and the title is therefore misleading. Although she is the root of the tragedy, Atalanta stands by as a spectator, not at all returning Meleager's love, and responding to his final passionate speech only with the words that she is sad and must go home.

Despite these minor shortcomings, this is a truly great poem, fittingly hailed as the greatest English achievement in the classical vein and the nearest approach to classical mood and tone. In *Atalanta* Swinburne found his true voice. Most of the story is told in blank verse, with variant meters used in the songs; but the blank verse has a new surge and accent—it is no longer imitative of Elizabethan blank verse but truly Swinburnian. He himself was aware that he had found new power. In a letter to his sister Alice on December 31, 1863, Swinburne told of his delight in listening to Mary Gordon play Handel's music on the organ at "Northcourt" while he wrote *Atalanta:* "It crams and crowds me with old and new verses, half-remembered and half-made, which new ones will hardly come straight afterwards: but under their influence I have done some more of my Atalanta which will be among my great doings if it keeps up with its own last scenes throughout." [15]

Since the great Christmas music of Handel is his *Messiah,* a reasonable conjecture is that this was the music played. A musical epic whose theme is the birth of Christ and the Redemption of man, its music surges with triumph and jubilation. Many of its choral and solo tempos are in three-four, three-eight, six-eight, and twelve-eight time, musical equivalents of the dactyl and spondee, necessitated in the *Messiah* by a libretto which favors such meters. For instance, the opening chorus is, "And the glory of the Lord shall be revealed, and all flesh shall see it together"; the next, "And he shall purify the sons of Levi, that they may offer unto the Lord an offering in righteousness"; the next, "O thou that tellest good tidings to Zion, arise, say unto the cities of Judah, Behold your God!" and so on.

Swinburne's blank verse has the same epic quality, the same

organ roll, the same triumphant stride and exuberance. *Atalanta* opens with this prayer of the chief huntsman to Artemis:

> *Maiden, and mistress of the months and stars*
> *Now folded in the flowerless fields of heaven,*
> *Goddess whom all gods love with threefold heart,*
> *Being treble in thy divided deity,*
> *A light for dead men and dark hours, a foot*
> *Swift on the hills as morning, and a hand*
> *To all things fierce and fleet that roar and range*
> *Mortal, with gentler shafts than snow or sleep. . . .*[16]

He increases the anapests, shortens the line to tetrameter, and employs rhyme to give the effect of boundless joy in the greatest lyric he ever wrote, a lyric which equals the best of Shelley or Burns:

> *When the hounds of spring are on winter's traces,*
> *The mother of months in meadow or plain*
> *Fills the shadows and windy places*
> *With lisp of leaves and ripple of rain;*
> *And the brown bright nightingale amorous*
> *Is half assuaged for Itylus,*
> *For the Thracian ships and the foreign faces,*
> *The tongueless vigil, and all the pain.*[17]

As we said before, in *Atalanta* he stood on the threshold of a new world of great promise and achievement. But like Meleager, he saw his dreams vanish in the dark clouds of a bitter fate, and his hopes burnt to ashes like the fatal brand that ended his hero's life. With bitterness in his heart he descended once again and with greater desperation into the corrosive life of London.

IV   Chastelard

Although Swinburne had begun *Chastelard* at Oxford and had completed it by the spring of 1863, he did not publish it until August, 1865.[18] The reason for the delay was that several of his friends—Ruskin, Meredith, possibly even Rossetti and Lord Houghton—to whom he had shown *Chastelard* and the poems he later gathered together into *Poems and Ballads* (1866), strongly advised against publication. Ruskin's opinion that they would give him a bad reputation was shared by the others.[19] Swinburne put *Chastelard* aside and wrote *Atalanta*.

The accolade that greeted *Atalanta* filled him with confidence that the time was ripe for a frontal assault on the ramparts of British Philistinism, or Utilitarianism—such an assault as had been made in France by Gautier and Baudelaire. Swinburne saw the Philistines as more than enemies of art; they also were his personal foes. They represented the forces of political Toryism and religious orthodoxy against which he had rebelled since his days at Eton. They were the conservatives who sat smugly by while the Austrians tyrannized Italy and while Louis Napoleon declared himself emperor of France. They were the blunt-spoken pragmatists who demanded of everything, art included, "What good is it? What can it be used for?" They were the snobs—at Eton, at Oxford, in his own family—who regarded Algernon Swinburne as an absurd oddity and listened to his tirades with amused derision. They represented the spirit which led Mary Gordon to reject him in favor of a "solid" man many years older. They were, in short, just about everyone and everything in Britain that Swinburne hated.

His warfare against the Philistines was nothing new. At least since his first year at Oxford he had berated the Philistine spirit in his verse, and several letters from 1860 to 1866 show his mounting scorn. Writing to William Bell Scott in 1865, he sneers at Browning as a "Philistine idol" and promises that " '. . . that twice-battered God of Palestine,' Dagon-Caliban, shall 'wear my stripes impressed on him, and bear my beating to his grave.' " [20] The letter defending Meredith's *Modern Love* sonnets and the articles on Hugo in the *Spectator* in 1862 had denied the validity of moral purpose in literature. The article on Baudelaire's *Les Fleurs du Mal* had, as we have seen, gone a step further with a bold acceptance of the beauty of evil. Now, the almost unanimous praise of *Atalanta* and the spirit of defiance that grew great through 1865 led him to abandon caution altogether.

His next step was probably suggested to him by *Les Fleurs du Mal*. Up to now he had been an English disciple of Baudelaire. But why remain a disciple? Why not become the English Baudelaire in very fact and perhaps even go beyond the master? Why not "poke up" the British Philistines with a whole series of "evil flowers" of his own—works in poetry and prose which would drag into the open the evil side of human nature and flaunt it before the hypocritical Philistines? Swinburne's *Les Fleurs du Mal* was to be five works in four different types of literature: the drama *Chastelard*, the *Poems and Ballads*, the novels *Love's Cross-Currents* and *Lesbia Brandon*, and the critical work about William Blake.

Chastelard made a good opening gun in the campaign. Its plot centers around the love of the French courtier Chastelard for Queen Mary of Scotland, whom he has followed from France to her native land. Two subplots—the affair between Darnley and Mary Hamilton, one of Queen Mary's maids-in-waiting, and that of the love of Mary Beaton, another of the queen's maids, for Chastelard—complicate the structure. After a love scene with Chastelard, the unpredictable queen announces her intention of marrying Darnley and of making him king of Scotland.

Chastelard secretes himself under the queen's bed on the night of her wedding to Darnley, and, when she is alone and undressing, he announces himself. At first very angry with the youth, the queen soon relents, confesses her love for him, and they embrace violently. He refuses her pleas to leave before Darnley comes; Darnley's arrival begins a tempestuous scene in which he accuses the queen of infidelity with Chastelard and in which Chastelard threatens to kill Darnley. The scene ends with Darnley partially convinced of the queen's innocence and with Chastelard arrested and imprisoned. Then follows a bewildering number of contradictions and vacillations on the part of the queen, who permits Chastelard's execution and who leans forward with evident joy as his head falls.

Told in five acts and employing blank verse, *Chastelard* has no discernible theme except for the strange love of a rather abnormal youth for a most abnormal woman. In the play Swinburne gave free reign to his passion for being hurt by a beautiful female: In one scene the queen tells Chastelard of her dream of dancing with him wearing a mask and his lips "sewn up close/ With scarlet thread all dabbled wet in blood." [21] And when Mary Beaton points out the probable consequences of his hiding under the queen's bed, he replies that to shed his blood for her would be an ideal death. All in all, *Chastelard* is a worthless work, filled, as William Bell Scott said, with "insaneness of the impulses." [22] We could wish that a great poet had found better employment for his time.

The reception of *Chastelard* proved the wisdom of Ruskin's original advice not to publish it. The *Spectator* took Swinburne to task for reveling in the bestial passions of lust and confessed that it laid *Chastelard* down "with a sense of profound thankfulness that we have at last got out of the oppressive atmosphere in that forcing-house of sensual appetite into the open air." [23] James Russell Lowell, in the *North American Review,* sneered that it was only "the school exercise of a young poet learning to write." [24] In the *Fortnightly* Lord Houghton admitted that the play showed "faults of sensuousness, even of coarseness," but insisted that these were counterbalanced by "exceeding tenderness and refined emotion." [25] At a gathering of noted men in London, Tennyson said his objections to it were "as deep as Heaven and Hell." [26]

Such comments did not constitute a nest of aroused hornets, but they were the rumblings of a threatening storm that a cautious man would have heeded. Instead, Swinburne set about the publication of *Poems and Ballads.*

V Byron

Following the success of *Atalanta,* Bertram Payne of Moxon's asked Swinburne to edit a book of selections from the poems of Byron for the series called *Moxon's Miniature Poets.* Swinburne did so, wrote a critical introductory essay, and *Byron* appeared in March, 1866. As in almost all Swinburne's critical writings, his appraisal of Byron contains a strong personal note. Certainly he was thinking of himself and of his rough handling by the reviewers of *Chastelard* when he wrote that Byron had three handicaps: "youth, and genius, and an ancient name," and that ". . . every hound and every hireling lavished upon him the loathsome tribune of their abuse; all nameless creatures that nibble and prowl, upon whom the serpent's curse has fallen, to go upon his belly and eat dust all the days of his life, assailed him with their foulest venom and their keenest fangs." [27]

Nevertheless, as criticism his essay on Byron is one of Swinburne's better efforts, for he strives to be impartial. He scores Byron's faulty sense of meter, his too great love of applause, the lack of grace and wit in the early satires; he finds him supreme in the later satires like *Don Juan* and "The Vision of Judgment." As a poet, he rates him below Wordsworth and Landor; but Swinburne finds Byron's treatment of his material superior to Wordsworth's. Wordsworth, he says, is guilty of misusing nature for didactic purposes.

Almost the only notice of the *Byron* was in the *Spectator,* which took issue with Swinburne for praising Byron and for condemning the Philistines who warred against him. Byron, said the *Spectator,* had brought down upon his own head the just wrath of the so-called Philistines; then it observed somewhat ominously that Swinburne appeared to desire a like fate.[28]

VI Poems and Ballads (*1866*)

"I went to see Swinburne yesterday and heard some of the wickedest and splendidest verses ever written by a human creature," wrote John Ruskin to Lady Trevelyan on December 8, 1865. "He drank three bottles of porter while I was there. I don't know what to do with him or for him, but he mustn't publish these things. He speaks with immense gratitude of you—please tell him he mustn't." [29] Ruskin didn't know it, but Lady Trevelyan had already written Swinburne on December 6, begging him to be cautious of what poems he included in *Poems and Ballads* and reminding him how near he had come to disaster in *Chastelard*. "Don't give people a handle against you now," she warned. "And do mind what you say for the sake of all to whom your fame is dear, and who are looking forward to your career with hope and interest. . . ." [30]

Her admonition to guard his talk is in reference to a letter she wrote him on or about December 1, 1865, a letter which we do not have but the content of which we can easily deduce from his answering letters to her on December 4 and 5. Her missing letter warned him against publicly expressing his approval of the ancient Greek practice of pederasty, with either a direct statement or a strong implication that he had proclaimed his own participation in such a practice and saw nothing wrong with it. His letters to her are violent denials of such charges—too violent to be completely convincing—coupled with almost tearful gratitude for her friendship and kindness.[31]

But by December 10 he had regained his composure. His letter to her of that date is aloof. He has written nothing to be ashamed of, he tells her. No two of his friends agree on their criticism of his poems; almost everything he has written he has been advised by somebody or other to suppress. Ruskin, when he heard the poems, seemed to enjoy and accept them—could there be a fairer judge? If all Swinburne's friends disapproved of any poem, it would be omitted; otherwise, he implies, he will have to learn to live with the conviction that anything he writes will displease somebody. He will therefore follow his own judgment.[32]

Poems and Ballads should have come out in May, 1866, but the printers' errors and other delays of one sort or another deferred it till the end of July. The die was irrevocably cast, and in short order Swinburne was to learn the wisdom of Lady Trevelyan's disregarded advice.

Sixty-two poems make up the historic book. They range from verses he had composed at Oxford in 1858-1859 to some written as late as 1865 or early 1866; in length they vary from "Dolores" of fifty-five stanzas and 440 lines to the "Rondel" of twelve lines. The classification of content is somewhat complex and involved, as might be expected in a catchall volume of verse. Two of them, "A Song in Time of Order. 1852" and "A Song in Time of Revolution. 1860," express his republican hatred of Napoleon III, the Pope, and the Emperor of Austria, as well as his hope that they would be overthrown and liberty won through revolution. "In Memory of Walter Savage Landor," "To Victor Hugo," and "Dedication" ("To my friend, Edward Burne Jones") pay his respects to a dead idol, a living one, and a warm friend. Two poems, "Itylus" and "At Eleusis," are settings of classical myths. "Hendecasyllabics" is a poetic exercise on the death of summer and the onset of winter; possibly it is an allegory about the death of love and the rise of despair. Ten poems—"St. Dorothy," "The Two Dreams," "Aholibah," "Love and Sleep," "The King's Daughter," "After Death," "May Janet," "The Bloody Son," "Sea-Swallows," "The Year of Love," and "Before the Mirror"—are more or less Pre-Raphaelite in character.

These add up to eighteen poems, leaving forty-four still to be accounted for. These forty-four are the meat of the book: Among them are some of the greatest lyrics Swinburne ever wrote, lyrics which, with each passing year, emerge more and more clearly as the major basis for his fame. Among them also are the "shockers" which most clearly express his abnormal sexuality and his savage rejection of religion.

Taken together, the forty-four relate a coherent and comprehensible story. Twenty-two of them tell of a great love experience progressing through several stages. In "Hesperia" he stands in autumn on the shore of the sea, welcoming love as a bird borne on the wind from the west; this love and the beautiful sea, he hopes, will release him "from love that recalls and represses,/ That cleaves to my flesh as a flame, till the serpent has eaten his fill. . . ." [33] He confesses that he has had too much of this evil, lustful love in his life, and prays that it may not again seize his soul. Perhaps if he and the "daughter of sunset and slumber" can flee together on the swift horses of love or fear, they may escape the baneful "Lady of Pain." In "Madonna Mia," "Rondel" ("Kissing her hair I sat against her feet"), "A Match," "August," "The Sundew," and perhaps in "Love at Sea," he tells of his courtship and worship of her, apparently not without some encouragement from her. In the "Rondel," for instance, he sits against her feet kissing her hair and playfully binding her hands with the longer strands. She is his Madonna in "Madonna Mia," a poem which describes her as living in a house under apple trees and between two bowers of "Red roses full of rain," for her bondwomen are all kinds of flowers.[34]

A plaintive note is struck in "Erotion," "Satia te Sanguine," "Before Dawn," and "A Leave-Taking," though in "Erotion" (possibly for camouflage) the complaining one is a girl whose lover has rejected her and leaves her wishing for death. The deathwish motif continues and rises in acrimony in "Satia te Sanguine," in which he wishes they both were dead so that he could know whether her heart is a stone or a snake.[35] The bitterness continues in "Rococo" with his wondering what the "mad gods" will do further to vent their hatred upon him or to shower their love upon her. If she wishes, she may dream that "March may wed September"—a sneering reference to her engagement to a man twenty-one years her senior—but she will not remember nor he forget their love affair.

> The snake that hides and hisses
> In heaven we twain have known;
> The grief of cruel kisses,

> The joy whose mouth makes moan;
> The pulse's pause and measure,
> Where in one furtive vein
> Throbs through the heart of pleasure
> The purpler blood of pain.
>
> We have done with tears and treasons
> And love for treason's sake;
> Room for the swift new seasons,
> The years that burn and break,
> Dismantle and dismember
> Men's days and dreams, Juliette;*
> For love may not remember
> But time will not forget.³⁶

Acrimony gives way to a pose of defiant indifference in "Before Parting," where, gazing upon her, he marvels that he no longer loves her; her features, once so fair, now seem no longer so, and love is not even worth regretting. In "An Interlude" he recalls their love and their final parting. Now, after a lapse of time, she has forgotten his kisses and he her name. In "Félise" they meet after a year on the seashore where they had once loved and laughed. But now grown wise, he finds her no longer beautiful even though she, his "snake with bright bland eyes," now loves him and wants him to love her. But it is too late; love has vanished and cannot be recalled. Prayers and entreaties to the gods will avail nothing; for the gods are cruel and delight in scourging men. Not one dead thing have they ever restored to life, nor will they revive the dead love of Swinburne for this girl. However, he tells her cynically and ominously, it is good to look upon many loves:

> Mutable loves, and loves perverse;
> But there is nothing, nor shall be,
> So sweet, so wicked, but my verse
> Can dream of worse.³⁷

The end of this episodic love story comes in one of Swinburne's greatest and also one of his most biographically significant po-

* The full name of Swinburne's cousin was Mary Julia Charlotte Gordon. "Juliette" might disguise her identity from the world; she would know well enough whom Swinburne meant.

ems—"The Triumph of Time." In it his mood is nostalgic as he exclaims that had she but loved him, they would have "grown as gods. . . . Filled from the heart to the lips with love. . . ."[38] In the mood of the confessional, he adds that with her love he would have "grown pure as the dawn and the dew,/ You had grown strong as the sun or the sea." [39] But alas! She need have no fear of meeting him in heaven, he cries, for he will not be there:

> But you, had you chosen, had you stretched hand,
> Had you seen good such a thing were done,
> I too might have stood with the souls that stand
> In the sun's sight, clothed with the light of the sun;
> But who now on earth need care how I live?
> Have the high gods anything left to give,
> Save dust and laurels and gold and sand?
> Which gifts are goodly; but I will none.[40]

No, he adds, he will reject all such vanities and return to the evil life:

> Your lithe hands draw me, your face burns through me,
> I am swift to follow you, keen to see;
> But love lacks might to redeem or undo me,
> As I have been, I know I shall surely be;
> "What should such fellows as I do?" Nay,
> My part were worse if I chose to play;
> For the worst is this after all; if they knew me,
> Not a soul upon earth would pity me.
>
> And I play not for pity of these; but you,
> If you saw with your soul what man am I,
> You would praise me at least that my soul all through
> Clove to you, loathing the lives that lie;
> The souls and lips that are bought and sold,
> The smiles of silver and kisses of gold,
> The lapdog loves that whine as they chew,
> The little lovers that curse and cry.[41]

"As I have been, I know I shall surely be"—this despairing cry of a man frustrated in the one great love of his life was at once a confession and a prophecy. Leaving Mary Gordon and "North-court" in February, 1864, he journeyed to Italy to pay his respects to nonagenarian Walter Savage Landor and then returned to London. True to his promise in "Félise," he showed to what lengths he could go in his search for the "sweet" and "wicked" in his verse. "Anactoria," "Hermaphroditus," "Phaedra," "Dolores," "Faustine," "Fragoletta," "The Leper," "A Cameo," "Laus Veneris," "A Ballad of Life," "A Ballad of Death," "In the Orchard," and "Sapphics"—these poured from his pen; and, despite the misgivings of such friends as Lady Trevelyan, he insisted on their being included in *Poems and Ballads.* "Faustine," of course, had appeared in the *Spectator* in 1862, but in theme and mood it belonged with the others.

These were his *Flowers of Evil.* That Swinburne was consciously following Baudelaire's lead is manifested by the recurring image of the evil flower scattered through these poems dealing with abnormal love. In the "Ballad of Life" the sinful and voluptuous Lucrezia Borgia is described as having a mouth like a "sad red heavy rose." [42] In "Anactoria" Sappho wishes that her lips were pressed "to the bruised blossom of thy scourged white breast!"— the breast of her female love.[43] A few lines further she speaks of the "flower-sweet fingers, good to bruise or bite" and "blood like purple blossom at the tips/Quivering." In "Hermaphroditus" Swinburne asks: "To what strange end hath some strange god made fair/The double blossom of two fruitless flowers?" [44] In "Fragoletta" he exclaims:

> *Thou hast a serpent in thine hair,*
> *In all the curls that close and cling;*
> *And ah, thy breast-flower!*
> *Ah love, thy mouth too fair*
> *To kiss and sting!* [45]

"Dolores" is described as having a "cruel/Red mouth like a venomous flower." [46] He addresses her as "O mystical rose of the mire" and asks fearfully:

> *Could you hurt me, sweet lips, though I hurt you?*
> *Men touch them, and change in a trice*
> *The lilies and languors of virtue*
> *For the raptures and roses of vice;*
> *Those lie where thy foot on the floor is,*
> *These crown and caress thee and chain,*

> *O splendid and sterile Dolores,*
> *Our Lady of Pain.*[47]

In "Sapphics" Sappho in a vision sees Aphrodite, who asks her to turn to her and normal love. Instead Sappho turns toward the Lesbian women loving each other, and sings her beautiful and terrible song.

> *Then rejoiced she, laughing with love, and scattered*
> *Roses, awful roses of holy blossom;*
> *Then the Loves thronged sadly with hidden faces*
> *Round Aphrodite. . . .*[48]

The outcome is such that even the gods grow pale, and all flee from Sappho with revulsion, leaving the land barren and full of fruitless women. These are only a few of many such examples that could be cited, but they illustrate the Baudelairean character of the songs of abnormal love.

The "Laus Veneris," perhaps the most noted of them all, is too closely allegorical of Swinburne's unfortunate love experience to be coincidental. His version of the medieval Tannhauser story begins with the knight feasting on the evil pleasures of the Venusberg, the wicked court of Venus in the Horsel Mountain of Thuringia. Cloyed with such evil fruits, he goes to Rome to seek pardon for his sins from the Pope. But the Pontiff is so horrified at the enormity of his offenses that he tells Tannhauser there is no more possibility of his being forgiven by God than of the Pope's staff bearing a blossom. In bitter despair the knight returns to the sexual sins of Venus. The miracle of the blossoming of the papal staff takes place; but, before the news can reach Tannhauser, he has once again vanished into the sinister caverns of the Horsel Mountain. He concludes gloomily by saying that Venus will cling to him even after death, for he is cast out of God's sight until Judgment Day.

If we imagine London as the Horselberg, the life of abnormal sexual excesses there as Venus, Swinburne as Tannhauser, Mary Gordon's rejection as the Pope's, and Swinburne's return to the evil life as Tannhauser's reentry into the Venusberg, the parallel is almost perfect—almost, except for the belated forgiveness that comes with the blooming of the Pope's staff. And this is supplied, in Swinburne's case, by "Félise," with its story of Mary Gordon's too-late love of him and his scornful rejection of her because his love is dead and cannot be revived.

The only obstacle to our complete acceptance of "Laus Veneris" as the allegorical account of Swinburne's own love affair is his statement that he had completed the poem before he received Baudelaire's pamphlet on Wagner's *Tannhauser* toward the end of 1863,[49] which is tantamount to saying that the poem was finished before Mary Gordon's rejection of him in early 1864. His statement, however, may be discounted on three counts. First, he made it in his gusty *Notes on Poems and Reviews,* where he was more interested in defending *Poems and Ballads* than in telling the truth, and where his chief defense was that the poems were merely works of art and had no autobiographical significance. Second, Swinburne did not scruple to lie in order to conceal the identity of his love, as is evidenced by his telling Edmund Gosse that his love affair was with "Boo" Faulkner, rather than with Mary Gordon. Finally, his first direct allusion to the Tannhauser story occurs in his letter to Lord Houghton on March 31, 1864,[50] suggesting that he was only then planning and perhaps beginning to write "Laus Veneris." Since this was almost two months after his bitter departure from Mary Gordon, this letter—with the other evidence presented above—warrants not only setting aside Swinburne's statement that "Laus Veneris" was written before the end of 1863 but holding to our conviction that "Laus Veneris" is the poetic rendering of his unhappy love experience.

The final group of poems reject the Christian ideal of a kind and merciful God, who is loving of His children, aware of their needs, and responsive to their prayers. Among those are the "Hymn to Proserpine," "Ilicet," "A Litany," "A Lamentation," "Anima Anceps," "A Ballad of Burdens," "The Garden of Proserpine," "A Christmas Carol," "Félise," and "The Masque of Queen Bersabe." Because they also contain the idea of the rejection of God, such poems as "Anactoria" and "Laus Veneris" could have been included in this classification; but, since their chief emphasis is upon abnormal love, they are more appropriately placed in that category. "Félise," because it rejects both love and God, belongs with both the love poems and with the antitheistic group.

His mood in these poems varies from the despairing nihilism of

"Ilicet," "A Lamentation," "Anima Anceps," and "The Garden of Proserpine" to the mockery of "A Litany," "Hymn to Proserpine," "Félise," and "A Christmas Carol"—a mockery so savage that a Christian could consider it as nothing short of blasphemy. In the "Carol" and the "Litany" the mockery is subtle, the "Carol" casting the suspicion of illegitimacy on the birth of Jesus, and the "Litany" being a tongue-in-cheek satire on the cruel treatment of man by God. But in "Félise," his scorn is unmistakable when he exclaims that prayer is useless because there are no gods to hear it:

> Behold, there is no grief like this;
> The barren blossom of thy prayer,
> Thou shalt find out how sweet it is.
> O fools and blind, what seek ye there,
> High up in the air?
>
> Ye must have gods, the friends of men,
> Merciful gods, compassionate,
> And these shall answer you again.
> Will ye beat always at the gate,
> Ye fools of fate?
>
> Ye fools and blind; for this is sure,
> That all ye shall not live, but die.
> Lo, what thing have you found endure?
> Or what thing have you found on high,
> Past the blind sky? [51]

VII   William Blake

Swinburne's interest in William Blake sprang from his association with Dante Gabriel Rossetti, who assisted his friend Alexander Gilchrist in editing the Blake manuscripts.[52] When Gilchrist took suddenly ill and died in 1861, Dante Gabriel offered to assist Gilchrist's widow in completing her husband's *Life of Blake,* and he enlisted the aid of Swinburne and William Michael Rossetti.[53] In October, 1862, Swinburne, learning that such a purist as Macmillan had been agreed upon as the publisher, refused to have anything more to do with the Gilchrist work and set about his own appreciative *William Blake,* which was ready for publication in 1866 but was delayed until January, 1868, because of the storm raised by *Poems and Ballads.*[54] In words of deep gratitude, Swinburne dedicates his book to William Michael Rossetti, dating the dedication as "November 1866." Since early in that month William had published his pamphlet *Swinburne's Poems and Ballads*, defending Swinburne in his hour of dire need in the storm that followed the publication of *Poems and Ballads,* the reason for the heartfelt tone of the dedication is obvious. Prefacing the book is a quotation from Baudelaire to the effect that all great poets are inevitably critics because it is necessary for them to examine their art, to discover its profoundest rules, and to derive from such a study the principles and guidelines which lead to perfection in the production of poetry. Baudelaire closes with the epigram that, though it is remarkable for a critic to become a poet, it is impossible for a poet not to have within him the genius of a critic.

Quite probably, this statement was the inspiration for Swinburne's own critical writings, especially this one on Blake. For what we find is not so much reasoned, objective criticism but lyrical bursts of praise. Written under the aegis of Baudelaire and Dante Gabriel Rossetti and at a time (1862-1865) when Swinburne was steeped in *l'art pour l'art*, the book is one of the most emphatic statements of the principles of "art for art's sake" in English literature. Of course he discovers in Blake a precursor of the aesthetic ideal: "To him, as to others of his kind, all faith, all virtue, all moral duty or religious necessity, was not so much abrogated or superseded as summed up, included and involved, by the one matter of art." [55] Once launched on his favorite subject, Swinburne digresses from Blake in a fervent sermon:

The contingent result of having good art about you and living in a time of noble writing or painting may no doubt be this: that the spirit and mind of men then living will receive on some points a certain exaltation and insight caught from the influence of such forms and colours of verse or painting; will become for one thing incapable of tolerating bad work, and capable therefore of reasonably relishing the best; which of course implies and draws with it many other advantages of a sort you may call moral or spiritual. But if the artist does his work with an eye to such results or for the sake of bringing about such improvements, he will too probably fail even of them. Art for art's sake first of all, and afterwards we may suppose all the rest shall be added to her (or if not she need hardly be overmuch concerned); but from the man who falls to artistic work with a moral purpose shall be taken away even that which he has—whatever capacity for doing well in either way he may have at starting. A living critic [Baudelaire] of incomparably delicate insight and subtly good sense, himself "impeccable" as an artist, calls this "the heresy of instruction" . . . one might call it, for the sake of a shorter and more summary name, the great moral heresy. Nothing can be imagined more futile; nothing so ruinous. Once let art humble herself, plead excuses, try at any compromise with the Puritan principle of doing good, and she is worse than dead.[56]

Obviously, this statement is nothing more than a paraphrase of Baudelaire's paraphrase of Poe. Ironically, by the time Swinburne's *Blake* was published, Swinburne had done an about-face and was figuratively marching in the opposite direction by writing verses once more for the cause of Italian freedom.

VIII Love's Cross-Currents *and* Lesbia Brandon

Although Swinburne never walked down Bond Street with a red rose in hand to show his contempt for the Philistines, as Oscar Wilde did at a later date,[57] he wrote one complete novel and an extensive fragment of another for the same purpose. Even today the complete novel, first published in 1877 as *A Year's Letters* but later changed to *Love's Cross-Currents,* would be considered short, for it runs to about fifty-five thousand words. By the Victorians, so short a piece of fiction as this would not be considered a novel at all, but a tale. *Lesbia Brandon,* the fragmentary novel Swinburne wrote in spurts from 1864 into the early 1870's, runs to about seventy-five thousand words, substantially longer than *Love's Cross-Currents,* but still far short of what was considered the proper length of the novel.

I believe the significance of this matter of length is that Swinburne did not take his novels seriously, but tossed them off in the spirit of burlesque and with the idea of "poking up" the Philistines—the same spirit in which he did the fake reviews of Ernest Clouet and Félicien Cossu. Actually it would have been strange if he had taken the novel seriously as a literary form; for, though Scott had elevated at least the historical novel in Victorian esteem, the novel in general still partook of the same stigma it had acquired in medieval days by reason of its descent from the French *nouvelle*. Of course, the advent of such great Victorian novelists as Dickens, Thackeray, George Eliot, and Thomas Hardy did much to overcome traditional prejudice against the novel and to raise it to such a level of respectability that even a serious poet could turn out an occasional novel without serious loss of prestige. But this turning point was not reached till the 1880's and 1890's when Swinburne had lost interest in the novel.

In the early part of his career Swinburne used the novel exclusively for such burlesques as *La Fille du Policeman, La Soeur de la Reine,* and the fiction of flagellation which he did with Lord Houghton. In something of this same spirit he wrote *Love's Cross-Currents* and *Lesbia Brandon,* or at least he began them in this spirit, though as they developed, he, like Fielding in *Joseph Andrews,* abandoned the burlesque and took them more seriously. Likewise, as he grew older, he, like most other Victorians, acquired more respect for the novel generally. His changing attitude toward *Love's Cross-Currents* illustrates the point. On February 17, 1866, he scolded Payne of Moxon's for revealing his authorship of *Cross-Currents.*[58] In 1877 he published it under the pseudonym "Mrs. H. Manners" in installments in *The Tatler.*[59] In 1905 he published it under his own name with a dedication to Watts-Dunton, styling it as "this buried bantling of your friend's literary youth," [60] and suppressing the satirical preface with which it had appeared in *The Tatler.*

This preface of 1877 reveals clearly Swinburne's anti-Philistine design. In the form of a publisher's letter of rejection, it upbraids Mrs. Manners for impugning the sanctity of English marriages, an error of judgment into which she has fallen by living too long in immoral France. In England, the irate "publisher" continues with heavy irony, things are happily different:

Marriage in England is indissoluble, is sacred, is fortunate in every instance. Only a few—happily a very few—perverse and fanciful persons still venture to imagine or suggest that a British household can be other than the chosen home of constancy and felicity. We know, if you do not, that all husbands, all wives, and all children, born or bred or married within the boundary of the three seas, are in consequence good and happy.[61]

That she does not recognize such an obvious truth is proof of her lack of "any sufficient sense of moral beauty. Without this you can achieve no success, you can perform no work worthy of an earnest thinker in a Christian age." [62]

The satire on Philistine morality is carried out beautifully in the novel, a completely cynical tale of philandering and intrigue in an English aristocratic family like the Swinburnes and Ashburnhams. The leading character and prime mover of most of the action is old Lady Midhurst, born in 1800 and now in her early sixties; completely pagan and completely frank, she has a profound contempt for Victorian hypocrisy and prudery. Superbly intelligent and realistic, she manipulates the lives and fortunes of the other members of the family with consummate finesse and resourcefulness. Her antagonist is her niece Mrs. Clara Radworth, who, born in 1836, is a complete Victorian Philistine and a whited sepulcher. Beneath a mask of piety and altruism, she attempts to conceal a character both ruthless and devious.

The bone of contention between these two strategists is the welfare of Reginald Harewood (Swinburne himself) and his half-sister Amicia Cheyne, wife of Lord Cheyne. Both grandchildren of Lady Midhurst, they are the objects of her affection and concern. During the course of the story, Reginald becomes involved in a love affair with Mrs. Clara Radworth, who, outwardly pretending to resist his affections, subtly draws him on. Sensing the potential damage to Reginald from such an affair and divining the true role of Clara, Lady Midhurst strives unsuccessfully to free him from the clutches of her niece. When she finally comes into possession of a packet of letters revealing a former love affair of Clara's with a French philanderer named M. de Saverny, she threatens to send them to Reginald unless Clara crushes his love for her with a cold, blunt statement that she wishes to have no more to do with him. This Clara does.

The other strand of the plot concerns the story of Amicia, married lovelessly and childlessly to the Philistine humanitarian, Lord Cheyne. Frank Cheyne, Clara Radworth's brother, visits Lord Cheyne and Amicia at "Lidcombe," the family seat. Frank and his cousin Amicia, reviving their old love affair, commit adultery; almost immediately afterward Lord Cheyne drowns accidentally. Lord Cheyne's death without issue leaves Frank heir to the family title. In due course the widowed Amicia leaves "Lidcombe," and Frank takes possession as the new Lord Cheyne. Triumphant because her brother has replaced Amicia's husband in the title, Clara Radworth writes Lady Midhurst a letter overflowing with malicious sympathy.

Then comes the catastrophe. Lady Midhurst lets it be known that Amicia is pregnant. In due course she gives birth to a son whom all the family know to be Frank's; but, for the sake of family honor, they dare not say so. This illegitimate child is therefore recognized as Lord Cheyne's son and as the proper heir to the title. Frank, through his adulterous act, has cheated himself of his birthright. There is nothing else for him to do but to resign the title and move from "Lidcombe." He does so, and Amicia and her infant heir take possession. Clara's triumph over Lady Midhurst and her granddaughter is therefore short lived. Lady Midhurst quickly seizes the opportunity to even the score with Clara by writing her a letter in which the venom and *double entendre* are masterfully injected. So skillfully does Swinburne weave together the threads of his narrative that it is the same letter in which she tells Clara of the acquisition of her love letters to the Frenchman, by means of which she forces her to dismiss Reginald. Not satisfied even with this, the ruthless old campaigner visits Clara and gloats over her chagrin, conveying her impressions to Amicia with relish in her letter which is the concluding one of the novel:

They get on well enough again by this time, I believe. To use her own style, she is *dead beat*, and quite safe; viciously resigned. I think we may look for peace. She would have me racked if she could, no doubt, but received me smiling from the tips of her teeth outwards, and with a soft dry pressure of the fingers. Not a hint of anything kept back. Evidently, too, she holds her brother well in leash. Frank pleased me: he was courteous, quiet, without any sort of affectation, dissembled or displayed.[63]

Lady Midhurst is of course the great creation of the story and one of the great characters of fiction; she is worthy of standing beside Becky Sharp, Lady Castlewood, and Elizabeth Bennet. The English novel has nobody quite like her, though Miss Crawley in *Vanity Fair* is cut from the same stout oak. Her character does not change during the story, but it is of such complexity and depth that it would be an achievement for any novel. For a work as short as *Love's Cross-Currents* and for one so restricted by the limitations of the epistolary style, her portrait is truly a work of great art. She is not only Swinburne's spokesman for "art for art's sake" in her frequent gibes at the affectations of moral and religious hypocrites, but is Swinburne himself in her paganism and religious nihilism. And yet she is still more: fierce old virago though she is, she epitomizes the indomitable British courage which conquered Napoleon's battalions and shot Hitler's Luftwaffe out of the skies. In words reminiscent of Churchill's "blood, sweat, and tears," she writes to Amicia, who is distraught and conscience stricken after the death of Lord Cheyne:

I could wish to write you a softer-toned letter of comfort than this; but one thing I must say: do not let your grief hurry you even for one minute beyond the reach of advice. As for comfort, my dearest child, what can I well say? I have always hated condolence myself: where it is anything, it is bad—helpless and senseless at best. A grievous thing has happened; we can say no more when all comment has been run through. To us for some time—I say to us, callous as you are now thinking me—the loss and misfortune will seem even greater than they are. You have the worst of it. Nevertheless, it is not the end of all things. The world will dispense with us some day; but it shall not while we can hold out. Things must go on when we have dropped off; but, while we can, let us keep up with life.⁶⁴

Lesbia Brandon shows the effects of being written during Swinburne's dark period after the unfortunate love affair with Mary Gordon. In the mood and spirit of the worst poems of *Poems and Ballads*—to which it has many similarities—and of the most frenetic scenes of *Chastelard*, this novel is a prose *Flowers of Evil*. Swinburne's purpose in it also was to roil the Philistine, but in a much more coarse and brutal fashion than in *Love's Cross-Currents*. In January, 1867, while he was still smarting from the debacle of *Poems and Ballads*, he wrote Richard Burton: "I have in hand a scheme of mixed verse and prose—a sort of étude à la Balzac *plus* the poetry—which I flatter myself will be more offensive and objectionable to Britannia than anything I have yet done. You see I have now a character to keep up, and by the grace of Cotytto I will endeavour not to come short of it—at least in my writings." ⁶⁵

Although longer than *Love's Cross-Currents*, *Lesbia* is so fragmentary that the reader is hard put to make a coherent story of it.

Swinburne introduces himself into this novel also—as Bertie Seyton, who at the beginning is a youngster prepping for Eton
chiefly by being flogged by his psychotic tutor Denham. Besides
flagellation, the novel offers other evidences of abnormal sexuality
in the suggestion of incestuous love between Bertie and his sister
Lady Wariston and between Lady Wariston and Tutor Denham,
who turns out to be her and Bertie's half-brother. Lesbianism enters the story with the name "Lesbia Brandon." Lesbia is a soul-
less beauty lacking femininity, who is like Atalanta, Mary Stuart,
or perhaps Mary Gordon as Swinburne describes her in some of
the love poems of *Poems and Ballads*. Homosexuality is present
in Bertie Seyton, who Swinburne said was himself, who enjoys
being flogged, dresses up in girls' clothes, and is described as
having such "a strong feminine element" that ". . . he ought to
have been a pretty . . . girl." [66]

Significantly, as Bertie matures, he falls in love with the strange
creature, Lesbia Brandon, who, like Mary Gordon, is interested in
writing, though she writes verse rather than fiction. But, when he
presses his suit, he suffers the same fate described in "The Triumph of Time," "Satia te Sanguine," "A Leave-Taking," and several others of *Poems and Ballads*. Sadly she tells him she would
love and marry him if she could love and marry anyone, but she
is unmarriageable. Henceforth they must be as brother and sister,
not lovers.

Lesbia commits suicide through the prolonged use of eau de
cologne and opium. Bertie sits by her bed as she describes a
dream which bears a strong resemblance to "The Garden of
Proserpine." In her dream Lesbia sees Proserpine standing in a
field of poppies and surrounded by ghostly figures. Sympatheti-
cally, Bertie holds Lesbia's hand until she finishes the story of her
dream. Addressing him as her brother, she wonders what love
with him would have been like, and she asks him to kiss her. As
he does so, he loses control and kisses her so violently that she
pushes him away and begs him to let her die in peace. Subdued,
he sits till dawn; then she bids him goodby, turns her face to
the pillow, and dies.

One thing is certain: In *Lesbia Brandon*, as in *Chastelard* and
in *Poems and Ballads*, Swinburne was doing more than baiting
the Philistines; he was expressing and exhibiting the abnormal
side of his nature, the side to which, as he had threatened in

Poems and Ballads, he would give free rein as a retaliatory measure for his defeat in love. Such a reaction by the person abnormally inclined is entirely in accord with the findings of Dr. Bieber and his associates in the study we have referred to before. Homosexual proclivities being at variance with nature, the victim is impelled by nature, at various times in his life, to reach for normalcy. If the attempt meets with frustration, he falls back all the more deeply and hopelessly into abnormality. Such a reach did Swinburne make toward Mary Gordon; *Chastelard, Poems and Ballads,* and *Lesbia Brandon* are the fruits of his defeat.

In *Love's Cross-Currents* and in *Lesbia Brandon* Swinburne proved that he could have been a very good or perhaps a very great novelist. He would have had to work at the craft, for he obviously had much to learn. The cumbersome "Prologue" to *Love's Cross-Currents* is so obscure that the reader needs a character chart to straighten out the interrelationships of the characters, while the ill-advised use of the epistolary framework precludes necessary comments and interpretations by the author. Still, both novels have an immediacy, a skillful handling of scene and dialogue, depth of understanding of life, and an ability to portray character that indicate talents of a high order. The only obstacle lying athwart the path of success was that his interests lay in other directions.

CHAPTER 6

Turnabout

THE literary detonation following immediately upon the publication of *Poems and Ballads* was the greatest in England
since the days of Byron and Shelley. The proliferation of magazines and newspapers brought about during the 1830's and 1840's
by the improvements in printing added many journalistic voices
to the harsh chorus that burst forth in condemnation of Swinburne's book.

As it happened, the first blasts at *Poems and Ballads* came to
him in a fashion both dramatic and unfortunate. Out strolling
with Bertram Payne, head of Moxon's publishing house since the
death of Moxon, Swinburne saw the issue of the *Saturday Review*
for August 4, 1866, bought it, and read it while standing in the
street. So furious did he become and so violent was his language
that Payne steered him into a tea room, begging him to do his
cursing in French.

Within a day or so, Payne discontinued the publication and
circulation of *Poems and Ballads*. Sir William Hardman, a publisher himself, quotes a rumor that Dallas of *The Times* notified
Payne that he had written an article denouncing both Swinburne
and Payne, that the article was already in type, and that it would
be printed in the "Thunderer" shortly unless Payne killed the
book.[1] Payne, fearful that such a denunciation from such an august source might lead to prosecution and humiliation, stopped
publication immediately.

The story might be true, or it might be an invention of Payne's,
who was not overly scrupulous and who might have invented it
as an excuse for his breach of contract with Swinburne. For a
breach of contract it was. The proper time for Payne to have de-
murred and to have demanded the excision of questionable ma-

terial from the book was before he accepted it for publication. As the publisher of *Chastelard*, he not only knew the bent that Swinburne's work was taking, but was also aware of the unfavorable reaction it had stirred up. If he had doubts of his own judgment, he could have done what Chapman did earlier when the manuscript of *Poems and Ballads* was submitted to him—consulted Browning or someone equally qualified to judge it.[2]

One other possibility deserves consideration in this matter. Moxon's was also the publisher for Tennyson, the Laureate. Tennyson's condemnation of *Chastelard* had been so emphatic that we can imagine his choler when he read *Poems and Ballads*. He could have written Payne a note or else have stormed into his office demanding the discontinuance of the offending book on the threat of transferring his patronage to another publisher if it were not done. And, of course, Tennyson would have insisted that Payne not mention his name as the reason for the withdrawal.

Two facts suggest Tennyson's connection with Payne's decision: A short two years later, Tennyson did break with Moxon's and made an agreement with the eminently proper Alexander Strahan to publish him. Even before Payne announced his decision to withdraw Swinburne's book, the bruised and smarting Swinburne received an invitation from Edward Bulwer-Lytton to visit him at "Knebworth." [3] And the invitation came to Swinburne on August 4, the day when the blow fell. Curiously enough, no close tie existed between Swinburne and Lytton; in fact, before the invitation only two other letters between the two are recorded: one from Lytton to Swinburne, congratulating him on *Atalanta*, and a grateful response from Swinburne on January 16, 1866.[4]

On the other hand, no love existed between Tennyson and Lytton. Promoted by a mutual antipathy, the two men satirized each other publicly and privately, making no attempt to conceal their disdain. Since *Poems and Ballads* was published about July 16, 1866, it is possible that Lytton had heard through the literary grapevine of Tennyson's angry fulminations and of the inimical reviews shortly to appear, suspected that Tennyson was one of the instigators of the reviews, and decided to aid the victim. At any rate, the arrival of Lytton's invitation simultaneously with the appearance of the reviews in the *Saturday* and the *Athenaeum* is a singular coincidence unless he was in London on that day, read the review, dashed off a note, and sent it immediately.

The review in the *Saturday* was by John Morley, later Lord Morley, who in 1866 was twenty-eight, one year younger than Swinburne. A disciple of John Stuart Mill and an agnostic, as well as something of a snob, Morley had turned to journalism when his father, angry because his son would not become an Anglican clergyman, cut off his allowance.[5] Quite possibly, Morley's savage review was at least partially the result of the views of John Douglas Cook, editor, Tory, and High Church Anglican, and of the Reverend William Scott, assistant editor and High Churchman also.[6] Certainly it was in accordance with the Tory character of the *Saturday*, which, though it had been founded as recently as 1855 by Beresford Hope, represented the ultraconservative viewpoint.[7]

Morley's review runs over two thousand words and is tinged with heavy irony. Implicit in it is the suggestion that Swinburne was a homosexual who could not help dwelling on the unnatural aspects of sex.[8] Admitting the futility of lecturing any artist on his material, Morley says Swinburne has to go in the direction his "character" forces him: "If the character of his genius drives him pretty exclusively in the direction of libidinous song, we may be very sorry, but it is of no use to advise him and preach to him. What comes of discoursing to a fiery tropical flower of the pleasant fragrance of the rose or the fruitfulness of the fig-tree?"[9]

With an ironic shrug of the shoulders he continues: "It is of no use, therefore, to scold Mr. Swinburne for grovelling down among the shameless abominations which inspire him with such frensied delight. They excite his imagination to its most vigorous efforts, they seem to him the themes the most proper for poetic treatment, and they suggest ideas which, in his opinion, it is highly to be wished that English men and women should brood upon and make their own."[10]

Then, mockingly, he affects to praise his victim, but actually he scorns him for revealing his abnormality: "And at all events he deserves credit for the audacious courage with which he has revealed to the world a mind all aflame with the feverish carnality of a schoolboy over the dirtiest passages in Lemprière. It is not every poet who would ask us to go hear him tuning his lyre in a stye. It is not everybody who would care to let the world know that he found the most delicious food for poetic reflection in the practices of the great island of the Aegean, in the habits of Messalina, of Faustina, of Pasiphäe." [11]

Morley drops the mask of sympathy to say that, if Swinburne had rebelled only against the prudes, no one would find fault with him. "But there is an enormous difference between an attempt to revivify among us the grand old pagan conceptions of Joy, and an attempt to glorify all the bestial delights that the subtleness of Greek depravity was able to contrive." [12]

Unquestionably, Morley's is one of the great reviews in English literary history. Its length, artistry, and subtlety indicate that he had worked on it for a week or two at least. One can readily see why it drove Swinburne into a frenzy: he could not have failed to understand the veiled allusions and to realize that perceptive readers would likewise understand them.

Like Morley's, Buchanan's review in the *Athenaeum* contains the implication of homosexuality, but, couched in classical terms, its full meaning would have been understood only by the well educated. [13] Buchanan must have been aware of Swinburne's abhorrence of being called boyish, for he remarks patronizingly that these poems are too puerile to do any serious moral damage to anybody because they are so insincere and affected. Then, like a rapier thrust to the vitals, comes the damaging allusion: "They are too juvenile and unreal for that. The strong pulse of true passion beats in no one of them. They are unclean, with little power; and uncleanness repulses. Here, in fact, we have Gito, seated in the tub of Diogenes, conscious of the filth and whining at the stars." [14]

Now in the ancient Roman novel, the *Satyricon*, written by Petronius Arbiter, one of the prominent officials at the court of Nero, Gito is the boy with whom the narrator Encolpius has sexual relations. This was not uncommon among the ancients. Only now is the *Satyricon* easy to get here, but in England in 1862 a German edition of it is advertised in the respectable *Publishers' Circular*. It is safe to assume that Swinburne was familiar with it, what with his wide classical reading at Oxford and his browsing in Lord Houghton's library at Fryston. It is equally safe to assume that most of the Victorian intelligentsia who were male and university educated would get the full drift of the Gito reference. Buchanan's article ends significantly with advice that Swinburne should "cast his evil advisers aside" and turn to wisdom. After this book, Buchanan predicts, even the "parasites" will avoid him; and the best course for him is to "seek out Nature" and to "try to think seriously on life and art." [15]

The reference to the "evil advisers" and to Swinburne as Gito shows that Buchanan was well informed about the facts of Swinburne's private life. As Lady Trevelyan had warned Swinburne, his wild and loose talk in gatherings of literary men had given him a bad reputation that did him no good now. A person in private life may get away with all manner of immorality without news of it getting about, but writers, actors, and outstanding politicians are regarded as public property, and word of their shenanigans soon becomes universal knowledge.

Almost the next day after Payne announced his withdrawal of *Poems and Ballads*, Dante Gabriel Rossetti and Frederick Sandys called on him in an effort to persuade him to reconsider. He was, they reported, so terrified at the prospect of prosecution that their efforts were in vain. Swinburne availed himself of Bulwer-Lytton's invitation to withdraw from the London scene to think. Enraged at Payne's breach of contract, he was determined to republish *Poems and Ballads* without any changes. To do anything else, he wrote Lord Lytton, would be deserting his colors.[16] But how? Who would now take it, a foundling of evil repute?

Through the offices of either Howell, Lord Houghton, or perhaps Joseph Knight, he entered into an agreement with an unsavory publisher, John Camden Hotten, who had built his business largely on the publishing and selling of pornographic books to a carefully selected clientele. Hotten paid Swinburne £200 for the first thousand copies of *Poems and Ballads*, bought up the remainder of Moxon's unsold stock, and reissued the book around November 1, 1866.[17] Before doing so, he persuaded Swinburne to write and publish a pamphlet, *Notes on Poems and Reviews*, in which he defended himself against the charges hurled against him on the ground that his poems in *Poems and Ballads* were objective studies and commentaries, not the expression of his personal opinion or belief. "Hermaphroditus," for instance, was simply a study of the statue in the Louvre, nothing more, and "Laus

Veneris" was a new treatment of an old medieval legend. That the reviewers had discerned anything objectionable in such poems was evidence only of their own evil minds.

Simultaneously with Swinburne's defense, Hotten published also William Rossetti's lengthy essay, *Swinburne's Poems and Ballads,* which he had first hoped to publish in the *North American Review.* It was rejected there, largely through the influence of James Russell Lowell, who had published in that journal strongly disapproving reviews of *Chastelard* and *Poems and Ballads.* Few men have ever surpassed William Rossetti in the art of seeming to say something without saying it, of casting aspersions and vicious suggestions while apparently striving to be fair and impartial. Likewise, when he wanted to be, he was a master at obfuscating an issue or a question. His essay begins with the bland statement that his purpose is to examine Swinburne's poems in order to assign him his proper place among poets—a high place, Rossetti feels certain. The so-called "indecencies" of *Poems and Ballads* he finds to be only literary frankness on classical subjects, a line of argument close to Swinburne's and as specious; for William Rossetti knew as well as did Swinburne that the objectionable poems were largely autobiographical. Answering the charges of indecency, he delivers this piece of gobbledygook: "Of positive grossness or foulness of expression there is none—nor yet of light-hearted, jocular, jovial libertinism. The offences to decency are in the subjects selected—sometimes too faithfully classic, sometimes more or less modern or semiabstract —and in the strength of phrase which the writer insists upon using on these as on other topics." [18]

These circuitous defenses might have fooled the gullible—but not anybody who had read *Poems and Ballads* with understanding. Under the caption "Calling a Thing by its Right Name," *Punch* lived up to its name with this heavy blow: "Having read Mr. Swinburne's defence of his prurient poetics, *Punch* hereby gives him his royal licence to change his name to what is evidently its true form—SWINEBORN." [19]

Many more notices appeared in the press, but their tenor followed generally the lead of the *Saturday* and the *Athenaeum.* Here and there a friend raised his voice to try to stem the tide of condemnation, as Lord Houghton did in an unsigned letter to the *Examiner;*[20] but such attempts only brought forth even more harsh rejoinders such as Carleton Greene's in the Cambridge University magazine, *The Light Blue*.[21]

The effect on Swinburne of his catastrophe and of all the obloquy heaped upon his name can be imagined. He had become increasingly bolder in the expression of the abnormal side of his nature because of the encouragement of such people as Dante Rossetti and Lord Houghton—despite their denials, they did encourage him, as is borne out by the accounts of Henry Adams, William Hardman, and Lady Ritchie. Association with such men as Charles Howell and Simeon Solomon had increased his boldness because it dispelled any lingering doubts he might have had as to the necessity of restraining and concealing his abnormality. And of course, as we have already noted, the doctrine of "art for art's sake," supported by the example of Baudelaire's *Les Fleurs du Mal,* had given him a complete rationale for letting himself go.

He had done just this. He had told the secret longings of his soul; he had laid bare the tragedy of his personal defeat in love; and what had happened? The friends who had encouraged him, on whom he had counted, had withdrawn from him: Lord Houghton betook himself to Vichy; Meredith was away; the Rossettis were at best lukewarm. Swinburne was left to fight alone in a joyless battle in which even a partial victory brought him small satisfaction. True, he had succeeded in republishing *Poems and Ballads,* but, to do so, he had been forced into association with the disreputable Hotten and to resort to a mass of lies—and what he and his friends well knew were lies—in his *Notes.* The whole affair caused him untold anguish.

Nor can we forget that this man did not stand alone in his suffering. A member of two of England's old aristocratic families and bearing a proud old name, he could not be unmindful that many others were affected by what happened to him, especially anything as disgraceful as this. We can imagine the letters that flitted around among the Swinburnes and Ashburnhams at the spectacle that Cousin Hadji was making of himself in London. We can imagine, too, the angry letters that came to him from his harassed parents, uncles, aunts, and cousins because of the humiliation he had brought upon them.

Rumors persist that, shortly after the republication of *Poems and Ballads,* a conference atended by Jowett and others took place to discuss what had best be done with Swinburne. I think it much more likely that it was a conference at "Holmwood" during the Christmas season, when the Swinburnes always gathered anyway, and that it was attended principally by the Admiral, Lady Jane, Swinburne, and possibly an uncle or aunt. I believe that what we know of Swinburne provides us with ample material for a conjecture on how they handled the problem of stopping him in his mad career and of turning him into safer channels.

To have threatened, scolded, and commanded would have only made him more rebellious. But Lady Jane knew her son, his love for her, and his pride in his name and family. All she would have had to do would be to point to the ignominious sneer in *Punch* to illustrate the damage he was doing them all. Then she could remind him that any marriage prospects his sisters Alice, Charlotte, and Isabel—all at home and in their middle or late twenties—might have would be worsened or perhaps ruined forever by his antics. I think it highly possible that the Admiral added a flat warning that unless Swinburne changed his literary course, he would discontinue the £200 he had been giving him every year. Without this money and with now no certain prospect of literary earnings, Swinburne could hardly have continued in London.

The Admiral and Lady Jane could have pointed out to him that his name was a proud one because of the luster his ancestors had given it, luster he could add to or detract from by his own life and work. Such considerations were enough, I believe, to make him pause to reconsider the course of his career and perhaps to give at least a halfway promise that he would stir up no more hornets' nests right away.

But it is not enough to take something away; something must be added to take its place. If such idols as Dante Rossetti and Lord Houghton were overturned and if the old religion of "art for art's sake" were abandoned, what was to fill the void? The ideal of republicanism had never been completely forgotten, but it had been thrust into the background by de Sadism and aestheticism. Italy was still struggling for her freedom against the forces of reaction, and France still lived under the autocratic rule of Napoleon III. As early as October 9, 1866, Swinburne wrote William Rossetti that, after many months of inactivity, he was able to write verse again and was working on his "A Song of Italy" in which he intended to express his reverence for Mazzini. He

added: "After all, in spite of jokes and perversities . . . it is nice
to have something to love and to believe in as I do in Italy." [22]

Nor had his enthusiasm for Victor Hugo and for the cause of
French republicanism ever waned. His review of *Les Miserables*
in the *Spectator* had led to exchanges of complimentary letters
with Hugo and to the dedication of *Chastelard* to him. He fed
his mind with Hugo's thought and philosophy, eagerly devouring
each new work as soon as it came out. From Hugo's *Les Contemplations* and from the first part of his *La Légende des Siècles*
(1859), Swinburne made his first acquaintanceship with Auguste
Comte's Positivism, a philosophy which came prominently to the
fore in England in the middle and late 1860's, largely through
the writings of John Stuart Mill and of Harriet Martineau, who
translated Comte's *Cours de Philosophie Positive* in 1852. Briefly
put, Comte's Positivism denies the existence of a personal God,
metaphysics, and revealed religion, and sets up humanity as God.
Through his intelligence, man will in time solve all his problems
and achieve a utopian civilization on earth. The shackles which
have held man back and retarded his progress through the ages
are the kings and priests who enslaved man's mind and robbed
him of his freedom. All human history is but the story of how
man, slowly and painfully, has broken one bond after another as
he has plodded upward. Though much has been done, much remains to do; and the duty of the Positivist is to expound his doc-
trines to the ignorant masses so as to dispel darkness and hasten
the advent of the Positivist heaven.

Essentially this was the philosophy Hugo expounded in *Les
Contemplations* and in the first part of *La Légende des Siècles.*
Swinburne seems not to have fully grasped the philosophy when
he published his article "Victor Hugo's Philosophy" in the *Spectator* in 1862, for he complains therein that Hugo will not accept
human meanness or adopt any philosophy which accepts it. Actually, Hugo's Positivism accepts human perversity as the evil
against which man struggles but which he finally conquers. However, Swinburne soon comprehended and accepted the tenets of
Positivism, for in "A Song of Italy," read to Mazzini at the end
of March, 1867, Positivistic thought is unmistakable in the de-
piction of kings' wailing and priests' growing pale before the
advent of freedom.

Postivism was easy for Swinburne to turn to because it included much that he already believed, as well as adding some new and optimistic touches which, as he wrote William Rossetti, were a welcome relief to the cheerless nihilism and despair under which he had lived for the past ten years. It commanded him to despise any form of political tyranny; it scorned Christianity and other forms of religion as mere absurd superstitions; it gave him a God in which he could believe, the limitless possibilities of man's intellect; it promised him a final great day of triumph in the future. After the bleak despair of pagan nihilism he had expressed in such poems as "Laus Veneris," "Anactoria," and "The Garden of Proserpine," he must have felt like one who had come out of a dank mausoleum into the warm sunshine.

Events shaped themselves so opportunely toward the new end that we cannot throw off the suspicion that the Admiral and Lady Jane did enlist the aid of Jowett and perhaps, through him, Aurelio Saffi—a former associate of Mazzini and Swinburne's old Italian teacher at Oxford—to supply the one ingredient necessary to complete his conversion: an idol. The idol came forward in the person of Mazzini, who on March 10, 1867, wrote Swinburne a belated thanks for the gift copy of *Atalanta* he had received two years earlier but had never acknowledged, praised his recently published "Ode to Candia," and included a fervent piece of rhetoric urging him to abandon "songs of egotistical love and idolatry of physical beauty" and to turn out "a series of 'Lyrics for the Crusade.'" [23]

Things progressed rapidly. On March 30, 1867, Swinburne, all atremble, went with his friend Thomas Purnell to the house of Karl Blind, a German exile, and waited in a crowded room until the great man entered. As Swinburne wrote his mother next day, Mazzini walked up to him, said, "I know you," and Swinburne went down on his knees, seized the idol's hand, and kissed it. Then he read him "A Song of Italy," which Mazzini praised highly, inviting the poet to call on him whenever he wished. The conversion was an accomplished fact.

I A Song of Italy

Mazzini commented to Swinburne, after he had finished reading the poem, that there was too much about him in it. We are bound to admit that he is right. A poem of some 840 lines, almost a third of it is in praise of "the Chief," as Swinburne calls him;

and the chorus of praise rises until it becomes an ecstatic litany, calling upon the Italian cities to praise Mazzini as the savior. We can imagine that Mazzini went through an ordeal in that crowded room as he listened to the singsong voice of Swinburne apotheosizing him. In alternating lines of iambic pentameter and trimeter with each two lines rhyming, the poem is much longer than it needs to be and has too much use of alliteration.

The effect upon the reader is one of tedium. We suspect that the poet was trying to huff and puff himself into an emotion which he did not really feel and to cover up with words a barrenness of feeling and a poverty of thought. It is almost as if Swinburne has turned the clock back to his early days at Oxford and the "Ode to Mazzini."

II Songs before Sunrise

The *Songs before Sunrise* are based on the hope of both Mazzini and Swinburne that Italian freedom would grow out of the repudiation of any form of monarchy and of the temporal power of the Pope, and that the form of government finally set up would be republican. By 1867, when Swinburne met Mazzini, King Victor Emmanuel had secured control of almost all of Italy with the exception of Rome. Mazzini's hope was that Rome would be the nucleus of the republic, and that the republican spirit would then spread over all Italy and unseat the monarchy. This, of course, did not take place until the mid-twentieth century, following World War II, when Umberto was denied the throne and Italy became what she is today—a republic.

Mazzini's and Swinburne's dream of an Italian republic was doomed because they were a century ahead of their time. The Italians wished to be rid of foreign intervention and exploitation, but they had for so many centuries been used to monarchical government that the extent of their desires was only to supplant the foreign monarch with one of their own, not to do away with the system altogether. Likewise, although they had long been cynical toward the temporal aspects of the papacy and the governmental structure of the Catholic Church, they had no doctrinal quarrel with it, and no thought of repudiating it, as Swinburne and many other Englishmen hoped.

Had Swinburne fully realized the innate conservatism of the Italian people, his enthusiam would have been considerably lessened. As it was, he plunged into the cause with all the verve of a zealot. In the "Dedication" to Mazzini he sings: "I bring you the sword of a song,/ The sword of my spirit's desire. . . ." [24] Plainly he saw himself as a warrior in verse, perhaps something of a vicarious realization of an ideal as old as his youthful desire to become a soldier in the Crimean War. He must have been aware that he had done a complete about-face from the principles of "art for art's sake," for as a verse-soldier he was writing poetry to serve a cause.

He carries this militant spirit into the "Prelude," a poetic repudiation of *Poems and Ballads.* The "fierce flute," the cymbal, and the "clamorous kettledrum" that had once acclaimed "dim goddesses of fiery fame" are now silent; pleasure and passion have passed and there yet remains

> *A little time that we may fill*
> *Or with such good works or such ill*
> *As loose the bonds or make them strong*
> *Wherein all manhood suffers wrong.*[25]

His first "good work" was "Super Flumina Babylonis," a poem in honor of Mazzini's manifesto of 1831 to "Young Italy," calling upon youth to rise in the cause of liberty. The weeping "by the waters of Babylon" gives way to triumphant joy as the light of freedom dawns. The mood changes to one of grief for the capture of Garibaldi by Rattazzi in September, 1867. England is blamed for her indifference and the Pope execrated for perfidy, while Garibaldi, who had escaped before the poem could be published, is reminded that his name will be famous in free Italy.

Two poems sound the strong note of Postivism: "Hertha," which Swinburne considered the best verse he had ever written, and the "Hymn of Man," a solemn note of warning on the occasion of the Ecumenical Council of 1870. Hertha, the old German goddess of the earth, represents growth or nature. In language borrowed from the Book of Job, she says:

> *Before ever land was,*
> *Before ever the sea,*
> *Or soft hair of the grass,*
> *Or fair limbs of the tree,*
> *Or the flesh-coloured fruit of my branches, I was, and thy soul was in me.*[26]

God speaks, but He is a Positivist God who comdemns as false all other concepts of Him; He does not need prayer or supplication; His only command is to live. But He sadly upbraids men for worshiping false gods and for neglecting Him. He closes with a proclamation that He and man are identical:

> *One birth of my bosom;*
> *One beam of mine eye;*
> *One topmost blossom*
> *That scales the sky;*
> *Man, equal and one with me, man that is made of me, man that is I.*[27]

"The Hymn of Man" jeers at the heads of the Catholic Church for having created God for their own sakes, and warns them that their God is about to die the same death that all false gods have suffered. In "Before a Crucifix" and in "Tenebrae" Swinburne also uses the terminology of Catholicism to condemn Christianity and to extol Positivism—much in the same fashion that he had done in the most blasphemous poems of *Poems and Ballads.* The chief difference is that there is no reference to sex in the *Songs before Sunrise.*

France comes in for a share of attention in "Mater Dolorosa," "Mater Triumphalis," and "A Marching Song"—in all of which the poet grieves that the mother of freedom is content to sit in bondage. But in the "Ode on the Proclamation of the French Republic," dated September 4, 1870, his joy is delirious with the realization of his dreams.

Included among the *Songs* is "To Walt Whitman in America," asking the American poet to send overseas a song of freedom to Englishmen too steeped in greed and error to compose such songs for themselves; and "Cor Cordium," a sonnet in tribute to Shelley, "for whom / The lyrist liberty made life a lyre." [28] The sentiment is sincere and beautiful; the verse suffers from too much alliteration.

The final item in the volume of the Bonchurch Edition containing the *Songs* is a series of seventeen sonnets, most of which were published in the *Examiner* during 1873. As savage as anything Swinburne ever wrote, they underscore the fact that Positivism had not extinguished his love of invective. They consign to hell such of his pet hates as Ferdinand II, Pius IX, and Napoleon III, over whom he gives thanks that he has lived long enough to say, ". . . The dog is dead." [29] The seventeenth sonnet is titled "Apologia." The bitterness of his verse, he says, is not his fault, but theirs whose wrongdoings have raised such bitterness within him.

Right here might be the place to point out the complete lack of compassion in Swinburne's poems. A great poet, ever mindful of the essential tragedy of human life, has a measure of pity even for an Iago, a Pardoner, a Creon, or a Satan. And most men are so keenly conscious of their own faults that they can view the sins of others with some tolerance and even forgiveness, if not before, at least after their deaths. Swinburne was curiously incapable of such tolerance and forgiveness, even long years after the dissolution of those he had hated.

CHAPTER 7

The Literary Gamecock

IN ALL cases Swinburne's literary quarrels came about because of his inability to believe that criticism of him and his works could ever be impartial and objective. In his view, critics were either friends or enemies: If friends, they praised; if enemies, they attacked. There was no middle ground.

In part, of course, this conviction came from the peculiarities of his own history and temperament. But in great part it came from an awareness of the puffery and antipuffery underlying much of Victorian reviewing. Biographies of such literary figures as Tennyson, Thackeray, Dante Rossetti, Robert Buchanan, and Thomas Hardy, to mention only a few, offer ample testimony that the Victorian reviewer was often motivated by considerations other than literary merit and demerit. This is not to say that honest criticism did not exist, for it did, and to a remarkable extent; but too often it existed side by side with mercenary criticism.

Toward the end of his *Notes on Poems and Reviews* Swinburne says: "I have never been able to see what should attract men to the profession of criticism but the noble pleasure of praising." [1] He was probably not fully aware that he did not practice his own rule; for, even when engaged in praising, as in the *Blake*, he could not forbear making invidious comparisons to the disadvantage of others. It is safe to assume that he followed the same procedure in his verbal remarks, often more dangerous than the written in that they are not usually pondered over beforehand and cannot be erased afterward.

Throughout his career his criticisms of others and theirs of him involved him in a series of imbroglios that he could well have done without. Besides the quarrel with Hutton of the *Spectator* that we have already mentioned, he had brushes with George

Eliot, Dr. Furnivall of the New Shakespeare Society, Emerson, Browning, Lowell, and his old friend Whistler; and, aligned with William and Dante Rossetti, Swinburne engaged in a prolonged and climactic quarrel with Robert Buchanan in the Fleshly Controversy, one of the most far-reaching and significant literary wars in English literary history. The others we can pass by with mere mention; the Fleshly Controversy, because of its profound significance to Swinburne's life and writings, deserves full treatment.

I *The Fleshly Controversy*

We do not know the initial cause of the ill feeling between Robert Buchanan and Swinburne, but it could not have been Payne's taking from Buchanan and giving to Swinburne the edition of Keats for which Buchanan had already written an introduction. Swinburne's letter of January 4, 1866, to William Rossetti on the matter shows that even then he had no love for the Scotsman. Recounting Payne's proposal that he take over the edition for £10, the amount already paid Buchanan, Swinburne says with evident malice: "This sum the publisher is willing to lose, and to cancel the poor devil's work, if I will do Keats instead on those terms: and won't I? and wouldn't I gratis? This forthcoming Scotch edition of Keats, who hated the Scotch as much as I do . . . has long been a thorn in my side: and apart from the delight of trampling on a Scotch Poetaster, I shall greatly enjoy bringing out a perfect edition of Keats with all his good verses and none of his bad." [2]

A curious mixture of feelings is evinced here. He has a grain of sympathy for Buchanan because of the loss of the edition, but he scorns him as a Scot and rejoices that Keats is out of his hands. The personal note implies that the two had met, perhaps at a gathering at Moxon's; had found each other distasteful; but were not active enemies. In his letter to Payne on January 5, 1867, Swinburne insists that Payne make it clear to Buchanan that the transfer of the Keats was in no way Swinburne's doing but had been done by Payne without any request or suggestion from Swinburne. Evidently he was apprehensive of reprisals. He had good reason to be, for Buchanan was also redheaded, short tempered, and as quick to take offence as Swinburne.

Born in 1841 of humble Scottish-Welsh parentage, Buchanan

had fought his way up the London literary ladder by dogged determination since his arrival in the metropolis in May, 1860. He eked out an uncertain living by writing poems, articles, and reviews for the *Athenaeum, Good Words,* and *Temple Bar.* In 1863, Moxon's published his first volume of poetry, *Undertones;* and, in 1865, Alexander Strahan brought out his second, *Idylls and Legends of Inverburn,* a book of poems dealing mostly with humble Scottish fisher folk. In the spring of 1866 he readied his third and most successful volume of poems, *London Poems,* for the press, and then moved himself and his family to the Scottish resort town of Oban for rest and recuperation.

We wonder why Payne had the poor judgment to take the Keats from Buchanan, who had apparently filled his part of the bargain, and give it to Swinburne. Payne obviously had little respect for a contract of any kind, as his later violation of contract in the case of Swinburne's *Poems and Ballads* shows. From what we know of the affair of the edition of Keats, Payne's conduct was highly unethical.

The next item in the quarrel is Buchanan's review of *Poems and Ballads* in the *Athenaeum* for August 4, 1866. The patronizing tone and the implication of Swinburne's homosexuality, along with the advice that he put behind him his evil advisers, show that Buchanan had accurate knowledge of Swinburne's private life and was using it to pay off an old score. Although Buchanan admitted in later years that he had been unfair in comparing Swinburne to Gito,[3] in 1866 he had no such compunction; for in September he published pseudonymously in the *Spectator* his mocking poem "The Session of the Poets," apparently based upon a gathering Moxon's had had for its authors on or about December 13, 1865. At that affair Swinburne's conduct had been so obnoxious that Lord Houghton, also present, later took him to task for being drunk and for insulting Tennyson.[4] In the poem, written cleverly in Swinburne's favorite anapests, Swinburne leaps to his feet at the dinner hour, and shocks the company with his wild talk:

> *Up jumped, with his neck stretching out like a gander,*
> *Master Swinburne, and squeal'd, glaring out thro' his hair,*
> "*All Virtue is bosh! Hallelujah for Landor!*
> *I disbelieve wholly in everything!—There!*" [5]

So great is the consternation of the others that Tennyson, red with embarrassment, leaps to his feet, pounds the table with his fist, and commands: "To the door with the boy! Call a cab! He is tipsy!" and Swinburne is carried out.

Presumably, Buchanan, also one of Moxon's authors, was at the dinner, witnessed the same scene Lord Houghton complained of, and reported the details with basic accuracy; but he also used enough exaggeration and caricature to make the chief actor more ridiculous. Some time later Swinburne learned that Buchanan had authored the *Athenaeum* review, probably through his friend Joseph Knight, also on the staff of the *Athenaeum*. But to crack the inner councils of the *Spectator* to learn who had written the "Sessions" was much more difficult because of Editor Hutton's continuing animosity to his former reviewer. Dante Rossetti's letters show that he knew by the end of December, 1871, that the "Sessions" was Buchanan's, so it is safe to assume that Swinburne and William also knew it at that time. How much earlier they may have been aware of it, we do not know.

Swinburne hardly knew Buchanan as his assailant in the poem, but he may have been informed of him as the *Athenaeum* reviewer when he wrote his *Notes*. The tone of the *Notes* is, for him, quite mild. In the midst of some satirical remarks about the current popularity of idyls in poetry, he permitted himself a sneer at the Scotsman's expense: "If the Muse of the minute will not feast with 'gig-men' and their wives, she must mourn with costermongers and their trulls." [6] In a later essay Buchanan referred to "a gifted young contemporary, who . . . upbraids me for writing 'Idyls of the gallows and the gutter,' and singing songs of 'costermongers and their trulls.'" [7] Swinburne admitted in *Under the Microscope* that the reference was to him.[8]

Much more truculent was William Rossetti's attitude in his *Swinburne's Poems and Ballads*, published, according to the *Publishers' Circular*, between November 15-30, 1866, a week or two later than Swinburne's *Notes,* and at the same time as the republication of *Poems and Ballads*. William opens his essay with a vicious slash at the reviewer-poet: "The advent of a new great poet is sure to cause a commotion of one kind or another; and it would be hard were this otherwise in times like ours, when the advent of even so poor and pretentious a poetaster as a Robert Buchanan stirs storms in teapots." [9]

In the *Memoir* of his brother, William said he wrote this insult because he already knew of Buchanan's attack on Swinburne; but, if so, it was the review, not the poem, because we have no letters from him informing Swinburne, still at "Holmwood" on November 12, about who wrote the "Session." [10] However, when Buchanan published his joshing riposte to Swinburne's *Notes* in the *Athenaeum* of November 3, 1866,[11] Swinburne's letter to William Rossetti on November 12 revealed that he knew Buchanan had written it, but that he had taken no great offense.[12] His mood was still somewhat mild when he published his article "Mr. Arnold's New Poems" in the *Fortnightly Review* in October, 1867, because he contented himself with a slightly disparaging reference to David Gray, a dead Scottish poet and former close friend of Buchanan and a protégé of Lord Houghton. In connection with his disapproval of Wordsworth's doctrine that, if a poet were inspired he did not need to master the technique of his craft, Swinburne remarked: "Such talk as this of Wordsworth's is the poison of poor souls like David Gray." [13] When Swinburne published this essay in *Essays and Studies* (1875), he added a lengthy footnote attacking Gray with the utmost scorn and ill feeling.[14] Buchanan later cited this footnote as his reason for attacking Dante Rossetti and Swinburne in his "The Fleshly School of Poetry" of 1871, but he is in error. The note was not printed until after the attack.

Indeed the feeling between Buchanan and Swinburne in 1867-1869 amounted to little more than aversion. On January 26, 1869, Swinburne wrote Buchanan a courteous note regretting his inability to attend the Scotsman's public reading of his poems in London on the previous day because the invitation and complimentary ticket Buchanan had sent had arrived too late.[15] The tone of the letter is formal, but civil and also somewhat complimentary since Swinburne expresses his regret at missing the pleasure of hearing Buchanan read.

In 1868 Buchanan published his *David Gray and Other Essays* with the reference to the "gifted young contemporary" we have already noted, and in January, 1870, he evened his score with William Rossetti with a harsh review in the *Athenaeum* of his edition of Shelley. Buchanan stated that Rossetti had mistaken his vocation because he lacked sufficient material, critical insight, and the good taste necessary to an editor of such a project.[16]

Then came the climax in which Dante Gabriel Rossetti, who had buried his manuscript volume of poems in the coffin of Elizabeth Siddal Rossetti in 1862 as an act of penance, allowed himself to be persuaded by the scapegrace Charles Augustus Howell to exhume and publish them. The exhumation took place in the fall of 1869 without Rossetti's informing his family or Swinburne until it was done. Swinburne assisted Rossetti in readying the volume for the press, and it came out in the latter part of April, 1870, containing not only the exhumed poems but many others Rossetti had written in the intervening years. Several of the additions, as Oswald Doughty shows in his biography of Rossetti, dealt with his singular affair with Mrs. Jane Morris wife of William Morris, especially many of the "House of Life" sonnets.

Rossetti was not unmindful of what had happened to Swinburne's *Poems and Ballads,* nor was he unaware that several of the poems in his own volume were so frank in their expression of sexual passion and desire as to violate Victorian standards of morality. Moreover, he had a psychotic fear of adverse criticism. Therefore he "worked the oracle," as the phrase was, by arranging ahead of time that his book would be reviewed in most of the leading reviews by his friends. When the *Poems* came out, it met with a chorus of praise with, here and there, a few off-key notes from the magazines he had been unable to reach.

Two factors need to be taken into account here. Since 1868, Rossetti had been showing signs of the same mental trouble that had plagued his father's last years—increasing melancholy, a persecution complex coupled with suspicion of others, and a growing tendency to hallucinations. His Bohemian life, with its irregular hours, use of alcohol, and sexual excesses, only hastened the schizophrenia that unmistakably afflicted him; and when, in 1869 or 1870, he began to use chloral in increasing doses to overcome insomnia, he was indeed in a bad way.

The other factor is that at least since Swinburne's debacle in 1866, word had been getting about literary London that

Rossetti's influence was chiefly responsible. Such exhibitions as the one told by Sir William Hardman of Swinburne extolling de Sade at Rossetti's smoker helped create the impression.[17] Gossip of Rossetti's philanderings at his studio with a veritable procession of women from Jane Morris to Fanny Cornforth intensified it. In the view of many he was an evil Italian Svengali who had hypnotized and vitiated a promising young English poet of noble lineage. Something should be done about it.

While the furor about *Poems and Ballads* was at its height, Tennyson remarked publicly that Rossetti and possibly Lord Houghton were responsible for encouraging Swinburne in this direction. On October 6, 1866, Rossetti wrote Tennyson a letter denying the charge and claiming that he had struggled against this tendency in Swinburne.[18] As we know, his statement is untrue. By precept and example he had contributed materially to the worsening of Swinburne's character. Nor is it likely that Tennyson was befooled by Rossetti's disavowal. Ruskin knew most of the details of Rossetti's unsavory life and character, and he was in a position to gauge accurately his effect upon Swinburne. Ruskin met frequently and talked with Tennyson, Browning, Jowett, and other leading men of the time. It is reasonable to assume that he told them what he knew of the case and that they believed him rather than Rossetti.

Rossetti's reputation suffered also from the fact that though Swinburne's verse took a new direction in March, 1867, the downhill trend of his personal life continued and even accelerated in the years from 1866 to 1871. His alcholism and abnormal sexual excesses increased to such a degree that the trips of his father to London to take him home for rest and medical treatment became more and more frequent. Mazzini felt certain that Swinburne's death was imminent and grew impatient for the Italian songs to be published before it was too late.

His condition was dramatized and advertised by several events of a public character. His excesses increased his susceptibility to a form of epilepsy which manifested itself in fainting fits. In, July 1867, he toppled over at one of Lord Houghton's breakfasts; in October, he cut his face in what he described as a fall from a hansom which could have been caused by another fit. In 1867 and 1868 he had a well publicized affair with the notorious Adah Isaacs Menken, an American equestrienne who rode a horse bareback around the stage in a dramatization of Byron's *Mazeppa*. Like Chaucer's Wife of Bath, she had been married five times and had had many affairs, the best known being with the elder Alexander Dumas and with Swinburne. Swinburne apparently enjoyed the affair and even permitted pictures of Adah Menken and himself together to be posted in shop windows around London, possibly with the notion of offsetting rumors of his homosexuality. The casual fashion in which he tells George Powell of her death in Paris in August, 1868, shows how little she meant to him.

The fainting fits continued. On July 10, 1868, he blacked out in the British Museum, cut his forehead in a fall, and was carried out unconscious. The event appeared in the papers with such pessimistic accounts of his health that Jowett wrote him a friendly letter advising him to mend his ways and offering him money if he needed it. Swinburne, struck with this kindness from an unexpected source, immediately wrote his gratitude to his old master. From this time his friendship with Jowett grew until the scholar's death in 1893, and it led to vacation trips together. The probability is that Jowett's reentry into his life was no accident, but was only one result of a widespread anxiety about Swinburne and a determination to save him from the baneful influences into which he had fallen in London. I suspect Ruskin as the intermediary, maybe at the request of the Admiral or Lady Jane.

The sensational publicity continued when Swinburne was nearly drowned at Étretat on the French coast in October, 1868, while vacationing with the sinister George Powell. Caught by an undertow, he was carried out to sea and would surely have been drowned but for the timely arrival of a French fishing boat.

Swinburne's publication in 1868 of the *Blake* and "Ave Atque Vale," the poetic obituary to Baudelaire, both of which had been written when he had been under the influence of "art for art's sake," only confirmed the public impression that he was still devoted to the aesthetic ideals of *Poems and Ballads*. Moreover, his "Notes on Some Pictures of 1868" paid glowing tributes to several of Rossetti's pictures: "the sweet luxurious mouth" of "Lilith," expressive of "the warm repose of passion sure of its delight"; the "glorious bosom" of the "Venus Verticordia"; and

[134]

the praise of both Whistler and Rossetti for their devotion to beauty.[19] All these stray bits of evidence could be linked together in a cause and effect relationship indicting Rossetti for a major share in the corruption of Swinburne.

The final touch to Rossetti's image as Swinburne's seducer was provided by Swinburne's ecstatic review of Rossetti's *Poems* in the *Fortnightly Review* in May, 1870. John Morley, author of the *Saturday Review* blast at *Poems and Ballads* in 1866, had become editor of the *Fortnightly* in 1867. Swinburne had been introduced to him by Joseph Knight, a friend of both, and the two had become such good friends that Swinburne became a regular contributor to the *Fortnightly*. Morley never summoned sufficient courage to tell Swinburne that he had written the review, nor did Swinburne ever tell Morley that he knew he had written it; however, they got along so well that, when Swinburne asked Morley's permission to review Rossetti's book, it was given at once.

"It is my devout intention to cut it fat. . . ." Swinburne wrote Dante Rossetti on February 24, 1870, using a butcher's terminology for cutting meat with plenty of suet to describe his review of Rossetti's book.[20] He cut it too fat and did Rossetti more harm than good. The review runs to about fifteen thousand words, a staggering total even for those days. It is a continuous panegyric in lyrical prose with showers of adjectives and extravagant claims. Rossetti is compared not unfavorably with Shakespeare as a sonneteer. No English poet of the day stands higher and few as high—Tennyson, Browning, and Arnold, possibly. Two-thirds of the way through the review he proudly acknowledges Rossetti to be ". . . the great artist by the light of whose genius and kindly guidance he [Morris] put forth the first fruits of his work, as I did afterwards."[21]

To shield Rossetti from the charges of paganism fastened upon *Poems and Ballads*, Swinburne claims that much of Rossetti's verse is Christian and even Catholic, but of a sincere kind, much superior to that of Browning or Newman. Unfortunately, when he gets down to particulars, he forgets this claim; reveling in the sensuous qualities of Rossetti's verse, he describes it as "fleshly." Of the "House of Life" sonnets: "No nakedness could be more harmonious, more consummate in its fleshly sculpture, than the imperial array and ornament of this august poetry."[22] Of the "Songs" following the "House of Life": "In all the glorious poem built up of all these poems there is no great quality more notable than the sweet and sovereign unity of perfect spirit and sense, of fleshly form and intellectual fire." [23] The poem "Lilith," written for Rossetti's picture, makes the reader "feel face to face the very vision of the old tale, and no symbol or shadow, but a bodily shape and a fleshly charm, dominant in ear and eye." [24]

Still in Scotland during 1870-1871 and in ill health, Buchanan did not get around to attacking Rossetti and Swinburne till eighteen months after the publication of *Poems*. In the *Contemporary Review* for October, 1871, appeared his "The Fleshly School of Poetry: Mr. D. G. Rossetti," filling some seventeen pages of that journal. He is unquestionably following the lead of James Russell Lowell in his review of Rossetti's *Poems* in the *North American Review* for October, 1870, six months after the publication of the book and *one year* before the appearance of Buchanan's article. Buchanan, in fact, quotes Lowell in the final paragraph of his article, prefacing the quotation with the remark that he agrees "substantially" with the opinion of the reviewer.

Lowell's article is truly great criticism. The public, he says, is skeptical of the claims of Swinburne, Morris, and William Rossetti that Dante Rossetti is a great poet, because he has hitherto refused to publish and because they were known to be close to him and not reliable judges in such matters. Rossetti he thinks a second rate poet because ". . . he is all feelings and desires . . ." but ". . . of thought and imagination he has next to nothing." [25] He is self-centered, is fond of clothing himself in a false medieval garb, and refuses to deal with contemporary life. Lowell finds a note of morbid eroticism in many of the poems, especially in "Jenny," and he accuses Rossetti of using "a set of properties" to delude the unsuspecting reader. [26] The love which Rossetti deals with is "a sensuous and sexual love, refined to some extent by that sort of worship of one's mistress as saint and divinity which the early Italians made a fashion, certainly, whether or not it was ever a faith by which they lived." [27] Lowell's final opinion is that Rossetti's eventual poetic rating will fall much below what his friends have claimed and that the world will consider him to be ". . . a man of the temperament of genius lacking power to give effect, in words at least, to a nature and gifts rare rather than strong or valuable, nevertheless it will be admitted that he is an

elaborately skilful love-poet of narrow range who affords an occasional touch that makes the reader hesitate and consider
whether he has not now and again struggled out and really
emerged as a poet worthy of the name." [28]

Buchanan obviously had Swinburne's and Lowell's reviews before him when he wrote his article. Like Lowell, he minimizes
Rossetti's importance, saying that in a cast of *Hamlet* he would
play Osric to Tennyson's and Browning's Hamlet, and he accuses
Rossetti, Morris, and Swinburne of having formed a "Mutual Admiration School" to praise each other's works. He quotes from
Morris's and Swinburne's reviews to prove his point. Like Lowell,
too, he finds Rossetti's chief fault to be sexuality disguised as love,
his emphasis centering upon the sonnet "Nuptial Sleep," quoted
in full. And he agrees with Lowell that the disguise for the persistent strain of lust is a "grotesque mediaevalism," imitated from
Dante, though the style is taken from Tennyson, Browning, and
Mrs. Browning. With evident gusto he takes both Rossetti and
Swinburne to task for having their lovers of both sexes "bite,
scratch, scream, bubble, munch, sweat, writhe, twist, wriggle,
foam" in their lovemaking.[29] His opinion coincides with Lowell's
that Rossetti's verse has infrequent passages of real beauty, but
such passages are marred by the recurrent note of illicit sexuality.
Like Lowell also, he accuses Rossetti of being completely absorbed in himself and his emotions. But he goes beyond the American critic in two notable particulars: He objects to the heart-
lessness of the monologuist in "Jenny" and to the irregularity of
rhythm which forces the reader to put the accent on the wrong
syllable in such words as "Haymar*ket*" and "li*ly*."

From Swinburne's review he took the word "fleshly" and flung
it like a stone at Rossetti, using it as the key word of his title as
well. The phrase Swinburne employs to praise Rossetti's diction,
"the golden affluence of words," recurs mockingly throughout the
review. And Swinburne comes in for minor attention as one
who has recently written several novels, the statement being followed by an exclamation point in parentheses, manifestly an
oblique reference to the content of *Lesbia Brandon* and of *A
Year's Letters*. In the *Hamlet* cast Buchanan has Swinburne and
Morris in the unflattering roles of Rosencrantz and Guildenstern;
as a poet Swinburne is "transcendently superficial"; in *Poems and*

Ballads he is "only a little mad boy letting off squibs; not a great strong man, who might be really dangerous to society," and his review of *Poems* is "a hysteria of admiration." [30]

Buchanan knew the fury his review would raise, so he took pains to avert suspicion by scattering a few false leads through it. He includes himself as Cornelius in the *Hamlet*, whereas anyone knowing him would suppose that his vanity would have had him at least as Horatio; and he speaks of himself as having been accused of "maudlin sentiment and affected tenderness" in his "quasi-lyrical" poems.[31] The review was signed "Thomas Maitland."

The dodge worked well for a time. However, even as early as mid-October Rossetti heard rumors that Buchanan was the author, and by December he was fairly certain.[32] An insulting article in the *Athenaeum* for December 9, 1871, by Sidney Colvin brought an angry admission from Buchanan and a denial from Publisher Strahan. Buchanan's letter was dated from London, but he had apparently replied in such hot haste that he and Strahan had been unable to work out a unified strategy, and their contradictory letters to the *Athenaeum* were the embarrassing result.

Quick to capitalize on the windfall, the *Athenaeum* printed both letters on December 16, adding the caustic comment that Buchanan's was "an edifying comment" on Strahan's and that Buchanan should have signed his own name to the article and not have delayed his admission until he had been found out. The implication of the comment is that Buchanan and Strahan are liars tripped up by their own falsehoods.

Buchanan's letter denied that he had had anything to do with the addition of the pseudonym or with the "suppression" of his name, and promised that he would reissue the article "with many additions," under his own name, and published by Strahan. He added that "The grave responsibility of not agreeing with Mr. Rossetti's friends . . . will thus be transferred . . . to my own shoulders." [33]

The same issue of the *Athenaeum* carrying the fiasco of the letters had a two-thousand-word defense of his *Poems* by Rossetti. Writing it in the form of a letter also and titling it "The Stealthy School of Criticism," Rossetti denies the charge of sensuality, and countercharges that Buchanan has quoted him out of context and distorted his meaning. On the question of the sensuality of "Nuptial Sleep," he dodges the issue by asserting that it is not a whole poem, but only one item in a cycle of sonnets; that it should be considered only in the context of the cycle, and that on no ground should it be taken as his own view of love.[34] (Basically, this last is the same argument Swinburne used in his defense of *Poems and Ballads*.) In proof of his assertion Rossetti quotes in full his sonnet "Love-Sweetness" and adds: "Any reader may bring any artistic charge he pleases against the above sonnet; but one charge it would be impossible to maintain against the writer of the series in which it occurs, and that is, the wish on his part to assert that the body is greater than the soul." [35]

Now the sonnet in question has a quite sensuous description of a voluptuous lady, her hair loosened and falling about the lover's face, and his kissing of her cheeks, neck, and eyelids in the first eight lines; the last six voice the sentiment that without the fervor of her heart and "the swift beat / And soft subsidence of the spirit's wing" all her physical attractions "would lose their sweet. . . ." [36]

This sonnet does not stultify the charge of sensuality against Rossetti—not at all. But he claims that it does. And this is his method throughout the defense: first, state the charge; second, give a quotation from the *Poems;* third, assert that he has disproved the charge. After much lengthy quotation, he closes by remonstrating against the use of the pseudonym by one poet attacking another. Rossetti asserts piously that, for justice, he would leave Buchanan to his conscience, for he was obviously disturbed or he would not have used the pseudonym in the first place (a clever way of branding as a lie Buchanan's denial that he had affixed the pseudonym). He then remarks caustically that this was the very man who "from behind his mask" had accused him of insincerity.[37]

Rossetti's protestations of the innocence of his "House of Life" sonnets and of his intentions in them acquire a hollow sound and a touch of Voltairean irony from the fact that when Buchanan's Fleshly article appeared in October, 1871, Rossetti was just completing three months of cohabitation at "Kelmscott Manor" with Mrs. Jane Morris, to whom, we now know, many of the sonnets were written. Husband William Morris had the curious notion that if he could not hold his wife's love, he had no right to interfere with her transferring it to another man. With full knowledge that Rossetti was with his wife, Morris remained away for most of the time.[38]

We wonder how Rossetti could have had the effrontery to accuse Buchanan of insincerity and of not telling the truth. Yet it must be admitted that repetition of the accusation of falsehood, as well as the suggestion of treason in one poet's attacking another, was clever. It kept Buchanan where the *Athenaeum* had put him when it printed his and Strahan's letters—squarely on the defensive; and it dragged a red herring across the trail to divert him and the public from the main question of the morality or immorality of Rossetti's poems. Buchanan attempted to revive the central issue with his booklet *The Fleshly School of Poetry and Other Phenomena of the Day,* published by Strahan in the first week of May, 1872. But instead of helping matters, he played into the hands of his foes by going to such ridiculous lengths in his pursuit of fleshliness that he completely stultified both himself and his case. Everywhere he goes in London, he says, he sees evidence of the growing menace of fleshliness: on drawingroom tables, in poems read by girls, in confectionery stores with "models of the female Leg, the whole definite and elegant article as far as the thigh, with a fringe of paper cut in imitation of the female drawers and embroidered in the female fashion!" [39]

While all this controversy was going on, Swinburne was having his troubles. His dissipations were increasing, and the periods of time he was able to be in London before his health broke down and he had to be taken to "Holmwood" for care grew ever shorter. In London early in 1871 he soon got into such a condition that, his father being ill, his parents had to enlist Rossetti's aid in getting him to "Holmwood." They kept him there until August, when he took a vacation trip to Scotland with Jowett which lasted into mid-September. Then back to London, he was in such bad shape in early October that the Admiral came, closed out his tenancy of his apartment, moved his goods into storage, and took him home, apparently intending that he should not return.

On February 11, 1871, his worried mother wrote Rossetti a most revealing letter with clear implications that she and the Admiral well knew the exact cause of his trouble. Above all, she says, they wish he would stay away from London and remain at "Holmwood"; and they have urged him to have his books and other necessaries brought there. Then she adds: "I fear his having his books would not keep him here—it is impossible but a mind like his should require the society of persons with minds and pursuits similar to his own, unless he could make up his mind to remain here as a means of conquering his fearful propensity—for a time he is perfectly happy and his health as good as possible, he says how much better he can work here and how much better he feels." [40] But their only way of keeping him there against his will was to go to court, prove him mentally incompetent, and have him committed either to an institution or to their care. This they were not willing to do—yet.

While at "Holmwood," he received a letter early in November, 1871, from Frederick Locker with the news that Buchanan was the author of the *Contemporary* article. On November 13 he passed the word along to Rossetti, urging him to write and publish a reply. Either he was not satisfied with Rossetti's defense, or Buchanan's threat to expand his article into a booklet prodded him into action. He had also learned by this time of Buchanan's authorship of "The Session." At any rate he set about his own reply in *Under the Microscope,* and it appeared in the bookstalls by early July, 1872.

Swinburne begins by explaining that since it is a scientific age, he plans to spend an hour in scientific research and to set forth his findings in this book. The two "bugs" he examines are Alfred Austin—whose *Poetry of the Period* contains some caustic strictures on Swinburne—and Robert Buchanan. The first half of the essay deals with Austin by way of warm-up for the main bout with Buchanan. Swinburne does not argue with Buchanan, as Rossetti makes a show of doing in "The Stealthy School"; he belabors him with epithets, insults, and scurrilous insinuations, leaving him not a shred of dignity as a human being, but casting him aside at the end as a foul serpent too loathsome to touch.

He begins by rating Buchanan as far below Austin as Austin is beneath Tennyson and Browning; and he insinuates that, like Petronius, the Scotsman is a homosexual. Noting the hope of some critics that Buchanan might develop into a major poet, Swinburne says positively: "The tadpole poet will never grow into anything bigger than a frog; not though in that stage of development he should puff and blow himself till he bursts with windy adulation at the heels of the laurelled ox." [41]

Raging in this vein through many pages of violent rhetoric, he gives free rein to the sadistic side of his nature and aptly illustrates his mother's later criticism of him that he never knew when to stop. His friends had often flattered him on his ability to annihilate with words; in the Fleshly article Buchanan had remarked on his genius for fashioning "alliterative thunderbolts." [42] Plainly Swinburne saw himself here as an angry schoolmaster cutting to bloody shreds the back and bottom of a vile boy. But he rages so long, so loud, and so uncontrollably that he is unconvincing. The Anglo-Saxon image of an angry man is of one who says only a few words but makes those few count because he is ready to back them up with action if necessary. In *Under the Microscope* Swinburne was demonstrating his lack of manly self-control.

This was precisely the weakness Buchanan played up in a squib called "The Monkey and the Microscope" he wrote by way of reply and published in *St. Paul's Magazine* for August, 1872:

> *A clever Monkey—he can squeak,*
> *Scream, bite, munch, mumble, all but speak;*
> *Studies not merely monkey-sport*
> *But vices of a human sort;*
> *Is petulant to most, but sweet*
> *To those who pat him, give him meat;*
> *Can imitate to admiration*
> *Man's gestures, gait, gesticulation;*
> *Is amorous, and takes no pain*
> *To hide his Aphrodital vein;*
> *And altogether, trimly drest*
> *In human breeches, coat, and vest,*
> *Looks human, and upon the whole*
> *Lacks nothing, save perchance a Soul.*[43]

The controversy lay dormant till 1875, when Swinburne published his *Essays and Studies*, including his "Matthew Arnold's New Poems" with the addition of the patronizing footnote on Gray we have discussed earlier. The note enraged Buchanan far more than *Under the Microscope*. He vowed revenge and waited his opportunity. It came in the summer of 1875 with the publication of an anonymous poem *Jonas Fisher*, really by James Carnegie, the Earl of Southesk, but with so many of the characteristics of Buchanan's verse—humanitarianism, anti-Catholicism, strictures on literary and artistic immorality—that Swinburne felt sure it was his. He was quick to retaliate with four lines of scornful verse to the *Examiner:*

> EPITAPH ON A SLANDERER
> *He whose heart and soul and tongue*
> *Once above-ground stunk and stung,*
> *Now less noisome than before,*
> *Stinks here still, but stings no more.*
> A. C. Swinburne.[44]

A week later the *Examiner* reviewed *Jonas Fisher*, devoting its first paragraph to a satirical speculation that Buchanan was the probable author. On December 4, Buchanan published in the *Athenaeum* a flat disavowal, and in the *Examiner* for December 11, Swinburne burlesqued the whole matter of the original Fleshly article and the pseudonym and the pseudonymous *Jonas Fisher* with a letter titled "The Devil's Due" and signed "Thomas Maitland." The letter opens with a long paragraph imitating the style of Buchanan's critical essays with a bewildering number of reservations, insinuations, and definitions. Then it turns to the question of authorship and observes that *Jonas Fisher* could as well be attributed to Satan as to "the polypseudonymous lyrist and libeller in question." [45]

However, Swinburne continues, the author does not seem to be Buchanan because he has not learned to praise his own works and throw dirt on the works of others. Moreover, *Jonas* is in the style of the "Bab Ballads," a style not yet mastered by Buchanan. Here he adds a lengthy note instructing his publisher to add still another note, heavily satirizing all of Buchanan's and Strahan's notes to the *Athenaeum:*

The writer of the above being at present away from London, on a cruise among the Philippine Islands, in his steam yacht (the *Skulk*, Captain Shuffleton master), is, as can be proved on the oath or the solemn word of honour of the editor, publisher, and proprietor, responsible neither for an article which might with equal foundation be attributed to Cardinal Manning, or to Mr. Gladstone, or any other writer in the *Contemporary Review*, as to its actual author; nor for the adoption of a signature under which his friends in general . . . have thought it best and wisest to shelter his personal responsibility from any chance of attack.[46]

II *The Trial*

This time Swinburne had gone too far, and Buchanan had him at last on a charge of libel. The trial took place in London on June 29, 30, and July 1, 1876. Buchanan sued P. A. Taylor, owner of the *Examiner*, for £5,000 for libel. At the outset, Taylor's lawyers attempted to have the suit transferred to Swinburne; but MacClymont, one of Buchanan's lawyers, was a friend of John Nichol, who successfully interceded with him to have the suit remain against Taylor. Buchanan's Fleshly School article and book were brought into the case, as were "The Session of the Poets" and his essay praising Whitman. Buchanan unblushingly insisted that his remarks in the poem were against Swinburne's writings, not his person. When a book of Whitman's poems was submitted to the judge and the jury for silent examination because they were too evil to be read aloud, the Scotsman replied that he had not condemned Whitman as he had the Fleshly writers because he considered the American fundamentally "a spiritual person." [47]

Swinburne did not escape unscathed. When Justice Archibald demanded the reason Buchanan's attorneys had sued Taylor instead of Swinburne, they answered that the poet was a "man of straw" who had not the money to pay the damages, so they had taken Taylor instead. Likewise when several of Swinburne's and Rossetti's poems were read, Archibald said the world would have been better off if they had never been written.

In his summation to the jury, Justice Archibald indicated quite clearly that he favored the defendant, but the jury took only twenty minutes to bring in a verdict of £150 for Buchanan, hardly enough to pay his attorneys' fees. Watts-Dunton, who acted as Swinburne's adviser, tried to persuade him to pay part or all of the damages, perhaps on the ground that William Minto, editor of the *Examiner*, had not realized the libelous nature of Swinburne's satirical letters because he had not been familiar with the background of the Fleshly Controversy, whereas Swinburne did know their full import. Swinburne refused.

For him the trial had been a dreadful ordeal that scarred his soul. He had been taught a lesson that he never forgot. His proud name had been dragged into court and made ridiculous; his poems had been read aloud in public and scoffed at; he had been scorned as an ineffectual creature too mean to prosecute.

For Swinburne the Fleshly Controversy was at an end. Not one word more did he publish about Buchanan. But, as his letters show, his hatred continued to burn fiercely until his death in 1909.

CHAPTER 8

The Recluse of Putney

AS STATED in the preface, the purpose of this book is to render Swinburne's work understandable to the modern reader. For him, more than for most men of letters, the achievement of such an aim necessitates an examination of the various aesthetic and philosophical influences affecting him and leaving their impress upon his writings. We have followed him through such stages as classicism, republicanism, Pre-Raphaelitism, Baudelaireism, and Positivism. In all of these he was, of course, dominated by others whose personalities captured his fancy. Their ideas became so completely and implicitly his that he accepted them in most cases without apparent reservation or question. And, since he wrote as he thought, we can readily follow the parade of ideas in his works.

He was to undergo one final transformation in his life and thought, a transformation so comprehensive, so far-reaching in its consequences, that it must be taken into consideration in discussing the works of the latter half of his life. Unlike the other stages in his career, this one has no convenient label. It is a period of growing conservatism, of increasing patriotism, of angry repudiation of some of his earlier enthusiasms, and, finally, of lessening interest in the world about him.

The proclamation of the French Republic in 1870, the completion of Italian unification in the same year, the deaths of Mazzini in 1872 and of Napoleon III in 1873, left Swinburne without a cause to serve, a leader to follow, or a political tyrant to denounce. He was even more left high and dry when William Rossetti wrote him early in July, 1872, that Dante's condition was so bad that Swinburne should on no account try to see him. Even though Dante recovered and went about almost as usual, their friendship was completely at an end; the two men never thereafter met nor had any kind of correspondence with each other. Swinburne was hurt and bewildered by such conduct on the part of his old friend, and he remained in the dark as to the reason for it. And, although he and William remained as close friends as ever, William never threw any light on the matter.

But, as we have shown, the answer may well lie in the fact that Dante and William concluded that Buchanan's attack on Dante had come about because of the widespread suspicion that Dante had corrupted Swinburne and seduced him into evil paths. The best preventive for such attacks in future, therefore, was the complete severance of all relations between Rossetti and his erstwhile disciple.

From 1872 to 1877 a number of factors contributed to keeping Swinburne at "Holmwood" and out of the dangerous environment of London. As his dissipations increased, the periods of time he could be in London before it became necessary for his father or someone else to take him to "Holmwood" for recuperation grew progressively shorter. Likewise he was short of money because Hotten, with whom his difficulties had been mounting, paid him very little; also, as a necessary measure toward keeping him out of the metropolis, Swinburne's father may have either curtailed or discontinued altogether the allowance of £200 he had been paying him since 1861. Under the circumstances who could blame him?

Furthermore, Swinburne was both shocked and frightened in 1873 when scandalous rumors of abnormal sexual practices attached themselves to Simeon Solomon's name and circulated widely throughout London. No man who cared for his own good name, he wrote Watts, could afford to have anything to do with such a person. But for the past ten years or more he had had only too much to do with Solomon, publicly and privately, having gone so far as to publish an article on the young painter's poems in *The Dark Blue* in July, 1871.[1] Better, then, to stay out of London while the wave of scandal was at the crest.

Another quieting influence had entered actively into Swinburne's life in 1872 in Walter Theodore Watts (later Watts-Dunton). A country solicitor who yearned for a literary career, he took up residence in London and made himself extremely useful to both Dante Rossetti and Swinburne in handling and straightening out their tangled financial affairs. He took over negotiations with the slippery Hotten, and he had already instituted legal action to force him to settle with Swinburne when the publisher died suddenly in June, 1873. Thereupon Watts effected a much more amicable and profitable arrangement with Andrew Chatto, Hotten's reputable successor, who became henceforth Swinburne's publisher. From this time on, Watts exerted a steady, subtle influence to bring Swinburne back into the paths of respectability and to rule out of his life anything of a disturbing or unsettling nature. For the rest of Swinburne's life, Watts served without pay as his literary agent, shrewdly marketing his wares for the best possible prices.

After the Fleshly School trial of 1876, in which Watts again acted as Swinburne's adviser, the poet returned to "Holmwood" until the death of Admiral Swinburne at the age of eighty on March 5, 1877, brought him back to London with his inheritance of £5,000 at his disposal. As might be expected, he returned with such a will to his old life of dissipation and excess that on May 31, 1878, he was too ill to accept Hugo's invitation to be his guest at the festival in honor of Voltaire. Swinburne's landlady at Great James Street, Mrs. Jane Magill, kept Lady Jane informed of what was going on. Lord Houghton, who visited him in July, 1878, found him in such dire straits that he wrote Lady Jane recommending medical supervision, but she answered helplessly that she had no power to enforce it. Instead, she wrote Watts, who lived only a few doors away from Swinburne's apartment, to investigate and report to her.[2]

Finally, in June, 1879, Watts carried Swinburne from his rooms in what biographers agree was a nearly dying condition, and, in due course, moved him to "The Pines" at Putney, a suburb of London, where they took a house together and continued to live until Swinburne's death in 1909. Under Watts' watchful eye and gentle but determined persuasion, the poet was weaned away from alcohol and guided into a regular and progressively reclusive existence. More and more he came to rely upon Watts and to defer to his judgment until it finally became almost impossible to see Swinburne without first securing Watts' permission.

To say, as some biographers do, that Swinburne became little more than Watts' puppet and that his writings during these final years were, to use Shakespeare's phrase in *Hamlet,* "weary, stale, flat, and unprofitable," is not to state the whole truth. Undoubtedly, Watts's influence was pronounced, as was that of the other older men whom Swinburne trusted and admired; but it was not absolute. On some notable occasions Swinburne overruled Watts, as he did in October, 1882, to drag him to Paris for the fiftieth anniversary of Hugo's *Le Roi s'Amuse*. Generally, the two got along very well and grew gracefully old in the quiet repose of "The Pines." Swinburne became noticeably more conservative and much more of an English patriot instead of an objector to English complacency, even going so far as to praise Queen Victoria in his poem "Euonymos" for her courage in the assassination attempt of 1882. His conservatism is also apparent in his disavowal of "art for art's sake" in the essay "Mr. Whistler's Lecture on Art" of 1887 and in "The Armada," the tricentennial poem of 1888 hailing England as the "Mother more beloved than all who bear not all their children free." [3]

But to say that all this was solely the result of Watts's influence is going to an unwarranted extreme. In great part, I believe, it was the manifestation of the natural conservatism that comes with age, as well as the natural tendency, now that his father was dead and the antagonism between them ended, to adopt more and more the father's conservative viewpoint and outlook. For, like many other men, Swinburne, as he grew older, developed an understanding and appreciation of his father that he had been incapable of during the Admiral's lifetime.

Much has been made of the many poems Swinburne wrote after 1879 to Bertie Mason, Watts-Dunton's five-year-old nephew and the son of his sister, who lived close by. Generally, it has been cited as an evidence of the childish and rather spiritless personality that Swinburne is supposed to have become under the domination of Watts-Dunton. I can find no conclusive evidence that Swinburne developed such a personality, but I am willing to admit that he did lean heavily upon Watts-Dunton. His great love for children is one of the interesting phenomena of these later years. Even Watts-Dunton and Lady Jane were uneasy about it, obviously fearful that it might be one more manifestation of Swinburne's abnormal tendencies. But his love was not just for Bertie; it was for any child he came across, even two little girls he met in one of his morning walks about Putney. His emotion, however, is all love and tenderness rather than the former psychotic gloating over the prospect of beating them until they bled. My conjecture is that his relationship with Bertie Mason was a vicarious fatherhood that opened the floodgates and let his love flow as it never had before—not even when he was paying court to Mary Gordon in 1863-1864.

The extent of his literary production from 1872 to 1909 is truly remarkable, approximately four times the volume of that for the period from 1856 to 1872. As before 1872, it lies in the areas of drama, poetry, and criticism. It includes some of his best work and some of his poorest. In drama it ranges from the high point of *Erechtheus* to the nadir of *The Duke of Gandia;* in poetry, from the supreme beauty of *Tristram of Lyonesse* to the greeting-card bathos of "Babyhood"; in criticism, from the noble "Recollections of Professor Jowett" to the ignoble and lamentable "The New Terror," in which he exhumed and belabored the corpse of William Bell Scott. Its subject matter is truly catholic. Much of it is of a memorial character, with poetic tributes to a great number of friends, associates, and prominent persons who preceded him in death. Generally speaking, we find the focus of his attention increasingly upon things British, with a corresponding decrease of emphasis on foreign subjects and topics. He hadn't forgotten to hate, as his fierce denunciations of Russia, Germany, the Pope and the Catholic Church, Carlyle, and Furnivall show quite clearly; nor how to love and admire, as is evidenced by his devoted tributes to Hugo, Shelley, Charlotte and Emily Bronte, Landor, Dickens, Coleridge, and Mazzini. Newly present in the poetry is an almost Wordsworthian love of nature, with especial emphasis upon the sea, and considerably lessened are any traces of the abnormal sexuality so prominent in the earlier works.

I *The Drama*

We could wish that Swinburne had not wasted his time in attempting to write dramas. To begin with, he had no knowledge of dramatic technique or of the requirements of the drama. Like Browning, Tennyson, and most of the other Victorian poets who tried their hands at the drama, he labored under the Shakespeare-complex that all dramas must be in blank verse, in five acts, and in the heroic tone and pattern. With such handicaps, realism and immediacy were precluded and artificiality insured. Nor did he have any notion of a central theme or core of meaning around which to build his dramas. Therefore organization and proportion are woefully absent from Swinburne's attempts, and some grotesque malformations occur. Nor did he have any idea of the practical demands and limitations of the stage. What he needed to do was what Shakespeare, Eugene O'Neill, or any other who has successfully written for the stage has had to do— get a job with an acting troupe and master the lore of the stage in the only way it can be mastered, by practical experience. For Swinburne this was, of course, out of the question, and his dramas, except for occasional passages of good poetry and some plausible dialogue, are failures.

The first drama of this period, and one of the worst, is *Bothwell* (1874), a huge monstrosity running to five hundred and thirty pages in the Bonchurch Edition, about five times as long as the uncut *Hamlet*. Swinburne was obviously overawed by history, including much that should have been omitted. In spots the poetry is excellent, but it is lost in a futile cause. An excellent example of Swinburne's total lack of dramatic know-how occurs in Act III when, after Bothwell tells Queen Mary that the battle is lost because the troops have deserted and left them hopelessly outnumbered by the approaching enemy, she launches into a bitter speech of about four hundred words—and this with disaster upon them and the speediest kind of action necessary!

In *Erechtheus* (1876), he returned to the classical material that had served so well in *Atalanta*. This time the result was not so happy, possibly because he wrote under the influence of Jowett and gave more attention to the classical tone and style of his verse than to its music. Swinburne wrote it almost like a school exercise, with little of "the fever and the fret" of real life anywhere in evidence.

Mary Stuart (1881) ends the trilogy which begins with *Chastelard,* and is dedicated to Victor Hugo, as are the two earlier dramas dealing with the unfortunate Scottish queen. Only about a third as long as *Bothwell,* this play deals with the imprisonment and execution of Mary Stuart at the hands of Elizabeth. Once again, the characters are cardboard figures stiffly going through their assigned roles with very little action, external or internal; and, as usual in Swinburne's dramas, the plot has no suspense.

Marino Faliero (1885), a play patterned after Byron's tragedy of the same title, is the story of an old man with a young wife.

The play deals with an octogenarian who takes the law into his hands to avenge an insult to his honor and ends up being beheaded for treason to the state. Swinburne makes him into a precursor of Mazzini with republican ideals and hatred of the Catholic clergy. Some suspense is injected with the villain's vow to have revenge upon Marino, but the insult to Marino is so casually reported that the old man's resorting to treason to avenge it seems highly improbable.

Of the four remaining tragedies—*Locrine* (1887), *The Sisters* (1892), *Rosamund, Queen of the Lombards* (1899), and *The Duke of Gandia* (1908)—the most interesting is *The Sisters* because of the autobiographical material it contains. Swinburne casts himself as Reginald Clavering, a hero of the battle of Waterloo. Two of Reginald's cousins, Mabel and Anne Dilston, are in love with him. He chooses Mabel to be his bride; and then jealous Anne poisons the both of them. *The Duke of Gandia* is the most regrettable of all the plays and a "throwback" to *Chastelard* (1865) and the worst of *Poems and Ballads* (1866). Consisting of only four scenes, *The Duke* is a playlet dealing with Pope Alexander VI; his concubine Vannozza Catanei; and their three children, Francesco, Caesar, and Lucrezia Borgia. Francesco, the duke, is murdered by an assassin hired by Caesar, who makes it clear to their grieving father than Francesco's death was expedient and that it will not cause Caesar to lose any sleep. Replete with suggestions of incest, absolute immorality, and dealing with characters who are monsters, not humans, the play is the kind of thing Swinburne should neither have written nor published.

II *The Criticism*

In the field of criticism Swinburne's publications during his final period include *Essays and Studies* (1875), *George Chapman* (1875), the *Note on the Muscovite Crusade* (1876), *A Note on Charlotte Bronte* (1877), *A Study of Shakespeare* (1880), *Miscellanies* (1886), *A Study of Victor Hugo* (1886), *A Study of Ben Jonson* (1889), *Studies in Prose and Poetry* (1894), and *The Age of Shakespeare* (1908). Like the dramas, most of Swinburne's critical works were misspent efforts marred by extravagant praise or fierce blame, depending upon whether the subject met with his approval or censure. But, as always, he showed that "the pleasure of praising" could not be enjoyed without drawing those unfortunate comparisons at the expense of others of whom he did not approve. A good example of this unfortunate propensity is the *Note on Charlotte Bronte,* which could as well be titled "An Attack on George Eliot," for that is what it equally is. He designates Charlotte Bronte as "one of the greatest among women" and then adds that her works will be read "with reverence and admiration . . . when even *Daniel Deronda* has gone the way of all waxwork, when even Miss Broughton no longer cometh up as a flower, and even Mrs. Oliphant is at length cut down like the grass." [4] What better way to call forth the Erinyes in all their fury?

The voluminous works about Shakespeare and the other Elizabethan playwrights and about such figures as Hugo, Landor, Shelley, and Coleridge we may pass over hurriedly because they are paeans of praise and nothing more. The criticism of the dramatists is further nullified by the fact, well illustrated by Swinburne's own dramas, that he lacked sufficient knowledge of the drama to criticize it intelligently.

In writing about the novel, it is interesting to note that he fell into the usual Victorian error with regard to Emily Bronte's *Wuthering Heights,* failing to understand it as a prose poem of a love so great that it transcends the grave, and regretting its ferocity and violence. But he does insist that its "noble purity" will more than offset such faults. Dickens he hails as the supreme Victorian literary figure, with *Great Expectations* and *David Copperfield* as his greatest novels.

In "Whitmania" he can find little to praise in the American bard whom he had admired in his "art-for-art's-sake" days except his views of death, his abundant sympathies, and his usually good intentions. Otherwise, the American often mistakes rhetoric for song, and he is frequently guilty of treating sex in a very coarse fashion! Whether Swinburne realized how far he had departed from his "not-for-girls" argument in *Notes on Poems and Reviews* of 1866 is debatable.

The *Note of an English Republican on the Muscovite Crusade* is a determined attack on Gladstone and Carlyle for their support of Russia in her dispute with Turkey. Swinburne had been angered by a comment made by Carlyle in 1874 that Swinburne's poetry showed that he was standing in a cesspool up to his chin and also contributing to its contents. He evened the score now by taunting Carlyle for supporting Russia because she had kept in subjection the "anarchic populations" in her part of the world, and sneered that Carlyle had never spoken or written a word in support of Italian freedom.

Perhaps the most regrettable piece of all is the essay "The New Terror" (1892), his enraged response to what he thought were traitorous and envious remarks made about him by his dead friend William Bell Scott in his *Autobiographical Notes*. Because William Minto, former editor of the *Examiner* when Swinburne's libelous remarks had been published therein, was also editor of Scott's autobiography, he shared in the attack. Scott, said Swinburne, was an "unspeakable Caledonian" who was guilty of "malignant impertinence of senile invention." And Minto, by his folly in permitting such scurrilous remarks to appear in print, had only succeeded in "stripping and gibbeting" the dead author.[5] It was a deplorable affair altogether, and, as in the case of *The Duke of Gandia*, one regrets that he wrote what he did.

Quite otherwise is his noble testimonial to Jowett, perhaps the finest essay he ever wrote. The tone and style are dignified and wholly appropriate to the subject. He testifies to Jowett's courage, enthusiasm, and modesty, praising him for rarely letting pedagogical formality displace the *bonhomie* of the cheerful friend and companion. It is a touching tribute from a devoted pupil to a great teacher.

III *The Poetry*

As always, Swinburne's best work in his final period was in his poetry. Although he was out of his proper metier in the drama and criticism, in poetry he was supremely at home. He might not have the patience, the analytical objectivity, the technical competence to construct a long drama or a major work of criticism; but he did possess the fire, the imagination, the supreme and intuitive genius with rhythm and rhyme to create good and often truly great poetry.

His production in the last period is truly remarkable. Beginning with *Songs of Two Nations* (1875), it includes *Poems and Ballads, Second Series* (1878), *Songs of the Springtides* (1880), *Studies in Song* (1880), *The Heptalogia* (1880), *Tristram of Lyonesse* (1882), *A Century of Roundels* (1883), *A Midsummer Holiday*

(1884), *Poems and Ballads, Third Series* (1889), *Astrophel and Other Poems* (1894), *The Tale of Balen* (1896), *Rosamund, Queen of the Lombards* (1899), and *A Channel Passage and Other Poems* (1904). In addition to these, many other poems, some of them written during his Oxford days, were posthumously published by the noted literary forger, Thomas J. Wise, to whom Watts-Dunton, Swinburne's sole heir, sold them following the poet's death.

Perhaps the best of these are the autobiographical poems "Thalassius" and "On the Cliffs," and a new rendering of the Tristram and Isolde story, entitled *Tristram of Lyonesse*. "Thalassius," literally "the sea-man" in Greek, tells the story of Swinburne's life in its relations to the sea. The child of Apollo and Cymothoe, the sun and the sea, Swinburne says he was found lying on the beach by one "born of man's most highest and heavenliest birth"—Landor—whose songs teach him to despise tyranny, to love liberty, and to aspire to sing songs "goldener than gold." The boy encounters love but learns bitterly that it is only death in disguise. Disillusioned, he turns to lust and dissipation only to learn that these make him feel unclean. He returns to the sea, which purges his soul and restores his faith so that he is enabled once again to sing his songs joyfully.

The setting of "On the Cliffs" is also by the sea, for Swinburne, standing at twilight on a cliff, looks out over the calm sea and meditates upon the great mysteries of life and death. This poem was written in July and August, 1879, while he was at "Holmwood," shortly after Watts-Dunton had saved him from certain death. His mood is therefore understandably pensive and introspective. Like Matthew Arnold in "Dover Beach," Swinburne stands apart and views himself, in relation to the rest of mankind and to the enigma of existence.

Nowhere else does he discuss the effect of his physical peculiarity upon his life and poetry with the frankness that is here. All pretense, all "front," all borrowed philosophies and enthusiasms, all the defenses that Swinburne's intrinsically shy spirit had erected between itself and the world are gone. He reveals his naked soul as he asks the eternal question "why?" He poses the question to Sappho, the ancient Greek poetess, whom he calls "sister" because, he says, they are alike in their poetic genius and in their abnormality:

Thee only of all; yet can no memory say
How many a night and day
My heart has been as thy heart, and my life
As thy life is, a sleepless hidden thing,
Full of the thirst and hunger of winter and spring,
That seeks its food not in such love or strife
As fill men's hearts with passionate hours and rest.
From no loved lips and on no loving breast
Have I sought ever for such gifts as bring
Comfort, to stay the secret soul with sleep.
The joys, the loves, the labours, whence men reap
Rathe fruit of hopes and fears,
I have made not mine; the best of all my days
Have been as those fair fruitless summer strays,
Those water-waifs that but the sea-wind steers,
Flakes of glad foam or flowers on footless ways
That take the wind in season and the sun,
And when the wind wills is their season done.[6]

She it was, he says, who first inspired him to sing the song of
their longings.

As brother and sister were we, child and bird,
Since thy first Lesbian word
Flamed on me, and I knew not whence I knew
This was the song that struck my whole soul through,
Pierced my keen spirit of sense with edge more keen,
Even when I knew not,—even ere sooth was seen,—
When thou wast but the tawny sweet winged thing
Whose cry was but of spring.[7]

He pleads with her to tell him what it is that the gods have given
him and her. She can supply the answer, he feels certain, because,
as a Lesbian, she is capable of more profound perceptions of love
and pain than he is. Then, from the night, the wind, and the sea
he fancies he hears her song, and his soul rises in lyric ecstasy.

Ah, then, what song is this, that here
One ear fulfilled and mad with music, one
Makes all the night one ear,
Heart kindling as the heart of heaven, to hear
A song more fiery than the awakening sun

[156]

> *Sings, when his song sets fire*
> *To the air and clouds that build the dead night's pyre?*
> O thou of divers-coloured mind, O thou
> Deathless, God's daughter subtle-souled—*lo, now,*
> *Now to the song above all songs, in flight*
> *Higher than the day-star's height,*
> *And sweet as sound the moving wings of night!*
> Thou of the divers-coloured seat—*behold,*
> *Her very song of old!*—
> O deathless, O God's daughter subtle-souled! [8]

Lafourcade calls "On the Cliffs" "the high-water mark" of Swinburne's poetry. Along with *Atalanta*, "The Triumph of Time," "Thalassius," and *Tristram of Lyonesse*, it may stand among the high peaks of his achievement. Nowhere in world literature is there a more inspired revelation of the innermost soul of the artist in his eternal struggle with the mysteries of life and self.

In long narrative poetry *Tristram of Lyonesse* is one of the supreme achievements of Swinburne's genius. Lafourcade says Swinburne began the poem in 1868, but lost his manuscript in a cab and had to start over.[9] In 1870, perhaps disgusted with Tennyson's publication of "The Grail," he worked on it again.[10] Lafourcade is also our authority for the statement that Watts-Dunton, before it was published in 1882, toned down some of the passages that he thought overly sensual.[11] His later version of the Tristram legend runs to about four thousand lines and one hundred and forty-four pages in the Bonchurch Edition. Divided into nine books, it is epic in character and style. The meter is iambic pentameter rhymed couplets, a device that is happily suited to the medieval story.

Nothing gives a more accurate indication of the growth of Swinburne's poetic genius than a comparison of this poem with the early version of the same story he had done at Oxford under the title *Queen Iseult*. The more masculine title is indicative of the much more masculine approach to the old love story in *Tristram of Lyonesse*. Gone are most of the algolagnia and the other suggestions of abnormality that mar *Queen Iseult*. The later Tristram does not yearn to be killed or tortured by Iseult, as had his earlier model. He prefers to love her in some of the most sensual scenes in English poetry. Nor is he so silly as to fall in love with her hair; he now loves the whole woman. Nor, after they arrive in

Cornwall, does Iseult have to carry him to her room. She sends her maid and companion Brangwain to sleep with King Mark (who, in the darkness, fancies his companion is Iseult) while she steals to Tristram's room and spends the night there.

Was this more masculine approach the result of Watts-Dunton's advice? Was it attributable to Swinburne's nature at this time making another effort toward normality—the same kind of response that had evidently led him to Mary Gordon in 1863? Or was there some other cause? We don't know. At any rate, the love theme in *Tristram of Lyonesse* is more authentically treated than in any other of Swinburne's poems. There are a few touches of algolagnia in that their love is mixed with some pain—their kisses, for instance, are described as "burning"—but, for the most part, this is a great and convincing story of the love of a man and a woman, told with sympathy and deep feeling.

The story is likewise handled with far greater skill than in the Oxford poem. *Tristram* begins on shipboard with Tristram and Iseult leaving Ireland for Cornwall. Iseult's mother's giving Brangwain the goblet with the love philter and instructing her to make sure that King Mark and Iseult drink it on their wedding night is skillfully worked into the narrative in a flashback, instead of being a major scene as it was in the early poem. And the business of Tristram's parentage and birth are handled in a few swift lines without stopping the chief movement of the story. Tristram's wanderings after leaving his angry uncle are omitted altogether. We end Book II with Tristram and Iseult making love in the forest in Cornwall, and we begin Book III with him in Brittany pining for her. When the scenes of sensual love between Tristram and Iseult become a bit tedious, Swinburne relieves them by injecting the hate motif with Iseult of the white hands— the wife Tristram abandons when he returns to Iseult of Cornwall.

The central theme of the poem is the intensity of the love between the chief protagonists. Here Swinburne rises to the heights in bursts of lyric fervor. After Iseult drinks the love potion, she is transformed from an innocent girl to a woman desperately in love:

> . . . *yea, she felt*
> *Through her own soul the sovereign morning melt,*
> *And all the sacred passion of the sun;*

> *And as the young clouds flamed and were undone*
> *About him coming, touched and burnt away*
> *In rosy ruin and yellow spoil of day,*
> *The sweet veil of her body and corporal sense*
> *Felt the dawn also cleave it, and incense*
> *With light from inward and with effluent heat*
> *The kindling soul through fleshly hands and feet.*[12]

After rescuing Iseult from the evil Palamede, Tristram takes her to a cave in the forest where their lovemaking rises to ecstasy:

> *Here he caught up her lips with his, and made*
> *The wild prayer silent in her heart that prayed,*
> *And strained her to him till all her faint breath sank*
> *And her bright limbs palpitated and shrank*
> *And rose and fluctuated as flowers in rain*
> *That bends them and they tremble and rise again*
> *And heave and straighten and quiver all through with bliss*
> *And turn afresh their mouths up for a kiss,*
> *Amorous, athirst of that sweet influent love;*
> *So, hungering towards his hovering lips above,*
> *Her red-rose mouth yearned silent, and her eyes*
> *Closed, and flashed after, as through June's darkest skies*
> *The divine heartbeats of the deep live light*
> *Make open and shut the gates of the outer night.*[13]

But there is more to *Tristram in Lyonesse* than sensuous verse. Swinburne tells his story and depicts his characters with a subtlety that reminds the reader of *Love's Cross-Currents*. Iseult of the white hands is, at the beginning of the poem, an innocent girl of sixteen. She is puzzled and hurt when Tristram does not consummate their marriage on their wedding night. But she grows into a fury when he leaves her for the Iseult in Cornwall. Vowing vengeance, she waits until he returns sick and wounded; then she administers the death stroke by lying to him that Iseult of Cornwall is not coming to him in answer to his dying request.

The charm of the story is heightened by Swinburne's philosophical comments upon, and interpretations of, the events. Quite in contrast to his earlier anger at God for permitting evil and injustice is his philosophical acceptance of fate when Tristram lies dying:

> . . . *Fate, that is fire to burn and sea to drown,*
> *Strength to build up and thunder to cast down;*
> *Fate, shield and screen for each man's lifelong head,*
> *And sword at last or dart that strikes it dead;*
> *Fate, higher than heaven and deeper than the grave,*
> *That saves and spares not, spares and dothe not save;*
> *Fate, that in gods' wise is not bought and sold*
> *For prayer or price of penitence or gold. . . .*[14]

The most serious flaw in *Tristram* lies in the fact that the love passion appears to be purely sensual. The lovers desire each other's physical being, nothing more. There is no tenderness, no deep sympathy, no delight in companionship—nothing of the spiritual grandeur that raises the love of man and woman to the sublime. Of course, Swinburne could have excused this fault on the ground that the love was caused by the philter, which inspired Tristram and Iseult with an insatiable physical longing for each other. But the events of the story imply that this was a love beyond the senses. It was more than sensual love that impelled a dying Tristram to ask Iseult to come to him; it was certainly more than sensual love that brought her over the sea to his deathbed.

Oddly enough, *Tristram of Lyonesse* is seldom anthologized. Yet it is a truly fine poem which throbs with life and drama. To omit it is to deny to a truly great poet, who all his life struggled against almost insuperable handicaps, the honor that is his due.

IV   *The Burlesques*

Perhaps here is as good a place as any to discuss Swinburne's truly great sense of humor and his humorous writings. He seems to have considered such writings beneath the dignity of a great poet, for, with the exception of his parodies in verse, his most notable efforts in this direction he did not publish. Instead, he circulated them privately among his friends. Because of their intrinsic merit and because they present a side of Swinburne that the world knows little of, they should be published. It is hoped that they will be in the near future.

The verse parodies are delectable. They include tongue-in-cheek takeoffs on Tennyson ("The Higher Pantheism in a Nutshell" from the original "The Higher Pantheism"), Browning

("John Jones's Wife"—from the original "James Lee's Wife"), Elizabeth Browning ("The Poet and the Woodlouse" from her poem by the same title), Coventry Patmore ("The Person of the House" from his poem of that same title), Robert Lytton ("Last Words of a Seventh-Rate Poet" also from the original of the same title), Dante Rossetti ("Sonnet for a Picture" is from "Sonnets for a Picture"), and Swinburne himself ("Nephelidia"). In this last, Swinburne shows his good sportsmanship by wickedly parodying his weakness for adjectives and alliteration. All the parodies are so penetrating and so skillfully contrived that they constitute probably the greatest literary criticism Swinburne ever wrote.

Added to these should be such works as *La Fille du Policeman,* the fake reviews of Cossu and Clouet, *The Sister of the Queen,* perhaps the *Cannibal Catechism,* the dialogue in French in which Queen Victoria describes to her mother her seduction by Wordsworth, and numerous other quips from his letters. Essentially, of course, all these are in the spirit of that defiance of Victorian prudery and pomposity that had inspired his espousal of Pre-Raphaelitism and Baudelaireism and that underlay *Chastelard* and the *Poems and Ballads* of 1866. We can only regret that he had not always been able to temper his rebellion with the delicious humor that these works exhibit. His life would have been happier and his works would have benefited inestimably.

V *Swinburne's Contribution*

What is the true measure of Swinburne's achievement? What has been his effect upon English literature? Physically and psychologically handicapped by his personal shortcomings, he was unable to comprehend the whole of life or to treat of it convincingly. The happiness of true love, the expansion of identity that comes with marriage, the deeper understanding of the cycle of life that comes with having children and watching them mature—these were experiences that were never his. He was further restricted by the loss of his religious faith and by his consequent denial of mysticism. For all these reasons his verse never plumbed the profundities of life explored by Browning and Arnold, nor did he attain the lyrical heights of the verse of Keats or Tennyson. He must, therefore, take rank below all of them.

His chief services to English literature lay in two directions. He thrust aside the smug prudery of his times and dared to sing of the body and the senses as no one before him had done. He prepared the way for modern frankness in literature by making the love passion the subject of lyrical verse. As no one had before him, he turned into beautiful song the longings and frustrations of the sexually abnormal. His second contribution lay in his incomparable mastery of prosody. Even Tennyson acknowledged that he envied Swinburne's lyrical gift, and well he might. In his songs Swinburne taught the poets who followed him new lyrical possibilities of English verse. His resources for achieving rhythmical variety were apparently boundless. Perhaps nowhere are they better displayed than in his "The Triumph of Time," "Dolores," "Thalassius," and *Tristram of Lyonesse.*

Certainly Swinburne was one of the most learned of the English poets. Endowed with a remarkable memory, he ranged over the length and breadth of the history and literature of both ancient and modern times as few English poets ever did, but he carefully avoided Browning's obscurity and did not clutter up his works with abstruse references. What Swinburne had to say was sometimes said with verbosity, but it was always said artistically and clearly. With remarkable facility he could write a Latin satire or a French song or essay. His translations of the poems of Villon into English cause us to regret that he did not do more in this direction, for he had a real knack of catching the mood and flavor of the original in his translation.

Watts-Dunton's remark that Swinburne invented Walter Pater is, of course, an exaggeration, but it points up the fact that Pater learned much from Swinburne. So did Rossetti, Lord de Tabley, Ezra Pound, and many others, most of whom have not acknowledged their indebtedness. Even James Joyce, in his experimentation with the meaning that may be extracted from the sounds of words, was following Swinburne's lead. For if Swinburne proved nothing else, he aptly demonstrated that words have not only meanings but sounds which may be combined into music and rhythm to achieve a higher meaning than any lexicographer can express or than any mere message-hunting reader of poetry can ever comprehend.

Notes and References

Chapter One

1. Georges Lafourcade, *Swinburne: A Literary Biography* (London, 1932), p, 6.
2. Georges Lafourcade, *La Jeunesse de Swinburne* (London, 1928), I, 63-64.
3. Mrs. Disney Leith, *Algernon Charles Swinburne* (New York, 1916), pp. 8-9.
4. Cecil Y. Lang, ed., *The Swinburne Letters* (New Haven, 1959-1962), II, 82-83; hereafter referred to as *Letters*.
5. Irving Bieber, *et al.*, *Homosexuality: A Psychoanalytic Study* (New York, 1962), p. 117.
6. *Ibid.*, p. 41.
7. *Letters*, III, 10-11.
8. Edmund Gosse, *The Life of Algernon Charles Swinburne* (London, 1917), p. 26.
9. *Letters*, IV, 321.
10. Gosse, pp. 13-14.
11. *Ibid.*, p. 26.
12. Humphrey Hare, *Swinburne* (London, 1949), p. 15.
13. Photoduplicated from the manuscript in the British Museum by permission of William Heinemann Ltd.
14. Gosse, pp. 26-27.
15. *Letters*, VI, 6-7.
16. James Pope-Hennessy, *Monckton Milnes* (London, 1951), p. 146.
17. *Letters*, I, 256.
18. *Ibid.*, 78.
19. *Ibid.*, VI, 6.
20. Lafourcade, *Swinburne*, p. 47.

Chapter Two

1. A. C. Swinburne, *Two Unpublished Manuscripts* (San Francisco, 1927); these are in the Lilly Library at Indiana University.
2. *Letters*, III, 13, 14.

3. Oswald Doughty, *Dante Gabriel Rossetti* (New Haven, 1949), pp. 99-101.

4. *Ibid.*, p. 102.

5. John G. Millais, *The Life and Letters of Sir John Everett Millais* (London, 1899), I, 52, 55.

6. Helen Rossetti Angeli, *Dante Gabriel Rossetti* (London, 1949), pp. 217-24.

7. Charles Baudelaire, "Salon de 1859," *Curiosites Esthetiques,* ed. M. Jacques Crepet (Paris, 1923), p. 267.

8. Théophile Gautier, "Preface by the Author," *Mademoiselle de Maupin* (New York, 1944), p. xxvii.

9. *Letters,* II, 75.

10. Mrs. Georgiana Burne-Jones, *Memorials of Edward Burne-Jones* (London, 1906), p. 149.

11. *Letters,* I, 195.

12. *Ibid.,* V, 207.

Chapter Three

1. Lafourcade, *La Jeunesse*, II, 17-18. For most of Swinburne's unpublished works I am indebted to Professor Lafourcade's second volume of *La Jeunesse,* where extensive summaries are given with ample quotations.

2. *The Complete Works of Algernon Charles Swinburne,* Bonchurch Edition, eds. Sir Edmund Gosse and Thomas J. Wise (London, 1925), I, 118. Hereafter given as *Works.*

3. *Ibid.*

4. Lafourcade, *La Jeunesse*, II, 41. In the title the name is spelled "Iseult," but in the poem it is given as "Yseult."

5. *Ibid.*

6. Doughty, pp. 637-38.

7. Cecil Y. Lang, "Swinburne's Lost Love, *PMLA,* LXXIV (March, 1959), 123-30.

8. Lang, *Letters,* II, 342-43, dates this letter as 1874, but indicates uncertainty. Lafourcade, *La Jeunesse,* II, 128, dates it as 1873.

9. Lafourcade, *La Jeunesse,* II, 132.

10. *Ibid.,* 171.

11. *Ibid.,* 169.

12. *Ibid.,* 223.

13. *Ibid.,* 165.

Chapter Four

1. Lafourcade, *Swinburne,* p. 83.

2. *Ibid.,* p. 81.

3. Bieber, *et al.,* p. 28.

4. *Ibid.,* pp. 39-40.
5. Doughty, p. 323.
6. Ford Madox Hueffer, *Ancient Lights* (London, 1911), p. 26.
7. *Letters,* I, 46.
8. Bieber, *et al.,* p. 303.
9. Lafourcade, *Swinburne,* p. 191n.
10. Angeli, *Rossetti,* p. 77.
11. *Ibid.,* p. 216.
12. William Bell Scott, *Autobiographical Notes of the Life of William Bell Scott* (New York, 1892), I, 289-90.
13. *Letters,* VI, 92.
14. Lafourcade, *Swinburne,* p. 83.
15. *Ibid.,* p. 127.
16. Helen Rossetti Angeli, *Pre-Raphaelite Twilight* (London, 1954), p. 178.
17. *Letters,* VI, 245.
18. *Ibid.,* I, 51-53.
19. *Works,* XX, 436.
20. *Ibid.,* XIII, 419.
21. *Ibid.*
22. *Ibid.,* 423.
23. *Ibid.,* 426.
24. *Letters,* I, 88.
25. Pope-Hennessy, p. 134.
26. Marquis de Sade, *Selected Writings,* trans. Leonard de Saint-Yves (London, 1953), p. 10.
27. *Letters,* I, 53-54.
28. *Ibid.,* 66-67.
29. *Ibid.,* 75.
30. *Ibid.,* 78.
31. *Ibid.,* 44n., 223n.
32. Lafourcade, *Swinburne,* p. 129.
33. Hare, pp. 111-12.
34. Gosse, pp. 95-96.
35. Henry Adams, *The Education of Henry Adams* (Boston, 1918), p. 139.
36. *The Times,* (London) May 3, 1866, p. 14.
37. *Letters,* III, 278-79.
38. Lang, "Swinburne's Lost Love," 123-30.
39. *Letters,* I, 125.
40. *Ibid.,* 135.
41. *Ibid.,* 143.
42. *Ibid.,* 155n., 161n.
43. *Ibid.,* 183.

44. Gosse, p. 119.
45. William Meredith, ed., *Letters of George Meredith* (London, 1912), I, 55.

Chapter Five

1. *Works*, XIII, 159.
2. *Ibid.*, 163-64.
3. Lafourcade, *La Jeunesse*, II, 375-76.
4. *Ibid.*
5. Hare, p. 73.
6. *Spectator*, XXXV (June 7, 1862), 632-33.
7. *Letters*, I, 55, 58.
8. *Works*, VII, 351.
9. *Letters*, I, xxxii.
10. *Ibid.*, VI, 236-37.
11. *Works*, VII, 293.
12. *Ibid.*, 299.
13. *Ibid.*, 300.
14. *Ibid.*, 307.
15. *Letters*, I, 93.
16. *Works*, VII, 269.
17. *Ibid.*, 271.
18. Lafourcade, *Swinburne*, p. 130.
19. *Ibid.*, pp. 112-13.
20. *Letters*, I, 114.
21. *Works*, VIII, 38.
22. *Letters*, I, 136.
23. *Spectator*, XXXVIII (December 2, 1865), 1343-44.
24. *North American Review*, CII (April, 1866), 545.
25. Lord Houghton, "Mr. Swinburne's 'Chastelard,'" *Fortnightly Review*, IV (April 15, 1866), 543.
26. Charles Tennyson, *Alfred Tennyson* (New York, 1949), p. 359.
27. *Works*, XV, 122-23.
28. *Spectator*, XXXIX (March 31, 1866), 357.
29. *Letters*, I, 141n.
30. *Ibid.*, 140n.
31. *Ibid.*, 137-39.
32. *Ibid.*, 141.
33. Swinburne, *Poems and Ballads* (London, 1889), p. 197.
34. *Ibid.*, p. 305.
35. *Ibid.*, pp. 102-4.
36. *Ibid.*, pp. 133-34.
37. *Ibid.*, p. 217.
38. *Ibid.*, p. 46.

39. *Ibid.*, p. 50.
40. *Ibid.*, p. 51.
41. *Ibid.*, p. 54.
42. *Ibid.*, p. 7.
43. *Ibid.*, p. 73.
44. *Ibid.*, p. 96.
45. *Ibid.*, p. 100.
46. *Ibid.*, p. 174.
47. *Ibid.*, pp. 175, 176.
48. *Ibid.*, p. 230.
49. Lafourcade, *Swinburne*, p. 109; also *Works*, XVI, 365.
50. *Letters*, I, 99.
51. *Poems and Ballads*, p. 220.
52. Doughty, p. 281.
53. *Ibid.*, and Lafourcade, *Swinburne*, p. 106.
54. Lafourcade, *Swinburne*, p. 193.
55. *Works*, XVI, 132-33.
56. *Ibid,.* 137-38.
57. Hueffer, *Ancient Lights*, p. 148.
58. *Letters*, I, 156.
59. Lafourcade, *La Jeunesse*, II, 285.
60. *Works*, XVII, 67.
61. *The Novels of A. C. Swinburne*, ed. Edmund Wilson (New York, 1962), pp. 43-44.
62. *Ibid.*, p. 44.
63. *Works*, XVII, 251-52.
64. *Ibid.*, 180-81.
65. *Letters*, I, 224.
66. Swinburne, *Lesbia Brandon*, ed. Randolph Hughes (London, 1952), p. 30.

Chapter Six

1. *Letters*, I, 172.
2. *Ibid.*, 84-85.
3. *Ibid.*, 169-70. Swinburne's letter to Joseph Knight on August 3, 1866, shows that he had already read the *Athenaeum* review. I assume that the *Saturday* also came out on August 3, and that Lytton's letter arrived on that date.
4. *Ibid.*, 151.
5. J. W. R. Scott, *The Life and Death of a Newspaper* (London, 1952), pp. 14, 48, 49.
6. T. H. S. Escott, *Masters of English Journalism* (London, 1911), pp. 231-32.
7. *Ibid.*

8. Merle Mowbray, *The Saturday Review, 1855-1868* (New York, 1941), p. 221.
9. [John Morley] "Mr. Swinburne's New Poems," *The Saturday Review,* XXII (August 4, 1866), 145.
10. *Ibid.*
11. *Ibid.*
12. *Ibid.*
13. *Athenaeum* (August 4, 1866), 137-38.
14. *Ibid.*
15. *Ibid.*
16. *Letters,* I, 173.
17. *Ibid.,* 176-77.
18. William Michael Rossetti, *Swinburne's Poems and Ballads, A Criticism* (London, 1866), p. 36.
19. *Punch,* LI (November 10, 1866),189.
20. *The Examiner* (October 6,1866), p. 627.
21. [Carleton Green] "Mr. Swinburne and His Poetry," *The Light Blue* (January, 1867), pp. 10-15.
22. *Letters,* I, 195.
23. Lafourcade, *Swinburne,* p. 149.
24. *Works,* II, 67.
25. *Ibid.,* 72, 75.
26. *Ibid.,* 137.
27. *Ibid.,* 145.
28. *Ibid.,* 233.
29. *Ibid.,* 363.

Chapter Seven

1. *Works,* XVI, 372.
2. *Letters,* I, 146.
3. Harriet Jay, *Robert Buchanan* (London, 1903), p. 161.
4. *Letters,* I, 143.
5. *Spectator,* XXXIX (September 15, 1866), 1028.
6. *Works,* XVI, 371.
7. Robert Buchanan, "On My Own Tentatives," *David Gray and Other Essays* (London, 1868), p. 291.
8. *Works,* XVI, 430.
9. William M. Rossetti, *Swinburne's Poems and Ballads* (London, 1866), p. 7.
10. William M. Rossetti, *Dante Gabriel Rossetti: His Family Letters with a Memoir* (Boston, 1895), I, 295.
11. *Athenaeum* (November 3, 1866), pp. 564-65.
12. *Letters,* I, 212.

13. Swinburne, "Matthew Arnold's New Poems," *Fortnightly Review*, n. s. II (October 1, 1867), 428.

14. *Works*, XV, 90n.

15. *Letters*, VI, 264.

16. *Athenaeum* (January 29, 1870), pp. 154-56.

17. Sir William Hardman, *A Mid-Victorian-Pepys* (New York, 1923), pp. 78-79.

18. *Letters*, I, 192.

19. *Works*, XV, 212, 214, 215.

20. *Letters*, II, 101.

21. *Works*, XV, 29.

22. *Ibid.*, 7.

23. *Ibid.*, 13.

24. *Ibid.*, 39.

25. *North American Review*, CXI (October, 1870), 471-74.

26. *Ibid.*, 457-79.

27. *Ibid.*, 479.

28. *Ibid.*, 480.

29. Robert Buchanan, "The Fleshly School of Poetry: Mr. D. G. Rossetti," *Contemporary Review*, XVIII (October, 1871), 343.

30. *Ibid.*, 337, 338.

31. *Ibid.*, 343.

32. *Letters of Dante Gabriel Rossetti to William Allingham*, ed. George B. Hill (London, 1897), p. 292.

33. *Athenaeum* (December 16, 1871), p. 794.

34. *Ibid.*, 792-93.

35. *Ibid.*, p. 793.

36. Dante Gabriel Rossetti, *Poems* (London, 1870), p. 201.

37. *Athenaeum* (December 16, 1871), pp. 793-94.

38. Doughty, pp. 469-85 *passim*.

39. Robert Buchanan, *The Fleshly School of Poetry* (London, 1872), p. 3.

40. *Letters*, II, 137-38.

41. *Works*, XVI, 425.

42. Buchanan, "The Fleshly School of Poetry," 337.

43. Robert Buchanan, "The Monkey and the Microscope," *St. Paul's Magazine*, XI (August, 1872), 240.

44. *The Examiner* (November 20, 1875), p. 1304.

45. *The Examiner* (December 11, 1875), p. 1388.

46. *Ibid.*

47. *Athenaeum* (July 8, 1876), pp. 50-51.

Chapter Eight

1. *Letters*, II, 143n.
2. *Ibid.*, IV, 55-56.
3. *Works*, III, 171.
4. *Ibid.*, XIV, 3.
5. *Ibid.*, XVI, 12-14.
6. *Works*, III, 307.
7. *Ibid.*, 311.
8. *Ibid.*, 313.
9. Lafourcade, *Swinburne*, p. 195.
10. *Ibid.*, p. 202.
11. *Ibid.*, p. 292.
12. *Works*, IV, 46.
13. *Ibid.*, 70.
14. *Ibid.*, 151.

Selected Bibliography

PRIMARY SOURCES

The most complete collection of the works is the Bonchurch Edition of *The Complete Works of Algernon Charles Swinburne,* edited by Sir Edmund Gosse and Thomas J. Wise, 1925-1927, and published in London by William Heinemann Ltd. Because of Wise's reputation an accurate edition should be prepared. Several of the early works and some of the later works of an off-color character have been omitted from the Bonchurch Edition; its title is, therefore, misleading. When the complete works are reedited, all the strays should be included.

As things now stand, the best account of the early unpublished works, together with extensive quotations, is given in Georges Lafourcade, *La Jeunesse de Swinburne,* II, published in London in 1928 by William Heinemann Ltd. The first publication of the novel *Lesbia Brandon* is that edited by Randolph Hughes and published in London in 1952 by the Falcon Press. Hughes' voluminous commentary makes extravagant claims that have never been substantiated. An edition of the two novels *Love's Cross-Currents* and *Lesbia Brandon* was done in 1962 by Edmund Wilson and published in New York by Farrar, Straus & Cudahy.

The six-volume edition of *The Swinburne Letters,* edited by Cecil Y. Lang for the Yale University Press, was published from 1959 to 1962. It includes hundreds of letters never before published and is indispensable. In the preface to the first volume Professor Lang makes it clear that there are still many letters outstanding which may still appear. It is presumed that Mrs. Disney Leith's statement in the preface to her *Algernon Charles Swinburne* (New York: G. P. Putnam's Sons 1917), that she destroyed the family letters of Swinburne after the publication of her book, is correct.

BOOKS BY SWINBURNE

I. Collected Editions
Poems. 6 vols. London: Chatto and Windus, 1904.

Tragedies. 5 vols. London: Chatto and Windus, 1905.
Complete Works. 20 vols. Bonchurch Edition. London: William Heinemann Ltd., 1925-27.

II. Individual Works

The Queen Mother and Rosamond. London: Edward Moxon and Co., 1860.
Atalanta in Calydon. London: Edward Moxon and Co., 1865.
Chastelard. London: Edward Moxon and Co., 1865.
Poems and Ballads. London: John Camden Hotten, 1866.
Notes on Poems and Reviews. London: John Camden Hotten, 1866.
A Song of Italy. London: John Camden Hotten, 1867.
William Blake. London: John Camden Hotten, 1868.
Notes on the Royal Academy Exhibition. John Camden Hotten, 1868.
Songs before Sunrise. London: F. S. Ellis, 1871.
Under the Microscope. London: D. White [F. S. Ellis], 1872.
Bothwell. London: Chatto and Windus, 1874.
George Chapman. London: Chatto and Windus, 1875.
Essays and Studies. London: Chatto and Windus, 1875.
Songs of Two Nations. London: Chatto and Windus, 1875.
Note on the Muscovite Crusade. London: Chatto and Windus, 1876.
Erechtheus. London: Chatto and Windus, 1876.
A Year's Letters. Epistolary novel published in installments in *The Tatler*, August 25 to December 29, 1877, under pseudonym "H. Manners."
A Note on Charlotte Bronte. London: Chatto and Windus, 1877.
Poems and Ballads, Second Series. London: Chatto and Windus, 1878.
A Study of Shakespeare. London: Chatto and Windus, 1880.
Songs of the Springtides. London: Chatto and Windus, 1880.
Studies in Song. London: Chatto and Windus, 1880.
Tristram of Lyonesse and Other Poems. London: Chatto and Windus, 1882.
Mary Stuart. London: Chatto and Windus, 1882.
A Century of Roundels. London: Chatto and Windus, 1883.
A Midsummer Holiday and Other Poems. London: Chatto and Windus, 1884.
Marino Faliero. London: Chatto and Windus, 1885.
Miscellanies. London: Chatto and Windus, 1886.
A Study of Victor Hugo. London: Chatto and Windus, 1886.
Locrine. London: Chatto and Windus, 1887.
The Whippingham Papers. London: Chatto and Windus, 1888.
Poems and Ballads, Third Series. London: Chatto and Windus, 1889.
A Study of Ben Jonson. London: Chatto and Windus, 1889.
The Sisters. London: Chatto and Windus, 1892.

Selected Bibliography

Astrophel and Other Poems. London: Chatto and Windus, 1894.
Studies in Prose and Poetry. London: Chatto and Windus, 1894.
The Tale of Balen. London: Chatto and Windus, 1896.
Rosamond, Queen of the Lombards. London: Chatto and Windus, 1899.
A Channel Passage and Other Poems. London: Chatto and Windus, 1904.
Love's Cross-Currents. London: Chatto and Windus, 1905.
The Age of Shakespeare. London: Chatto and Windus, 1908.
The Duke of Gandia. London: Chatto and Windus, 1908.
Lesbia Brandon, ed. Randolph Hughes. London: The Falcon Press, 1952.

SECONDARY SOURCES

I. Bibliographical
Bateson, F. W. *The Cambridge Bibliography of English Literature.* Vol. III, 317-322. New York: The Macmillan Company, 1941.
Lafourcade, Georges. *La Jeunesse de Swinburne.* Vol. III, 583-600. London: Oxford University Press, 1928. Especially good for the early works, many of which have not yet been published. Must be used with caution because Lafourcade got much of his information from Thomas J. Wise, who is extremely unreliable. Must be checked against John Carter and Graham Pollard, *An Enquiry into the Nature of Certain Nineteenth Century Pamphlets* (New York: Scribner, 1934) to weed out the Wise forgeries.
Lang, Cecil Y. *The Swinburne Letters.* Vol. VI, 420-431. New Haven: Yale University Press, 1962. Though only a portion of the index, and with the information scattered throughout the six volumes of the letters, this is a good listing of the works.
Wise, Thomas J. *Bibliography of the Writings in Prose and Verse of Algernon Charles Swinburne.* Vol. XX of the Bonchurch Edition of *The Complete Works of Algernon Charles Swinburne.* London: William Heinemann Ltd., 1927. The most complete and detailed bibliography, but for reasons given above it must be used with caution and checked against Carter and Pollard's *Enquiry.*

II. Critical and Biographical
Adams, Henry. *The Education of Henry Adams.* Boston: Houghton Mifflin Co., 1918.
Allingham, William. *A Diary.* London: Macmillan and Co., Ltd., 1907. Personal recollections of Dante Gabriel Rossetti.
Angeli, Helen Rossetti. *Dante Gabriel Rossetti.* London: Hamish

Hamilton, 1949. The daughter of William Rossetti gives new information on both Dante Rossetti and Swinburne.

——. *Pre-Raphaelite Twilight*. London: The Richards Press, 1954. Though primarily a defense of Charles A. Howell and Dante Rossetti, this work adds still newer information on Dante Rossetti, Swinburne, and Howell. Because of the author's strong family bias, one must weigh carefully her unsubstantiated information.

Ashbee, Henry Spencer. *Index Librorum Prohibitorum*. London: [No publisher given], 1877. Not to be confused with the Catholic *Index*, this book gives private information on London publishers, especially John Camden Hotten.

Austin, Alfred. "Mr. Swinburne," *Temple Bar*, XXVI (July, 1869), 457-74. A strongly negative article on Swinburne which he answered in *Under the Microscope*.

Baudelaire, Charles. "Notes Nouvelles sur Edgar Poe," Introduction to Baudelaire's French edition of Poe's short stories in Vol. VI of *Nouvelles Histoires Extraordinaires*. Paris: Calmann-Lévy Éditeurs, 1857.

——. *Oeuvres Complètes*. Paris: Louis Conard, Libraire-Éditeur, 1923.

Beerbohm, Max. *Rossetti and his Circle*. London: William Heinemann Ltd., 1922.

Bevington, Merle M. *The Saturday Review*. New York: Columbia University Press, 1941. Explains the editorial policy that led to attack on *Poems and Ballads*.

Bieber, Irving, et. al. *Homosexuality: A Psychoanalytic Study*. New York: Basic Books, Inc., 1962. A psychoanalytic case study of abnormal sexuality.

Browning, Oscar. *Memories of Sixty Years*. London: John Lane, the Bodley Head, 1910. Gives personal recollections of life at Eton in Swinburne's time.

"Buchanan *versus* Taylor," *The Examiner* (July 8, 1876), 763. Gives a jocular account of the trial of 1876.

Burne-Jones, Mrs. Georgiana. *Memorials of Edward Burne-Jones*. London: Macmillan and Co., Ltd., 1906. Firsthand material on Swinburne's early days in London by the wife of one of his close friends.

Caine, Hall. *Recollections of Rossetti*. London: Cassell and Co. Ltd., 1928. Important anecdotes of Rossetti's last years.

Chew, Samuel C. *Swinburne*. Boston: Little, Brown, and Co., 1929. Excellent criticism.

Child, Ruth C. *The Aesthetic of Walter Pater*. New York: The Macmillan Company, 1940. Since Pater took many ideas from Swinburne and was closely associated with him, this affords a secondhand approach to Swinburne's aesthetic and philosophical principles.

De Sade, Marquis. *Selected Writings.* Trans. Leonard de Saint-Yves. London: Peter Owen Ltd., 1953.

Doughty, Oswald. *Dante Gabriel Rossetti.* New Haven: Yale University Press, 1949. Still the best, most comprehensive biography.

Friswell, James Hain. "Mr. Algernon C. Swinburne." *Modern Men of Letters Honestly Criticized.* London: Hodder and Stoughton, 1870. Contemporary criticism, mostly harsh.

Gautier, Théophile. *Charles Baudelaire.* London: Greening and Co., 1915. Good account by a contemporary.

———. *Mademoiselle de Maupin.* New York: The Heritage Press, 1944. Swinburne's first introduction to "art for art's sake" came through this novel.

Gilman, Margaret. *Baudelaire the Critic.* New York: Columbia University Press, 1943. An excellent critical biography and explanation of Baudelaire's critical and artistic philosophy.

Gosse, Sir Edmund. *The Life of Algernon Charles Swinburne.* London: The Macmillan Company, Ltd., 1917. The first full-length biography, it contains much source material. Somewhat biased and not always reliable because of Gosse's love of dramatization.

———. "Swinburne: an Essay," originally written in 1925 but first published in Vol. VI of Lang's edition of *The Swinburne Letters* (New Haven: Yale University Press, 1962), 233-48.

Hardman, Sir William. *A Mid-Victorian Pepys.* New York: George H. Doran Co., 1923. Personal anecdotes of Swinburne and others by a London publisher.

Hare, Humphrey. *Swinburne.* London: H. F. and G. Witherly Ltd., 1949. Interestingly written but not always reliable.

Hueffer, Ford Madox. *Memories and Impressions.* New York: Harper and Brothers, 1911. A breezy account of Rossetti, Swinburne, and the Pre-Raphaelites by a cousin of the Rossettis.

Hunt, W. Holman. *Pre-Raphaelitism and the Pre-Raphaelite Brotherhood.* 2 vols. London: Macmillan and Co., Ltd., 1905. An account of the early ideals of the movement by its founder.

Hyder, C. K. *Swinburne's Literary Career and Fame.* Duke University Press, 1933. Contains indispensable source materials.

Lafourcade, Georges. *La Jeunesse de Swinburne.* 2 vols. London: Oxford University Press, 1928. The best account of the years to 1866 in Vol. I and the most complete account as well as the best criticism of the early works in Vol. II.

———. *Swinburne.* London: Oxford University Press, 1932. The best biography, but it does not include recent and indispensable material.

Lang, Cecil Y. "Swinburne's Lost Love," *PMLA* (March, 1959), 123-

130. This most important essay presents a strong case to show that Swinburne's love affair was with his cousin Mary Gordon (Mrs. Disney Leith) rather than "Boo" Falkner.

Leith, Mrs. Disney. *Algernon Charles Swinburne*. New York: G. P. Putnam's Sons, 1917. Account by Swinburne's cousin who knew him as a child. Personal recollections.

Millais, John G. *The Life and Letters of Sir John Everett Millais*. 2 vols. London: Methuen and Co., 1899. An account of the early days of Pre-Raphaelitism.

Moore, George. *Confessions of a Young Man*. London: T. Werner Laurie, 1904. Personal recollections of Swinburne by a later member of the aesthetic movement.

Nicolson, Harold. *Swinburne (EML)*. London: The Macmillan Company, Ltd., 1926. A good critical study.

Pope-Hennessy, James. *Monckton Milnes*. London: Constable, 1951. Good recent biography of Lord Houghton; somewhat laudatory.

Rossetti, William M. *Dante Gabriel Rossetti: His Family Letters with a Memoir*. 2 vols. Boston: Roberts Brothers, 1895. Fiercely defensive of his brother; must be read with caution.

————. *Rossetti Papers, 1862-1870*. London: Sands and Co., 1903. Personal material but also to be read with caution.

————. *Swinburne's Poems and Ballads*. London: John Camden Hotten, 1866. A clever, strongly biased defense of Swinburne.

Satyricon of Petronius Arbiter. London: [No publisher given], 1899. This explains the insult in Buchanan's Gito reference to Swinburne in the *Athenaeum* review of *Poems and Ballads* on August 4, 1866.

Scott, William Bell. *Autobiographical Notes of the Life of William Bell Scott*. 2 vols. New York: Harper and Brothers, 1892. Candid and unbiased accounts of Swinburne and the Rossettis by personal friend; occasionally inaccurate.

Stedman, E. C. *Victorian Poets*. Boston: James R. Osgood and Co., 1876. Criticism biased in favor of Swinburne by one of his friends.

Tennyson, Charles. *Alfred Tennyson*. New York: The Macmillan Company, 1949. Gives new material on Tennyson's reaction to Swinburne.

Watts-Dunton, Clara. *Home Life of Swinburne*. London: A. M. Philpot, 1922. Account of home life at "The Pines" by Watts-Dunton's secretary, whom Watts-Dunton married.

Waugh, Evelyn. *Rossetti*. New York: Dodd, Mead and Co., 1928. An interpretive, witty biography written by a novelist.

Welby, T. Earle. *A Study of Swinburne*. New York: George H. Doran Company, 1926. Excellent criticism.

Wilde, Oscar. *Letters*. Ed. Rupert Hart-Davis. London: Harcourt, Brace & World, 1962. Shows closer association with Swinburne than Swinburne acknowledged.

Index

Index

Index

Index